SOURCE BOOK
of a Study of Occupational Values
and the Image of the Federal Service

SOURCE BOOK

of a Study of Occupational Values
and the Image of the Federal Service

Franklin P. Kilpatrick
Milton C. Cummings, Jr.
M. Kent Jennings

The Brookings Institution
Washington, D.C.

© 1964 by

THE BROOKINGS INSTITUTION

Published January 1964

Library of Congress Catalogue Card Number 64-13906

THE BROOKINGS INSTITUTION is an independent organization devoted to nonpartisan research, education, and publication in economics, government, foreign policy, and the social sciences generally. Its principal purposes are to aid in the development of sound public policies and to promote public understanding of issues of national importance.

The Institution was founded December 8, 1927, to merge the activities of the Institute for Government Research, founded in 1916, the Institute of Economics, founded in 1922, and the Robert Brookings Graduate School of Economics and Government, founded in 1924.

The general administration of the Institution is the responsibility of a self-perpetuating Board of Trustees. The Trustees are likewise charged with maintaining the independence of the staff and fostering the most favorable conditions for creative research and education. The immediate direction of the policies, program, and staff of the Institution is vested in the President, assisted by the division directors and an advisory council, chosen from the professional staff of the Institution.

In publishing a study, the Institution presents it as a competent treatment of a subject worthy of public consideration. The interpretations and conclusions in such publications are those of the author or authors and do not purport to represent the views of the other staff members, officers, or trustees of the Brookings Institution.

Foreword

THIS BOOK REPORTS THE BASIC DATA obtained for a large-scale study of occupational values and of public attitudes toward the federal service in the United States. Launched in 1959, the study had two broad objectives: (1) to analyze the occupational values and attitudes toward work that prevail in American society today; and (2) to ascertain the attitudes of various groups in the American public toward the federal civilian service generally and toward the federal service as an employer. The study was prompted by an interest in exploring the dimensions of the government's personnel problem—to identify and to explain the government's strengths and weaknesses as it competes for talented manpower in the 1960's. To do this, personal interviews based on standardized questionnaires were conducted with more than 5,000 people—including a cross section of the general working public outside the federal government; federal civilian employees; high school and college students and teachers; graduate students; natural scientists, social scientists, and engineers in business, the academic world, and the federal government; and top-level business and federal executives.

The interpretation of this material and some of the implications to be drawn from it will be found elsewhere: in *The Image of the Federal Service,* a volume published at the same time as this *Source Book,* and in a planned publication on occupational values in American life, on which work is still progressing. The purpose of this *Source Book* is different: to present the detailed findings with respect to each of the groups interviewed, and to provide a detailed account of the study's methodology. It is hoped that the material in this volume will provide a fund of information of interest to people concerned with the public's attitudes toward the federal service, with occupational values and attitudes toward work, and with personnel matters, policies, and procedures, both in and out of government.

This study is one of a series that the Brookings Institution is undertaking in the general field of leadership, management, and the public service. An Advisory Committee, consisting of James A. Bayton, Professor of Psychology, Howard University, Harvey C. Mansfield, Professor of

Political Science, Ohio State University, and James M. Mitchell, Director of the Advanced Study Program, the Brookings Institution, read the manuscript and made numerous helpful suggestions to the authors.

The authors, Franklin P. Kilpatrick, a social psychologist, Milton C. Cummings, Jr., a political scientist, and M. Kent Jennings, a political scientist now at the University of Michigan, were all staff members of the Governmental Studies Division of the Brookings Institution when the study was made.

The opinions and conclusions presented in this volume are those of the authors, and do not purport to represent the views of the trustees, officers, or other staff members of the Brookings Institution.

ROBERT D. CALKINS
President

November 1963
The Brookings Institution
1775 Massachusetts Avenue N.W.
Washington, D.C.

Authors' Acknowledgments

MANY PEOPLE HELPED US with this book, but we owe a special debt of gratitude to the large group of unnamed individuals whose aid was truly indispensable—the more than 5,000 people who gave an hour or more of their time to be interviewed, and the numerous officials and personnel officers in business firms, schools, and federal installations who facilitated the work of our interviewers.

Among the many federal officials who assisted us in our research, four were especially helpful: Warren B. Irons, Executive Director, U. S. Civil Service Commission; John W. Macy, Jr., Chairman of the Commission; Dale Rogers, then Executive Vice Chairman of the Interagency Advisory Group, the Civil Service Commission, and now with the Office of Industrial Relations, Department of the Navy; and James E. Smith, then in the Personnel Division of the Civil Service Commission, and now with the Philadelphia Region of the Commission. The other members of the Interagency Advisory Group also made a substantial contribution to the study by helping to prepare the way for our interviews with federal employees in their departments and agencies.

Others whom we wish to thank are: Jane M. O'Donnell and Sidney Binder, both of National Analysts, Inc., who contributed in many ways to the interviewing and the coding and tabulating of the questionnaires; and Edwin E. Olson, now at the University of Southern California, who served as a research assistant during much of the project. For help at various stages of the work, our thanks also go to George A. Graham, Director of the Governmental Studies Division, the Brookings Institution, and to Robert D. Calkins, President of the Institution.

At Brookings, we also received much valuable assistance from Amy R. Reeves, who did the major share of the secretarial work throughout the project, and from Virginia J. Baxter, whose prolonged exposure to the hundreds of tables and figures contained in this volume failed to dim the enthusiasm and energy with which she checked and rechecked them for accuracy. To Kathleen Sproul, who edited the manuscript for publication, we are especially grateful. Scarcely a page of the book has not been improved by her deft and perceptive editorial touch.

The members of our Advisory Committee, already mentioned in the Foreword, gave us the benefit of their careful reading of the manuscript and made numerous helpful suggestions for improving it. Like all the others whose aid is acknowledged in these pages, however, they should not be taxed for any shortcomings of the material that follows. For those, we alone are responsible.

FRANKLIN P. KILPATRICK
MILTON C. CUMMINGS, JR.
M. KENT JENNINGS

Contents

xi

List of Tables

PART ONE

Chapter 3. The Conduct of the Study

PART TWO

Chapter 4. Occupational Satisfaction and the Appeal of Federal Employ-ment

Chapter 5. Elements of the Ideal and the Worst Occupation

Chapter 6. The Occupational Value Scale Items

Chapter 7. Positive and Negative Features Seen in Own Occupations

Chapter 11. The Image of the Federal Employee

Chapter 12. Image of the Federal Employee: Ratings on Five Character-istics

Chapter 13. Image of the Federal Employee: Perceived Motives and Work Activity

to the question, "What do you picture a (federal civil service employee) (person employed by a large private business or industry) as doing—that is, what sort of work?"   378-391

Chapter 15. General Employed Public: Images of Federal Employment and Employees

Chapter 16. General Federal Employees: Occupational Ratings and Values

Chapter 17. General Federal Employees: Images of Federal Employment and Employees

Chapter 18. Federal Employees: Further Attitudes and Values

Chapter 19. Student Populations: Occupational Ratings and Values

Chapter 20. Student Populations: Images of Federal Employment and Employees

Chapter 21. College and High School Teachers

Chapter 22. Business Executives

Chapter 23. Federal Executives

Chapter 24. Natural Scientists, Social Scientists, and Engineers

Appendix A

Appendix C

PART ONE

1

Introduction

THE RESEARCH DESCRIBED in this volume was launched in 1959 to explore two broad questions: What values and goals do present-day Americans seek to realize in their occupations? In this context, how do they perceive the federal government as an employer and how does working for the government compete in attractiveness with other employment?

To try to find the answers to these questions and a host of more specific queries generated by them, we undertook a national sampling survey of occupational and other groups throughout the continental United States. Personal interviews based on a standardized questionnaire were conducted with more than 5,000 people—including members of the general adult working force; federal employees; high school and college students and teachers; natural and social scientists and engineers; business executives. In designing the survey and all other phases of the study, one of our research objectives was to ensure that our methods would permit comparative analysis of the findings from group to group and also provide base lines for comparative trend analysis in future research.

When the survey information was finally codified and tabulated, we were in possession of a very large amount of new data. It seemed clear that other researchers and public and private administrators might find this material, in itself, useful in many ways, quite aside from our own analysis of it. Furthermore, we were sure that the patterns and implications with which our written analyses were to be concerned would emerge much more clearly and usefully for a reader if they could be viewed against a fairly comprehensive background of data.

Consequently, this *Source Book* was prepared to document two shorter interpretive companion volumes, *The Image of the Federal Service* and

3

Occupational Values in American Life.[1] It describes the study's design methodology, and—mainly without analysis and in considerable detail—findings, and sets forth much of the conclusive data in tabular form. Researchers and other readers who care to do so can thus examine the whole process and assess the implications of the data for their individual purposes and from their specific viewpoints. Those researchers who may wish to repeat all or any part of the study in a sample survey of their own and compare their results with ours will find most of the necessary procedural details provided here, along with the tabular showing of the precise results we obtained.[2]

Background of the Study

Why did we choose occupational values and public attitudes toward government service as research subjects? The case for a study of occupational values in American life can be easily made. Aside from their intrinsic human importance, they are extremely revealing of the general nature of the American society. If one discovers what characteristics the members of any society believe they want in their jobs, one also learns by implication a great deal about their attitudes toward other aspects of the society. In a free society like that of the United States, where individual preferences often control the choice of jobs, people's occupational values have a profound effect on how human effort, skills, and talent are distributed among the various major enterprises that are important to the progress and welfare of the society.

Our focus on the relative appeal of federal employment was motivated by a specific concern, which relates to the above-mentioned distribution

[1] *The Image of the Federal Service* is published simultaneously with the *Source Book;* the second companion volume will be issued later. Both of the shorter books, because of the detailed documentation furnished in this present volume, present their analyses in nontechnical terms and with a minimum of tabular material. In them we stress and summarize what we consider to be the most important findings of the research, and recommendations are made and conclusions drawn. In the *Image of the Federal Service* recommendations are especially emphasized concerning federal personnel policies, procedures, and organization, as well as public information and education on the federal service.

[2] Because of their length, we have not included in the *Source Book* the coding instructions for the open-end questions (described in Chapter 3) or the general instructions for the interviewers (touched on in Chapter 3). These materials would of course be needed by anyone who wished to use the questions in a sample survey; mimeographed copies of them can be obtained by arrangement with the Brookings Institution.

of skills. For some years, presumptive evidence has been accumulating that the United States government increasingly faces a problem of critical proportions in staffing certain kinds of positions in the federal service.[3] In part, our study was designed to identify the nature and the extent of this problem, particularly as it relates to the values that condition individual choice of a job, and to serve as the basis for various policy recommendations that might enable the federal government to compete more effectively for talented manpower.

Both occupational values and attitudes toward federal public service in the United States have been the subjects of much prior published discussion and a considerable amount of previous research. These discussions and earlier investigations were highly instructive when we were formulating the plan for our study, and again helpful when we were interpreting our results. The following section summarizes briefly the kinds of approaches that have characterized research in these two areas. (A more detailed presentation of the investigations and discussions will be found in Appendix A.)

Previous Views and Evaluations

The earliest information concerning American occupational values stems from observations made by visitors from abroad and by Americans themselves. Charles Dickens, for example, was repelled during his first visit to the United States in 1842 by what he regarded as the excessive commercialism of American life—a reaction which prompted him to belabor the "national love of trade" in his account of his journey.[4] And Alexis de Tocqueville, perhaps the most acute foreign observer American society has ever had, early perceived a link between the nation's political institutions and the commercial ventures into which an increasing number of Americans were being drawn.

> Democracy not only swells the number of working-men, but leads men to prefer one kind of labor to another; and while it diverts them from agriculture, it encourages their tastes for commerce and manufactures. . . . A similar observation is likewise applicable to all men living in democracies, whether they are poor or rich. Those who live in the midst of democratic

---

[3] The presumptive evidence of the problem is discussed at some length in the first chapter of *The Image of the Federal Service.*

[4] Dickens, *American Notes and Pictures from Italy* (Oxford University Press, 1957), p. 246.

fluctuations have always before their eyes the image of chance; and they end by liking all undertakings in which chance plays a part. They are therefore all led to engage in commerce, not only for the sake of the profit it holds out to them, but for the love of the constant excitement occasioned by that pursuit.[5]

Americans also drew attention in various ways to their work ethic during the country's early years. As Max Lerner has pointed out, the great folk myths of America—such as the stories of Paul Bunyan and Mike Fink and John Henry—are tales of mighty workers and their work prowess.[6] Before long, men of letters were writing of the particular kinds of occupations that began to flourish in America. In *The Confidence Man*, Herman Melville turned a critical eye on the arts of the salesman and the advertiser. And in the years of industrial expansion that followed the Civil War, the nation's speculative and acquisitive spirit came in for pungent criticism, perhaps best documented in the novel by Mark Twain and Charles Dudley Warner, *The Gilded Age*.

Throughout much of American history, sources like these provided the main fund of information about occupational values in the United States, and even today the first-hand impressions of perceptive observers of the American scene are of primary importance. After World War I, however, new ways of studying occupational values began to take root.

There followed a whole series of new approaches and insights into man's attitudes toward his work: studies of the prestige enjoyed by different occupations; investigations of employee morale and related problems by those concerned with human relations in industry; examination of particular motives, such as a desire for high pay, that were believed to be of prime importance; investigation of the entire process by which the individual chooses an occupation; studies by business corporations designed to indicate the steps that should be taken to attract high quality personnel; studies of the full range of occupational values common to particular social classes or groups and of the distribution of these values among different groups in the society; general interpretive works such as C. Wright Mills' *White Collar* or William H. Whyte's *The Organization Man;* works that attempted to synthesize the now extensive literature on occupational values; and the cross-cultural comparisons that have been made in recent years of occupational values in a number of different societies.

[5] Tocqueville, *Democracy in America* (Vintage Books, 1958), Vol. 2, pp. 163-165.
[6] Lerner, *America as a Civilization* (Simon and Schuster, 1957), pp. 238-239.

The evolution in investigations of occupational values was paralleled by a similar development in studies of the government service. Evaluations began as early as 1789 in journals, letters, and other statements of those who were involved in the business of government. There were also continuous early comments of contemporary observers—both Americans and foreigners. From then on we have had internal reviews, both by the Executive branch and by the Congress, of the government's operations; documents, steeped in controversy, prepared by those who sought to change the nation's administrative system and those defending the *status quo;* the testimony of experts; scholarly studies of specific aspects of the public service; statistical profiles of the composition of the federal bureaucracy; projections of future manpower needs.

All of this enlarged the body of knowledge about the public service of the United States. Recently, industrial psychologists and sociologists have made contributions to an understanding of the workings of large-scale organizations, and social surveys have been designed to probe into the attitudes of the public toward the politician, public employment, and the role of the public servant in American society.

This listing of the various kinds of appraisals and studies indicates something of the variety of the subject matter and methodology that these two main streams of previous research contain. Even in these brief summaries, the thread of development in the way Americans have studied their public service and occupational values can be detected. Over the years, the appraisals of the nation's administrative system and of the public's attitudes toward work have increasingly been supplemented by more systematic investigations of these topics. Nevertheless, given the advances of recent years in the methods of social analysis, the gap between what could be studied with profit and what has been studied remains large.

Prior to the research reported in this volume, for example, there has been no detailed study of the standing and appeal of the federal service which was based on a survey of a national sample of the American population. Nor has there been a comprehensive analysis that presents an over-all view of the strengths and weaknesses of the federal government as it competes for talented manpower in the job markets of the 1960's, in relation to the context of general occupational values. It is this kind of new data and findings that we have tried to provide in this volume and its two companion volumes.

The Scope of the Source Book

The next two chapters, which complete Part One, describe the methodology for the study, with sufficient precision and detail to make our research path clear, step by step, both to permit duplication by other researchers of all or any part of our research (see footnote 2) and to show other readers exactly how we obtained the data presented in Parts Two and Three. Three Appendixes supplement this methodological description. As noted, Appendix A summarizes the previous research on occupational values and public attitudes toward the federal service on which we were able to draw in formulating the plans for the study. In Appendix B the content of our questionnaires is reprinted. Appendix C provides brief statistical descriptions of our samples of the various groups studied, in terms of such factors as age, income, education, and the like.[7]

In Part Two the patterns of the research results are described in topical chapters. For each of the topics, standardized tables present the results for each of the populations studied, as well as by sex and by educational level for the general employed public and for the general sample of federal employees.

Part Three supplements the over-all results for each of the sample populations shown in Part Two with information concerning variations within groups. For each sample population the major findings are presented that resulted from further analyses by such factors as age, sex, income, political party preference, occupational level, geographic region, and so on. Also detailed are the results of certain questions which were asked only of particular groups; one chapter, for example, is devoted entirely to supplementary questions asked only of federal employees.

The data assembled here have been selected by a severe winnowing process. When the survey information was first put together, we found ourselves in possession of more than 5,000 tables, most of them forbiddingly complex. In choosing from this vast amount of material what to describe in text and what to offer in tabular form, we have tried to exercise our best analytic and interpretive judgment. We hope that the pages which follow bear out our judgment, and that readers may find the information there contained important and rewarding.

---

[7] The book does not carry an index, because we believed that the great amount of data it presents could be more usefully mapped for the reader by means of a more than usually detailed table of Contents and a List of Tables.

2

The Design of the Study

THE OVER-ALL DESIGN of any study involves a resolution of conflict between the researcher's desire to fulfill the study's objectives to the greatest envisioned extent and the actual availability of necessary resources—time, money, personnel, and an adequate state of the art of relevant theory and methodology. At the outset of the present research we were fully aware that its objectives were ideal goals, not completely attainable. At the same time we were confident that the state of theory and methodology was such that, given the other resources available to us, a significant contribution could be made to knowledge in areas of critical importance.

Objectives

In pursuit of the two broad goals of the study, as stated in Chapter 1, our six specific objectives were:

1. *To learn what image people have of the federal government as an employer.* What occupational values do people see as being fulfilled and not fulfilled by the federal government in its role as an employing enterprise?

2. *To learn what image people have of federal public servants.* Do people have generalized "pictures in their heads" concerning the qualities and traits of civil servants, appointive officials, and members of Congress? How do they perceive these public servants in terms of character, ability, and occupational values? This information is important for two reasons. First, it provides a picture of an important aspect of how Americans view their government. Second, since an individual's perception of the kind of people he would become identified with if he accepted

9

a particular type of employment may play a large part in his occupational decisions, the image has direct bearing on federal personnel problems.

3. *To learn what occupational values are of concern to people and what occupational values are of basic importance.* What aims, immediate and long-range, are people trying to realize? What are they striving for occupationally and what are they trying to avoid? Again, there are two reasons for obtaining this information. First, it provides important general insights into the nature of American society. Second, only through knowing the society's prevailing pattern of occupational values can we properly evaluate the prevailing images of the federal government as an employer and of public servants in their occupational roles.

4. *To ascertain the pattern of these images and values among the general public, among federal employees, and among a wide variety of occupational, educational, age, sex, and other subgroups in our society.* Ideally, the patterns should be ascertained for all groups which are significant to the productivity and future welfare of American society, but for practical reasons we concentrated on the several groups which have special relevance to the personnel problems of the federal government.

5. *To be able to compare the findings for any one group selected for study with those for any other such group, and with the employed public in general.* Only through such comparative analysis can we understand the factors that go into the occupational decision patterns of given groups.

6. *To assemble our data in such a way that they provide a base line for subsequent trend analysis.* Social research too often ignores the probable needs of future research. A single study provides only a snapshot, a picture of what *is* at a given point in time that yields few clues as to the direction in which things are moving. But a study can be designed to be repeatable and thus offer a reliable comparative base for data obtained at later points in time.

General Design

The nature of these objectives in combination suggested a standardized personal interview questionnaire as the basic instrument to be used. In this type of questionnaire the wording and order of the questions and the method of recording the answers are prescribed, and all interviewers operate under the same set of instructions. It was clear that the most nearly perfect standardization possible was needed if we were to do either comparative analysis or trend analysis successfully. Without it we would not know whether variations in our results were due to differences in questions and procedure, or to actual differences in images and values.

During the planning stage we were often asked, "Wouldn't it be better to use techniques that provide greater depth, that get at the 'real' underlying images and values?" Such techniques include projective tests—e.g. Rorschach or TAT; numerous variations of prolonged, intensive interviewing; role-playing; psychologically or chemically induced hypnosis; and so on. Our reasons for not using any of these were both conceptual and practical.

Conceptually speaking, the depth of the data obtained in a study should be appropriate to the level of their analytical use. For example, a survey interview might typically reveal that "self-determination"—that is, relative freedom of personal choice and absence of coercion and regulation on the job—is an important occupational value. More intensive methods might reveal that "self-determination" is merely one surface manifestation of a basic, unconscious pattern of authority rejection laid down in early childhood.

For our intentions of analyzing, not individual, but group patterns and of making policy recommendations, it was more important to learn the crystallized, verbalizable, occupationally related outcome ("self-determination") of the childhood pattern than the admittedly more basic motive deeply buried at its root. However, in employing the survey method and assessing the data, one must maintain a sharp awareness of the level of information that has been produced; even when the most advanced methods of question wording and of probing are used and rapport is established with maximum skill, there are limits to the amount and kinds of information people can, or will, provide in such a situation.

On the practical side, application of any of the "depth" techniques calls for high professional training and skill—and controlled or at least prearranged conditions. Some of the procedures require weeks and possibly years with each individual under study and even the least time-consuming take many hours. Thus their mechanics make them poorly adapted to research that demands coverage of large numbers of people under a wide variety of conditions in a relatively short period of time. In addition, the very characteristic that makes them valuable in dealing with individual cases—their necessary variability in application from one individual to another—is reason for doubt concerning their reliability and validity as instruments for group research.

We were also asked, "If large numbers of cases and broad coverage are needed, and time and money are limited, wouldn't it be better to use a mail questionnaire?" Generally speaking, questionnaires sent by mail must be both brief and categorical—and especially so when they are being administered to heterogeneous populations. As a consequence they could not provide either the breadth or depth of information needed in this study. Further, the response rate within large heterogeneous populations, except under special conditions which do not apply here, is almost certain to be so low as to make the probability of marked bias in the sample very great.

The Nature of the Questions

Once we had decided to rely on standardized personal interviews, the objectives of the study told us certain things about the necessary content and form of the questionnaire. Moreover, they told us that if we were to carry out analysis according to various groups and segments in the population we must obtain the background information necessary to place people in their proper categories and groups.

Certain broad decisions concerning the composition of the questions were also possible at this point. We knew that categorical questions— questions which do not permit free response but instead offer a range of prescribed alternatives—have certain marked advantages in securing information of the kind we needed, and in the considerable range of areas we had to cover. They take relatively less interviewing time than free-answer questions; are very easy to code and tabulate; are more susceptible to precise statistical treatment; and in some forms are an aid in obtaining information which people either cannot verbalize, or prefer not to.

On the other hand, their outstanding characteristic of limiting the respondent to choosing an answer from a certain number of preformulated alternatives is often a disadvantage, and would be especially so for this study. In never permitting the respondent to state his answer in his own way, the categorical question in effect presumes that all the important categories or classes of response are known, and that research need only show how people sort themselves out in their choices of these predetermined alternatives.[1] In the area of images and values being investi-

---

[1] Certain types of highly refined statistical analysis of categorical responses (factor analysis, latent structure analysis, etc.) can yield "new" information, such as common underlying variables, patterns that are differentially characteristic of the individual as opposed to what is being judged, and the like.

gated, we would have been foolhardy to assume that we knew enough to be sure of including all of the important categories of questioning and response. But to use all free-answer or open-end questions would be immensely time-consuming and would diminish the analytic precision of the entire study.

The solution was to make the questioning procedure a blend of open-end and categorical questions. This had several advantages. In the first place, if both open-end and closed-end questions are asked about the same general topic, each type of answer furnishes a check for the other. Internal consistency analysis of this kind helps to provide an estimate of the reliability of the responses, and of the degree of caution one must use in interpretation.

The dual approach also afforded us the possibility of cross-checking "concern" and "importance." Open-end questions tend to yield responses which reveal the matters that are of present concern to the individual in his day-to-day transactions with his environment. They can, and often do, miss entirely other matters which are basically important to him, but which over indefinite periods of time may not be of immediate concern.

The distinction can be illustrated by noting that the act of breathing is important, but we are rarely concerned with it. Yet if something interferes with breathing, it immediately assumes a high priority of concern. In response to an open-end question, we would not be likely to mention "continuing to breath" as a value, but if a categorical question referred to breathing and asked for a rating of its importance, we would probably rate it very high. Similar considerations apply with respect to occupational values. Security of employment, for example, may be of little concern to many people during an era of continued high demand for the kinds of skills they have to offer, but the conclusion should not therefore be that security is not important to them.

In the study of human behavior, it is useful to ascertain both saliency (concern) and importance. Behavior tends to be regulated in terms of what is of concern. Thus, knowing the pattern of present concerns assists greatly in understanding behavior; it also aids in predicting behavior, provided there is little or no change in the situation. Changes can elevate considerations which are important—but were of little or no concern before the change—to the highest order of saliency and effect on behavior. Thus the onset of an economic recession can alter the saliency of employment security very markedly.

This consideration is especially critical to our objective of learning about occupational values. If in answer to open-end questions people rarely mention financial security as an occupational value, this suggests that it is not a matter of immediate present concern but indicates nothing about its importance. Here the categorical rating, which does help to assess importance, is a useful supplement.

A specific imperative was imposed on the nature of the questions by our desire to make the data serve as an adequate basis for trend analysis, should the study be repeated by ourselves or other researchers at a subsequent time. The questions could not be "time-bound." Their wording must be such that they could be asked in exactly the same form, and with the same meaning, five, ten, or even twenty years from now. Otherwise, one would not know whether differences observed at a later time were due to changes in the values and images or simply to alterations in question form or meaning. It is difficult to be certain that one has eliminated all topical aspects from a group of questions, but it is possible to use only the kinds of questions which are likely to change very little in meaning over a number of years.

The Interviewees

Next on the design agenda was the problem of who should be interviewed and how they were to be selected. Our objectives made it clear that we must sample members of the general employed public. Data from them concerning their occupational values and images of the public service were necessary (1) as a base line for comparison with other groups and (2) as a take-off for generalized statements about the distribution of these values and images in American society. Similar considerations dictated the necessity for obtaining a general sample of civilians presently employed by the United States government.

In addition, since the federal personnel problem is basically a shortage, not of numbers, but of skills and talent, separate analyses should be made of high-level occupational groups such as natural scientists, social scientists, engineers, and business executives. However, no reasonable size sample of the general employed public would yield enough cases in any of these categories to make separate analyses possible. Consequently, we drew supplementary subsamples in each of the desired categories.

Important also to the purposes of the study was an understanding of the values and images of young people still in school, who would be missing from the above samples. Thus we needed to draw special subsamples of high school students, college students, and college graduate students.

The question of how many interviews, over all, should be conducted was resolved arbitrarily by relating the known approximate cost per interview to the time and money available for the study. This established a limit of roughly 5,000 to 6,000 interviews. This left us with the question of how many groups, which groups, and how to allocate the total number of interviews among them. It was decided to make the samples of the general employed public and of federal employees large enough to support analysis of each of them by such breakdowns as age, sex, geographic region, amount of education, general type of occupation, income, and the like.

The minimum number of cases which will permit such subcategories and still allow meaningful (though gross) analysis is approximately 1,000. Out of our total of some 5,000 interviews, then, we concluded we would have to allocate 2,000 to 2,500 cases between our two general samples; the balance must be distributed among the several special subgroups—natural scientists, teachers, executives, students, and so on. This imposed restrictions: in each of our special subgroups there would be too few cases to support any very complex breakdowns by age, school grades, amount of education, and the like; we would also be unable to obtain samples of all the special groups ideally desirable to the study, simply because there were not enough interviews to go around.

We had known from the outset that respondents must be selected through proper probability sampling procedures and that the manner of drawing the sample must be clearly specified.[2] Only when probability sampling is carefully performed in this way, can one safely generalize from the sample to the population from which it was drawn, safely make comparisons among various special populations, insure that the results of the study constitute a proper basis for subsequent repetition and comparative trend analysis, and estimate statistically the probable degree of error involved.

In summary, then, certain broad decisions as to study design were made in the beginning by taking into account the nature of the problem, the nature of the study objectives, the present state of knowledge about methodology and sampling, estimated costs for various procedures, and available resources of time, money, and personnel. But these decisions

---

[2] The sampling framework that was used for the study is described in Chapter 3.

constituted only a general prescription. There were specific further pre-scriptions—the design of the questionnaire and of the interviewing, sampling, and analytic procedures—still to be decided upon the basis of empirical evidence from small-scale preliminary research.

Developmental and Pilot Phases

Conducting a sample survey is not a matter of writing out a few questions and plunging ahead. It must be preceded by a certain amount of developmental and pilot research, during which a questionnaire adequate for the study's purposes can be carefully constructed; the amount required depends upon the nature and complexity of the study. In addition, almost every social survey presents some unique problems, the solution of which calls for considerable methodological ingenuity and even innovation. Nevertheless, over time a set of generally understood, standardized procedures, applicable to most survey operations, has been developed in both academic and commercial survey research. We have made every effort to follow these procedures with care. Thus, this study went through five successive stages of developmental and pilot reesarch carried out over a period of six months.

Developmental Research

Systematic, carefully done developmental research for a complex sample survey involves six essential steps.

1. The problems to be investigated are stated in a clearly understandable way, so that the purpose of the research is completely explicit at the outset. This step may appear simple but is characteristically difficult to carry out. Unless it is done properly, however, the entire study will suffer.

2. Ideas of what may be true about various factors that are directly relevant to the problems of the study are written down. These hunches or hypotheses can be drawn from a number of sources—analyses of relevant research, the opinions of knowledgeable people, preliminary unstructured interviews, personal hunches, and so on. They must be set down in such a fashion that their truth or falsehood, or their degree of truth or falsehood, can be tested by data.

3. For each such hypothesis, the exact nature of the data that would

be needed to test it is determined. This should be done whether or not one believes it possible to obtain the necessary data.

4. Provisional methods that might secure the required information are set down beside each type of data needed. The decision can be straight-forward, if one knows from the past research that a specific procedure will secure the information with the required reliability and validity. In other instances, two, three, or four possible procedures must be set down, because one does not yet know which one will be best for the purpose. In still other cases, no suitable method is known, but one sets down certain notions about *inventing* a new method. And, finally, there will be some data (and thus hypotheses) that must be abandoned, because there are no known ways of securing the needed information, and no realistic prospects of inventing anything that will do the job.

5. The provisional analytic plan is now set down. This includes all the ways in which the data will have to be manipulated and analyzed to test the hypotheses.

6. The entire procedure is reviewed and assessed in terms of the problem statement and the available time, money, and personnel.

After these six steps have been carried out as a procedural and analytic exercise, all of the varieties of provisional data collection and analytic methods that have been specified are subjected to empirical tests by trying them out in actual interviewing and analysis. Very often this phase raises more questions than it answers; it may suggest a number of new hypotheses, yield ideas concerning methods, and even suggest new types of data that might be relevant. So one must again go through the entire six-step procedure and try out the results in another small-scale survey, and, if necessary, keep on repeating the sequence until arriving at what seems to be the best possible balance between what is feasible and what one ideally would like to do.

Pilot Study

Even then the product is not yet final. It must now be tried out in a pilot study, i.e., a small-scale replica of the actual conditions under which it will be used. In this phase, the questionnaire is used on a sample of respondents which is sufficiently large and heterogeneous to subject the procedure to as wide a variety of different levels of understanding, geographic distribution, social environment, and the like, as is possible in a small trial run. Tested at the same time is a booklet of interviewer instructions which prescribes step by step and question by question the precise procedure that must be employed by every interviewer in asking questions and recording answers.

The pilot study provides a final check on a number of essential matters, and the check is conducted both by analyzing the resulting data and by interviewing the interviewers. Are the questions perfectly clear and do they mean the same thing to all types of people who are to be included in the survey? Is there any bias in the wording of any of the questions: that is, does the form of the question itself predispose people to give a certain type of answer, rather than some other answer which more truly reflects their attitude or feeling? Is there any evidence of order bias in the interview; that is, is the pattern of questioning such that the asking of one question, or series of questions, predisposes the respondent to answer any of the following questions in a certain way?

Are there any unusual and correctible difficulties in the actual interviewing procedure itself? For example, is there something about the form of the questionnaire that makes recording of answers difficult? Are there any awkward phrasings that make the questions seem unnatural and set up tensions in the interview situation? How does the questionnaire flow? Does it proceed naturally from topic to topic, maintaining interest at a high level, and minimizing respondent resentment and fatigue?

Is the interviewing instruction booklet adequate? Does it clearly prescribe all the necessary procedures? Does it include some things which are unnecessary or even impossible in actual practice?

And most important of all, does the interview obtain the needed data?

The Result: Three Forms of a Questionnaire

In developing the basic questionnaire we had to take into account that three different types of populations would be included in our total sample: people who are presently employed but not by the federal government, people presently employed by the federal government, and high school and college students who have not yet entered upon full-time employment. This meant that we had to prepare three forms of the questionnaire, but the differences between them would be kept to an absolute minimum. The questionnaire for the nonfederal employed public would be the basic form, and then the necessary modifications and additions for federal employees and for students would be made.

To arrive at the basic form, we went through the six-step procedure four different times, performing interviewing and extensive analysis each time. Approximately two hundred interviews of from one to four hours in length were conducted during this stage. Finally, the tentative questionnaire was subjected to a pilot study carried out by a staff of field interviewers at ten different points in the United States; what this involved can be seen from the few following instances.

The section of the questionnaire designed to reveal occupational values originally contained twenty different questions that consumed over two hours of interviewing. Through successive refinements we finally arrived at four questions, together taking an average of less than fifteen minutes of interviewing time, which elicited all the essential information. Similarly, in the section on the image of the federal government as an employer, the number of questions was reduced from eighteen to three, without appreciable loss of essential information. The pilot study also helped us in the construction of the categorical questions on occupational values. We needed to be reasonably sure that the questions related objectively to the major occupational values. A large number of open-end questions were asked of a wide variety of people, and the results were analyzed. Each occupational value mentioned was listed and the frequency of mention was tallied. The items of high frequency were turned into categorical questions, which were then tested for clarity, lack of ambiguity, discrimination value, and reliability before being accepted for the final form.

The final product was in some respects a compromise, dictated by the inescapable fact that there is a limit to how much one can discover in a single interview. For example, we found it impractical to use questions about all major divisions of federal employment, and therefore arbitrarily eliminated consideration of the military and the judiciary. The developmental research had also shown that responses to open-end questions concerning members of the United States Senate and of the House of Representatives were virtually identical, save for the fact that respondents tended to accord somewhat greater respect to senators than to representatives. Consequently, we saved valuable time by referring to "United States congressmen." Nevertheless, we retained the assessment of some of the differences in attitude by including a number of categorical questions that dealt directly with senators and representatives.[3] Categorical

---

[3] The results of those portions of the questionnaires that concerned appointed and elected federal officials and politics are not reported in this volume. They will appear in a forthcoming book, *The Public's Image of Politics and Politicians*.

questions take only several seconds each of interviewing time, whereas open-end questions can take a good many minutes each.

Despite such necessary compromises, however, the final pre-test showed that the three forms of the questionnaires were now clear, unambiguous, had little or no bias due to question order or content, and were capable of eliciting information that would go far toward fulfilling our research objectives.

The Standardized Questionnaires

The basic form—the questionnaire for the nonfederally employed public—takes an average of one hour and twenty minutes to administer. It consists of twenty-two open-end questions, eighty-five questions in the form of items or statements which the respondent sorts on a ten-point response scale, four self-anchoring scale ratings, six categorical questions, and forty brief classification questions concerning the status and background of the respondent. Since its contents are reprinted—along with the variations in content of the other two forms—in Appendix B, our discussion here will be confined to those aspects of purpose and procedure which may not be immediately apparent from an examination of the appendix.

Self-Anchoring Scaling

Items 1 through 12 of the questionnaire require comment because they are built around the device of self-anchoring scaling, a procedure which has been developed during the past few years in connection with a number of international and national surveys.[4] Briefly, a self-anchoring scale is one in which each respondent is asked to describe, in terms of his own perceptions, goals, and values, the top and bottom or anchoring points of the dimension on which scale measurement is desired. The respondent is then asked to employ this self-defined continuum as a measuring device and as a basis for further questioning concerning his values and goals.

[4] The theoretical basis and general areas of usefulness of the method have been described elsewhere. See. F. P. Kilpatrick and Hadley Cantril, "Self-Anchoring Scaling: A Measure of Individuals' Unique Reality Worlds," *Journal of Individual Psychology*, Vol. 16 (November 1960), pp. 158, 173. Also available as Brookings Reprint No. 47.

The device, as adapted to probe into occupational values, is so central to this study that a description of how it was used is in order. The interviewer opened the procedure as follows (Item 1):

"First, I would like you to think of what really matters most to you in your own life. Tell me what kind of a way of earning a living would be ideal for you—that is, the very best way of doing it from your point of view. Maybe no occupation could fit your ideal. But just let yourself dream a bit and tell me the various things *about* an occupation which would make it *absolutely ideal* for you. I am not asking for the name of a specific occupation, but for the *kinds of things about* an occupation which would make it *absolutely ideal* for you."

The interviewer encouraged as detailed a response as possible and recorded it as nearly verbatim as possible, then said (Item 2):

"Now about the worst sort of occupation. What kinds of things *about* an occupation would make it the worst or least satisfying to you?" Again, elaboration was encouraged and the response was recorded as fully as possible.

At this point the respondent was handed an 8½ by 11 inch card showing a ladder scale with numbers (see Figure 1, page 22, for reproduction). The interviewer said (Item 3): "Here is a picture of a ladder. Suppose we say at the *top* of the ladder is the *very best*, the absolutely ideal sort of occupation you have just described. At the *bottom* is the *very worst* sort of occupation. Where on this ladder would you put your present occupation, that is, what you are doing now?" The interviewer recorded the step number pointed to by the respondent.

The interviewer then said (Item 4): "Now think of what you were doing five years ago. Where on this ladder would you put what you were doing as an occupation five years ago?" The step number was recorded, and the respondent was asked (Item 5): "Thinking now of your occupational future. Where on the ladder do you expect to be five years from now?" The step numbers chosen by the respondent for these two questions revealed, in numerical fashion and in terms of his own occupational values, his feeling of occupational advancement over the past five years and his anticipation concerning his future.

Next, the ladder rating which the respondent had given his present occupation was employed as a means of further eliciting values in terms of the pluses and minuses he perceived in his current occupation. Pointing to the present occupation rating, the interviewer asked, "What kinds of things" about it kept the respondent from putting it higher or lower on the ladder (Items 6 or 7 and 8 or 9).

FIGURE 1.

*Occupational Value
Ladder Scale*[a]

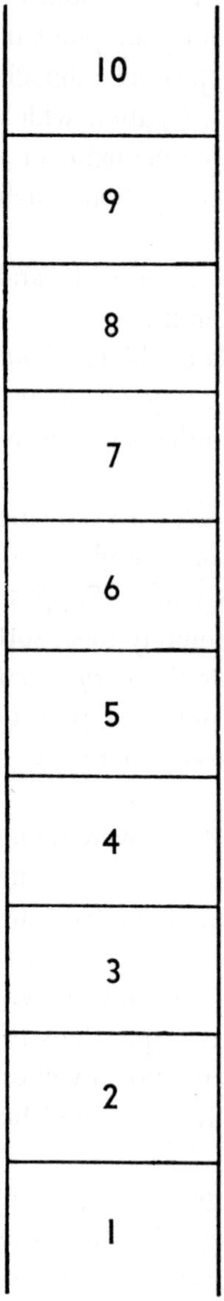

FIGURE 2.

*Ten-Interval
Agree-Disagree Scale*

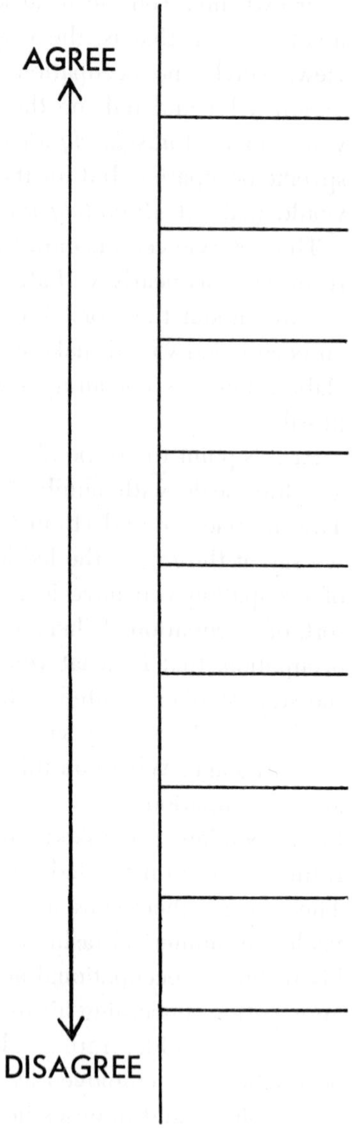

| 10 |
| 9 |
| 8 |
| 7 |
| 6 |
| 5 |
| 4 |
| 3 |
| 2 |
| 1 |

AGREE

DISAGREE

[a] Figure 1 reduced from 10 by 1½ inches; Figure 2 from 22 by 6¾ inches.

Now came the first key question concerning federal employment and the image of the federal service (Item 10). The interviewer said, "Suppose your work or occupation stayed the same but you worked for the federal government—that is, the United States government—how much better or worse would that be? Show me on the ladder, please." The step number pointed to by the respondent was recorded. In this way we obtained a numerical representation of the degree to which the person felt he would move up or down the scale, in terms of his own occupational values, if he were to continue in the same sort of work but for the federal government.

To learn the reasons for this numerical judgment and to explore the individual's image of federal employment, the interviewer then asked (Items 11 and 12): "What things would be likely to be better?" and "What things would be likely to be worse?" Thus we obtained the individual's feeling about the federal government as an employer, in the context of *continuing to perform the same sort of work.* Our preliminary research had shown that this context was necessary; otherwise a respondent's reply tended to be a confusing blend of how he would feel about working for the government, and how he would feel about changing occupations.

When federal employees were interviewed, occupational values and ratings of their own occupations were secured in the same fashion as for nonfederal employees. Then they were asked, if they continued to do the same sort of work but went to work *outside* the federal government, how much better or worse that would be on the ladder rating, and what things would be likely to be better and what things worse.

In the case of students, the questionnaire used a certain amount of supposition. Since students had no present regular occupation to rate on the ladder scale, they were asked, "Now thinking of the time when you start to work at a regular occupation, where on this ladder do you think you are apt to be when you start?" To get at the longer-range expectations concerning occupation, the next question was, "How about five years after you start? Where on this ladder do you expect to be then?" The ladder rating of where one was occupationally five years ago was of course eliminated.

The initial question in the series designed to secure the image of the federal government as an employer was, "Suppose your first occupation was with the U. S. government. Would this be better or worse from your point of view?" This was followed by, "How much (better) (worse)?

Show me on the ladder." The nature of the positive and negative values associated with federal employment were then obtained by asking "What things would be likely to be better?" and, "What things would be likely to be worse?"

Open-End Questions

The purpose of an open-end question is not always apparent from simply reading the question. For example, all respondents were asked (Item 21), "If you were to describe your general idea of a United States civil service employee, what sort of a person would that be?" This may appear to be a bad question. The only really logical answer to it is simply to say that there are all kinds of employees, and perhaps express a little anger that such a stupid question has been asked. But the fact remains that, in varying degrees, most people do have evaluative pictures or stereotypes of civil servants in their minds, and they did express them in response to the question. Since the question was intended to reveal the degree and content of stereotyping in various segments of the population, and whether the stereotypes or images are predominantly favorable, unfavorable, or neutral, the individuals who responded, "That is a stupid question; there are all kinds and types of people in the civil service," also supplied us with valuable information directly relevant to the objectives of the study.

Similar considerations apply to almost all of the series of open-end questions concerned with the nature, type of work, and motivations attributed to civil service employees, people employed by a large private business or industry, U. S. congressmen, and appointive officials. The entire series succeeded very well in revealing the amount, nature, and positive or negative direction of the stereotyping present in the groups interviewed concerning these various categories of personnel.

Scale Sorts

A third matter requiring some discussion is the scale sort used in Item 17 of the questionnaire. This scale sort does not involve scaling in the technical sense of the term, but is simply a way of getting reliable numerical responses to fifty-five separate statements in a very short amount of interviewing time. The statements were concerned with such matters as the importance of certain occupational values, the evaluation of certain aspects of federal employees and federal employment, and attitudes toward government and politics.

To elicit this kind of information questions offering several categories of response are commonly used. For example, questions such as the following (which are adapted from three of our scale-sort statements) would be asked and recorded one at a time by the interviewer:

> Would you say that a young man of ability who starts work in the federal civil service has an extremely good chance, a fairly good chance, a fairly poor chance, or hardly any chance of ending up in one of the top-level jobs?
>
> Would you say that after you are making enough money to get along, then making more money in an occupation is still extremely important, fairly important, fairly unimportant, or extremely unimportant?
>
> Would you say that most people who work for the federal government try very hard, try somewhat, or don't try at all to do their best to serve the public?

In our scale-sorting procedure, these three declarative statements were among the fifty-five used:

> A young man of ability who starts work in the federal civil service has a good chance of ending up in one of the top-level jobs.
>
> After you are making enough money to get along, then making more money in an occupation isn't very important.
>
> Most people who work for the federal government do their best to serve the public.

Each statement was printed on a separate card about 2 by 4 inches. (For the full series of statements, see Appendix B.) Each interviewer was supplied with a deck of the fifty-five cards and a large printed scale with ten spaces, each space being slightly larger than the dimensions of a card. As Figure 2 shows, the spaces form a vertical ten-interval scale labeled "Agree" at the top and "Disagree" at the bottom.

In the actual interview situation, the interviewer shuffled the small cards to insure random presentation, thus eliminating possible order bias due to presenting the items in the same order time after time. The interviewer then said to the respondent:

> Please take the small cards and place each one in turn on the large card according to how much you agree or disagree with the statement on it. You have ten different positions available to you. There are, of course, no right or wrong answers. Now, let's take the first small card, where would you place it? Now, just go on from there, please, as quickly as you can. We are just interested in your first impressions.

When the sorting operation had been completed, the interviewer picked up the items that had been placed on each scale space and put them in the appropriate one of ten numbered envelopes, and went on with the interview. When it was over, the interviewer completed the form in the questionnaire for recording the scale sort. The deck of cards was then reassembled and shuffled, and was ready for re-use.

The procedure has several major advantages. The most apparent is its speed in comparison with laborious question-by-question interrogation and recording: the sorting of the fifty-five statements took an average of twelve to thirteen minutes of interviewing time, whereas questions with categories presented verbally would have consumed a minimum of forty minutes of interviewing time. Further, the scale sorts yield a numerical representation of the response to each item which is comparable from item to item. It is a statistically simple procedure to derive average scores on each of the items for various groups in the populations being studied, and, using measures of dispersion, one may also measure amounts of agreement or disagreement on the placement of an item.

Another advantage is that answers derived in this way tend to be more reliable than answers obtained as categorical responses to individual questions, first of all because people tend to use all, or almost all, of the ten intervals of the scale in their responses. This yields higher reliability than the smaller number of three, four, or at most five intervals which are practical for a verbally presented set of categorical responses. The non-verbal ten-interval scale seems also to avoid much of the semantic confusion and misunderstanding commonly engendered by a set of verbal categories. Most people find it quite easy to place a certain item in a certain place on the ten-interval scale. They seem to feel there is a "natural" place on the scale for the item.

A slightly modified version of the scaling procedure, this time with thirty items on individual small cards, was used at a later point (Item 34) in the questionnaire. It, too, requires some explanatory comment. The cards were sorted and shuffled as in the earlier version. The large printed ten-point scale on which the respondent placed the cards was similar to that shown in Figure 2 except that it was labeled "Extremely High" at the top and "Extremely Low" at the bottom. Two dimensions of judgment were involved: the respondent was asked first to consider a particular category of people and then to rate them on a prescribed personal quality. For example, one card read, "Consider: People in the top-level jobs in the federal civil service. On the average, how would you rate them on *honesty?*" Another, "Consider: People in the top-level jobs in private business. On the average, how would you rate them on *ability?*" (For the full series, see Appendix B.)

In this fashion respondents rated six categories of people on five qualities on the ten-point scale. People in the top-level jobs in private business, federal civil service employees in general, appointees to top-level jobs in the administrative branch of the government, members of the Senate, members of the House of Representatives, and people in the top-level jobs of the federal civil service—all of these were rated on ability, honesty, drive to get ahead, how well respected they are, and how interested in serving the public.

3

The Conduct of the Study

Interviewing

THE STANDARDIZED QUESTIONNAIRES were administered to 5,158 respondents in the continental United States. The personal interviews ranged in length from slightly less than one hour to as much as two and a half hours, averaging, as expected from pilot study results, about one hour and twenty minutes. They were conducted by the interviewing staff of National Analysts, Inc., a commercial research organization which has specialized in "custom design" survey research, rather than in simple, routine, repetitive polling.

The firm's interviewing staff includes about 500 people living in various regions of the country and for the most part in or near the locations that constitute the 100 sampling points in National Analysts' master sample. They have been personally selected and trained either by local supervisors or by the staff of the central office in Philadelphia. Although they are part-time employees, the organization's volume of research is such that the majority of them are kept busy for a large share of their available time. Most of them are housewives with some college education. They are paid, not by the interview, but by the hour—a practice demonstrated experimentally to facilitate quality interviewing. On the average, they have had approximately five years of interviewing experience, as well as a great deal of interviewing training conducted as a routine matter and as a means of acquainting them with novel assignments which involve new or modified procedures.

At all locations where there are several interviewers, local field supervisors oversee their operations; all interviewers are subject to the supervision of central office traveling field supervisors. In addition, the field department staff in the central office checks constantly through liberal use of the mails, telegraph, telephone, and personal visits to make sure that all assignments are being conducted according to specifications and to high standards of quality and completeness.

The interviewing for our study was done in two phases, each phase being conducted by about 100 interviewers, who were among the most experienced and highly skilled on the company's roster. Most of them had had experience with the general types of scaling and card-sorting procedures used in the study; nevertheless, they were given further personal instruction and practice in the use of our questionnaire.

In accordance with standard practice, each interviewer was provided with the instruction booklet that had already been tested for clarity, accuracy, and completeness in the pilot study phase of the research. It described the general purpose of the study, told exactly how sampling procedures were to be carried out, and gave specific instructions for asking each question and recording the answer or answers. Finally, the interviewers were assembled in small groups at various conveniently located points around the country and given two days of personal training by central office staff members. These sessions involved not only general instructions, but practice interviews, review of them, and individual corrective instruction.

The first phase of the survey involved all the nonfederal employed populations, including students. Interviewing began in April 1960 and was almost entirely completed in May, with a small residue completed in early June. The second phase, in which 1,502 interviews with federal employees were carried out, was conducted from the middle of November 1960 through January 1961, with a very small residue carrying over into February. About 60 of the 100 interviewers employed had had experience with the first phase. Instruction booklets revised to accommodate the special problems of interviewing federal employees were provided, and once again personal training sessions were held.

Our own study group at Brookings and others on the Brookings staff played a large role in paving the way for the interviews with federal employees: contacts were made, either by mail or in person, with the head officer, and generally also the personnel officer, of each of the 205 federal installations throughout the United States in which we wished to conduct interviews. At all stages in this effort, the Brookings Institution had the active and inventive support of the Interagency Advisory Group, the Civil Service Commission, and the chief personnel officers of almost all the major departments and agencies in the federal government. Without the courteous support of these officials, it would have been impossible to carry out this phase of the research.

Sampling

A carefully devised, up-to-date, national (continental United States) general purpose sample provided the basic framework for all the samples for the various populations in the study.[1] This is a two-stage, stratified random sample in which each primary sampling unit (a county or group of counties) has a known probability of selection. The stratification is based on population size classes as well as the geographic regions defined by the U. S. Census. There are 130 primary sampling units, 60 of them from 32 metropolitan strata, 1 each from 16 strata in cities of population size 10,000 to 50,000, and 54 from other city and rural strata.

The Nonfederal Populations

GENERAL EMPLOYED PUBLIC SAMPLE. This part of the study was designed to obtain approximately 1,200 interviews, one per household, with regularly employed persons, male and female, 18 to 60 years of age inclusive, either self-employed or working for an employer (35 hours per week or more) other than the federal government.

In the 130 primary units, 509 sample segments were selected through the use of census block statistics in cities of over 50,000 population, and through Census Enumeration Districts in other areas. The interviewer listed the dwelling units in each segment on a prepared sheet that incorporated a random selection device whereby an average cluster of slightly over five occupied dwelling units per segment was identified for interviewer contact and for listing of individuals within the household. In households with only one eligible respondent, that one person was selected for interview; in those with more than one eligible person, the interviewee was selected by a random device incorporated in the household listing sheet.

Interviewers were limited to three personal calls per household to secure an interview. Of the 1,374 contacts made with eligible respondents, 1,142 (83 percent) resulted in satisfactorily completed interviews; 83 (6 percent) of the contacts were ineffective because of respondent illness,

[1] The National Analysts, Inc., National General Purpose Sample, 1960.

TABLE 3-1. *Sample of General Employed Public Compared with Census Data on Four Characteristics*

Characteristics	Sample	Census Data
Sex		
Males	77%	76%[a]
Females	23	24
Region (household figures)		
Northeast	26	26[b]
North Central	33	29
South	27	30
West	14	16
Occupation		
Professional, technical, and kindred workers	12	11[c]
Farmers and farm managers	7	4
Managers, officials, and proprietors, except farm	14	11
Clerical and kindred workers	10	15
Sales workers	6	7
Craftsmen, foremen, and kindred workers	16	13
Operatives and kindred workers	22	18
Private household workers	1	3
Service workers, except private household	6	9
Farm laborers and foremen	1	4
Laborers, except farm and mine	4	5
Median Income[d]	$4,700	$4,800[e]

[a] Based on figures drawn from U. S. Bureau of the Census, *Current Population Reports*, Series P-60, No. 37 (January 1962), pp. 43–44, Table 25. All percentages in this and subsequent tables in the book are rounded to the nearest whole figure.

[b] Drawn from U. S. Bureau of the Census, *Statistical Abstract of the United States: 1961*, p. 40, Table 35.

[c] *Ibid.*, p. 215, Table 287.

[d] Figures here and in subsequent tables are rounded to the nearest hundred dollars. The sample figure refers to money earnings, whereas the Census figure represents total money income of full-time workers (over fourteen years of age).

[e] *Current Population Reports*, No. 37, p. 38, Table 21.

language difficulty, etc., 18 (1 percent) because central office review showed the interviews to be incomplete or in error, and 131 (10 percent) because the potential respondent refused to be interviewed.

Although there is no published Census Bureau data which cover the precise specifications of the present sample, comparisons may be made on some basic demographic features between the sample and several Census populations which are very similarly defined (Table 3-1).

THE HIGH SCHOOL STUDENT AND TEACHER SAMPLES. The universe for the samples of high school juniors and seniors, high school teachers, and high school vocational advisers was defined as all high schools, public, private and parochial, in the continental United States.[2] Within the general sample framework, a random subsample of 100 segments was drawn. Within each, the interviewer determined the location of the high school or schools; if the area was served by more than one school, the one closest to the interviewer was designated as the sample school. The interviewer listed the number of 11th- and 12th-grade home rooms, then followed detailed instructions for random selection of home rooms and of the actual students to be interviewed. Similar procedures of listing and random selection were carried out in choosing the respondents for the teacher and vocational adviser samples.

Cooperation by the high schools was excellent; of the 100 schools, only 1 refused to participate. From the 296 teachers selected for interview, 283 (96 percent) satisfactory interviews were obtained, 80 of them with vocational counselors. From the 396 juniors and seniors chosen for interview, 359 (91 percent) satisfactory interviews were obtained. Of the remaining 37 cases, student absence accounted for 14 (3 percent), central office rejection for error or incompleteness for 12 (3 percent), and refusals for 11 (3 percent). The student sample was designed to provide the same proportion of males to females that is found in the general work force—about two thirds men and one third women.[3] The final sample showed a distribution of 238 boys (66 percent) and 121 girls (34 percent).

We discovered no readily obtainable data with which to compare relevant demographic characteristics of the high school juniors and seniors. However, four points of comparison are available for the high school teachers (Table 3-2).

THE COLLEGE SENIOR, GRADUATE STUDENT, TEACHER, NATURAL SCIENTIST, SOCIAL SCIENTIST, AND ENGINEER SAMPLES. The listing of four-year degree-granting colleges and universities in the United States, as given in *Education Directory: Higher Education*,[4] permitted the identification of 186

[2] Schools teaching grades 10, 11, and 12 were included, whether they taught one or more other grades or no other grades.

[3] This was done to insure large enough numbers of male students for subanalyses, as well as to facilitate direct comparisons of the results for the total high school student sample with those for the total general employed public. A consequence of the procedure is that the results for boys and girls combined may be generalized to all high school students *only* if the figures are statistically adjusted (reweighted) from the 2 to 1 boy-girl ratio obtained to the roughly 1 to 1 sex ratio which actually prevails in United States high schools.

[4] U.S. Office of Education, *Education Directory, 1958-1959: Part 3, Higher Education*, edited by Theresa Birch Wilkins (1960).

TABLE 3-2. *Comparisons Between the Brookings Sample of High School Teachers and NEA Sample of Public High School Teachers on Four Characteristics*

Characteristics	Sample	NEA Data[a]
Sex		
Males	55%	57%
Females	45	43
Marital status		
Married	63	70
Single	31	24
Other	6	6
Median Age	39 years	36 years
Median Occupational Income[b]	$5,600	$5,300

[a] Based on data from National Educational Association, *The American Public-School Teacher, 1960–61* (1963), Appendix A, pp. 84–101. The NEA sample included only public high schools whereas the Brookings sample included a small proportion of nonpublic high schools.

[b] These are income figures from teaching salaries.

colleges and universities in the national sample framework. For use in the survey, a subsample of 100 of them, adjusted to the distribution of colleges in the United States, was selected. At each school, interviews were conducted with samples of college seniors and faculty. In those schools offering postgraduate training, samples of graduate students also were interviewed. For faculty members, a differential sampling rate was applied to secure larger proportions of teachers of natural sciences, social sciences, and engineering than actually exist in the college teacher population.

College seniors and graduate students were defined as students so classified by their educational institutions. College teachers of natural science, social science, and engineering were defined as teachers of the subjects listed in Table 3-3.

The number of satisfactorily completed interviews was 404 for college seniors, 383 for graduate students, and 470 for faculty. Completion rate was 96 percent or higher for all three populations.

The 470 faculty members consisted of 121 natural scientists, 106 social scientists, 87 engineers, and 156 in other disciplines, including 56 teaching the humanities. Figures obtained from this purposely unbalanced sample could not, of course, simply be added up and generalized to the entire population of college teachers. First, reweighting according to the known distribution of natural scientists, social scientists, engineers, and others

TABLE 3-3. *Subject Lists Used in Defining Natural Scientists, Social Scientists, and Engineers in Colleges, Business, and the Federal Government*

Natural Sciences	Hydrology	Demography
Anatomy	Oceanography	Sociology
Pharmacology	Meteorology	Anthropology
Physiology	Climatology	
Nutrition and Metabolism	Geography	*Engineering*
Pathology	Physics	Aeronautical Engineering
Biophysics	Optics	Electrical Engineering
Microbiology	Acoustics	Electronics
Genetics	Astronomy	Architectural Engineering
Zoology	Chemistry	Marine Engineering
Entomology	Biochemistry	
Ecology	Medicine[a]	Civil Engineering
Hydrobiology		Agricultural Engineering
Botany	*Social Sciences*	Sanitary Engineering
Phytopathology	Psychology	Chemical Engineering
Horticulture	Archeology	Ceramic Engineering
Biometrics and Biostatistics	Economics	Mechanical Engineering
Biology	Political Science	Engineering Mechanics
Geophysics	Government	Mining Engineering
Geochemistry	Politics	Metallurgy and Metallurgical Engineering
Geology	Public Administration	
	International Relations	Industrial Engineering

[a] Only when individual is engaged primarily in medical research.

had to be performed. Through machine replication, the proportions were adjusted to the distribution of full-time teachers in institutions of higher education in 1958-59 as follows: natural sciences 14 percent, social sciences 10 percent, engineering 7 percent, humanities 26 percent, all other 43 percent.[5] The resulting replicated sample of 1,186 cases was used in all tabulations for the general "college teacher" population. All tables, however, show in the "number answering" column a figure based on the actual number of cases, that is, 470.

A comparison of the sample of college seniors with a large sample employed in a recent National Opinion Research Center (NORC) mail questionnaire study may be useful (Table 3-4).

[5] See National Education Association, *Teacher Supply and Demand in Universities, Colleges, and Junior Colleges, 1957-58 and 1958-59* (1959), p. 51, Table 30. The figures include data for junior colleges; however, no percentage differs more than 1% from the 1954 data for degree-granting institutions only provided in National Education Association, *Teacher Supply and Demand in Colleges and Universities, 1955-56 and 1956-57* (1957), p. 44, Table A.

TABLE 3-4. *Brookings and NORC Samples of College Seniors Compared on Three Characteristics*

Characteristics	Sample	NORC Data[a]
Sex[b]		
Males	66%	60%
Females	34	40
Marital Status[c]		
Single	83	75
Married (and other)	17	25
Father's Education		
High school completed, or less	58	60
Some college or college completed	25	26
Graduate or professional	15	13
Other	2	—

[a] Data are drawn from *Great Aspirations: Career Plans of America's June 1961 College Graduates: A Preliminary Report of a National Survey* (National Opinion Research Center, University of Chicago, Report No. 82, September 1961), Section VII, Table 1. The study employed mail questionnaires; the completion rate was 85%.

[b] Preliminary tabulations obtained on November 21, 1962, from the Educational Statistics Branch of the U. S. Office of Education show 61% males and 39% females among students earning 4-year degrees between July 1, 1960, and June 30, 1961.

[c] NORC data were obtained during the second semester of the students' senior year; ours were obtained during the first semester. Thus, one would expect the "married" percentage to be somewhat higher in the NORC sample.

A recent study of graduate students in the arts and sciences conducted by NORC supplies a roughly similar sample with which to compare the present sample in terms of a few basic characteristics (Table 3-5). It should be kept in mind, however, that our sample was of all graduate students, while that of NORC was of arts and sciences graduate students only.

Although we know that the college teacher sample was replicated in accordance with certain known distributions in the field of teaching, there is a scarcity of data in other studies with which to compare the kind of college teacher sample drawn. Comparison of income figures would be misleading because available sources gave them on a nine-or-ten-month basis, whereas our respondents were reporting on all income derived from their primary occupation of college teacher. On sex distribution, however, there is matching data from the National Education Association.[6] In our sample 79 percent of the college teachers were males,

[6] See NEA, *Salaries Paid and Salary Practices in Universities, Colleges, and Junior Colleges, 1959-60* (1960), p. 11, Table 4.

TABLE 3-5. *Brookings Sample of Graduate Students and NORC Sample of Graduate Students in Arts and Sciences Compared on Four Characteristics*

Characteristics	Sample	NORC Data[a]
Sex		
Males	78%	82%
Females	22	18
Marital status		
Single	55	50
Married (and other)	45	50
Age		
20–23	33	22
24–26	27	27
27–29	15	23
30–39	21	23
40 and older	4	5
Father's Education		
High school completed, or less	58	56
Some college or college completed	26	26
Graduate or professional	16	18

[a] Based on data found in James A. Davis, *Stipends and Spouses* (University of Chicago Press, 1962). The figures for sex and marital status come from p. 170, Table 3.20; those on age from p. 159, Table 3.1; those on father's education from p. 160, Table 3.2.

21 percent females; the NEA data showed 80 percent males to 20 percent females.

THE SAMPLES OF BUSINESS EXECUTIVES, AND NATURAL SCIENTISTS, SOCIAL SCIENTISTS, AND ENGINEERS IN BUSINESS ENTERPRISES. Again using the basic sampling framework, names and addresses of a random sample of businesses from a random sample of pages in the *McKittrick Directory of Advertisers* were identified in 22 metropolitan primary sampling units.[7] The names and addresses of 375 businesses were provided to the interviewers, 100 of which were designated as the primary sample. The additional businesses were for use in locating enough cases in the relatively scarce business population of natural scientists and social scientists. Respondents within business organizations were selected by the interviewers, who followed the prescribed listing and sampling procedure.

A business executive was defined for sampling purposes as one whose duties are primarily administrative (e.g. supervising, planning, organizing,

[7] *McKittrick Directory of Advertisers Classified,* 1960 Volume (George McKittrick and Co., 1959).

coordinating, reporting, delegating). In organizations with more than 20 employees, only those personnel above the supervisory or foreman level were included. In organizations with 20 employees or less, only those at the level of manager or vice president and above were included. From the business executives, 287 satisfactorily completed interviews were secured, the completion rate being 96 percent.[8]

A natural scientist in business was defined as a person in a business organization who has had more than four years of college with a major or graduate degree in one of the natural sciences listed in Table 3-3, and no higher degree in any subject not on that list. Social scientists were defined in the same way, but in terms of the social sciences listed in Table 3-3; the definition for engineers required only a four-year degree in one of the listed engineering disciplines, and no higher degree in another subject.

The interviewers obtained satisfactory completed interviews from 85 natural scientists, 73 social scientists, and 90 engineers. In all three instances, the completion rate, calculated against the numbers of eligible respondents selected by the sampling system, was 95 percent or higher. Our intention had been to get nearer to 100 cases in each sample, but the eligible respondents in the sample organizations were not numerous enough or distributed in such a way as to make this possible without abandoning proper proportional sampling procedures.

Because of the definitions of the universe from which the business samples were drawn, it is virtually impossible to compare demographic characteristics of the samples with those of any known populations.

The Federal Populations

GENERAL FEDERAL EMPLOYEE SAMPLE. The initial sample of federal employees was made available to the Brookings Institution by the U. S. Civil Service Commission. It consisted of the names and installation addresses of 5,000 federal civilian employees in the continental United States drawn by a random sampling procedure from the St. Louis Central Registry.[9]

The names and installation addresses were identified with respect to the locations of the primary sampling units in the master sample. A sam-

[8] We are inclined to believe that random selection *within* the organizations may have been carried out somewhat less well for the business sample than for the high school, college, and special federal samples. The feeling stems from reading a large number of the interviews, but cannot be confirmed empirically.

[9] CIA and FBI employees were omitted from the list.

ple of 1,500 names located within 50 miles of the primary sampling units was drawn, and its percentage distribution according to departments and agencies was checked against the known percentages of federal employees in the departments and agencies. It was found that the 50-mile rule resulted in some imbalance; the Air Force especially showed substantial under-representation. The rule was altered (to 250 miles for Air Force installations) and a new sample of 1,427 names was drawn. It was found to be in balance except for about a 5 percent under-representation of postal employees due to the exclusion of a substantial number of very small, widely scattered postal installations. To correct this imbalance was not economically feasible for us.

The sample of 1,427 names was used as a base list for personally checking a subsample of 1,297 potential respondents at their places of employment or immediate headquarters of employment. Of these, 166 were ineligible (not employed 35 hours per week or more, or no longer employed at the installation), and 41 were unavailable (on leave or on field assignment). Of the remaining 1,090, contact was not made with 126 within the three visits to which interviewers were limited; 16 others refused to be interviewed. The result was 948 satisfactorily completed interviews, a completion rate of 88 percent.

Unfortunately, the 88 percent rate conceals a pattern of differential completion which compounded the under-representation of postal employees. Because we succeeded in almost all cases in obtaining permission for interviews to be conducted on site and during working hours, completion rates were highest among those employees whose jobs did not make them difficult to reach and who could take time from their work to be interviewed. Completion, therefore, was extremely high for classification act employees and very high for wage board employees, but there

TABLE 3-6. *Unweighted Sample of General Federal Employees Compared with U. S. Civil Service Commission Data on Type of Employment*

Type of Employment	Sample	CSC Data[a]
Classification Act	62%	46%
Wage Board	26	28
Postal	11	23
Other	2	3

[a] Figures from U. S. Civil Service Commission, Federal Employment Statistics Office, *Pay Structure of the Federal Civil Service: June 30, 1960* (1961), p. 14, Table 3.

TABLE 3-7. *Unweighted and Weighted Samples of General Federal Employees Compared with U. S. Civil Service Commission Data on Four Characteristics*

Characteristics	Unweighted Sample	Weighted Sample	CSC Data[a]
Sex			
Males	70%	75%	76%
Females	30	25	24
Departments			
Army	20	17	17
Navy	17	16	15
Air Force	12	11	13
Post Office	13	24	22
Agriculture	3	3	4
Health, Education, and Welfare	3	3	3
Treasury	6	4	3
Veterans' Administration	11	10	7
Other	15	12	16
Classification Act Grades Only			
1–5	44	44	48
6–11	41	41	37
12–18	15	15	14
Median Income	$5,500	$5,500[b]	$5,400

[a] Sex distribution figures from U. S. Bureau of the Census, *Statistical Abstract of the United States: 1961* (1961), p. 394, Table 520. Other figures drawn from U. S. Civil Service Commission, *Pay Structure of the Federal Civil Service, June 30, 1960* (1961): departmental data from p. 12, Table 5; classification act grades from p. 11, Table 4; and median income figures from p. 10, Table 3.

[b] The unrounded median figure was $5,451.

was a large loss among postal employees, particularly mail carriers. A major share of the 126 eligibles who could not be contacted were in the postal group. When we compared the distribution in our sample with the actual distribution, we obtained the results shown in Table 3-6. Consequently, machine replication was employed to bring the sample into the proper known balance according to this type of classification; the replicated sample was used in all tabulations. All general federal employee tables, however, show in the "number answering" column a figure based on the actual number of cases (948).

Except for the underweighting of postal employees, the original federal sample was similar to other known distributions of federal employees. The weighted sample, as one might expect, is in even closer accord (Table 3-7).

THE FEDERAL EXECUTIVE, NATURAL SCIENTIST, SOCIAL SCIENTIST, AND EN-
GINEER SAMPLES. Since there existed no accurate or complete lists of any
of these four federal populations for use in sampling, a two-stage procedure based on our general sample of federal employees was devised.
In the first stage, when interviewers called for the first time at an installation in connection with our general federal sample, they also asked the
personnel officer for the numbers of executives, natural scientists, social
scientists, and engineers in that installation—having provided him with
the definitions of the four populations. Reports on the numbers were sent
by the interviewers to our research headquarters, where they were consolidated for the total number of installations contacted in the general
federal sample. Using the consolidated figures as a base, a random systematic sample was applied at differential rates to designate the number
of executive, natural scientist, social scientist, and engineer interviews to
be obtained at a given installation. These assignments were then sent to
the interviewers.

In the second stage, the interviewer visited the installation and with the
aid of the personnel officer drew from the personnel files by a specified
random procedure the required number of names in each category. Careful screening was performed to insure that respondents fitted the category
definitions. A federal executive was defined as a GS-12 (or equivalent
based on salary), or above, whose duties were primarily administrative.
Definitions of federal natural scientists, social scientist, and engineers were
the same as those for the comparable groups in business.

The interviews were conducted in 205 federal installations, and were
satisfactorily completed for 273 executives, 92 natural scientists, 90 social
scientists, and 99 engineers. In all four instances, the completion rate
calculated against the number of respondents which were eligible within
the rules of the sampling system was over 95 percent.

We looked for other data that defined these four populations as we
defined them and would therefore be useful for comparison with our
samples; we discovered none.

Sampling Error

In evaluating the results of this survey, it should be borne in mind that
all figures are subject to sampling error. Because any given figure is
derived from a sample and not from the total population, it is an *estimate*
of the "true" figure, and sampling error in turn provides an estimate of

the range above and below the sample figure within which the true figure is likely to fall. The size of the error depends upon the sample figure being assessed, the distribution of the sample figures, the number of cases in the sample, the way in which the sample was drawn, and how sure one wants to be that the true figure falls within the estimated range. The same considerations apply to the difference between any two sample figures, with the exception that the characteristics of *both* samples must enter into the calculations.

Separate statistical evaluations of all the figures in this study, or even just separate rule of thumb tables for the nineteen samples individually and in their various possible combinations, would lead to almost endless complications and confusion. They also would tend to obscure the fact that in evaluating results one should consider not only sampling error, but also such matters as the nature of the question, the accuracy of the interviewing, the consistency of the coding, and the patterning of related results. Consequently, we offer here only some general guides for the evaluation of percentages, the differences between percentages, and the differences between means (scale scores). The figures are conservative and take into account the general characteristics of the sampling plan.

Table 3-8 gives figures useful in evaluating various percentages for samples approximating the sizes of those used in this study. For example, 37 percent of 301 college teachers sampled cited poor financial reward as a negative feature of their work. In Column 1 of the table the nearest figure to 37 percent is 40 percent in the next to the bottom row; the nearest sample size to 301 is the 250 figure heading Column 4. At the

TABLE 3-8. *Percentage Allowances at the 95 Percent Probability Level for Sampling Errors of Percentages for Various Sample Sizes*[a]

Percentages Near	Sample Size				
	1,000	500	250	100	50
5 or 95	2	2	3	5	7
10 or 90	2	3	5	6	9
15 or 85	3	4	5	8	11
20 or 80	3	4	6	8	12
30 or 70	3	5	6	10	13
40 or 60	4	5	7	10	14
50	4	5	7	10	15

[a] The chances are 95 in 100 that sampling errors are not larger than the figures shown.

intersection of the next to the last row and the fourth column, we find the figure 7. Thus, we may say that the chances are 95 in 100 that, had we interviewed all college teachers, the percentage of those citing financial reward would have been within 7 percent of the figure obtained—i.e., between 30 and 44 percent.

Table 3-9 is similarly useful in evaluating differences between percentages. For example, 39 percent of the general employed public (N = 1,113) as compared to 27 percent of high school teachers (N = 270) said they would be moving "up the ladder" if they went to work for the federal government. How much faith can we place in this 12 percent difference? To be conservative, we use the larger percentage as the criterion and use the section of the table headed "For percentages near 40 or 60." At the intersection of sample sizes 1,000 and 250 we find the figure 7. Thus we may say that the odds are 95 in 100 that had we inter-

TABLE 3-9. *Percentage Allowances at the 95 Percent Probability Level for Sampling Errors of Differences Between Percentages for Various Sample Sizes*[a]

Sample Size	Sample Size				
	1,000	500	250	100	50
For Percentages Near 10 or 90:					
1,000	3	4	5	7	9
500		4	6	7	9
250			6	8	10
100				9	11
50					13
For Percentages Near 20 or 80:					
1,000	4	5	6	9	12
500		6	7	9	12
250			8	10	13
100				12	14
50					16
For Percentages Near 40 or 60:					
1,000	5	6	7	11	15
500		7	8	11	15
250			9	12	16
100				14	17
50					20

[a] The chances are 95 in 100 that the sampling errors are not larger than the figures shown.

viewed all of the general employed public and all high school teachers, we would have found a difference of 12 percent, plus or minus 7 percent —i.e., a difference of at least 5 percent but not more than 19 percent.

For a number of questions results are presented, not as percentages, but as mean scale scores. Our primary interest is in evaluating the significance of the differences *between* scale scores. On the self-anchoring scale ratings of the present, five years ago, five years from now, working for the federal government (nonfederal populations), and working outside the federal government (federal populations), the rule of thumb for a significant difference at the 95 percent level is:

.5 where both N^s are 100 or more;
.7 where either N is less than 100.

The same figures apply to the scale ratings of federal civil service employees in general, people in the top-level jobs in the federal civil service, and people in the top-level jobs in private business on honesty, interest in serving the public, how well respected they are, ability, and drive to get ahead.

For all other scale scores (e.g., occupational value items, ratings of federal employment on various attributes, etc.) the rule of thumb for a significant difference at the 95 percent level is:

.7 where both N^s are 100 or more;
1.0 where either N is less than 100.

Treatment of the Data

Preparation of the Code

When more than a small number of questionnaires are used in a research project, it is impossible to analyze the results simply by examining the questionnaires. The information on them must be classified, tabulated, and manipulated, in order to extract its meaning. Therefore, once enough interviews to provide a good sample had been returned from the field and had been checked and edited for quality and completeness, work began at the Brookings Institution on the next phase in the research—the preparation of the code. The purpose of coding is simply to identify and assign numbers to the relevant, discrete items of information in the completed interviews. Our task was one of turning the questionnaire data into a number code so it could be punched on standard 80-column IBM cards for machine reading and manipulation.

The categorical questions presented few problems beyond the relatively simple ones of managing the coding procedure with care so that the rate of error was kept within an acceptable limit. A large percentage of these items had already been assigned code numbers, which were printed on the questionnaire. The 55-item scale sort is an example of material that could be coded in straightforward fashion. The interviewers had already recorded in the proper spaces in each questionnaire the numbers of the scale boxes into which the items had been sorted by the respondent. The numbers constituted the code and were simply punched directly into the appropriate assigned columns on an IBM card. The 30-item scale sort was handled in the same way. Similar coding considerations also applied to such categorical information as respondent's income, number of years of schooling, and the like.

The coding of the free-response questions presented an entirely different problem. Since open-end questioning permits the emergence of new information, many of the codes for such questions must emerge from the responses. But the responses alone do not dictate the categories. Instead, any given code must strike a balance between the hypotheses to be tested and the answers contained in the interviews. In some cases, the proper code may be dictated almost entirely by the nature of the hypotheses; in others, the content of the answer plays a dominant role. In all cases, however, the underlying nature of the code is a function of the hypotheses to be tested.

For example, the responses to the questions on occupational values could have been coded on the basis of the *number* of occupational values mentioned, without regard to their content, the *kinds of names* used to describe the values, for the *quality or nature* of the values, and so on. How to decide among these possibilities? If one of our hypotheses had been that "fullness of response to questions on occupational values is associated with level of education, age, and other factors," we would have constructed a code based on the length of response, or on the number of different occupational values mentioned, without regard to the qualitative nature of the responses. But the hypothesis was not a part of our study; thus such a code would have been irrelevant.

We had hypothesized, however, that the *kind* of occupational values mentioned in response to open-end questions would be differentially patterned according to occupation, age, education, and other factors. This meant that we had to construct a code based on the different *kinds* of values described by the respondents, the dimension for categorization thus being distinctions in their qualitative nature. But we could not completely know in advance the nature of the occupational values that would be mentioned by people as matters of concern. Therefore, we had to let the code emerge from an analysis of actual responses. The procedure used in deriving the code is recounted below.

First, we drew a sample of about 300 interviews for analysis, turning our attention to all the questions which were designed to elicit occupational values. In the questionnaire for the nonfederal employed populations, the eight items built around the self-anchoring scaling device were of this kind. (See Chapter 2.) Item 1, for instance, asked for the kinds of things about an occupation which would make it absolutely ideal for the individual, and Item 2 for the kinds of things about an occupation that would make it the worst or the least satisfying to the individual.

For coding purposes, the responses to each of the eight questions were broken down into individual statements which described a single occupational value. For example, one respondent had answered Item 1 as follows:

> Well, pleasant work, that is, not all kinds of noise and dirt. I want it to pay fairly well. There would have to be variation in work; not monotonous. I would want pleasant companions around me. A good place to eat at work would be important, as well as good working hours, and interesting work.

Each of the seven values mentioned in the statement was entered on a 3-by-5 inch card: 1) Pleasant work: that is, not all kinds of noise and dirt; 2) I want it to pay fairly well; 3) Variation in work, not monotonous; 4) I would want pleasant companions around me; 5) A good place to eat at work would be important; 6) Good working hours; 7) Interesting work.

From the eight occupational value questions on the 300 sample questionnaires, over 7,200 of these individual cards were prepared, each containing a statement about a discrete occupational value, using the same phrasing as in the recorded responses. The next step was to use the cards to prepare a set of categories and a set of coding instructions with concrete examples. Two people, both thoroughly acquainted with the aims of the study, independently sorted, combined, and recombined the cards to obtain a set of occupational value categories. Following this independent sorting and assignment, they compared and reviewed their results and resolved their differences in consultation with the third member of the study team.

The final result was a fifty-category code of occupational values, which made it possible to classify virtually all of the responses to the free-answer questions concerning occupational values according to the same set of categories and to identical criteria. The nature and variety of the values is illustrated in the listing that follows, which gives the summary headings of the thirty-seven mentioned most frequently.

Financial Reward—the amount of money an occupation provides

Financial Reward—qualified by an explicit statement that it is not of primary importance

Social Motives—considerations involving interpersonal relations:

Relations with supervisors

Passive personal relations—having co-workers and other people around one who are congenial

Active personal relations—having a chance to work or deal with other people in an active, positive sense as part of one's occupation

Doing Work That Is Worthwhile or Useful—without specifying the way in which it is worthwhile or useful

Doing Work That Is Worthwhile or Useful, in the Sense of Serving Others—without specifying the exact nature of the contribution to others that is to be made

Doing Work That Is Worthwhile or Useful to Others—in the sense of making others happy or giving them pleasure

Doing Work That Is Worthwhile or Useful to Others—in the sense of contributing to their training, or to their mental, social, or physical development

Doing Work That Provides a Sense of Achievement or Accomplishment—seeing the results of your own work

Obtaining Recognition from Others for One's Work

Doing Work of a Religious, Spiritual, or Ethical Nature

Doing Work That Is Interesting or Enjoyable—without specifying a particular type of work

Doing Work of a Specific Type That Is Interesting or Enjoyable

Having Adequate Time Off for Leisure or Recreation

Doing Work That Affords Security, Stability, or Fringe Benefits

Doing Work That Contributes to One's Self-Development—doing work through which one can develop one's own capacities, talents, or knowledge

Doing Work That Calls for Self-Expression and Creativity—doing something original, to which one personally makes a unique contribution

Having Freedom from Restrictions Affecting One's Work—having control over the work which one does or over the way in which one does it

Avoiding Work Where There Is Excessive Pressure or Tension

Avoiding an Excessive Work Load—having too much to do

Doing Work That Is Challenging—overcoming obstacles, keeping goals ahead

Having Work with Responsibility and Authority—the power to make decisions

Avoiding Work with Responsibility and Authority—avoiding the necessity to make decisions

Doing Work That Has Prestige

Doing Work That Provides Opportunities for Self-Advancement and Progress

Doing Work That Fits One's Capacities or Training

Having the Equipment, Facilities, or Wherewithal To Do the Job

Avoiding Work That Is Too Hard

Having Good General Working Conditions—including a satisfactory physical environment in which to work

Working in a Desirable Location

Doing Work That Is Routine and Ordered

Doing Work That Is Varied and Not Routine

Doing Work That Provides Opportunities for Travel

Doing Mental Work

Avoiding Physical or Manual Work

Doing Physical or Manual Work

We knew, of course, that a fifty-category code was too lengthy and too complex for use in many parts of the final tabulation and analysis. We also knew that for the most part the values would have to be further clustered into a smaller number of categories which would be more inclusive and less specific, but we did not want to decide a priori what the clusterings should be. First we wanted to code in a highly fractionated manner, then let the decision as to further clustering be based upon initial tabulations of a very large number of questionnaires.

A highly fractionated code would also be more "universal," in that there would be a logical category for any occupational value mentioned in response to any kind of open-end question about occupational values. Only with a code of this kind could we make proper comparisons among the responses to different questions. For example, the code we derived permitted the direct comparison of the occupational values which respondents associate with the the image of the federal government as an employer with the occupational values they regard as ideal. If we had used different code categories for the two questions, and thus different criteria for assigning responses to categories, the value of the comparison would have been severely limited.

The next step was to create the coding instructions.[10] This involved setting down in words the nature and content of each category, along with concrete examples drawn from the questionnaires, so that a trained coder would be able to classify any response in the intended way. It was recognized that a certain amount of slippage from one category to another is inevitable, but every effort was made to provide instructions that would be so clear and unambiguous as to reduce slippage to a small percentage of the total.

The same over-all procedure was followed in creating the codes for all the other open-end questions where the nature of the code was not completely dictated by the nature of the hypotheses. In the entire operation, over 14,000 cards were prepared, sorted, and classified as a means of preparing the code and the instructions. The result was a coding instruction booklet of more than 200 pages, the major portion of it devoted to the open-end question codes.

Examples of Open-End Question Codes

The qualitative content of the instructions can be illustrated by a quotation from the occupational values section of the coding booklet, dealing with (1) three categories of economic values; (2) four categories of social motives; (3) a motive to which we applied the term "self-determination."

   1. ECONOMIC
      a. Financial reward—not further qualified

      Explanation: Responses in this category constitute a clear statement, made without signficant qualification, that the amount of money earned by an occupation is important to the respondent. There is no statement to indicate that money is seen as a means to some other end, nor that money is seen as being of secondary importance to other goals. It is seen as an important aspect of the "ideal occupation," standing in its own right.

      Illustrative examples contained in completed questionnaires:

      "I like (the challenge) and the money, too, of course."

      "If you mean about money—do you?—well, in sales, the sky's the limit."

[10] Both the creation of the codes and the preparation of the coding instructions were done by the Brookings Institution. However, much invaluable help and advice were given by Mrs. Genevieve Timm, of National Analysts, Inc.

"Be in a competitive industry where the financial rewards are significant."
"Good money."

b. Financial reward—qualified as to use for which desired

Explanation: In responses in this category, money is instrumental; it is a means to some other end explicitly stated by the respondent. Typically, the interviewee says that an occupation should yield "enough money for" something, should make him "financially independent for" something, or should provide money that is "adequate for" something.

Illustrative examples contained in completed questionnaires:
"A job by which I'd be financially independent so I could pursue these other things."
"Something that would give me a good living and enough to take care of my old age."
"Of course, I'd like the salary to be sufficient to support a family."

c. Financial reward—money qualified as to the extent of its importance

Explanation: The importance of money is qualified quite explicitly by statement or by context. It may be seen as being secondary, or not of prime importance. Alternatively, the respondent may say that he wants an income that is *just* adequate to provide a living so that he can pursue other goals that are more important to him.

Illustrative examples contained in completed questionnaires:
"There is the question of salary but that should not be the primary consideration."
"Would want a good salary (but personal satisfaction and enjoyment of my work would be first)."
"You have to eat so there is salary—but it is secondary."

2. SOCIAL MOTIVE—CONSIDERATIONS INVOLVING INTERPERSONAL RELATIONS
   a. Relations with supervisors

Explanation: Any statements referring to the importance of the respondent's supervisor fall in this category. The relationship between the respondent and his supervisor may be either passive or active. That is, the respondent may want a supervisor who is congenial or nice to him; on the other hand, the respondent may value an active relationship with his superior. He may in the latter case, for example, like to "be able to talk with his boss easily."

Illustrative examples contained in completed questionnaires:
"I mean by working conditions, conditions where the men you worked under (and with) were easy to get along with and did their share of the work."
"Who you have to work under."
"I like to be able to talk to my superiors."

b. Passive personal relations

Explanation: Statements in this category refer to relations between the respondent and other people (supervisors excepted) which are of a passive nature. Typically the respondent speaks of "getting along with" the people with whom he works, or of "being with nice people." He does *not* speak of working with or having the chance to meet people, which implies a more active approach to interpersonal relations.

Illustrative examples contained in completed questionnaires:

"With pleasant and agreeable people."

"The environment—I like people who don't look down on others."

"Of course, I'd want to like the fellow workers—not have petty troubles bother me."

c. Active personal relations

Explanations: Statements in this category refer to relations between the respondent and other people (supervisors excepted) which are of an active nature. Typically the respondent speaks of "dealing with" people, or of participating with other people in an active, positive sense.

Illustrative examples contained in completed questionnaires:

"I would like to work with young people."

". . . have good contacts with people you'd like to associate with—people who are fundamentally nice, not necessarily by income but by personality." (Note that here the respondent stresses the desirability of having *contacts with* other people.)

"Preferably people who like to talk about ideas either with connection to the job, coffee break, or whatever." (Here a strong interest in sharing common interests with other people is implied.)

"To work with people (so that I could help to make them happy)."

3. SELF-DETERMINATION—FREEDOM FROM RESTRICTIONS AFFECTING ONE'S WORK

Explanation: In statements that fall into this category, the respondent emphasizes the importance of having control over the work which he does or over the way in which he does it. Frequently the respondent speaks of having freedom to determine what he works on, and when and how he works on it.

Illustrative examples contained in completed questionnaires:

"I would like to be my own master—not a 'Yes man,' "

"I'd say the prime element is a certain amount of independence. [How do you mean this?] I mean no heavy supervision. I like to set my own pace."

"Freedom of thought."

"Academic freedom."

Coding

The coding operation, that is, the reading of the responses and the assignment of code numbers to the responses, was carried out jointly by National Analysts, Inc., and the Brookings Institution. The contractor utilized six coders and one full-time supervisor, and the Brookings Institution employed ten coders and two full-time supervisors. All coders were at the college or graduate-student level, were employed full time, and were paid by the hour.

The coding staff was divided into teams, each team specializing in a particular set of questions. A 96 percent check of all coding was carried out.[11] A large proportion of the work of each organization was checked by the other organization. In all cases the checking operation was performed by a different coder than the one who had performed the original coding. On the average, each questionnaire took two hours to code and one hour and twenty minutes to check. Thus the entire operation, not counting approximately 1,000 hours of initial training time and approximately 1,000 hours of pilot testing of the codes, took about 16,000 hours to complete.

The important question arises—"How accurate was the coding?" Unfortunately, this cannot be answered with a single set of statistics, because two different considerations are involved. In the case of the categorical questions, which require no judgment in assigning a code number, one can check the accuracy of the operation against an objective standard quite easily. Errors of this kind were kept well below 1 percent.

In the case of the open-end responses, both interpretation and judgment are involved and there is no objective standard with which to compare the results in order to get an absolute measure of error. The appropriate measure for evaluating such coding, therefore, is the amount of agreement between two sets of coders who have each performed the entire coding and checking operation independently. Independent tests of intercoder agreement were performed on two samples of questionnaires for all of the open-end coding. In Table 3-10 the question-by-question results are given in the form of percentages of agreement, when disagreement is defined as the assignment of a response to a different classifica-

[11] Not 100 percent, because in a few instances random spot checks showed that the error rate was so near zero as to make complete checking unnecessary.

TABLE 3-10. *Intercoder Agreement on Two Independent Codings of the Open-End Questions in Two Samples of Questionnaires*[a]

Question Number[b]	Sample I		Sample II	
	Number of Coded Responses	Percentage of Agreement	Number of Coded Responses	Percentage of Agreement
1	137	100%	149	96%
2	111	99	104	95
6 and 9	28	89	57	82
7 and 8	39	100	91	93
11	42	95	62	87
12	57	88	63	87
15	20	90	47	92
16	18	94	42	90
19	48	95	68	96
20	72	97	87	100
21	107	89	110	86
22	92	97	115	95
23	60	100	65	92
25	108	89	134	91
28	105	87	93	87
29	62	92	84	93
30	150	89	150	95
31	69	94	69	100
32	78	94	99	98
33	132	92	127	98
	1,535	93%	1,807	93%

[a] Each sample contained twenty-five questionnaires.
[b] Sample II contained questionnaires used in interviewing federal employees. Sample I contained nonfederal questionnaires. In some instances, an identical question had a different number in the federal questionnaire than in the nonfederal questionnaires. The question numbers listed in this column identify the questions by the number given them in the nonfederal questionnaire used for interviewing adults.

tion or category by two different coders. For each question, the percentage base is the total number of coded responses to that question.

The average of 93 percent agreement for all of the codes combined is excellent. One may note, however, that the agreement varies widely from question to question, in one instance dropping as low as 82 percent, in other instances rising as high as 100 percent. This variation is accounted for primarily by the differences among the questions in terms of the precision with which the coding categories could be described and differentiated. In the case of those few questions where the agreement was below 90 percent, the distribution of disagreements was widely scattered among the categories and could not be expected to make a major difference in the relative proportions of responses found in each category. Nevertheless, in analyzing and interpreting the tabulated results, it is important to keep in mind that not all questions can be relied upon to the same degree. We have tried to exercise proper caution in our analysis.

Punching and Tabulating

Once the coding operation was completed, the coded responses to all of the questions were punched onto standard 80-column IBM cards.[12] A complete verification of all key punching was performed. Each questionnaire required 8 IBM cards to record all the information; hence a total of approximately 40,000 cards was used.

Tabulation was done on an IBM 101. As a beginning step, question-by-question tabulations of responses were performed on all the questions for each sample population separately. They showed, as was expected, that many of the free-response code categories were mentioned too infrequently to permit analysis by smaller subgroups (e.g., age, income, etc.), even if the analysis were confined to the two large general samples (non-federal-employed public and federal employees). Consequently, some of the codes were combined into more inclusive categories, and others which could not logically be combined were eliminated from further tabulation.

Following this, numerous further tabulations were performed, to permit analysis and comparison of the patterns of responses in a considerable number of subdivisions of the sample populations (e.g., by age, patterns of occupational values, attitudes toward federal civil servants, educational levels, geographic regions, occupations, income levels, etc.). Since the number of subgroup tabulations that are *possible* in a study of this kind is almost astronomical, judgment and restraint had to be exercised to avoid a deluge of data, most of it of little or no value. In general, cross tabulations were performed only when they offered a chance of providing enough cases in the various subcategories to make analysis statistically feasible, and when at the same time they had a clear bearing on significant hypotheses. Consequently, we made only about twenty sets of subgroup tabulations for each of the two large samples, and two or three

[12] The punching and machine tabulating were performed under contract by National Analysts, Inc.

additional sets of subbreaks for each of the smaller samples. Even so, the result was approximately 5,000 complex tables.

These tables were examined for analytic value; then they were abstracted, summarized, and finally reduced to the minimum amount of material that we believed was needed to reveal the significant results with force and clarity. In the pages of Parts Two and Three the basic data of this material are presented in tabular form and the major findings are described.

PART TWO

4

Occupational Satisfaction and
the Appeal of Federal Employment

THIS CHAPTER IS CONCERNED with the over-all evaluations people make of their occupational situations and with their judgments of the appeal of federal employment. The results of these two sets of global assessments provide a framework helpful in evaluating and analyzing the balance of the study. They also set the stage for subsequent chapters that explore in considerable detail why people feel as they do about their present employment and why they rate the appeal of federal employment as they do.

Occupational Satisfaction

Our attention turns first to the general measures of occupational satisfaction, sense of progress, and expectation—measures which are derived from the judgments respondents made on the ten-point self-anchoring scale, as described in Chapter 2. The three scale questions, the results of which are shown in Table 4-1 (see pages 60 and 61), are reviewed briefly here. After respondents were asked to describe both the things about an occupation that would make it absolutely ideal for them and the things that would make it the worst or least satisfying, the ten-point self-anchoring scale was used to obtain three different sorts of occupational ratings in answer to the following questions:

Question 1: "Where on this ladder would you put your present occupation, that is, what you are doing now?" The means of the ratings given by the respondents in the various nonfederal and federal groups are shown in Column 3 of Table 4-1. Since the three student groups had no present occupation to rate they were asked instead where they expected to start out occupationally; the resulting mean figures are shown in the "present occupation" column of the table.

Question 2: "Now think of what you were doing five years ago. Where on this ladder would you put what you were doing as an occupation five years ago?" Mean scale ratings given by the various groups are shown in Column 2 of the table. The question was not asked of the student groups.

Question 3: "Thinking now of your occupational future. Where on the ladder do you expect to be five years from now?" The mean scale ratings given in response to this question are shown in Column 4 of the table.

An additional score was derived to obtain some rough measure of the average amount of occupational progress experienced over the past five years. For each group the "five years ago" score was subtracted from the "present occupation" score; the resulting mean difference scores are shown in Column 5. Difference scores were then derived to indicate expectations for the future. In each group the average rating given to "present occupation" was subtracted from the average rating of "five years from now"; the resulting scores are shown in Column 6.

A certain amount of care should be exercised in interpreting the difference scores, as they suffer from a methodological limitation. The higher a person rates his present occupation, the less room is left above it on the scale for rating "five years ago" and "five years from now" and the more latitude there is for rating both of these below it, and vice versa. The problem here, however, is mainly confined to the difference between "present occupation" and "five years from now," because most respondents used the upper half of the scale for all three ratings and tended to rate "five years from now" above "present occupation," and "five years ago" below it.

On the average, the general nature of the findings indicate, for all of the federal and nonfederal groups studied, a high level of occupational satisfaction, a sense of having progressed occupationally, and a strong positive expectation for the future. These indications have several important implications for the research as a whole.

It is clear, for example, that most of the respondents answered the questions in a frame of mind that was the reverse of occupational unhappiness, disillusionment, and negative expectation. Our results also suggest that when people are considering a change in employment they are apt to think of the positive appeal of a new job far more than of escape from the old one. In addition, it appears that basic occupational values are being satisfied to a considerable degree, and therefore the range of occupational values with which people can concern themselves is greatly broadened. The findings further suggest that the average nonfederal employee, when asked to appraise federal employment, and the average federal employee, when asked to appraise nonfederal employment, are both likely to judge on the basis not only of how each perceives his *present* occupational standing, but also of a marked sense of occupational progress in the past and a strong positive expectation for the future. Finally, the findings pose major subsidiary questions about the nature of the occupational values and perceptions which give rise to the pattern obtained.

Another general finding of importance concerns the federal employee populations. On the whole these groups show fairly high occupational satisfaction, sense of progress, and expectation for the future, but the patterning by educational and occupational level is significantly different from that found among respondents outside the government. In the general employed public all three basic scale ratings show marked positive correlation with educational level. Among general federal employees there is scarcely any relationship at all. For the lower educational groups in federal employment, the three ratings are equal to or slightly higher than those of their counterparts outside the federal government. However, a similar comparison at the higher educational and occupational levels indicates that upper-level federal employees tend to give ratings that are somewhat lower in all three respects than those of their counterparts outside government—and little, if any, higher than those of federal employees at the lower educational levels. These facts place an explanatory burden on the results presented in subsequent chapters.

Discussion of Specific Group Data

GENERAL EMPLOYED PUBLIC. In examining the data of Table 4-1 for the general employed public, one is struck first of all by the steplike progression in scale scores from "five years ago" to "present occupation" to "five years from now" (6.4, 7.1, and 8.1). On the average, people feel they have progressed occupationally over the past five years to a fairly high present level, and expect as much or more progress during the next five years.

(Text continued on page 62)

Table 4-1

The mean ratings shown on this table were derived from the use of the self-anchoring occupational value scale. After a respondent had described what would be the characteristics of the ideal occupation and of the worst from his point of view, he was told that his descriptions formed the top and bottom of a ten-point ladder scale, shown to him on a separate card. He was then asked where on the scale he would put his present occupation, he would put what he was doing five years ago, and where he expected to be occupationally five years from now. Students were asked where on the scale they expected to start out occupationally and where they expected to be five years later.

Highlights: Ratings of occupation at present, 5 years ago, and 5 years from now.

. . . . All employed populations show high occupational satisfaction (all "present occupation" ratings are in the upper third of the ten-point scale); marked sense of past progress (all "present occupation" ratings significantly exceed "5 years ago" ratings); and positive expectation for the future (all "5 years from now" ratings are high and significantly exceed "present occupation" ratings.)

. . . . In the general employed public, both sense of progress ("present" minus "5 years ago") and expected amount of progress ("5 years from now" minus "present") are positively related to level of education; this is not the case with general federal employees.

. . . . Students ratings of where they expect to start occupationally ("present occupation" column) are relatively low, and positively related to educational level. Their expected amounts of progress ("5 years from now" minus "present") are higher than any other group, and inversely related to their present educational level, mainly due to their relatively low ratings of where they expect to start.

. . . . Groups employed in education, especially those in colleges, give the highest ratings on present occupation, 5 years ago, and 5 years hence.

. . . . On none of the measures do general federal employees differ significantly from the general employed public, but (1) college-educated federal employees rate their present occupations and "5 years from now" lower than do their counterparts in the general employed public and (2) federal employees who have not completed high school rate "5 years from now" markedly higher than their counterparts in the general employed public.

. . . . Federal executives and business executives yield almost identical ratings on all measures.

. . . . Natural scientists, social scientists, and engineers in federal employment rate their present occupations somewhat lower than do those in industry, and markedly lower than do those in colleges; the same tendency appears in the "5 years from now" ratings, being most marked for engineers.

Table 4-1

espondents' ratings of where, occupationally, they are now, were 5 years ago, and
xpect to be 5 years hence. Average (mean) ratings on the 10-point self-anchoring,
Ideal occupation" scale; the higher the score, the nearer to "ideal."

	Average number answering	5 years ago	Present occupation	5 years from now	Difference: "present" minus "5 years ago"	Difference: "5 years from now" minus "present"
Nonfederal Populations						
General employed public	1063	6.4	7.1	8.1	+0.7	+1.0
By sex						
Men	837	6.3	7.1	8.0	+0.8	+0.9
Women	226	6.8	7.4	8.3	+0.6	+0.9
By educational level[a]						
High school not completed	308	6.4	7.0	7.4	+0.6	+0.4
High school completed	478	6.2	6.9	8.1	+0.7	+1.2
Some college	120	6.5	7.4	8.5	+0.9	+1.1
College graduate	129	6.9	8.0	8.9	+1.1	+0.9
Students						
High school students	358	(Does	5.5	8.0	(Does	+2.5
College seniors	404	not	6.3	8.2	not	+1.9
Graduate students	381	apply)	6.8	8.4	apply)	+1.6
Groups in education						
High school teachers	259	7.4	8.4	9.0	+1.0	+0.6
Vocational counselors	76	7.5	8.4	9.1	+0.9	+0.7
College teachers	448	7.7	8.7	9.2	+1.0	+0.5
Natural scientists	115	7.7	8.8	9.3	+1.1	+0.5
Social scientists	101	7.2	8.3	8.9	+1.1	+0.6
Engineers	81	7.5	8.4	9.1	+0.9	+0.7
Groups in business						
Executives	270	6.8	8.1	8.9	+1.3	+0.8
Natural scientists	82	7.0	8.0	8.9	+1.0	+0.9
Social scientists	72	6.2	8.0	9.1	+1.8	+1.1
Engineers	86	6.9	8.1	9.0	+1.2	+0.9
Federal Employee Populations						
General federal employees	896	6.1	7.0	8.1	+0.9	+1.1
By sex						
Men	633	6.0	6.9	8.0	+0.9	+1.1
Women	263	6.4	7.1	8.3	+0.7	+1.2
By educational level						
High school not completed	181	6.1	6.9	8.0	+0.8	+1.1
High school completed	339	5.9	6.8	7.9	+0.9	+1.1
Some college	172	6.1	6.8	8.1	+0.7	+1.3
College graduate	152	6.7	7.4	8.4	+0.7	+1.0
Executives	262	7.0	8.0	8.9	+1.0	+0.9
Natural scientists	85	6.5	7.9	8.7	+1.4	+0.8
Social scientists	85	6.5	7.7	8.8	+1.2	+1.1
Engineers	89	6.4	7.6	8.4	+1.2	+0.8

[a]Here and in subsequent tables the number of respondents by educational level is less
than the number for the general population as a whole, because a small percentage of respondents could not be safely fitted into any of the four levels.

61

There are differences, however, by sex and by educational level. Women rate themselves slightly higher than do men on all three measures. In addition, all three show a positive relationship with educational level. For the rating of "five years ago" the differences are not great: the lower three educational groups give scores of 6.4, 6.2, and 6.5; the score for college graduates is 6.9. Concerning "present occupation" the differences are somewhat greater: for the two lower groups the scores are 7.0 and 6.9; for the two upper the ratings rise to 7.4 and 8.0. The scores for "five years from now" show the strongest positive relationship with educational level: they climb sharply and progressively, moving up from 7.4, to 8.1, to 8.5, and finally, for college graduates, to 8.9.

Sense of progress over the past five years also shows a positive relationship with educational level. Respondents who have not completed high school rate their present occupation 0.6 ahead of what they were doing five years ago; college graduates yield a difference score of 1.1. Expectation for the future shows a somewhat different pattern: the high difference scores of 1.2, 1.1, and 0.9 for the high school completed, some college, and college graduate levels respectively, are in sharp contrast to the score of only 0.4 for the less than high school completed group.[1] Thus it would appear that those who are in the least-educated group in the general employed public, in comparison with people of more education, have less optimism about their occupational future, both in absolute terms and relative to where they feel they are now occupationally.

HIGH SCHOOL STUDENTS, COLLEGE SENIORS, AND GRADUATE STUDENTS. As mentioned earlier, the figures for students shown in Table 4-1 are incomplete, and not entirely comparable to those shown for other groups. The student groups were not asked to rate either where they were occupationally five years ago or their present occupations; the figures under "present occupation" are the ratings of where they expect to start out.

All three groups are relatively modest in their estimates of their occupational starts. The figures are lower than the ratings of "present occupation" given by any other group, nonfederal or federal: 5.5 for the high school students, 6.3 for college seniors, and 6.8 for graduate students. However, each group is far from pessimistic about where it expects to be

[1] The lack of positive correlation between educational level and the "five years from now" minus "present occupation" scores at the three upper educational levels may be due in large part to the methodological limitation previously described. In these three groups, ratings of "present occupation" move progressively upward from 6.9 to 8.0, thus progressively reducing the amount of possible positive difference when subtracting "present occupation" from "five years from now."

five years later, and there is little difference by present educational level; the 8.0 figure for high school students is only slightly below the 8.2 and 8.4 figures for college seniors and graduate students. Thus, on the average, high school students expect to move ahead 2.5 scale points during the five-year period after they begin their occupation; college seniors and graduate students yield difference scores of 1.9 and 1.6.[2]

HIGH SCHOOL TEACHERS AND VOCATIONAL COUNSELORS. The mean scores of these two groups on any of the measures shown in Table 4-1 are virtually identical; any differences are insignificant. The ratings are slightly higher than those of college graduates in the general employed public on all three basic measures but not as high as the college teachers' scores. In comparison with the business groups the high school groups rate themselves slightly higher on "present occupation" as well as "five years ago," and roughly the same on "five years from now." They show the same strong sense of occupational progress and optimism characteristic of all groups studied—evidenced by the upward movement of their mean scores for "five years ago," "present occupation," and "five years from now" from about 7.5, to 8.4, to about 9.0.

COLLEGE TEACHERS, NATURAL AND SOCIAL SCIENTISTS, AND ENGINEERS. Considering college teachers in general first, we note that they are very high in their ratings on where they were five years ago, their present occupation, and where they expect to be five years from now. Their scores of 7.7, 8.7, and 9.2 are higher than those of any other group, federal or nonfederal, with the single exception of college natural scientists, whose scores are the highest of all—7.7, 8.8, and 9.3. And on all three measures the ratings of this group of natural scientists are higher than those of their counterparts either in business (7.0, 8.0, 8.9) or in government (6.5, 7.9, 8.7).

College social scientists yield scores which are somewhat lower than those of their natural scientist colleagues. However, compared to their counterparts in business and government, they too show higher scores on where they were five years ago and where they are now, and roughly equal scores on their expectations for five years from now. The absolute figures for college engineers are quite similar to those for the social scientists; however, the favorable differences they show in comparison to their counterparts in business and government are even more marked. Their ratings (7.5, 8.4, 9.1) are higher than business engineer ratings

[2] See footnote 1.

(6.9, 8.1, 9.0), and much higher than the ratings given by government engineers (6.4, 7.6, 8.4).

GROUPS IN BUSINESS. The business executives, natural and social scientists, and engineers are remarkable in the similarity of their ratings for their occupational past, present, and future. Scores on nearly all the measures are virtually identical for all four groups; however, the social scientists rate their situation of five years ago substantially lower than do the other three groups. In general, the business scores almost perfectly parallel the ratings given by college graduates in the general employed public, and are substantially lower than those given by college faculty members. The ratings given by natural scientists, social scientists, and engineers in business are, on the average, somewhat higher than those given by their government counterparts. Business executive and federal executive scores are approximately the same.

GENERAL FEDERAL EMPLOYEES. The over-all scores for general federal employees and for the general employed public are almost exactly alike: "five years ago" ratings are 6.1 (federal) and 6.4; "present occupation" ratings are 7.0 and 7.1; and the "five years from now" figures are identical at 8.1. Breakdowns by sex in the general federal and nonfederal populations show a similar parallel, with women giving slightly higher scores in both instances. However, the similarity between the two general populations disappears when we compare the patterns by educational levels, especially on the ratings given to "present occupation" and to "five years from now."

First let us examine the figures according to educational level on "present occupation." As noted earlier, people in the general employed public with some college and especially college graduates rate their present occupations substantially higher than do people at the two lower educational levels. Among general federal employees only the college graduates show a rise in mean score. The scores, moving up the four educational levels, are 6.9, 6.8, 6.8, and 7.4, compared to 7.0, 6.9, 7.4, and 8.0 in the general employed public. Thus, federal employees with some college experience rate their present occupation no higher than do their less-educated colleagues. The general federal employees at the two lower educational levels rate their present occupations as high as their counterparts in the general employed public do; federal employees at the some college and college graduate levels rate their present occupations over one half a scale point lower than their counterparts outside the government.

The comparative results are even more extreme in the case of the mean scale ratings for "five years from now." In the general employed public there is a sharply graduated rise in scores from 7.4 at the less than high school completed level to 8.1, 8.5, and 8.9 at the high school completed, some college, and college graduate levels. Comparable figures for general federal employees are 8.0, 7.9, 8.1, and 8.4. Thus federal employees with less than a high school education rate where they expect to be five years from now 0.6 *higher* than do their counterparts in the general employed public; college graduates in the federal government give a rating for "five years from now" which is 0.5 *below* the rating given by college graduates in the general employed public.

In sum, federal employees at the two lower educational levels yield scores equal to or above those given by people of comparable educational level in the general employed public on occupational past, present, and future. However, only federal employees at the college graduate level show ratings appreciably higher than those given by their less-educated fellow employees in the government, and both the some college and college graduate groups show ratings of occupational past, present, and future that are markedly lower than those of their counterparts in the general employed public.

FEDERAL EXECUTIVES, NATURAL AND SOCIAL SCIENTISTS, AND ENGINEERS. Compared with the college graduate group among general federal employees, the four special federal populations rate themselves roughly the same on "five years ago," but significantly higher on where they are now occupationally and where they expect to be five years from now. The executives show the greatest favorable difference on both of these latter scores in comparison to federal college graduates in general; engineers show the least difference; and the natural and social scientists have very similar scores, which fall between those of the two other groups. We mentioned earlier that the scores of federal executives and business executives parallel one another very closely on all three measures. It should also be noted that the federal executive population yields the highest scale scores on past, present, and future of any of the federal populations—7.0, 8.0, and 8.9.

The scores of federal natural scientists roughly parallel those of natural scientists in business, but are markedly lower than those of natural scientists in colleges, as pointed out earlier. The situation is quite similar for the social scientists; that is, their scores are roughly the same as those of the business group and lower than those of the college group.

In the case of engineers, however, we have the consistent pattern of ratings that are lower than those given by engineers in *both* business and colleges. On the average, the federal engineers on all three measures yield scores which are lower than those of the three other special federal groups; lower than those of business engineers; and markedly lower than those of college engineers. However, their scores are roughly equal to those given by college graduates in the general sample of federal employees.

The Appeal of Federal Employment

One of the central purposes of this research is assessment of the appeal of federal employment to the various groups studied. Therefore, believing it unwise to rely on a single measure, we obtained a variety of measures, by which we could check the consistency of the results. The figures thus derived are shown in Tables 4-2 to 4-4 (pages 70-75). Even a cursory examination reveals that the *pattern* of results is highly consistent from measure to measure. Consequently, statements can be made with a great deal of confidence about the relative appeal of federal employment to one population group compared to another. But statements about the absolute appeal of federal employment cannot be made with the same degree of surety.

For example, consider the results nonfederal employees give (Table 4-2) on the self-anchoring occupational value scale when they are asked, "Suppose your work or occupation stayed the same but you worked for the federal government—that is, the United States government—how much better or worse would that be? Show me on the ladder, please."[3] For the general employed public, the table shows that, on the average, doing the same work for the federal government is rated about one half a scale point below the rating given to present occupation. Thus one might conclude that in absolute terms the over-all reaction to going to work for the federal government is negative.

On the other hand, Table 4-3, which involves a direct question approach rather than a scale rating, would lead to a slightly different conclusion. Respondents were simply asked, "Suppose you were to change

---

[3] Federal employees were asked, "Suppose your work or occupation stayed the same but you no longer worked for the U.S. government—that is, suppose you continued in your present occupation, but went to work outside the federal government—how much better or worse would that be? Show me on the ladder, please."

now and go to work for the federal government, doing the same thing you are doing now, how do you think your family might feel about it? Would they feel you were moving up the ladder or down?" Replies were recorded as "up," "down," and "no difference." In the general employed public 39 percent say "up the ladder," 21 percent "down," and 38 percent "no difference"—figures which suggest that, on the average, the idea of going to work for the government has a slight positive appeal. One can rationalize the slight difference between the two results by saying that the 21 percent who answer "down the ladder" probably feel much more strongly about it than the 39 percent who say "up the ladder," and that this intensity variation is reflected in the scale measures in Table 4-2. It is, however, equally probable that the difference is due to the difference in form of the questions and to the categorical question's introduction of the family factor.

Table 4-4 is derived from still another approach to the assessment of the appeal of federal employment, one that is also more useful in assessing comparative, rather than absolute, appeal. Among the fifty-five statements printed on individual cards and sorted by respondents onto the ten-point agree-disagree scale was the item, "All things considered, working for the federal government appeals to me." The mean scale scores assigned to this by each of the groups are recorded in Column 3 of the table. To permit group-by-group comparisons of the appeal of working for the government vs. working for a large private business, Column 2 records the mean scale scores of each group for the item, "All things considered, working for a large private business appeals to me." Column 4 shows the difference scores obtained by subtracting the latter mean scores from the former.

Table 4-4 also illustrates the problem of determining in any absolute sense the appeal of federal employment. We find that the general employed public's mean score for the statement concerning the appeal of federal employment is 5.3. Because the score is slightly above the middle of the ten-point scale, we might conclude that the rating is a little bit on the favorable side—a conclusion which accords with the results of Table 4-2. On the other hand, we still have no strong assurance that a score of 5 is actually the psychological dividing line between favorable and unfavorable judgments, even though it seems reasonable and there is some supporting evidence.[4] The difficulty of making judgments is further com-

[4] Jan Stapel, *Scales Without Tears* (International Institute of Public Opinion, Amsterdam, February 1953; mimeographed).

pounded by the fact that the question in most instances unavoidably suggests a change in employer and a slight negative reaction to the idea of change per se tends therefore to intrude upon all the measurements.

Nevertheless, while such considerations introduce a note of caution about making absolute judgments, they do not invalidate judgments concerning the relative appeal in one group as compared to another. Here we are on firm ground, because all the measures show the same general pattern.

In general, in the nonfederal populations the appeal of federal employment is negatively related to educational level, is higher for women than for men, and is especially low among groups in business. Among federal employees the appeal of nonfederal employment, both absolutely and in comparison to their own employment, increases with rising education; the appeal of federal employment is about the same at all educational levels, and is higher for women than for men. However, all groups of federal employees rate the appeal of large private business employment far lower than that of federal employment.

These are generalizations, of course. The important variations found in the groups studied are shown in Tables 4-2, 4-3, and 4-4, and discussed in the following group-by-group description of the findings.

Discussion of Specific Group Data

GENERAL EMPLOYED PUBLIC. When people in this group are asked to scale the appeal of federal employment in relation to their present employment the result is slightly negative (Table 4-2), but this may be mainly a reaction to the idea of change. When they are asked how their families would feel about it (Table 4-3), the results are slightly on the positive side. When the ratings of the appeal of large private business are compared to those of the appeal of federal employment (Table 4-4), the result is a slightly higher rating for business. One might generalize —but with caution—that in the general employed public as a whole the appeal of federal employment is slightly on the positive side, but below the appeal of present occupation and of large private business. The differences are, however, not great.

All three of the tables show that the appeal of federal employment is greater for women than it is for men. In Table 4-2 women give federal employment the same rating as their present occupation; men rate it 0.8 of a scale point lower on the average. In Table 4-3, 47 percent of the women say that their families would feel that they were going up the ladder if they went to work for the federal government, and only 12 percent say that they would be thought to go down the ladder; figures for men are 37 and 24 percent. Table 4-4 shows the same pattern. Men rate the appeal of federal employment at 5.2; women rate it at 6.0.

Of very great significance is the patterning of the figures by educational level for the general employed public—a strong negative relationship between the appeal of federal employment and educational level. Table 4-2 shows that, on the average, those who did not complete high school rate federal employment 0.1 of a scale point higher than their present occupation, those who completed high school rate it 0.4 lower, and those with some college and college graduates rate it 1.7 scale points lower.

A similar shift is shown in the percentage distributions in Table 4-3. In the high school not completed group 49 percent say "up the ladder" and 15 percent "down the ladder"; for college graduates the figures are 17 percent "up the ladder" and 35 percent "down." Also (Table 4-4), scale ratings on the statement "All things considered, working for the federal government appeals to me" decline from 6.1 at the lowest educational level to 4.2 at the college graduate level. It is worth noting that the scores on "All things considered, working for a large private business appeals to me" do not show the same negative relationship with educational attainment. The least-educated respondents rate federal employment almost exactly the same as business employment (0.1 higher), whereas the college graduates rate it 1.6 scale points lower.

HIGH SCHOOL STUDENTS, COLLEGE SENIORS, AND GRADUATE STUDENTS. For students the results are more equivocal than for any of the other populations, because the ratings were not for present occupation, but for where they expected to start out occupationally; the figures are entered under "present occupation" in Table 4-2 (Table 4-3 shows no figures for students, because it made no sense to ask the question of this group.)

The most useful figures appear in Table 4-4. They suggest that the over-all appeals of federal employment and of large private business employment are not significantly different. The ratings for both, however, show a tendency to be negatively related to educational level. In part, this may be due to a tendency for college seniors and graduate students, more than high school students, to see the professions and teaching as other alternatives. But we also find (Table 4-2) that high school students rate federal employment about equal to where they expect to start out.

(Text continued on page 76)

Table 4-2

"Same occupation in federal government" ratings were obtained from the nonfederal populations by asking, "Suppose your work or occupation stayed the same, but you worked for the federal government--that is, the United States government--how much better or worse would that be? Show me on the ladder, please." "Same occupation outside federal government" ratings were obtained from federal employee populations in the same way, substituting the words, "Suppose you continued in your present occupation, but went to work outside the federal government," etc.

<u>Highlights</u>: Present occupation vs. federal (nonfederal) employment.

. . . . Difference scores (last column) are almost all negative. The general employed public and general federal employees yield almost identical scores, showing about the same amounts of negative reaction (-.6 and -.9 respectively). An unknown amount of this general negative reaction probably should be attributed to an over-all tendency to react negatively to suggested change. Thus, the patterning of scores is more significant than the general negativism.

. . . . Women in the general employed public do not show an average negative reaction to federal employment (difference score = 0).

. . . . Of great significance are the comparative score patterns by educational level in the general employed public and the general federal employees. In the former, the higher the educational level the more negative the reaction to federal employment. Among federal employees, the higher the educational level, the less negative the reaction to changing to nonfederal employment.

. . . . High school students, on the average, do not react negatively to the idea of federal employment. College seniors and graduate students do react negatively.

. . . . High school teachers show significantly less negative reaction to federal employment than do college teachers.

. . . . Business executives show marked negativism to the idea of changing to federal employment; federal executives show hardly any negative reaction to changing to nonfederal employment.

. . . . Natural scientists, social scientists and engineers in education show strong negative reaction to changing to federal employment; those in industry are even more negative; but those in government show only slight negative reaction to changing to nonfederal employment.

Table 4-2

Present occupation vs. doing the same work, but for the federal government
(vs. "outside the federal government" for federal employees). Average (mean)
ratings on the 10-point self-anchoring "ideal occupation" scale; the higher
the score, the nearer to "ideal."

	Average number answering	Present occupation	Same occupation, but for the federal government	Difference: "federal (outside)" minus "present"
Non-federal Populations				
General employed public	1120	7.1	6.5	-0.6
By sex				
Men	862	7.1	6.3	-0.8
Women	258	7.4	7.4	0.0
By educational level				
High school not completed	324	7.0	7.1	+0.1
High school completed	503	6.9	6.5	-0.4
Some college	128	7.4	5.7	-1.7
College graduate	137	8.0	6.3	-1.7
Students				
High school students	359	5.5	5.6	+0.1
College seniors	404	6.3	5.3	-1.0
Graduate students	382	6.8	5.7	-1.1
Groups in education				
High school teachers	278	8.4	7.5	-0.9
Vocational counselors	78	8.4	7.3	-1.1
College teachers	453	8.7	7.1	-1.6
Natural scientists	115	8.8	7.0	-1.8
Social scientists	101	8.3	6.6	-1.7
Engineers	86	8.4	6.9	-1.5
Groups in business				
Executives	281	8.1	5.5	-2.6
Natural scientists	83	8.0	5.9	-2.1
Social scientists	73	8.0	5.3	-2.7
Engineers	89	8.1	5.6	-2.5
			Same occupation, but outside federal government:	
Federal Employee Populations				
General federal employees	927	7.0	6.1	-0.9
By sex				
Men	646	6.9	6.2	-0.7
Women	281	7.1	6.0	-1.1
By educational level				
High school not completed	188	6.9	5.7	-1.2
High school completed	346	6.8	5.9	-0.9
Some college	177	6.8	6.1	-0.7
College graduate	160	7.4	7.1	-0.3
Executives	264	8.0	7.8	-0.2
Natural scientists	90	7.9	7.4	-0.5
Social scientists	88	7.7	7.4	-0.3
Engineers	96	7.6	7.5	-0.1

Table 4-3

The wording of the question is given in the table heading. The question is nonspecific with respect to where in the federal government or in what kind of nonfederal enterprise one might work, and has a "projective" element in that it invites self-evaluation in the eyes of one's family.

Highlights: Judgments of family's reactions to one's being employed by the federal government.

. . . . In the general employed public, the over-all reaction to changing to federal employment is favorable (39% "up," 21% "down.") This is more true of women than men.

. . . . Among general federal employees, the over-all reaction to changing to nonfederal employment is strongly negative (18% "up," 46% "down,") especially among women.

. . . . Comparison of figures for the general employed public in this table and in Table 4-2 illustrates the danger of too-literal interpretation of absolute percentages or scores, i.e. this table shows an overall favorable reaction, while Table 4-2 shows a slight negative reaction. However, the relative patterning of scores by sex, by education, and for the various groups parallels Table 4-2 very closely. Thus, for example:

. . . . In the general employed public, the higher the education the more are there negative reactions to federal employment. Among general federal employees, the higher the education, the less the percentage of negative reactions to nonfederal employment.

. . . . High school teachers show higher percentages of positive reactions to federal employment than do college teachers.

. . . . Natural scientists, social scientists, and engineers in education show high percentages of negative reaction to changing to federal employment; those in industry are even higher in percentages of negative response. Those in the federal government show a balance favoring nonfederal employment. This is especially true of federal engineers.

. . . . Business executives show a high percentage reacting negatively to the idea of changing to federal employment; among federal executives, more of them react positively than negatively to the idea of changing to nonfederal employment.

. . . . The large "no difference" percentages suggest that large numbers of people in every group do not regard the federal vs. nonfederal aspect of employment as being, by itself, a crucial factor. The "no difference" percentages are highest among those groups in education.

Table 4-3

"Suppose you were to change now and go to work for the federal government ("outside the federal government" asked of federal employees) doing the same thing you are doing now, how do you think your family might feel about it? Would they feel you were moving up the ladder or down?"

	Number answering	Up the ladder	Down the ladder	No difference	Don't know
		If for the federal government:			
Nonfederal Populations					
General employed public	1113	39%	21%	38%	1%
By sex					
Men	854	37	24	38	1
Women	259	47	12	40	2
By educational level					
High school not completed	324	49	15	35	1
High school completed	498	42	19	37	1
Some college	128	30	32	37	1
College graduate	133	17	35	47	2
Groups in education					
High school teachers	270	27	14	59	0
Vocational counselors	75	16	11	72	1
College teachers	435	15	33	50	2
Natural scientists	116	12	32	53	3
Social scientists	100	11	32	57	0
Engineers	83	10	27	64	0
Groups in business					
Executives	276	12	47	40	1
Natural scientists	82	16	40	44	0
Social scientists	69	6	58	36	0
Engineers	85	11	39	49	1
		If outside the federal government:			
Federal Employee Populations					
General federal employees	913	18	46	36	1
By sex					
Men	631	20	45	34	1
Women	282	10	48	41	1
By educational level					
High school not completed	181	13	58	28	1
High school completed	341	16	46	37	1
Some college	176	20	43	36	0
College graduate	159	26	28	45	1
Executives	260	31	22	47	1
Natural scientists	89	37	23	40	0
Social scientists	86	24	27	49	0
Engineers	94	29	14	57	0

73

Table 4-4

This table, in contrast to Tables 4-2 and 4-3, which were based on questions dealing with the general concept of "nonfederal employment," introduces ratings of the relative appeal of "working for a large private business" vs. "working for the federal government."

Highlights: Appeal of large business vs. federal employment.

. . . . In the general employed public, large business employment ratings are very slightly higher than federal; a difference due to men, as women show a slight tendency to rate federal employment higher than large business employment.

. . . . In the general employed public, the appeal of large business is unrelated to educational level, but the appeal of federal employment shows a strong negative relation with educational level—the higher the educational level, the lower the appeal rating of federal employment.

. . . . Students rate large business employment and federal employment about equal in appeal.

. . . . Groups in education rate federal employment higher than large business employment, with the exception of engineers in college who show a preference for large business.

. . . . Groups in business rate very high the appeal of large business employment and rate very low the appeal of federal employment; federal employee groups without exception return the compliment, rating the appeal of large business employment very low, and that of federal employment very high.

. . . . Federally employed women show a larger difference score in favor of federal employment (+4.2) than do federally employed men (+3.4).

. . . . Engineers in the federal government, in business and in colleges rate higher the appeal of large business employment than do their natural scientist and social scientist colleagues.

. . . . Federal executives rate the appeal of federal employment higher (8.7) than does any other group.

Table 4-4

Occupational appeal of the federal government vs. large private
business. Average (mean) ratings of statements on the 10-point
agree-disagree scale; the higher the score, the more agreement.

	Average number answering	All things considered, working for a large private business firm appeals to me	All things considered, working for the federal government appeals to me	Difference: "government" minus "business"
Nonfederal Populations				
General employed public	1081	5.7	5.3	-0.4
By sex				
Men	832	5.8	5.2	-0.6
Women	248	5.6	6.0	+0.4
By educational level				
High school not completed	301	5.8	6.1	+0.3
High school completed	495	5.6	5.4	-0.2
Some college	122	5.9	4.6	-1.3
College graduate	134	5.8	4.2	-1.6
Students				
High school students	354	5.6	5.6	0.0
College seniors	400	5.1	5.2	+0.1
Graduate students	380	4.8	5.0	+0.2
Groups in education				
High school teachers	279	4.4	5.2	+0.8
Vocational counselors	79	4.2	5.0	+0.8
College teachers	463	4.4	4.7	+0.3
Natural scientists	118	4.1	4.7	+0.6
Social scientists	105	4.1	5.1	+1.0
Engineers	87	5.1	4.3	-0.8
Groups in business				
Executives	272	7.2	3.4	-3.8
Natural scientists	84	6.7	3.9	-2.8
Social scientists	70	7.1	4.0	-3.1
Engineers	90	7.6	3.1	-4.5
Federal Employee Populations				
General federal employees	932	4.5	8.0	+3.5
By sex				
Men	650	4.5	7.9	+3.4
Women	282	4.3	8.5	+4.2
By educational level				
High school not completed	182	4.2	7.7	+3.5
High school completed	354	4.4	8.2	+3.8
Some college	179	4.9	7.8	+2.9
College graduate	162	4.5	8.0	+3.5
Executives	271	4.8	8.7	+3.9
Natural scientists	90	4.1	8.3	+4.2
Social scientists	90	4.3	8.4	+4.1
Engineers	98	5.3	8.1	+2.8

In contrast, college seniors and graduate students rate it a full scale point below where they expect to start out. These results indicate that, on the average, the appeal of federal employment, both absolutely and in relation to expected initial employment, is negatively related to the student's present level of education—graduate students are slightly less favorably inclined toward federal employment than college seniors, and both see it less favorably than high school students do.

HIGH SCHOOL TEACHERS AND VOCATIONAL COUNSELORS. For these groups the results are conditioned by the fact that a high proportion of the respondents in them are employed in public schools and thus consider themselves to be in the employ of state and local government. This probably helps account for the high proportions (59 and 72 percent) that say "no difference" when asked how their families would feel if they changed to federal employment (Table 4-3) and for the somewhat greater number who say "up the ladder" (27 and 16 percent) rather than "down the ladder" (14 and 11 percent). When an intensity measure is introduced, as in the case of the figures derived from the ladder rating (Table 4-2), response to the idea of changing to federal employment is on the negative side, but less so than for the other presently employed groups at a similar educational level. Thus, one can say that high school teachers are more favorably disposed toward the idea of federal employment, or at least less unfavorably disposed, than are other employed groups with comparable education. This is substantiated by the ratings they give to the scale statement on the appeal of federal employment (Table 4-4), which are higher than the scores of other employed groups with similar education.

Worth noting also in Table 4-4 is that teachers rate the appeal of private business employment considerably lower than that of federal employment. However, to the teacher the statement itself—"All things considered, working for a large private business appeals to me"—probably implies a change, not only of employer, but also of occupation, to a greater degree than the statement on federal employment does. But this does not invalidate the general conclusion that the slightly negative reaction of high school teachers and vocational counselors to federal employment—in comparison to their present employment—is not strong and is not as pronounced as it is for the other employed populations with comparable education.

COLLEGE TEACHERS, NATURAL AND SOCIAL SCIENTISTS, AND ENGINEERS. All of the college teaching groups show a sharp negative reaction to the idea of working for the federal government. They rate it from 1.5 to 1.8 scale points lower than their present employment (Table 4-2), and, in response to the question on how their families would feel (Table 4-3), give more replies of "down the ladder" (27 percent or more) than "up the ladder" (15 percent or less). However, judgment of this result must be tempered; to the family question 50 to over 60 percent respond "no difference." Furthermore, all of the groups except the engineers rate the appeal of business employment even lower than the appeal of federal employment (Table 4-4).

GROUPS IN BUSINESS. The four business groups display the most extreme negative reaction, by all measures, to the idea of federal employment. They rate it from 2 to 2.5 scale points below their present occupation (Table 4-2); from 40 to almost 60 percent of them say, "down the ladder" (Table 4-3); the scale ratings they give to the appeal of working for the government are lower than those of any other group sampled (Table 4-4). As one might expect, these low ratings are accompanied by ratings of private business employment that are higher than any given by the other nonfederal or federal populations.

From the figures in the three tables, we may say that the natural and social scientists in business, while generally negative toward federal employment, are less so than the executives and engineers. For the engineers the results shown in Table 4-4 are particularly extreme: they rate the appeal of business employment higher (7.6), and the appeal of federal employment lower (3.1) than the other three groups do; their difference score is 4.5 scale points in favor of business employment.

GENERAL FEDERAL EMPLOYEES. Tables 4-2 and 4-3 show reactions of federal employees to *nonfederal employment*. Thus, here, the appeal of federal employment has to be judged by the relative appeal of nonfederal employment.

General federal employees on the average show as much (or even slightly more) negative reaction to the idea of shifting to nonfederal employment as the general employed public shows to the idea of shifting to federal employment. Table 4-2 suggests that the amount of negative reaction is about equal; Table 4-3 suggests that on the average the negative reaction is somewhat more marked among federal employees, and there is some indication that the women among them react more negatively than men.

The most important finding, however, is the pattern of association with educational level. Here we find (Tables 4-2 and 4-3) that the higher his educational level the less inclined is the federal employee to rate his present employment above outside employment. Table 4-2 shows a positive relationship between educational level and ratings of the same occupation outside the federal government, climbing from 5.7 for those not completing high school to 7.1 for college graduates. The difference scores show those with less than a complete high school education rating nonfederal employment 1.2 lower than their present employment; those with a high school diploma 0.9 lower; those with some college 0.7 lower; and college graduates only 0.3 lower, a difference which is not significant. These results are in sharp contrast to the pattern displayed by respondents in the general employed public: the higher their educational level, the more negative is their reaction to the idea of federal employment relative to present employment.

Table 4-4 confirms that federal employment seems to appeal more positively to the women presently in government work than to the men. It also shows that its absolute appeal is fairly high and about the same at all four educational levels, with scale values falling in a narrow range from 7.7 to 8.2. The ratings given to the appeal of business employment are also consistent but rather low, clustering around a scale value of 4.4; thus, general federal employees exhibit a decided preference for federal employment with difference scores of roughly 3.3 to over 4 scale points. Women show a stronger relative preference than men (difference scores of 4.2 vs. 3.4), but variation by educational level is small and inconsistent.

FEDERAL EXECUTIVES, NATURAL AND SOCIAL SCIENTISTS, AND ENGINEERS. In general, all four of the high-level federal groups react with little if any negativism to the idea of shifting to nonfederal employment in the same occupation. In Table 4-2 the difference scores for executives, natural and social scientists, and engineers, on ratings of "same occupation outside federal government" and of "present occupation" are only 0.2, 0.5, 0.3, and 0.1 in favor of "present occupation." As to how their families would feel if they went to work outside the government, "up the ladder" has higher percentages than "down" except in the case of social scientists, who show about equal percentages. These reactions of the four special groups are in sharp contrast to the strong negativism that their counterparts in business and in colleges show, on the average, toward the idea of shifting to the federal payroll.

However, when the appeal of federal employment is contrasted specifically with the appeal of large private business employment (Table 4-4), rather than nonfederal employment in general, the results are different. All four special federal groups give a very marked advantage to the government, with difference scores ranging from almost 3 scale points to over 4. Worth noting is that the engineers show the smallest difference score: they appear to be more favorably inclined toward large business employment and somewhat less favorably inclined toward federal employment than the other three high-level groups. This same tendency is seen also among the engineers in private business and in colleges.

5

Elements of the Ideal
and the Worst Occupation

THE TWO SERIES OF TABLES in this chapter, 5-1a through 5-1j and
5-2a through 5-2j (pages 84-123), present the results of the analyses of
two free-response questions which elicited descriptions of positive and
negative occupational concerns, and anchored the top and bottom of the
self-anchoring occupational value scale (see Chapter 2). The first question
asked for "the kinds of things about an occupation which would make it
absolutely ideal for you"; the second asked for "the kinds of things about
an occupation which would make it the worst or least satisfying." Both
questions tended to elicit positive and negative values that are of *concern*
to people. Thus the results should not be interpreted as reflecting the
importance people attach to the occupational values tabled. (The distinction between the two concepts was discussed in Chapter 2.)

The reader will find (Tables 5-1a and 5-2a) that there is a positive relationship, in both the nonfederal and federal populations, between educational level and average numbers of responses to the two questions—
especially to the one referring to positive values. Therefore the normal
expectation for all the values is that they will show a slight positive relationship between frequency of response and education. This is not surprising, since there is no reason to suppose that it reflects anything except a
tendency for higher educational attainment to be associated with a greater
number, variety, and complexity of occupational concerns, coupled with
a somewhat higher average verbal level.

Nevertheless, we cannot be as sanguine about the fact that federal
employees, on the average, give a higher number of replies than their
nonfederal counterparts do. Examining the average number of replies per
respondent in the federal and nonfederal samples, we find that general

federal employees on the average mention about 4.7 positive occupational values and 3.6 negative occupational values—compared to 3.5 and 2.9 in the general employed public; federal executives mention, on the average, 6.5 positive and 4.8 negative values—compared to 4.2 and 3.2 for business executives. Federal natural and social scientists and engineers show similar, though less extreme, differences in comparison with their business and college counterparts.

These results may be a true reflection of the existence of a greater number of occupational concerns among government employees, compared to people outside the federal establishment. We are, however, inclined to believe that they reflect methodological artifacts. Most of the federal employees were interviewed during their working hours, and after arrangement with superiors; most important of all, they knew that one of the main concerns of the research was federal employment and the federal employee. Since one or more of these factors may very possibly account for the greater volubility of federal employees, we have exercised restraint in comparing the responses of the nonfederal and federal populations to these two questions.[1] We have concentrated attention most heavily on the patternings within the nonfederal populations, and within the federal populations. (Fortunately, the scale items on occupational values presented in Chapter 6 are not subject to this methodological difficulty, and differences between nonfederal and federal groups are explored there in considerable detail.)

When both series of tables are considered as a whole, the wide variety of positive and negative occupational values with which people are concerned is impressive, as are also the extreme variations from group to group in the patterning of the values. It is clear that no single short list can validly characterize the nature of occupational aspirations and fears. An ordered list which would be valid for one group has little validity for any other group that differs in education or occupational level.

Certain values—financial reward, the general physical aspects of the working environment, personal relationships with other people at work, and the amount of self-determination and freedom—rank near the top in frequency of mention by almost all groups, although the precise rank order usually differs from one group to another. Beyond these four there is little consensus. The amount of challenge offered by the work, for

[1] In making comparisons, we considered not only the percentages shown in the tables but also the relative rank orders of the responses in the various groups, as well as percentages calculated by using total *responses* as a base.

example, ranks very high among highly educated groups but is hardly mentioned by those with little education. Similar group variability is seen concerning worthwhileness of the work, amount of variety afforded, and the degree of opportunity for self-development and self-expression.

Notable also is the almost uniformly high proportion of respondents in all groups who mention as a positive value the interest, enjoyment, satisfaction, and pleasure in doing work one is interested in, wants to do, or likes to do. As Table 5-1a shows, the factor is volunteered by three fourths of the respondents, regardless of occupation or educational level. The category admittedly tells us little about what people regard as interesting and satisfying. Nevertheless, the results are valuable in showing clearly that the majority of people in the United States feel that an ideal occupation should satisfy individual occupational aims. This large amount of free mention of personal, self-oriented motivation suggests a broad cultural acceptance of the legitimacy of having personal occupational aims apart from those of any organization or of the society as a whole.

The most commonly mentioned negative occupational value reflects a similar attitude. As Table 5-2a shows, one third to one half of the respondents mention that the "worst or least satisfying" aspect of an occupation would be doing work one especially dislikes, or being blocked off from the occupation one finds especially interesting and satisfying. (The latter aspect is emphasized more by the upper occupational and educational groups.)

It is of considerable interest that the patterns of the negative and positive values are not simply mirror images of each other. A rough parallel does exist, but there are also many extremely significant differences. A case in point is the value of personal relationships with people at work. All groups give considerable emphasis to the positive value of "active" personal relations—that is, being around stimulating, interesting people. On the negative side, however, this concern with the active aspect hardly appears, and the focus of concern becomes, not the *lack* of stimulating personal relationships, but the factor of being around unpleasant, disagreeable people. Concern with the nature of supervision differs in like manner. In all groups more people express concern about bad supervision (negative) than about good (positive). Again, the mention of routine as a negative value has a high frequency in all groups, ranging from about 20 percent to over 60. Yet variety and lack of routine and monotony are hardly ever mentioned in any of the groups as a positive value.

Perhaps most significant of all, both positive and negative occupational values show marked differential patterning by educational and occupational levels. At the lower levels, security and protective fringe benefits, general physical environment and the physical aspects of working conditions, and the nature of supervision receive the highest frequencies of mention, whereas self-expression, active personal relationships, self-development, creativity, worthwhileness of the work, challenge, and opportunity for personal achievement are scarcely mentioned. But as the respondents move progressively up the educational and occupational ladders these latter factors are mentioned with greater and greater frequency. The opportunity to do worthwhile, constructive work, for example, is mentioned as a positive value by one tenth of those in the general public who have not completed high school—and by one third of the college graduates. Concern with the lack of opportunity for self-expression, self-development, and creativity is mentioned by only 3 percent (or less) of those in the general public below the college graduate level. Among college graduates and the other upper educational and occupational groups, frequency of mention ranges from 13 to 25 percent.

Another point of interest is that, over all, occupational security is not ranked high as a concern, especially among the upper educational and occupational groups. However, this must not be construed to mean that security is *unimportant* to people as an occupational value. Rather, given the general occupational and economic situation that has prevailed for many years, the respondents apparently have little need to express concern with security, either as a positive aspiration or a negative lack.

Discussion of Specific Group Data

General Employed Public

The over-all pattern of positive and negative occupational values described above fails to convey significant variations by sex and by education in the general employed public. Men, for instance, tend to stress security, opportunity for self-advancement, and amount of self-determination and freedom on the job as positive values. Women, significantly more often than men, mention personal relationships with people at work, good and understanding supervision, and doing work that is worthwhile.

(Text continued on page 124)

The question quoted in the table title serves to anchor the high end of the self-anchoring scale. It tends to elicit positive occupational values which are of <u>concern</u>; percentages should not be interpreted as reflecting the <u>importance</u> people attached to the occupational values tabled. In examining the tables, the reader should keep in mind the average number of responses per respondent (column 2). They are higher in the federal employee populations than in comparable nonfederal populations, and are positively related to education in both populations. Thus, the <u>normal</u> expectation for any category would be: 1) a somewhat higher percentage figure for a federal population than for the comparable nonfederal population; 2) a moderate positive relationship between percentages and educational level. Thus, percentages which are higher for federal groups or show positive relationships with education should be slightly discounted; percentages which are higher for non-federal groups or show negative relationships with education should be given slightly greater weight than usual.

Table 5-1a

<u>Highlights</u>: Interest, enjoyment, satisfaction.

. . . . In one sense, this is a grab-bag category, high in all groups because for many people it is a convenient opening response gambit which summarizes positive values which they then discuss individually.

. . . . In another sense, however, it is significant that a high percentage of all groups mention interest, enjoyment, satisfaction. Such a high level of concern with personal, self-oriented motivation, while invited by the wording of the question, nevertheless suggests a broad cultural acceptance of the legitimacy of individual occupational aims.

Table 5-1a

Occupational values: what people describe as the attributes
of the "ideal" occupation.

Percentage distribution[a] of responses in each group to the question, what
are ". . . the kinds of things about an occupation which would make it
absolutely ideal for you?"

	Number answer- ing	Average number of responses per respondent	Interest, enjoyment, satisfaction, pleasure through doing work one is interested in, wants to do, likes to do
Nonfederal Populations			
General employed public	1136	3.5	72%
By sex			
Men	872	3.5	71
Women	264	3.5	73
By educational level			
High school not completed	330	3.1	78
High school completed	508	3.5	69
Some college	129	4.0	68
College graduate	139	4.1	69
Students			
High school students	359	4.0	79
College seniors	404	5.1	70
Graduate students	383	4.7	70
Groups in education			
High school teachers	282	4.4	65
Vocational counselors	80	5.2	69
College teachers	470	4.5	75
Natural scientists	121	4.6	84
Social scientists	105	4.6	75
Engineers	87	4.6	75
Groups in business			
Executives	286	4.2	71
Natural scientists	85	4.6	67
Social scientists	73	5.1	58
Engineers	90	4.3	72
Federal Employee Populations			
General federal employees	946	4.7	71
By sex			
Men	659	4.6	70
Women	287	4.8	75
By educational level			
High school not completed	190	3.9	74
High school completed	357	4.7	69
Some college	180	4.9	75
College graduate	163	5.4	71
Executives	273	6.5	63
Natural scientists	92	5.8	78
Social scientists	90	6.3	59
Engineers	99	6.0	70

[a] Percentage base = number of respondents answering in each group.
Percentages do not add to 100 in each group due to multiple replies.

85

Table 5-1b

Highlights: High or good financial reward.

. . . . Of major interest is the over-all similarity of percentages in all groups, ranging from about 30% to about 50%.

. . . . Fewer women than men, especially among federal employees, mention financial reward.

. . . . Among general federal employees, a slightly higher percentage of college graduates mention financial reward than is the case among those with less education.

. . . . Federal executives, natural scientists, social scientists and engineers mention financial reward with higher frequency than do their counterparts in either colleges or industry.

Highlights: Financial reward-importance explicitly qualified.

. . . . Explicit mention of limited, qualified financial reward, though not high in any group, is high enough to merit notice among college seniors and graduate students, among college teachers, and perhaps among natural scientists, social scientists, and engineers generally.

Highlights: Security.

. . . . In the general employed public, any aspect of security is mentioned by only 15%, and frequency of mention is unrelated to educational level.

. . . . Men mention security more often than do women, among both non-federal and federal employees.

. . . . All groups of federal employees show higher mention of security than their nonfederal counterparts. The differences are generally small, but consistent from group to group.

Table 5-1b

Occupational values: what people describe as the attributes
of the "ideal" occupation (cont'd.)

	High or good financial reward (e.g., make good money, high pay, etc.)	Financial reward-- importance explicitly qualified (e.g., secondary, just adequate)	Security, stability, protection, fringe (retirement, illness, income protection) benefits
Nonfederal Populations			
General employed public	43%	2%	15%
By sex			
Men	44	2	17
Women	38	2	7
By educational level			
High school not completed	40	2	12
High school completed	44	1	17
Some college	39	5	15
College graduate	44	5	12
Students			
High school students	42	6	12
College seniors	40	14	13
Graduate students	35	14	7
Groups in education			
High school teachers	39	7	11
Vocational counselors	40	6	5
College teachers	37	12	4
Natural scientists	34	12	3
Social scientists	44	12	3
Engineers	33	8	2
Groups in business			
Executives	34	6	9
Natural scientists	41	15	15
Social scientists	40	8	6
Engineers	40	9	3
Federal Employee Populations			
General federal employees	40	4	20
By sex			
Men	44	3	22
Women	26	4	16
By educational level			
High school not completed	38	2	17
High school completed	39	4	24
Some college	38	5	16
College graduate	47	5	21
Executives	52	10	20
Natural scientists	52	12	21
Social scientists	48	8	8
Engineers	50	10	17

87

Table 5-1c

Highlights: Good physical environment and working conditions.

. . . . Concern with the physical aspects of the working environment is high in the general employed public (41%) and among general federal employees (44%).

. . . . In both the general employed public and general federal employees there is a marked inverse relation with educational level. Paralleling this, high school students show more concern (40%) than do college seniors (27%) or graduate students (21%).

. . . . Federal executives cite it more often (31%) than do business executives (19%).

. . . . Federal natural scientists, social scientists and engineers mention it more often than do their counterparts in either business or colleges.

Highlights: Having the equipment, facilities, wherewithal to do the job.

. . . . This matter is mentioned more frequently by those in federal employment (all groups) than by those outside, where the percentages are, generally speaking, quite low.

. . . . About one fourth (26%) of federal natural scientists mention it, a higher proportion than is shown by any other group, in or out of government.

Highlights: Good superior, supervisor, boss.

. . . . References to good immediate superiors as an attribute of the "ideal" occupation are about twice as high in the federal employee populations as in the nonfederal.

. . . . In both the federal and nonfederal populations there is a tendency for women to mention it more than do men.

Table 5-1c

Occupational values: what people describe as the
attributes of the "ideal" occupation (cont'd.)

	Good physical environment and working conditions (e.g., clean, pleasant, not dangerous)	Having the equipment, facilities, wherewithal to do the job	Good superior, supervisor, boss (e.g., understanding, fair, nice, gives support)
Nonfederal Populations			
General employed public	41%	6%	11%
By sex			
Men	40	6	10
Women	43	7	15
By educational level			
High school not completed	39	6	12
High school completed	48	7	13
Some college	35	6	10
College graduate	25	5	4
Students			
High school students	40	7	11
College seniors	27	5	10
Graduate students	21	13	6
Groups in education			
High school teachers	28	9	10
Vocational counselors	31	5	13
College teachers	13	9	5
Natural scientists	12	9	3
Social scientists	6	7	4
Engineers	8	12	5
Groups in business			
Executives	19	5	9
Natural scientists	20	7	7
Social scientists	10	12	7
Engineers	10	8	4
Federal Employee Populations			
General federal employees	44	11	20
By sex			
Men	44	9	19
Women	46	14	24
By educational level			
High school not completed	47	9	22
High school completed	50	10	22
Some college	35	9	17
College graduate	35	13	15
Executives	31	19	18
Natural scientists	32	26	19
Social scientists	20	16	14
Engineers	29	14	22

Table 5-1d

Highlights: Good personal relations with people at work.

. . . . Personal relations are of major concern in all groups, with
percentages of mention clustering in the 30% to 60% range ("Total"
column).

. . . . The percentages for women are markedly higher than for men,
both in the general employed public and among general federal employees.

. . . . In the general employed public, total percentages are positively
related to educational level, accounted for mainly by the positive
relation of "active" personal relations (column 2) with educational
level. Among general federal employees, this relationship with educational level does not appear.

. . . . Mention of personal relations is markedly higher among general
federal employees than in the general employed public, most heavily contributed to by twice as high a mention of passive personal relations.

. . . . In all nonfederal populations, active personal relations are
mentioned more frequently than passive, and in most of these groups the
difference is great. This pattern of emphasis on active personal relations is not so apparent in the federal employee populations.

. . . . The high percentages in the "active" column for groups in education is partially accounted for by the fact that these people, as
teachers, are likely to mention active, stimulating contact with
students.

. . . . The emphasis of active over passive relations is especially
high for social scientists, whether in government, business, or
colleges.

Table 5-1d

Occupational values: what people describe as the attributes
of the "ideal" occupation (cont'd.)

| | Good personal relations with people at work (e.g., co-workers, the public, students | | | |
	Passive (e.g., be around pleasant, agreeable people)	Active (e.g., meet stimulating people; make good contacts)	Mis-cella-neous	Total
Nonfederal Populations				
General employed public	12%	19%	1%	30%
By sex				
Men	9	17	1	25
Women	19	26	2	44
By educational level				
High school not completed	10	12	2	22
High school completed	13	18	-	29
Some college	15	26	1	37
College graduate	9	34	1	42
Students				
High school students	15	33	3	46
College seniors	20	40	4	56
Graduate students	14	35	6	49
Groups in education				
High school teachers	18	50	2	61
Vocational counselors	30	54	3	73
College teachers	14	45	4	56
Natural scientists	13	49	3	60
Social scientists	8	44	9	52
Engineers	13	45	5	54
Groups in business				
Executives	21	27	2	44
Natural scientists	7	26	6	38
Social scientists	8	33	1	40
Engineers	6	23	3	28
Federal Employee Populations				
General federal employees	23	25	3	47
By sex				
Men	18	22	3	41
Women	35	33	5	63
By educational level				
High school not completed	24	20	2	43
High school completed	23	28	4	49
Some college	23	30	5	50
College graduate	20	21	4	40
Executives	22	35	5	54
Natural scientists	17	19	12	45
Social scientists	17	44	8	63
Engineers	20	31	9	52

Table 5-1e

It is likely that for all three occupational values (self-advancement, prestige, and recognition) shown in this table, the percentages under-state the degree of concern in all groups. People tend not to be candid about their desires for personal advancement, prestige and recognition, resulting in low frequencies of clear-cut statements about these mat-ters. To an unknown degree, respondents tend to transform such feelings into expressions about such matters as self-development, self-expression, creativity, and self-determination (Tables 5-1f and 5-1g). Better absolute measures of concern with self-advancement, prestige, and recognition are provided by the scale items (shown in the tables of Chapter 6) designed to help overcome the above limitations. However, in this table some attention to the relative amounts of concern in the various groups is warranted.

Highlights: Self-advancement and progress.

. . . . The general picture is one of somewhat more concern, over-all, in the federal than in the nonfederal populations.

. . . . Among general federal employees, frequency of mention is posi-tively related to educational level, accounted for in considerable part by the low figure (6%) for "high school not completed." A similar contrastingly low figure (4%) appears for the "high school not com-pleted" group in the general employed public.

. . . . All groups in education show very low percentages.

Highlights: Prestige.

. . . . Mention of prestige is very low for the general employed public over-all and at all four levels of education, and the same is true for general federal employees.

. . . . Perhaps worth noting is the 14% figure for federal executives compared to the 4% figure for business executives.

. . . . Social scientists yield the highest figures in government, business, and colleges.

Highlights: Recognition for one's work.

. . . . Percentages are quite low among all nonfederal populations except natural scientists, social scientists, and engineers in business.

. . . . All federal populations, with the exception of natural scien-tists, show higher percentages than do comparable nonfederal popula-tions.

. . . . About one fourth (26%) of the federal social scientists mention recognition.

Table 5-1e

Occupational values: what people describe as the attributes
of the "ideal" occupation (cont'd.)

	Self-advancement and progress (e.g., be promoted; get ahead)	Prestige (e.g., do work that is respected, not looked down on)	Recognition for one's work (e.g., have work appreciated; be given credit)
Nonfederal Populations			
General employed public	8%	2%	3%
By sex			
Men	10	2	2
Women	3	2	3
By educational level			
High school not completed	4	2	1
High school completed	10	2	2
Some college	9	2	4
College graduate	12	5	6
Students			
High school students	13	4	1
College seniors	16	11	7
Graduate students	9	9	7
Groups in education			
High school teachers	6	6	5
Vocational counselors	5	8	6
College teachers	2	7	5
Natural scientists	1	3	5
Social scientists	5	11	5
Engineers	3	9	5
Groups in business			
Executives	11	4	7
Natural scientists	15	5	13
Social scientists	11	14	11
Engineers	9	6	11
Federal Employee Populations			
General federal employees	13	4	8
By sex			
Men	14	4	8
Women	13	3	10
By educational level			
High school not completed	6	4	7
High school completed	14	3	6
Some college	18	4	11
College graduate	20	7	16
Executives	16	14	16
Natural scientists	9	9	11
Social scientists	13	18	26
Engineers	13	12	16

Table 5-1f

Self-development and self-expression and creativity were added together (total column) because, although they appear to be quite different logically, respondent replies yield few clear-cut differentiations between these two categories. The replied suggest that, psychologically, what is being expressed are two facets of a more basic concept which might be called a desire for personal emergence. Separate percentage distributions for self-development and for self-expression and creativity were retained, however, because they are helpful in revealing relative emphasis on the two aspects.

Highlights: Self-development, self-expression, and creativity.

. . . . This value is of moderate to major concern to all groups, federal and nonfederal, except for the two lowest educational levels in the general employed public.

. . . . Among both the general employed public and general federal employees, there is a marked positive relation of frequency of mention with level of education, with a very sharp rise in percentages from those with no college to those with some college.

. . . . The figures for college seniors and graduate students are roughly double those for high school students.

. . . . The figures for general federal employees are roughly double those for the general employed public, and this tends to be true for both men and women, and at all four educational levels (with some convergence at the some college and college graduate levels).

. . . . Federal executives mention this value much more frequently (41%) than do business executives (24%).

Table 5-1f

Occupational values: what people describe as the
attributes of the "<u>ideal</u>" occupation (cont'd.)

| | Self-development, self-expression, and creativity | | |
	Self-development (e.g., learn; develop; grow personally and professionally)	Self-expression and creativity (e.g., innovate; express own ideas)	Total
<u>Nonfederal Populations</u>			
General employed public	4%	6%	10%
By sex			
Men	4	7	10
Women	5	3	9
By educational level			
High school not completed	2	4	6
High school completed	4	4	7
Some college	9	7	16
College graduate	7	17	22
Students			
High school students	9	6	15
College seniors	18	15	31
Graduate students	20	18	33
Groups in education			
High school teachers	12	10	21
Vocational counselors	15	13	26
College teachers	19	18	33
Natural scientists	23	17	36
Social scientists	22	21	40
Engineers	16	22	33
Groups in business			
Executives	7	18	24
Natural scientists	13	22	33
Social scientists	4	29	36
Engineers	3	28	31
<u>Federal Employee Populations</u>			
General federal employees	12	9	20
By sex			
Men	11	9	19
Women	14	8	20
By educational level			
High school not completed	8	2	11
High school completed	10	7	16
Some college	14	12	25
College graduate	17	18	33
Executives	24	24	41
Natural scientists	21	14	29
Social scientists	21	29	43
Engineers	26	25	42

Table 5-lg

<u>Highlights</u>: Self-determination.

. . . . Mention of self-determination as a positive occupational value is high in all groups, federal and nonfederal.

. . . . Men cite self-determination significantly more often than do women.

. . . . There is a step-like increase in references from high school students, to college seniors, to graduate students.

. . . . There is some tendency for percentages to increase with educational level, both in the general employed public and the general federal employee populations.

. . . . Highest frequencies come from natural scientists, social scientists, and engineers in colleges. Also very high are natural scientists and social scientists in industry, and natural scientists in the federal government.

<u>Highlights</u>: Responsibility and authority, the power to make decisions.

. . . . In general, frequency of mention is not high in the general employed public, among students, and among groups in education.

. . . . College seniors show a fairly high percentage (16%).

. . . . Executives, social scientists, and engineers in business and in the federal government show quite high percentages (roughly 20% to 30%); comparatively speaking, the figures for natural scientists are low (17% and 12%).

<u>Highlights</u>: Sense of challenge, overcoming obstacles, keeping goals ahead.

. . . . In the general employed public, the percentage is low (7%), accounted for by the low figures for the high school not completed groups (1%) and the high school completed (5%) groups.

. . . . Relationship with educational level is sharply positive in both the general employed public and among general federal employees.

. . . . The figure for general federal employees is double that for the general employed public (14% to 7%).

. . . . Roughly one fifth to one fourth of students mention this value.

. . . . The figures are high for executives, natural scientists, social scientists, and engineers--federal or nonfederal (roughly in the 20% to 35% range).

96

Table 5-1g

Occupational values: what people describe as the
attributes of the "ideal" occupation (cont'd.)

	Self-determination (e.g., be my own master; no heavy supervision; freedom of thought, action)	Responsibility and authority, power to make decisions	Sense of challenge, overcoming obstacles, keeping goals ahead
Nonfederal Populations			
General employed public	29%	5%	7%
By sex			
Men	32	5	8
Women	22	4	3
By educational level			
High school not completed	24	2	1
High school completed	30	4	5
Some college	36	9	16
College graduate	31	7	18
Students			
High school students	14	3	8
College seniors	28	16	21
Graduate students	41	9	23
Groups in education			
High school teachers	19	6	15
Vocational counselors	28	11	20
College teachers	38	4	19
Natural scientists	48	6	17
Social scientists	48	7	26
Engineers	56	3	26
Groups in business			
Executives	29	21	26
Natural scientists	42	17	33
Social scientists	47	32	34
Engineers	27	27	28
Federal Employee Populations			
General federal employees	23	9	14
By sex			
Men	24	8	14
Women	20	10	12
By educational level			
High school not completed	19	5	4
High school completed	23	7	11
Some college	21	13	23
College graduate	31	13	23
Executives	33	28	39
Natural scientists	44	12	20
Social scientists	34	20	39
Engineers	36	20	28

Table 5-1h

<u>Highlights</u>: Sense of achievement or accomplishment through seeing
    results of own work.

. . . . Although the general employed public yields a figure of only 8%,
all other nonfederal groups except high school students (10%) and
college seniors (13%) show percentages two to three times as high;
federal employee populations show figures two to five times as high.

. . . . Percentage mentioning among general federal employees is twice
that in the general employed public.

. . . . Among general federal employees, percentages show a slight positive relation with educational level.

. . . . The figure for federal executives (41%) is more than double that
for business executives (18%).

<u>Highlights</u>: Do work that is worthwhile, useful, constructive.

. . . . The general pattern for this value is one of high frequency of
mention by all groups, federal and nonfederal.

. . . . Percentages are markedly higher for women than men in both
federal and nonfederal employment.

. . . . Percentages show a marked positive relation with educational
level among both federal and nonfederal employees.

. . . . The figures for college seniors and graduate students are much
higher than for high school students.

. . . . Mention is very high among high school teachers (49%) and especially among vocational counsellors (66%).

. . . . The figures for groups in business, while high, are considerably
lower than those for their counterparts in both the federal government
and in colleges.

. . . . The percentage for federal executives (45%) is almost double
that for business executives (24%).

. . . . Over half (56%) of the social scientists in the federal government mention this value.

Table 5-1h

Occupational values: what people describe as the
attributes of the "ideal" occupation (cont'd.)

	Sense of achievement or accomplishment through seeing results of own work	Do work that is worthwhile, useful, constructive
Nonfederal Populations		
General employed public	8%	14%
By sex		
Men	9	12
Women	5	23
By educational level		
High school not completed	7	9
High school completed	7	10
Some college	9	22
College graduate	15	32
Students		
High school students	10	26
College seniors	13	40
Graduate students	17	38
Groups in education		
High school teachers	22	49
Vocational counselors	18	66
College teachers	16	47
Natural scientists	18	47
Social scientists	16	44
Engineers	24	48
Groups in business		
Executives	18	24
Natural scientists	24	20
Social scientists	25	38
Engineers	21	31
Federal Employee Populations		
General federal employees	15	18
By sex		
Men	15	15
Women	16	26
By educational level		
High school not completed	9	11
High school completed	14	15
Some college	21	22
College graduate	20	30
Executives	41	45
Natural scientists	30	35
Social scientists	33	56
Engineers	24	34

Table 5-1i

Highlights: Do work that fits one's capacities and/or training.

. . . . The percentages are quite high in all groups, nonfederal and federal, with the general order from highest to lowest being federal employee populations, groups in business, groups in education, students, and the general employed public.

. . . . There is no relationship with educational level, either in the general employed public or among general federal employees.

. . . . Percentages for federal executives (34%) and natural scientists (24%) are roughly double those for their counterparts in business and in colleges.

. . . . Percentages for federal social scientists (32%) and engineers (24%) are about double those for their counterparts in colleges.

Highlights: Have variety in the work, absence of monotony and routine.

. . . . Desire for variety is mentioned with moderately high frequency by all groups except the high school not completed, both nonfederal and federal.

. . . . Groups in education show lower percentages than groups in business and the federal government.

Table 5-1i

Occupational values: what people describe as the
attributes of the "ideal" occupation (cont'd.)

	Do work that fits one's capacities and/or training	Have variety in the work, absence of monotony and routine
Nonfederal Populations		
General employed public	14%	10%
By sex		
Men	14	10
Women	14	9
By educational level		
High school not completed	19	5
High school completed	10	10
Some college	15	18
College graduate	14	15
Students		
High school students	15	12
College seniors	18	17
Graduate students	14	15
Groups in education		
High school teachers	17	11
Vocational counselors	25	14
College teachers	16	10
Natural scientists	12	10
Social scientists	19	9
Engineers	12	9
Groups in business		
Executives	18	16
Natural scientists	12	17
Social scientists	25	15
Engineers	26	19
Federal Employee Populations		
General federal employees	22	15
By sex		
Men	21	14
Women	23	19
By educational level		
High school not completed	23	7
High school completed	22	17
Some college	22	18
College graduate	20	21
Executives	34	19
Natural scientists	24	19
Social scientists	32	16
Engineers	24	22

101

Table 5-1j

Highlights: Leisure, recreation, time off.

. . . . Percentages are moderately low for the general employed public and for general federal employees, and do not differ significantly.

. . . . Frequency of mention among groups in business is somewhat lower than among their counterparts in the federal government or in colleges.

Highlights: Desirable location of work.

. . . . In general, the percentages are low, with a tendency to be somewhat higher for federal than nonfederal populations, especially among federal natural scientists, social scientists, and engineers, who mention desirable work location with moderately high frequency.

Highlights: Travel.

. . . . Travel as a positive occupational value is infrequently mentioned, except for a general pattern of moderate comment among federal executives, natural scientists, social scientists, and engineers.

. . . . Perhaps worth noting is the 7 to 9% mention of travel in the student groups.

Table 5-1j
Occupational values: what people describe as the
attributes of the "ideal" occupation (cont'd.)

	Leisure, recreation, time off, vacations	Desirable location of work (e.g., in nice area; convenient; where I prefer to live)	Travel (e.g., not stay in one place; see the country, the world)
Nonfederal Populations			
General employed public	10%	6%	4%
By sex			
Men	10	6	4
Women	10	8	2
By educational level			
High school not completed	6	6	3
High school completed	11	8	4
Some college	12	5	4
College graduate	14	5	5
Students			
High school students	10	8	9
College seniors	16	13	9
Graduate students	11	11	7
Groups in education			
High school teachers	17	5	3
Vocational counselors	20	3	1
College teachers	17	8	3
Natural scientists	19	8	3
Social scientists	15	5	3
Engineers	10	13	1
Groups in business			
Executives	7	7	6
Natural scientists	8	9	4
Social scientists	10	7	11
Engineers	6	7	2
Federal Employee Populations			
General federal employees	12	9	5
By sex			
Men	12	9	6
Women	12	9	5
By educational level			
High school not completed	9	8	4
High school completed	12	9	6
Some college	14	8	6
College graduate	17	14	5
Executives	15	14	11
Natural scientists	13	17	9
Social scientists	14	18	14
Engineers	14	22	15

Tables 5-2a Through 5-2j

The question quoted in the table title serves to anchor the low end of the self-anchoring scale. It tends to elicit negative occupational values which are of concern; percentages should not be interpreted as reflecting the importance people attach to the negative occupational values tabled. In examining the tables, the reader should keep in mind the average number of responses per respondent (column 2). They are higher in the federal populations than in comparable nonfederal populations, and are positively related to education in both populations. Thus, the __normal__ expectation for any category would be: 1) a somewhat higher percentage figure for a federal population than for the comparable nonfederal population; 2) a moderate positive relationship between percentages and educational level. Thus, percentages which are higher for federal groups or show positive relationships with education should be slightly discounted; percentages which are higher for nonfederal groups or show negative relationships with education should be given slightly greater weight than usual.

Table 5-2a

__Highlights__ (both categories): 1. Unable to follow the occupation one finds interesting, enjoyable, satisfying; 2. Have to do work (specified) one especially dislikes.

. . . . In one sense, these categories have the same meaning in that they both reflect a concern with generalized, __personal__, __self-oriented__ occupational motivation. While this type of concern is invited by the wording of the question, the high percentages (considering the two categories together) in all groups suggest a broad cultural acceptance of the legitimacy of personal occupational aims.

. . . . Neither category delineates specific negative occupational values. Both are ways in which many respondents tend to summarize negative values which they also discuss more specifically.

. . . . Mention of having to do work one especially dislikes shows a marked inverse relationship with education in the general employed public and among students.

. . . . Mention of being __blocked off__ from one's occupation (first category) tends to be higher among the most highly educated groups, except for groups in business.

Table 5-2a

Occupational values: what people describe as the attributes
of the "worst" occupation.
Percentage distribution[a] of responses in each group to the
question, "What kinds of things about an occupation would
make it the worst or least satisfying to you?"

	Number answering	Average number of responses per respondent	Unable to follow the occupation one finds interesting, enjoyable, satisfying	Have to do work (specified) one especially dislikes
Nonfederal Populations				
General employed public	1135	2.9	7%	48%
By sex				
Men	871	2.8	7	47
Women	264	3.1	9	50
By educational level				
High school not completed	327	2.7	6	56
High school completed	512	2.8	6	46
Some college	129	3 0	6	43
College graduate	137	3.2	12	39
Students				
High school students	358	3.3	20	52
College seniors	403	4.0	14	36
Graduate students	383	3.8	15	35
Groups in education				
High school teachers	283	3.6	17	39
Vocational counselors	80	3.9	15	46
College teachers	470	3.5	12	40
Natural scientists	121	3.4	12	34
Social scientists	105	3.5	11	34
Engineers	86	3.3	9	31
Groups in business				
Executives	283	3.2	8	38
Natural scientists	85	3.6	8	26
Social scientists	73	3.8	7	34
Engineers	90	3.4	10	39
Federal Employee Populations				
General federal employees	940	**3.6**	8	40
By sex				
Men	654	3.5	8	41
Women	286	3.8	8	38
By educational level				
High school not completed	189	3.0	7	39
High school completed	355	3.6	8	42
Some college	179	3.7	5	43
College graduate	161	4.2	13	36
Executives	272	4.8	13	29
Natural scientists	92	4.2	15	32
Social scientists	90	5.1	16	27
Engineers	99	4.2	13	32

[a] Percentage base = number of respondents answering in each group.
Percentages do not add to 100 in each group due to multiple replies.

105

Table 5-2b

Highlights: Poor or inadequate financial reward.

. . . . Poor financial reward is mentioned by about one fourth of the respondents both in the general employed public and among general federal employees.

. . . . Percentages are somewhat higher for men than for women, both nonfederal and federal.

. . . . In the general employed public, there is a tendency for mention of poor financial reward to be inversely related to educational level; among general federal employees, this is not the case.

. . . . Among students, the relationship with present educational level is negative--the higher the education, the lower the percentage who mention poor financial reward.

. . . . For those employed in colleges the percentages compared to the general level of other groups are somewhat lower.

. . . . Worth noting is the fact that federal engineers yield the highest percentage (35%).

Highlights: Absence of, or insufficient, security, protection, fringe benefits.

. . . . The major point worth noting is the absence of high percentages in any group, federal or nonfederal.

. . . . Percentages are higher (about double) for men than for women, both nonfederal and federal.

. . . . In the general employed public, to the extent that security is mentioned, frequency of mention is inversely related to educational level. The same is true of students with respect to present educational level. Among general federal employees, this relationship does not appear.

Table 5-2b

Occupational values: what people describe as the attributes of
the "worst" occupation. Percentage distribution[a] of responses
in each group to the question, "What kinds of things about an
occupation would make it the worst or least satisfying to you?"

	Poor or inadequate financial reward	Absence of or insufficient security, stability, protection, fringe (retirement, illness, income protection) benefits
Nonfederal Populations		
General employed public	27%	9%
By sex		
Men	28	11
Women	23	5
By educational level		
High school not completed	30	11
High school completed	29	9
Some college	20	7
College graduate	20	5
Students		
High school students	26	9
College seniors	20	7
Graduate students	16	3
Groups in education		
High school teachers	21	10
Vocational counselors	19	6
College teachers	16	3
Natural scientists	17	3
Social scientists	14	3
Engineers	14	1
Groups in business		
Executives	17	6
Natural scientists	25	8
Social scientists	25	4
Engineers	22	1
Federal Employee Populations		
General federal employees	24	12
By sex		
Men	27	14
Women	16	6
By educational level		
High school not completed	22	14
High school completed	26	12
Some college	23	9
College graduate	26	13
Executives	25	11
Natural scientists	28	5
Social scientists	26	9
Engineers	35	9

a Percentage base = number of respondents answering in each group.
Percentages do not add to 100 in each group due to multiple replies.

107

Table 5-2c

<u>Highlights</u>: Bad physical environment and working conditions.

. . . . Frequency of mention is high, almost half of both the general employed public and general federal employees mention some aspect of physical environment and working conditions.

. . . . Percentages show a negative relationship with educational level in both the general employed public and among general federal employees, a sharp drop in "percentage mentioning" occurring at the college level in both groups.

. . . . College seniors and graduate students yield percentages roughly half the percentage for high school students.

. . . . Federal executives, natural scientists, social scientists, and engineers mention this from two to three times as frequently as their counterparts in industry or colleges.

<u>Highlights</u>: Absence of or insufficient equipment, facilities, where-with&l to do the job.

. . . . The general picture is one of very low frequency of mention except for federal executives and social scientists.

<u>Highlights</u>: Bad superior, supervisor, boss.

. . . . All federal employee populations show markedly higher concern about relations with superiors than do the nonfederal populations, roughly one third mentioning it in all federal groups.

. . . . Women note this somewhat more often than do men, both in federal and nonfederal employment.

. . . . The 7% and 8% for social scientists in colleges and business respectively are in sharp contrast to the 32% for federal social scientists.

Table 5-2c

Occupational values: what people describe as the attributes
of the "worst" occupation (cont'd.)

	Bad physical environment and working conditions (e.g., dirty, unpleasant, dangerous)	Absence of or insufficient equipment, facilities, wherewithal to do the job	Bad superior, supervisor, boss (e.g., unfair, unpleasant, fails to give support)
Nonfederal Populations			
General employed public	48%	3%	18%
By sex			
Men	50	3	16
Women	41	4	24
By educational level			
High school not completed	54	3	16
High school completed	51	4	20
Some college	46	2	16
College graduate	24	2	14
Students			
High school students	48	3	17
College seniors	27	2	18
Graduate students	21	5	15
Groups in education			
High school teachers	28	7	18
Vocational counselors	29	8	16
College teachers	13	4	11
Natural scientists	12	3	7
Social scientists	9	1	11
Engineers	13	4	15
Groups in business			
Executives	19	4	16
Natural scientists	20	8	17
Social scientists	11	4	8
Engineers	12	9	11
Federal Employee Populations			
General federal employees	48	8	31
By sex			
Men	48	7	29
Women	46	11	36
By educational level			
High school not completed	51	6	32
High school completed	50	10	31
Some college	50	7	28
College graduate	34	8	34
Executives	35	20	34
Natural scientists	39	13	24
Social scientists	23	18	32
Engineers	36	11	27

Table 5-2d

Highlights: Bad or inadequate relations with people at work.

. . . . Nearly one third of general federal employees mention bad personal relations, whereas only about one fifth of the general employed public do so.

. . . . Percentages for women are double those for men in both nonfederal and federal employment; one half of federally employed women mention bad personal relations.

. . . . When thoughts about negative personal relationships are expressed, passive rather than active aspects tend to dominate, i.e., concern is more with being around personal unpleasantness than with lack of opportunity to enjoy stimulating personal relationships.

Table 5-2d

Occupational values: what people describe as the attributes
of the "worst" occupation (cont'd.)

| | Bad or inadequate relations with people at work (e.g., co-workers, the public, students) | | | |
	Passive (e.g., be around unpleasant, disagreeable people)	Active (e.g., not meet stimulating, worthwhile people)	Miscellaneous	Total
Nonfederal Populations				
General employed public	11%	3%	7%	19%
By sex				
Men	8	3	5	15
Women	18	4	13	32
By educational level				
High school not completed	7	3	6	15
High school completed	12	2	5	18
Some college	13	2	16	26
College graduate	12	6	8	24
Students				
High school students	18	3	11	29
College seniors	20	6	18	41
Graduate students	18	2	15	32
Groups in education				
High school teachers	21	1	18	38
Vocational counselors	21	3	21	41
College teachers	10	1	22	30
Natural scientists	12	1	21	32
Social scientists	10	1	27	35
Engineers	8	0	16	21
Groups in business				
Executives	13	3	7	23
Natural scientists	9	14	12	32
Social scientists	12	1	16	29
Engineers	10	3	9	20
Federal Employee Populations				
General federal employees	20	2	9	29
By sex				
Men	16	1	7	23
Women	33	3	14	47
By educational level				
High school not completed	18	1	4	22
High school completed	23	1	8	31
Some college	22	2	14	34
College graduate	13	1	13	26
Executives	19	3	17	36
Natural scientists	23	8	14	42
Social scientists	23	11	10	42
Engineers	12	1	22	32

Table 5-2e

<u>Highlights</u>: Lack of self-advancement and progress.

. . . . Lack of self-advancement and progress is not, over-all, accorded very high notice as one of the "worst" aspects of an occupation.

. . . . In general, federal employees show higher percentages than nonfederal.

. . . . Percentages for students and for groups in business are somewhat higher than are those for groups in education and for the general employed public.

<u>Highlights</u>: Little or no recognition for one's work.

. . . . While none of the figures for lack of recognition is high, there is a sharp nonfederal, federal contrast. Nonfederal groups mention it hardly at all; on the average, over 10% of federal employees mention it.

. . . . That 17% of the federal executives mention it is worth noting.

Table 5-2e

Occupational values: what people describe as the attributes
of the "worst" occupation (cont'd.)

	Lack of self-advancement and progress (e.g., no promotions; no chance to get ahead)	Little or no recognition for one's work (e.g., no appreciation, credit for one's work)
Nonfederal Populations		
General employed public	6%	2%
By sex		
Men	6	2
Women	4	2
By educational level		
High school not completed	3	2
High school completed	6	2
Some college	7	2
College graduate	9	4
Students		
High school students	13	3
College seniors	14	7
Graduate students	13	6
Groups in education		
High school teachers	5	4
Vocational counselors	4	5
College teachers	4	4
Natural scientists	3	3
Social scientists	6	5
Engineers	2	5
Groups in business		
Executives	12	9
Natural scientists	15	9
Social scientists	15	7
Engineers	9	3
Federal Employee Populations		
General federal employees	12	11
By sex		
Men	13	10
Women	8	12
By educational level		
High school not completed	5	12
High school completed	14	9
Some college	15	12
College graduate	15	13
Executives	19	17
Natural scientists	10	9
Social scientists	20	11
Engineers	14	14

113

Table 5-2f

Highlights: Lack of self-development, self-expression, and creativity.

. . . . In this table, there is a sharp contrast between all groups,
federal and nonfederal, who have educational levels of some college or
less, and all groups who have four years or more of college. In the
former, concern over lack of self-development, self-expression, and
creativity is mentioned hardly at all; in the latter, frequency of
mention is relatively high.

. . . . Among those groups who mention the matter with higher frequency,
replies tend to be couched in terms of lack of self-expression and
creativity, rather than lack of self-development.

. . . . The 21% and 23% figures for college seniors and graduate
students, respectively, deserve notice.

Table 5-2f

Occupational values: what people describe as the attributes
of the "worst" occupation (cont'd.)

| | Lack of self-development, self expression and creativity | | |
	Lack of self-development (e.g., unable to learn; develop; grow personally, professionally)	Lack of self-expression and creativity (e.g., unable to inovate; express own ideas	Total
Nonfederal Populations			
General employed public	1%	2%	3%
By sex			
Men	1	2	3
Women	1	2	3
By educational level			
High school not completed	0	1	1
High school completed	1	1	2
Some college	2	2	3
College graduate	3	10	13
Students			
High school students	3	4	7
College seniors	7	15	21
Graduate students	9	16	23
Groups in education			
High school teachers	4	10	13
Vocational counselors	3	13	15
College teachers	7	12	17
Natural scientists	6	18	23
Social scientists	5	9	13
Engineers	1	15	15
Groups in business			
Executives	1	14	15
Natural scientists	7	14	21
Social scientists	10	15	25
Engineers	2	22	24
Federal Employee Populations			
General federal employees	3	4	6
By sex			
Men	3	4	6
Women	4	4	8
By educational level			
High school not completed	1	1	2
High school completed	3	3	6
Some college	3	4	8
College graduate	7	11	15
Executives	9	17	24
Natural scientists	2	9	11
Social scientists	14	13	24
Engineers	7	7	14

Table 5-2g

<u>Highlights</u>: Lack of self-determination.

. . . . Mention of lack of self-determination as one of the worst
aspects of an occupation is fairly high in both the general employed
public and among general federal employees.

. . . . Frequency of mention is positively related to educational level.
Figures for the most highly educated groups, especially those in
colleges, are very high, ranging from about 25% to almost 50%.

. . . . 24% of natural scientists in business mention self-determination, compared to 39% in federal employment and 43% in colleges.

<u>Highlights</u>: Lack of responsibility and authority, lack of power to make
     decisions.

. . . . Despite its almost complete lack of mention by most groups, this
category was tabled primarily in order to show the contrasting 16%
figure for federal executives.

. . . . Worth noting also is the 16% figure for social scientists in
business.

<u>Highlights</u>: Lack of challenge; no sense of overcoming obstacles,
     keeping goals ahead.

. . . . Lack of challenge is mentioned hardly at all by the general
employed public (even college graduates), high school students, and
general federal employees with no college; all other groups mention it
with moderate frequency. Thus, the general picture is one of positive
association with educational level.

. . . . 13% of college seniors and graduate students cite lack of challenge as one of the worst aspects of an occupation.

. . . . One fourth (26%) of federal social scientists mention lack of
challenge.

116

Table 5-2g

Occupational values: what people describe as the attributes
of the "worst" occupation (cont'd.)

	Lack of self-determination (e.g., not my own master, rigid supervision; no freedom of thought, action)	Lack of responsibility and authority, lack of power to make decisions	Lack of challenge; no sense of overcoming obstacles, keeping goals ahead
Nonfederal Populations			
General employed public	15%	1%	2%
By sex			
Men	16	1	2
Women	13	0	2
By educational level			
High school not completed	13	0	0
High school completed	13	0	0
Some college	23	0	5
College graduate	23	4	4
Students			
High school students	11	1	4
College seniors	31	6	13
Graduate students	32	5	13
Groups in education			
High school teachers	21	4	8
Vocational counselors	19	3	9
College teachers	38	4	16
Natural scientists	43	2	12
Social scientists	48	2	14
Engineers	42	2	15
Groups in business			
Executives	24	6	10
Natural scientists	24	7	19
Social scientists	38	16	15
Engineers	26	11	18
Federal Employee Populations			
General federal employees	14	3	4
By sex			
Men	14	3	4
Women	15	3	5
By educational level			
High school not completed	8	1	1
High school completed	12	2	3
Some college	19	4	7
College graduate	25	9	10
Executives	26	16	15
Natural scientists	39	2	9
Social scientists	32	9	26
Engineers	20	8	8

117

Table 5-2h

<u>Highlights</u>: Little or no sense of achievement or accomplishment
    through seeing results of own work.

. . . . Frequency of mention is low in the general employed public and
among general federal employees, but tends to be positively related to
educational level in the general employed public.

. . . . The figure for federal executives is somewhat higher (18%) than
for business executives (10%).

. . . . Percentages for social scientists in business and the federal
government are highest of all (21% and 22%).

<u>Highlights</u>: Work that violates or does nothing to fulfill religious,
    spiritual, or ethical values.

. . . . Of interest is the over-all low attention paid this matter as a
"worst" feature of an occupation.

. . . . Percentages for groups in education are, in general, somewhat
higher than for other groups, except for social scientists in government
and business.

<u>Highlights</u>: Be unable to do work that is worthwhile, useful, construc-
    tive.

. . . . This matter is scarcely mentioned by the general employed public
and by general federal employees.

. . . . 15% of the graduate students mentioned it.

. . . . Groups in education show moderate frequency of mention.

. . . . Percentages for federal executives, natural scientists, social
scientists, and engineers are higher than for their counterparts in
business.

. . . . Over one fourth (27%) of federal social scientists mention it;
also, the 16% figure for social scientists in business is higher than
the figures for other business groups.

Table 5-2h

Occupational values: what people describe as the attributes
of the "worst" occupation (cont'd.)

	Little or no sense of achievement or accomplishment through seeing results of own work	Work that violates or does nothing to fulfill religious, spiritual, or ethical values	Be unable to do work that is worthwhile, useful, constructive
Nonfederal Populations			
General employed public	3%	4%	1%
By sex			
Men	3	3	1
Women	3	4	2
By educational level			
High school not completed	0	3	0
High school completed	3	2	0
Some college	4	6	2
College graduate	11	7	7
Students			
High school students	3	2	5
College seniors	9	7	8
Graduate students	11	6	15
Groups in education			
High school teachers	10	11	10
Vocational counselors	9	14	11
College teachers	10	16	14
Natural scientists	5	13	12
Social scientists	9	16	15
Engineers	9	16	13
Groups in business			
Executives	10	9	7
Natural scientists	4	5	9
Social scientists	21	12	16
Engineers	13	2	3
Federal Employee Populations			
General federal employees	6	2	3
By sex			
Men	6	2	3
Women	5	2	3
By educational level			
High school not completed	6	1	3
High school completed	4	1	1
Some college	7	2	3
College graduate	9	9	6
Executives	18	10	14
Natural scientists	12	2	14
Social scientists	22	17	27
Engineers	19	5	12

Table 5-2i

<u>Highlights</u>: Work that does not fit one's capacities and/or training.

. . . . Such statements are not numerous in the general employed public, except for college graduates, for whom the figure (15%) is twice the over-all figure.

. . . . One fourth (27%) of the federal social scientists mention this factor.

<u>Highlights</u>: Physical work; work that is physical, menial, or manual.

. . . . Percentages do not vary much from group to group, and show moderate frequency of mention (roughly 10% to 15%).

. . . . Among general federal employees, mention is higher among men (15%) than among women (8%); in the general employed public the figures for men (9%) and women (13%) suggest that the reverse may be true.

<u>Highlights</u>: Too much routine in the work; monotonous; not enough change, variety.

. . . . Monotony and routine as a "worst" feature of an occupation is mentioned with moderately high to extremely high frequency by all groups except those who have not completed high school (nonfederal 7%, federal 14%).

. . . . Percentages for general federal employees are higher than for the general employed public especially at the high school not completed levels and some college levels.

. . . . Percentages show a marked positive relationship with educational level in the general employed public, among general federal employees, and for students.

. . . . Characteristic figures for groups with four years or more of college are 45% or higher.

Table 5-2i

Occupational values: what people describe as the attributes
of the "worst" occupation (cont'd.)

	Work that does not fit one's capacities and or training	Physical work; work that is physical, menial or manual	Too much routine in the work; monotonous; not enough change, variety
Nonfederal Populations			
General employed public	7%	10%	21%
By sex			
Men	7	9	20
Women	9	13	24
By educational level			
High school not completed	7	9	7
High school completed	5	9	22
Some college	9	12	30
College graduate	15	14	45
Students			
High school students	10	12	34
College seniors	12	17	57
Graduate students	15	16	59
Groups in education			
High school teachers	10	10	44
Vocational counselors	16	11	50
College teachers	12	17	53
Natural scientists	7	17	53
Social scientists	11	13	57
Engineers	11	15	52
Groups in business			
Executives	12	13	46
Natural scientists	13	18	66
Social scientists	18	12	51
Engineers	12	17	57
Federal Employee Populations			
General federal employees	11	13	29
By sex			
Men	11	15	28
Women	14	8	34
By educational level			
High school not completed	8	13	14
High school completed	12	13	25
Some college	12	14	45
College graduate	15	16	49
Executives	19	11	54
Natural scientists	11	16	49
Social scienitsts	27	13	52
Engineers	18	10	52

Table 5-2j

<u>Highlights</u>: Little or no leisure, recreation, time off.

. . . . This category was tabled simply to display the low percentages of mention characteristic of all groups.

<u>Highlights</u>: Too much pressure or tension.

. . . . Mention of pressure is moderately low in all groups, but is somewhat more characteristic of women than men, especially among general federal employees (nonfederal 12% to 8%; federal 15% to 6%).

. . . . Neither federal executives nor business executives refer to it very often.

<u>Highlights</u>: Excessive work load; hard work.

. . . . Excessive work is pointed out hardly at all except by the two lowest educational groups in the general employed public and among general federal employees. Thus, frequency of mention is negatively associated with educational level, especially in the general employed public, where the figure for the high school not completed group is 20% in contrast to 4% for college graduates.

<u>Highlights</u>: Bad location of work.

. . . . This category was tabled to show the higher, but still moderate percentages among federal executives, natural scientists, and engineers.

Table 5-2j

Occupational values: what people describe as the attributes
of the "worst" occupation (cont'd.)

	Little or no leisure, recreation, time off	Too much pressure or tension	Excessive work load; hard work	Bad location of work (e.g., in unpleasant area; inconvenient; not where I want to live)
Nonfederal Populations				
General employed public	4%	9%	12%	4%
By sex				
Men	4	8	11	3
Women	4	12	14	6
By educational level				
High school not completed	3	10	20	3
High school completed	4	9	10	4
Some college	3	8	5	4
College graduate	4	7	4	5
Students				
High school students	3	4	8	4
College seniors	8	9	4	6
Graduate students	4	8	4	6
Groups in education				
High school teachers	6	12	4	3
Vocational counselors	5	14	3	4
College teachers	5	9	1	4
Natural scientists	3	9	3	4
Social scientists	7	8	0	1
Engineers	1	7	0	8
Groups in business				
Executives	3	6	3	4
Natural scientists	2	6	5	4
Social scientists	4	1	4	3
Engineers	1	8	3	2
Federal Employee Populations				
General federal employees	5	8	8	7
By sex				
Men	5	6	7	6
Women	5	15	12	8
By educational level				
High school not completed	4	5	13	5
High school completed	5	11	8	8
Some college	6	8	4	5
College graduate	4	7	3	8
Executives	7	10	2	12
Natural scientists	5	8	3	15
Social scientists	11	9	8	5
Engineers	4	5	1	18

123

In discussing negative aspects, men mention lack of employment security more often than women do; women emphasize far more the factors of being around unpleasant, disagreeable people and being subject to bad or unfair supervision.

Variations in response pattern by educational level are even more marked. The higher the level, the *less* frequently are good physical environment and working conditions and having a good and understanding supervisor or boss mentioned as aspects of an ideal occupation—and the *more* frequently such matters as associating with stimulating worthwhile people, having opportunity for self-advancement and for self-development, self-expression, and creativity, being in an occupation that offers challenge, and being able to do worthwhile, constructive work. With respect to the last-mentioned value, for instance, frequency rises from 9 percent at the high school incomplete level to 32 percent at the college graduate level. Mentions of concern for having stimulating associates rise from 12 percent at the lowest level to 34 percent at the highest.

Similar variations by educational level occur in the description of the factors characterizing the worse sort of occupation. The higher the level, the less likely are mentions of such negative values as a specific kind of work especially disliked, poor physical environment on the job, and an excessive workload; on the other hand, the more likely are mentions of being unable to follow the particular kind of work liked, being unable to engage in worthwhile, constructive work, lacking opportunity for self-determination, freedom, self-development, self-expression, and self-advancement, and being compelled to do routine, monotonous work. For this last negative value the range is from 7 percent at the high school incomplete level to 45 percent among college graduates. The other factors in general show less dramatic shifts, but the differences are still highly significant.

High School Students, College Seniors, and Graduate Students

Among the student populations the differential patterns of positive and negative occupational values by present educational level are roughly similar to those found in the general working population. Between college seniors and graduate students the differences are relatively small; between these two college groups and the high school students the differences are fairly large. The college groups, for example, in discussing the ideal occupation emphasize self-development, self-determination, sense of achievement, and sense of worthwhileness in the work far more than do high school students. Worth noting also is that 14 percent of each of the college groups, compared to 6 percent of high school students, explicitly qualify their statements that financial reward is a positive value by saying that money is not of primary importance, and that one needs only to be paid enough for an adequate standard of living.

The pattern of student replies about the characteristics of the worst sort of occupation is also related to educational level. High school students, in comparison to college students, more frequently mention inadequate financial reward and bad physical environment and general working conditions; they also mention significantly less frequently lack of opportunity for self-expression, self-determination, challenge, achievement, and worthwhile work. Monotony and routine as a negative feature is mentioned with high frequency by all three student populations, but there is still a marked difference between the high schoolers (34 percent) and the college seniors and graduate students (57 and 59 percent).

A comparison of high school students with respondents in the general public who have completed high school reveals that the students place considerably more emphasis on the positive occupational values of personal relationships on the job, especially active, outgoing relationships, on opportunity for self-development, on challenge in the job, and on opportunity to do worthwhile, constructive work. For example, 26 percent of high school students mention this last factor, whereas only 10 percent of the comparable group in the general public do. Comparison of the two groups with respect to negative values shows an essentially similar picture. Thus, in general, the high school students of today seem to show a configuration of positive and negative occupational values which resembles the pattern of the college educated in the general public rather than the pattern of those with lesser education. How much of this is due to age differences, intergenerational culture change, or the fact that our high school sample contains a high proportion of potential college-level people is not revealed by these data.

High School Teachers and Vocational Counselors

The responses of high school teachers and vocational counselors are very similar to those of college graduates in the general employed public. There are, however, certain significant differences.

The high school teachers emphasize good personal relationships far more than the college graduates do—and especially relationships that are active and stimulating rather than merely passive and agreeable. This is not surprising in view of their teaching function and the importance of relationships with their students, but it is worth noting that this group emphasizes the factor even more than college teachers do. The positive value of experiencing a sense of achievement or accomplishment through seeing the results of one's own work is also stressed more by high school teachers than by college graduates in the general population. In addition, 49 percent of the teachers and 66 percent of the counselors mention the positive value of being able to do worthwhile, constructive work, compared to 32 percent of the college graduates.

College Teachers, Natural and Social Scientists, and Engineers

In general, the population of college teachers shows the pattern we have already found to be associated with a high level of education, but the group is also unique in some of its responses. There is, for example, scarcely any mention of occupational security as a positive or a negative concern, and little attention is given to either the good or the bad features of supervision. Further, only 2 percent of college teachers cite opportunity for self-advancement as a positive value, in contrast to up to 20 percent citing it in other upper-level educational and occupational groups. They show especially high concern with opportunity for self-development, self-expression, and creativity; on the negative side, the concern is high about loss of self-determination, lack of challenge, and lack of opportunity to do worthwhile, constructive work. Statements about financial reward as a positive feature are qualified by 12 percent, who say that money is important only to the extent that it meets a certain specified minimum.

The pattern for the natural and social scientists and the engineers is essentially the same as that of the general college teacher population, in which they are included in their proper proportions. However, all three of these groups differ significantly from the general teacher population in being markedly more concerned with self-determination and freedom. Self-determination as an aspect of the ideal occupation is mentioned by 48 percent of both the natural and the social scientists and by 56 percent of the engineers, whereas the figure for the general group is 38 percent. The natural scientists, in describing the "worst" occupation, note the loss of opportunity for self-development, self-expression, and creativity significantly more often than do the social scientists and engineers.

Groups in Business

In general the business groups show relatively few common traits that can be attributed with certainty to the fact that they are in business rather than in some other type of employment. Their patterns of positive and negative occupational values are largely characteristic of other well-educated groups, but a few other tentative generalizations can be made.

The groups emphasize slightly less than do their counterparts elsewhere a concern with occupational security and the nature of supervision. On the chance to do worthwhile, useful, or constructive work their figures are fairly high, ranging from 20 to almost 40 percent, but tend over all to be somewhat lower than for comparable groups in education or government. The business respondents also seem to express somewhat less concern with personal relationships on the job, but again the figures are fairly high; those who do mention the factor emphasize active, as opposed to passive, relationships very strongly. In discussing features of the "worst" occupation, they give less emphasis to disagreeable personal relationships; the range is roughly from 20 to 30 percent, whereas for almost all of the comparable groups the figures are well above 30 percent. But references to routine and monotony as negative occupational features are frequent among the business groups—the percentages ranging from 46 to 66.

General Federal Employees

A comparative review of the figures for general federal employees indicates a configuration of occupational values that differs significantly in many ways from that of the general employed public. It is impossible, however, from these data to say whether the differences result from the type of people that select, or are selected for, federal employment or from acculturation on the job. It is likely that both factors are operating.

In comparison with the general employed public, federal employees on the average show significantly more concern about the positive values of job security, good equipment and facilities, good supervision, good personal relationships—especially passive relationships—and opportunities for self-advancement and for recognition. Of particular interest are their more frequent references to supervision and to personal relationships: whereas 11 percent of the general employed public mention supervision, 20 percent of the federal employees do so; for personal relationships the figures are 30 and 47 percent. Relative consideration of passive versus active personal relationships presents a further contrast: federal employees, compared to nonfederal, tend to stress the passive—that is, simply being around pleasant agreeable people rather than having contact with stimulating, interesting people.

A similar pattern of differences is shown in the responses about the worst possible features of an occupation. For mention of bad supervision as an occupational drawback the federal figure is 31 percent, compared to 18 percent for the general employed public. Federal employees also evince especially high concern with bad personal relations on the job—29 percent, compared to 19 percent in the general employed public—and place significantly more emphasis on lack of self-advancement, lack of recognition, and the disadvantages of routine and monotony.

The structuring of values shows a number of significant differences by sex. In discussing the positive values, men place significantly more emphasis than women on financial reward and security, and slightly more on self-determination. Women are much more likely to emphasize worthwhile and constructive work and supervision that is good, understanding, and sympathetic. And approximately two thirds of them mention the factor of personal relationships whereas only about 40 percent of the men do so.

The pattern of sex differences concerning negative values is similar. Men devote considerably more attention to poor financial reward and to lack of security on the job; women place much greater emphasis on poor personal relationships and bad and unsympathetic supervision. The disparities regarding personal relationships are again especially significant: 23 percent of the men vs. 47 percent of the women.

Frequency of mention and educational level are positively related for a large number of values. In general the higher the level, the more often are the values associated with personal emergence and ego-satisfaction mentioned. Opportunity for self-advancement and progress as a positive value rises from 6 percent at the high school not completed level to 20 percent for college graduates; receiving recognition for one's work increases from 7 to 16 percent; opportunity for self-development, self-expression, and creativity from 11 to 33 percent; self-determination and autonomy from 19 to 31 percent; doing work that offers a sense of challenge and keeps goals ahead from 4 to 23 percent; having a sense of achievement or accomplishment through seeing the results of one's own work from 9 to 21 percent; and doing work that is worthwhile, useful, and constructive from 11 to 30 percent.

The patterning of negative concerns shows a roughly similar relationship to educational level. Here, however, certain other values enter into the picture and are similarly positively related to educational level. Particularly important is the negative concern with having to do routine or monotonous work: 14 percent of the general federal employees who have not completed high school mention this factor, compared to 49 percent of the college graduates.

The concern with the nature of personal relationships on the job is especially worth noting. Frequency of mention of this factor, whether positive or negative, is very high and shows little difference by educational level. Approximately one half of all general federal employees at all educational levels say that good personal relationships are an attribute of an "ideal" job, and one fourth to one third mention the lack of them when discussing the "worst" occupation. In contrast, the general public's references to personal relationships as a positive value show a sharp positive relationship to educational level—ranging from 22 percent at the lowest level to 42 percent among college graduates. Furthermore, federal employee college graduates mention the passive and the active aspects of relationships as positive values about equally often; among college graduates in the general public only 9 percent mention the passive aspect, while 34 percent mention the active aspect.

Federal employees at the college graduate level cite high or good financial reward as a positive value significantly more often than federal employees with less education; this is not the case in the general employed public. And among general federal employees mention of poor or inadequate financial reward as a negative concern shows no association with educational level, whereas in the general public there is a definite negative association with education.

Federal Executives, Natural and Social Scientists, and Engineers

The occupational values of the four special federal groups are similar in most important respects to those found in the groups with the highest educational and occupational attainments outside federal employment. In their descriptions of the things which characterize the best sort of occupational situation, all four groups mention good financial reward with very high frequency, the figures ranging from 48 to 52 percent. Sharing the honors for first place in frequency of mention is the nature of personal relationships on the job: from 45 to 63 percent of the respondents cite it. Also accorded high attention are the positive values of being able to do worthwhile, constructive work; having a sense of achievement or accomplishment in connection with one's work; opportunity for self-development and self-expression; doing work that offers a challenge and keeps goals ahead; self-determination and autonomy; doing work that fits one's capacities and abilities; having good physical environment and general working conditions.

When these respondents describe the characteristics of the worst occupational situation, references to routine and monotony top the list in every case, with figures of 49 to 54 percent. Having bad personal relationships with people on the job is second in frequency of mention for all except the federal engineers, for whom it is fifth. Bad physical environment and general working conditions, poor or inadequate supervision, having to do a specific kind of work one especially dislikes, lack of self-determination, lack of self-development, self-expression, and creativity, having little or no sense of achievement, and lack of self-advancement also stand in the forefront of the factors mentioned. It is of interest that poor or inadequate financial reward, which receives fairly high notice in all groups, ranks seventh for the federal natural and social scientists—well below bad personal relations, bad supervision, and lack of self-determination. Only in the case of the engineers is poor financial reward accorded a frequency of mention which ranks it near the top as a negative characteristic.

Relative to comparable groups outside of government, these four special federal populations characteristically place significantly more stress on personal relationships on the job—with particular stress on passive relationships—the nature of supervision, and good financial reward. It is worth noting also that, although they do not mention security with high frequency, they do cite it significantly more often than do the comparable nonfederal groups.

In describing "worst" features, all of the four groups emphasize more than do their nonfederal counterparts bad personal relationships on the job, bad supervision, and bad physical environment and general working conditions. Poor or insufficient security is mentioned with low frequency (5 to 11 percent), but there is a suggestion that the federal groups are a bit more concerned with security than are their nonfederal counterparts, whose comments rarely include the lack of security.

The four special federal populations are not homogeneous in their patterning of values. The executives—in comparison to the other three groups—tend to give special emphasis to the positive value of work that is challenging and that allows one a sense of achievement or accomplishment through seeing its results. Discussing the worst features of an occupation, they give relatively more emphasis to lack of self-advancement and to lack of self-development, self-expression, and creativity.

The natural scientists, for their part, give significantly more emphasis to the positive factors of self-determination and autonomy, as well as the equipment or facilities to do the job. The percentage mentioning the importance of finding interest, enjoyment, satisfaction, and fun in the work is also appreciably higher. However, they seem to place less emphasis on personal relationships and, insofar as they do mention them, are less likely to emphasize the active aspect. Similarly, their percentages are relatively somewhat lower for the values of self-development and self-expression, challenge, and the worthwhileness of the work. When they consider the "worst" occupation they seem to place less emphasis on bad supervision, lack of self-advancement, lack of a sense of achievement through being unable to see the results of their work, and doing work that does not specifically fit their capacities. In contrast, they give especially high mention to the absence of self-determination.

The federal social scientists are of particular interest because of their strong emphasis on the positive feature of being able to do work that is worthwhile and constructive, as well as their stress on good personal relationships on the job—especially those that are stimulating and worthwhile. They rank these relationships first (63 percent mention them), followed by worthwhileness of the work (56 percent), and by good financial reward (48 percent). On the negative values the social scientists also show some differences. They tend to deplore, more than the other three groups, doing work that is not fitted to their capacities and training and doing work that lacks opportunity for self-advancement and self-development.

The engineers distinguish themselves from the other three high-level groups, not so much by their descriptions of the ideal job, but by the differential frequency with which they mention certain features of the "worst" occupation. A significantly higher percentage of them mention poor financial reward: this ranks number three as a negative feature and is almost tied for second place; in none of the other three groups does it rank higher than sixth place. Engineers also give considerably more emphasis to working in a bad location—almost a fifth of them cite this. But they mention lack of self-determination as a negative feature considerably less than the other three groups do.

The number of federal and business executives interviewed was sufficiently large to make it worthwhile to compare the two groups. Caution is needed, however, because, as noted earlier, the federal group was much the more voluble in discussing occupational values; therefore they mentioned practically all positive and negative values with higher frequencies than did their business counterparts. Thus it is especially important in comparing the two groups to attend more to the relative rank orders of values than to the relative percentages.

When we do this, we find that the rank orders for both groups do not greatly differ. The federal executives display a little more concern with supervision, financial reward, and worthwhileness of the work, while business executives show a little more concern with self-determination, challenge, and not having to do work they especially dislike.

6

The Occupational Value Scale Items

THE ELEVEN TABLES IN THIS CHAPTER present the results from the scaling of thirty occupational value statements by the respondents in all of the federal and nonfederal populations.[1] Each statement was placed where the respondent thought it belonged on the ten-point agree-disagree scale. (The scaling method is discussed in detail in Chapter 2.) The results tabled here show the mean scores each group gave each item; the higher the mean score, the higher the average amount of agreement with the item by the group.

Most of the statements fall into related value clusters of items. In Table 6-1a (pages 138-139) three items deal with occupational involvement. The first, "A person has a right to expect his work to be fun," is designed to measure the degree to which a person believes he has a right to this sort of positive involvement in his occupation. The second, "To me work is nothing more than a way of making a living," is oriented to the present. A low level of agreement suggests that the respondent sees his work as providing, not merely a living, but many other positive values. Strong agreement with the third item, "I like the kind of work you can forget about after the work day is over," suggests that the individual prefers to place work in one compartment and the rest of his activities in another; disagreement suggests that a more complete integration of work with other aspects of living is preferred.

The two items of Table 6-1b concern two important aspects of financial reward in relation to occupational values. The scaling of the first item "To be really successful in life, you have to care about making money," suggests the degree to which people see money as an ingredient of success; the second item, "After you are making enough money to get

[1] The thirty statements were among the total fifty-five items to be sorted on the agree-disagree scale; see Appendix B, Item 17.

along, then making more money in an occupation isn't very important," poses the relationship between money and other values more directly.

The cluster of items in Table 6-1c is concerned with three different aspects of status as an occupational value. It was particularly important to introduce these three measures of status. People seem to feel that stating their direct concern with status as an occupational value is socially unacceptable, and therefore we found very little direct mention of it in the answers to free-response questions. In the scaling procedure, however, despite the fact that the status implications of the items are not well concealed, all three aspects are given moderately high to very high ratings by all groups, indicating that, to some degree at least, the items penetrated the "social cover-up." The status aspects touched upon are respect ("To me, gaining the increased respect of family and friends is one of the important rewards of getting ahead in an occupation"), keeping up with the Joneses ("I would like my family to be able to have most of the things my friends and neighbors have"), and personal recognition ("Getting recognition for my work is important to me").

Table 6-1d is concerned with personal relationships on the job. The first statement, "To me, a very important part of work is the opportunity to make friends," emphasizes the positive seeking out of friendships in a context, not merely of concern or desire, but of importance. The second, "Sometimes it may be right for a person to lose friends in order to get ahead in his work," deals with the competitive aspect of interpersonal relations, with friendship put in opposition to getting ahead. The third statement, "It is satisfying to direct the work of others," deals with the authority aspect of job relationships.

The four items in Table 6-1e are designed to get at aspects of the closely related values of occupational striving and competitiveness. The first, "It is more important for a job to offer opportunity than security," pits opportunity against security in terms of their importance to the person; the higher the score, on the average, the more is the group oriented to opportunity rather than to security. The second concerns the importance of having a chance to get to the top; the third, competitiveness as it relates to feelings about being passed up occupationally by others; and the fourth, competitiveness as it relates to the feeling that it is important to do a better job than the next person.

The cluster in Table 6-1f might be called "perceived avenues to success." The three items measure the degrees to which people feel that luck, knowing the right people, and hard work are avenues to success.

In Table 6-1g the items were designed to measure subscription to altruistic social goals as occupational aims. The first, "The main satisfaction a person can get out of work is helping other people," is a strong statement, implicitly pitting help to other people against all the other possible occupational motives. The response can be made in very personal terms, since the respondent may have in mind helping people with whom he is closely associated. The second item, "To me, almost the only thing that matters about a job is the chance to do work that is worthwhile to society," is an equally strong statement (or perhaps even stronger), but has less of the personal-association element in it and is broadly oriented to society.

The two items in Table 6-1h are not related, although both deal with a personal or ego-oriented view of one's work. The first, "To me, it's important in an occupation that a person be able to see the results of his own work," involves a significant occupational value. The second, "To me, it's important to have the kind of work that gives me a chance to develop my own special abilities," involves an aspect of self-development and personal emergence—also a highly significant value.

The two statements in Table 6-1i are also not closely related conceptually. The first, "Work is most satisfying when there are hard problems to solve," is concerned with one aspect of occupational challenge. The second, "To me, it's important in an occupation for a person to be able to carry out his own ideas without interference," gets at the value of personal autonomy and self-determination.

The cluster of statements in Table 6-1j deal with a value that might be called duty, or obligation towards one's work. The first, "A person should constantly try to succeed at work even if it interferes with other things in life," certainly touches upon occupational involvement, but also implies duty or obligation, as does the second, "Even if you dislike your work, you should do your best"; in the latter instance, however, duty is pitted against negative perceptions of one's job. The third statement, "If a person doesn't want to work hard it's his own business," is considerably more abstract than the others and broaches the idea of occupational duty as an ethic.

The items in Table 6-1k constitute three different aspects of a generalized attitude toward work which is reputed to prevail in the United States as a heritage of the Puritan and Calvinist traditions. The general concept could be characterized as "work is a positive thing, essential to and compatible with the nature of man." The first item, "Work helps you forget about your personal problems," deals with work as a feature of positive personal adjustment. The second and third items, "Work is a good builder of character" and "Work is a way of being of service to God," have strong ethical overtones.

In general, the group patterning of the scores on the thirty statements is highly consistent with the pattern of the responses to the free-answer questions on occupational values (with the exception, mentioned earlier, of the status ratings). This high degree of consistency between the results of these two methods of assessment—the "open-end question" and "item-scaling"—adds to surety of interpretation.

Discussion of Specific Group Data

In this description of group-to-group results a minimum of attention is paid to fine comparisons between the average amount of agreement or disagreement with one statement and the average amount with another. The scaling procedure does not lend itself to precise distinctions of this kind. Some of the statements are worded positively and some negatively, and we have no ready method for equating a degree of positive feeling with a degree of negative feeling. There is some research which indicates that a score of five may be regarded roughly as the dividing line between agreement and disagreement.[2] Even if we accept this, we know from experience that subtle differences in item wording can very often make a significant difference in the average amount of agreement or disagreement accorded.

However, in comparing the mean score of one group of respondents to that of another group on any given item we are not faced with the same difficulties. Each respondent in every group responded to the same items on the same scale; therefore we may more safely compare the relative scores of one group to those of another. This type of between-group comparison is emphasized in the following discussion.

General Employed Public

For the reasons given above, the average item-by-item scores in the general employed public are not enumerated here. We turn directly to a

[2] Jan Stapel, *Scales Without Tears* (International Institute of Public Opinion, Amsterdam, February 1953; mimeographed).

comparison of the relative scores of groupings within this population.

COMPARATIVE PATTERNS BY SEX. With respect to occupational involvement, women show a somewhat greater tendency than men to agree with the statement "I like the kind of work you can forget about when the work day is over," suggesting less desire to integrate work with other activities. They also place less emphasis on the importance of being respected by others as an attribute of the work they do; are significantly less oriented toward opportunity as opposed to security; subscribe less to the idea that it is important to have a chance to get to the top; place less emphasis on doing a better job than the next person; are less apt to see the challenge of hard problems as a satisfying aspect of work; and are perhaps slightly less inclined to believe it important to be able to carry out their own ideas without interference.

On the other hand, women subscribe more than men to the statement, "To me, a very important part of work is the opportunity to make friends," and agree significantly less with the ideas that it may be right for a person to lose friends in order to get ahead in his work and that it is satisfying to direct the work of others. There appears to be no significant sex difference concerning the importance of doing work that is worthwhile to society, but when the idea of commitment to social goals is put in the potentially personal context of "helping other people," the average score for women is significantly higher than that for men. Women also see work as a means of forgetting personal problems to a greater degree than men.

The over-all pattern suggests that women, as compared to men, see work somewhat more in terms of security (as opposed to opportunity), interpersonal relationships, and perhaps somewhat more as an escape partially divorced from other activities. Men appear to be somewhat more oriented in the direction of opportunity, drive to get ahead, competitiveness, challenge, and autonomy.

COMPARATIVE PATTERNS BY EDUCATIONAL LEVEL. Most of the occupational values touched upon by the thirty scale statements show a marked difference in patterning by educational level. In some instances the differences between the mean scores of those who did not complete high school and of the college graduates are as great as 3 scale points, and differences exceeding 1½ scale points are extremely common; the scores proceed in steps, upward or downward, from high school not completed, to high school completed, to some college, and to college graduates.

(Text continued on page 160)

Tables 6-1a Through 6-1k

The figures in this series of tables show the average amounts of agreement or disagreement in the nonfederal and federal population groups with each of a number of statements covering a wide range of occupational values. The statements were printed on small cards; respondents manually sorted them on to a 10-point ladder scale, placing them according to the amount of agreement or disagreement they felt.

Column 1 of Table 6-1a gives the average number of respondents in each group who sorted the items presented in Tables 6-1a through 6-1k. In every group the variation in the number who sorted each of the items was so small that it was felt that tabling the actual number for each of the items would be a waste of space.

Table 6-1a

Highlights: "A person has a right to expect his work to be fun."

. . . . The over-all picture is one of mild agreement with this statement in all groups.

. . . . College seniors and graduate students show more agreement than high school students.

. . . . In general those employed by the federal government indicate less subscription than those outside the government.

Highlights: "To me, work is nothing more than a way of making a living."

. . . . The average scores for all groups except the high school not completed group in the general employed public show mild to very strong disagreement.

. . . . The figure for the general employed public is higher than the figure for general federal employees, accounted for mainly by the markedly higher figures at the high school completed and high school not completed levels in the general employed public.

. . . . In the general employed public and among general federal employees there is a strong negative relationship between degree of agreement and educational level--the higher the educational level the less agreement.

. . . . High school students concur slightly more than college seniors and graduate students.

Highlights: "I like the kind of work you can forget about after the work day is over."

. . . . The ratings range from moderate agreement to moderate disagreement.

. . . . Agreement is slightly higher in the general employed public than among general federal employees; in both groups women show a stronger agreement than do men.

. . . . In the general employed public and among general federal employees mean scores are negatively related to educational level--the higher the educational level the less agreement.

. . . . Disagreement is stronger for college seniors and graduate students, than for high school students. In general, natural scientists, social scientists, and engineers in the federal government, in business, and especially in colleges disagree with the statement.

Table 6-1a

Occupational values: average (mean) ratings of "occupational value" statements on the 10-point agree-disagree scale; the higher the score, the more agreement

	Average number answering	"A person has a right to expect his work to be fun."	"To me, work is nothing more than a way of making a living."	"I like the kind of work you can forget about after the work day is over."
Nonfederal Populations				
General employed public	1087	6.2	4.2	6.7
By sex				
Men	835	6.1	4.2	6.6
Women	252	6.3	4.4	7.2
By educational level				
High school not completed	304	6.4	5.6	7.5
High school completed	495	6.0	4.0	6.7
Some college	123	6.1	3.2	6.0
College graduate	135	6.5	2.6	5.3
Students				
High school students	354	6.1	2.8	4.9
College seniors	400	7.0	2.1	3.8
Graduate students	380	6.9	2.1	3.5
Groups in education				
High school teachers	279	6.1	2.6	5.3
Vocational counselors	79	5.9	2.5	4.6
College teachers	470	6.5	2.0	3.5
Natural scientists	118	7.1	1.9	3.2
Social scientists	104	6.1	2.1	3.8
Engineers	86	6.5	2.0	3.1
Groups in business				
Executives	272	5.9	2.8	4.7
Natural scientists	84	6.4	2.2	3.8
Social scientists	70	6.0	2.0	4.0
Engineers	89	6.5	2.6	4.5
Federal Employee Populations				
General federal employees	930	5.2	3.3	6.2
By sex				
Men	647	5.4	3.4	6.0
Women	283	4.9	3.0	6.6
By educational level				
High school not completed	182	5.9	3.9	6.8
High school completed	353	5.1	3.3	6.6
Some college	179	4.7	3.0	5.6
College graduate	162	5.4	2.7	5.1
Executives	271	5.5	2.1	4.4
Natural scientists	91	6.2	1.9	4.1
Social scientists	90	6.1	2.0	4.0
Engineers	98	5.8	2.6	4.8

Table 6-1b

Highlights: "To be really successful in life, you have to care about making money."

. . . . There is more agreement with this statement in the general employed public than among general federal employees, and in both populations the scores show a negative relationship with educational level; the higher the education the more disagreement.

. . . . In general the scores for students and for groups in education are quite low.

. . . . Business executives show markedly higher concurrence than do federal executives. The same is true of engineers in business compared with engineers in the federal government or in colleges.

. . . . In general the ratings for natural scientists and social scientists are quite low, indicating substantial disagreement, but they are somewhat higher for those in business than for those in the federal government or in colleges.

Highlights: "After you are making enough money to get along, then making more money in an occupation isn't very important."

. . . . Scores are about the same for the general employed public and for general federal employees. In both groups there is a suggestion that the high school not completed and the college graduate levels subscribe a little more strongly than the two middle educational levels.

. . . . The amoung of agreement is positively related to present educational level among students.

. . . . The greatest amount of agreement is shown among the college groups.

. . . . Federal executives, natural scientists, social scientists, and engineers give higher ratings to the statement than their counterparts in business.

Table 6-1b

Occupational values: average (mean) ratings of "occupational value" statements on the 10-point agree-disagree scale; the higher the score, the more agreement (cont'd.)

	"To be really successful in life, you have to care about making money."	"After you are making enough money to get along, then making more money in an occupation isn't very important."
Nonfederal Populations		
General employed public	5.8	4.9
By sex		
Men	5.8	5.0
Women	5.8	4.7
By educational level		
High school not completed	6.6	5.2
High school completed	5.7	4.7
Some college	5.5	4.8
College graduate	4.6	5.5
Students		
High school students	4.3	5.0
College seniors	3.8	5.9
Graduate students	3.6	6.4
Groups in education		
High school teachers	4.2	5.4
Vocational counselors	4.3	5.6
College teachers	3.3	6.8
Natural scientists	3.2	6.9
Social scientists	3.4	6.4
Engineers	3.6	7.3
Groups in business		
Executives	5.7	5.0
Natural scientists	4.1	5.6
Social scientists	4.4	5.2
Engineers	5.9	5.2
Federal Employee Populations		
General federal employees	5.0	4.8
By sex		
Men	5.2	4.9
Women	4.3	4.5
By educational level		
High school not completed	6.1	4.8
High school completed	4.9	4.4
Some college	4.4	4.6
College graduate	4.1	5.8
Executives	4.0	5.8
Natural scientists	3.4	6.9
Social scientists	3.6	6.2
Engineers	4.2	5.8

Table 6-1c

The three statements in this table were designed to get at aspects of occupational status and recognition. This was thought to be particularly important because in general people do not admit readily to status striving per se in response to open-end questions. This same sort of reluctance probably operates to some extent in the manual sorting used in connection with these items. Nevertheless, the scores in general are quite high on all three items for all groups and reveal some of the positive feeling toward various aspects of status.

Highlights: "To me, gaining the increased respect of family and friends is one of the important rewards of getting ahead in an occupation."

. . . . Scores are about equal for general employed public and general federal employees; in both groups there is a tendency for men to rate the item higher than do women.

. . . . Among students the scores are negatively related to present educational levels.

Highlights: "I would like my family to be able to have most of the things my friends and neighbors have."

. . . . The ratings for the general employed public and for general federal employees, both over-all and with respect to educational level, are about the same. However, among general federal employees men give the item a higher rating than do women.

. . . . Executives and engineers in the federal government agree more with the item than do natural scientists and social scientists in government; the same pattern is shown by these groups in business.

Highlights: "Getting recognition for my own work is important to me."

. . . . In general the scores are quite consistently high for all groups, being highest for groups in business and for all federal employee populations. High school teachers and vocational counselors, as well as high school students, deviate somewhat toward the low side.

Table 6-1c

Occupational values: average (mean) ratings of "occupational value" statements on the 10-point agree-disagree scale; the higher the score, the more agreement (cont'd.)

	"To me, gaining the increased respect of family and friends is one of the important rewards of getting ahead in an occupation."	"I would like my family to be able to have most of the things my friends and neighbors have."	"Getting recognition for my own work is important to me."
Nonfederal Populations			
General employed public	7.6	7.4	7.6
By sex			
Men	7.7	7.4	7.7
Women	7.2	7.2	7.6
By educational level			
High school not completed	7.6	7.7	7.6
High school completed	7.6	7.3	7.6
Some college	8.1	7.3	7.6
College graduate	7.4	7.1	7.7
Students			
High school students	8.2	7.4	7.0
College seniors	7.3	6.8	7.7
Graduate students	6.9	6.8	7.7
Groups in education			
High school teachers	7.6	7.1	7.3
Vocational counselors	7.3	7.3	7.3
College teachers	7.1	6.6	7.6
Natural scientists	7.6	6.8	7.9
Social scientists	7.0	6.6	8.0
Engineers	7.1	6.8	7.7
Groups in business			
Executives	7.9	7.5	8.4
Natural scientists	7.4	7.1	8.2
Social scientists	7.4	7.1	8.1
Engineers	8.0	7.6	8.3
Federal Employee Populations			
General federal employees	7.7	7.2	8.2
By sex			
Men	7.9	7.5	8.3
Women	7.0	6.0	7.9
By educational level			
High school not completed	7.9	7.7	8.2
High school completed	7.8	7.2	8.3
Some college	7.5	6.7	8.0
College graduate	7.7	7.0	8.2
Executives	7.9	7.7	8.2
Natural scientists	7.2	6.9	8.4
Social scientists	6.8	6.5	8.2
Engineers	7.4	7.4	8.6

Table 6-1d

The items in this table were designed to get at three aspects of occupationally related personal relationships: positive seeking out of friendships, the competitive aspect, and the authority aspect.

Highlights: "To me, a very important part of work is the opportunity to make friends."

. . . . All groups indicate moderate to high concurrence.

. . . . In the general employed public women agree slightly more than men; among general federal employees the reverse is true.

. . . . Students' scores show a slight negative relationship with present educational levels--the higher the level the less agreement.

. . . . In both government and business, natural and social scientists assign lower ratings than do engineers and executives.

Highlights: "Sometimes it may be right for a person to lose friends in order to get ahead in his work."

. . . . All groups show mild disagreement. Figures for the general employed public and general federal employees differ little--over-all, by sex, and by educational level.

. . . . In the two general employee groups men agree slightly more than women.

. . . . The general employed public's scores have a slight negative relationship with educational level.

Highlights: "It is satisfying to direct the work of others."

. . . . Among all groups agreement is moderate to high.

. . . . The general employed public subscribes somewhat less than general federal employees do--owing mainly to differences at the two lower educational levels.

. . . . In the two general employee groups men concur more than women.

. . . . Agreement is positively related to educational level in both the federal and nonfederal populations.

. . . . Business engineers and executives assign high ratings to a lesser extent as do engineers and executives in the federal government.

Table 6-1d
Occupational values: average (mean) ratings of "occupational
value" statements on the 10-point agree-disagree scale; the
higher the score, the more agreement (cont'd.)

	"To me, a very important part of work is the opportunity to make friends."	"Sometimes it may be right for a person to lose friends in order to get ahead in his work."	"It is satisfying to direct the work of others."
Nonfederal Populations			
General employed public	7.4	4.1	6.6
By sex			
Men	7.3	4.2	6.8
Women	7.8	3.7	5.8
By educational level			
High school not completed	7.6	4.5	6.0
High school completed	7.2	4.0	6.5
Some college	7.6	4.1	7.1
College graduate	7.4	3.8	7.6
Students			
High school students	8.2	3.5	6.5
College seniors	7.8	3.9	7.5
Graduate students	7.2	3.7	7.3
Groups in education			
High school teachers	7.8	4.1	7.9
Vocational counselors	7.5	3.8	7.8
College teachers	7.2	4.0	7.6
Natural scientists	7.4	3.9	7.9
Social scientists	6.6	4.5	7.0
Engineers	6.9	3.6	8.1
Groups in business			
Executives	7.4	4.0	8.4
Natural scientists	6.1	4.0	7.6
Social scientists	6.3	4.2	7.6
Engineers	7.4	4.1	8.7
Federal Employee Populations			
General federal employees	7.2	4.0	7.1
By sex			
Men	7.3	4.1	7.3
Women	6.8	3.8	6.4
By educational level			
High school not completed	7.4	4.4	6.9
High school completed	7.3	3.7	7.0
Some college	6.8	3.8	7.2
College graduate	7.2	4.0	7.5
Executives	7.3	4.3	8.3
Natural scientists	6.6	3.6	7.4
Social scientists	6.4	4.1	7.7
Engineers	7.1	4.3	8.1

Table 6-1e

The four items in this table were designed to get at aspects of occupational striving and competitiveness.

<u>Highlights</u>: "It is more important for a job to offer opportunity than security."

. . . . Ratings show mild to strong agreement in all groups, with scores for the two general employee groups differing little either over all, or by sex and educational level.

. . . . In both general groups agreement is higher for men than for women. There is also a strong positive correlation between scores and educational levels. Among the student groups scores are positively related to present educational level.

. . . . Scores of natural and social scientists and engineers in business are somewhat higher than those of their federal and college counterparts. This tendency is also shown for the three items below.

<u>Highlights</u>: "To me, it's important in an occupation to have a chance to get to the top."

. . . . All groups indicate strong affirmation of this item.

. . . . The general employed public agrees somewhat less than general federal employees; this is also true by sex and educational level. In both groups men subscribe more than women.

. . . . Scores for business executives and federal executives do not differ significantly; both are high.

<u>Highlights</u>: "It would be hard to live with the feeling that others are passing you up in your occupation."

. . . . In all groups agreement is moderate to fairly high, with the general employed public agreeing slightly less than general federal employees.

<u>Highlights</u>: "It is important to do a better job than the next person."

. . . . All groups show moderate to strong agreement, with students and groups in education agreeing somewhat less than most other groups.

. . . . Business executives give higher ratings than federal executives.

Table 6-1e

Occupational values: average (mean) ratings of "occupational value" statements on the 10-point agree-disagree scale; the higher the score, the more agreement (cont'd.)

	"It is more important for a job to offer opportunity than security."	"To me, it's important in an occupation to have a chance to get to the top."	"It would be hard to live with the feeling that others are passing you up in your occupation."	"It's important to do a better job than the next person."
Nonfederal Populations				
General employed public	5.9	7.8	6.1	6.9
By sex				
Men	6.1	8.0	6.1	7.0
Women	5.3	7.2	6.0	6.4
By educational level				
High school not completed	5.3	7.6	5.8	7.0
High school completed	5.7	8.0	6.2	6.9.
Some college	6.6	7.9	6.3	7.0
College graduate	7.2	7.8	5.9	6.7
Students				
High school students	5.5	7.9	6.4	6.3
College seniors	7.2	7.7	6.5	6.0
Graduate students	7.6	7.3	6.4	5.9
Groups in education				
High school teachers	6.6	7.4	6.2	6.0
Vocational counselors	7.2	7.2	6.0	5.9
College teachers	7.5	7.2	6.1	6.2
Natural scientists	7.6	7.4	6.5	6.1
Social scientists	7.4	7.4	6.4	5.8
Engineers	7.7	7.4	6.2	6.5
Groups in business				
Executives	7.7	8.5	7.0	7.7
Natural scientists	8.1	8.0	6.6	7.0
Social scientists	8.1	8.4	6.6	7.1
Engineers	8.4	8.9	7.6	7.7
Federal Employee Populations				
General federal employees	5.7	8.3	6.4	7.0
By sex				
Men	5.8	8.5	6.4	7.2
Women	5.5	7.6	6.5	6.6
By educational level				
High school not completed	5.1	8.3	5.8	7.6
High school completed	5.4	8.4	6.5	7.1
Some college	6.3	8.3	6.8	6.8
College graduate	7.1	8.2	6.4	6.8
Executives	7.9	8.6	6.9	6.8
Natural scientists	7.3	7.5	6.5	6.5
Social scientists	7.8	7.7	6.8	5.6
Engineers	7.4	8.3	7.1	6.8

Table 6-1f

The three items in this table are designed to measure how people feel
about the relative roles of luck, personal influence, and hard work in
occupational success. In every group the order of mean scores is invariant, with luck being accorded the least importance, personal influence
next, and hard work being accorded the most important role of all.
Despite this invariant order there are some interesting variations from
group to group with respect to individual items.

Highlights: "Success in an occupation is mainly a matter of luck."

. . . . On the average luck is assigned a slightly more positive role by
the general employed public than it is by general federal employees;
the difference occurs mainly at the two lower educational levels.

. . . . In both the general employed public and among general federal
employees the scores show a slight negative correlation with educational
level. The higher the educational attainment the less tendency to agree
with the item.

Highlights: "Success in an occupation is mainly a matter of knowing the
    right people."

. . . . On the average, agreement is higher in the general employed
public than it is among general federal employees. This is true at all
four educational levels, especially at the lowest educational step.

. . . . College seniors and graduate students agree more with the
statement than do high school students.

Highlights: "Success in an occupation is mainly a matter of hard
    work."

. . . . Agreement is moderate to fairly high in all groups.

. . . . Scores for the general employed public and general federal
employees do not differ over-all, by sex or by educational level.

. . . . Among students there is a slight negative relationship of
scores with present educational level; the higher the educational level
the less tendency to agree with the item.

. . . . Social scientists in the federal government and in colleges
agree somewhat less with the item than do other groups.

Table 6-1f

Occupational values: average (mean) ratings of "occupational value" statements on the 10-point agree-disagree scale; the higher the score, the more agreement (cont'd.)

	"Success in an occupation is mainly a matter of luck."	"Success in an occupation is mainly a matter of knowing the right people."	"Success in an occupation is mainly a matter of hard work."
Nonfederal Populations			
General employed public	3.6	5.0	7.3
By sex			
Men	3.5	5.0	7.3
Women	3.7	5.1	7.2
By educational level			
High school not completed	4.2	5.9	7.3
High school completed	3.5	4.8	7.3
Some college	2.8	4.4	7.2
College graduate	3.1	4.4	7.3
Students			
High school students	2.3	3.7	8.2
College seniors	2.6	4.5	7.5
Graduate students	3.0	4.4	7.2
Groups in education			
High school teachers	2.5	3.9	7.1
Vocational counselors	2.6	3.6	6.8
College teachers	2.6	3.9	6.7
Natural scientists	2.4	3.8	7.1
Social scientists	3.3	4.2	6.4
Engineers	2.8	3.8	7.3
Groups in business			
Executives	3.1	3.8	7.2
Natural scientists	2.6	3.8	6.6
Social scientists	2.8	3.4	6.8
Engineers	3.5	4.1	7.6
Federal Employee Populations			
General federal employees	2.9	4.1	7.2
By sex			
Men	3.0	4.2	7.3
Women	2.9	4.1	7.1
By educational level			
High school not completed	3.2	4.0	7.3
High school completed	2.8	4.2	7.5
Some college	3.0	4.2	6.8
College graduate	2.8	4.0	7.0
Executives	2.6	3.3	7.2
Natural scientists	2.7	3.7	7.1
Social scientists	2.7	3.7	6.2
Engineers	3.1	4.5	7.3

Table 6-1g

Both items in this table were designed to provide some measure of people's subscription to social goals as occupational aims. The second item invites a lower level of agreement than the first because of the more restricted wording "almost the only thing that matters," and because it uses the rather broad word, "society."

Highlights: "The main satisfaction a person can get out of work is helping other people."

. . . . The scores for the general employed public and for general federal employees are about the same over-all, by sex and by educational level. In the general employed public there is a tendency for women to assign higher scores than men do.

. . . . Among students, level of agreement shows a negative relationship with educational level.

. . . . High school students show especially strong agreement, as do high school teachers and vocational counselors.

. . . . Groups in business have ratings that are somewhat lower than those characteristic of other groups.

Highlights: "To me, almost the only thing that matters about a job is the chance to do work that is worthwhile to society."

. . . . This item invites the evaluation of contribution to social benefit as a dominant occupational goal. The over-all pattern is one of agreement ranging from mild to moderately high.

. . . . Agreement is slightly higher among general federal employees than in the general employed public; this is true at all four educational levels. Among general federal employees men show somewhat stronger agreement than women.

. . . . Business executives agree less with the statement than do federal executives.

. . . . Federal natural scientists, social scientists, and engineers have slightly higher average scores than comparable groups in business, but their scores are somewhat lower than for comparable groups in colleges.

Table 6-1g

Occupational values: average (mean) ratings of "occupational value" statements on the 10-point agree-disagree scale; the higher the score, the more agreement (cont'd.)

	"The main satisfaction a person can get out of work is helping other people."	"To me, almost the only thing that matters about a job is the chance to do work that is worthwhile to society."
Nonfederal Populations		
General employed public	6.9	5.6
By sex		
Men	6.8	5.6
Women	7.4	5.6
By educational level		
High school not completed	7.1	5.8
High school completed	6.7	5.3
Some college	6.9	5.5
College graduate	7.3	6.4
Students		
High school students	8.1	6.5
College seniors	7.7	6.8
Graduate students	7.3	6.7
Groups in education		
High school teachers	8.1	6.9
Vocational counselors	8.1	6.8
College teachers	7.8	7.2
Natural scientists	7.5	7.0
Social scientists	6.8	6.7
Engineers	7.7	7.0
Groups in business		
Executives	6.7	5.7
Natural scientists	6.3	6.1
Social scientists	6.6	6.2
Engineers	6.6	6.1
Federal Employee Populations		
General federal employees	7.0	6.2
By sex		
Men	6.9	6.4
Women	7.2	5.6
By educational level		
High school not completed	7.0	6.2
High school completed	7.0	6.1
Some college	6.5	6.1
College graduate	7.5	6.7
Executives	7.1	6.3
Natural scientists	7.0	6.9
Social scientists	6.8	6.5
Engineers	6.5	6.3

Table 6-1h

<u>Highlights</u>: "To me, it's important in an occupation that a person be able to see the results of his own work."

. . . . Agreement with this statement is extremely high in all groups, nonfederal and federal.

. . . . Scores for the general employed public and general federal employees do not differ significantly.

. . . . There is a slight suggestion of a positive relationship between level of agreement and level of education in the general employed public and among students; however, the dominant picture is one of strong agreement at all educational strata.

<u>Highlights</u>: "To me, it's important to have the kind of work that gives me a chance to develop my own special abilities."

. . . . The main picture is one of very strong agreement, especially in all those groups with higher education.

. . . . Scores for the general employed public and general federal employees do not differ much, although agreement is slightly higher among general federal employees, accounted for mainly by differences at the lowest educational level.

. . . . In the general employed public there is a fairly strong positive relationship between level of agreement and educational level; among general federal employees the same sort of positive relationship occurs but not so strongly. In the student populations there is also a slight positive relationship of scores with present educational level.

152

Table 6-1h

Occupational values: average (mean) ratings of "occupational value" statements on the 10-point agree-disagree scale; the higher the score, the more agreement (cont'd.)

	"To me, it's important in an occupation that a person be able to see the results of his own work."	"To me, it's important to have the kind of work that gives me a chance to develop my own special abilities."
Nonfederal Populations		
General employed public	8.4	8.1
By sex		
Men	8.5	8.2
Women	8.4	7.9
By educational level		
High school not completed	8.2	7.6
High school completed	8.4	8.1
Some college	8.6	8.5
College graduate	8.9	8.9
Students		
High school students	8.4	8.7
College seniors	8.7	9.1
Graduate students·	8.7	9.2
Groups in education		
High school teachers	8.6	8.9
Vocational counselors	8.3	8.8
College teachers	8.4	9.1
Natural scientists	8.9	9.2
Social scientists	8.1	9.0
Engineers	8.5	8.9
Groups in business		
Executives	8.8	8.9
Natural scientists	8.9	9.1
Social scientists	8.6	9.1
Engineers	8.8	8.7
Federal Employee Populations		
General federal employees	8.6	8.5
By sex		
Men	8.7	8.5
Women	8.5	8.4
By educational level		
High school not completed	8.6	8.4
High school completed	8.8	8.5
Some college	8.5	8.5
College graduate	8.7	8.7
Executives	9.0	9.0
Natural scientists	9.0	9.3
Social scientists	8.5	9.0
Engineers	8.9	8.9

153

Table 6-1i

Highlights: "Work is most satisfying when there are hard problems to solve."

. . . . This statement, designed to measure an important aspect of "challenge," is accorded a high level of agreement by all groups having a high level of education.

. . . . Subscription is higher over all among general federal employees than in the general employed public and for both men and women and at three of the four educational levels.

. . . . In the general employed public, agreement is higher among men than women; the reverse is true among federal employees.

. . . . In the two general employee groups the positive relationship of scores with educational level is very strong. Student scores also show a positive relationship with level of present education.

. . . . Federal executives agree more with the statement than do business executives.

Highlights: "To me, it's important in an occupation for a person to be able to carry out his own ideas without interference."

. . . . The statement, designed to measure an important aspect of "self-determination," is accorded moderate to high agreement by all groups.

. . . . Over-all scores for the general employed public and for general federal employees are about the same.

. . . . Among general federal employees agreement is stronger for men than for women; the same is true in the general employed public but to a less degree.

. . . . Among students there is a positive relationship between level of agreement and level of education.

. . . . Agreement is higher among business executives than among federal executives.

. . . . Ratings for social scientists and engineers in the federal government are lower than for these groups in business and especially in colleges.

. . . . The score for natural scientists in government is especially high in comparison to all other groups in the federal government.

Table 6-1i

Occupational values: average (mean) ratings of "occupational value" statements on the 10-point agree-disagree scale; the higher the score, the more agreement (cont'd.)

	"Work is most satisfying when there are hard problems to solve."	"To me, it's important in an occupation for a person to be able to carry out his own ideas without interference."
Nonfederal Populations		
General employed public	6.5	6.7
By sex		
Men	6.7	6.8
Women	6.0	6.4
By educational level		
High school not completed	5.6	6.8
High school completed	6.4	6.5
Some college	7.6	6.8
College graduate	7.8	7.2
Students		
High school students	7.0	6.9
College seniors	7.9	7.6
Graduate students	8.2	8.0
Groups in education		
High school teachers	7.6	7.2
Vocational counselors	7.1	7.1
College teachers	8.1	8.1
Natural scientists	8.4	8.3
Social scientists	7.9	8.2
Engineers	8.5	7.9
Groups in business		
Executives	8.1	7.6
Natural scientists	8.4	7.6
Social scientists	8.6	7.6
Engineers	8.7	7.7
Federal Employee Populations		
General federal employees	7.2	6.4
By sex		
Men	7.2	6.7
Women	7.4	5.6
By educational level		
High school not completed	6.6	7.0
High school completed	7.0	6.1
Some college	7.6	6.0
College graduate	8.2	6.8
Executives	8.7	6.7
Natural scientists	8.7	8.1
Social scientists	8.4	7.1
Engineers	8.5	7.4

155

Table 6-1j

The three items in this table were designed to explore aspects of "duty" as an occupational value. Over-all, they indicate a somewhat stronger subscription to duty as an occupational value in the federal employee populations than in the nonfederal populations.

Highlights: "A person should constantly try to succeed at work, even if it interferes with other things in life."

. . . . Agreement with the statement is lower in the general employed public than among general federal employees. This is true over all, and for both men and women and at all four educational strata.

. . . . In the two general employee groups agreement is slightly higher at the high school not completed level than at the other three levels. The student groups show a similar pattern with high school students agreeing more than college seniors or graduate students.

Highlights: "Even if you dislike your work you should do your best."

. . . . The over-all pattern is one of extremely high agreement, with all federal employee populations scoring higher than comparable nonfederal populations.

. . . . While students show strong agreement, the ratings are lower than for other groups.

. . . . The score for social scientists in college is lower than the scores for all other populations.

Highlights: "If a person doesn't want to work hard, it's his own business."

. . . . There is markedly less subscription to this among general federal employees than in the general public, and thus holds regardless of sex or educational level. The difference is particularly great at the college graduate level.

. . . . Ratings for high school teachers and vocational counselors are atypically low among the nonfederal populations.

. . . . The business executive score is considerably higher than the federal executive score.

. . . . In general, scores for federal natural and social scientists and engineers are lower than for the comparable business and college groups.

156

Table 6-1j

Occupational values: average (mean) ratings of "occupational value" statements on the 10-point agree-disagree scale; the higher the score, the more agreement (cont'd.)

	"A person should constantly try to succeed at work, even if it interferes with other things in life."	"Even if you dislike your work, you should do your best."	"If a person doesn't want to work hard, it's his own business."
Nonfederal Populations			
General employed public	6.0	8.3	5.4
By sex			
Men	6.1	8.3	5.5
Women	5.8	8.3	5.2
By educational level			
High school not completed	6.3	8.4	5.6
High school completed	6.0	8.2	5.2
Some college	6.0	8.4	5.4
College graduate	5.8	8.2	5.6
Students			
High school students	5.8	7.9	5.1
College seniors	5.1	7.7	5.5
Graduate students	5.2	7.7	5.5
Groups in education			
High school teachers	6.1	8.3	4.2
Vocational counselors	6.1	8.3	4.2
College teachers	5.9	8.4	4.9
Natural scientists	6.0	8.6	5.3
Social scientists	5.4	7.6	5.0
Engineers	5.5	8.6	5.3
Groups in business			
Executives	6.2	8.3	5.3
Natural scientists	6.1	8.2	4.7
Social scientists	5.6	8.3	5.1
Engineers	6.2	8.4	5.6
Federal Employee Populations			
General federal employees	6.6	8.8	4.3
By sex			
Men	6.6	8.8	4.4
Women	6.5	8.8	4.1
By educational level			
High school not completed	7.2	8.8	4.7
High school completed	6.5	9.1	4.1
Some college	6.1	8.6	4.5
College graduate	6.5	8.6	4.2
Executives	6.6	9.1	4.1
Natural scientists	5.8	8.6	4.6
Social scientists	5.8	8.4	4.7
Engineers	6.0	8.7	4.7

Table 6-1k

The statements in this table were designed to get at three facets of the occupational "ethic" which looks upon work as good in the sense of being essential to and compatible with the nature of man. The general pattern is one of moderate to high agreement with all three statements.

Highlights: "Work helps you forget about your personal problems."

. . . . The level of agreement is about the same for the general employed public and for general federal employees; however, general federal employees at the some college and college graduate levels show somewhat less agreement than the same groups in the general employed public.

. . . . Scores are lower for students than for most other populations, federal or nonfederal.

. . . . Federal social scientists indicate less agreement than do other federal populations; the same tendency is shown by social scientists in colleges in comparison to the other college populations.

Highlights: "Work is a good builder of character."

. . . . Figures for the general employed public and for general federal employees do not differ significantly over-all by sex or by educational level.

. . . . College seniors and graduate students agree less with the item than do high school students.

. . . . Ratings for social scientists--whether in the federal government, in business, or in college--are, relatively speaking, low.

Highlights: "Work is a way of being of service to God."

. . . . In general, subscription is quite high and does not differ significantly between the general employed public and general federal employees. However, there is some indication that general federal employees with some college or college degrees agree slightly less than their counterparts in the general employed public.

. . . . College seniors, and especially graduate students, agree less than high school students.

. . . . Social scientists in the federal government, in business, and in colleges register a low level of agreement.

Table 6-1k

Occupational values: average (mean) ratings of "occupational value" statements on the 10-point agree-disagree scale; the higher the score, the more agreement (cont'd.)

	"Work helps you forget about your personal problems."	"Work is a good builder of character."	"Work is a way of being of service to God."
Nonfederal Populations			
General employed public	7.2	8.2	7.7
By sex			
Men	7.0	8.2	7.6
Women	7.9	8.4	7.9
By educational level			
High school not completed	7.4	8.3	7.9
High school completed	7.1	8.2	7.5
Some college	7.4	8.4	7.9
College graduate	7.2	8.3	7.3
Students			
High school students	6.1	8.5	7.9
College seniors	6.1	7.9	6.8
Graduate students	6.2	7.3	6.4
Groups in education			
High school teachers	7.6	8.1	7.8
Vocational counselors	7.3	7.5	7.4
College teachers	6.8	7.4	7.2
Natural scientists	7.3	7.7	7.0
Social scientists	6.1	6.3	5.7
Engineers	6.6	7.6	6.7
Groups in business			
Executives	7.2	8.2	6.9
Natural scientists	6.0	7.9	6.0
Social scientists	6.4	7.3	5.6
Engineers	7.1	8.1	6.5
Federal Employee Populations			
General federal employees	7.1	8.4	7.4
By sex			
Men	7.0	8.4	7.4
Women	7.5	8.6	7.7
By educational level			
High school not completed	7.5	8.5	7.7
High school completed	7.3	8.6	7.7
Some college	6.3	8.2	7.3
College graduate	6.9	8.1	6.9
Executives	6.8	8.0	7.4
Natural scientists	6.3	7.8	7.1
Social scientists	5.5	7.0	5.3
Engineers	6.8	8.2	6.9

159

These results, in association with similar configurations that emerge from the free-answer responses, leave little doubt that there is a significant difference in the patterning of occupational values according to educational background.

The groups with higher education, for example, show a much stronger tendency toward positive occupational involvement than those with less education. The average scores accorded the statement "To me work is nothing more than a way of making a living" by the four educational levels in the general employed public are as follows: high school not completed, 5.6; high school completed, 4.0; some college 3.2; college graduate 2.6. A similar pattern is shown regarding the desire to separate work from, or to integrate it with, other activities: mean scores for the statement "I like the kind of work you can forget about when the work day is over" range from 7.5 at the high school not completed level to 6.7, 6.0, and 5.3, proceeding up the educational ladder.

There are also parallel significant increases in emphasis on opportunity vs. security; on the desire to see the results of one's work; on the importance of having the opportunity to develop one's own special ability; on the degree to which the challenge of hard problems to solve is seen as an important and satisfying aspect of work; and on the degree to which the opportunity to direct others is perceived as a satisfying aspect of work. And the higher the educational level, the less are money and keeping up with the Joneses emphasized as ingredients of success and status. Those at the upper educational strata are also less likely to attribute success to either luck or influence.

For the college graduate group, compared to the other three groups, there is a somewhat stronger subscription to social goals as occupational aims, especially in the broad context of doing work that is "worthwhile to society." Competitiveness in its various aspects (drive to get to the top, desire not be passed up in one's occupation, and urge to do a better job than the next person) is quite high over-all and shows little difference by educational level. The same appears to be true of the desire for self-determination and autonomy, as measured by the average agreement with the statement "To me, it's important in an occupation for a person to be able to carry out his own ideas without interference."

There is also substantial agreement, regardless of educational level, with the idea that work helps one forget about personal problems. And all levels tend strongly to perceive work as a good builder of character and as a way of being of service to God.

High School Students, College Seniors, Graduate Students

The three student populations reveal a score patterning by present educational level that very closely parallels the pattern in the general employed public. There is, however, a general tendency for the average scores of the high school students to resemble those of people with some college in the general public rather than those at the high school completed level. Thus, even though the student *pattern* is similar to the general public *pattern*, the two sets of scores tend to differ quite widely in absolute magnitude. In response to the statement "I like the kind of work you can forget about after the work day is over," the mean scores at the high school completed, some college, and college graduate levels in the general employed public are 6.7, 6.0, and 5.3. Among students, direction by educational level was the same, but the scores of high school students, college seniors, and graduate students are all considerably lower —4.9, 3.8, and 3.5. Also, the differences between scores of college seniors and of graduate students are not great, in most cases paralleling the direction of differences according to education found in the general population.

In general, then, we find that college seniors and graduate students, as compared to high school students, show a greater desire for involvement in their work, and put less emphasis on respect and keeping up with the Joneses as aspects of status; show a stronger desire to direct the work of others; place far more emphasis on opportunity than on security; show greater inclination to see satisfaction in the challenge of hard problems; indicate a significantly greater desire for autonomy and the opportunity to carry out their own ideas; and are less inclined to see money as a necessary ingredient of success and more inclined to agree that once you are making enough money for an adequate living standard other occupational values are more important.

Among college students, as compared to high school students and to college-level people in the general work force, there is an interesting pattern, various parts of which seem to be related. The data show that college students agree more with the idea that one has a right to expect his work to be fun; give higher ratings to influence and luck as avenues to success, and lower ratings to hard work as an avenue to success; subscribe significantly less to the notion that one should try to succeed even if it interferes with other things in life; and agree slightly more that if one doesn't want to work hard, it's own business. College students also show significantly less agreement with the idea that work is a good builder of character and a way of being of service to God.

These results strongly suggest that, on the average, college students—as compared to high school students and to college-level people in the general employed public—approach work with more of an idea of fun and personal satisfaction, less dedication and determination to work hard, perhaps an equal, or greater, desire for opportunity, but possibly less willingness to strive and be dedicated to work at the expense of other things. In the absence of trend data it is impossible to say whether the difference in value patterns of college students and of college-level people now at work is a product of social change or merely a reflection of the different situation in which college students find themselves as compared to people who are presently employed.

Perhaps worth noting, as a related factor, is the finding that the high school students rate exceptionally high the opportunity to help other people through one's work, while college seniors and especially graduate students rate it significantly lower. However, when social goals are defined as "a chance to do work that is worthwhile to society," all three student groups tend to agree and their scores do not differ significantly.

Focusing on the high school students we find that, relative to college students, they tend to give slightly more emphasis to money in its various aspects; are far less oriented to opportunity and more to security; show stronger desire to get to the top and more perception of hard work as the way to get there; subscribe more to helping others as an occupational value; display a somewhat stronger attitude of dedication to work; and subscribe more to the idea that work is a good thing in itself.

High School Teachers and Vocational Counselors

The scores of high school teachers and vocational counselors on the various statements in general parallel very closely the scores of college graduates in the general employed public. Certain exceptions are worth noting, however. Compared to the college graduates, they agree somewhat less that money is a necessary ingredient of success. They also agree somewhat less with two aspects of competitiveness—that it is important to have a chance to get to the top and important to do a better job than the next person—but they are about equal to college-level people in the general public in their distaste for seeing others pass them by occupationally. They have a greater tendency to see hard work as a duty; their average score for the item "If a person doesn't want to work hard, it's his own business" is 4.2 as compared to 5.6 for the college graduates.

As one might expect, they also subscribe strongly to the value of an occupation in which one can both help others and do something worthwhile for society in general. They tend to agree a little less than other comparably educated populations with the importance of the various aspects of status as an occupational value, but their scores on this are not as low, on the average, as those of the college teachers.

College Teachers, Natural and Social Scientists, and Engineers

The college faculty populations show a score pattern that is typical of highly educated groups. The differences between them and other such groups are less of kind than of degree—with the college teacher's scores, in the main, being extreme. Their occupational involvement is especially high, as evidenced by a uniformly strong rejection of the idea that work is nothing more than a way of making a living and of the statement "I like the kind of work you can forget after the work day is over." Thus, they appear to like work that interpenetrates other activities. They also agree moderately more that a person has a right to expect his work to be fun; the natural scientists are especially outstanding in this regard.

These groups are extreme, too, in comparison to all other groups in or out of government, in disagreeing that to be really successful you must care about making money, and agreeing that when one makes enough money to get along, making more isn't important. We can only speculate to what degree this set of attitudes represents conviction rather than rationalization.

On the three status statements, the college faculty groups yield especially low average scores on wishing for the possessions one's friends and neighbors have, but put especially strong emphasis on the importance of recognition for one's work. Natural scientists depart somewhat from the general pattern in the degree to which they see increased respect as one of the important rewards of getting ahead: their average score is 7.6, compared to 7.1 for college teachers in general, 7.0 for the social scientists, and 7.1 for the engineers. All of the groups seem to be somewhat low in competitiveness, compared to similar groups in business and government. In general, they agree less that it is important to have a chance to get to the top, that it would be hard to live with the feeling that others are passing you by in your occupation, and that it is important to do a better job than the next person. On the other hand, as a group they appear to be very concerned with the value of autonomy and self-determination. Their scores were particularly high on the statement "To me, it's important in an occupation for a person to be able to carry out his own ideas without interference."

Natural scientists tend to give stronger emphasis than the other faculty groups to the right to expect their work to be fun; to respect as a reward of getting ahead; to rejection of luck as an avenue to success; to the importance of being able to see the results of their own work; and to the idea that work helps one forget personal problems.

Social scientists, on the other hand, tend to differ from the others in their stronger agreement that after one is making enough money to get along, making more isn't very important; in their lower agreement that it is satisfying to direct the work of others; in their lower agreement that success in an occupation is mainly a matter of hard work—coupled with a greater agreement that it is a matter of luck and influence; and, somewhat surprisingly, in their lower subscription to social goals as occupational aims, whether by helping other people or by doing work that is worthwhile to society. They also agree somewhat less that one should try to succeed in work even if it interferes with other things in life, and that even if you dislike your work you should do your best. Their agreement is relatively high on the proposition "Sometimes it may be right for a person to lose friends in order to get ahead in his work," and relatively low on the ideas that work helps you forget your personal problems, is a good builder of character, and is a way of being of service to God.

The responses of engineers follow the pattern of the general college teachers rather closely, with perhaps slightly more emphasis on hard work as an ingredient in success.

Groups in Business

The patterning of scores revealed by all the business groups is again typical of highly educated groups. In general, however, compared with their counterparts in colleges and the government, these respondents rate the importance of financial reward considerably higher. They subscribe much more strongly to the statement "To be really successful in life you have to care about making money," and agree significantly less that after you are making enough money to get along making more isn't important. They also appear to rate status a little higher as an occupational value; this is definitely true in comparison to the college teachers, but the case is more doubtful in comparison to their counterparts in government or to the college graduate group in the general public. The ratings further suggest that the business groups subscribe somewhat less to social goals as occupational values: their mean scores on the item "To me, almost the only thing that matters about a job is the chance to do work that is worthwhile to society" are consistently lower than those of other comparable groups.

Further over-all generalizations on the results are impossible, because there appears to be a major cleavage within the business groups. For the executives and engineers there seems to be one rather consistent pattern, for the natural scientists and social scientists, another, equally consistent. The executives and engineers, for example, as compared to the natural and social scientists, show a lower degree of occupational involvement; they subscribe more strongly to the idea that work is nothing more than a way of making a living, and to the statement "I like the kind of work you can forget after the work day is over." They place greater emphasis on money as a necessary ingredient of success: on the statement "To be really successful in life you have to care about making money" they score 5.7 and 5.9; the natural and social scientists score 4.1 and 4.4.

The same cleavage is apparent in respect to status; the executives and engineers give significantly higher scores to the aspects of respect and material possessions. They also score higher on the opportunity to make friends at work and on finding satisfaction in directing the work of others; on all three aspects of competitiveness; on seeing hard work as an avenue to success; and on the degree to which they see work as an aid in forgetting personal problems, as a builder of character, and as a way of being of service to God.

General Federal Employees

The average scores of federal employees differ from those of the general employed public by significant amounts on a large share of the items.

Again, whether this is due to the type of people who select or are selected for, federal employment, or to acculturation and adjustment of attitudes to a group norm, cannot be determined on the basis of this research. The most reasonable assumption is that both factors are operating and tend to reinforce one another. The fact remains that federal employees show a pattern of emphasis significantly different in many ways from the value pattern found in the general public.

Particularly striking is the higher degree of occupational involvement and spartan approach to work shown by federal employees over-all, by both men and women, and by all four educational levels. This group disagrees much more strongly with the idea that work is nothing more than a way of making a living, and scores significantly lower on the statement "I like the kind of work you can forget about after the work day is over." Coupled with this, however, are significantly lower scores on the statement "A person has a right to expect his work to be fun." And in evaluations of avenues to success, federal employees place far less emphasis on luck and influence, and equal the general employed public in the emphasis on hard work.

They subscribe more strongly to duty as an occupational value than do members of the general public—both by sex and by educational levels. In response to the statement "A person should constantly try to succeed at work even if it interferes with other things in life" they give an average score of 6.6, compared to the general employed public's average score of 6.0; on the item "Even if you dislike your work you should do your best" the comparative scores are 8.8 and 8.3. But on the statement "If a person doesn't want to work hard it's his own business" the federal employees' average score is 4.3; that of the general employed public is 5.4.

Federal employees are also far less likely to see money as a necessary ingredient of success; this is true both by sex and by educational level. The average score for general federal employees is 5.0, for the general employed public, 5.8. On the other hand, on the statement "After you are making enough money to get along, then making more money in an occupation isn't very important," the scores for the two groups are almost the same, both of them tending to disagree with the statement, or at least not agreeing very strongly. On status as an occupational value, the two also differ little on the respect and material possession aspects, but federal employees place somewhat more emphasis on getting recognition for one's work.

Some of our findings (for example, in Chapter 12) show that many people tend to stereotype federal employees as lacking in competitiveness. It is interesting, therefore, to note that federal employees score as high as the general employed public on all three items on competitiveness, and slightly higher on two of them. Average scores for the statement "To me, it's important in an occupation to have a chance to get to the top" are 8.3 for federal employees and 7.8 for the general employed public; for "It would be hard to live with the feeling that others are passing you up in your occupation," 6.4 and 6.1; and for "It's important to do a better job than the next person," 7.0 and 6.9.

For the statement pitting opportunity against security as an occupational value, we find that the scores for both groups are almost identical, with no apparent significant differences by sex or by educational level. These results obviously do not fit the stereotype of the federal employee who is primarily interested in security rather than opportunity.

Particularly striking also are the comparative scores on the statement "Work is most satisfying when there are hard problems to solve." If we compare the scores of federal employees—over-all, by sex, and by educational level—with those of the general employed public we find the federal employee agreement with the statement to be consistently higher. The over-all scores are 7.2 for the federal group and 6.5 for the nonfederal group. Thus, federal employees appear to be more likely than comparable employees outside of government to respond positively to the challenge of difficult problems.

Another significant comparison is the relative subscription of the two groups to social goals as an occupational aim. Here we find about equal amounts of agreement on "The main satisfaction a person can get out of work is helping other people." However, federal employees show significantly stronger agreement with the broader, less personalized statement "To me, almost the only thing that matters about a job is the chance to do work that is worthwhile to society." Differences between the two populations on this are especially great for men, and for the three lower educational levels.

In sum, general federal employees, compared with the general employed public, show a high degree of occupational involvement, a greater subscription to duty as an occupational value, put less emphasis on money and on the material aspects of status, indicate a somewhat stronger desire for personal recognition in their work, and put more emphasis on challenge and worthwhile social goals as occupational values.

COMPARATIVE PATTERNS BY SEX. We find that the differential patterning of occupational values roughly parallels the differences by sex in the general employed public. Federally employed women agree markedly less than men that they have a right to expect their work to be fun; express stronger liking for work that can be forgotten about after the work day is over; score significantly lower on all three status items; agree less that it is satisfying to direct the work of others; accord less importance to an opportunity to get to the top; agree less with "It's important to do a better job than the next person"; and assign less importance to self-determination and autonomy—indicated by substantially lower agreement with the statement "To me, it's important in an occupation for a person to be able to carry out his own ideas without interference."

Regarding the value of financial reward, there is a difference by sex not found in the general employed public. The federal scores on the statement "To be really successful in life you have to care about making money" are 5.2 for men and 4.3 for women; in the general population the scores are 5.8 and 5.8. On the statement "To me, almost the only thing that matters about a job is the chance to do work that is worthwhile to society" women score 5.6, men 6.4; in the general public the scores are even at 5.6. It should be noted that the difference between the two populations on this item is entirely due to the markedly higher scores of federally employed men.

COMPARATIVE PATTERNS BY EDUCATIONAL LEVEL. While the absolute values of the scores are different for the federal and nonfederal populations, as described above, the relationships between the scores according to educational level almost perfectly parallel one another in the two populations—with only the three exceptions noted in the paragraphs below. On most statements where scores rise or decline with educational level in the nonfederal population, a similar rise or decline appears in the federal population.

The first exception concerns the statement "Success in an occupation is mainly a matter of knowing the right people." In the general employed public, subscription declines with increasing educational level—5.9 for the high school not completed group and 4.4 for college graduates. Among federal employees the scores are uniformly lower and not significantly related to educational background, being 4.0, 4.2, 4.2, and 4.0 from the lowest to the highest level.

Exception two: "To me it's important in an occupation that a person be able to see the results of his own work." The general employed public's scores are positively related to educational level—8.2 for the high school not completed group, 8.9 for college graduates. But federal employees give almost uniformly high agreement with the item at all educational levels, the scores being 8.6, 8.8, 8.5, and 8.7 from the lowest to the highest.

Exception three: "Work helps you forget about your personal problems." In the general employed public there is no relationship between scores and educational level. Among federal employees agreement with the item appears to be negatively associated with educational status; scores decline from 7.5 at the lowest level to 6.9 for college graduates.

The near-perfect paralleling of scores by educational level found among the two groups indicates that we may place a high degree of faith in the differential patterning of occupational values according to education. This belief in the reliability of the findings is encouraged by the high degree of consistency between the results obtained from two entirely independent populations.

Federal Executives, Natural and Social Scientists, and Engineers

In our earlier examination of the scores of business executives, natural and social scientists, and engineers, it was seen that on many statements the executive and engineer scores tended not only to be alike but also to differ substantially from the scores of the natural and the social scientists, which also tended to be alike. The same phenomenon is found in these comparable groups in the government with respect to exactly the same items.

Federal executives and engineers, in comparison to the federal natural and social scientists, agree somewhat more with the statement "I like the kind of work you can forget about after the work day is over." They are more likely to see money as a necessary ingredient of success and less likely to agree that money isn't very important after you are making enough to get along; agree more strongly with the status item "I would like my family to be able to have most of the things my friends and neighbors have"; place higher value on the opportunity to make friends at work; agree more that it is satisfying to direct the work of others; and give higher ratings to the statement "To me, it's important in an occupation to have a chance to get to the top." They also agree somewhat more strongly that work helps one to forget personal problems, and appear to agree a little more strongly that work is a good builder of character, but in this instance the score of the natural scientists is almost as high.

In comparing federal executive and business executive scores, we find that the federal executives are slightly less inclined to feel that work is nothing more than a way of making a living; markedly less likely to see money as a necessary ingredient of success and more inclined to agree that making more money is not important once you have enough to get along; subscribe more strongly to the occupational value of helping other people and doing work that is worthwhile to society; are less inclined to see luck and influence as means of getting ahead; and somewhat more likely to agree that work is a way of being of service to God.

The federal executives are more inclined also to see duty as an occupational value: they score 9.1 on the item "Even if you dislike your work you should do your best," and business executives score 8.3; on "If a person doesn't want to work hard, it's his own business" they score 4.1, business executives, 5.3. With respect to the challenge statement, "Work is most satisfying when there are hard problems to solve," the federal executives agree more (8.7) than the businessmen (8.1).

There is, however, strong indication that federal executives are less inclined to subscribe to the competitive idea of doing a better job than the next person; their average score is 6.8, that of business executives 7.7. A similar difference is found on the item designed to get at the value of self-determination and autonomy: federal executives agree less with "To me, it's important in an occupation for a person to be able to carry out his own ideas without interference"; their score is 6.7, and that of the businessmen is 7.6.

It is notable that executives both in and out of government appear to differ little in their responses to the statement "It is more important for a job to offer opportunity than security." Both groups yield opportunity-oriented scores, and there is no significant difference between them. There is also no significant difference on their desire for various aspects of status; on various factors of interpersonal relationships on the job; on hard work as an avenue to success; on desire to see the results of their own work; on desire for the kind of work that will develop their own special ability; or on perception of work as a means of forgetting problems and as a builder of character.

Concerning certain values, the scores of federal executives differ outstandingly from those of the federal natural and social scientists and engineers. The executives score somewhat higher on the status factors of respect and of having the possessions their friends and neighbors have, but it is on the duty or obligation aspects of work that they show the sharpest cleavages from the other three groups. They agree more with the statements "A person should constantly try to succeed at work even if it interferes with other things in life" and "Even if you dislike your work, you should do your best," and show much stronger disagreement with the statement "If a person doesn't want to work hard it's his own business." They also agree less with the self-determination statement, "To me, it's important in an occupation for a person to be able to carry out his own ideas without interference." Their mean score on this is lower than that of any group, federal or nonfederal, at a comparable educational or occupational level; although in some instances the differences are not great, they are all in the same direction.

When we turn to the federal natural scientists, two generalizations are called for: considerably more similarities are found in the various value scores of the three groups of natural scientists (federal, business, and college) than differences; what significant differences there are tend to be between the federal and business groups, not between the federal and college groups. The occupational values of federal natural scientists seem to approximate those of college natural scientists more closely than those of natural scientists in business. There are three exceptions to this, how-ever. Federal natural scientists do resemble their business counterparts on the duty item—"If a person doesn't want to work hard, it's his own business." Scores are 4.6 (federal), 4.7 (business), and 5.3 (college). On the item "Work helps you forget about your personal problems" the scores are 6.3 (federal), 6.0 (business), and 7.3 (college). And the federal natural scientists also resemble natural scientists in business in scoring appreciably lower than their college counterparts on involvement in their work—agreeing less with "A person has a right to expect his work to be fun" and more with "I like the kind of work you can forget about after the work day is over."

On nearly all other matters where there are significant differences among the natural scientist groups, however, the ratings of the federal natural scientists are roughly the same as those of the academic group—and both are significantly different from those of natural scientists in business. This is more apparent for the financial reward items. On "To be really successful in life, you have to care about making money," the federal and college groups score 3.4 and 3.2; the business group shows stronger agreement with 4.1. For "After you are making enough money to get along, then making more money in an occupation isn't very important," the federal and college groups both score 6.9, the business group, 5.6. A similar pattern is shown on the "striving" and "competitive" items involving the importance of having an opportunity to get to the top and the importance of doing a better job than the next person; on the statement "To me, almost the only thing that matters about a job is the chance to do work that is worthwhile to society"; and on the statement "It is more important for a job to offer opportunity than security." On this last item the business natural scientists show substantially greater agreement. indicating a strong opportunity orientation, but the federal group shows slightly more security orientation than its college counterpart. In agreeing with the statement "Work is a way of being of service to God" the federal and college groups are again similar—scoring 7.1 and 7.0; the business score is 6.0.

On some statements the federal natural scientists stand out as scoring either appreciably higher or lower than the three other federal groups. They rate the statement "After you are making enough money to get along, then making more money in an occupation isn't very important" at 6.9, compared to 5.8, 6.2, and 5.8 for executives, social scientists, and engineers. They also are less inclined to agree that sometimes it may be right for a person to lose friends in order to get ahead in his work, and that directing the work of others is satisfying. They show distinctively stronger subscription to the value of self-determination and autonomy, scoring 8.1 on the statement "To me, it's important in an occupation for a person to be able to carry out his own ideas without interference," compared to 6.7, 7.1, and 7.4 for executives, social scientists, and engineers.

For the most part, social scientists in government, college, or business show a high degree of homogeneity in their scores. There are differences, but even though they are significant and merit description they are not extreme. In many ways, federal social scientists resemble social scientists in college more than those in business. On the two items involving financial reward, for example, the federal and college groups are alike in agreeing less than their counterparts in business with the statement "To be really successful in life, you have to care about making money," and in agreeing more that after you are making enough money to get along, making more isn't too important. The pattern also prevails on the statement "It's important to do a better job than the next person," with the federal and college scores more than a scale point lower than the business score, and to a lesser degree on the item concerning hard work as an avenue to success—in this case with business social scientists scoring higher than the other two groups.

On the other hand, federal and business social scientists agree more than the college group that it is satisfying to direct the work of others, that you should do your best even though you dislike your work, and that work is a good builder of character.

On a few values the federal social scientists seem to differ substantially from *both* the business and college groups. They score lower than either on the self-determination item, "To me, it is important in an occupation for a person to be able to carry out his own ideas without interference," and agree substantially less that work helps one to forget personal problems.

In comparing federal social scientists with their federal colleagues, we find that they agree somewhat less that gaining the increased respect of family and friends is one of the important rewards of getting ahead in an occupation, and with the statement "I would like my family to be able to have most of the things my friends and neighbors have." Thus it appears that they place less emphasis on these two aspects of status although the differences are small. The case is less doubtful for "It's important to do a better job than the next person," on which they score 5.6, compared to 6.8, 6.5, and 6.8 for the executives, natural scientists, and engineers. The pattern is similar for "Success in an occupation is mainly a matter of hard work." The social scientists' score is 6.2; executives, natural scientists, and engineers give ratings of 7.2, 7.1, and 7.3. Social scientists also agree markedly less that "Work helps you to forget about your personal problems"; their average score is 5.5, compared to scores of 6.8, 6.3, and 6.8 for executives, natural scientists, and engineers. They show similar lower agreement of about the same magnitude with the ideas that work is a good builder of character and a way of being of service to God.

The results found for federal engineers are more like those for engineers in business than for engineers in colleges. Thus, federal and business engineers are very much alike in their higher agreement that work is nothing more than a way of making a living; in showing somewhat more liking for the kind of work one forgets about after the work day is over; in putting generally greater emphasis on status; and in giving lower ratings to doing the kind of work in which you can help other people.

Wherever the three engineer populations show other differences, the scores of the federal group seem to fall approximately halfway between those of the other two. This is true of the two items on financial reward; the federal engineers appear to value financial reward more highly than the college group, but not as highly as the business group does. They also stand midway between the other two on opportunity versus security, and on the three statements that concern the more competitive aspect of striving.

With respect to only two of the scale items can it be said that neither of the above two patterns holds for engineers. On "It is satisfying to direct the work of others" we find that the federal and college engineers yield identical scores of 8.1; the business group's score is 8.7. On "If a person doesn't want to work hard, it's his own business" the federal engineers showing markedly less agreement than either of the two other groups.

7

Positive and Negative Features
Seen in Own Occupations

AFTER RESPONDENTS HAD RATED their present occupations on the ten-point self-anchoring occupational value scale (see Chapters 2 and 4), they were asked two follow-up questions designed to reveal the positive and negative features they saw in their own jobs. Responses to the first question—"What kinds of things about your present occupation kept you from placing it lower on the ladder?"—are shown in Tables 7-1a through 7-1h (pages 180 to 195).[1]

Negative features were elicited by asking, "What kind of things about your present occupation kept you from placing it higher on the ladder?" The question could not be asked of those who rated their jobs at the top of the ladder (position 10); thus the figures shown in Tables 7-2a through 7-2g record the responses of people who gave their jobs a ladder rating of 9 or lower (pages 196 to 209).[2]

The tables reveal an impressive variety of positive and negative occupational values, with marked variation from group to group. Despite the over-all variability, however, certain values tend to be emphasized by all groups, federal and nonfederal. In describing the positive features of their present jobs, a fairly high percentage of respondents in all groups mention that they find in their work a considerable amount of general interest, enjoyment, satisfaction, and pleasure, as well as a general sense

[1] The question was not asked of respondents who rated their occupations at the bottom of the ladder (position 1). However, since very few people did rate their occupations that low, nearly all respondents in all groups were asked the question. The number responding in each group is shown in Column 1 of Table 7-1a.

[2] The number responding in each group is shown in Column 1 of Table 7-2a. Neither question was asked of the student populations, since they had no present occupations to rate or evaluate.

of fulfillment and well-being. Substantial percentages mention good financial reward and good personal relationships with people at work. Moderate percentages note that their work has a pleasing amount of self-determination and autonomy and that it is also well suited to their personal capacities and abilities. Even in these values, however, the percentages vary markedly from group to group, and on still other values there is little agreement.

Concerning the negative aspects people see in their work, there are substantial percentages in all groups who say that their financial reward is inadequate. Otherwise there appears to be no general agreement among the various groups on the negative features.

Once more we find that the patterning of positive and negative values often differs by educational and occupational level, paralleling in many ways the hierarchical arrangement of values which appeared when people were asked to describe what would make an occupation the most and the least ideal for them. In describing the positive features of present occupations, the lower educational and occupational groups tend to emphasize security, financial reward, physical environment, and general working conditions. The higher-level groups tend to give more emphasis to self-development, self-expression, and creativity, self-determination, challenge, general sense of achievement and accomplishment, and the feeling that their work is worthwhile, useful, and constructive. On the negative side, the lower educational groups emphasize bad physical environment and bad working conditions in general; the higher-level groups emphasize lack of self-determination, responsibility, and authority, and lack of sufficient equipment to do the job.

The two series of tables also illustrate that people mention more positive than negative features about their jobs. Asked to discuss the good features, most respondents were more voluble than when asked about the bad features. These results accord well with our earlier findings of the generally high occupational satisfaction and optimism which appear to be characteristic of all groups.

A number of other significant matters stand out in the over-all results. Of considerable interest is the small amount of systematic variation from group to group in the percentages that mention good financial reward as a positive feature of their occupations: in nearly all groups these replies fall in the 20 to 30 percent range. This suggests that people tend to see the financial reward offered by their jobs in relation to standards which vary considerably from group to group, and not in terms of some absolute amount. That groups in education depart somewhat from the general pattern and show significantly lower mentions of good financial reward as a positive aspect of their occupation does not invalidate the conclusion. Rather, it suggests that members of these groups, because of their higher educational and occupational status levels, have high standards which are not being met in a large percentage of cases.

Also worth noting is the almost complete lack of mention in any group of insufficient occupational security as a negative feature. In the general employed public only 8 percent mention it; in all other groups typical figures are 1 and 2 percent.

Another rather striking finding is the considerably greater emphasis that federal employees, compared to nonfederal groups, give to supervision, both as a positive and negative feature of their work. Federal employees appear to have a greater awareness of, and sensitivity to, relationships to superiors than employees outside government.

Two answers somewhat unrelated to specific characteristics of a job are offered in substantial numbers by most groups as negative attributes: (1) that a person did not rate his job higher because he feels there is always room for improvement in an occupation, that nothing is ever perfect; (2) that he did not rate his job higher because of personal limitations or the lack of choice on his part. Clearly, these responses are more indicative of a state of mind and of circumstances than of negative attributes seen in the job.[3]

[3] One response pointing out a positive attribute of work is also not directly relevant to the particular characteristics of a person's occupation: that the person did not rate his job any lower because in a comparative or relative sense he feels it is better than other jobs of which he is aware. In other words, "things could be worse." Not only is it fairly obvious that this answer does not deal with particular positive aspects of the work itself, but a later examination of some of the questionnaires in which this response was used also indicated that the reply was sometimes a "brush-off" answer. For these two reasons we have not tabled the incidence of the catgory. It may be of interest to note, however, that the statement is considerably more common among the two general work forces (12 percent for the nonfederal and 16 percent for the federal) than in the special populations, and that it is particularly infrequent among high school and college teachers (around 1 percent). In the general employed public the percentages vary directly and strongly with educational level, but among general federal employees the differences according to education are virtually nonexistent.

Discussion of Specific Group Data

General Employed Public

As positive features of their work, people in the general employed public tend to emphasize factors of interest, enjoyment, satisfaction, and general sense of fulfillment, as well as good financial reward, good physical environment and general working conditions, and good personal relationships on the job. After these values, for which the figures range from 21 to over 40 percent, there is a sharp drop to 15 percent for self-determination and autonomy; for other values the percentages are even lower. On the negative side, only poor financial reward (32 percent) and bad physical environment and general working conditions (23 percent) are accorded appreciably high frequencies. A considerable variety of other negative attributes are mentioned, but by only 10 percent or less.

COMPARATIVE PATTERNS BY SEX. Women in the general employed public, compared to men, are especially likely to mention as positive features of their jobs such matters as general interest and satisfaction and good physical environment and working conditions. They are almost twice as likely as men to mention good personal relationships on the job and having understanding and sympathetic supervision. They also more often cite the worthwhileness of the work—11 percent of them do so vs. 4 percent of the men. Men give somewhat higher frequency of mention to good financial reward (35 vs. 26 percent) and occupational security (14 vs. 6 percent). Men seem also to be a little more likely to mention self-determination, self-advancement, and doing work that fits one's capacities, although the percentages in all instances are not high and the sex differences of borderline significance.

Concerning negative features of their work, women are a little more likely than men to speak of bad or unsympathetic supervision and bad personal relationships on the job, although the frequency does not exceed 8 percent for either factor. Mention of excessive work load is made by only 14 percent of the women, but even this is in marked contrast to the 5 percent figure for men.

COMPARATIVE PATTERNS BY EDUCATIONAL LEVEL. For many of the positive features people see in their work, there is not a smooth upward or downward progression in percentages as we proceed from the low of the high school not completed group to the high of the college graduate level.

Instead, the break tends to be sharp between the some college and college graduate levels, resulting in a pattern for college graduates that is distinctive from the patterns of the other three groups. The college graduate percentages are markedly higher on the general value of interest, enjoyment, and satisfaction; on sense of achievement; on doing work that fits their capacities and abilities; and on the worthwhileness of the work. Almost one fourth (23 percent) of the college graduates mention the worthwhileness factor as a positive feature, compared to 3, 2, and 6 percent for the other three groups. College graduates also differ from the other groups in their significantly lower mentions of suitable financial reward, good physical environment and working conditions, and good supervision. They show higher percentages for the positive features of self-determination, challenge, and having responsibility and authority, but on these values the downward trend in percentages from the highest to the lowest levels tends to be more evenly graduated.

The figures on the negative aspects of work show first of all that the people at the two upper educational levels mention negative aspects with less high frequency than do those at the two lower educational levels.[4] In particular, there is significantly less frequency of mention of poor financial reward: about a fourth of those with some college or with a college diploma mention poor financial reward, compared to a third or more of those on the two lower levels. The difference is even more marked in regard to bad physical environment and general working conditions: college graduates and those with some college have identical figures of 9 percent, compared to 28 percent for the high school not completed and 27 percent for the high school completed groups. Complaints of excessive work load decline from 11 percent at the lowest level to 1 percent among college graduates.

On the other hand, frequency of complaints about lack of self-determination, although not exceeding 14 percent in any of the four groups are somewhat higher at the two upper educational levels. It is also significant, although the response does not pertain to a negative factor as such, that (1) twice as many men as women say they did not rate their job higher because they believe nothing is ever perfect and (2) this response increases markedly with rise in education.

[4] This is particularly noteworthy in view of our earlier findings which indicate that, in general, frequency of reply and complexity of occupational value patterns tend to increase with educational level.

(Text continued on page 210)

Tables 7-1a Through 7-1h

"What kinds of things about your present occupation kept you from placing it lower on the ladder?" This question was very effective in eliciting from respondents thoughtful evaluations of the positive aspects of their own jobs. Students do not appear in the tables because they had no "present occupation" to be asked about. The question was also not asked of the small number of respondents who rated their present occupation at the bottom of the ladder.

Table 7-1a

Highlights: Interest, enjoyment, satisfaction, pleasure through doing work one is interested in, wants to do, likes to do.

. . . . The over-all picture is one of a high percentage of people in all groups reporting a feeling that their work is suited to their interests and tastes.

. . . . In the general employed public the 50% figure for college graduates is significantly higher than the figures for the other three educational levels.

. . . . All groups in education have extremely high entries, perhaps partly because they are less inclined to mention "general sense of fulfillment" (last column).

. . . . General federal employees and the general employed public have roughly the same percentages except at the "some college" educational level, where the federal percentage is higher (48% compared to 32%).

. . . . The figures for federal executives, natural scientists, and engineers are about the same as for the same groups in business, but the 22% figure for social scientists in business is only half that for federal social scientists.

Highlights: General sense of fulfillment, of well-being, of goals being met.

. . . . While this response is given with moderate frequency by most groups, it is most common among executives, natural scientists, and engineers in business, and least common among groups in education.

. . . . The figure for social scientists in business (10%) is markedly lower than the percentages for the other business groups.

Table 7-1a

Occupational values: the _positive_ attributes people see in their own jobs. Percentage distribution[a] of responses in each group to the question, "What kinds of things about your present occupation kept you from placing it lower on the ladder?"

	Number answer-ing	Interest, enjoyment, satisfaction, pleasure through doing work one is interested in, wants to do, likes to do	General sense of fulfillment, of well-being, of goals being met
Nonfederal Populations			
General employed public	1093	37%	16%
By sex			
Men	840	35	15
Women	253	42	19
By educational level			
High school not completed	308	32	17
High school completed	493	36	13
Some college	127	32	18
College graduate	135	50	17
Groups in education			
High school teachers	277	65	4
Vocational counselors	79	65	6
College teachers	466	64	7
Natural scientists	121	70	6
Social scientists	103	60	8
Engineers	85	65	8
Groups in business			
Executives	284	41	27
Natural scientists	84	39	24
Social scientists	73	22	10
Engineers	90	37	38
Federal Employee Populations			
General federal employees	925	41	12
By sex			
Men	644	38	11
Women	281	48	13
By educational level			
High school not completed	185	36	11
High school completed	349	40	12
Some college	176	48	9
College graduate	159	42	12
Executives	272	36	15
Natural scientists	90	47	9
Social scientists	89	44	14
Engineers	99	41	14

[a] Percentage base = number of respondents answering in each group.
Percentages do not add to 100 in each group due to multiple replies.

181

Table 7-1b

Highlights: High or good financial reward.

. . . . One third of the general employed public cite good pay as a positive attribute of their own jobs, whereas less than one fourth (23%) of general federal employees do so. This difference is present at each educational level except "college graduate," where the figures are about equal (24% and 20%).

. . . . In the general employed public women mention good pay somewhat less often than men; this is not true among general federal employees.

. . . . Groups in education mention good pay less frequently than any other groups.

. . . . Figures for executives, natural scientists, social scientists, and engineers in business and in federal employment are about the same.

Highlights: Security, stability, protection, fringe benefits.

. . . . Some aspect of security is noted as a positive feature of their jobs by only 12% of the general employed public; men cite it more than twice as often as women do, and lower educational groups more frequently than higher ones.

. . . . Groups in education and business refer to security scarcely at all.

. . . . The figure for general federal employees (25%) is double that for the general employed public (12%); this relationship holds at all four educational levels.

. . . . Among general federal employees, as in the general employed public, men cite security more often than women, and mention is more frequent among lower educational groups than among higher.

. . . . Mention of security is more frequent among federal executives, natural scientists, social scientists, and engineers than among the same groups in business.

182

Table 7-1b

Occupational values: the _positive_ attributes people
see in their own jobs (cont'd.)

	High or good financial reward (e.g., make good money, high pay)	Security, stability, protection, fringe (retirement, illness, income protection) benefits
Nonfederal Populations		
General employed public	33%	12%
By sex		
Men	35	14
Women	26	6
By educational level		
High school not completed	33	12
High school completed	36	14
Some college	31	8
College graduate	24	7
Groups in education		
High school teachers	14	5
Vocational counselors	10	1
College teachers	13	1
Natural scientists	13	2
Social scientists	13	1
Engineers	9	2
Groups in business		
Executives	25	4
Natural scientists	31	2
Social scientists	25	4
Engineers	18	3
Federal Employee Populations		
General federal employees	23	25
By sex		
Men	23	28
Women	23	16
By educational level		
High school not completed	27	27
High school completed	26	31
Some college	18	15
College graduate	20	19
Executives	20	11
Natural scientists	27	8
Social scientists	23	9
Engineers	21	9

Table 7-1c

<u>Highlights</u>: Good physical environment and working conditions.

. . . . Figures for the general employed public and for general federal employees are almost the same over-all (22% and 23%) and at all educational levels except college graduate; the figure for nonfederally employed college graduates drops to 13%.

. . . . College and business groups have low percentages.

. . . . Figures for federal executives, natural scientists, social scientists, and engineers are lower than for federal employees in general; and, for the most part, are somewhat higher than for the same groups in business and in colleges.

<u>Highlights</u>: Having the equipment, facilities; wherewithal to do the job.

. . . . Though this attribute is rarely mentioned in most groups, it was tabled to show that it is cited by roughly 10% of federal natural scientists, social scientists, and engineers.

<u>Highlights</u>: Good superior, supervisor, boss.

. . . . Women, both in nonfederal and federal employment, refer to a good supervisor or superior more often than do men.

. . . . Federal employee populations in general show a pattern of somewhat higher percentages than nonfederal populations.

184

Table 7-1c

Occupational values: the _positive_ attributes people
see in their own jobs (cont'd.)

	Good physical environment and working conditions (e.g., clean, pleasant, not dangerous)	Having the equipment, facilities, wherewithal to do the job	Good superior, supervisor, boss (e.g., understanding, fair, nice, gives support)
Nonfederal Populations			
General employed public	22%	2%	12%
By sex			
Men	20	1	10
Women	26	3	19
By educational level			
High school not completed	20	3	14
High school completed	25	2	12
Some college	22	1	12
College graduate	13	0	7
Groups in education			
High school teachers	13	7	8
Vocational counselors	13	6	9
College teachers	8	5	9
Natural scientists	5	7	10
Social scientists	9	6	8
Engineers	6	1	2
Groups in business			
Executives	6	4	9
Natural scientists	8	6	8
Social scientists	6	4	12
Engineers	10	2	9
Federal Employee Populations			
General federal employees	23	4	16
By sex			
Men	23	4	13
Women	21	5	23
By educational level			
High school not completed	20	4	16
High school completed	28	4	15
Some college	18	4	14
College graduate	21	4	16
Executives	11	3	11
Natural scientists	8	8	17
Social scientists	15	9	16
Engineers	17	11	24

Table 7-1d

Highlights: Good personal relations with people at work.

. . . . Good personal relations is mentioned with moderately high to high frequency in all groups, percentages ranging roughly from 20% to 50% (Total column).

. . . . Women, much more frequently than men, comment on good personal relations. The figure for federally employed women is especially high (42%).

. . . . Percentages for groups in education, except for college engineers, are especially high, and these groups emphasize active over passive relations (ratio of roughly 3 to 1).

. . . . Among general federal employees, for both men and women and at all educational levels, the active/passive ratio is approximately 1 to 2, in contrast to an approximate 1 to 1 ratio in the general employed public.

. . . . For federal natural scientists and engineers, the active/ passive ratio is about 1 to 4; for those in business the ratio is about 1 to 1; for those in colleges it is about 2.5 to 1.

Table 7-1d

Occupational values: the <u>positive</u> attributes people
see in their own jobs (cont'd.)

| | Good personal relations with people at work (e.g., co-workers, the public, students) | | | |
	Passive (e.g., around pleasant, agreeable people)	Active (e.g., meet stimulating people, make good contacts)	Miscel- laneous	Total
<u>Nonfederal Populations</u>				
General employed public	11%	11%	0%	21%
By sex				
Men	8	10	1	18
Women	19	16	0	32
By educational level				
High school not completed	8	6	0	14
High school completed	12	11	0	22
Some college	13	17	2	28
College graduate	7	19	1	25
Groups in education				
High school teachers	13	41	2	51
Vocational counselors	19	46	1	54
College teachers	16	31	3	44
Natural scientists	15	38	1	49
Social scientists	10	28	3	39
Engineers	6	22	1	28
Groups in business				
Executives	11	13	1	23
Natural scientists	16	14	1	30
Social scientists	8	21	0	27
Engineers	11	8	1	20
<u>Federal Employee Populations</u>				
General federal employees	18	10	1	28
By sex				
Men	15	8	1	23
Women	28	14	2	42
By educational level				
High school not completed	20	9	1	28
High school completed	16	10	1	27
Some college	19	9	3	31
College graduate	18	8	1	25
Executives	16	15	0	29
Natural scientists	27	7	0	32
Social scientists	25	20	1	45
Engineers	24	6	0	30

Table 7-1e

<u>Highlights</u>: Self-advancement and progress.

. . . . Of particular interest are the over-all low references in almost all groups to seeing self-advancement and progress as a positive attribute of one's own occupation.

. . . . The 17% figure for the "some college" group in the general employed public stands out.

. . . . In the nonfederal populations frequency of mention by groups in education is very low. Among groups in business it is, relatively speaking, fairly high (except, perhaps, for social scientists).

<u>Highlights</u>: Self-development, self-expression, and creativity.

. . . . The figure (total column) for the general employed public is low (5%), higher for general federal employees but still not very high (9%), and fairly substantial for natural scientists, social scientists, and engineers in colleges, business, and the federal government (roughly 15% to 25%).

. . . . There is a positive relationship between mention of self-development, self-expression, and creativity and educational level, especially among general federal employees.

Table 7-1e

Occupational values: the _positive_ attributes people
see in their own jobs (cont'd.)

	Self-advancement and progress (e.g., promotion good; good chance to get ahead)	Self-development, self-expression, and creativity		Total
		Self-develop-ment (e.g., learn; develop; grow personally, professionally)	Self-expres-sion and cre-ativity (e.g., innovate; ex-press own ideas)	
Nonfederal Populations				
General employed public	6%	3%	2%	5%
By sex				
Men	7	4	2	6
Women	2	3	0	4
By educational level				
High school not completed	2	2	0	3
High school completed	6	5	1	6
Some college	17	3	4	7
College graduate	8	3	6	9
Groups in education				
High school teachers	2	7	4	11
Vocational counselors	4	9	5	13
College teachers	2	14	11	22
Natural scientists	1	19	6	24
Social scientists	3	10	10	16
Engineers	2	19	4	22
Groups in business				
Executives	12	1	10	11
Natural scientists	13	11	13	20
Social scientists	8	16	7	22
Engineers	16	3	11	14
Federal Employee Populations				
General federal employees	7	6	3	9
By sex				
Men	6	6	3	9
Women	9	7	2	8
By educational level				
High school not completed	4	6	1	7
High school completed	6	7	1	8
Some college	10	7	4	10
College graduate	9	7	9	15
Executives	10	8	8	15
Natural scientists	6	10	6	14
Social scientists	14	23	14	30
Engineers	8	12	5	15

Table 7-1f

Highlights: Self-determination.

. . . . The figures for self-determination are moderately high, ranging roughly from 10% to 20%.

. . . . In the general employed public and among general federal employees the percentages are related to level of education.

. . . . Mention of self-determination as a positive attribute of one's occupation is noticeably low among high school teachers, including vocational counselors.

. . . . Natural scientists and social scientists in colleges, business, and the federal government register approximately the same figures.

. . . . The percentage for engineers in the federal government (17%) is about the same as that for engineers in business, but markedly lower than that for engineers in colleges (41%).

Highlights: Responsibility and authority, power to make decisions.

. . . . Responsibility and authority are scarcely mentioned as positive attributes of one's job in the general employed public and among groups in education.

. . . . In the general employed public, despite the low over-all frequencies, there is a slight positive relationship with level of education. Among general federal employees the positive relationship is even more marked.

. . . . In general, claims of responsibility and authority as a positive attribute of their own jobs are moderately high among executives, natural scientists, and engineers in the federal government. The figures do not differ appreciably from those for the same groups in business.

Highlights: Sense of challenge, overcoming obstacles, keeping goals ahead.

. . . . Challenge is listed infrequently by the general employed public, somewhat more often by general federal employees.

. . . . Percentages are positively related to level of education in the general employed public and among general federal employees.

. . . . Figures for natural scientists, social scientists, and engineers are roughly the same in the federal government, in business, and in colleges (slightly lower in colleges).

. . . . Federal executives mention a sense of challenge as a positive attribute of their own jobs with moderately high frequency and somewhat more often than do business executives.

Table 7-1f

Occupational values: the _positive_ attributes people
see in their own jobs (cont'd.)

	Self-determination (e.g., I am my own master; no heavy supervision; freedom of thought, action)	Responsibility and authority, power to make decisions	Sense of challenge, overcoming obstacles, keeping goals ahead
Nonfederal Populations			
General employed public	15%	4%	4%
By sex			
Men	16	4	4
Women	12	4	3
By educational level			
High school not completed	13	2	1
High school completed	14	3	3
Some college	19	7	7
College graduate	21	9	11
Groups in education			
High school teachers	9	4	13
Vocational counselors	10	5	13
College teachers	31	4	14
Natural scientists	36	3	7
Social scientists	44	5	11
Engineers	41	4	13
Groups in business			
Executives	17	22	13
Natural scientists	33	17	17
Social scientists	30	23	18
Engineers	20	16	19
Federal Employee Populations			
General federal employees	12	8	7
By sex			
Men	11	8	8
Women	14	10	7
By educational level			
High school not completed	8	6	3
High school completed	12	8	6
Some college	11	9	9
College graduate	16	13	18
Executives	21	30	20
Natural scientists	37	12	17
Social scientists	37	19	18
Engineers	17	19	22

Table 7-1g

<u>Highlights</u>: Sense of achievement, accomplishment through seeing results of own work.

. . . . The general employed public and general federal employees, with the exception of college graduates in both groups, cite sense of achievement infrequently.

. . . . For natural scientists frequencies are somewhat higher in colleges than in business or in the federal government.

. . . . Engineers in business note sense of achievement as a positive attribute of their own jobs more often than do engineers in either colleges or in federal government.

<u>Highlights</u>: Do work that is worthwhile, useful, constructive.

. . . . Such references are quite low in both the general employed public and among general federal employees, with the exception of those at the college graduate level, especially in the general employed public.

. . . . College graduates in the general employed public have a markedly higher figure (23%) than that for college graduates among general federal employees (12%).

. . . . In general, groups in education register higher figures than groups in business and in the government, with the exception of federal social scientists.

. . . . Natural scientists in government show a figure of only 8% in comparison to 12% for those in business and 23% for those in colleges.

. . . . The figure for federal executives, while only moderately high (20%), is double that of business executives (9%).

Table 7-1g

Occupational values: the _positive_ attributes people
see in their own jobs (cont'd.)

	Sense of achievement, accomplishment through seeing results of own work	Do work that is worthwhile, useful, constructive
Nonfederal Populations		
General employed public	4%	6%
By sex		
Men	5	4
Women	3	11
By educational level		
High school not completed	4	3
High school completed	3	2
Some college	4	6
College graduate	10	23
Groups in education		
High school teachers	17	31
Vocational counselors	10	34
College teachers	16	29
Natural scientists	17	23
Social scientists	15	18
Engineers	8	20
Groups in business		
Executives	15	9
Natural scientists	11	12
Social scientists	16	14
Engineers	24	11
Federal Employee Populations		
General federal employees	6	7
By sex		
Men	6	6
Women	6	9
By educational level		
High school not completed	5	6
High school completed	5	4
Some college	7	7
College graduate	12	11
Executives	12	20
Natural scientists	9	8
Social scientists	18	27
Engineers	10	12

Table 7-1h

<u>Highlights</u>: Do work that fits one's capacities and/or training.

. . . . The general employed public and general federal employees cite this feature fairly often and in about the same proportions.

. . . . The 22% figure at the high school not completed level among general federal employees is markedly higher than the figures for the other three educational levels among general federal employees, and higher than the figure (16%) for the comparable group in the general employed public.

. . . . College graduates in the general employed public have a somewhat higher figure than the college graduates among general federal employees --21% versus 13%.

. . . . Social scientists in the federal government mention this factor considerably more frequently than do their counterparts in business and in colleges.

<u>Highlights</u>: Variety in the work, absence of monotony and routine.

. . . . This factor is cited infrequently in the general employed public; the figure for general federal employees is somewhat higher.

. . . . The figures for college groups are especially low.

. . . . Women in the general federal employee group mention variety more frequently than do men.

. . . . Federal executives, natural scientists, social scientists, and engineers have about the same percentages as their counterparts in business.

<u>Highlights</u>: Leisure, recreation, time off, vacation.

. . . . This category was tabled simply to show the low notice in all groups of leisure and time off as a positive attribute of one's job.

Table 7-1h

Occupational values: the _positive_ attributes people
see in their own jobs (cont'd.)

	Do work that fits one's capacities and/or training	Variety in the work, absence of monotony and routine	Leisure, recreation, time off, vacations
Nonfederal Populations			
General employed public	14%	7%	4%
By sex			
Men	15	7	4
Women	11	6	3
By educational level			
High school not completed	16	4	4
High school completed	11	8	3
Some college	13	9	3
College graduate	21	8	4
Groups in education			
High school teachers	9	9	8
Vocational counselors	13	13	4
College teachers	10	3	6
Natural scientists	14	5	5
Social scientists	5	5	5
Engineers	9	6	2
Groups in business			
Executives	11	11	3
Natural scientists	16	13	1
Social scientists	8	16	6
Engineers	12	12	0
Federal Employee Populations			
General federal employees	14	10	10
By sex			
Men	14	9	10
Women	14	16	8
By educational level			
High school not completed	22	5	10
High school completed	11	14	12
Some college	12	8	5
College graduate	13	12	9
Executives	12	13	3
Natural scientists	11	13	1
Social scientists	20	15	6
Engineers	10	14	5

Tables 7-2a Through 7-2g

The question quoted in the table title was designed to elicit the negative attributes people see in their own jobs. It was not asked of
people who rated their present occupation at the top of the ladder (10),
that is, at the very top of the "ideal occupations"; nor of students,
because they had no "present occupation" to discuss.

Table 7-2a

Highlights: Just dislike present job.

. . . . Mention of generalized, nonspecific dislike of one's occupation
occurs with relatively low frequency in all groups, both nonfederal and
federal. There is a tendency for it to be somewhat higher among the
general employed public, especially at the high school not completed
level, and among high school teachers.

Highlights: This is not the occupation I prefer; not the one I find
    most (or highly) interesting, enjoyable, satisfying.

. . . . This response, which suggests that the respondent has another
more interesting or satisfying occupation in mind, occurs with very low
frequency in all groups, although there is some indication that slightly
higher percentages of federal employees feel this way.

Table 7-2a

Occupational values: the <u>negative</u> attributes people see in their own jobs. Percentage distribution[a] of responses in each group to the question, "What kinds of things about your present occupation kept you from placing it higher on the ladder?"

	Number answer-ing	Just dislike present job (not further elaborated)	This is not the occupation I prefer; not the one I find most (or highly) interesting, enjoy-able, satisfying
Nonfederal Populations			
General employed public	909	10%	2%
By sex			
Men	716	10	2
Women	193	11	2
By educational level			
High school not completed	258	15	2
High school completed	428	8	2
Some college	102	10	2
College graduate	100	10	1
Groups in education			
High school teachers	201	9	3
Vocational counselors	59	12	2
College teachers	302	4	3
Natural scientists	75	9	0
Social scientists	78	3	1
Engineers	67	0	2
Groups in business			
Executives	208	8	3
Natural scientists	70	3	10
Social scientists	67	0	8
Engineers	75	8	0
Federal Employee Populations			
General federal employees	814	6	6
By sex			
Men	574	5	6
Women	240	9	7
By educational level			
High school not completed	153	6	6
High school completed	308	7	6
Some college	158	6	5
College graduate	151	4	7
Executives	242	3	3
Natural scientists	87	6	6
Social scientists	82	9	5
Engineers	96	4	5

[a] Percentage base = number of respondents answering in each group. Percentages do not add to 100 in each group due to multiple replies.

197

Table 7-2b

<u>Highlights</u>: Poor or inadequate financial reward.

. . . . All groups cite poor or inadequate financial reward with moderate to high frequency.

. . . . Complaints about financial reward are higher in the general employed public than in the general federal work force.

. . . . In the general employed public, the two upper educational groups cite poor financial reward significantly less often than do the two lower groups. Among general federal employees this is true of the some college group, but to a lesser extent, and complaints among college graduates are not significantly less than among the two lower educational groups.

. . . . In the general employed public, frequencies for men and women are about equal; but in the general federal work force, mention of poor financial reward is higher for men.

. . . . Mentions are higher among groups in education than among their counterparts in business or the federal government.

. . . . Federal executives and engineers do not diverge appreciably from their counterparts in business. However, natural scientists in federal employment mention poor financial reward somewhat more frequently than do natural scientists in business. For social scientists the reverse is true.

<u>Highlights</u>: Absence of, or insufficient security, stability, protection, fringe (retirement, illness, income protection) benefits.

. . . . This category was tabled to show that it is mentioned only infrequently by the general employed public (and there, primarily in the two lower educational groups); and that all the other populations, nonfederal and federal, cite it hardly at all.

198

Table 7-2b

Occupational values: the negative attributes people see
in their own jobs (cont'd.)

	Poor or inadequate financial reward	Absence of or insufficient security, stability, protection, fringe (retirement, illness, income protection) benefits
Nonfederal Populations		
General employed public	32%	8%
By sex		
Men	31	9
Women	35	5
By educational level		
High school not completed	36	8
High school completed	34	11
Some college	25	6
College graduate	26	4
Groups in education		
High school teachers	36	2
Vocational counselors	36	2
College teachers	37	2
Natural scientists	36	1
Social scientists	32	4
Engineers	31	2
Groups in business		
Executives	14	2
Natural scientists	14	4
Social scientists	25	2
Engineers	19	1
Federal Employee Populations		
General federal employees	24	1
By sex		
Men	27	1
Women	16	1
By educational level		
High school not completed	27	2
High school completed	25	1
Some college	19	1
College graduate	24	1
Executives	17	2
Natural scientists	22	1
Social scientists	17	0
Engineers	20	2

Table 7-2c

<u>Highlights</u>: Bad physical environment and working conditions.

. . . . The frequency of this complaint is quite high in the general employed public, but is confined mainly to the lower educational groups. Among general federal employees the over-all figure is lower, but is distributed more evely through all four educational levels.

. . . . Groups in education and in business scarcely mention bad physical environment and working conditions.

. . . . Federal executives, social scientists, natural scientists, and engineers comment on this factor with higher frequency than do comparable groups outside the government. However, the absolute figures among these federal groups is still not very high.

<u>Highlights</u>: Absence of or insufficient equipment, facilities, wherewithal to do the job.

. . . . This type of reply occurs with very low frequency in the general employed public, but with moderate to high frequency among general federal employees, especially those at the college graduate level.

. . . . All groups in education respond in this fashion moderately often.

. . . . Federal executives, natural scientists, social scientists, and engineers mention insufficient equipment and facilities more frequently than do their counterparts in business.

<u>Highlights</u>: Bad superior, supervisor, boss.

. . . . The most significant feature to note is that comments about the quality of the immediate supervision is in general much higher among federal groups than nonfederal groups.

. . . . Worth noting also is that in the federal employee populations the percentages are moderately high and do not vary a great deal from group to group.

Table 7-2c

Occupational values: the <u>negative</u> attributes people see
in their jobs (cont'd.)

	Bad physical environment and working conditions (e.g., dirty, unpleasant, dangerous)	Absence of or insufficient equipment, facilities, wherewithal to do the job	Bad superior, supervisor, boss (e.g., unfair, unpleasant, fails to give support)
<u>Nonfederal Populations</u>			
General employed public	23%	5%	5%
By sex			
Men	22	5	4
Women	28	6	8
By educational level			
High school not completed	28	5	5
High school completed	27	5	5
Some college	10	9	5
College graduate	9	4	2
Groups in education			
High school teachers	6	15	5
Vocational counselors	2	12	2
College teachers	5	14	3
Natural scientists	1	17	9
Social scientists	1	13	3
Engineers	0	12	8
Groups in business			
Executives	2	6	9
Natural scientists	4	14	11
Social scientists	2	6	15
Engineers	1	5	3
<u>Federal Employee Populations</u>			
General federal employees	17	12	17
By sex			
Men	16	11	16
Women	20	15	19
By educational level			
High school not completed	16	8	21
High school completed	17	12	15
Some college	21	8	17
College graduate	11	19	13
Executives	7	14	16
Natural scientists	12	24	12
Social scientists	7	12	20
Engineers	10	10	15

Table 7-2d

<u>Highlights</u>: Bad or inadequate personal relations with people at work.

. . . . References to this factor are extremely low in the general employed public, somewhat higher among general federal employees.

. . . . Among general federal employees women cite bad personal relations more frequently than men.

. . . . Social scientists in the federal government and in colleges mention this factor a little more frequently than do other groups.

<u>Highlights</u>: Lack of self-advancement and progress.

. . . . In the general employed public mention of lack of self-advancement and progress is fairly low and there is a slight tendency for it to be negatively related to level of education. Among general federal employees on the other hand mention is much more common, occurring moderately often. Also, there is a suggestion that among general federal employees frequency of mention is <u>positively</u> related to level of education, the figures for the some college groups and college graduate groups being almost double the figure for the high school not completed stratum.

. . . . Groups in education note the lack of self-advancement and progress scarcely at all.

. . . . Federal executives, natural scientists, social scientists, and engineers register somewhat lower figures than federal employees in general.

. . . . The figures for federal executives, natural scientists, and engineers are relatively low and do not differ significantly from those shown by their counterparts in business. There is some indication that social scientists in the federal government mention lack of self-advancement and progress more often than do their counterparts in business.

<u>Highlights</u>: Lack of self-development, self-expression, and creativity.

. . . . This factor is scarcely cited by any group except social scientists in the federal government and by natural scientists in business.

Table 7-2d

Occupational values: the _negative_ attributes people see
in their own jobs (cont'd.)

	Bad or inadequate personal relations with people at work (e.g., co-workers, the public, students)	Lack of self-advancement and progress (e.g., no promotions, no chance to get ahead)	Lack of self-development, self-expression, and creativity
Nonfederal Populations			
General employed public	4%	9%	2%
By sex			
Men	3	9	2
Women	7	6	2
By educational level			
High school not completed	3	8	2
High school completed	4	10	1
Some college	8	7	3
College graduate	5	4	2
Groups in education			
High school teachers	12	4	2
Vocational counselors	9	2	2
College teachers	10	0	5
Natural scientists	4	1	3
Social scientists	14	1	6
Engineers	8	0	2
Groups in business			
Executives	5	9	5
Natural scientists	10	13	14
Social scientists	8	8	9
Engineers	9	7	3
Federal Employee Populations			
General federal employees	8	16	3
By sex			
Men	6	17	3
Women	12	14	4
By educational level			
High school not completed	7	11	1
High school completed	7	17	3
Some college	8	19	5
College graduate	6	18	4
Executives	7	8	4
Natural scientists	7	10	7
Social scientists	17	15	12
Engineers	2	8	3

Table 7-2e

Highlights: Lack of self-determination.

. . . . The general employed public and general federal employees mention the lack of self-determination with low and equal frequency. However, in the general employed public there is a very slight positive relationship with level of education; among general federal employees the relationship with level of education is very strongly positive, rising from 4% at the high school not completed level to 17% at the college graduate level.

. . . . Approximately one fourth of the college teachers as a whole and natural scientists, social scientists, and engineers in colleges mention lack of self-determination.

. . . . Figures for the groups in business are lower than for comparable groups in the federal government and especially in colleges.

. . . . Federal executives say lack of self-determination much more frequently (26%) than do business executives (11%).

Highlights: Lack of responsibility and authority, of power to make decisions.

. . . . The general employed public and groups in education scarcely mention this negative occupational attribute. Among general federal employees the two highest educational levels mention it with low to moderate frequency.

. . . . Lack of responsibility and authority is noted by groups in business with moderate to moderately high frequency. Roughly similar figures occur for executives, social scientists, and engineers in the federal government.

Table 7-2e

Occupational values: the _negative_ attributes people see
in their own jobs (cont'd.)

	Lack of self-determination (e.g., not my own master, rigid supervision; no freedom of thought, action)	Lack of responsibility and authority, lack of power to make decisions
Nonfederal Populations		
General employed public	7%	2%
By sex		
Men	7	2
Women	5	2
By educational level		
High school not completed	6	0
High school completed	5	2
Some college	14	2
College graduate	9	4
Groups in education		
High school teachers	9	3
Vocational counselors	9	5
College teachers	21	1
Natural scientists	27	3
Social scientists	24	0
Engineers	27	2
Groups in business		
Executives	11	11
Natural scientists	20	11
Social scientists	12	19
Engineers	13	15
Federal Employee Populations		
General federal employees	7	6
By sex		
Men	8	5
Women	5	7
By educational level		
High school not completed	4	2
High school completed	4	6
Some college	10	9
College graduate	17	7
Executives	26	15
Natural scientists	24	5
Social scientists	16	15
Engineers	17	13

Table 7-2f

Highlights: Work does not fit capacities and/or training.

. . . . This factor is given very scant notice by most of the nonfederal populations with the exception of social scientists and engineers in business, who give it slightly more notice.

. . . . Figures for general federal employees are somewhat higher than for the general employed public, but still low.

Highlights: Too much routine in the work; monotonous, not enough change, variety.

. . . . This item was tabled to demonstrate its low prominence in all groups. One exception is the moderate figure of 15% for general federal employees with some college training.

Highlights: Excessive work load; hard work.

. . . . In the general employed public, frequency of mention is low. However, women mention excessive work almost three times as often as do men, and such references are negatively related to educational level.

. . . . High school teachers and high school vocational counselors mention excessive work load fairly often, as do college teachers in general and social scientists in colleges.

. . . . Groups in business and all groups in federal employ barely mention excessive work load.

Table 7-2f

Occupational values: the <u>negative</u> attributes people see
in their own jobs (cont'd.)

	Work does not fit capacities and/or training	Too much routine in the work; monotonous, not enough change, variety	Excessive work load; hard work
Nonfederal Populations			
General employed public	2%	4%	7%
By sex			
Men	2	4	5
Women	2	5	14
By educational level			
High school not completed	2	3	11
High school completed	1	4	7
Some college	3	7	2
College graduate	3	7	1
Groups in education			
High school teachers	3	3	12
Vocational counselors	5	3	12
College teachers	3	3	11
Natural scientists	0	0	4
Social scientists	4	4	12
Engineers	3	0	8
Groups in business			
Executives	5	3	4
Natural scientists	4	7	4
Social scientists	12	10	2
Engineers	11	7	4
Federal Employee Populations			
General federal employees	7	7	3
By sex			
Men	6	7	2
Women	10	9	8
By educational level			
High school not completed	9	2	1
High school completed	6	7	4
Some college	7	15	5
College graduate	7	7	5
Executives	4	3	2
Natural scientists	5	6	1
Social scientists	6	7	0
Engineers	7	10	2

207

Table 7-2g

<u>Highlights</u>: Personal limitation or lack of choice.

. . . . Replies falling in this category reflect the tendency to turn inward upon oneself the blame for any deficiencies in job or occupation. They suggest a feeling of unfulfillable aspiration to better oneself occupationally.

. . . . Such comments occur moderately often in the general employed public and show little relationship with sex or educational level.

. . . . Frequencies are moderate in groups in education and in business and show little variability.

. . . . The over-all figure for general federal employees is not significantly different than that for the general employed public. But among general federal employees, frequency of response is negatively related to educational level, with figures of 20% for the high school not completed group versus only 8% for college graduates.

. . . . Federal executives have a somewhat lower figure than business executives.

<u>Highlights</u>: Didn't rate the job higher because there is always room for improvement; nothing is perfect.

. . . . Responses of this kind suggest an over-all high level of satisfaction with one's job or occupation, coupled with a feeling that things can or will get even better.

. . . . The percentages for the general employed public and for general federal employees are about the same and fairly high. However, in the general employed public this reply runs twice as high for men as for women; this is not the case for general federal employees. In addition, in the general employed public there is a strong positive relationship between frequency of mention and educational level. No such strong positive relationship occurs among general federal employees, but the 25% figure for the some college group does stand out.

. . . . This kind of generalized satisfaction and optimism is highest among executives, social scientists, and engineers in business; it is markedly higher for these three groups than for their counterparts in federal employment.

Table 7-2g

Occupational values: the negative attributes people see
in their own jobs (cont'd.)

	Answers unrelated to particular characteristics of person's job	
	Personal limitation or lack of choice (e.g., my job is as good as I can get with my circumstances, education, training)	Didn't rate the job higher because there is always room for improvement; nothing is perfect
Nonfederal Populations		
General employed public	12%	20%
By sex		
Men	12	22
Women	14	11
By educational level		
High school not completed	14	13
High school completed	11	19
Some college	8	30
College graduate	12	36
Groups in education		
High school teachers	10	14
Vocational counselors	12	15
College teachers	10	10
Natural scientists	12	17
Social scientists	15	19
Engineers	10	19
Groups in business		
Executives	13	39
Natural scientists	14	19
Social scientists	13	28
Engineers	8	33
Federal Employee Populations		
General federal employees	15	18
By sex		
Men	15	19
Women	13	17
By educational level		
High school not completed	20	18
High school completed	15	15
Some college	16	25
College graduate	8	20
Executives	7	22
Natural scientists	13	18
Social scientists	10	12
Engineers	9	19

High School Teachers and Vocational Counselors

In discussing the positive aspects of their occupations, high school teachers give particularly strong emphasis to the interest, enjoyment, satisfaction, and pleasure they find in doing the kind of work they are interested in and like to do. This emphasis is characteristic of the teacher population, as shown by the high percentage of college teachers who also mention this factor. In nonteacher populations the figures range from 30 to 50 percent, whereas about two thirds of all teachers volunteer it as a positive feature in their work.

The high school groups also strongly emphasize good personal relationships—over 50 percent mention it—and stress is placed on the active aspects of such relationships. The ratio of frequency of mention of active vs. passive is about 3 to 1, and undoubtedly stems from the satisfaction teachers find in their positive relationships with their students. About one third of the two groups also mention the worthwhile and constructive nature of their work.

These three factors are the most outstanding positive features seen by the teachers and vocational counselors in their work. Frequency then drops sharply to the 17 percent that mention a feeling of achievement or accomplishment, after which no positive factor is mentioned by more than 9 percent. Scarcely any in the two groups point out either financial reward or security as positive features.

The only negative feature of their work cited with any great frequency is poor financial reward; 36 percent of both groups mention it, and the figure is 10 percent above the finding among college graduates in the general employed public. And, although the absolute figures are not high, these teachers mention excessive work load (12 percent) and lack of sufficient equipment and facilities (15 percent) slightly more often than other populations do.

College Teachers, Natural and Social Scientists, and Engineers

In describing the positive features of their work, the general college teachers refer most often to interest, enjoyment, and satisfaction through doing the kind of work they are interested in and like to do. Approximately two thirds volunteer this response; this is followed by 44 percent who mention good personal relationships, with an emphasis of about 3 to 1 on the active vs. passive aspects. Third in frequency of mention—31 percent—is the feeling that college teaching offers a high degree of personal freedom, self-determination, and autonomy. But almost as many— 29 percent—say that the work they do is worthwhile and constructive, and over one fifth also say that their occupation offers opportunity for self-development, self-expression, and creativity. The percentage mentioning good financial reward as a positive feature is markedly lower than for any other group, within or outside government, except the high school teachers.

On the other hand, about one third of the group cites poor financial reward as a negative aspect of their work. And it is interesting, since self-determination is a highly positive feature for this group, that mention of its lack as a negative feature is also high. This suggests that the college teacher population is particularly sensitive to and aware of personal freedom and self-determination as an occupational value.

Among the special college groups, the natural scientists' responses parallel quite closely those of the general college teachers. In general this is also true of the social scientists, who do, however, show a slight tendency to mention self-determination and autonomy somewhat more frequently as a positive feature, and to cite somewhat less frequently opportunity for self-development, self-expression, and creativity. The engineers differ from the general college teachers in making somewhat less reference to good supervision, good personal relationships, and sense of achievement or accomplishment, and in paying somewhat more attention to self-determination and autonomy.

Groups in Business

The pattern of positive and negative features that business executives, natural and social scientists, and engineers see in their occupations is in many ways similar to the college graduate pattern in the general employed public. For some reason which we do not presently understand, however, these groups—with the exception of the social scientists—are considerably more likely than others to mention as positive features a general sense of fulfillment, pervasive well-being, and goals being met. They are also somewhat more likely than comparable groups to mention opportunity for self-advancement and progress, and the feeling that they have responsibility and authority and the power to make decisions. On the average, they appear to speak somewhat less often of doing something worthwhile and constructive. While they seem to be no more apt than other comparable groups to cite good financial reward as a positive factor, they are considerably less likely to mention the lack of it as a negative factor. Finally—except for the natural scientists—they are more inclined to say they rated their jobs no higher because there is always room for occupational improvement.

On two positive values, engineers in business are distinguishably different from their natural and social science colleagues: they are considerably less likely to describe their work as offering opportunity for self-expression, self-development, and creativity, and for self-determination and autonomy. There are also a few other exceptions to the general pattern of similarity among the four groups. A smaller percentage of the engineers see good financial reward in their work. Social scientists place much emphasis on active, rather than passive, personal relationships. The natural scientists complain a bit more frequently than the other three groups about lack of self-advancement and progress, lack of self-development, self-expression, and creativity, and especially (20 percent) about the lack of self-determination. The natural scientists are also much less inclined to say they rated their jobs no higher because there is always room for improvement.

General Federal Employees

Although the major positive features that general federal employees see in their occupations are roughly the same as those mentioned by people in the general employed public, the pattern of emphasis among federal employees is somewhat different. The descending rank order of positive occupational attributes for federal workers begins with the general factor of interest, enjoyment, satisfaction, and pleasure through doing work one is interested in, wants to do, and likes to do: about 40 percent of the respondents mention this. Then there is a sharp drop to the mentions of good personal relationships on the job (28 percent); then to a cluster—general physical environment and working conditions (23 percent), good financial reward (23 percent), and security and protective fringe benefits (25 percent). The next drop is to the 16 percent citing good supervision.

Thus, we see that federal employees are less apt (23 percent) than the general employed public (33 percent) to see good financial reward as a positive feature. On the other hand, federal employees mention job security and protective fringe benefits twice as frequently (25 vs. 12 percent). They also emphasize good supervision and good personal relationships on the job slightly more, with far more emphasis on passive than active relationships. Their passive/active ratio is approximately 2 to 1; the general employed public's is 1 to 1.

Concerning the negative features they see in their jobs, general federal employees are less likely than members of the general work force to point to poor financial reward. Careful examination of the results indicates that this difference is due mainly to two facts: federally-employed women are far less likely than women in the general employed public to mention poor financial reward; and federal workers at the three lower educational levels are less likely than their opposite numbers in the general work force to cite it. Federal employees are somewhat less likely to mention bad physical environment as a negative feature, but complain somewhat more frequently—especially at the two upper educational levels—about bad supervision and lack of self-advancement and progress.

COMPARATIVE PATTERNS BY SEX. Federally employed men, in discussing the good aspects of their employment, give considerably more emphasis (28 percent) than women (16 percent) to job security and protective fringe benefits. Women pay much higher attention to the two factors of good supervision (23 percent vs. 13 percent for men) and good personal relationships (42 vs. 23 percent). Women also mention variety and lack of monotony as a good feature of their work somewhat more than men.

Concerning the bad features of their occupations, men are much more apt to cite poor financial reward (27 percent vs. 16 percent for women). (This difference is not apparent in the general employed public, where about one third of both men and women mention poor financial reward as a negative feature.) Women speak more frequently than men about bad personal relationships; coupled with their frequency of mention of good relationships as a positive feature, this suggests that they have a differentially higher sensitivity to personal relationships on the job. (In the general employed public women also place far more emphasis than men on this factor.)

COMPARATIVE PATTERNS BY EDUCATIONAL LEVEL. Mention of security, stability, and protective fringe benefits as positive features declines with increasing educational level; here federal employees parallel the nonfederal, although *frequency* of mention is markedly higher at all four educational levels among the federal employees. The figures for good physical environment and general working conditions are parallel at the various educational levels for both general populations—with the exception of the college graduate level, where 21 percent of federal employees mention the factor and only 13 percent of the general public. The college graduates differ also on the factor of good supervision—16 percent of those who are federal employees mention it as a positive feature, and only 7 percent of those in the general public.

We noted earlier that federal employees, in their perception of good personal relationships as a positive feature, are more apt than the non-federal to emphasize the passive aspect of the relationships. Interestingly, this relative emphasis appears to be equally strong at all four levels.

As also in the general employed public, a number of positive factors receive increasing notice from federal employees as educational level rises. These include opportunity for self-development, self-expression, and creativity; for responsibility, authority, and the power to make decisions; for self-determination and autonomy; and a sense of challenge in the job. For most of these factors the federal figures at all educational levels are somewhat higher than the nonfederal figures.

One figure for federal employees who have not completed high school, is worth special notice: 22 percent mention as a good aspect of their work that the job fits their capacities and training. This is double the frequency among federal employees at the other three levels, and also substantially higher than the figure for the nonfederal group that did not complete high school. Relatively speaking, a large percentage of the less-educated federal employees appear to believe that their work is especially suited to their capacities and training.

Concerning the occupational complaints of federal employees by educational level, it is notable, because of the manner in which the finding supplements other findings, that at no level is there more than 2 percent mention of the absence of job security and protective fringe benefits. Perhaps equally important, the percentage distribution of complaints about poor financial reward does not differ a great deal by educational levels: at each level one fifth to one fourth of the respondents mention the factor. In the general employed public references to it decline from 36 percent at the lowest level to 26 percent at the highest.

It is worthwhile to compare the federal and nonfederal groups by educational level in their comments about bad physical environment and general working conditions. In the nonfederal group the complaints are especially common at the two lower levels, and rather low at the upper two. Among federal employees mention of the factor is about equally common at all four levels; in general for the two upper educational levels, the figures are slightly higher than those for the same levels in the general employed public, but for the two lower levels they are markedly less than for the counterpart nonfederal groups. Thus it appears that federal employees in general are less disgruntled about bad physical environment and general working conditions, but what dissatisfaction does exist is about as frequent among the highly educated as among the less educated.

Outstanding is the 19 percent of federal college graduates who mention lack of sufficient equipment, facilities, and wherewithal to do the job. This is substantially higher than the percentages for federal personnel at the other three levels, and five times as high as the figure for college graduates (4 percent) in the general employed public.

The factor of lack of self-advancement and progress also presents an interesting comparative picture. At all four educational levels, there are substantially more federal than nonfederal employees making this complaint. The nonfederal percentages also decline slightly with increasing educational level, but the federal figures rise from 11 percent at the lowest level to 18 percent at the highest. Federal comments about the lack of self-determination and autonomy also rise sharply with educational level —from 4 percent at the lowest to 17 percent at the highest. A similar pattern of positive relation with education is shown by the federal complaints on lack of responsibility, authority, and the power to make decisions, although at all four levels the figures are low.

Finally, it is significant that the federal and nonfederal percentage distributions are at variance on two other factors. The federal statements about personal limitations or lack of choice decline as educational attainments rise; in the general public the percentages differ little by education. And while federal employees differ only slightly by educational level in saying they rated their jobs no higher because they believe nothing is ever perfect, among the nonfederal employees there is a strong positive association between education and this response.

Federal Executives, Natural and Social Scientists, and Engineers

These special groups of federal employees are distinguished by a number of over-all differences from similar groups in business and in colleges. They seem to be about as likely as their counterparts in business to mention financial reward as a positive feature, and much more likely than comparable college teacher groups. In general, they mention security more often as a positive feature than do their counterparts in either business or colleges, but their absolute percentages are not high—8 to 11 percent. They are also somewhat more likely than either of the other groups to mention general physical environment and working conditions as being a good feature. The natural and social scientists and, especially the engineers mention good supervision with higher frequency. All four groups—but especially natural scientists and engineers—strongly emphasize passive over active relationships. For federal natural scientists and engineers, the active/passive ratio is about 1 to 4; for those in business, about 1 to 1; for those in colleges, about 2½ to 1.

Concerning negative features of their occupations, the four special federal groups are less likely than the college teacher populations to complain about financial reward; in comparison to their business counterparts, however, there is no consistent pattern. Federal natural scientists mention poor pay more frequently than business natural scientists do; social scientists in business complain more frequently about it than do federal social scientists; and for the two sets of executives and engineers the figures do not differ significantly.

When we examine the positive and negative features federal and business executives see in their employment, the parallel in most respects is very close. Federal executives, however, are considerably more likely to mention responsibility and authority, security, and especially, the opportunity for challenging work and for worthwhile, constructive work. Challenge, for example, is cited by 20 percent of the federal executives as a positive feature, and by 13 percent of the businessmen; on the worthwhile, constructive nature of the work, the federal figure is 20 percent, the nonfederal 9 percent. Concerning occupational complaints, there is one further, outstanding difference between the two groups: lack of self-determination and autonomy is cited by 26 percent of the federal executives and by only 11 percent of the business executives.

Comparing federal natural scientists with their counterparts in business and in colleges, we find few differences in the over-all patterns for positive features seen in their jobs. One exception is the low mention by the federal group (8 percent) of their work as being worthwhile, useful, and constructive—compared to 12 percent for the natural scientists in business and 23 percent for those in colleges. On the negative side, about a fourth of the federal natural scientists refer to lack of equipment and facilities to do the job, a substantially higher figure than that for natural scientists in business (14 percent) and in colleges (17 percent). The federal scientists are also more likely (22 percent) than their business counterparts (14 percent) to complain about poor financial reward, but not as likely as the college natural scientists (36 percent).

Social scientists in the government, in comparison to their counterparts in business and in colleges, are especially prone to emphasize good personal relationships on their jobs, opportunity for self-development, self-expression, and creativity, and opportunity to do worthwhile and constructive work. Negatively, however, in comparison to the other two groups, they make more complaints about bad supervision, bad personal relationships, and the lack of opportunity for self-advancement.

Federal engineers, in comparison to the other special federal groups— and especially in comparison to both business and college engineers— display more concern with the nature of supervision, positively and negatively. Almost one fourth of them cite good supervision as a positive feature of their work, compared to 9 and 2 percent of business and college engineers. On the other hand, 15 percent of them mention bad supervision as a negative feature, compared to 3 and 8 percent in the business and college groups. It should be noted, however, that the engineers' 15 percent is paralleled by the 12 to 20 percent of the federal executives and natural and social scientists who make the same complaint.

8

Federal and Nonfederal Employment: "Better" and "Worse" Features

THE TEN-POINT SELF-ANCHORING SCALE was further employed to elicit a general comparison of federal and nonfederal employment, which would reflect the image of the government as an employer. Respondents in the nonfederal populations were asked: "Suppose your work or occupation stayed the same but you worked for the federal government—that is, the United States government—how much better or worse would that be? Show me on the ladder please. The place you pointed to before is marked in red." They were then asked two free-response questions: "What things would be likely to be better?" and "What things would be likely to be worse?"

In considering the responses, special attention should be paid to the phrase "suppose your work or occupation stayed the same." In the developmental research we had found that unless such a phrase was included people were apt to assume that their occupations would be different if they became federal employees. Careful analysis of pre-test interviewing indicated that the phrasing finally used was successful in focusing respondents' attention on the relative evaluation of the federal government as an employer, and not on the idea of changing occupations.

Federal employees were asked a similar question: "Suppose your work or occupation stayed the same but you no longer worked for the U.S. government—that is, suppose you continued in your present occupation, but went to work outside the federal government—how much better or worse would that be? Show me on the ladder, please." The free-response questions were then posed. Since the phrase "outside the federal government" is nonspecific, respondents were free to consider any type of nonfederal employment.[1]

The results of the two questions are presented in Tables 8-1a through 8-1e ("Better") and 8-2a through 8-2e ("Worse"), and the two sets of findings are discussed according to the nonfederal and federal populations. The chapter concludes with a section in which direct comparisons are made between the two populations regarding both of the factors.

In one particular respect the reader is urged to exercise caution in interpreting results: one should not conclude that the figures reveal the *over-all* positive attraction of federal employment to nonfederal respondents or of nonfederal employment to federal respondents. Such an evaluation can be approximated only by including also the relative appeal to the various groups of the values they mention. For example, the finding that a high percentage of the nonfederal population sees security as being better in federal employment does not necessarily indicate that federal employment is highly attractive. The relatively low degree of concern with security as an occupational value shown by the nonfederal populations must also be taken into account, especially at the upper educational and occupational levels.

Discussion of Nonfederal and Federal Population Data

Nonfederal Groups

"BETTER" FEATURES OF FEDERAL EMPLOYMENT. When asked what things might be better about federal employment, a good many people in the nonfederal groups simply reply that nothing would—20 percent of the general employed public, for instance, and 39, 45, and 44 percent of business executives, social scientists, and engineers. At the higher educational levels the reply is more common than at the lower. Nevertheless, many respondents do see certain values that would be better in a federal job.

---

[1] Ratings of federal and of large business employment on the basis of selected occupational values are presented and compared in Chapter 9.

(Text continued on page 240)

Tables 8-1a Through 8-1e

This series of tables shows what people who are not federal employees say would be "better" about federal employment, and what federal employees say would be "better" about nonfederal employment, assuming that the nature of their work stayed the same. The responses should not be interpreted as revealing the relative appeal of federal and nonfederal employment. For example, many nonfederal respondents see security as better in federal employment, but one should not conclude that federal employment is therefore attractice to them, without taking into account the low degree of concern with security as an occupational value that is evidenced in replies to other questions.

Table 8-1a

Highlights: Interest, enjoyment, satisfaction, pleasure in being able to do work one is interested in, wants to do, likes to do.

. . . . Very few people in the nonfederal populations see federal employment as intrinsically more interesting than what they are doing now. Worth noting, however, are the 16% and 15% for college seniors and graduate students, and the 10% for college natural scientists.

. . . . By the same token very few federal employees see work outside the government as intrinsically more interesting or satisfying.

Highlights: High or good financial reward.

. . . . About one fourth of the general employed public feels that pay would be better in the government. Almost twice as many women as men say so, and there is a very strong negative relationship with educational level.

. . . . Among students mention of better financial reward also shows a strong negative relationship with present educational level.

. . . . About one fourth to one third of the people in the education groups say that federal financial reward would be better.

. . . . The business groups scarcely mention financial reward.

. . . . General federal employees looking at nonfederal employment mention better pay much more often than does the general employed public looking at federal employment, and their pattern of percentages by sex and education is almost a mirror image of the pattern in the general employed public. Federally employed men mention the factor almost twice as often as do the women; the reverse is true in the general employed public. Also, relationship with the level of education is strongly positive, in contrast to the negative relationship in the general employed public.

. . . . A substantial majority of federal executives, natural and social scientists, and engineers cite financial reward as better outside government.

220

Table 8-1a

The image of the federal government as an employer: the positive attributes people not federal employees see in federal employment, and federal employees see in nonfederal employment. Percentage distrubution[a] of the responses in each group to the question, "Suppose your work stayed the same, but you worked for the federal government, ('outside the federal government' asked of federal employees). What things would be likely to be better?"

	Number answering	Better in federal employment:	
		Interest, enjoyment, satisfaction, pleasure through being able to do work one is interested in, wants to do, likes to do	High or good financial reward (e.g., make good money, high pay, etc.)
Nonfederal Populations			
General employed public	1077	1%	26%
By sex			
Men	822	1	22
Women	255	0	39
By educational level			
High school not completed	307	1	38
High school completed	490	1	24
Some college	117	1	15
College graduate	134	1	16
Students			
High school students	347	8	32
College seniors	394	16	20
Graduate students	376	15	17
Groups in education			
High school teachers	277	1	34
Vocational counselors	79	1	34
College teachers	458	6	32
Natural scientists	121	10	25
Social scientists	104	6	30
Engineers	83	6	21
Groups in business			
Executives	279	2	3
Natural scientists	85	6	6
Social scientists	71	3	1
Engineers	87	0	0
		Better in nonfederal employment:	
Federal Employee Populations			
General federal employees	906	2	40
By sex			
Men	632	3	45
Women	274	2	24
By educational level			
High school not completed	184	1	35
High school completed	340	3	34
Some college	171	3	44
College graduate	159	5	55
Executives	264	2	58
Natural scientists	89	9	75
Social scientists	87	8	62
Engineers	96	6	66

[a] Percentage base = number of respondents answering in each group. Percentages do not add to 100 in each group due to multiple replies.

221

Table 8-1b

<u>Highlights</u>: Security, stability, protection, fringe, (retirement, illness, income protection) benefits.

. . . . Among the nonfederal populations, the percentages who mention security as better in federal employment are remarkably consistent from group to group, ranging roughly from 35% to 45%. Exceptions are the groups in education, where the percentages drop to a level of roughly 15% to 20%.

. . . . There is a slight tendency in the general employed public and among students for frequency of mention to be negatively related to level of education.

. . . . Of the five components of security shown in the table, the general work force cites job security most often (18%) with retirement security being a close second.

. . . . References to job security show a moderately negative association with educational attainment in the general public and among students.

. . . . Very few federal employees in any group say that security would be better outside federal employment.

Table 8-1b

The image of the federal government as an employer: the <u>positive attributes</u> people not federal employees see in federal employment, and federal employees see in nonfederal employment (cont'd.)

| | Better in federal employment: | | | | | |
| | More security, stability, protection, fringe benefits | | | | | |
	Not further speci- fied	Job secur- ity	Finan- cial secur- ity	Retire ment security (e.g., pension)	Other protec- tive benefits (e.g., sick leave, insur- ance, etc.)	Total
Nonfederal Populations						
General employed public	6%	18%	6%	15%	11%	42%
By sex						
Men	7	18	7	16	11	44
Women	2	17	4	12	12	36
By educational level						
High school not completed	5	24	8	13	9	46
High school completed	6	16	6	16	14	43
Some college	6	15	4	19	14	41
College graduate	8	12	4	10	5	34
Students						
High school students	10	27	6	7	8	45
College seniors	19	15	6	9	12	43
Graduate students	14	16	3	10	11	38
Groups in education						
High school teachers	7	5	1	5	7	21
Vocational counselors	8	4	1	3	10	18
College teachers	5	5	4	7	5	19
Natural scientists	6	5	4	7	3	18
Social scientists	7	4	0	4	4	14
Engineers	4	10	1	5	4	16
Groups in business						
Executives	12	10	3	13	8	35
Natural scientists	14	15	5	8	9	37
Social scientists	14	6	4	9	9	32
Engineers	14	7	5	13	5	32
	Better in nonfederal employment:					
Federal Employee Populations						
General federal employees	0	1	0	1	3	5
By sex						
Men	0	1	0	1	3	5
Women	0	1	0	1	3	4
By educational level						
High school not completed	0	0	0	1	2	3
High school completed	0	1	0	1	2	4
Some college	1	3	0	1	6	9
College graduate	0	1	2	1	5	8
Executives	1	0	0	0	5	6
Natural scientists	0	1	0	0	8	9
Social scientists	0	0	0	3	3	5
Engineers	0	3	0	2	5	7

223

Table 8-1c

<u>Highlights</u>: Good physical environment and working conditions.

. . . . 16% of the general employed public cite physical environment and working conditions as better in federal employment. Mention is equally common among men and women, but shows a sharp negative correlation with educational level--such comments being confined almost entirely to the two lower educational levels.

. . . . The figures for students are low, but the indication of negative relationship with educational level is worth noting.

. . . . References to physical environment and working conditions are lower among general federal employees looking outside than in the general employed public looking at federal employment. However, among general federal employees the distribution by educational level is extremely flat.

. . . . Frequency of mention among federal executives, natural and social scientists, and engineers is similar to that among general federal employees and higher than the figures for comparable groups in colleges and in business.

<u>Highlights</u>: Having the equipment, facilities, wherewithal to do the job.

. . . . Figures for the general employed public looking at federal employment and for federal employees looking at nonfederal employment are very low and at the same level.

. . . . That 12% of graduate students mention federal equipment and facilities is of interest.

. . . . Groups in education tend to have higher frequencies than other nonfederal populations.

. . . . 25% of college natural scientists and 17% of business natural scientists mention equipment and facilities as better in the government.

. . . . Federal executives, natural and social scientists, and engineers mention this factor from two to three times more often than other federal populations. However, the figures range from only 10% to 19%.

224

Table 8-1c

The image of the federal government as an employer: the <u>positive</u>
<u>attributes</u> people not federal employees see in federal employment,
and federal employees see in non-federal employment (cont'd.)

	Better in federal employment:	
	Good physical environment and working conditions (e.g., clean, pleasant, not dangerous)	Having the equipment, facilities, wherewithal to do the job
<u>Nonfederal Populations</u>		
General employed public	16%	5%
By sex		
Men	16	5
Women	15	5
By educational level		
High school not completed	22	4
High school completed	18	5
Some college	6	4
College graduate	5	6
Students		
High school students	11	7
College seniors	8	8
Graduate students	4	12
Groups in education		
High school teachers	4	22
Vocational counselors	3	18
College teachers	2	15
Natural scientists	1	25
Social scientists	1	10
Engineers	2	10
Groups in business		
Executives	8	4
Natural scientists	2	17
Social scientists	3	4
Engineers	3	7
	Better in nonfederal employment:	
<u>Federal Employee Populations</u>		
General federal employees	11	5
By sex		
Men	10	6
Women	15	3
By educational level		
High school not completed	12	5
High school completed	12	6
Some college	10	6
College graduate	11	5
Executives	10	17
Natural scientists	11	19
Social scientists	16	14
Engineers	12	10

Table 8-1d

Highlights: Self-advancement and progress.

. . . . Scarcely any of the respondents in the nonfederal populations mention self-advancement and progress as being better in federal employment. Exceptions are the 18% of high school students and 15% of college seniors.

. . . . A significant percentage of all federal employee populations say that self-advancement and progress would be better outside federal employment. The figures for those who have not completed high school is somewhat lower than for other federal groups.

Highlights: Self-development.

. . . . This category was tabled principally to show the 12% and 11% figures for high school students and college seniors.

Highlights: Self-determination.

. . . . Among the nonfederal populations there is scarcely any mention of self-determination as relatively better in federal employment.

. . . . A small percentage of general federal employees comment that self-determination would be relatively better in nonfederal employment. The figures rise to 13% for college graduates.

. . . . Significant proportions of federal executives, social and natural scientists, and engineers cite self-determination as being relatively better in nonfederal employment; about one fourth of the executives and social scientists say this.

Highlights: Less bureaucracy.

. . . . In none of the nonfederal populations do respondents perceive bureaucracy as less in federal employment than in their own situation.

. . . . A small but significant percentage of general federal employees mention a feeling that bureaucracy would be less outside government, and frequency of mention shows a positive correlation with educational level, rising to 11% for the college groups.

. . . . Significant percentages of the four special federal groups, especially the engineers, executives, and social scientists feel that bureaucracy would be less outside government.

Table 8-1d

The image of the federal government as an employer: the positive attributes people not federal employees see in federal employment, and federal employees see in non-federal employment (cont'd.)

		Better in federal employment:		
	Self advancement and progress (e.g., be promoted; get ahead)	Self-development (e.g., learn; develop; grow personally, professionally)	Self-determination (e.g., be my own master, no heavy supervision; freedom of thought; action)	Less bureaucracy (e.g., red tape, unwieldiness, waste motion)
Nonfederal Populations				
General employed public	5%	1%	2%	0%
By sex				
Men	5	1	1	0
Women	4	2	3	0
By ecucational level				
High school not completed	5	2	2	0
High school completed	6	1	1	0
Some college	3	0	3	0
College graduate	5	1	2	0
Students				
High school students	18	12	1	0
College seniors	15	11	4	0
Graduate students	8	5	4	0
Groups in education				
High school teachers	3	4	1	0
Vocational counselors	1	4	0	0
College teachers	2	3	1	0
Natural scientists	2	3	1	0
Social scientists	0	6	3	0
Engineers	2	5	6	0
Groups in business				
Executives	4	1	0	0
Natural scientists	2	2	6	0
Social scientists	1	1	0	0
Engineers	1	0	1	0
		Better in nonfederal employment:		
Federal Employee Populations				
General federal employees	12	1	6	7
By sex				
Men	13	1	6	6
Women	10	1	4	8
By educational level				
High school not completed	6	1	5	3
High school completed	16	1	5	5
Some college	14	1	4	11
College graduate	10	1	13	11
Executives	11	3	24	18
Natural scientists	9	5	14	10
Social scientists	13	1	25	22
Engineers	17	1	10	17

227

Table 8-1e

<u>Highlights</u>: Do work that is worthwhile, useful, constructive.

. . . . This category was tabled to show the 9% and 10% figures for high school students and college seniors, in contrast to the very low figures for other populations, federal and nonfederal.

<u>Highlights</u>: Leisure, vacation, leave, recreation, time off.

. . . . A small but significant percentage of the general employed public, both men and women and at all educational levels, see leisure and vacation as being better in federal employment.

. . . . Significant percentages in the business groups also mention leisure and time off in federal employment.

. . . . Scarcely any federal employees feel that leisure and time off would be better outside government.

<u>Highlights</u>: Nothing would be better.

. . . . One fifth of the general employed public maintains that nothing would be better about federal employment; more men than women say this, and the frequency of the response shows a positive relationship with educational level.

. . . . Somewhat more of the general federal employees (27%) say that nothing would be better about nonfederal employment, and women say this slightly more often than men. In sharp contrast to the situation in the general employed public, the frequency shows a very strong negative relationship with educational level: the figures fall from 34% at the lowest level to 11% for college graduates.

. . . . Among the student groups the positive relationship of mention frequency with present educational level and the comparatively low figures are worth noting.

. . . . For business executives, social scientists, and engineers and for college engineers the proportions are especially high, ranging from one third to almost one half.

. . . . The 21% figure for natural scientists in business is low compared to the other business groups.

. . . . The very low percentage of federal executives, natural and social scientists, and engineers who say that nothing would be better outside federal employment contrasts sharply with the high percentage of the business and college counterpart groups who claim that nothing would be better in federal employment.

Table 8-1e

The image of the federal government as an employer: the <u>positive attributes</u> people not federal employees see in federal employment, and federal employees see in non-federal employment (cont'd.)

	Better in federal employment:		
	Do work that is worthwhile, useful, constructive	Leisure, vacation, leave, recreation, time off	Nothing would be better
Nonfederal Populations			
General employed public	1%	10%	20%
By sex			
Men	1	10	22
Women	3	10	13
By educational level			
High school not completed	1	8	15
High school completed	2	12	19
Some college	1	9	29
College graduate	2	7	28
Students			
High school students	9	2	6
College seniors	10	9	10
Graduate students	7	9	17
Groups in education			
High school teachers	3	3	18
Vocational counselors	1	8	17
College teachers	3	1	23
Natural scientists	1	3	22
Social scientists	2	1	27
Engineers	1	4	36
Groups in business			
Executives	3	13	39
Natural scientists	6	15	21
Social scientists	6	14	45
Engineers	9	8	44
	Better in nonfederal employment:		
Federal Employee Populations			
General federal employees	0	2	27
By sex			
Men	0	1	26
Women	0	3	30
By educational level			
High school not completed	0	1	34
High school completed	0	1	31
Some college	0	2	21
College graduate	1	2	11
Executives	1	3	8
Natural scientists	2	1	3
Social scientists	2	3	7
Engineers	0	2	4

This series of tables shows what people who are not federal employees say would be "worse" about federal employment, and what federal employees say would be "worse" about nonfederal employment.

Table 8-2a

Highlights: Poor or inadequate financial reward.

. . . . In the general employed public mention of financial reward as being worse in the government is fairly low. But men cite it much more often than women, and the figures show a positive relationship with educational level.

. . . . About one fifth of high school students and about one fourth of college seniors and graduate students state that financial reward would be worse in federal employment.

. . . . Groups in education scarcely mention the factor, with the exception of the engineers, whose figure is low but significant.

. . . . In general, the business groups mention poor or inadequate financial reward with the highest frequencies of all: roughly one fourth to one third say that government pay would be worse.

. . . . The percentage of general federal employees who refer to financial reward as worse outside of government is slightly higher than that of the employed public who feel that it would be worse in the government. The higher percentage is accounted for mainly by an extremely high figure for women (31%) and by the fairly high figures (22% and 20%) for the two lower educational levels.

. . . . Very few federal executives, natural and social scientists, or engineers say that financial reward would be worse outside the government.

Highlights: Bad physical environment and working conditions.

. . . . In the nonfederal populations very few people say that physical environment and working conditions would be worse in federal employment.

. . . . Federal employees say fairly often that such conditions would be worse outside government. Mention of the factor is especially high among men and at the high school not completed level.

Table 8-2a

The image of the federal government as an employer: the <u>negative attributes</u>
people not federal employees see in federal employment, and federal employees
see in nonfederal employment. Percentage distribution[a] of the responses in
each group to the question, "Suppose your work stayed the same, but you worked
for the federal government ('outside the federal government' asked of federal
employees). What things would be likely to be worse?"

| | Number answer-ing | Worse in federal employment: | |
		Poor or inadequate financial reward	Bad physical environment and working conditions (e.g., dirty, unpleasant, dangerous)
Nonfederal Populations			
General employed public	1100	13%	5%
By sex			
Men	844	15	4
Women	256	6	6
By educational level			
High school not completed	309	8	5
High school completed	497	13	4
Some college	128	19	5
College graduate	136	18	4
Students			
High school students	347	19	5
College seniors	397	26	5
Graduate students	380	25	6
Groups in education			
High school teachers	279	5	4
Vocational counselors	78	6	6
College teachers	470	5	0
Natural scientists	121	6	1
Social scientists	104	5	1
Engineers	87	13	0
Groups in business			
Executives	286	30	1
Natural scientists	85	33	0
Social scientists	73	32	1
Engineers	88	23	3
		Worse in nonfederal employment:	
Federal Employee Populations			
General federal employees	932	19	19
By sex			
Men	648	14	21
Women	284	31	14
By educational level			
High school not completed	190	22	27
High school completed	347	20	17
Some college	179	15	12
College graduate	161	11	18
Executives	265	5	12
Natural scientists	90	8	11
Social scientists	86	8	7
Engineers	96	5	15

a Percentage base = number of respondents answering in each group.
Percentages do not add to 100 in each group due to multiple replies.

Table 8-2b

Highlights: Security, stability, protection, fringe benefits.

. . . . The figures in this table present a dramatic contrast. Practically no one outside the government claims that security would be worse in federal employment. On the other hand, a substantial majority of federal employees say that security would be worse in nonfederal employment.

. . . . The figures for federal college graduates, executives, and natural and social scientists are high, but those for the other federal groups who state that security would be less outside the government are even higher.

. . . . The component of the whole security response cited most often by general federal employees is "other protective benefits" (37%) with "job security" second in frequency (29%). Men cite the latter more than women; women cite the former more than men. Among the special federal groups, all but the engineers mention "job security" most often.

Table 8-2b

The image of the federal government as an employer: the <u>negative attributes</u> people not federal employees see in federal employment, and federal employees see in nonfederal employment (cont'd.)

| | <u>Worse in federal employment:</u> | | | | | |
| | Less security, stability, protection, fringe benefits | | | | | |
	Not further speci-fied	Job secur-ity	Finan-cial secur-ity	Retire-ment se-curity (e.g., pension)	Other protec-tive benefits (e.g., sick leave, insur-ance, etc.)	Total
<u>Nonfederal Populations</u>						
General employed public						3%
By sex						
Men						3
Women						2
By educational level						
High school not completed						1
High school completed						4
Some college						5
College graduate						2
Students						
High school students						5
College seniors						4
Graduate students						2
Groups in education						
High school teachers						2
Vocational counselors						5
College teachers						3
Natural scientists						4
Social scientists						4
Engineers						2
Groups in business						
Executives						3
Natural scientists						5
Social scientists						4
Engineers						3
	<u>Worse in nonfederal employment:</u>					
<u>Federal Employee Populations</u>						
General federal employees	9	29	3	17	37	66
By sex						
Men	9	32	3	17	35	66
Women	8	19	1	16	43	63
By educational level						
High school not completed	7	30	4	15	37	63
High school completed	10	26	2	19	43	71
Some college	10	33	2	16	36	69
College graduate	9	31	2	17	21	52
Executives	8	35	3	23	22	57
Natural scientists	3	29	6	9	18	46
Social scientists	11	29	2	11	8	42
Engineers	8	31	2	18	30	62

Table 8-2c

<u>Highlights</u>: Lack of emphasis on merit in promotion.

. . . . Moderate percentages of college seniors, graduate students, groups in business, and college engineers say that emphasis on merit in promotion would be worse in federal employment.

. . . . Scarcely any federal employees cite this factor as being worse outside of federal employment.

<u>Highlights</u>: Lack of incentive, loss of drive, initiative, ambition.

. . . . No one in any federal group mentions this factor as something which would be worse in nonfederal employment, but significant percentages in a number of nonfederal groups do mention it about federal employment. People in the business groups, with moderate to fairly high percentages, are particularly apt to cite such a feature.

<u>Highlights</u>: Lack of self-advancement and progress.

. . . . Although the over-all percentage in the general employed public is very low, there is a suggestion of a positive relationship with level of education.

. . . . The 13% to 17% figures for students contrast sharply with the almost complete lack of mention by groups in education.

. . . . The 10% to 18% figures for groups in business looking at the federal government diverge noticeably from the 2% to 4% figures for comparable groups in the federal government looking at outside employment.

234

Table 8-2c

The image of the federal government as an employer: the negative attributes
people not federal employees see in federal employment, and federal employees
see in nonfederal employment (cont'd.)

| | Worse in federal employment: | | |
	Lack of emphasis on merit in promotion (e.g., get ahead by seniority, pull; not merit, ability)	Lack of incentive; loss of drive, initiative, ambition	Lack of self-advancement and progress (e.g., no promotions; no chance to get ahead)
Nonfederal Populations			
General employed public	3%	5%	3%
By sex			
Men	4	6	4
Women	2	4	2
By educational level			
High school not completed	1	1	0
High school completed	2	3	3
Some college	6	7	5
College graduate	8	9	9
Students			
High school students	3	0	14
College seniors	13	6	17
Graduate students	13	11	13
Groups in education			
High school teachers	2	1	2
Vocational counselors	1	3	4
College teachers	5	4	1
Natural scientists	8	5	2
Social scientists	8	3	2
Engineers	12	12	1
Groups in business			
Executives	13	21	10
Natural scientists	14	22	14
Social scientists	11	18	18
Engineers	9	15	15
	Worse in nonfederal employment:		
Federal Employee Populations			
General federal employees	2	0	4
By sex			
Men	2	0	4
Women	2	0	4
By educational level			
High school not completed	1	0	4
High school completed	2	0	3
Some college	2	1	8
College graduate	1	0	4
Executives	4	0	2
Natural scientists	2	0	3
Social scientists	8	0	4
Engineers	4	0	3

235

Table 8-2d

Highlights: Lack of self-determination.

. . . . High percentages of most of the nonfederal populations feel that self-determination would be worse in federal employment. This is particularly true for the more highly educated groups—and especially college teachers as a whole (57%) and social scientists in business (53%).

. . . . General federal employees scarcely mention the feeling that nonfederal employment would be worse in terms of self-determination. The figure is only slightly higher for federal executives.

. . . . 30% of federal natural scientists state that nonfederal employment would offer less self-determination. Approximately the same percentage of natural scientists in business make the statement about federal employment. However, both figures are much lower than the 57% of the natural scientists in college who say that self-determination would be less in federal employment.

. . . . The 17% and 18% figures for federal social scientists and engineers are significant, but much lower than the figures for their counterparts in business and especially in colleges.

Highlights: Bureaucracy.

. . . . References to bureaucracy in its many ramifications as being worse in federal employment are only moderately high over all in the general employed public, but range from high to extremely high in the more highly educated groups, with figures of roughly 25% to 50%.

. . . . The 29% figure for high school teachers and especially the 40% figure for vocational counselors provide a significant contrast with the 3% figure for high school students.

Highlights: Too much politics.

. . . . This category was tabled to show its low mention in all groups except those in business where mention is only moderate.

Table 8-2d

The image of the federal government as an employer: the negative attributes people not federal employees see in federal employment, and federal employees see in nonfederal employment (cont'd.)

	Worse in federal employment:		
	Lack of self-determination (e.g., would not be my own master; rigid supervision; no freedom of thought, action)	Bureaucracy (e.g., red tape, involvement in waste motion, too large, unwieldy)	Too much politics (e.g., subject to political control, pressures, etc.)
Nonfederal Populations			
General employed public	22%	16%	4%
By sex			
Men	22	17	4
Women	18	9	3
By educational level			
High school not completed	19	10	2
High school completed	20	12	3
Some college	28	24	6
College graduate	29	32	6
Students			
High school students	18	8	2
College seniors	28	22	6
Graduate students	33	29	6
Groups in education			
High school teachers	33	29	5
Vocational counselors	35	40	9
College teachers	57	32	6
Natural scientists	57	28	4
Social scientists	54	29	9
Engineers	49	31	6
Groups in business			
Executives	33	35	11
Natural scientists	32	38	8
Social scientists	53	41	14
Engineers	31	50	11
	Worse in nonfederal employment:		
Federal Employee Populations			
General federal employees	4	1	1
By sex			
Men	4	1	1
Women	4	0	0
By educational level			
High school not completed	2	1	2
High school completed	4	0	0
Some college	2	1	1
College graduate	6	1	2
Executives	9	3	3
Natural scientists	30	1	3
Social scientists	17	4	2
Engineers	18	0	3

Table 8-2e

Highlights: Not as much leisure, vacation, leave, recreation, time off.

. . . . Practically no one outside the government feels that provisions for leisure and vacation would be worse in federal employment in comparison to their present situations.

. . . . In contrast more than one fourth of the general federal employees mention that leisure and leave would be less favorable outside federal employment. Women say this especially often. College graduates mention it somewhat less than other general federal employees.

Highlights: Too much pressure or tension.

. . . . Virtually no one outside the government mentions seeing too much pressure or tension in federal employment as compared to their own occupations.

. . . . Among general federal employees there is very little mention of seeing too much pressure or tension in nonfederal employment, although the 9% figure for the college graduate level is worth noting.

. . . . Over one fourth of the federal natural scientists and almost one fifth of the federal engineers cite pressure or tension as being worse in nonfederal employment, as also do 10% of federal executives and 11% of federal social scientists.

Highlights: Nothing would be worse.

. . . . Over one fourth of the general employed public respondents claim nothing would be worse about federal employment, suggesting that they feel everything about it would be as good or better than their present situation. About one third of the women say this, and about one fourth of the men.

. . . . Frequency of mention in the general employed public shows a very strong negative relationship with educational level, declining from 41% at the high school not completed level to 7% at the college graduate level. Similarly, there is a sharp break among students; a fifth of those in high school mention it, whereas scarcely any college seniors and graduate students do so.

. . . . In very sharp contrast to the above are the consistently low figures for all federal employee populations. Very few people in any of the government groups feel that nothing would be worse outside federal employment. When interpreting these figures, the very high percentages in all federal groups who say that there would be less security in nonfederal employment should be kept in mind.

238

Table 8-2e

The image of the federal government as an employer: the <u>negative attributes</u> people not federal employees see in federal employment, and federal employees see in nonfederal employment (cont'd.)

	Worse in federal employment:		
	Not as much leisure, vacation, leave, recreation, time off	Too much pressure or tension	Nothing would be worse
Nonfederal Populations			
General employed public	1%	1%	26%
By sex			
Men	1	1	24
Women	0	2	33
By educational level			
High school not completed	0	1	41
High school completed	2	1	26
Some college	0	2	14
College graduate	0	2	7
Students			
High school students	1	1	20
College seniors	3	2	4
Graduate students	1	1	8
Groups in education			
High school teachers	1	2	13
Vocational counselors	3	1	5
College teachers	4	1	5
Natural scientists	3	2	6
Social scientists	0	3	4
Engineers	0	0	10
Groups in business			
Executives	0	2	6
Natural scientists	2	2	4
Social scientists	0	1	3
Engineers	0	3	2
	Worse in nonfederal employment:		
Federal Employee Populations			
General federal employees	27	5	5
By sex			
Men	25	6	4
Women	33	3	6
By educational level			
High school not completed	24	4	5
High school completed	33	5	4
Some college	26	4	7
College graduate	17	9	3
Executives	13	10	5
Natural scientists	8	27	3
Social scientists	6	11	5
Engineers	19	18	5

Dominant are the replies centering on aspects of occupational security and on financial reward. Over 40 percent of the general employed public mention security, and nearly all of the nonfederal groups give it high mention, although the frequency for those with more education tends to be somewhat lower. Only among high school and college teachers is mention merely moderate—ranging from about 15 to 20 percent. The feeling that financial reward would be better in federal employment is held by about one fourth of the general employed public; frequency of mention is negatively related to educational level, moving from 38 percent for those not completing high school to 16 percent for college graduates. Substantial percentages of students—especially in high school—and of high school and college teachers cite financial reward, but almost no one in the business groups does.

Women appear to view the relative characteristics of federal employment slightly more favorably than men; only 13 percent of them say nothing would be better, compared to 22 percent of the men. Better financial reward is mentioned by 39 percent of the women and by only 22 percent of the men.

When we turn to other occupational values, not many are seen by the nonfederal groups as better in government employment. Such factors as the opportunity for self-development, self-expression, and creativity, for facing challenges, or for doing worthwhile constructive work receive very little notice. Special exceptions occur, however; 18 percent of the high school students and 15 percent of the college seniors volunteered that opportunities for self-advancement would be better in a federal job, and 12 and 11 percent, respectively, cited self-development. And among high school and college teachers and, to some extent, graduate students, 10 to as high as 25 percent cited the equipment, facilities, and wherewithal to do the job as likely to be better. The college natural scientists and the high school teachers are especially outstanding here: 25 percent of the former and 22 percent of the latter make this statement.

"WORSE" FEATURES OF FEDERAL EMPLOYMENT. Slightly over one fourth of the general employed public say that nothing would be worse about a federal job, implying that everything would be as good as or better than their present situation. However, it is instructive to look at the pattern of the replies by educational level. From 41 percent at the lowest level, the figures decline sharply: high school completed, 26 percent; some college, 14 percent; college graduates, 7 percent. Similarly, 20 percent of high school students say nothing would be worse, but only 4 percent of college seniors and 8 percent of graduate students say so. For high school and college teachers and for all four business groups the figures are also fairly low. Thus, the likelihood of seeing federal employment as equal to or better than one's present employment is strongly and negatively related to educational and occupational level.

Paralleling this is the finding that most of the occupational features seen as being "worse" in a federal job (Tables 8-2a through 8-2e) show higher frequencies of mention at the upper educational and occupational levels. The negative factors cited are lack of self-determination, in the sense of being under more rigid supervision and having less freedom of thought and action; bureaucracy, variously described as waste motion, large, complicated, unwieldy organizational procedures and more involvement in red tape; and poor financial reward.

Less self-determination is mentioned by 22 percent of the general employed public, with a range from 19 percent at the high school not completed level to 29 percent at the college graduate level. Among students mention ranges from 18 to 33 percent, from high school to graduate students. The factor is cited by 57 percent of the general college teachers, and by 57, 54, and 49 percent of the college natural and social scientists and engineers. About one third of the business respondents mention it, and the business social scientists are outstanding with 53 percent.

Bureaucracy as a "worse" feature is cited by 16 percent of the general public. Here again frequency is sharply related to education—rising from 10 percent at the lowest level to 32 percent for college graduates. For the student populations the figures are 8 (high school), 22 (college seniors), and 29 percent (graduate students). Roughly 30 percent of both high school and college teachers mention bureaucracy, but vocational counselors show a figure of 40 percent. In general, the highest mention occurs among the business groups, all the figures exceeding 35 percent and rising to the business engineers' 50 percent.

Poor financial reward is mentioned by 13 percent of the general public, and there is a rise from the lowest level's 8 percent to the college graduates' 18 percent. The student populations mention the factor markedly more often than do people at the comparable educational levels in the general employed public: 19 percent for high school students and 26 and 25 for college seniors and graduate students. The only higher figures are those for the business groups; approximately one third of these respondents mention the factor. The pattern is different, however, for high school and college teachers; very few of them—some 6 percent or less—feel that financial reward would be worse in federal employment.

In general, all of the business groups show an over-all pattern of much higher frequency of mention of factors that would be "worse" about federal employment. In addition to being high on the three factors discussed above (the only ones noted with substantial frequency by most other nonfederal populations), the business respondents cite a number of other negative factors in significant proportions. From 15 to over 20 percent mention the comparative lack of chance to use initiative. From 10 to almost 20 percent mention lack of self-advancement and progress; roughly 10 to 15 percent cite lack of emphasis on merit in promotion and speak of undesirable political controls and pressures. Somewhat smaller, but still significant, percentages of college seniors and graduate students also mention the same negative features. High school students, however, are less critical; of the additional negative features only lack of self-advancement and progress is mentioned by a significant number (14 percent).

Again we find that the response pattern of women is slightly more favorable toward federal employment: 33 percent of the women and 24 percent of the men say that nothing would be worse about a federal job. And fewer women cite financial reward as worse (6 percent) and bueaucratic red tape, waste motion, and unwieldy procedures (9 percent); the figures for men are 15 and 17 percent.

Federal Groups

"BETTER" FEATURES OF NONFEDERAL EMPLOYMENT. When asked what would be better about working outside the government, about one fourth of the general federal employees say nothing would be. The answer is, however, heavily concentrated in the lower educational groups; frequency declines from 34 percent at the lowest level to 31 at high school completed; 21, some college; 11, college graduates. Figures for federal executives, natural and social scientists, and engineers are even lower, ranging from the executives' 8 percent to the natural scientists' 3 percent. Thus it appears that the higher a federal employee's educational and/or occupational level, the more likely is he to see some features of nonfederal employment as better than his present situation.

Of the specific "better" features cited, financial reward is dominant: 40 percent of general federal employees say that pay would be better outside the government. The reply shows a positive relation with educational level, the frequency rising from 35 percent at the high school not completed level to 55 percent among college graduates. In the four special personnel groups the figures are even higher: better pay is mentioned by 58 percent of the executives, and by 62, 66, and 75 percent of the social scientists, engineers, and natural scientists.

Just how high the visibility of the comparative pay factor is to the general federal employee is underlined by the lower frequencies of the next most mentioned factors, which are only half as high, on the average, as the frequencies for financial reward. Roughly 10 to 15 percent of the general group says that self-advancement and progress, as well as general physical environment and working conditions. would be better outside government.

The high-level federal groups tend markedly to feel that nonfederal employment would offer opportunity for more self-determination and freedom of thought and action, and involve less red tape, unwieldiness, and waste motion. Specifically, 13 percent of the college graduates and 24, 14, 25, and 10 percent of executives, natural scientists, social scientists, and engineers mention self-determination. Less bureaucracy is mentioned by 11 percent of the college graduates, and by 18, 10, 22, and 17 percent of the executives, natural scientists, social scientists, and engineers. The executives and the social scientists appear to be particularly likely to see more self-determination in the private sphere and also—here joined by the engineers—less bureaucracy.

The difference between men and women concerning comparative financial reward is sharp. The probable higher pay of nonfederal jobs is mentioned by 45 percent of the men and by 24 percent of the women.

Occupational security is notable for its low frequency of mention as being better outside the government. Highest frequency of mention by any group is 9 percent (some college), and the figures range downward to 3 percent (high school not completed). We have noted that extremely high percentages of nonfederal employees see security as being better in federal employment; federal employees seem to share this view, or at least feel that security is no better outside the government.

"WORSE" FEATURES OF NONFEDERAL EMPLOYMENT. The emphasis on security as a better aspect of federal employment is underlined when federal employees are asked what would be "worse" about working outside the government. Two thirds of the general employees say that a nonfederal job would offer less security, stability, job protection, and protective fringe benefits; only at the college graduate level does the percentage fall lower—to 52 percent. For executives and engineers the figures are 57 and 62 percent, for the natural and social scientists, 46 and 42 percent.

No other negative category approaches these frequencies of mention. However, a number of other features are seen as being worse outside the government. Leading the list for general federal employees—27 percent— is leisure, vacation, and time off. Mention of the factor is more likely for women than men, and less likely for upper-level employees, especially the natural and social scientists, for whom the figures are 8 and 6 percent.

Significant percentages of general federal employees also feel that financial reward would be worse in nonfederal employment. This is far more characteristic of women (31 percent) than men (14 percent), and is negatively related to educational level—22 percent for high school not completed to 11 percent for college graduates. Mention by all four special groups is low—their figures are 8 percent or less.

About one fifth of general federal employees say that physical environment and general working conditions would be worse in nonfederal jobs. Men (21 percent) are more likely than women (14 percent) to mention this. By education, the concentration of the statement is at the high school not completed level—27 percent. For executives, natural and social scientists, and engineers the frequencies range downward from 15 to 7 percent. Thus it appears that a federal employee with lower education, and especially a man, is most apt to see general physical environment and working conditions as worse outside government.

The pattern of replies concerning lack of self-determination outside federal employment is especially interesting. Among the general employees its mention occurs with very low frequencies, ranging down from 6 percent. Even among executives, mention is only 9 percent. For the natural and social scientists and engineers, however, the figures are 30, 17, and 18 percent. The figure for the natural scientists is especially significant. We noted earlier that 14 percent of this group felt that self-determination would be better outside of government; now we find that twice that percentage says the opposite.

Another factor mentioned with significant frequency by upper-level federal employees is pressure or tension. Very few at the three lower educational levels feel that this factor would be worse in nonfederal employment, but 9 percent of the college graduates say that it would. Among the four special groups, greater pressure or tension outside government is cited by 10 percent of executives, 11 percent of social scientists, 18 percent of engineers, and 27 percent of natural scientists.

Some Federal-Nonfederal Comparisons

For a number of the occupational values discussed earlier, it is instructive to make direct comparisons between the federal and nonfederal populations. Of particular interest is financial reward. As we have seen, in the general employed public about one fourth of the respondents say that financial reward would probably be better in federal employment, and almost twice as many women (39 percent) as men (22 percent) make this reply. The higher the educational level, the fewer are the respondents who cite the factor; the percentages decline from 38 at the lowest level to 16 at the highest. Among general federal employees, we find a markedly higher percentage saying that financial reward would be better outside the government—40 percent vs. 26 percent in the general employed public looking at federal employment. The results by sex and educational level for general government employees are virtually the mirror image of the general employed public pattern: nearly twice as many federally employed men (45 percent) as women (24 percent) mention financial reward, and the educational level percentages climb from 35 at the lowest level to 55 for college graduates.

The pattern of the "What would be worse" figures in Table 8-2a, which is the reverse of the configuration found in the "What would be better" responses, confirms the preceding results. In the general employed public, for example, more than twice as many men as women state that financial reward would be worse in federal employment; whereas among general federal employees more than twice as many women as men say that it would be worse outside government. A similar relationship appears by educational level. In the general employed public, the higher the level the *more* likely is the respondent to say that pay would be worse in federal employment; among general federal employees, the higher the level the *less* likely is the respondent to say that pay would be worse outside government.

These results suggest several generalizations. Among both federal and nonfederal employees there appears to be a common core of feeling, differentiated by sex and by educational level, concerning the federal pay schedule. Relatively, it looks better to women than to men, and to those of lower education than to those of higher education. The picture for the populations other than the two general employed groups is primarily corroborative. Thus, the government pay schedule looks better to high school students than to college seniors and graduate students. And it looks definitely worse to executives, natural and social scientists, and engineers both in business and in government than to the two general employee populations. The groups in education, however, more nearly resemble the general employed public—especially its two lower educational levels—in their view of federal financial reward.

We find another common core of agreement between the federal and nonfederal populations on the high degree of security offered by federal employment. With the exception of the high school and college teachers, roughly one fourth to almost one half of the people in the nonfederal groups volunteer that security is better in federal employment; the response is a little more common on the lower educational levels than on the higher. Coupled with this is the finding (Table 8-2b) that scarcely anyone in the nonfederal populations says that security would be worse in government employment. Among the federal employee populations almost no one says that security would be better in nonfederal employment (Table 8-1b) and roughly two thirds (Table 8-2b) say that it would be worse outside the government.

Somewhat similar, but less extreme, results are shown for the categories of bureaucracy, self-determination, self-advancement and progress, leisure and vacation, and physical environment and working conditions. Substantial proportions of the nonfederal populations, especially men and employees at the upper educational levels, say that the degree of bureaucracy in federal employment would be greater, and no one says it would be less. Among federal employees, almost no respondents cite bureaucracy as worse outside the government, and moderate percentages of federal college graduates, executives, and the scientific and engineering populations feel that there would be less bureaucracy.

Concerning self-determination, one fifth to over one half of all nonfederal respondents speak of less self-determination in federal employment, and scarcely any say that it would be greater. Among general federal employees, we find relatively little mention of this factor as being either better or worse in nonfederal employment; however, 13 percent of the federal college graduates say that nonfederal employment would be better in this regard. For the federal executives, natural and social scientists, and engineers the picture is more complex; substantial proportions of them do mention self-determination, both positively and negatively. About one fourth of the executives and social scientists favor nonfederal employment for this factor. But among the engineers and natural scientists, self-determination is cited as worse in nonfederal employment by more (18 and 30 percent) than say it would be better (10 and 14 percent).

Mention of opportunity for self-advancement and progress as either better or worse is fairly low in both federal and nonfederal populations. However, there is a significant tendency for the nonfederal student and business groups to see less opportunity for advancement in a federal job. Further, very few of the nonfederal respondents, except high school students and college seniors (18 and 15 percent), feel that federal employment would be better in this regard. Paralleling this is the scarcity of mention by federal employees that chances for self-advancement would be less in nonfederal employment, whereas roughly 10 to 15 percent in all federal groups say that the chances would be greater.

On the factor of vacation and leisure, both nonfederal and federal populations favor federal employment. Almost no one outside government says federal employment would be worse in this regard, and modest percentages of some groups say it would be better. Very few federal employees indicate that leisure and vacation would be better in nonfederal employment, and approximately one fourth of them say that it would be worse.

Concerning good physical environment and general working conditions, the "What would be better" results are rather complicated. In the general employed public, 16 percent feel that the factor would be better in federal employment, but the reply is most common at the two lower educational levels and occurs infrequently at the two higher. Among federal employees, however, we have a very flat distribution: from 10 to 15 percent in *all* the groups say that physical environment and working conditions would be better outside government. But equal or higher percentages of all but one group (social scientists) state that the factor would be *worse* outside government, the reply being a little more common at the lower educational levels and especially among men (21 percent) compared to women (14 percent). On the other hand, scarcely any nonfederal respondents cite the factor as worse in federal employment.

Certain categories of responses appear only in the "What would be better" tables—8-1 series—because their frequency as responses to "What would be worse" was not sufficient to warrant tabling in the 8-2 series. Of these, the category of equipment, facilities, and wherewithal to do the job is especially worth noting (Table 8-1c). Only 5 to 6 percent of the general employed public and general federal employees offered this response. However, of the nonfederal graduate students, high school and college teachers, and college and business natural scientists, 10 to 25 percent volunteer that federal employment would have more to offer on this factor. We must also note that 10 to 17 percent of federal engineers, social and natural scientists, and executives say the same thing about employment *outside* government.

Another "What would be better" response concerns worthwhile, useful, and constructive work (Table 8-1e). Significantly, almost none of the federal populations say that opportunity for this kind of work would be better outside government, whereas in some of the nonfederal groups small but significant percentages feel that such opportunity would be better in federal employment; these groups include the students (7 to 10 percent) and the business natural and social scientists (6 percent) and engineers (9 percent).

There were also a number of responses whose frequencies merited tabling only in the "What would be worse" series. Lack of incentive and loss of drive, initiative, and ambition (Table 8-2c) is cited as a negative feature of federal employment by all the business groups (15 to 22 percent) and to a lesser extent by college engineers and graduate students, and by college graduates in the general employed public (12, 11, and 9 percent). In contrast, virtually no federal employee says this about nonfederal employment. A similar pattern is shown concerning lack of emphasis on merit in promotion. Among the business groups, college engineers, college seniors and graduate students, and college graduates in the general employed public, from 8 to 14 percent feel that the lack would be worse in government work. Very few federal employees make the comment about nonfederal employment. The too much pressure or tension category, however, shows an entirely different pattern (Table 8-2e). There is almost no mention by the nonfederal populations that a government job would be worse in this respect. Yet among the federal college graduates, executives, natural and social scientists, and engineers, 9 to 27 percent say pressure or tension would be worse outside government; the figures for the natural scientists and engineers—27 and 18 percent—are especially outstanding.

9

Evaluations of Federal and
Large Private Business Employment

THE IMAGE OF THE FEDERAL GOVERNMENT as an employer is reflected in some of the results we obtained from the scale-sort procedure in which respondents evaluated fifty-five statements by placing them on the ten-point agree-disagree scale. Among the statements were five pairs that concerned five different aspects of employment: opportunity for being really successful; chance of getting ahead; chance of winding up in a top-level job; security; and routine and monotony. One item for each pair asked for evaluation of its specific occupational attribute relative to working for a large private business, the other for evaluation relative to working for the federal government.

The paired ratings are shown in Tables 9-1a through 9-1e. Each table displays the results for one attribute: the mean ratings given by each group for federal employment and for large private business employment, then the difference (net) scores obtained by subtracting the business ratings from the government ratings.

Discussion of Specific Group Data

The results for the fourth and fifth pairs of items are much less complex than for the other three. Since they therefore require only brief discussion, we will consider them first.

(Text continued on page 260)

This series of tables shows the scale ratings that the various groups give to statements about working for the U.S. government compared to working for a large private business. As with all scale items, the variation from item to item in the number answering in each group was so small as to make it a waste of space to present the number answering each individual item. Instead, the average number answering is presented in the first column of this series of tables.

Table 9-1a

Highlights: "For a young man of ability, his best chance for being really successful lies in (working for the federal government) (working for a large private business corporation)." The concept "best chance for being really successful" is intentionally general, contains several components, and involves the respondent's personal feelings of what constitutes both "chance" and "real success."

. . . . In the general employed public working for the federal government is rated below large private business. This is true for both men and women, and at all educational levels.

. . . . In the general employed public there is a very strong negative relationship between ratings of federal employment and educational level; ratings of large private business drop slightly with increased educational level, but only slightly. The result is that at the some college and college graduate levels, federal employment is rated 1.5 to 2 scale points below private business.

. . . . High school students rate federal work only slightly below private business. However, college seniors and graduate students both place it 1.4 points below private business.

. . . . High school teachers' and vocational counselors' ratings disfavor government by 1.0 and 1.5 points respectively.

. . . . The four college teacher populations score private business markedly lower than do other nonfederal populations, but still from .9 to 1.3 points higher than they rate the federal government.

. . . . Groups in business rate the federal government lower than do other nonfederal populations and give high ratings to large private business. The result is that the federal government is rated from 2.7 to 3.6 scale points below large private business.

. . . . In general, federal employees rate working for the federal government from one-half to one full scale point below working for a business corporation. Only for the high school not completed group does the difference score favor the government, and there by only a small amount (.3).

Table 9-1a

The image of the federal government as an employer: average (mean) ratings of evaluative statements on the 10-point agree-disagree scale; the higher the score, the more agreement.

| | Average number answering | "For a young man of ability, his best chance for being really successful lies in _____." | | |
		Working for the federal government	Working for a large private business corporation	Difference: "government" minus "business"
Nonfederal Populations				
General employed public	1087	4.4	5.4	-1.0
By sex				
Men	835	4.3	5.4	-1.1
Women	252	4.6	5.3	-.7
By educational level				
High school not completed	304	5.6	5.9	-.3
High school completed	495	4.3	5.1	-.8
Some college	123	3.4	5.1	-1.7
College graduate	135	3.1	5.2	-2.1
Students				
High school students	354	4.4	4.8	-.4
College seniors	400	3.6	5.0	-1.4
Graduate students	380	3.5	4.9	-1.4
Groups in education				
High school teachers	279	3.6	4.6	-1.0
Vocational counselors	79	3.5	5.0	-1.5
College teachers	470	3.2	4.3	-1.1
Natural scientists	118	3.1	4.4	-1.3
Social scientists	104	3.6	4.5	-.9
Engineers	86	3.1	4.2	-1.1
Groups in business				
Executives	272	3.0	5.9	-2.9
Natural scientists	84	2.7	5.4	-2.7
Social scientists	70	2.9	5.6	-2.7
Engineers	89	2.8	6.4	-3.6
Federal Employee Populations				
General federal employees	930	4.4	5.0	-.6
By sex				
Men	648	4.5	5.2	-.7
Women	283	4.0	4.6	-.6
By educational level				
High school not completed	182	5.7	5.4	+.3
High school completed	353	4.1	5.1	-1.0
Some college	179	4.2	4.9	-.7
College graduate	162	3.6	4.3	-.7
Executives	271	3.8	4.7	-.9
Natural scientists	91	3.7	4.0	-.3
Social scientists	90	4.0	4.3	-.3
Engineers	98	4.0	4.7	-.7

Table 9-1b

Highlights: "A person who works for (a large private business) (the federal government) generally has a good chance to get ahead.

. . . . In these judgments of a person's chances of getting ahead, ratings by the general employed public of large private business and the federal government are about equal, with women rating the government somewhat higher than business. However, there is a marked negative relationship between ratings of the federal government and educational level. The two lower educational levels rate federal employment slightly above private business employment, and the two higher educational levels place government work below private business.

. . . . A similar association with educational level is shown among students. High school students rate the federal government and large private business approximately equal. College seniors and graduate students assign a lower rating to government.

. . . . Among groups in education ratings of large private business and the federal government are approximately equal.

. . . . Groups in business give very low ratings to the federal government and high ratings to large private business, with the result that their ratings favor private business by roughly 1.5 to 2.5 scale points.

. . . . All groups but one (the some college group) in federal employment score the federal government higher than large private business in this regard. This is slightly more true of women than it is of men.

Table 9-1b

The image of the federal government as an employer: average (mean)
ratings of evaluative statements on the 10-point agree-disagree
scale; the higher the score, the more agreement (cont'd.)

| | "A person who works for the _____ generally has a good chance to get ahead." | | |
	The federal government	A large private business	Difference: "government" minus "business"
Nonfederal Populations			
General employed public	6.5	6.4	+.1
By sex			
Men	6.3	6.5	-.2
Women	7.0	6.3	+.7
By educational level			
High school not completed	7.2	6.8	+.4
High school completed	6.5	6.2	+.3
Some college	5.6	6.0	-.4
College graduate	5.3	6.4	-1.1
Students			
High school students	6.6	6.5	+.1
College seniors	5.7	6.2	-.5
Graduate students	5.5	6.0	-.5
Groups in education			
High school teachers	6.0	5.7	+.3
Vocational counselors	6.0	5.7	+.3
College teachers	5.9	6.0	-.1
Natural scientists	5.9	6.1	-.2
Social scientists	6.0	5.7	+.3
Engineers	6.0	6.0	0.0
Groups in business			
Executives	5.0	6.9	-1.9
Natural scientists	5.1	6.7	-1.6
Social scientists	4.9	6.6	-1.7
Engineers	4.8	7.2	-2.4
Federal Employee Populations			
General federal employees	6.7	6.1	+.6
By sex			
Men	6.8	6.2	+.6
Women	6.5	5.6	+.9
By educational level			
High school not completed	7.2	6.2	+1.0
High school completed	6.6	6.2	+.4
Some college	6.2	6.3	-.1
College graduate	6.7	5.6	+1.1
Executives	7.2	6.1	+1.1
Natural scientists	6.8	5.6	+1.2
Social scientists	7.0	5.6	+1.4
Engineers	6.9	5.9	+1.0

Table 9-1c

Highlights: "A young man of ability who starts work in (a large private business corporation) (the federal civil service) has a good chance of ending up in one of the top-level jobs."

. . . . In the general employed public, the federal civil service is rated lower than the business corporation. Women rate them about equal as do the two lowest educational groups. Differences in the government's disfavor are especially great at the some college and college graduate levels, due to the markedly lower ratings these groups give to the federal civil service.

. . . . Student ratings slightly favor large private business.

. . . . All groups in education assign roughly equal ratings to large private business and the federal civil service.

. . . . Among all groups in business there is a quite consistent difference in favor of large private business, ranging from roughly about 1.5 to 2 scale points.

. . . . General federal employees rate large private business and the federal civil service approximately equal over-all, by sex, and at three of the four educational levels. At the some college level, ratings slightly favor private business.

. . . . Federal executives rate the federal civil service somewhat higher than private business, as do federally-employed natural scientists and, especially, social scientists. For federal engineers, on the other hand, the scores do not differ significantly.

Table 9-1c

The image of the federal government as an employer: average (mean)
ratings of evaluative statements on the 10-point agree-disagree
scale; the higher the score, the more agreement (cont'd.)

	"A young man of ability who starts work in _____ has a good chance of ending up in one of the top level jobs."		
	The federal civil service	A large private business corporation	Difference: "federal" minus "business"
Nonfederal Populations			
General employed public	6.4	7.0	-.6
By sex			
Men	6.3	7.0	-.7
Women	6.8	6.9	-.1
By educational level			
High school not completed	7.1	7.2	-.1
High school completed	6.6	6.9	-.3
Some college	5.4	6.7	-1.3
College graduate	5.3	6.9	-1.6
Students			
High school students	6.4	7.0	-.6
College seniors	5.9	6.5	-.6
Graduate students	5.8	6.3	-.5
Groups in education			
High school teachers	6.1	6.3	-.2
Vocational counselors	6.0	6.3	-.3
College teachers	5.8	5.9	-.1
Natural scientists	5.9	6.2	-.3
Social scientists	5.7	5.7	0.0
Engineers	6.2	6.3	-.1
Groups in business			
Executives	5.5	7.2	-1.7
Natural scientists	5.5	7.0	-1.5
Social scientists	5.6	6.9	-1.3
Engineers	5.3	7.2	-1.9
Federal Employee Populations			
General federal employees	7.0	7.1	-.1
By sex			
Men	7.0	7.1	-.1
Women	7.1	6.9	+.2
By educational level			
High school not completed	7.9	7.6	+.3
High school completed	7.0	7.1	-.1
Some college	6.2	6.9	-.7
College graduate	6.5	6.3	+.2
Executives	7.6	6.9	+.7
Natural scientists	6.5	6.0	+.5
Social scientists	7.1	6.0	+1.1
Engineers	6.5	6.4	+.1

255

Table 9-1d

Highlights: "Employment with (a large private business) (the federal government) offers a high degree of security."

. . . . Among all populations, federal and nonfederal, ratings on security overwhelmingly favor the federal government in comparison to a large private business. In the nonfederal populations the differences in favor of the government range from about 1 to 2.5 scale points; among the federal employee populations differences favor the federal government by 3 to almost 4 scale points.

. . . . In both the federal and nonfederal populations women give somewhat higher ratings to the federal government, and somewhat lower ratings to large private business, than do men.

. . . . Among students, there is a slight positive relationship of present educational level with difference scores--the higher the education, the more the net scores favor government.

Table 9-1d

The image of the federal government as an employer: average (mean)
ratings of evaluative statements on the 10-point agree-disagree
scale; the higher the score, the more agreement (cont'd.)

	"Employment with _____ offers a high degree of security."		
	The federal government	A large private business	Difference: "government" minus "business"
Nonfederal Populations			
General employed public	7.4	6.1	+1.3
By sex			
Men	7.3	6.1	+1.2
Women	7.5	5.8	+1.7
By educational level			
High school not completed	7.6	6.3	+1.3
High school completed	7.3	5.9	+1.4
Some college	7.1	6.1	+1.0
College graduate	7.1	5.9	+1.2
Students			
High school students	7.4	5.9	+1.5
College seniors	7.7	5.8	+1.9
Graduate students	7.8	5.6	+2.2
Groups in education			
High school teachers	7.5	5.3	+2.2
Vocational counselors	7.5	5.2	+2.3
College teachers	7.7	5.4	+2.3
Natural scientists	7.8	5.2	+2.6
Social scientists	7.4	5.4	+2.0
Engineers	7.8	5.8	+2.0
Groups in business			
Executives	7.7	5.9	+1.8
Natural scientists	7.6	5.8	+1.8
Social scientists	7.7	5.9	+1.8
Engineers	7.3	6.1	+1.2
Federal Employee Populations			
General federal employees	8.1	4.8	+3.3
By sex			
Men	8.1	4.9	+3.2
Women	8.3	4.4	+3.9
By educational level			
High school not completed	8.2	4.8	+3.4
High school completed	8.4	5.0	+3.4
Some college	7.8	4.6	+3.2
College graduate	7.6	4.5	+3.1
Executives	7.8	4.6	+3.2
Natural scientists	8.0	4.6	+3.4
Social scientists	7.9	4.8	+3.1
Engineers	7.9	4.8	+3.1

Table 9-1e

Table 9-1e

Highlights: "Most jobs in (private business) (the federal government) are routine and monotonous."

. . . . In the general employed public ratings of private business and federal government on routine and monotony are approximately equal. Ratings of the federal government are positively related to educational level. The group with some college and the college graduates rate the federal government about one point higher than private business.

. . . . A similar pattern is apparent among students. High school students rate private business and federal government about the same; but college seniors and graduate students consider the federal government higher on monotony and routine.

. . . . Groups in education rate the federal government, characteristically, a little bit higher than they do private business.

. . . . Among groups in business the difference scores are very marked, with the federal government being placed higher on routine and monotony by approximately 1 to somewhat over 2 scale points.

. . . . The ratings of federal employee populations on routine and monotony in private business and the federal government are roughly the same. The scores assigned to the federal government are quite consistent for all federal employee populations and are lower than the ratings assigned to the federal government by the nonfederal populations. There is some indication that general federal employees at the some college level see private business employment as being a little less monotonous and routine than federal employment.

Table 9-1e

The image of the federal government as an employer: average (mean)
ratings of evaluative statements on the 10-point agree-disagree
scale; the higher the score, the more agreement (cont'd.)

| | "Most jobs in _____ are routine and monotonous." | | |
	The federal government	Private business	Difference: "government" minus "business"
Nonfederal Populations			
General employed public	4.9	4.7	+.2
By sex			
Men	5.1	4.8	+.3
Women	4.3	4.4	-.1
By educational level			
High school not completed	4.9	5.2	-.3
High school completed	4.6	4.5	+.1
Some college	5.3	4.2	+1.1
College graduate	5.6	4.6	+1.0
Students			
High school students	4.3	4.2	+.1
College seniors	5.1	4.4	+.7
Graduate students	5.3	4.4	+.9
Groups in education			
High school teachers	4.7	4.4	+.3
Vocational counselors	4.3	3.6	+.7
College teachers	5.0	4.7	+.3
Natural scientists	5.0	4.6	+.4
Social scientists	5.1	5.1	0.0
Engineers	4.5	3.7	+.8
Groups in business			
Executives	5.9	3.9	+2.0
Natural scientists	4.7	3.5	+1.2
Social scientists	5.3	4.2	+1.1
Engineers	6.3	4.2	+2.1
Federal Employee Populations			
General federal employees	4.2	4.0	+.2
By sex			
Men	4.3	4.2	+.1
Women	3.9	3.5	+.4
By educational level			
High school not completed	4.2	4.4	-.2
High school completed	4.3	4.2	+.1
Some college	4.6	3.6	+1.0
College graduate	4.0	3.7	+.3
Executives	3.8	3.7	+.1
Natural scientists	3.7	4.0	-.3
Social scientists	4.6	4.2	+.4
Engineers	3.8	3.9	-.1

Security

The statements to be rated on this factor read, "Employment with the federal government [a large private business] offers a high degree of security." The results (Table 9-1d) are entirely unequivocal and completely in line with the findings on security obtained in response to the free-answer questions discussed in Chapter 8. In every federal and nonfederal group the average scale ratings given to federal employment on security are not only very high in absolute terms, but also significantly higher than those given to large private business.

The difference scores favoring the government range for the nonfederal populations from 1.0 to 2.6, and for the federal employee populations from about 3 to almost 4. That the federal employees' *difference* scores are larger than those of the nonfederal groups is somewhat accounted for by their higher ratings for federal job security but largely by their lower ratings for private business employment.

Routine and Monotony

Comparative ratings of this factor were obtained with the statements, "Most jobs in the federal government [private business] are routine and monotonous" (Table 9-1e). For the most part, the scores for both private and government employment are fairly low and, except in a few cases, differ only slightly. The nonfederal populations consider government employment somewhat more routine and monotonous than the federal groups do, and this tendency is positively related to educational level. The higher the level, the higher are the ratings for government employment on the factor in relation to the scores for private business; at the college graduate level, the difference score is 1.0. In the student population there is a similar positive relationship, but again the scores are not large. Of all the nonfederal populations, those most inclined to rate routine and monotony in government employment higher than in private employment are the business groups—especially the executives and engineers, whose net scores are 2.0 and 2.1.

The federal populations give approximately equal scores to federal and to private employment; in most cases, the differences are not significant or are of borderline significance. For the employees at the some college level, however, the net score shows more of a feeling that private employment is somewhat less monotonous than federal employment.

The results on this factor are of particular interest because, on the basis of limited developmental work at the beginning of this study, we felt that routine and monotony were an important aspect of the image of federal employment, in comparison to the image of nonfederal employment. The scale evaluations presented here show that the hypothesis is in some degree correct, but not overwhelmingly so. To the extent that such stereotyping occurs, it occurs most in the four business groups and at the two upper educational levels in the general employed public. It is seen also in some measure among the federal employees with some college experience, but hardly at all among other federal groups.

Opportunity for Success

The three pairs of statements for which the results are more complex are revealing when considered one pair at a time, but even more revealing in their relationships to one another. The first pair (Table 9-1a) read, "For a young man of ability, his best chance for being really successful lies in working for the federal government [a large private business corporation]."

The scale ratings given to both federal and private employment by the general employed public and general federal employees decline with increasing educational level. At this point, we can only speculate about the reason for this over-all negative relationship. It may, however, result from a tendency of the more highly educated to define both the quality and level of attainment of "real success" in a more restricted way than the less educated do. In any case, it suggests that attention should be focused, not so much on the absolute scores given to each of the scale items, as shown in Table 9-1a, but on the difference scores in the last column of the table. Here we find that, with only one exception, all of the federal and nonfederal groups rate the large private corporation higher than the government on the chances it offers for success. The single exception is the federal employee group that did not complete high school; its net score favors the government, but only by 0.3 of a scale point.

Looking at the difference scores for each of the groups, we find that the general employed public favors private business by 1 scale point, and that women give slightly less advantage to private business than do men. We also find that educational levels relate sharply to the difference scores: for respondents not completing high school the difference in favor of private business is 0.3; for college graduates it is 2.1. Among the student populations, the relationship between net scores and educational level is similar but the pattern is less extreme. For high school students the difference is 0.4; for both college seniors and college graduate students it is 1.4.

The results for the groups in education show only slight group-to-group variation. High school teachers, vocational counselors, college teachers, and college natural and social scientists and engineers place private business 1 to 1.5 scale points higher than federal employment.

On the average, the business groups rate private employment somewhat higher and the federal government somewhat lower than the other nonfederal groups do. The result is that the difference scores for the executives, natural and social scientists, and engineers are very high—2.9, 2.7, 2.7, and 3.6 respectively.

As previously mentioned, the net scores for the federal employee populations—with the one exception noted—consistently favor the private business corporation, although in general not extremely so and in some cases with only borderline significance.

In sum, the results on this pair of items concerning the chances of *real success* for a young man of ability are unequivocal. The scores show overwhelmingly, in both the nonfederal and federal populations, that federal employment is rated lower than large private business corporation employment in this regard. What the respondents might have had in mind in giving these ratings is not, however, quite so unequivocal.

Two significant variables may be involved here. The first is the factor of chance—embodied in the statement as "his best chance." Respondents may have given the ratings they did because they considered the *chances* for getting ahead or reaching the top to be less in federal employment than in corporate employment. On the other hand, there is the factor of success—embodied in the statement as "being really successful." Respondents possibly regarded the chances of getting ahead or reaching the top in federal and corporate employment as being about equal, but considered the upper levels of federal employment less well endowed with the ingredients of *real success* than the upper levels of corporate employment.

That either explanation is exclusively true is unlikely. The question is, however, which of the two variables plays the greater role in the respondents' judgments. The next two pairs of items help to answer this question; they provide comparable ratings of federal and corporate employment on the two "chance" factors—chance to get ahead, and chance of getting to the top.

Chance of Getting Ahead

The first pair of these sets of items (see Table 9-1b) was stated thus: "A person who works for the federal government [a large private business] generally has a good chance to get ahead." For the nonfederal populations, the results show only a few strong consistent patterns. The over-all ratings in the general employed public for government employment and for private business are about equal; however, women assign a slight advantage to federal employment, and respondents with higher education rate private employment higher than federal, especially at the college graduate level where private business is favored by 1.1 scale points.

Among the student populations, high school students rate the two forms of employment approximately the same. College seniors and graduate students give a slight advantage to private business.

Among high school teachers, vocational counselors, and the four college teacher groups, any variations in judgment about the government and large private business are nonsignificant and form no consistent pattern. It appears that it is characteristic of teachers to feel that there is little difference between business and federal employment in this regard.

As might be expected, all the business groups rate large private business as significantly better than federal employment in offering chances for advancement. These larger disparities come about because, as noted before, the respondents tend to rate private business higher and government lower than the other nonfederal populations characteristically do. The result is that the business executives, natural and social scientists, and engineers favor business employment by net scores of 1.9, 1.6, 1.7, and 2.4.

The above pattern for nonfederal populations strongly suggests that when the various groups judged federal employment to be less advantageous than private employment as an avenue for becoming "really successful," it was not primarily because they felt the chances for promotion and for getting ahead were poorer. On the getting ahead factor, only in the general college graduate and business groups do we find marked differences favoring private business, and even these, substantial as they are, are not nearly as great as the differences favoring private business on the "being really successful" factor.

The ratings given by the federal employee population to this pair of scale items show that virtually every group—men and women, three of the four educational levels, and executives, natural and social scientists, and engineers—rates federal employment higher than the business corporation on opportunity to get ahead. It is true that the difference scores for federal employment are not markedly higher, but they are consistent from group to group and most are large enough to be significant. This pattern is directly opposite to what one would expect if these groups rated federal employment lower on chances for being "really successful" simply because they saw it lacking, relatively, in opportunity to get ahead. Thus, it appears that federal employees on the average rate government employment lower on chances for "real success" *in spite of the fact* that they perceive it as better in terms of getting ahead.

It is possible that, even though differential perceptions of chances for promotion do not account for the large differences favoring private business employment as an avenue for "real success," the results may still be accounted for by perceived discrepancies between corporate and federal employment in relation to the way people see another aspect of promotion possibility—the eventual opportunity to reach the top. It may be that people see greater chances for "real success" in private employment, not because they see its promotional opportunity in general as better, but because they think it offers greater access to top-level jobs.

Chance of Getting to the Top

The pair of scale items dealing with this factor were stated thus: "A young man of ability who starts work in the federal civil service [a large private business corporation] has a good chance of ending up in one of the top-level jobs." Examining the net scores, we see that none of the nonfederal populations score the civil service higher than the business corporation. For the two lower educational levels, women in the general employed public, high school teachers, and all groups of college teachers, the differences are so small as to be insignificant. For the student populations they are also small and of borderline significance.

For college graduates and those with some college in the general employed public, and for the business groups, negative scores are sufficiently large—with a range from about 1.5 to 2.0 scale points—to show that the business corporation is unequivocally being rated higher than the civil service on this factor. These results suggest that, for some groups, the estimation that chances of getting into a top-level job are better in the large corporation does play some role in the much higher ratings given to private business on the chances for "real success." Nevertheless, it is unlikely that all of the higher scores can be accounted for in this way.

Among the federal populations the average ratings assigned to each type of employment on the chances of getting to a top-level job are not appreciably different. General federal employees, and both men and women, rate corporations and the civil service approximately the same. By educational level, we find no consistent pattern in the difference scores. Among federal executives, natural and social scientists, and engineers, the divergencies, by and large, are not significant, even though they slightly favor the civil service.

We must conclude that federal employees do not perceive a great deal of difference between the top-level opportunities offered by federal employment and by large private business, but tend to favor federal employment slightly. Thus it appears that the higher ratings they gave to private business as an avenue to "real success" cannot be accounted for by their general feeling that the civil service is more restricted in the opportunities it offers to reach the top.

In summary, all groups, nonfederal and federal, rate federal employment lower than private business employment on chances for "real success," and this cannot be fully accounted for by the perceived differences in either promotional opportunity or chances of winding up in one of the top-level jobs. For some of the nonfederal populations, it is possible that the combination of the two "opportunity" factors may account for a considerable amount of the advantage accorded large business on chances for "real success." But, for most of the nonfederal populations and for all of the federal, some other major elements of "real success" appear to be seen as lacking, relatively speaking, in federal employment.

10

Further Aspects of the Image of Federal Employment

THIS CHAPTER DEALS WITH the results of several questions which were designed to explore three further aspects of how the government is perceived as an employer: (1) the extent to which people employed outside government can or do differentiate among the employment opportunities offered by the federal establishment, and, to the degree that perception of this kind exists, what its nature is and what reasons people offer for saying that one federal agency might be better or more suitable than another to work in; (2) whether people believe that men may find more occupational satisfaction in federal service than women do, and vice versa; (3) how much people really know about the maximum salaries in the civil service, and what they think the maximum *should* be.

Differentiation of the Federal Service by Nonfederal Employees

All of the employed respondents in the nonfederal populations were asked, "Suppose a person in your line of work did go to work for the United States government. Are there any particular branches or parts that would be better to be in than others, from your point of view?" (Table 10-1). Those who answered "Yes" were then asked: "What particular branches or parts of the government would be better?" (Tables 10-2a through 10-2j.) And "Why do you think that?" (Tables 10-3a through 10-3d.)[1]

[1] This series was not asked of the high school and college students. A parallel series was asked of the federal populations; see Chapter 19.

Knowledge of Differentiation

In considering Table 10-1, one caution should be observed. The distribution of the categorical responses "Yes," "No," "Don't know" should not be interpreted to mean that certain percentages of respondents have or do not have the desire or the intention of changing employers. Instead, it suggests only the proportions of respondents whose perceptions of the federal establishment are sufficiently differentiated that they can designate the part or parts they would prefer.

Discussion of Differentiation Knowledge Data

"Yes" responses are made by 39 percent of the general employed public, but by fewer women than men—24 and 43 percent. The frequency of affirmations rises sharply with educational level, from the high school not completed 29 percent to 36, 50, and 60 percent at the three other levels.

The "No" responses vary little according to sex or educational level, being roughly 15 to 20 percent in all groups, whereas the "Don't know" responses vary a great deal. In the general group, 42 percent say they don't know whether any branch would be better than any other; more women than men make this response—58 versus 37 percent; and by educational levels the figures decline sharply from 53 percent at the lowest level to 26 at the highest.

The percentages for the high school teachers and vocational counselors almost perfectly parallel those for college graduates in the general public. Roughly 60 percent say "Yes," 16 to 20 percent "No," and 24 percent "Don't know." Among the college teachers, including the natural and social scientists and engineers, responses shift significantly away from "No" and "Don't know" to "Yes." About three fourths of the respondents in the college groups say that certain agencies would be better than others for them, less than 10 percent say "No," and roughly 15 to 20 percent, "Don't know."

The figures for the natural and social scientists and engineers in business roughly parallel those for their college counterparts, although the

(Text continued on page 270)

Table 10-1

This question, quoted in the table title on the facing page, was
designed to assess the degree to which nonfederal employees differentiated a certain part or parts of the federal government from the
whole in terms of its special suitability for them. The resulting
distribution of categorical responses should not be interpreted to
mean that certain percentages of respondents have or do not have
either the desire or the intention of changing employers. Instead,
it suggests only the proportions in the various groups whose perceptions of federal employment are sufficiently differentiated that
they can designate a part or parts which they would prefer.

Highlights: Categorical responses "Yes," "No," and "Don't know."

. . . . In the general employed public considerably less than half
of the respondents differentiate a part or parts of the federal
government as being more desirable for employment. The percentage
of women who do so is much smaller than the percentage of men who
do so. In addition, the percentages of "Yes" responses show a
sharp positive relationship with educational level.

. . . . Roughly three-fourths of the college teachers in general,
as well as natural scientists, social scientists, and engineers in
colleges respond affirmatively.

. . . . Percentages of "Yes" responses are very high among groups
in business with the exception of business executives. Only half
of them make such a differentiation.

Table 10-1

Extent to which nonfederal employees see certain parts of the government as being preferable to others. Percentage distribution of responses in each group to the question, "Suppose a person in your line of work <u>did</u> go to work for the United States government. Are there any particular branches or parts that would be better to be in than others, from your point of view?"

	Number Answering	Yes	No	Don't know
General employed public	1140	39%	20%	42%
By sex				
Men	875	43	20	37
Women	265	24	18	58
By educational level				
High school not completed	330	29	18	53
High school completed	513	36	23	41
Some college	128	50	16	34
College graduate	139	60	14	26
Groups in education				
High school teachers	282	60	16	24
Vocational counselors	79	56	20	24
College teachers	466	78	7	15
Natural scientists	118	77	8	15
Social scientists	104	79	9	12
Engineers	87	71	9	20
Groups in business				
Executives	287	50	16	34
Natural scientists	85	81	7	12
Social scientists	73	74	12	14
Engineers	90	63	20	17

engineers give a somewhat lower percentage of "Yes" responses than the college engineers. The business executives depart somewhat from the pattern characteristic of the other high-level nonfederal groups; fewer of them say "Yes" and many more say "Don't know."

Statements of Preference and Reasons for It

When one considers the group patterning of results discussed above, the first few words of the preamble to the question should be kept in mind: "Suppose a person in your line of work. . . ." A member of the general employed public whose "line of work" is not highly specialized may well be thereby predisposed to give a "No" or "Don't know" response. It seems reasonable, for example, that a laborer or even a clerical worker might see no more advantage for him in working in any one part of the government rather than in any other. Similarly, an executive might feel that his talents and capabilities would be quite broadly applicable in the federal service, and not more specifically suited to one part than another. But respondents who are more highly trained—particularly those who have specialized in teaching and in science—have better grounds for differentiation of branches that relate best to their own specialties.

Thus, care must be used in interpreting the "Don't know" answers as necessarily meaning a display of ignorance of differential employment opportunities. But when we find substantial percentages of highly trained or highly specialized people saying either "No" or "Don't know," we may suspect that these are people not sharply attuned to these features of the federal establishment.

Additional light is shed on the problem of interpretation when we examine the results of the two follow-up questions directed tc the respondents who replied "Yes" to the initial question. Tables 10-2a through 10-2j show the parts of the government designated as better to work in than others; Tables 10-3a through 10-3d show the reasons for the designations.

Discussion of Preference Data

In the general employed public, respondents indicated few preferences for any parts of the federal service. Certain divisions of the Defense Department received some mention, as did the Post Office Department, but even here the concentration of responses is not great—only 9 percent cite the Post Office, for instance. A somewhat similar picture of low percentages is presented by business executives. There is some slight concentration of choices on four Departments—Defense, State, Health, Education, and Welfare, and Agriculture—but in no instances are the frequencies high.

Among the high school and college teachers, certain agencies are preferred much more often than others. Furthermore, the agencies cited tend to be different from group to group. The high school teachers and vocational counselors more often cite the Department of Health, Education, and Welfare, and especially its Office of Education; they also refer fairly often to the State Department in general, and the Foreign Service and Diplomatic Corps in particular. The Federal Bureau of Investigation is mentioned by them more than by any other group, although the figures are not high—6 and 9 percent respectively.

All of the college teachers show a differential tendency to mention the State Department and Health, Education, and Welfare. Natural scientists, college and business alike, are especially apt to mention Health, Education, and Welfare, and its Office of Health is cited by 21 percent (college) and 22 percent (business). The Agriculture Department also receives high notice (19 and 16 percent) from these two groups, as does the Bureau of Standards in the Commerce Department (18 and 12 percent).

The social scientists, again both college and business, name the State Department especially often (27 and 19 percent). There is also a slight concentration of replies for the Commerce Department. The college group, but not the business group, refers fairly often to the Labor Department and also to Health, Education, and Welfare, especially its Office of Health.

College and business engineers show a pattern which characterizes them as engineers and differentiates them from the natural and social scientists. They mention the Defense Department often, the frequencies being particularly high for the Navy and for the Corps of Engineers. They also concentrate on the Department of Commerce, the college engineers being especially likely (11 percent) to mention its Bureau of Standards.

When respondents were asked why they felt the government branches they had named would be better than other branches, their answers for the most part fell into two general categories. Table 10-3a shows that roughly half say that the work fits their capacities and/or training.

(Text continued on page 290)

Tables 10-2a Through 10-2j

This series of tables shows the parts of the federal establishment mentioned by the respondents in the various groups as being
better for employment. No breakdowns of the responses of the
general employed public by sex or by educational level are shown,
because, generally speaking, the percentages in the general employed
public were too small to warrant such cross tabulation.

Table 10-2a

Highlights: Defense Department

. . . . The Army, Navy, Air Force, and Corps of Engineers were
accorded sufficient frequency of mention by at least some groups
to warrant separate presentation. As the next to the last
column shows, numerous other specific divisions were mentioned,
but none of them with sufficient frequency to justify separate
presentation.

. . . . Engineers, both in colleges and in business mention some
part of the Defense Department more often than any other group;
they mention Navy and Corps of Engineers with especially high
frequency.

Table 10-2b

Highlights: State Department

. . . . The general employed public mentions the State Department
quite infrequently. However, high school teachers -- especially
vocational counselors -- college teachers, and social scientists
both in colleges and in business have high frequencies of mention.
The strongest tendency is to simply mention the State Department,
without further specification. Exceptions, however, are Foreign
Service and Diplomatic Corps.

Table 10-2a

Parts of the federal government mentioned as better for
employment by respondents in nonfederal populations.
Percentage distribution in each group[a] of parts mentioned
by respondents who stated that certain parts of the federal
government would be better to be employed in than others,
and named one or more parts.

| | Number answer-ing | Defense Department | | | | | |
		Army	Navy	Air Force	Corps of Engineers	Other specific divisions	Not further specified
General employed public	435	2%	5%	4%	1%	6%	2%
Groups in education							
High school teachers	169	2	1	3	0	10	0
Vocational counselors	44	5	0	5	0	14	0
College teachers	361	2	5	2	1	5	0
Natural scientists	91	0	8	4	1	3	0
Social scientists	82	1	6	5	0	4	4
Engineers	62	8	29	10	15	13	0
Groups in business							
Executives	144	1	2	2	0	8	4
Natural scientists	69	1	7	3	0	9	3
Social scientists	54	0	4	0	0	4	11
Engineers	57	2	12	2	12	9	4

[a]Percentage base = number of respondents answering in each group. Percentages do
not add to 100 in each group due to multiple replies.

Table 10-2b

Parts of the federal government mentioned as better
for employment (cont'd.)

| | State Department | | | |
	Foreign service	Diplomatic Corps	Other specific divisions	Not further specified
General employed public	2%	2%	0%	3%
Groups in education				
High school teachers	5	7	0	9
Vocational counselors	9	11	0	14
College teachers	5	4	2	23
Natural scientists	2	0	0	2
Social scientists	5	0	0	27
Engineers	0	2	0	2
Groups in business				
Executives	6	4	2	6
Natural scientists	6	1	1	1
Social scientists	7	9	2	19
Engineers	0	2	2	2

Table 10-2c

<u>Highlights</u>: Health, Education, and Welfare Department.

. . . . The general employed public cites the Department of Health, Education, and Welfare infrequently. However, high school and college groups and natural scientists in business accord it moderately high notice.

. . . . High school teachers and vocational counselors who cite it are likely to mention either the Office of Education or simply the department without further specification.

. . . . Natural scientists, both in colleges and in business, are espcially likely to mention the Office of Health. Social scientists in colleges also name the Office of Health with moderate frequency, but are even more likely to cite the department without further specification.

. . . . References by college engineers and by executives, social scientists, and engineers in business are very low.

Table 10-2d

<u>Highlights</u>: Agriculture Department.

. . . . Whenever respondents mention the Agriculture Department they tend to do so without further specification. However, there is a slight inclination for natural scientists both in colleges and in business to mention the Agricultural Research Service.

. . . . The Agricultural Department in accorded low frequency of mention in the general employed public, but still receives slightly more than most other departments.

. . . . Natural scientists both in colleges and in industry cite the Agriculture Department with moderately high frequency.

274

Table 10-2c

Parts of the federal government mentioned as
better for employment (cont'd.)

| | Health, Education, and Welfare Department | | | |
	Office of Health	Office of Education	Other specific divisions	Not further specified
General employed public	1%	1%	1%	1%
Groups in education				
High school teachers	1	14	2	11
Vocational counselors	0	16	5	18
College teachers	6	9	2	14
Natural scientists	21	6	4	6
Social scientists	11	0	1	22
Engineers	3	3	0	2
Groups in business				
Executives	1	1	4	1
Natural scientists	22	0	10	1
Social scientists	0	0	4	4
Engineers	2	0	0	0

Table 10-2d

Parts of the federal government mentioned as
better for employment (cont'd.)

| | Agriculture Department | | |
	Agricultural Research Service	Other specific divisions	Not further specified
General employed public	1%	4%	6%
Groups in education			
High school teachers	0	5	2
Vocational counselors	0	2	0
College teachers	0	2	4
Natural scientists	3	4	19
Social scientists	0	1	4
Engineers	0	2	2
Groups in business			
Executives	1	3	4
Natural scientists	4	3	16
Social scientists	0	2	4
Engineers	0	2	5

Table 10-2e

<u>Highlights</u>: Commerce Department.

. . . . The Commerce Department is scarcely designated by the
general employed public, or by high school teachers and vocational
counselors. A slightly higher percentage of college teachers
mention it.

. . . . Natural scientists, both in colleges and in business,
accord the Bureau of Standards moderate to fairly high notice.
There is a similar tendency among engineers in colleges.

. . . . Social scientists name the Commerce Department moderately
often, but the tendency among them is to cite it without further
specification.

Table 10-2f

<u>Highlights</u>: Interior Department.

. . . . To the degree that the Interior Department is singled out
by any group, there is a tendency to refer to some specific division. However, the Bureau of Mines is the only division accorded
high enough frequency of mention by any group to justify showing
separately. In the case of the Bureau of Mines, college engineers
and natural scientists and engineers in business show quite low
frequencies, but high enough to warrant tabling.

. . . . Other specific divisions of the Interior Department are
mentioned with moderate frequency by college natural scientists
and engineers.

Table 10-2e

Parts of the federal government mentioned as
better for employment (cont'd.)

| | Commerce Department | | |
	Bureau of Standards	Other specific divisions	Not further specified
General employed public	0%	1%	1%
Groups in education			
High school teachers	1	0	0
Vocational counselors	0	0	0
College teachers	5	1	3
Natural scientists	18	0	2
Social scientists	0	4	10
Engineers	11	3	2
Groups in business			
Executives	1	1	10
Natural scientists	12	1	1
Social scientists	0	4	13
Engineers	5	7	5

Table 10-2f

Parts of the federal government mentioned as
better for employment (cont'd.)

| | Interior Department | | |
	Bureau of Mines	Other specific divisions	Not further specified
General employed public	0%	2%	1%
Groups in education			
High school teachers	0	1	2
Vocational counselors	0	2	0
College teachers	0	4	2
Natural scientists	0	9	2
Social scientists	0	4	1
Engineers	5	8	3
Groups in business			
Executives	0	1	2
Natural scientists	4	4	6
Social scientists	0	2	2
Engineers	5	4	4

Table 10-2g

<u>Highlights</u>: Treasury Department.

. . . . The only group that names the Treasury Department with
even moderate frequency is the business executive group. In that
group there is some mention of the Internal Revenue Service, and
of the Treasury Department without further specification.

Table 10-2h

<u>Highlights</u>: Justice Department.

. . . . There is some reference to the Justice Department among
the general employed public and among high school teachers and
vocational counselors. Such designations are confined almost
exclusively to the Federal Bureau of Investigation.

Table 10-2g

Parts of the federal government mentioned as
better for employment (cont'd.)

| | Treasury Department | | |
	Internal Revenue Service	Other specific divisions	Not further specified
General employed public	3%	1%	2%
Groups in education			
High school teachers	1	0	1
Vocational counselors	0	0	0
College teachers	1	1	0
Natural scientists	0	0	0
Social scientists	0	2	2
Engineers	0	0	0
Groups in business			
Executives	6	2	8
Natural scientists	0	1	0
Social scientists	0	0	2
Engineers	2	0	4

Table 10-2h

Parts of the federal government mentioned as
better for employment (cont'd.)

| | Justice Department | | |
	Federal Bureau of Investigation	Other specific divisions	Not further specified
General employed public	4%	1%	1%
Groups in education			
High school teachers	6	1	1
Vocational counselors	9	0	0
College teachers	0	0	1
Natural scientists	1	0	0
Social scientists	0	1	1
Engineers	0	0	0
Groups in business			
Executives	2	1	2
Natural scientists	0	0	0
Social scientists	2	4	2
Engineers	2	0	0

Table 10-2i

<u>Highlights</u>: Post Office Department.

. . . . 9% of the general employed public mention the Post Office
Department. It is scarcely mentioned at all by other groups.

<u>Highlights</u>: Labor Department.

. . . . There is some tendency for high school vocational counselors
and for social scientists, especially those in colleges, to nominate
the Labor Department.

Table 10-2j

<u>Highlights</u>: Foreign Technical Programs.

. . . . The frequency of mention of foreign technical programs
is extremely low in all groups; however, the 6% figure for college
teachers is worth noting.

<u>Highlights</u>: Miscellaneous specific agencies.

. . . . The figures in this column show that college teachers and
natural and social scientists and engineers both in colleges and in
business have a tendency to cite a considerable variety of specific
agencies. The number of agencies included in this category is
rather large and no agency is mentioned with enough frequency by
any group to warrant tabling separately. Thus it would appear that
among those college and business groups there is a perception of a
wide variety of special agencies of particular significance to the
individual.

Table 10-2i

Parts of the federal government mentioned as
better for employment (cont'd.)

	Post Office Department	Labor Department
General employed public	9%	0%
Groups in education		
High school teachers	1	2
Vocational counselors	0	7
College teachers	0	4
Natural scientists	0	0
Social scientists	0	12
Engineers	2	0
Groups in business		
Executives	1	1
Natural scientists	0	1
Social scientists	0	6
Engineers	4	2

Table 10-2j

Parts of the federal government mentioned as
better for employment (cont'd.)

	Foreign technical programs (e.g., USIA, Point Four)	Miscellaneous specific agencies (e.g., TVA, ICC)
General employed public	1%	5%
Groups in education		
High school teachers	1	4
Vocational counselors	0	7
College teachers	6	11
Natural scientists	1	12
Social scientists	2	13
Engineers	0	24
Groups in business		
Executives	1	8
Natural scientists	0	13
Social scientists	4	11
Engineers	2	12

281

Tables 10-3a Through 10-3d

This series of tables presents the reasons given by respondents in the nonfederal populations for selecting as better for employment a particular part of the federal government. The code categories used for tabling are those of the general occupational value code employed in all questions dealing with occupational values. Considered as a whole, the tables seem to show that the respondents' reasons for their selections are relatively nonspecific. The tendency appears to be to select a particular branch of government primarily because it is perceived a kind of work the individual is interested in performing and feels he has the capacity or training to do. Thus the responses tend to be a blend of the individual's own concerns, his estimate of the kind of work he can do, and a rather vague perception that a certain part of the government has that kind of work available. Some exceptions to this generalization will be pointed out in connection with specific tables.

Table 10-3a

Highlights: Interest, enjoyment, satisfaction, pleasure through doing work one is interested in, wants to do, likes to do.

. . . . High percentages of all populations give this as a reason for selecting a particular part of the government. This suggests that a dominant reason for selecting a particular part is because in it is perceived the availability of a particular job or kind of work which fits the individual's over-all value pattern.

Highlights: Work that fits one's capacities and/or training.

. . . . Here again the emphasis is on the availability of a particular kind of work, in this case work that is desirable because it fits one's own perceived capacity and training. This is the dominant reason given by most groups.

Table 10-3a

Reasons given by nonfederal employees for selecting as
better for employment a certain branch or part of the
federal government. Percentage distribution[a] of responses
of those in each group who named a selection and answered
the question, "Why do you think that?"

	Number answer- ing	Interest, enjoyment, satisfaction, pleasure through doing work one is interested in, wants to do, likes to do	Work that fits one's capacities and/or training
General employed public	440	35%	45%
By sex			
Men	377	35	44
Women	63	38	48
By educational level			
High school not completed	95	37	40
High school completed	185	37	40
Some college	64	39	48
College graduate	84	30	55
Groups in education			
High school teachers	167	38	42
Vocational counselors	43	44	47
College teachers	361	43	56
Natural scientists	90	54	48
Social scientists	80	54	50
Engineers	61	33	57
Groups in business			
Executives	144	23	65
Natural scientists	69	28	52
Social scientists	54	28	44
Engineers	56	27	55

[a]Percentage base = number of respondents in each group.
Percentages do not add to 100 in each group due to multiple replies.

283

Table 10-3b

Highlights: High or good financial reward.

. . . . In general, respondents tend not to differentiate the various parts of the federal government with respect to the financial reward available. There is some inclination for the general employed public to do so, especially the two lower educational groups, but the percentages are only moderate.

Highlights: Self-advancement and progress.

. . . . Only slight proportions of the populations differentiate parts of the government in terms of self-advancement and progress.

Highlights: Security, stability, protection, fringe benefits.

. . . . There is very little tendency for any population, with the exception of the two lower educational groups in the general employed public, to give this cluster of security factors as a reason for seeing one part of the federal government as better than another for employment.

Table 10-3b

Reasons given by nonfederal employees for selecting as
better for employment a certain branch or part of the
federal government (cont'd.)

	High or good financial reward (e.g., make good money, high pay)	Self-advancement and progress (e.g., be promoted, get ahead)	Security, stability, protection, fringe (retirement, illness, income, protection) benefits
General employed public	12%	8%	12%
By sex			
Men	11	9	13
Women	14	3	5
By educational level			
High school not completed	17	6	17
High school completed	16	10	14
Some college	3	6	6
College graduate	6	5	6
Groups in education			
High school teachers	6	2	2
Vocational counselors	7	2	0
College teachers	1	3	1
Natural scientists	1	1	2
Social scientists	4	0	0
Engineers	0	3	0
Groups in business			
Executives	1	4	1
Natural scientists	3	4	0
Social scientists	0	2	2
Engineers	4	2	4

Table 10-3c

<u>Highlights</u>: High standards.

. . . . Of special interest is the fact that 22% of natural
scientists in business and 18% of social scientists and engineers
in colleges see high standards as a particular appeal of certain
parts of the federal government.

<u>Highlights</u>: Active personal relations.

. . . . Worth noting are the moderately high percentages of high
school teachers and vocational counselors who offer active, stimulating, personal relations as a particular appeal of certain parts
of the federal government.

<u>Highlights</u>: Self-development, self-expression, and creativity.

. . . . Mention of this factor is relatively low. However,
college graduates in the general employed public, college teachers,
college social scientists, and engineers in business show moderate
figures of 10% to 13%.

Table 10-3c

Reasons given by nonfederal employees for selecting as
better for employment a certain branch or part of the
federal government (cont'd.)

	High standards (e.g., demand high skill; interested in progress)	Active personal relations (e.g., meet stimulating people, make good contacts)	Self-development, self-expression, and creativity
General employed public	4%	5%	7%
By sex			
Men	4	4	7
Women	2	8	8
By educational level			
High school not completed	2	1	8
High school completed	3	6	4
Some college	8	2	8
College graduate	4	10	11
Groups in education			
High school teachers	6	16	8
Vocational counselors	7	19	7
College teachers	10	9	10
Natural scientists	9	3	6
Social scientists	18	6	13
Engineers	18	7	5
Groups in business			
Executives	7	9	8
Natural scientists	22	0	7
Social scientists	2	7	9
Engineers	2	2	11

Table 10-3d

<u>Highlights</u>: Work that is worthwhile, useful, constructive;
   work that is significant for others (Columns 1 and 2 considered
   together).

. . . . Modest but significant percentages of the general employed
public mention these factors. References to work that is significant for others are positively related to educational level.

. . . . All groups in education and business display moderate to
moderately high mention of these two factors, with the exception
of college natural scientists and engineers for whom the figures
are quite low.

288

Table 10-3d

Reasons given by nonfederal employees for selecting as
better for employment a certain branch or part of the
federal government (cont'd.)

	Work that is worthwhile, useful, constructive	Work that is significant for others (e.g., affects welfare of all people; of country)
General employed public	5%	7%
By sex		
Men	5	7
Women	11	6
By educational level		
High school not completed	4	2
High school completed	6	8
Some college	2	8
College graduate	8	12
Groups in education		
High school teachers	11	10
Vocational counselors	14	9
College teachers	9	13
Natural scientists	2	7
Social scientists	4	11
Engineers	5	2
Groups in business		
Executives	7	8
Natural scientists	6	9
Social scientists	4	11
Engineers	9	20

And from 23 to over 50 percent say that it offers possibilities of the satisfaction or pleasure that comes from work one is interested in or likes to do. It appears, then, that most of the selections were made primarily on the basis of some general knowledge that the kind of work a respondent knows how to do or likes to do is in fact done in that part of the government. However, among the various groups there is an interesting scattering of other more specific replies.

Significant percentages of college teachers, college social scientists and engineers, and natural scientists in business say that their chosen branches maintain high standards in terms of the skills demanded and a demonstrated interest in progress. Particularly outstanding are the figures in this regard for the college social scientists and engineers and the natural scientists in business—18, 18, and 22 percent.

Among high school teachers and vocational counselors, 16 and 19 percent say their choices were made because the work would offer rewarding active personal relations—opportunities to meet stimulating people and to make good contacts. Small but significant numbers (11 and 14 percent) mention the opportunity to do work that is worthwhile, useful, and constructive, and 10 and 9 percent say that the chosen branch would offer work that affects the welfare of all the people and the country.

Certain other groups also stress the chance to do work that is significant for the people and the country: college teachers in general (13 percent), college and business social scientists (both 11 percent), and business engineers (20 percent).

A number of the more specific reasons given by people in the general employed public show an interesting positive relationship with educational level. None of the percentages are high, but their rise with the rise in educational level is in many instances of sufficient magnitude to be statistically significant. The category of active personal relations, for example, climbs in frequency from 1 percent at the high school not completed level to 10 percent among college graduates, and mention of doing work that is significant for the people and the country rises from 2 to 12 percent.

Mention of financial reward and security is infrequent in the upper-level educational and occupational groups. In the general employed public, however, 14 to 17 percent of the respondents at the two lower educational levels cite these factors as reasons for their choice.

Federal Employment:
More Satisfying to Men or to Women?

To explore another aspect of the image of federal service, this question was asked of both federal and nonfederal respondents: "On the whole who would be most likely to be satisfied with civil service employment— men or women?"[2] Replies were recorded under the categories of "Men," "Women," "No difference," and "Don't know." The results are shown in Table 10-4.

Discussion of Men-Women Data

In all groups either "No difference" or "Don't know" replies are made by 30 to more than 50 percent of the respondents, who thus indicate that the differential suitability of federal employment for men or women is not a significant factor in their perceptions of the civil service. On the other hand, 50 to 70 percent in the various group *do* make such a differentiation, and the patterning of their replies is of considerable interest.

In the general employed public, 31 percent say that men would be more satisfied with civil service employment; 18 percent maintain that women would. This result, however, conceals within it a pattern which is markedly different at the various educational levels. At the high school not completed level 34 percent answer "men"; the figures then decline sharply with increasing education to 16 percent among college graduates. Conversely, only 7 percent of those who have not completed high school answer "women," and the figures rise to 18, 28, and 37 percent as the levels rise.

The pattern for the student groups shows a similar relationship with level of education. Responses of high school students are equally divided —28 percent for both men and women. Among college seniors, the ratio of replies in favor of women is almost 2 to 1; among graduate students almost 3 to 1.

---

[2] The question as worded did not specify federal civil service, but the nature of the preceding questions could have left no doubt in respondents' minds that the federal civil service was meant.

(Text continued on page 294)

Table 10-4

Highlights: Judgments of whether federal civil service employment
is more satisfying to men or women.

. . . . In the general employed public, percentages favor men by
a ratio of about 3 to 2. However, among general federal employees
the percentages favor women by a ratio of about 4 to 2 1/2.

. . . . Among almost all the more highly educated groups, including
college students and teachers and groups in business as well as
federal executives, social scientists, and engineers, significantly
higher percentages of respondents see federal civil service employment as more likely to be satisfying to women than to men.

. . . . In all groups, from 30% to over 50% of respondents say
either "no difference" or "don't know," replies which indicate
that differential suitability for men or women is not a significant factor in their perceptions of the federal civil service.

. . . ... 52% of federally employed women say the federal civil service
is more satisfying for women; only 16% of them say it is more satisfying for men.

Table 10-4

The image of the federal government as an employer: judgments of
whether civil service employment is more satisfying to men or to
women. Percentage distribution of responses to the question,
"On the whole, who would be most likely to be satisfied with
civil service employment--men or women?"

	Number answering	Men	Women	No difference	Don't know
Nonfederal Populations					
General employed public	1139	31%	18%	33%	18%
By sex					
Men	873	31	19	33	17
Women	266	30	15	31	24
By educational level					
High school not completed	329	34	7	32	26
High school completed	512	32	18	33	16
Some college	129	30	28	29	13
College graduate	139	16	37	33	13
Students					
High school students	359	28	28	25	18
College seniors	403	21	41	25	13
Graduate students	382	14	39	30	16
Groups in education					
High school teachers	283	26	29	31	14
Vocational counselors	80	26	36	28	10
College teachers	470	15	33	35	17
Natural scientists	121	10	30	38	22
Social scientists	106	10	34	35	21
Engineers	86	11	35	35	20
Groups in business					
Executives	287	23	38	25	15
Natural scientists	85	11	38	35	16
Social scientists	73	14	45	30	11
Engineers	90	18	41	29	12
Federal Employee Populations					
General federal employees	947	24	39	30	7
By sex					
Men	661	27	35	30	8
Women	286	16	52	29	3
By educational level					
High school not completed	192	26	28	36	10
High school completed	356	27	40	28	5
Some college	180	20	50	24	5
College graduate	163	22	41	30	7
Executives	273	25	35	30	9
Natural scientists	92	25	25	23	27
Social scientists	90	19	36	30	16
Engineers	99	24	28	36	11

293

Among all of the college teaching and business groups, the figures for women are much higher than for men by ratios of 2 to 1 to as high as 3½ to 1. Only high school teachers depart from this pattern, which is characteristic of college graduate and high-level employee populations; their answers are about evenly split: 26 percent for men and 29 percent for women. The vocational counselors seem to favor women, but the number of cases is small; the conclusion cannot be drawn with certainty.

How do federal employees themselves feel about it? Among general federal employees the answer appears to be that more of them consider that the federal service would be more satisfying to women (39 percent) than to men (24 percent). Among men the responses slightly favor women —35 and 27 percent. Among women, however, the replies overwhelmingly favor women—52 and 16 percent. The response pattern is related to educational level. The replies of those who have not completed high school are almost equally split—26 (men) and 28 percent. At the other three levels, respondents saying "women" outnumber those saying "men" by ratios from 1½ to 1, to as high as 2½ to 1.

Among the special federal groups, the natural scientists and engineers say "men" and "women" with approximately equal frequency. The executives favor women slightly—35 and 25 percent. Social scientists also yield higher figures for women than men—36 and 19 percent.

The general picture, then, includes substantial percentages of the respondents in all groups, nonfederal and federal, who say they cannot or do not judge federal employment as being differentially satisfying by sex. However, there are also 50 to 70 percent of respondents in the various groups who do feel that differentiation can be made. Among these, the respondents at the upper educational and occupational levels reply "women" much more often than "men." The only groups reversing this are those at the two lower educational levels in the general public.

The results make it a matter of considerable interest to learn why the respondents made these judgments. Unfortunately, our developmental work had not led us to adequately anticipate these results, so that only one rather ineffective follow-up question was asked: "Why do you say that?" The replies did not lend themselves to the precise categorization and tabulation which would warrant presenting the results in tabular form. However, the answers did tell us something of what respondents had in mind when they said that men (or women) would be more satisfied or that there would be no difference.

The Reasons

Among the respondents who replied "No difference," many explained that it is impossible to make such a judgment, because there are so many different kinds of jobs and opportunities available in federal employment. A somewhat less common explanation was that, in general, men and women want about the same things from their jobs; thus the distinction being asked for simply could not be made. A considerable number of respondents contended that, even though men and women might want somewhat different things from their work, federal employment offers some features that men like especially and some that women like; since the factors are likely to balance out, there would be no real reason to believe that women would be more satisfied than men, and vice versa. The security provisions of federal employment were also seen as a leading reason for both sexes to be satisfied.

A sizable majority of those who replied "men" to the original question advanced two reasons for doing so, both of them relating to the feeling that federal employment offers an especially high degree of occupational security. In both the nonfederal and federal populations from 25 to about 75 percent of these respondents explained that men are more apt to be satisfied with federal employment since they value occupational security more highly than women do. From 40 to over 75 percent said that in general men are usually the real breadwinners, and that a job is a more central aspect of a man's life; therefore, men would be more satisfied by what federal employment has to offer. The chance to move ahead and the number of job opportunities available were also listed moderately often, particularly by federal groups, as reasons for men being more satisfied.

Four main reasons were given by the respondents who had replied "women." About a tenth to a third of the nonfederal respondents explained that they think the level of pay in the civil service is high enough to satisfy women—but not men to the same extent. Interestingly, this reason is also offered by 40 percent of the general federal employees and 49 percent of federal executives. One fifth to two fifths in various groups said that women are more likely than men to be satisfied with routine and clerical-type work, which these respondents see as characteristic of federal employment. A third reason was that government service offers the kind of clean, safe, nontiring work that is valued by women more than men. Thus, these three judgments are rooted in the common perception—especially prevalent among upper-level educational and occupational groups—that civil service employment is characterized by relatively low pay; by routine, monotonous, and clerical-type work; and by generally good, clean, and nontiring working conditions. The final reason was that the security of a government job would be better for women. This is interesting, since the security factor was cited also as a reason for men and for both sexes to prefer civil service.

Knowledge of the Top Salary
in the Civil Service

Salary is an important aspect of any employment and, as noted earlier, an important factor in evaluations of the federal government as an employer. Consequently, all of the groups were asked two questions bearing directly on this subject. The first was designed to provide some assessment of the individual's knowledge of what federal salaries actually are: "What is the top salary per year in the United States Civil Service—that is, not the salaries of elected and appointed officials, but the highest salary anyone in the regular United States Civil Service can get?" The second—an opinion question—was asked immediately after the first: "What do you think the highest salary per year *should be* for people who hold the top-level jobs in the United States Civil Service?" Tables 10-5 and 10-6 show the two sets of results (pages 298 to 301).

Table 10-7 utilizes the results of both questions. It presents for each of the groups the median of the replies on what the top salary is, the median of what respondents say it should be, and the difference between the two. The three sets of figures are of interest, not only because they show the degree to which people think the top federal salaries should be higher or lower—and thus indicate whether federal civil service personnel are seen as deserving of more or less financial reward—but because they shed indirect light on people's estimates of the financial consequences of reaching the top in the federal service.

Discussion of Civil Service Salary Data

Before turning to the group-by-group analysis, certain over-all findings should be considered. As Table 10-5 shows, a majority of the nonfederal groups lack even approximate knowledge about the top salary in the federal civil service.

To be sure, it is a little difficult to define "the correct answer" precisely. When the research was being conducted the top general schedule salary (GS-18 level) was $18,500. Some of the professional and scientific research and development salaries, however, were $19,000, and there were two or three jobs technically considered part of the career service at the $20,000 level. Since very few people could be expected to know of these $20,000 jobs, and since the most publicized figure is $18,500, for analytic purposes we have considered answers in the $17,000 to $19,999 range as "correct."

Using this as a criterion, we find only 4 percent of the general employed public giving an accurate response. The figures are similarly low for other groups: for high school students, college seniors, and graduate students, 1, 8, and 11 percent; for high school teachers and vocational counselors 5 and 8 percent. Even for the college teaching and businesss groups the figures range from only 11 to 26 percent. Further, substantial proportions of the general public, especially those at the lower educational levels and women, say they don't know or cannot guess what the top salary is. Among high school students, 24 percent also make this response. Among college students and groups in education and in business, however, such responses drop to 14 percent or less.

In general, most of the nonfederal populations markedly underestimate the top civil service salary. For the general employed public the median estimate is $10,000. Women, high school students, and respondents at the two lowest educational levels give the lowest estimates; the medians range from $8,000 to $9,500 for these groups. Only the business social scientists make a median estimate as high as $18,500. As a rule, the higher the educational and occupational level the higher is the estimated salary; nevertheless, the median for college graduates is only $15,000, with 42 percent giving figures under $17,000 and only 27 percent suggesting $20,000 and over. Comparable figures below $17,000 and above $20,000 for high school students, college seniors, and graduate students are 63 and 12, 62 and 21, and 57 and 24 percent, and the percentages for high school teachers and vocational counselors are about the same.

The college teaching groups and the groups in business all come closer to the mark and are about as likely to overestimate as to underestimate. But even here the balance is slightly toward underestimation by roughly $1,000 to $3,000. Exceptions are business executives, whose $14,500

(Text continued on page 304)

Table 10-5

This question was designed to assess the respondents' knowledge of
what the top salary actually is in the federal civil service. At
the time the question was asked, the maximum salary for the top
jobs in the General Schedule (GS-18) was $18,500. However, some
professional and scientific salaries were as high as $19,000, and
two (or three) jobs, technically considered part of the career
service, were at the $20,000 level. For analytic purposes, answers
in the $17,000-$19,999 interval are considered "correct."

Highlights: Distribution of estimates of what the top salary is in
    the United States civil service.

. . . . The general employed public has very little accurate
knowledge concerning the top salary in the civil service. Only
4% mention figures in the $17,000-$19,999 interval, with figures of
0%, 4%, 5% and 14% moving up the four educational levels. "Don't
know" responses are 29% over-all, almost twice as common for women
as men, and show a sharp negative relation with educational level.
Over-all, for both men and women, and at all educational levels,
percentages are higher for understatements than for overstatements
or the true figure. The lower the educational level, the greater
the understatement.

. . . . The students' pattern is similar to the general employed
public's. Among high school students, 24% say "don't know"; 13%
give answers at or above the true figure; 37% make estimates under
$10,000. "Don't know" responses are fewer and estimates higher
among college seniors and graduate students, but only 29% and 35%
estimate the true level or more.

. . . . The response patterns of high school teachers and vocational
counselors are similar to those of college seniors and graduate
students, and of college graduates in the general public.

. . . . The college teacher groups give very few "don't know"
answers, and about 45% to 55% of the replies are at or above the
true figure.

. . . . Of the business groups, executives and engineers have the
highest total percentages of underestimation; 26% of natural and
social scientists give answers falling in the "correct" interval.

. . . . 29% of general federal employees make estimates within the
"correct" interval. By educational level the figures for the
interval rise sharply from 14% at the lowest to 45% for college
graduates. For the group over-all, and by sex and educational level,
there are more answers below the true figure than above.

. . . . Roughly two thirds of the four special federal groups answer
within the correct interval, but 15% to almost 25% underestimate.

298

Table 10-5

Estimates of what the top salary _is_ in the United States civil service.
Figures based on responses to the following question: "What is the top
salary per year in the United States civil service--that is, not the
salaries of elected and appointed officials, but the highest salary
anyone in the regular United States civil service can get?"

	Number answering	Under $10,000	$10,000-13,999	$14,000-16,999	$17,000-19,999	$20,000 and over	Don't know/can't guess
Nonfederal Populations							
General employed public	1142	27%	17%	8%	4%	15%	29%
By sex							
Men	876	26	18	8	5	18	25
Women	266	30	14	6	1	7	42
By educational level							
High school not completed	331	28	13	5	0	9	45
High school completed	513	32	19	8	4	13	24
Some college	129	19	23	8	5	23	22
College graduate	139	12	17	13	14	27	17
Students							
High school students	359	37	17	9	1	12	24
College seniors	404	16	23	23	8	21	9
Graduate students	383	9	22	26	11	24	8
Groups in education							
High school teachers	283	16	23	18	5	24	14
Vocational counselors	80	12	20	16	8	32	12
College teachers	470	6	13	26	16	29	10
Natural scientists	121	7	15	30	17	27	4
Social scientists	106	6	11	28	22	31	2
Engineers	87	3	8	26	18	38	6
Groups in business							
Executives	287	15	18	17	11	30	9
Natural scientists	85	2	11	18	26	35	8
Social scientists	73	4	8	14	26	45	3
Engineers	90	6	14	22	12	40	6
Federal Employee Populations							
General federal employees	948	4	14	23	29	18	12
By sex							
Men	661	4	14	24	28	20	10
Women	287	3	13	22	28	16	18
By educational level							
High school not completed	192	9	15	19	14	17	26
High school completed	357	4	18	24	26	17	11
Some college	180	3	9	21	34	24	9
College graduate	163	1	7	23	45	21	3
Executives	273	0	1	19	65	15	0
Natural scientists	92	0	1	22	61	14	2
Social scientists	90	0	2	13	68	17	0
Engineers	99	0	2	21	60	16	1

Table 10-6

This question, which immediately followed the question of Table 10-5, was designed to assess what people feel the top civil service salary should be. It should be noted that the class intervals in this table range from "under $14,000" to "$30,000 and over," in contrast to the intervals in Table 10-5. The upward revision of intervals for this "should" table was made necessary by the fact that most respondents gave figures considerably higher than the "is" figures.

Highlights: Distribution of answers of what the top salary should be in the United States civil service.

. . . . Moderate to high percentages (13% to 43%) of respondents in all nonfederal populations say they don't know or cannot guess. In the general public such responses are much more common for women than men, and much more frequent at the lowest educational level than at the three higher levels.

. . . . Salary levels named show a strong positive relationship with educational level in the general employed public and among students.

. . . . Roughly 20% to almost 40% of college graduates, college seniors, graduate students, college teachers, and groups in business give a figure of $30,000 or higher. Roughly one third to over one half in these same groups offer answers of $24,000 or higher.

. . . . Federal employees at all levels give higher figures and fewer "don't know" responses than their counterparts outside the government.

. . . . 36% of the general federal employees name an amount of $24,000 or higher. More men (39%) than women (27%) do so. The percentages doing so rise from 17% at the high school not completed level to 66% for the college graduates--40% of whom say $30,000 or more.

. . . . From about 30% to 40% of the federal executives, natural scientists, social scientists, and engineers say $30,000 or more; two thirds to three fourths of them give replies of $24,000 or more.

Table 10-6

Estimates of what the top salary should be in the United States civil
service. Figures based on responses to the following question: "What
do you think the highest salary per year should be for people who hold
the top level jobs in the United States civil service?"

	Number answer- ing	Under $14,000	$14,000- 18,999	$19,000- 23,999	$24,000- 29,999	$30,000 and over	Don't know/ can't guess
Nonfederal Populations							
General employed public	1141	34%	11%	6%	8%	10%	31%
By sex							
Men	875	33	13	7	9	11	27
Women	266	37	7	4	5	5	42
By educational level							
High school not completed	331	36	9	4	4	4	43
High school completed	513	40	13	6	7	8	26
Some college	129	28	12	9	14	11	26
College graduate	138	16	13	12	12	24	23
Students							
High school students	359	44	13	7	5	6	25
College seniors	404	20	18	15	12	18	17
Graduate students	383	15	19	14	13	24	15
Groups in education							
High school teachers	283	22	18	11	14	11	24
Vocational counselors	80	18	10	6	21	15	30
College teachers	470	9	11	11	21	24	24
Natural scientists	121	11	15	15	18	28	13
Social scientists	106	7	12	14	24	29	14
Engineers	87	2	16	15	20	32	15
Groups in business							
Executives	286	13	16	10	19	19	23
Natural scientists	85	2	13	18	18	33	16
Social scientists	73	5	8	12	18	39	18
Engineers	90	10	11	8	18	34	19
Federal Employee Populations							
General federal employees	947	10	22	13	18	18	18
By sex							
Men	660	10	21	14	18	21	16
Women	287	10	27	12	16	11	24
By educational level							
High school not completed	191	18	23	13	8	9	29
High school completed	357	13	27	12	17	14	17
Some college	180	4	19	16	22	23	16
College graduate	163	2	10	13	26	40	9
Executives	273	0	7	18	36	32	7
Natural scientists	92	0	10	17	33	29	11
Social scientists	90	1	3	12	33	41	10
Engineers	99	0	7	11	33	42	7

Table 10-7

This table shows for the various groups the medians of what respondents say is the top salary in the federal civil service, what they say it should be, and the difference between the two medians. The figures exclude those in each group who say they didn't know and could not guess, and therefore did not make an estimate.

Highlights: Medians of what respondents say the top salary is and should be in the federal civil service.

. . . . In general, respondents in the nonfederal populations underestimate the top salary. The median estimate for the general employed public is only $10,000; women, the two lowest educational groups, and high school students place it even lower. Those with more education come closer to the true figure, but only college engineers, and natural and social scientists and engineers in business come to within $1,000 of the actual top salary of $18,500.

. . . . For all federal employee populations, the median estimates of present top salary are slightly below the actual top, but approximate reality quite closely. Only the two lowest educational groups show significant underestimates.

. . . . Among college faculty groups, business groups, federal employees at the some college and college graduate levels, and among the four special federal groups, medians of the top "should be" salary all fall in the $22,000 to $25,000 range, with the heaviest clustering near $25,000. The raw data, not tabled here, shows that in all these groups the most commonly mentioned (modal) figure is $25,000.

. . . . All of the difference scores are positive--that is, every group, on the average, gives a higher figure for "salary should be" than for "salary is."

. . . . In both of the two general employed populations (federal and nonfederal) differences are much higher for men than for women, and show strong positive relationship to educational level.

. . . . For the college and business groups, the four special federal groups, and the general federal employees at the two upper educational levels the differences range roughly from $6,000 to $8,000.

Table 10-7

Median estimates of what the top salary is and should be in the United States civil service. Figures based on responses to the following questions: "What is the top salary per year in the United States civil service--that is, not the salaries of elected and appointed officials, but the highest salary anyone in the regular United States civil service can get?" and "What do you think the highest salary per year should be for people who hold top-level jobs in the United States civil service?"

| | Number answering for: | | Top salary is[a] | Top salary should be[a] | Difference: "salary should be" minus "salary is" |
	Top salary is[a]	Top salary should be[a]			
Nonfederal Populations					
General employed public	811	788	$10,000	$14,000	+$4,000
By sex					
Men	657	635	10,500	14,500	+ 4,000
Women	154	153	8,000	9,500	+ 1,500
By educational level					
High school not completed	185	190	9,000	10,000	+ 1,000
High school completed	390	379	9,000	12,000	+ 3,000
Some college	100	95	12,000	16,000	+ 4,000
College graduate	115	106	15,000	20,000	+ 5,000
Students					
High school students	274	270	9,500	11,500	+ 2,000
College seniors	369	334	14,500	19,500	+ 5,000
Graduate students	351	325	15,000	19,500	+ 4,500
Groups in education					
High school teachers	243	214	14,000	17,500	+ 3,500
Vocational counselors	70	56	15,000	24,000	+ 9,000
College teachers	427	361	16,000	24,000	+ 8,000
Natural scientists	116	105	15,000	23,000	+ 8,000
Social scientists	104	91	17,000	23,500	+ 6,500
Engineers	82	74	17,500	23,500	+ 6,000
Groups in business					
Executives	261	222	14,500	22,000	+ 7,500
Natural scientists	78	71	17,500	24,500	+ 7,000
Social scientists	71	60	18,500	25,000	+ 6,500
Engineers	85	73	18,000	25,000	+ 7,000
Federal Employee Populations					
General federal employees	832	775	17,000	20,000	+ 3,000
By sex					
Men	596	555	17,000	21,000	+ 4,000
Women	236	220	17,000	19,000	+ 2,000
By educational level					
High school not completed	141	135	15,000	17,500	+ 2,500
High school completed	319	298	16,500	19,000	+ 2,500
Some college	164	151	17,500	24,000	+ 6,500
College graduate	158	149	18,000	25,000	+ 7,000
Executives	273	253	18,000	25,000	+ 7,000
Natural scientists	90	82	18,000	25,000	+ 7,000
Social scientists	90	81	18,000	25,000	+ 7,000
Engineers	98	92	18,000	25,000	+ 7,000

[a]Excludes those who did not make an estimate.
[b]Figures rounded to nearest $500.

median markedly underestimates, and business social scientists, whose $18,500 median, as noted before, is fairly accurate.

Federal employees show somewhat higher percentages of accurate estimates. Nevertheless, only 29 percent of the general federal employee replies fall in the $17,000-$19,999 range; if we broaden our criterion and accept any figure over $17,000 as "correct," we still find slightly less than half of this group giving correct answers. Slightly less than one third of those at the high school not completed level mention $17,000 or more; the comparable figures climb to 43, 58, and 66 percent for the three higher educational levels. Thus, about a third of those at the two highest educational levels and almost half of those at the two lower levels underestimate the salary.

General federal employees reply "Don't know" and "Cannot guess" considerably less frequently than members of the general employed public, but 12 percent of them do give those responses. This type of response is almost twice as common for women as for men; by educational level, it declines from 26 percent at the lowest to 3 percent at the highest.

Considering the median figures (Table 10-7) for general federal employees, we find that estimates of the top salaries are positively related to educational level, but college graduates still underestimate on the average by at least $500. The high school not completed level does so by at least $3,500.

The federal executives, natural and social scientists, and engineers are significantly more accurate than the general federal employees. Approximately two thirds of these special groups mention amounts in the $17,000 to $19,999 range, and roughly 75 to 85 percent say $17,000 or more. Almost no one says "Don't know." However, 15 to almost 25 percent of them give answers of under $17,000; the median figures in Table 10-7 show that the top salary is underestimated by a margin of about $500.

In summary, it appears clear that people in the nonfederal populations have very little accurate knowledge of the top salaries in the federal civil service. Underestimation of the true top salary ranges from roughly $8,000 to $9,000 at the lowest educational levels and from $500 to as much as $3,500 at the upper educational and occupational levels (with the single exception of the business social scientists). Federal employees are more accurate, with median estimates, in general, within $500 to $1,500 of the true level (with the exception of underestimation by as much as $3,500 at the lowest educational levels). Nevertheless, one third to over one half of the general federal employees and 15 to almost 25 percent of the executives, natural and social scientists, and engineers either reply "Don't know" or give estimates of under $17,000.

When people were asked what they thought the top salary in the federal civil service should be, their response patterns closely paralleled those for the "what is" question, again showing a positive correlation of level of estimates with educational and occupational strata in both the nonfederal and federal populations. However, all of the "should be" salaries are higher. In Table 10-5 the class intervals for "what is" salaries range from under $10,000 to $20,000 and over. In Table 10-6, however, to accommodate the "should be" results in five class intervals, the range is from under $14,000 to $30,000 and over. Table 10-7 shows that the "should be" medians range from $1,000 to as much as $9,000 higher than the "salary is" medians.

Another difference between the results shown in the two tables is the greater frequency, in general, of "Don't know" or "Cannot guess" replies in Table 10-6, although the relationship with educational level is still seen. Substantial percentages in all of the nonfederal populations give these replies, and on the average the percentages in the federal groups, although less than in the nonfederal, are higher than for the "what is" question. Since this is so, and since the results, as noted above, do parallel those from the first question, we will turn to a comparison of the two sets of responses, as shown in Table 10-7. The difference figures—the median figures for what the salary should be, minus the median figures for what it is thought to be—in the last column of Table 10-7 are especially interesting, as will be discussed in what follows, and are significant to the meaning of the absolute "should be" figures.

Especially to be noticed is that all of the difference scores are positive. Without exception, every group on the average says that the top salary in the federal civil service should be higher than what (they think) it actually is.

For the general employed public, the over-all difference figure is $4,000. It is higher for men ($4,000) than for women ($1,500). The higher the educational level, the greater are the differences between "salary is" and "salary should be" median figures; they rise from $1,000 at the lowest level to $5,000 at the college graduate level. Thus, not only do the absolute salary levels given in response to the two questions rise with educational level, but also, because the "should be" figures rise even more precipitously, the difference figures show an increase. The same thing is seen in the student populations. High school students give lower absolute amounts in response to both questions than do college seniors and graduate students, and they also show a lower difference score. The high school "salary should be" figure is $2,000 higher than the "salary is" figure; the difference figures are quite close for college seniors ($5,000) and graduate students ($4,500).

Comparisons of the results for high school teachers and for high school vocational counselors are particularly interesting. The "salary is" figures for the two groups are not greatly different, but the teachers say that the salaries should be $3,500 higher, whereas the vocational counselors on the average say they should be $9,000 higher; this is the most extreme difference between estimates found in any of the populations, nonfederal or federal. For the college faculty and business groups the median "should be" figures range from $6,000 to $8,000 higher than the median "salary is" estimates.

Federal employees also apparently think that the top salary should be higher than their estimates of what it is. The over-all difference figure for general federal employees ($3,000) is lower than that for the general employed public ($4,000). However, the figure for the federal employees is the difference between a $17,000 "salary is" figure and a $20,000 "should be" figure. The general employed public's comparable figures are $10,000 and $14,000. As in the general employed public, men in the federal service also yield a higher difference figure ($4,000) than women ($2,000), and the relationship between educational level and the figures in the difference column is positive—$2,500 at the lowest level and $7,000 for college graduates. For the four special federal groups the difference figures are the same as the college graduates'—$7,000.

Thus we may say that, in general, the higher people think the actual top salary is, the greater is the amount they think it should be increased, and these two judgments are positively related to educational and occupational levels in both the nonfederal and federal populations. Further, men name higher figures than women do for what the top salary should be and suggest a greater increase over what they think it is.

THE PRECEDING RESULTS present something of an analytic problem. On one hand, only the absolute figures might be considered, and it could be said, for example, that on the average the general employed public thinks that the top salary in the United States Civil Service should be about $14,000. However, if one adopts a literal interpretation of this kind, certain other generalizations must be set forth. In those nonfederal populations where most of the respondents may be presumed to have college degrees—e.g., college teachers and most of the business group—the median judgments of the "should be" top salary all fall in the $22,000 to $25,000 range. Also, on the average, general federal employees think that the top salary ought to be about $20,000, even though those at the lowest educational level say it ought to be $17,500. But college graduates among the general federal employees and all four of the special federal populations advance median figures of $25,000 as the desirable level for the top salary.

The problem of interpretation (using absolute figures) is not particularly acute for the high-level educational and occupational groups in either the nonfederal or federal populations. Their median estimates of what the top salary is are lower in general than the "real" top, but for the most part the difference is not great. In the same groups, those who have an approximately realistic picture of the "real" top show substantial agreement on a "should be" figure from $6,000 to $8,000 higher.

The main interpretive problem is presented by the respondents in the general employed public, especially those at the lower educational levels. It would be logical to emphasize a comparative interpretation of the figures these groups give. Members of the general employed public state, on the average, that the top salary should be $14,000—a figure, it would seem, that should be evaluated in relation to their unrealistic median "salary is" estimate of $10,000. Worth taking into account, also, is that the median annual family income for these respondents is $5,500. It is reasonable to suppose, then, that their guess at a top salary for the federal civil service represents a figure that is high by their own standards. This interpretation is supported by the positive correlation of "is" and "should be" estimates with educational level, since we know that both personal and family income tend to rise with increasing educational level.[3]

Thus the standards for a "high" salary will tend to rise with increasing educational level. If, then, we take the view that very few people in the general employed public have any real knowledge of the top salary in

[3] Supplementary analysis, not presented in this book, indicated that the median estimates of "is" and "should be" top salaries, while having a positive relationship with family income, did not vary quite as markedly as was the case by educational level. As with education, the association is more pronounced with the "should be" figures than with the "is" figures.

the federal service, and that they simply make a guess which is heavily affected by their own personal standards of what a good salary is, we arrive at a slightly different interpretation of the figures they give for "salary is" and "salary should be." We may say that, on the average, an individual in the general employed public estimates the top salary in the civil service to be almost twice as high as his own salary, and that he thinks it should be 40 percent higher than that.

11

The Image of the Federal Employee

THE TABLES IN THIS CHAPTER present the analyzed results of two free-response questions which were designed to discover to what degree people have general images or stereotypes of federal civil servants and of employees in large business firms and the nature or content of the images. Thus, the first question was: "If you were to describe your general idea of a United States civil service employee, what sort of person would that be?" Later in the questionnaire a parallel question was asked: "Turning away from government people for a moment, how about a person employed by a large private business or industry. If you were to describe your general idea of such a person, what would that be?"

For a comprehensive impression of the range and variety of data elicited by the two questions, the tables themselves and their highlights need to be read. A brief summary of the data, however, will serve as a useful introduction to the tables.

Perhaps the most striking finding is the extent to which people are willing to generalize about employees in both government and private business (Tables 11-3a through 11-3i). In the general employed public and among general federal employees an overwhelming majority—about 90 to over 95 percent—readily accept the idea of stereotyping and that these workers can be characterized as groups. Further, the respondents seem to be more willing to stereotype the civil servant than the employee of a large business firm.

Some groups, however, are less likely than others to generalize. Among the nonfederal populations (and to a lesser extent among federal) willingness to stereotype is inversely related to education and occupational attainments. College seniors and graduate students, college teachers, and the four special federal groups are especially averse to generalizing about either type of employee; in some cases, moreover, refusals to stereotype either one are about equal in frequency. Among business executives, natural and social scientists, and engineers, sizable numbers also refuse to generalize about business employees, but are somewhat more ready to stereotype the federal civil servant. Nevertheless, in every population interviewed, three fourths or more of the respondents are willing and able to generalize about both types of employees.

Favorable-Unfavorable Tone

The way in which people generalize about another group often reveals their basic attitudes toward that group. The adjectives they choose may be words that most Americans would consider "favorable," and would be happy to have applied to themselves. On the other hand, words can be used that have a neutral connotation—neither favorable nor unfavorable. There are also words that most Americans would consider clearly unfavorable and derogatory, especially when applied to themselves. Finally, there may be a roughly equal blending of favorable and unfavorable statements.

By analyzing a respondent's total reply when he is asked to describe his idea of a federal civil servant or an employee of a large business, it can usually be determined whether his over-all impression is generally favorable, unfavorable, neutral, or an ambivalent mixture of approximately equal favorable and unfavorable. The results of employing this classificatory scheme to the responses made to the open-end questions are presented in Tables 11-1 and 11-2.

Discussion of Favorable-Unfavorable Data

Concerning Federal Employees

An important finding is that substantial percentages of people in virtually all federal and nonfederal populations describe federal employees in such a way that, according to our criterion, the responses could not be classified as either clearly favorable or unfavorable. Approximately one fifth to two fifths of all groups shown in Table 11-1 give replies of this nature.[1] In general, this type of reply increases somewhat at the higher educational and occupational levels.

Nevertheless, the 60 to 80 percent of the respondents who reply in ways which are either clearly favorable or unfavorable produce some significant disparities among the groups. The data show that most respondents in the general employed public, among high school students, and in the federal employee populations give replies which, on balance, indicate a generally favorable image of the federal civil servant. But it is equally clear that some groups have a much less favorable view than others, and in a few of the high-level special groups the unfavorable views actually outnumber the favorable. Some of these variations are discussed below.

In the general employed public, women are somewhat more prone to give favorable comments than men—59 vs. 48 percent—and the proportion of favorable comments drops off as educational level rises: 60 percent of those who did not finish high school give favorable replies compared to 30 percent of the college graduates. Conversely, unfavorable comments rise sharply with increasing education: the figure is 3 percent at the lowest level and 27 percent at the highest.

This relationship with education also appears in the student populations. Among high school students, favorable descriptions of the civil servant outnumber the unfavorable by an overwhelming 63 to 7 percent. Among college seniors, favorable responses lead the unfavorable, but only by 33 to 24 percent; among graduate students, the unfavorable slightly outnumber the favorable—32 to 26 percent.

In the college teacher groups the division is fairly even between favorable and unfavorable. High school teachers and vocational counselors, however, predominantly give answers favorable to the federal civil servant, and thus resemble the general employed public rather than the other highly educated groups.

Of all the groups interviewed, the four business populations are the most critical of federal employees. Nearly one half of the business engineers, for example, give replies that are clearly unfavorable, and only 12 percent give clearly favorable replies.

[1] Responses coded in this fashion stem from two basic types of replies: (1) statements which maintain that generalizations cannot be made about the employee, and (2) replies in which the respondent generalizes, but in which the content of the reply is too ambiguous to permit a favorable, unfavorable, or partly favorable-unfavorable classification.

(Text continued on page 316)

Table 11-1

Highlights: The over-all tone of respondents' descriptions of federal civil service employees.

. . . . In the general employed public, slightly over half of the respondents give answers that could be fairly classified as favorable, in contrast to 10% of the replies that are unfavorable. This tendency to give favorable responses is slightly higher among women than among men.

. . . . The pattern in the general employed public by educational level is of special significance. Percentages of favorable responses decline sharply with increasing educational level, while unfavorable responses increase sharply with increasing educational level. Among college graduates the percentages of favorable and unfavorable replies are approximately equal.

. . . . The same pattern is shown in the student populations. Here the high school students give a 9 to 1 ratio of favorable replies; among college seniors and graduate students the ratio is approximately 1 to 1.

. . . . High school teachers and vocational counselors show a pattern of response quite similar to the over-all figure for the general employed public. College teachers, including natural and social scientists and engineers, on the other hand, show a higher level of unfavorable replies and a lower level of favorable replies, with the result that unfavorable and favorable replies are about equal.

. . . . Among groups in business, unfavorable responses outweigh the favorable by ratios of 1 1/2 to almost 4 to 1, the highest unfavorable ratio being shown by engineers.

. . . . The proportions of favorable responses are higher among general federal employees than in the general employed public. There is a slight tendency for this to be more true for women than men.

. . . . In contrast to the general employed public, there is no sharp relationship of responses with educational level among general federal employees. However, there is a slight suggestion that the percentage of favorable responses declines with increasing educational level.

. . . . More than two thirds of federal executives give favorable replies. The federal natural scientists, social scientists, and engineers show somewhat lower percentages of favorable replies than the executives.

Table 11-1

The image of the federal civil servant: the overall tone of respondents' descriptions of federal civil service employees. Percentage distribution in each group of responses to the question, "If you were to describe your general idea of a United States civil service employee, what sort of a person would that be?", classified according to favorable-unfavorable overall tone of response.

	Number answering	Favorable	Unfavorable	Partly favorable and partly unfavorable	Not clearly favorable or unfavorable	Don't know
Nonfederal Populations						
General employed public	1142	51%	10%	2%	30%	7%
By sex						
Men	876	48	11	2	32	7
Women	266	59	8	2	22	10
By educational level						
High school not completed	331	60	3	1	20	17
High school completed	513	52	9	2	33	5
Some college	129	42	16	5	37	1
College graduate	139	30	27	5	36	1
Students						
High school students	358	63	7	1	22	7
College seniors	401	33	24	8	32	2
Graduate students	378	26	32	1	40	0
Groups in education						
High school teachers	278	49	13	6	30	1
Vocational counselors	77	43	13	10	32	1
College teachers	470	30	24	9	34	3
Natural scientists	120	30	21	5	43	1
Social scientists	106	26	24	7	41	2
Engineers	87	24	29	5	41	1
Groups in business						
Executives	281	20	39	6	34	1
Natural scientists	83	20	31	6	40	2
Social scientists	73	15	37	10	38	0
Engineers	88	12	46	8	34	0
Federal Employee Populations						
General federal employees	939	66	6	2	26	0
By sex						
Men	653	64	6	2	27	0
Women	286	70	7	1	21	1
By educational level						
High school not completed	189	72	3	1	22	2
High school completed	355	66	7	1	25	0
Some college	179	61	9	2	28	0
College graduate	161	62	5	3	30	0
Executives	272	70	8	3	19	0
Natural scientists	92	59	8	4	28	0
Social scientists	90	56	16	4	24	0
Engineers	98	55	9	2	32	2

Table 11-2

This table presents the distributions of favorable and unfavorable over-all tones of descriptions of civil service employees and business employees. It is primarily of value for its comparative data.

Highlights: The favorable and unfavorable over-all tone of respondents' descriptions of civil service and large private business employees.

. . . . Over-all descriptions of business employees by the general employed public show little difference in either the favorable or unfavorable percentages, by educational level. This is in sharp contrast to the shift in an unfavorable direction with rising education for descriptions of federal workers, where the favorable drop from 60% to 30% while the unfavorable rise from 3% to 27%.

. . . . Among students, favorable images decrease and unfavorable ones increase as present educational status rises. This is much truer of descriptions of civil servants than those of business employees.

. . . . Among groups in education, the percentages of favorable replies are roughly the same for both types of employees. An exception is the college engineer group (43% favorable for business employees vs. 24% for civil servants. On the other hand, groups in education give fewer unfavorable replies for business employees than for civil servants.

. . . . Business groups give fewer favorable replies for business employees than comparable federal groups give civil servants. For example, 70% of the federal executives give favorable descriptions of civil servants; 58% of the business executives describe business employees favorably.

. . . . Among general federal employees the percentages of unfavorable responses about business employees are very small, some 50% or more giving responses that could be classified as favorable. The exception is the college graduate level, where favorable responses drop to slightly over one third.

. . . . Unfavorable descriptions of business employees by the special federal populations are much less frequent than the unfavorable characterizations of civil servants by comparable groups in business.

Table 11-2

The image of the federal civil servant: a comparison of favorable and unfavorable over-all tones of respondents descriptions of federal civil service employees and employees of large private business. Percentage distributions of favorable and unfavorable responses only.

	Number answering question		Favorable		Unfavorable	
	About civil service employees	About large business employees	Civil service employees	Large business employees	Civil service employees	Large business employees
Nonfederal Populations						
General employed public	1142	1139	51%	56%	10%	4%
By sex						
Men	876	874	48	56	11	4
Women	266	265	59	57	8	4
By educational level						
High school not completed	331	331	60	56	3	2
High school completed	513	510	52	57	9	5
Some college	129	129	42	61	16	5
College graduate	139	139	30	54	27	6
Students						
High school students	358	357	63	60	7	4
College seniors	401	400	33	49	24	12
Graduate students	378	377	26	34	32	13
Groups in education						
High school teachers	278	278	49	51	13	5
Vocational counselors	77	79	43	49	13	5
College teachers	470	464	30	34	24	9
Natural scientists	120	118	30	29	21	11
Social scientists	106	103	26	30	24	16
Engineers	87	86	24	43	29	5
Groups in business						
Executives	281	283	20	58	39	5
Natural scientists	83	85	20	41	31	2
Social scientists	73	72	15	46	37	4
Engineers	88	89	12	37	46	4
Federal Employee Populations						
General federal employees	939	892	66	50	6	6
By sex						
Men	653	619	64	48	6	6
Women	286	273	70	57	7	5
By educational level						
High school not completed	189	180	72	51	3	7
High school completed	355	338	66	52	7	6
Some college	179	171	61	55	9	5
College graduate	161	151	62	36	5	4
Executives	272	260	70	48	8	11
Natural scientists	92	91	59	34	8	14
Social scientists	90	86	56	41	16	13
Engineers	98	84	55	37	9	8

315

Federal employees themselves describe the civil servants in ways that are of special interest. Not surprisingly, they are generally the most charitable group of all. For the general employees as well as the executives, natural and social scientists, and engineers the number of favorable replies is large—55 percent or higher. However, those at the upper educational and occupational levels—except for the executives—yield somewhat fewer favorable replies than those at lower educational levels.

Comparative Favorable-Unfavorable Images

When the nonfederal populations' responses on both civil servants and business employees are analyzed for over-all tone, the comparative balance favors the business employee (Table 11-2). This is particularly true at the higher educational and occupational levels. The most extreme examples occur in the business groups, where 12 to 20 percent give favorable descriptions of the civil servant, compared to 37 to 58 percent for the business employee. None of the nonfederal populations shows a balance clearly on the side of the civil servant. There are a few cases, however, of roughly equal percentages—among the two lower educational groups and women in the general public, high school students, and high school and college teachers.

A comparison of the favorable descriptions reveals only part of the advantage accorded the business employees, especially by those groups whose percentages of favorable responses were roughly equal for the two types of employees. Looking at the unfavorable responses, we find that in each nonfederal group the percentages for civil servants are almost invariably higher than those for business employees. One fourth or more of the college graduates in the general employed public, the college seniors and graduate students, and all college teacher and business groups give responses about the civil servant that are clearly unfavorable in tone. But in no instance do unfavorable replies about business employees exceed 16 percent, and in all but one group the percentages are between 2 and 13. These two factors together—fewer favorable and more unfavorable descriptions for the civil servant vis-à-vis the business employee—document a generally less advantageous picture of the civil servant among virtually all the nonfederal populations, especially those at the higher educational and occupational levels.

On the part of the federal populations, the comparative favorable-unfavorable images as shown in Table 11-2 are quite another story. In every group the balance of favorable responses is on the side of the civil servant. Among the four special federal groups, for example, differences in favorable answers range from the social scientists' 56 percent (civil servant) vs. 41 percent (business employee) to the natural scientists' 59 and 34 percent. At the same time, all federal groups are less likely than their nonfederal counterparts to give unfavorable descriptions of civil servants, and about equally likely to describe business employees unfavorably. The net result is that federal employees accord a marked advantage to the civil servant in the over-all favorable-unfavorable tone of their replies.

Characteristics of the Images

In summarizing briefly the *content* of the answers (Tables 11-3a through 11-3i, pages 320 to 337) to our two open-end questions it is important to note that the images of the civil servant range widely from group to group. Thus it would be virtually impossible to give here a simple over-all picture of the characterizations; the picture seen by one group would not conform to pictures seen by others.

It is true, however, that for most groups certain characteristics of the image are of greater salience than others. The civil servant is described fairly often as a person of good personal character, who is capable of performing the work; he is also termed a good worker, and security conscious. And most groups only occasionally impute ambition and initiative to him or say that he desires material goods and a high salary. Beyond these generalizations, however, there is little consistency. For example, in the general employed public as a whole a lack of ambition and initiative is infrequently mentioned as an attribute, but the percentages of this ascription rise—sometimes dramatically—among the academic and business groups, as well as among the more highly educated in the general public. Many other response categories show similar variations according to formal schooling and occupational groupings.

Despite over-all basic similarities, the difference between the federal and the nonfederal employee responses concerning a number of traits is important to note. The federal populations are especially more likely than their counterparts outside government to describe the civil servant as a good worker, sincere and conscientious, having an agreeable personality, serving or wanting to serve others, and as being interested in and satisfied with his work. There are also specific differences between the views of the special federal groups and those of their counterparts in colleges and, particularly, in business.

The special groups in business take an extreme position. Of all the respondents, they are the most prone to characterize the civil servant as security conscious, lacking in ambition, a poor or mediocre worker, noncreative and dull, and liking, or adaptable to, routine work. And they register some of the *lowest* percentages on saying that he is personable, service oriented, and of good personal character.

When the traits attributed to the civil service employee and to the business employee are compared, striking differences are revealed on some points. For example, almost without fail all groups, nonfederal and federal, attribute security consciousness, lack of ambition, good personal character, and a service motive to the civil servant more often than to his business counterpart, whereas the business employee is more likely to be seen as desiring material goods and a high salary, and as being high on initiative and ambition. On a number of traits, however—such as good worker, capability, and above-average education and mental ability—most groups seem to perceive little difference between the two types of employees.

Discussion of Specific Attribution Data[2]

Nonfederal Populations

GENERAL EMPLOYED PUBLIC. The quality attributed most often to the civil servant by members of the general employed public is good personal character; over one fourth (28 percent) of these respondents describe the quality in various terms. From 12 to 16 percent mention capability for the work, being a good worker, having an agreeable personality, being security conscious, and being educated above the average level. Another 5 to

---

[2] For the most part, the characteristics attributed to each type of employee by the various groups will be discussed here in non-normative fashion. That is, we will not label a response category as being a favorable or an unfavorable comment about the employee. There are two reasons for this. First, there is enough variation among the groups interviewed concerning what is a "favorable" or "unfavorable" aspect of a person to warrant avoidance of such distinctions. Second, the specific context in which a given trait is attributed to a civil servant or a business employee may distort the apparent valence of the trait. What may be obviously commendatory in one context may be quite the reverse in another. This is the reason for our presentation earlier of the classificatory scheme which assessed the tone or valence of the *entire* response.

9 percent say that the civil servant is a sincere and conscientious worker, wants to serve others, lacks ambition and initiative, is a poor or mediocre worker, and is above average in mental ability. Less than 5 percent describe him as liking, or being adaptable to, routine work, noncreative and dull, finding satisfaction in his work, and having ambition and high initiative.

Some of these characteristics are offered about equally by people at all four levels of education. The lower levels, however, credit the civil servant with an agreeable personality and an above-average mental ability and educational background more frequently than the two higher levels do: on educational background, for example, the figures decrease from 18 percent at the high school not completed level to 12, 5, and 3 percent at the successively higher levels. The highly educated respondents are more likely than others to depict federal employees as security conscious, not very ambitious, liking or adaptable to routine work, poor or mediocre workers, and noncreative and dull: attributions of security consciousness rise from 5 percent at the lowest level to 13, 23, and 27 percent; those of liking, or being adaptable to, routine work climb from 0 to 9 percent.

Men and women in the general employed public are fairly similar in the characteristics they attribute. However, men (10 percent) are more inclined than women (3 percent) to describe the civil servant as lacking ambition and initiative.

The image of the business employee seen by people in the general employed public differs from their image of the civil servant in several important respects. The business employee is described moderately less often as having a good personal character (13 vs. 28 percent), being security conscious (2 vs. 13 percent), and lacking ambition (1 vs. 8 percent). There is also some very slight evidence that the business employee is less frequently thought of as a poor worker (1 vs. 5 percent); he is also more frequently credited with having ambition and high initiative (23 vs. 4 percent).

For the most part, such disparities become much more marked as the educational level rises. Among those who have not completed high school, security consciousness is attributed to civil service employees by 5 percent, to business employees by 1 percent, a net difference of 4 percent. Among college graduates the figures are 27 percent for the civil servant and 1 percent for the business employee, a net difference of 26 percent.

(Text continued on page 338)

Tables 11-3a Through 11-3i

This series of tables is designed to present in comparative fashion the major elements of the stereotypes of civil service employees and large business employees. Coding categories, procedures, and criteria were identical for the responses concerning civil service employees and the responses concerning large business employees. Therefore, the figures presented side by side are directly comparable.

Table 11-3a

Highlights: Good personal character.

. . . . The general picture is that all groups, except those in business, attribute good personal character to civil service employees two to four times more often than to business employees.

. . . . About one fourth of the general employed public, both men and women and at all educational levels, ascribe good personal character to civil service employees. This is also true of high school students and high school teachers; however, the figures for college seniors, graduate students, college teachers, and business groups are considerably lower, ranging from 6% to 14%.

. . . . Among general federal employees and federal executives, about a third attribute good personal character to civil service employees. The figures are about the same for both men and women, and at all four educational levels.

. . . . Federal natural and social scientists and engineers are somewhat less likely than most other federal employees to mention good personal character as an attribute of either federal employees or large business employees.

Table 11-3a

The image of the federal civil servant--a comparison with employees of large private business: characteristics attributed to federal civil service employees and to employees of large private business. Percentage distribution[a] of responses in each group to the question, "If you were to describe your general idea of (a United States civil service employee) (a person employed by a large private business or industry), what sort of a person would that be?"

	Number answering question		Good personal character (e.g., honest, ethical, loyal, high integrity, upright morally)	
	About civil service employees	About large business employees	Attributed to civil service employees	Attributed to large business employees
Nonfederal Populations				
General employed public	1142	1139	28%	13%
By sex				
Men	876	874	27	13
Women	266	265	30	12
By educational level				
High school not completed	331	331	30	16
High school completed	513	510	29	11
Some college	129	129	22	14
College graduate	139	139	24	9
Students				
High school students	358	357	22	10
College seniors	401	400	10	5
Graduate students	378	377	10	4
Groups in education				
High school teachers	278	278	25	9
Vocational counselors	77	79	25	6
College teachers	470	464	14	3
Natural scientists	120	118	12	1
Social scientists	106	103	8	1
Engineers	87	86	6	4
Groups in business				
Executives	281	283	9	7
Natural scientists	83	85	8	4
Social scientists	73	72	8	7
Engineers	88	89	6	1
Federal Employee Populations				
General federal employees	939	892	33	11
By sex				
Men	653	619	34	9
Women	286	273	32	17
By educational level				
High school not completed	189	180	36	10
High school completed	355	338	35	11
Some college	179	171	28	15
College graduate	161	151	31	8
Executives	272	260	33	12
Natural scientists	92	91	23	12
Social scientists	90	86	17	7
Engineers	98	84	18	5

a Percentage base = number of respondents answering in each group. Percentages do not add to 100 in each group due to multiple replies.

Table 11-3b

Highlights: Security conscious.

. . . . Security consciousness is attributed to civil service employees with moderate to very high frequency; it is attributed to large business employees scarcely at all.

. . . . In the general employed public, only about 13% mention security consciousness as a quality of civil service employees. Among women the percentage drops to 7. However, there is a very strong positive correlation of frequency of mention with level of education. The figures rise from 5% at the lowest level to 27% at the highest level.

. . . . The percentages of general federal employees who say civil servants are security conscious are not markedly different from the percentages of the general employed public who say so. This is true over all, and by sex and educational level.

. . . . Characterization of federal employees as being security conscious is quite low among high school students; among college seniors and graduate students, the figures are fairly high, being about one fourth and one third respectively.

. . . . About a fourth to a third of the respondents in the education groups mention security consciousness as characteristic of federal employees. For college engineers, however, the figure rises to 43%.

. . . . Groups in business are especially high in attributing security consciousness to federal employees.

. . . . Federal executives mention security consciousness as a characteristic of federal employees far less frequently than do their opposite numbers in business. The same is true for federal natural and social scientists and engineers, in comparison with their counterparts in colleges and especially in business.

Highlights: Capable of doing the work because of ability, training, background, qualifications.

. . . . In general, capability is attributed to civil service employees and large business employees about equally often by the respondents in all groups, with perhaps a very slight over-all advantage in favor of business employees. Exceptions to this general picture are college natural scientists, federal natural and social scientists, and college graduates among general federal employees, who give a slight edge to civil service employees.

Table 11-3b

The image of the federal civil servant--a comparison with employees of large
private business: characteristics attributed to federal civil service
employees and to employees of large private business (cont'd.)

	Security conscious (e.g., wants security, rates security high, places security above advancement)		Capable of doing the work because of ability, training, background, qualifications	
	Attributed to civil service employees	Attributed to large business employees	Attributed to civil service employees	Attributed to large business employees
Nonfederal Populations				
General employed public	13%	2%	16%	19%
By sex				
Men	15	2	15	19
Women	7	1	18	22
By educational level				
High school not completed	5	1	15	20
High school completed	13	2	16	18
Some college	23	2	15	17
College graduate	27	1	17	25
Students				
High school students	7	3	18	17
College seniors	24	6	13	12
Graduate students	31	7	9	10
Groups in education				
High school teachers	22	3	14	19
Vocational counselors	29	5	20	19
College teachers	32	5	17	13
Natural scientists	29	2	18	6
Social scientists	28	6	18	16
Engineers	43	5	13	11
Groups in business				
Executives	42	6	11	18
Natural scientists	42	8	6	11
Social scientists	47	6	11	11
Engineers	52	6	13	10
Federal Employee Populations				
General federal employees	16	3	11	15
By sex				
Men	18	3	10	15
Women	12	2	14	13
By educational level				
High school not completed	8	3	13	16
High school completed	15	3	8	13
Some college	23	2	10	19
College graduate	24	3	19	13
Executives	13	2	19	19
Natural scientists	17	3	17	11
Social scientists	22	2	27	14
Engineers	12	4	11	11

Table 11-3c

Highlights: Good worker.

. . . . A moderate number of respondents in the general employed public describe civil service employees and business employees as good workers, the figure being slightly higher for the latter. By sex there appear to be no differences. However, by education level, the figures show two opposing patterns: the figures for civil servants show a slight positive relation with educational level; those for business employees show a slight negative relationship.

. . . . Among students, being a good worker is attributed about equally often to civil service employees and to large business employees. In both instances, figures show a negative relationship with present educational level.

. . . . About one fourth of the high school teachers mention "good worker" in describing both types of employees. Among the college groups, however, the trait is ascribed more often to civil servants than to business employees. College engineers are an exception; for them the figures are about equal.

. . . . Among business executives, social scientists, and engineers, business employees are described as good workers more often than are civil servants, although the figures are not high in either case.

. . . . The percentage terming civil servants good workers is quite consistent for all groups of federal employees, and the figures are roughly twice as high as in the nonfederal populations.

. . . . In all the federal populations the percentages attributing "good worker" to civil servants are higher than the percentages attributing the quality to large business employees, ranging 26% to 42% in the former case and 13% to 28% in the latter.

. . . . Worth noting is that natural scientists, whether in government, business, or colleges, favor civil servants on this quality.

Highlights: Sincere and conscientious worker--tries to work well.

. . . . This quality is attributed hardly at all to business employees by any group, federal or nonfederal; it is attributed to civil service employees to a minor extent by the general employed public, students, and groups in business. There is a slight tendency for groups in education to see civil servants in this way, and a marked tendency for all federal populations to do so. Among general federal employees, the percentages are positively related to educational level, although not strongly.

Table 11-3c

The image of the federal civil servant--a comparison with employees of large
private business: characteristics attributed to federal civil service
employees and to employees of large private business (cont'd.)

	Good worker (e.g., works hard and willingly; efficient, dependable, steady)		Sincere and conscientious worker--tries to work well	
	Attributed to civil service employees	Attributed to large business employees	Attributed to civil service employees	Attributed to large business employees
Nonfederal Populations				
General employed public	15%	19%	5%	3%
By sex				
Men	15	19	4	3
Women	15	20	8	2
By educational level				
High school not completed	14	21	3	3
High school completed	14	20	5	3
Some college	16	14	8	2
College graduate	19	15	9	2
Students				
High school students	21	19	4	2
College seniors	16	17	7	3
Graduate students	10	14	4	1
Groups in education				
High school teachers	25	25	11	3
Vocational counselors	23	22	9	5
College teachers	15	9	10	2
Natural scientists	16	9	10	3
Social scientists	19	11	10	2
Engineers	14	16	6	6
Groups in business				
Executives	10	19	5	2
Natural scientists	19	11	10	4
Social scientists	11	18	7	1
Engineers	8	14	3	2
Federal Employee Populations				
General federal employees	30	22	15	6
By sex				
Men	29	22	14	4
Women	33	23	17	11
By educational level				
High school not completed	33	25	12	3
High school completed	30	22	15	7
Some college	30	24	15	7
College graduate	30	15	19	4
Executives	42	20	27	9
Natural scientists	39	11	24	4
Social scientists	36	28	30	5
Engineers	26	13	25	4

Table 11-3d

Table 11-3d

<u>Highlights</u>: Interested in, satisfied with, enjoys the work.

. . . . This category was tabled mainly to show that roughly 10% of all respondents in the federal employee populations assign this characteristic to civil service employees, in contrast to the nonfederal populations' very low figures for both types of employees and the federal populations' very low figures for business employees.

<u>Highlights</u>: Personality is agreeable.

. . . . Agreeable personality is mentioned with moderate frequency by all groups in the general employed public, by high school students, in contrast to college seniors and graduate students, and by high school teachers. All these groups attribute it about equally to both types of employees.

. . . . There is some indication that the tendency to attribute agreeable personality to civil service employees is negatively related to educational level in the general employed public.

. . . . One fourth of the general federal employees ascribe agreeable personality to civil servants; the figure rises to about one third in the case of federally employed women. There is a clear negative relationship between frequency of attributing agreeable personality to civil servants and educational level.

. . . . All groups of federal employees assign this quality more frequently to civil service employees than to business employees. These differences are especially marked at the two lowest educational levels.

. . . . The percentages of federal executives, natural and social scientists, and engineers who associate this quality with civil service employees are markedly lower than the percentages for general federal employees, and even slightly lower than the percentages among the general employed public.

Table 11-3d

The image of the federal civil servant--a comparison with employees of large
private business: characteristics attributed to federal civil service
employees and to employees of large private business (cont'd.)

	Interested in, satisfied with, enjoys the work		Personality is agreeable (e.g., friendly, nice, congenial, personable, neat)	
	Attributed to civil service employees	Attributed to large business employees	Attributed to civil service employees	Attributed to large business employees
Nonfederal Populations				
General employed public	3%	3%	15%	15%
By sex				
Men	3	3	15	15
Women	4	3	17	17
By educational level				
High school not completed	2	4	18	15
High school completed	4	3	15	18
Some college	3	2	12	11
College graduate	3	2	10	14
Students				
High school students	7	10	22	21
College seniors	6	7	9	12
Graduate students	4	5	6	5
Groups in education				
High school teachers	7	5	13	18
Vocational counselors	5	3	5	13
College teachers	6	4	10	9
Natural scientists	3	3	7	9
Social scientists	1	7	1	7
Engineers	5	5	3	6
Groups in business				
Executives	3	5	6	11
Natural scientists	4	2	5	4
Social scientists	7	6	1	7
Engineers	3	2	7	6
Federal Employee Populations				
General federal employees	10	5	25	15
By sex				
Men	9	5	22	13
Women	12	5	32	24
By educational level				
High school not completed	11	5	34	17
High school completed	10	4	24	16
Some college	10	6	16	17
College graduate	9	6	18	9
Executives	11	7	13	7
Natural scientists	12	4	12	8
Social scientists	12	2	7	4
Engineers	9	5	9	7

Table 11-3e

Highlights: Mental ability is above average.

. . . . The figures for both types of employees range from extremely low to moderately low, and in most instances are not significantly different for any of the groups, either federal or nonfederal. However, the 17% figure for high school students referring to civil service employees is worth noting.

Highlights: Educational level is above average.

. . . . The general employed public gives a slight advantage to civil service employees on this quality, but the frequency of such descriptions is negatively related to educational level.

Table 11-3e

The image of the federal civil servant--a comparison with employees of large
private business: characteristics attributed to federal civil service
employees and to employees of large private business (cont'd.)

	Mental ability is above average (e.g., intelligent, smart, high mentality)		Educational level is above average (e.g., well-educated; college experience)	
	Attributed to civil service employees	Attributed to large business employees	Attributed to civil service employees	Attributed to large business employees
Nonfederal Populations				
General employed public	9%	7%	12%	9%
By sex				
Men	9	7	11	9
Women	10	5	15	9
By educational level				
High school not completed	9	7	18	10
High school completed	11	6	12	8
Some college	7	12	5	12
College graduate	4	5	3	9
Students				
High school students	17	12	6	10
College seniors	10	10	3	7
Graduate students	6	7	2	4
Groups in education				
High school teachers	11	11	4	9
Vocational counselors	8	6	0	11
College teachers	10	8	5	7
Natural scientists	5	4	3	3
Social scientists	8	4	2	5
Engineers	2	7	0	0
Groups in business				
Executives	3	7	3	7
Natural scientists	5	6	2	4
Social scientists	6	7	4	7
Engineers	3	9	1	10
Federal Employee Populations				
General federal employees	8	5	4	7
By sex				
Men	8	5	4	5
Women	10	8	4	11
By educational level				
High school not completed	9	8	3	7
High school completed	6	6	3	9
Some college	10	6	3	7
College graduate	10	2	6	1
Executives	10	7	9	5
Natural scientists	3	2	2	2
Social scientists	9	6	12	5
Engineers	4	4	4	1

Table 11-3f

This table, taken as a whole, is particularly striking. It shows that ambition is frequently attributed to business employees by all populations, and that it is rarely attributed to civil service employees even by the federal employee populations. It also shows that lack of ambition is ascribed to civil servants with moderate to high frequency among all the better-educated groups, even those in the federal populations, and that none of these groups attribute this lack to business employees.

Highlights: Ambitious, high initiative.

. . . . Scarcely any respondents in any of the nonfederal populations mention ambition in connection with civil servants. In contrast, roughly 25% to 50% of these same people mention it in connection with business employees. The percentages are especially high for groups in business, but the 50% figure for college seniors is worth noting also.

. . . . The general employed public shows a positive relationship between educational level and frequency with which ambition is attributed to business employees. There is a suggestion that general federal workers show the same sort of positive relationship.

Highlights: Not very ambitious, low initiative.

. . . . The percentage of the general public that attributes lack of ambition to civil servants is fairly low (8%), but the breakdowns by sex and education show that the low figures are more typical of women than men, and that there is a very strong positive relationship with educational level. Only 1% at the lowest level attribute lack of ambition to civil service employees, but the figures rise to 6%, 19%, and 26% at the three successively higher levels. A similar positive relationship with present educational level is shown in the student groups.

. . . . The figures for the groups in business are especially high. From over one third to almost one half of them attribute lack of ambition to civil servants.

. . . . The over-all percentage of general federal employees who characterize civil service employees as lacking ambition is low, but it is worth noting that the figures rise to 12% and 8% at the some college and college graduate levels.

. . . . As high a percentage of federal executives assign lack of ambition to civil servants as attribute ambition to them (Column 1). Higher percentages of federal natural and social scientists and engineers attribute lack of ambition to civil servants than ascribe ambition to them (Columns 1 and 3).

Table 11-3f

The image of the federal civil servant--a comparison with employees of large private business: characteristics attributed to federal civil service employees and to employees of large private business (cont'd.)

	Ambitious, high initiative (e.g., aggressive, competitive, lots of drive; wants to advance, succeed)		Not very ambitious, low initiative (e.g., not very aggressive, competitive, little drive or effort to get ahead, succeed)	
	Attributed to civil service employees	Attributed to large business employees	Attributed to civil service employees	Attributed to large business employees
Nonfederal Populations				
General employed public	4%	23%	8%	1%
By sex				
Men	4	24	10	1
Women	4	18	3	1
By educational level				
High school not completed	4	14	1	0
High school completed	4	23	6	1
Some college	4	38	19	2
College graduate	6	32	26	2
Students				
High school students	5	30	5	3
College seniors	5	50	16	2
Graduate students	5	38	19	2
Groups in education				
High school teachers	5	37	10	0
Vocational counselors	5	43	17	0
College teachers	4	34	16	1
Natural scientists	4	35	16	1
Social scientists	5	40	14	0
Engineers	0	31	21	2
Groups in business				
Executives	3	52	38	2
Natural scientists	2	54	45	1
Social scientists	3	50	43	3
Engineers	1	47	40	2
Federal Employee Populations				
General federal employees	7	23	7	1
By sex				
Men	7	22	7	2
Women	9	25	5	0
By educational level				
High school not completed	6	13	2	1
High school completed	7	24	7	1
Some college	7	28	12	1
College graduate	8	28	8	2
Executives	11	27	11	2
Natural scientists	3	32	10	1
Social scientists	10	40	19	2
Engineers	3	25	12	1

331

Table 11-3g

: Serves or wants to serve others.

. . . . There is scarcely any tendency in any group, federal or non-federal, to attribute a service motive to business employees. On the other hand, moderate percentages of a number of nonfederal populations attribute the motive to civil servants, and the percentages among federal employees who do so range from moderate to fairly high.

. . . . About 10% of high school students and college seniors describe civil service employees in this way; the figures are slightly higher for high school teachers and vocational counselors.

. . . . Social scientists, both in business and in colleges, give civil service employees somewhat higher percentages than most nonfederal populations do.

. . . . The percentages of general federal employees (over-all, by sex, and by educational level) attributing a service motive to civil servants are almost three times as high as the comparable figures for the general employed public.

. . . . From one fifth to one fourth of federal executives, natural and social scientists, and engineers characterize civil service employees as being service oriented.

Highlights: Desires material goods, high salary; money is important.

. . . . Materialistic motives simply are not attributed to civil service employees by the respondents in any group, federal or nonfederal. However, they are attributed to business employees by moderate to moderately high percentages of students, groups in education, and groups in business, as well as by federal executives, natural and social scientists, and engineers.

. . . . Of the student groups, college seniors are especially inclined to attribute materialism to large business employees.

Table 11-3g

The image of the federal civil servant--a comparison with employees of large private business: characteristics attributed to federal civil service employees and to employees of large private business (cont'd.)

	Serves or wants to serve others (e.g., help, benefit others; dedicated to, interested in, serving others)		Desires material goods, high salary; money is important	
	Attributed to civil service employees	Attributed to large business employees	Attributed to civil service employees	Attributed to large business employees
Nonfederal Populations				
General employed public	5%	2%	1%	4%
By sex				
Men	4	2	1	5
Women	7	2	1	3
By educational level				
High school not completed	2	1	1	2
High school completed	6	2	1	4
Some college	7	2	0	8
College graduate	4	3	1	7
Students				
High school students	10	1	1	8
College seniors	9	3	2	17
Graduate students	5	2	2	19
Groups in education				
High school teachers	13	2	1	9
Vocational counselors	12	1	1	13
College teachers	9	3	2	12
Natural scientists	9	0	1	14
Social scientists	15	0	3	18
Engineers	6	2	1	12
Groups in business				
Executives	6	1	1	10
Natural scientists	7	0	2	22
Social scientists	11	1	0	17
Engineers	1	2	2	12
Federal Employee Populations				
General federal employees	14	1	1	8
By sex				
Men	13	1	1	10
Women	17	2	1	4
By educational level				
High school not completed	12	2	1	8
High school completed	14	2	1	8
Some college	16	1	2	8
College graduate	15	1	0	9
Executives	26	4	2	13
Natural scientists	20	1	2	21
Social scientists	24	0	3	20
Engineers	20	2	1	14

333

Table 11-3h

<u>Highlights</u>: Likes, or is adaptable to, routine work.

. . . . A liking for or adaptability to routine work is rarely attributed to civil service employees by the general employed public or by
any of the federal employee populations. However, there is such a tendency on the part of the more highly educated of the nonfederal populations. This shows up in the figures ranging from 8% to 18% for college
graduates in the general employed public, college seniors and graduate
students, groups in education, and groups in business. There is little
tendency for these same groups to attribute the quality to business
employees.

<u>Highlights</u>: Noncreative, dull, unimaginative.

. . . . Although the percentages of respondents who describe civil
service employees as dull and lacking imagination are not high in any
group, the fact that it is attributed to them in some degree and not
at all to business employees, is worth noting. College teachers, groups
in business, and social scientists seem slightly more inclined than
others to assign this characteristic to civil servants.

Table 11-3h

The image of the federal civil servant—a comparison with employees of large
private business: characteristics attributed to federal civil service
employees and to employees of large private business (cont'd.)

	Likes, or is adaptable to, routine work		Non-creative, dull, unimaginative	
	Attributed to civil service employees	Attributed to large business employees	Attributed to civil service employees	Attributed to large business employees
Nonfederal Populations				
General employed public	2%	1%	2%	0%
By sex				
Men	2	1	2	0
Women	1	1	2	0
By educational level				
High school not completed	0	1	0	0
High school completed	1	1	1	0
Some college	2	0	5	0
College graduate	9	1	6	0
Students				
High school students	3	1	1	0
College seniors	10	3	7	2
Graduate students	11	2	8	1
Groups in education				
High school teachers	10	2	5	0
Vocational counselors	8	1	7	0
College teachers	13	5	11	2
Natural scientists	8	3	5	2
Social scientists	16	3	11	3
Engineers	10	6	7	1
Groups in business				
Executives	12	0	9	0
Natural scientists	11	1	6	2
Social scientists	18	1	12	0
Engineers	11	2	10	1
Federal Employee Populations				
General federal employees	2	0	1	0
By sex				
Men	2	0	1	0
Women	2	0	0	0
By educational level				
High school not completed	1	0	1	0
High school completed	1	0	1	0
Some college	2	0	1	0
College graduate	3	1	1	1
Executives	2	0	4	0
Natural scientists	3	2	7	0
Social scientists	4	2	10	1
Engineers	3	0	2	2

Table 11-3i

Highlights: Poor or mediocre worker.

. . . . Scarcely any respondents in any group, federal or nonfederal, describe private business employees as being poor or mediocre workers. On the other hand, while such attributions to civil service employees are not excessive, the percentages are high enough to indicate a significant contrast.

. . . . The higher the educational level in the general employed public, the more this characteristic is attributed to civil service employees. The relationship with educational level is also shown among students; figures are 1% for high school students, 12% for college seniors and graduate students.

. . . . With the exception of natural scientists, respondents in the business groups are especially likely to describe civil service employees as poor or mediocre workers.

Highlights: Respondent does not generalize.

. . . . This category reveals the frequency with which respondents in the various groups refuse to stereotype civil service employees on the one hand and large business employees on the other. In general it shows that almost all of the groups, nonfederal and federal, are characteristically more willing to generalize about the civil servant than about the business employee. However

. . . . Refusal to generalize about civil service employees is fairly frequent among college seniors, graduate students and vocational counselors. Refusal is even higher among all the college teacher groups. However, in all these groups there are equal and generally higher percentages of refusals to generalize about business employees.

. . . . Among federally employed college graduates, executives, and natural and social scientists, the percentages refusing to generalize about civil service employees, while moderate, are somewhat lower than the percentages refusing to generalize about large business employees. For federal engineers the figures are about equal.

Table 11-3i

The image of the federal civil servant--a comparison with employees of large private business: characteristics attributed to federal civil service employees and to employees of large private business (cont'd.)

	Poor or mediocre worker (e.g., lazy, putting in time, undependable)		Respondent does not generalize about civil service employees (refuses to generalize; rejects idea that all are the same)	
	Attributed to civil service employees	Attributed to large business employees	In describing civil service employees	In describing large business employees
Nonfederal Populations				
General employed public	5%	1%	4%	11%
By sex				
Men	5	1	5	12
Women	4	1	2	10
By educational level				
High school not completed	2	1	2	8
High school completed	5	1	5	11
Some college	6	2	3	12
College graduate	12	0	6	20
Students				
High school students	1	0	3	7
College seniors	12	2	11	10
Graduate students	12	1	16	20
Groups in education				
High school teachers	6	1	7	17
Vocational counselors	4	1	13	22
College teachers	7	1	18	24
Natural scientists	4	2	22	28
Social scientists	4	3	22	22
Engineers	10	1	17	24
Groups in business				
Executives	18	0	5	15
Natural scientists	8	1	11	15
Social scientists	15	1	10	24
Engineers	21	0	8	26
Federal Employee Populations				
General federal employees	3	1	7	11
By sex				
Men	4	1	6	11
Women	3	1	9	11
By educational level				
High school not completed	3	1	6	9
High school completed	3	0	6	9
Some college	6	1	9	8
College graduate	1	1	9	22
Executives	4	3	10	18
Natural scientists	7	4	19	23
Social scientists	6	1	17	24
Engineers	8	1	18	16

Similarly, among those with the least education, 4 per cent attribute ambition and initiative to the civil servant, and 14 percent to the business employee, a difference of 10 percent; the comparable figures among college graduates are 6 and 32 percent, a difference of 24 percent.

A number of other response categories which the general public applies with little difference in frequency to either type of employee do show differences according to educational level. This is especially true for attributes that, over all, are mentioned rarely. Thus, the category of poor or mediocre worker is applied to the civil servant by 2 percent of those not completing high school and to the business employee by 1 percent; 12 percent of the college graduates apply it to the civil servant, and none to the business employee. And, while no one with the lowest education calls either type of employee noncreative and dull, 6 percent of the college graduates apply the term to the civil servant alone.

HIGH SCHOOL STUDENTS, COLLEGE SENIORS, AND GRADUATE STUDENTS. The link between respondents' educational status and their image of the federal civil servant is also found among the student groups. For example, college seniors and graduate students are less likely than high school students to credit the civil servant with an agreeable personality and above-average mental ability and education. They are also less inclined (10 percent of both groups) than high school students (22 percent) to mention good personal character and (10 and 16 percent vs. 21 percent for high school students) being a good worker. The percentages citing lack of ambition, security consciousness, being a poor or mediocre worker, liking for routine, and being noncreative and dull all tend to increase successively as we move from high school students to college seniors, and from them to graduate students.

In some cases the differences by education are more striking among the student populations than in the general employed public. Concerning the civil servant's capability for doing the work, for instance, the figures are 18 percent for high school students and 13 and 9 percent for college seniors and graduate students—a slightly negative relationship that contrasts with the lack of relationship with educational level in the general public on this factor.

When students' descriptions of civil servants and business employees are compared, the differences by educational level are minor on capability, good personal character, agreeable personality, being a good worker, being interested in and enjoying the work, and having above-average mental ability and education. For other response categories, the patterning by educational status resembles the general employed public's. Thus, the higher the students' educational level, the more the percentages give the edge to the civil servant over the business employee on security consciousness, liking for routine, lack of ambition, dullness and lack of creativity, and being a poor or mediocre worker.

HIGH SCHOOL TEACHERS AND VOCATIONAL COUNSELORS. In general, these two populations resemble the more highly educated members of the general employed public in the traits they ascribe to the federal employee. Certain exceptions are worth noting, however. The teachers and the counselors are slightly more inclined to credit the civil servant with above-average mental ability and with a desire to serve others. They also say somewhat less often that he is a poor or mediocre worker, or lacks ambition and initiative.

Their comparative judgments of the civil servant vis-à-vis the business employee are about the same as those of the college graduates in the general work force, but there is one significant variation on this theme. Whereas the college graduates attribute nearly equal service motives to the two types of employees (4 and 3 percent), 13 percent of the teachers and 12 percent of the vocational counselors see the civil servant as wanting to serve others, but only 1 and 2 percent see the business employee in this role.

COLLEGE TEACHERS, NATURAL AND SOCIAL SCIENTISTS, AND ENGINEERS. Although the college populations also show the pattern that in general prevails among other highly educated respondents, there are some interesting deviations from it. All of the college groups are less prone than the two high school groups and the respondents at all four educational levels in the general public to attribute good personal character to the civil servant. The figures are 14 percent for general college teachers as a whole (with lower percentages for the three special groups), 25 percent for the high school groups, and an average of 28 percent for the general employed public. The college teacher pattern is also different in its slightly less frequent mention of the civil servant's lack of ambition and initiative.

Certain of the groups, in comparison to other high-level groups, stand out for especially high or low mentions of particular characteristics. For example, when 43 percent of the college engineers describe the civil servant as security conscious and 3 percent of them cite his agreeable personality, the first figure is comparatively high and the second comparatively low. The social scientists' 1 percent on agreeable personality is also relatively low. Of particular interest is the definite inclination of the college teacher group to describe the business employee as desiring material goods and high salary: the figures range from 12 to 18 percent, in contrast to the range of 1 to 3 percent who attribute the same motive to the civil servant.

GROUPS IN BUSINESS. Business executives, natural and social scientists, and engineers, as the tables show, voice the most negative general impression of the federal civil servant. They ascribe good personal character, capability, sincerity and conscientiousness, and being a good worker to him slightly to moderately less often than other high-level groups. They are also noticeably more likely to assert that he is security conscious, a poor or mediocre worker, and adaptable to routine work. Especially outstanding is their inclination to say that he is low on ambition and initiative: the figures are 45 percent for the natural scientists and 43, 40, and 38 percent for the social scientists, engineers, and executives.

The comparative figures for a number of categories also reflect a more extreme view of the civil servant than is found among other high-level groups. Only 1 to 3 percent of the business groups, for example, cite ambition as a trait of the civil servant, whereas from 47 to 54 percent ascribe it to the business employee; the average difference is thus around 50 percent. The picture is similar for the category of low ambition and lack of initiative: about 40 percent mention this for the civil servant, and less than 4 percent for the business employee. While such disparities in the other populations are all heavily in this same direction, they are generally less extreme.

Federal Employee Populations

GENERAL FEDERAL EMPLOYEES. The descriptions of the civil servant given by the general federal employees are remarkably similar in a number of respects to those given by the general employed public. Differences are minor for such often-cited categories as good personal character—given first rank by the federal workers, just as it was by the general employed public—security consciousness, capability, presence of ambition and initiative, and lack of ambition and initiative. Differences are also minor for the more rarely mentioned categories of adaptability to, and a liking for, routine work, being noncreative and dull, and being a poor or mediocre worker. There are, however, demonstrable differences between the groups on several other characteristics.

The federal workers are considerably more likely to describe the civil servant as being a good worker (30 percent vs. the general public's 15 percent), a sincere and conscientious worker (15 vs. 5 percent), serving or wanting to serve others (14 vs. 5 percent), and as having an agreeable personality (25 vs. 15 percent). Thus, the meaningful differences between the two general populations usually show the federal employees more frequently investing the civil servant with "favorable" qualities; nevertheless, 12 percent of the general public, and only 4 percent of the general federal workers, say the civil servant has an above-average education.

Several items mentioned by general federal employees show a slight positive relation to educational level—among them security consciousness (8, 15, 23, and 24 percent, moving up the four levels), and lack of ambition (2, 7, 12, 8 percent). (In the general public these increases by educational level are also seen.) Educational level is negatively related to ascriptions of an agreeable personality, with percentages declining from 34 percent for those not completing high school to 18 percent for college graduates. (A similar decline is seen in the nonfederal group.) For virtually all the other response categories, the differences according to education are minor.

Similarities between the two general populations are revealed again when their descriptions of the civil servant and the business employee are compared. Both groups depict the civil servant, more often than the business employee, as having good personal character, being security conscious, lacking ambition, and (though the percentages are small) as being a poor or mediocre worker; both also say less often that the civil servant has ambition and desires material rewards. Finally, there is considerable intergroup agreement that the two types of employees are about equal in being capable of doing the work, having above-average mental ability and education, and (two infrequently mentioned categories) liking routine work, and being noncreative and dull. The comparative similarities are the more striking because the absolute figures of the federal group and of the nonfederal group are also in a number of cases very close to each other.

In at least four instances, however, the comparative perceptions of the two general populations diverge. Whereas the nonfederal group cites being a good worker about equally for the civil servant and the business employee (15 vs. 19 percent), the federal employees give the civil servant a slight edge (30 vs. 22 percent). And 15 percent of the respondents in the general public attribute agreeable personality to both types of employees, while the federal employees' figures for this are 25 percent (civil servant) and 15 percent (business employee). The general public gives the civil servant only a minute advantage for being a sincere and conscientious worker and for wanting to serve others, but the federal workers—with much higher absolute percentages for the civil servant—leave little doubt that they see the civil servant surpassing the business employee in these qualities.

In each instance of marked discrepancy between the figures of the two populations the pattern is plain. The discrepancy stems from the higher percentages of the federal group that accord "favorable" or "positive" characteristics to the civil servant rather than to the large business employee.

FEDERAL EXECUTIVES, NATURAL AND SOCIAL SCIENTISTS, AND ENGINEERS. The special federal groups' image of the civil servant is of special interest. The specific qualities which they assign to him diverge in many instances from the attribution patterns of general federal employees as a whole, but frequently resemble the patterns of those with some college experience and the college graduates.

The executives, natural and social scientists, and engineers (with occasional exceptions) are somewhat more likely than the general federal group to describe the civil servant as a sincere and conscientious worker, capable of doing the work, wanting to serve others, and lacking ambition and initiative. The service motive, for example, is cited by 20 to 26 percent of them, lack of ambition by 10 to 19 percent; the general employee figures are 14 and 7 percent on the two factors, respectively. There is also a hint that the special groups more often picture the civil servant as non-creative and dull, and a poor or mediocre worker. On the other hand, they attribute an agreeable personality to him much less often—13 percent or less vs. the general federal employees' 25 percent. Worth noting are the executives' particularly frequent references to good personal character (33 percent), and the engineers' especially low references to good workers (26 percent).

Compared with the college and business executives, natural and social scientists, and engineers, the special federal groups assert somewhat more often that the civil servant has good personal character, serves or wants to serve others, is a good and dependable worker, and a sincere and conscientious employee. On the sincerity category, for example, the range for the groups in colleges and business is 3 to 10 percent; for the federal groups it is 24 to 30 percent. In addition, except for the engineers, the federal groups are more likely than business groups to describe civil servants as capable.

A number of other attributes are mentioned by the special federal groups less often than by their counterparts; these include security orientation and liking for or adaptability to routine work. Further contrasts are provided when the business groups only are compared with the federal groups; the latter are much less likely to term the civil servant unambitious and lacking initiative, and (here omitting the business natural scientists) a poor, mediocre worker.

12

Image of the Federal Employee:
Ratings on Five Characteristics

To explore the perceived image of workers in the federal service further, ratings on specific personal characteristics were obtained by using one of the scale-sort procedures described in Chapter 2. Respondents were asked to consider how they would rate general civil service employees, top-level civil servants, and top-level private businessmen on five qualities: honesty, ability, drive to get ahead, interest in serving the public, and the degree of respect they inspired. Fifteen scale-sort item cards (five for each group being rated) were given to each respondent to place on one of the intervals of the ten-step scale, the top of which was labeled "extremely high," the bottom "extremely low."[1] (See Appendix B, Item 34 of the questionnaire for the nonfederal employed populations.)

Tables 12-1a through 12-1e present the mean ratings given to the items by each of the groups interviewed. Again, as in Chapter 11, the tables themselves and their highlights need to be read if one is to comprehend the range and variety of the data elicited by the scale-sort items.

Discussion of the Ratings

Honesty

All of the nonfederal populations rate top-level civil servants and general federal employees high on honesty, both absolutely and in comparison with people in top-level jobs in private business. Further, all of these

[1] In the questionnaire procedure, a total of thirty scale-sort items were used to rate six groups, three of which are not discussed here: top-level federal appointees, members of the Senate, and members of the House of Representatives. The complete findings on these three groups will be presented in a later book, *The Image of Politics and Politicians.*

groups, except for the business engineers, rank the top-level civil servant higher than the top-level businessman; by the majority of them, the general employee is ranked second highest, although by some respondents at the upper educational and occupational levels he is rated about equal to, or with only a slight advantage over, the businessman, and by all of the business groups he is given third ranking. But respondents at all educational levels and in all groups other than business executives and engineers rate the civil servant who has reached a top job approximately 0.5 to 1.0 scale points higher than his business counterpart.

The business executives, natural and social scientists, and engineers rate top-level businessmen much higher on honesty than does any other group, giving them scores more nearly equal to those of the top civil servants. This tendency is most marked among the business executives (only 0.1 advantage to the federal employee) and engineers (0.1 advantage to the businessman); the natural and social scientists give advantages of 0.4 and 0.5 to the top-level civil servant.

All federal employee groups give honesty ratings to both categories of civil servants that are substantially higher than those given by the nonfederal populations, the increases for both categories being roughly 0.5 to 1.0 scale points. At the same time, the ratings given to top-level businessmen are much the same as those given by the nonfederal populations —with the exception of the business groups themselves. Consequently, without exception, the federal populations put businessmen in third place. General federal employees are given somewhat higher ratings, and top-level civil servants the highest of all. The difference ratings for the two top-level groups are markedly in favor of the top civil servant—by scale points ranging from about 1 to as much as 2.

Interest in Serving the Public

When the nonfederal populations consider the public interest category, both types of federal employees again fare very well, though not quite as well as in the honesty ratings. By every group, however, top-level civil servants are rated highest, and the scale point advantage accorded them over the top-level businessmen by all groups—except the business populations—ranges from 0.5 to 2. Among the business groups, the executives and engineers give the top civil servant a very slight advantage—about 0.1 scale point—the natural and social scientists considerably more.

(Text continued on page 356)

During the course of the interview, each respondent was asked to sort 30 cards on a ten-point, high-low scale. In this way, scale ratings were obtained on five different personal characteristics of general civil service employees, top-level civil servants, and top-level businessmen. (Ratings were also obtained for members of the U.S. Senate, members of the House of Representatives, and top-level federal appointees, which will be presented in a later book.) The personal attributes on which each of these kinds of people were rated were honesty, ability, drive to get ahead, interest in serving the public, and how well respected they are. This series of tables presents the mean results on each of the five attributes.

Table 12-1a

Highlights: Scale ratings on honesty.

. . . . In general, all groups rate all three classes of employees rather high on honesty.

. . . . For the most part, both federal and nonfederal populations give the highest ratings to people in top-level jobs in the federal civil service, then to general civil service employees, and then to people in top-level jobs in private business. The exception to this pattern is found in ratings given by groups in business. They rate top-level civil servants at the top, give top-level businessmen slightly lower or equal ratings, and put general civil service employees in third place.

. . . . College seniors and graduate students assign lower than average ratings both to general civil service employees and to top-level businessmen.

. . . . The federal populations give considerably higher ratings to both types of civil service employees than do the nonfederal populations.

Table 12-1a

The image of the federal civil servant: "honesty" ratings given
to federal civil service employees in general and in top-level
jobs and to people in top-level jobs in private business. Average
(mean) ratings on the 10-point high-low scale; the higher the
score, the higher the rating on honesty.

		"On the average, how would you rate _____ on honesty?"		
	Average number answering	Federal civil service employees in general	People in the top-level jobs in the federal civil service	People in the top-level jobs in private business
Nonfederal Populations				
General employed public	1093	7.6	7.8	7.2
By sex				
Men	840	7.6	7.9	7.3
Women	253	7.7	7 7	7.1
By educational level				
High school not completed	308	7.7	7.7	7.2
High school completed	495	7.6	7.9	7.2
Some college	124	7.5	7.8	7.4
College graduate	137	7.4	7.9	7.4
Students				
High school students	356	7.7	8.1	7.1
College seniors	401	7.1	7.8	6.8
Graduate students	379	7.1	7.8	6.8
Groups in education				
High school teachers	277	7.5	8.0	7.4
Vocational counselors	78	7.4	8.0	7.6
College teachers	464	7.5	7.9	7.0
Natural scientists	118	7.7	8.0	7.2
Social scientists	103	7.5	8 0	7.1
Engineers	87	7.4	7.8	7.2
Groups in business				
Executives	273	7.7	8.2	8.1
Natural scientists	84	7.5	8.2	7.8
Social scientists	70	7.5	8.5	8.0
Engineers	88	7.6	8.3	8.4
Federal Employee Populations				
General federal employees	934	8.3	8.4	7.5
By sex				
Men	651	8.4	8.5	7.6
Women	284	8.0	8.2	7.3
By educational level				
High school not completed	184	8.3	8.5	7.6
High school completed	354	8.5	8.5	7.6
Some college	180	8.0	8.2	7.5
College graduate	162	8.3	8.6	7.3
Executives	271	8.7	9.1	7.7
Natural scientists	92	7.8	8.7	6.6
Social scientists	90	8.3	8.7	7.3
Engineers	98	7.9	8.7	7.2

347

Table 12-1b

Highlights: Scale ratings on interest in serving the public.

. . . . People in the top-level jobs in the federal civil service are rated above general civil service employees and top-level businessmen on this characteristic. The picture with respect to the latter two classes of employees is not so clear, however; the groups vary considerably on which of the two they rate higher.

. . . . In the general employed public, ratings of general civil service employees are negatively related to educational level. This negative relationship with educational level is not apparent in the ratings of the other two classes of employees. The result is that by respondents with some college and especially by the college graduates, general civil service employees are rated below people in the top-level jobs in private business.

. . . . The ratings given by college seniors and graduate students to general civil service employees are remarkably lower than those given by high school students. To a lesser extent this pattern appears also in the students' ratings of people in the top-level jobs in the federal service and in private business.

. . . . Federal employee populations tend to assign somewhat higher ratings to both classes of federal employees than do nonfederal groups.

. . . . Among general federal employees, ratings of general civil service employees and of top-level businessmen show a negative relationship with educational level. This is not apparent in their ratings of top-level civil servants.

. . . . Federal executives give general civil service employees and people in the top-level civil service jobs higher ratings than any other group, federal or nonfederal, gives, with one exception--the equal or higher ratings given to general civil servants by the two lower educational levels of the general federal employee group. Ratings given to people in the top-level business jobs by federal natural and social scientists and engineers are low in comparison with the ratings given by their colleagues in business.

Table 12-1b

The image of the federal civil servant: "interest in serving the public" ratings given to federal civil service employees in general and in top-level jobs, and to people in top-level jobs in private business. Average (mean) ratings on the 10-point high-low scale; the higher the score, the higher the rating on interest in serving the public.

	"On the average, how would you rate _____ on their interest in serving the public?"		
	Federal civil service employees in general	People in the top-level jobs in the federal civil service	People in the top-level jobs in private business
Nonfederal Populations			
General employed public	6.8	7.3	6.9
By sex			
Men	6.7	7.3	6.9
Women	7.1	7.4	6.9
By educational level			
High school not completed	7.1	7.3	7.0
High school completed	6.9	7.3	6.9
Some college	6.3	7.2	6.6
College graduate	5.9	7.2	6.8
Students			
High school students	7.1	7.6	6.3
College seniors	5.9	7.2	5.7
Graduate students	5.7	7.2	5.7
Groups in education			
High school teachers	6.4	7.4	6.4
Vocational counselors	6.2	7.3	6.2
College teachers	6.2	7.4	6.0
Natural scientists	6.2	7.6	5.8
Social scientists	6.1	7.7	5.8
Engineers	6.0	7.5	6.3
Groups in business			
Executives	5.9	7.2	7.1
Natural scientists	6.1	7.6	6.3
Social scientists	5.5	7.4	6.6
Engineers	5.4	7.1	7.0
Federal Employee Populations			
General federal employees	7.5	8.0	7.2
By sex			
Men	7.6	8.1	7.2
Women	7.3	7.6	7.4
By educational level			
High school not completed	7.9	8.1	7.8
High school completed	7.7	8.0	7.3
Some college	7.1	7.8	7.0
College graduate	7.3	8.0	6.8
Executives	7.7	8.7	6.7
Natural scientists	6.6	7.9	5.3
Social scientists	7.2	8.2	5.6
Engineers	7.2	8.1	6.1

349

Table 12-1c

Highlights: Scale ratings on how well respected they are.

. . . . In the nonfederal populations, the pattern is clearly one of
general civil service employees at the bottom, people in the top-level
civil service jobs in the middle, and people in the top-level business
jobs at the top. Differences in ratings are especially great for college seniors and graduate students, the college teacher groups, and the
business groups.

. . . . Ratings of general civil service employees are negatively
associated with educational level in the general employed public. To
a lesser extent this is true of ratings of top-level civil servants.
Ratings of the top-level businessmen, on the other hand, are positively
related to educational level. This same pattern of negative and positive relationships appears among students and, to some extent, among
general federal employees.

. . . . General federal employees give their lowest ratings to general
civil service employees, while giving people in the top-level jobs in
civil service and in business about equal ratings. However, in the
latter two instances, the negative and positive relationships with
educational level result in lower ratings being given to top-level
civil servants than to top-level businessmen by those at the two higher
levels.

. . . . Federal executives, natural and social scientists, and engineers accord lower respect ratings to top-level civil servants than to
top-level businessmen. Also, their ratings of general civil service
employees are lower than the average ratings given by all federal
employees.

Table 12-1c

The image of the federal civil servant: "how well respected they are"
ratings given to federal civil service employees in general and in top-
level jobs, and to people in top-level jobs in private business. Average
(mean) ratings on the 10-point high-low scale; the higher the score, the
higher the rating on how well respected they are.

	"On the average, how would you rate _____ on how well respected they are?"		
	Federal civil service employees in general	People in the top-level jobs in the federal civil service	People in the top-level jobs in private business
Nonfederal Populations			
General employed public	7.0	7.6	7.8
By sex			
Men	7.0	7.6	7.8
Women	7.3	7.7	7.7
By educational level			
High school not completed	7.4	7.7	7.6
High school completed	7.1	7.6	7.8
Some college	6.6	7.5	7.9
College graduate	6.2	7.3	8.2
Students			
High school students	7.0	7.5	7.6
College seniors	5.8	7.4	8.0
Graduate students	5.5	7.4	8.3
Groups in education			
High school teachers	6.6	7.6	8.0
Vocational counselors	6.3	7.5	8.0
College teachers	6.0	7.5	8.2
Natural scientists	6.0	7.7	8.1
Social scientists	5.7	7.3	8.2
Engineers	5.9	7.5	8.1
Groups in business			
Executives	6.0	7.5	8.6
Natural scientists	5.9	7.8	8.2
Social scientists	5.5	7.6	8.5
Engineers	5.6	7.6	8.6
Federal Employee Populations			
General federal employees	7.2	8.0	8.1
By sex			
Men	7.2	8.0	8.1
Women	7.2	7.9	8.0
By educational level			
High school not completed	7.6	8.2	7.8
High school completed	7.4	8.1	8.1
Some college	6.7	7.8	8.3
College graduate	6.6	7.8	8.2
Executives	6.7	8.1	8.5
Natural scientists	5.6	7.6	7.8
Social scientists	5.8	7.7	8.5
Engineers	6.1	7.9	8.3

Table 12-1d

<u>Highlights</u>: Scale ratings on ability.

. . . . Over all, general civil service employees are rated lowest on ability, followed by people in the top-level jobs in the civil service; people in the top-level business jobs are given the highest ratings of all. This holds true in the ratings given by the federal employee populations, although the differences between the three ratings are not so great as the differences seen in the nonfederal ratings.

. . . . Ratings of both general civil service employees and federal employees holding top-level jobs are negatively related to educational level in the general employed public. The opposite is true for the ratings of people in top-level jobs in private business. This same pattern holds in the student populations.

. . . . All federal populations rate both general civil service employees and top-level civil servants higher than any of the nonfederal populations do.

. . . . The particularly low ratings given to general civil service employees by college seniors, graduate students, groups in education, and especially by groups in business are of special interest.

Table 12-1d

The image of the federal civil servant: "ability" ratings given to federal civil service employees in general and in top-level jobs, and to people in top-level jobs in private business. Average (mean) ratings on the 10-point high-low scale; the higher the score, the higher the rating on ability.

	Federal civil service employees in general	"On the average, how would you rate _____ on ability?"	
		People in the top-level jobs in the federal civil service	People in the top-level jobs in private business
Nonfederal Populations			
General employed public	6.9	7.7	8.1
By sex			
Men	6.8	7.6	8.1
Women	7.3	7.9	7.9
By educational level			
High school not completed	7.3	7.8	7.8
High school completed	7.1	7.7	8.0
Some college	6.4	7.5	8.1
College graduate	6.0	7 5	8.6
Students			
High school students	7.2	8.0	8.1
College seniors	6.1	7.9	8.4
Graduate students	5.9	7.7	8.6
Groups in education			
High school teachers	6.5	7.9	8.5
Vocational counselors	6.2	7.7	8.6
College teachers	6.2	7.9	8.3
Natural scientists	6.2	7.9	8.4
Social scientists	6.1	8.0	8.3
Engineers	5.8	7.9	8.6
Groups in business			
Executives	5.9	7 6	8.8
Natural scientists	5.9	7.7	8.7
Social scientists	5.6	8.0	8.9
Engineers	5.7	7.6	8.9
Federal Employee Populations			
General federal employees	7.5	8.1	8.4
By sex			
Men	7.6	8.1	8.5
Women	7.3	8.1	8.2
By educational level			
High school not completed	7.8	8.2	8.2
High school completed	7.7	8.1	8.5
Some college	7.0	8.0	8.6
College graduate	7.0	8.1	8.4
Executives	7.4	8.7	8.8
Natural scientists	7.0	8.4	8.5
Social scientists	6.9	8.5	8.6
Engineers	7.0	8.2	8.6

353

Table 12-1e

<u>Highlights</u>: Scale ratings on drive to get ahead.

. . . . The differences between the three sets of ratings on this
factor are very great. General civil service employees are rated quite
low, people in the top-level civil service jobs fairly high, and people
in the top-level business jobs extremely high. The pattern is seen both
in the nonfederal and federal populations, though for the latter the
differences are not so extreme.

. . . . In the general employed public, ratings of both types of civil
service employees are negatively related to educational level. The
higher the education, the lower the rating given. The opposite tendency
is shown in their ratings of people in top-level jobs in business; the
higher the education, the higher the rating given. These patterns hold
for the student populations in their ratings of general civil service
employees and of top-level people in business. They also appear among
general federal employees in their ratings of general civil service
employees (negatively related to educational level) and top-level business people (positively related to educational level).

. . . . College seniors, graduate students, groups in education, and
groups in business render especially low ratings to general civil service employees, and especially high ratings to people in the top-level
jobs in business.

. . . . General federal employees rate both classes of civil service
employees higher than does the general employed public.

. . . . Federal natural and social scientists and engineers assign
ratings to general civil service employees that are lower than the
average ratings given by general federal employees.

354

Table 12-1e

The image of the federal civil servant: "drive to get ahead" ratings
given to federal civil service employees in general and in top-level
jobs, and to people in top-level jobs in private business. Average
(mean) ratings on the 10-point high-low scale; the higher the
score, the higher the rating on drive to get ahead.

	"On the average, how would you rate _____ on their drive to get ahead?"		
	Federal civil service employees in general	People in the top-level jobs in the federal civil service	People in the top-level jobs in private business
Nonfederal Populations			
General employed public	6.6	7.4	8.4
By sex			
Men	6.5	7.4	8.4
Women	7.1	7.6	8.4
By educational level			
High school not completed	7.1	7 5	8.1
High school completed	6.7	7.4	8.4
Some college	6.1	7.3	8.7
College graduate	5.6	7.1	9.0
Students			
High school students	6.7	7.4	8.2
College seniors	5.6	7.3	9.1
Graduate students	5.3	7.5	9.1
Groups in education			
High school teachers	6.1	7.6	8.9
Vocational counselors	5.8	7.5	9.0
College teachers	5.7	7.4	9.2
Natural scientists	5.5	7.6	9.2
Social scientists	5.8	7.6	9.2
Engineers	5.5	7.4	9.0
Groups in business			
Executives	5.4	7.1	9.2
Natural scientists	5.2	7.4	9.4
Social scientists	4.6	7.2	9.4
Engineers	4.9	7.4	9.2
Federal Employee Populations			
General federal employees	7.2	8.2	8.6
By sex			
Men	7.2	8.2	8.7
Women	7.3	8.1	8.5
By educational level			
High school not completed	7.6	8.3	8.3
High school completed	7.3	8.3	8.6
Some college	6.8	8.0	8.9
College graduate	6.7	7.9	8.9
Executives	7.1	8.5	9.2
Natural scientists	6.5	8.1	9.1
Social scientists	6.6	8.4	9.3
Engineers	6.5	7.9	9.1

355

For general civil servants the ratings assigned from group to group and by educational level vary. The scores given them by the general employed public, over all, and by the high school and college teaching groups put them on the average either slightly above or roughly equal to top-level businessmen. But by educational level in the general public the ratings decline with increasing education, moving from 7.1 for those not completing high school to 6.9, 6.3, and 5.9 for the three ascending levels. Thus, by the two higher levels, top businessmen are ranked markedly above the general civil servant on their interest in serving the public. All four business populations also rate general civil servants fairly low on this category. On the average, the scores they assign range from 1 point to over 1.5 points below those assigned to the two top-level groups.

The various populations of federal employees, as might be expected, rate both categories of civil servants higher than do the nonfederal groups. All of the federal groups rank the public interest of top businessmen at the bottom of the scale, with general civil servants in the middle, and top-level civil servants at the top. The most extreme differences in scores are recorded by federal college graduates and by the federal executives, natural and social scientists, and engineers, who rate general civil servants roughly 0.5 to as much as 1.6 higher than they do top-level businessmen, and top-level civil servants another 0.7 to 1.3 scale points higher. Upper-level federal employees score top civil servants from 2 to almost 3 scale points higher on interest in serving the public than they score top businessmen.

How Well Respected They Are

On the attribute of respect, neither federal group fares as well in comparison to top-level businessmen as it did on the preceding two qualities. The general employed public gives the two top-level groups about equally high ratings, but scores general civil servants more than half a scale point below both.

This over-all score in the general employed public, however, conceals an interesting patterning by educational level. For both types of federal employees the scores decline as the educational level rises. This is especially so for the general federal employees, whose scores move downward from 7.4 at the high school not completed level to 7.1, 6.6, and 6.2 at the three higher levels. Exactly the opposite occurs in the case of the scores given to the top-level businessmen, which rise with increasing education from 7.6 to 7.8, 7.9, and 8.2. The result is that the upper educational groups in the general public accord the top-level businessman a marked advantage over his counterpart in government. This holds true for the other nonfederal populations, with the exception of high school students. Thus, on the matter of respect, all the upper educational and occupational groups outside the government give top businessmen a scale point advantage ranging from 0.5 to 1.0 over top civil servants and from 1 to more than 2 over general civil servants.

In the federally employed population, exactly the same situation prevails. General federal employees rate people in the top levels of the civil service and of business about equal on being respected, with general civil servants being placed about 1 scale point lower than either. Here too the scores accorded both types of civil servants decline and the businessmen's scores rise slightly with increasing educational level. College graduates in federal employ—as well as the executives, natural and social scientists, and engineers—accord top businessmen a respect rating about 0.5 scale points above top civil servants and about 1.5 to 2.5 points above general civil servants.

Ability

Practically all of the populations rank civil servants well below top-level businessmen on ability. The businessmen are rated the highest; there is then a substantial drop to the ratings for top civil servants, and an even more marked drop to those for general federal employees. The only exceptions to this pattern occur among women employed in the government and among the general federal employees who have not completed high school: in these two instances, the two top-level groups are rated about equal on ability.

In the general employed public and among general federal employees, we again find a marked decline in the scores assigned to general civil service employees as the educational level ascends. The scores in the general employed public move downward from 7.3 (high school not completed) to 6 (college graduates); those among general federal employees, from 7.8 to 7.

The ability ratings of top-level civil servants given by either nonfederal or federal employees show no significant relationship with educational level. On the other hand, those given to their business counterparts by the general employed public show a marked positive relationship, with scores moving upward from 7.8 at the lowest level to 8.6 at the college graduate level. Among the nonfederal populations, the scores given top businessmen are 0.5 to 1 scale point above those for top civil servants, with the greatest differences being assigned by the upper educational and occupational groups. In all groups the businessman's advantage over the general civil servant is even more extreme, ranging from 2 to as much as 3 scale points.

Among federal employees at all levels the pattern is fairly similar, but the advantage accorded the businessman is less extreme. Here the scores assigned to the two top-level groups do not differ significantly; nevertheless, a slight but consistent advantage is given to the businessman. Both top groups are rated by all the federal populations roughly 1 to 1.5 scale points above general civil servants.

Drive to Get Ahead

Of all the five specified attributes, "drive to get ahead" shows the most extreme and consistent results in favor of the top-level businessman. Every nonfederal group ranks him at the top, with a large decline (roughly, 1 to 2 scale points) to the scores of top-level civil servants, and another similar decline to the scores of general civil servants. The pattern holds true even in the federal populations, but is somewhat less extreme.

Again, the more highly educated respondents—both federal and nonfederal—rate general civil servants lower than do the less-educated respondents. In the general employed public, the ratings on drive to get ahead move downward from 7.1 at the lowest educational level to 6.7, 6.1, and 5.6 for the three higher levels. Among general federal employees the downward move is from 7.6 to 7.3, 6.8, and 6.7.

The ratings assigned to top-level civil servants show a modest (but not significant) decline with increasing education in the general employed public and among general federal employees. By contrast, the general public's scores for top-level businessmen rise sharply with education—from 8.1 at the lowest level to 8.4, 8.7, and 9.0 at the progressively higher levels. A similar, but again less extreme, pattern prevails among general federal employees, with scores moving from 8.3 to 8.6, 8.9, and 8.9. The outcome of this patterning is that the upper educational and occupational levels among the nonfederal groups rate top businessmen about 1.5 to over 2 scale points above top civil servants, and about 3 to over 4 points above general civil servants. Among federal employees the results are similar, but with slightly lower difference scores.

The ratings given by the business groups depart from the general pattern, owing to the extremely low scores assigned to general federal employees—roughly 4 to almost 5 scale points below those given to top-level businessmen.

Summary

When the various ratings given by different populations to the three employee groups being considered are compared, certain general points emerge. The two types of civil servants fare well, both absolutely and in comparison with top-level businessmen, in the ratings on honesty and interest in serving the public—particularly on honesty. They do less well, especially among the upper educational and occupational groups, on ratings for the respect they inspire, and even less well for ability. They do least well of all on drive to get ahead, where there is a uniform pattern of highest ratings for businessmen, a substantial drop to top-level civil servants, and another very substantial drop to general civil servants.

Over all, the scores given to each of the federal groups (especially the general civil servants) tend to decline with the rise of the respondents' educational and occupational levels. Conversely, the scores given to top-level businessmen tend to move upward with rising educational and occupational levels. These differential positive and negative relationships are fairly strong for the attributes of respect and ability, and very strong for drive to get ahead. Understandably, the business populations rate top-level businessmen particularly high on all five qualities, but, to an even greater degree, they downgrade both types of civil servants. Finally, it is worth noting that, although the federal employee populations are inclined to rate both classes of civil servants somewhat higher than the nonfederal populations do, their over-all pattern of ratings given to the three groups of employees on the five attributes is substantially the same as the prevailing pattern among nonfederal respondents.

13

Image of the Federal Employee: Perceived Motives and Work Activity

THE TWO SERIES OF TABLES in this chapter stem from our analyses of responses to three open-end questions directed at uncovering additional aspects of the public's attitudes toward federal civil servants. The first question was: "What do you suppose would cause a person to become a United States civil service employee instead of something else?" The other two questions were interrelated: "What do you picture a federal civil service employee as doing—that is, what sort of work?" and, for comparison, "What do you picture a person employed by a large private business or industry as doing—that is, what sort of work?"

Motives for Becoming a Civil Servant

Although the various groups differ somewhat in their estimation of what motivates a person to become a federal civil servant, one response category elicited by the question is so pervasive that it tends to overshadow all of the other motives cited. With two only exceptions, over 50 percent of the respondents in the nonfederal groups say that a desire for the security, stability, protection, and fringe benefits found in civil service is the reason a person would choose to enter the federal service. The two exceptions are the high school students (36 percent) and the respondents in the employed public who have not completed high school (48 percent). Not only are the absolute percentages mentioning the security motive large—ranging as high as 83 percent among business executives —but vis-à-vis the percentages citing other motives they are also significant. For example, security is mentioned by 59 percent of the general employed public; high or good financial reward is this group's next most frequently mentioned reason—but by only 21 percent. The ratio of the security response to the next most frequently given reply is thus about 3 to 1. Comparable ratios for several other populations run even higher.

This global category of security consists of five components—job security, financial security, retirement security, other protective benefits (e.g., sick leave and insurance) and security in general (that is, not further specified). All replies dealing with security were allocated into one or more of these five components. For most nonfederal groups, the rank order of the responses was as follows: security in general, job security, retirement security, other protective benefits, and financial security. The employees in the general public constitute a prominent exception: they place a stronger emphasis on job security, especially women as compared with men, and the two lower educational strata as compared with the two higher.

Among the federal groups security is also by far the most popular reason advanced for becoming a federal civil servant instead of something else: 76 percent of the general federal employees and from 59 to 67 percent of the special federal groups volunteer this reply. And again the percentages are high, not only absolutely, but also when compared to the frequency with which other reasons are offered. Among general federal workers financial reward is the second-ranking reply, with a figure of 16 percent; the ratio of "security" responses to this is thus nearly 5 to 1. Among the special groups, the ratio is much less extreme, primarily because from 31 to 47 percent of the executives, natural and social scientists, and engineers cite the presence of specific job opportunities in the government as a motivating factor. Nevertheless, these groups, too, see security as the dominant motive attracting people into the federal service.

There are, however, various other motives mentioned for entering government work, and a number of these merit being brought into focus. The opportunity to serve others is seen as an important appeal of federal service, particularly by respondents in some of the more highly educated and special occupational groups. The range of social scientists in education, natural and social scientists in business, and all four of the special federal populations referring to the service motive is from 15 to 26 percent. And between 12 and 14 percent of the student groups also cite the service factor.

On the other hand, certain groups declare that a person seeks government employment because he lacks ambition and initiative or because he wants easy work. Mention of this motive rises slightly with increasing educational status among members of the employed general public—from 5 percent among the high school incompletes to 11 percent of the college graduates—and is more frequent among present college and graduate students than among high school students. But the groups most likely to assert that civil servants lack ambition and initiative or want easy work are the executives, social scientists, and engineers in business (12 to 16 percent). In contrast, very few people in the federal populations mention these motives.

Substantial numbers of people in certain groups say that a person might become a civil servant because he was unable to work or succeed elsewhere. The statement increases among the more highly educated nonfederal groups. In the general public, 4 percent of the high school incompletes and 11 percent of the college graduates make the statement, and in the college teacher groups, 10 to 14 percent of the natural and social scientists and engineers also make it. And once again the business groups are the most likely to attribute this motive to the person who becomes a federal civil servant: the range is 14 to 20 percent, with the business natural scientists furnishing the 20 percent. However, the business groups are joined in this appraisal by about one tenth of the respondents in most of the federal groups.

We have seen that a wide variety of motives are attributed to the person who becomes a federal civil servant. Two motives *not* much mentioned are also worthy of note. In nearly all groups, only a small number of people (generally between 2 and 7 percent) say that a person goes into a civil service job because of the influence of, or contacts with, other people; a salient exception is the 11 percent of the federal executives who do mention this factor. And the assertion that selfish or dishonest gain is a likely motive is made by almost no one—respondents in only five of the groups mention it, and the figures in no case exceed 1 percent.

The points of this summary are demonstrated in Tables 13-1a through 13-1e (pages 364 to 373).

Discussion of Motive Data

Nonfederal Populations

GENERAL EMPLOYED PUBLIC. We find that a small to moderate proportion (5 to 15 percent) of the general employed public mentions the following motives for entering the federal civil service: desire for self-advancement and success, appeal of good working conditions, desire to do work one is capable of doing or trained for, the presence of specific job opportunities, and desire for public service. Mentions of being capable for the work and of good working conditions are inversely related to educational status, but references to the service motive and to the presence of specific job opportunities increase slightly with the increasing education of the respondents.

Good financial reward and interest in the kind of work civil servants do are mentioned by somewhat larger proportions (21 and 18 percent). The frequency with which the federal pay scale is cited as an attractive feature, however, is inversely related to educational level, dropping from 25 percent among those not completing high school to 15 percent among college graduates. Mention of two other reasons—inability to work or succeed elsewhere and lack of initiative or a desire for easy work—increases with rising education: only 4 percent at the lowest educational level cite the first reason, compared to 11 percent at the highest; the figures on lack of ambition are 5 and 11 percent.

As pointed out earlier, the security of employment in the federal service is the motive most often volunteered by the members of all groups. About six out of every ten respondents in the general employed public cite it, yet certain differences in the figures within the general work population are worth noting: (1) concern for security is cited by over 60 percent of the respondents at each of the three upper educational levels, in contrast to 48 percent of those at the lowest level; (2) more men mention it than women (61 vs. 51 percent); (3) references to security without further elaboration increase markedly as education rises.

HIGH SCHOOL STUDENTS, COLLEGE SENIORS, AND GRADUATE STUDENTS. The response pattern among students is similar to the pattern by educational level in the general employed public. Security is cited by 68 percent of the college seniors and 71 percent of the graduate students, but by only 36 percent of the high school students. Both groups of college students are also considerably more likely than high school students to say that people may choose government service because of specific jobs open to them there or because they lack ambition and want an easy job, and are unable to work or succeed elsewhere. High school students are much more inclined (35 percent) than are college seniors and graduate students (22 and 18 percent) to cite interest and satisfaction in the work.

(Text continued on page 374)

This series of tables is concerned with a further aspect of stereotyping of civil service employees. They show the percentage distributions in the various groups of the responses given when the respondents were asked to give their opinions of what might be the motives causing a person to become a civil service employee instead of something else.

Table 13-1a

<u>Highlights</u>: Security, stability, protection, fringe benefits. (The only fringe benefits coded in this category were those which have a protective aspect, for example, sick leave insurance. These benefits, insofar as they can be specified, are coded in Columns 5 and 6 with the headings "retirement security" and "other protective benefits.")

. . . . The total column reveals the pervasiveness with which the security motive is attributed to civil service employees by respondents in all groups, nonfederal and federal. Figures range from about 50% to over 80%.

. . . . In the general employed public, the security motive is attributed somewhat less often by women than men and less by the high school not completed group than by the three upper educational levels. A parallel relationship with educational level is found in the student populations, where the figures for college seniors and graduate students are almost double the figure for high school students.

. . . . The 76% figure in the total column for general federal employees is significantly higher than the 59% figure for the general employed public. Among general federal employees, the percentages do not differ significantly for men and women. By educational level, the picture is a mild reversal of that shown in the general employed public; attribution of the security motive is negatively related to educational level, although the percentages are extremely high at all levels.

. . . . All groups of federal employees emphasize "other protective benefits" as a motive for becoming a civil service employee much more than do any of the nonfederal populations. In the nonfederal populations, there is a tendency to be less specific and simply to mention the general concept of security which is tabled under the "not further specified" heading.

Table 13-la

The image of the federal civil servant: the motives people see as causing
a person to become a federal civil servant. Percentage distribution[a] of
responses in each group to the question, "What do you suppose would cause
a person to become a United States civil service employee
instead of something else?"

	Number answering	Not further specified	Job security	Financial security	Retirement security (e.g., pension)	Other protective benefits (e.g., sick leave, insurance)	Total
						Security, stability, protection, fringe benefits	
Nonfederal Populations							
General employed public	1136	25%	28%	5%	17%	8%	59%
By sex							
Men	871	27	28	6	17	8	61
Women	265	17	27	5	17	9	51
By educational level							
High school not completed	329	15	28	4	16	6	48
High school completed	510	24	29	6	21	11	62
Some college	129	35	28	7	12	4	65
College graduate	138	43	20	8	11	7	67
Students							
High school students	358	17	16	2	5	3	36
College seniors	403	38	21	7	8	9	68
Graduate students	382	48	24	5	8	9	71
Groups in education							
High school teachers	282	45	22	7	10	5	69
Vocational counselors	79	51	19	10	10	8	73
College teachers	470	51	20	8	12	5	75
Natural scientists	121	55	23	3	13	9	78
Social scientists	105	53	20	8	10	5	74
Engineers	86	40	24	4	2	4	62
Groups in business							
Executives	284	46	32	7	16	10	83
Natural scientists	85	52	28	7	11	7	81
Social scientists	73	45	22	8	4	8	67
Engineers	89	43	28	5	11	6	76
Federal Employee Populations							
General federal employees	938	27	31	6	21	30	76
By sex							
Men	652	27	35	6	22	27	76
Women	286	29	20	5	20	37	75
By educational level							
High school not completed	189	21	34	7	22	27	76
High school completed	353	29	35	4	24	36	80
Some college	179	30	28	7	15	22	70
College graduate	163	26	25	3	20	24	67
Executives	272	24	30	2	16	15	62
Natural scientists	91	26	34	3	11	14	67
Social scientists	88	19	32	1	9	14	59
Engineers	97	27	23	2	12	21	62

a Percentage base = number of respondents answering in each group.
Percentages do not add to 100 in each group due to multiple replies.

Table 13-1b

Highlights: High or good financial reward.

. . . . In the general employed public attribution of the financial
reward motive is more common among women than men and is negatively
associated with level of education.

. . . . The 22% figures for high school teachers and vocational counselors are somewhat higher than might be expected from their educational
levels.

. . . . Groups in business show the lowest frequency of mention of
financial reward as a motive for becoming a federal civil servant.

. . . . The over-all percentage for general federal employees is
slightly lower than the figure for the general employed public. Here
too there is a tendency for women to mention this factor more often than
do men. The picture by educational level, however, is somewhat different: the lowest rather than the highest figure is given by the high
school not completed group.

. . . . The figures for federal executives, natural and social scientists, and engineers are consistent and moderately high.

Highlights: Good physical environment and working conditions.

. . . . In none of the groups is this motive named very often, but its
mention is high enough in the general employed public--especially at
the two lower educational levels--and in the general federal employed
population to indicate that it does play a role, even though minor, in
the over-all stereotype.

Highlights: Self-advancement and desire for success.

. . . . The attribution of this motive is rather low in the nonfederal
population, especially in groups in business, but the figures over all
are high enough to indicate that the factor is of some salience in the
general stereotype.

. . . . The federal and nonfederal figures do not differ appreciably,
with two exceptions: federally employed women are much more likely to
mention self-advancement than are women outside the government, and the
figure for the federal executives is higher than the general level for
most groups.

Table 13-1b
The image of the federal civil servant: the motives people see as
causing a person to become a federal civil servant (cont'd.)

	High or good financial reward	Good physical environment and working conditions	Self-advancement and desire for success
Nonfederal Populations			
General employed public	21%	10%	10%
By sex			
Men	19	9	10
Women	26	12	9
By educational level			
High school not completed	25	9	10
High school completed	20	12	9
Some college	19	5	10
College graduate	15	5	10
Students			
High school students	15	5	13
College seniors	15	4	14
Graduate students	13	2	10
Groups in education			
High school teachers	22	6	8
Vocational counselors	22	5	9
College teachers	14	2	10
Natural scientists	15	4	10
Social scientists	13	4	10
Engineers	19	1	7
Groups in business			
Executives	7	1	4
Natural scientists	5	5	8
Social scientists	10	3	4
Engineers	2	1	9
Federal Employee Populations			
General federal employees	16	9	10
By sex			
Men	13	9	8
Women	25	9	17
By educational level			
High school not completed	12	12	10
High school completed	16	8	10
Some college	20	5	12
College graduate	19	11	8
Executives	22	6	16
Natural scientists	22	12	9
Social scientists	22	8	9
Engineers	18	4	14

Table 13-1c

Highlights: Interested in, satisfied with, enjoys, or desires that type
of work.

. . . . This motive is noted moderately often in the general employed
public by both men and women and at all four educational levels.

. . . . Among students the figures are negatively related to present
educational level. Of particular interest is the fact that over a third
of the high school students mention this motive; of equal interest is
the decline to a figure of 18% at the graduate student level.

. . . . Mention of this motive is very low by all groups in business.

. . . . General federal employees cite the motive less than half as frequently as the general employed public. However, the figures for
federal executives, natural and social scientists, and engineers are
somewhat higher than the figures for general federal employees, and
about equal to those for the general employed public.

Highlights: Serves or wants to serve others, society, or certain parts
of society.

. . . . The general employed public only occasionally mentions a service
motive as a reason for becoming a federal civil servant.

. . . . The moderate percentage of students at all levels who attribute
this motive is worthy of note.

. . . . College teachers and college social scientists and natural and
social scientists in business mention service as a motive for becoming
a civil servant moderately often.

. . . . While general federal employees do not mention the service theme
very often, they do so significantly more than members of the general
employed public. This is especially true of those at the some college
and college graduate levels.

. . . . The percentages for federal executives, natural and social
scientists, and engineers are quite consistent, and significantly higher
than the over-all average for general federal employees.

Highlights: For selfish or dishonest gain.

. . . . This category was tabled simply to show that almost no one in
any group, nonfederal or federal, mentions selfish or dishonest gain
as a motive for becoming a federal civil servant.

Table 13-1c

The image of the federal civil servant: the motives people see as causing a person to become a federal civil servant (cont'd.)

	Interested in, satisfied with, enjoys, or desires that type of work	Serves or wants to serve others, society, or certain parts of society	For selfish or dishonest gain
Nonfederal Populations			
General employed public	18%	4%	0%
By sex			
Men	18	4	0
Women	19	4	0
By educational level			
High school not completed	19	3	0
High school completed	18	4	0
Some college	18	5	0
College graduate	22	7	1
Students			
High school students	36	14	1
College seniors	22	12	1
Graduate students	18	12	1
Groups in education			
High school teachers	13	9	0
Vocational counselors	9	10	0
College teachers	15	19	0
Natural scientists	22	12	0
Social scientists	16	26	0
Engineers	17	7	0
Groups in business			
Executives	8	10	0
Natural scientists	7	21	0
Social scientists	8	18	0
Engineers	5	9	1
Federal Employee Populations			
General federal employees	8	8	0
By sex			
Men	9	9	0
Women	6	8	0
By educational level			
High school not completed	11	7	0
High school completed	7	6	0
Some college	7	14	0
College graduate	11	11	0
Executives	18	16	0
Natural scientists	17	15	0
Social scientists	19	18	1
Engineers	22	16	0

Table 13-1d

Highlights: Capable of and qualified for the work.

. . . . While mention of this motive is in general quite low, it is significantly higher in the general employed public than among general federal employees. This is especially true for women in the general employed public, and there is a slight indication that frequency of mention in the general employed public is negatively related to educational level. Among general federal employees frequency of mention appears to be somewhat positively related to educational level.

. . . . Percentages for federal executives and natural and social scientists are slightly higher than the over-all average for general federal employees.

Highlights: Presence of job opportunities.

. . . . Mention of this factor is not high in the general employed public; however, there is a faint suggestion that it is positively related to educational level.

. . . . In the student populations the 21% figure for both college seniors and graduate students contrasts sharply with the 9% figure for high school students.

. . . . The figures for groups in education and in business, ranging as they do from about one fifth to about one third, are significantly higher than the over-all average for the general employed public.

. . . . Among general federal employees, frequency of mention is somewhat higher than in the general employed public. Also, the figures show a fairly strong positive relationship with educational level.

. . . . Mention of job opportunities as a motivating factor is very high among federal executives, natural and social scientists, and engineers, the proportions ranging from almost one third to nearly one half.

Highlights: Influence of, or contacts with, other people.

. . . . This category was tabled to show that the possession of influence and contacts as a motive is mentioned rarely by any group, nonfederal or federal. A possible exception is the 11% figure for federal executives, but this stands out only because of the extremely low percentages for all other groups.

Table 13-1d
The image of the federal civil servant: the motives people see as
causing a person to become a federal civil servant (cont'd.)

	Capable of and qualified for the work	Presence of job opportunities	Influence of, or contacts with, other people
Nonfederal Populations			
General employed public	11%	9%	4%
By sex			
Men	9	9	5
Women	16	9	3
By educational level			
High school not completed	13	5	4
High school completed	10	9	4
Some college	9	12	5
College graduate	8	11	4
Students			
High school students	8	9	6
College seniors	7	21	4
Graduate students	8	21	3
Groups in education			
High school teachers	8	16	5
Vocational counselors	9	20	9
College teachers	7	22	4
Natural scientists	4	24	3
Social scientists	9	25	4
Engineers	5	33	2
Groups in business			
Executives	6	12	5
Natural scientists	0	21	4
Social scientists	4	27	4
Engineers	2	15	5
Federal Employee Populations			
General federal employees	5	13	4
By sex			
Men	5	13	4
Women	4	14	5
By educational level			
High school not completed	3	10	1
High school completed	2	10	4
Some college	9	14	6
College graduate	7	27	5
Executives	9	38	11
Natural scientists	10	40	7
Social scientists	17	47	8
Engineers	7	31	4

Table 13-1e

<u>Highlights</u>: Lack of ambition and initiative; desire for easy work.

. . . . Very few respondents in the federal employee populations suggest
a lack of ambition and initiative as a motive for becoming a federal
servant. The figures are significantly higher in some of the nonfederal
populations.

. . . . This negative motive is mentioned by 7% of the general employed
public, and there is a suggestion that the higher the educational level,
the more likely the mention. The tendency toward a positive relationship with educational level, while not marked, is nevertheless also
present in the student population.

. . . . The generally higher figures for groups in business, with the
exception of natural scientists, are worth noting.

<u>Highlights</u>: Unable to work or succeed elsewhere.

. . . . In the general employed public the frequency with which people
say a person might become a civil servant because he could not work or
succeed elsewhere is not high, but that 6% do mention it is worth
noting. That such references are positively related to educational
level is also of interest. This same tendency toward a positive relationship with educational level is shown in the student populations.

. . . . From 10% to 14% of college natural and social scientists and
engineers mention inability to work or succeed elsewhere, and the
figures for groups in business rise as high as 20%.

. . . . Of particular interest is the 10% figure for general federal
employees; while not high, it is nevertheless higher than the figure for
the general employed public (6%). Among general federal employees the
figures are consistent for both sexes and at all four educational
levels.

. . . . There is a suggestion that federal natural scientists attribute
the motive somewhat less often than other federal employees.

Table 13-1e

The image of the federal civil servant: the motives people see as
causing a person to become a federal civil servant (cont'd.)

	Lack of ambition and initiative; desire for easy work	Unable to work or succeed elsewhere
Nonfederal Populations		
General employed public	7%	6%
By sex		
Men	7	6
Women	4	6
By educational level		
High school not completed	5	4
High school completed	6	6
Some college	9	9
College graduate	11	11
Students		
High school students	3	7
College seniors	8	12
Graduate students	9	11
Groups in education		
High school teachers	5	6
Vocational counselors	3	10
College teachers	8	7
Natural scientists	5	10
Social scientists	5	14
Engineers	13	12
Groups in business		
Executives	16	14
Natural scientists	6	20
Social scientists	16	18
Engineers	12	17
Federal Employee Populations		
General federal employees	2	10
By sex		
Men	2	10
Women	4	8
By educational level		
High school not completed	2	10
High school completed	1	11
Some college	4	10
College graduate	2	8
Executives	2	10
Natural scientists	3	4
Social scientists	0	13
Engineers	3	8

All the student groups mention the service motive (12 to 14 percent) rather more often than do members of the general public. Compared with the general public and a number of other groups, all of them place less emphasis (a range of 5 to 8 percent) on the retirement benefits aspect of the security motive.

HIGH SCHOOL TEACHERS AND VOCATIONAL COUNSELORS. Most of the groups in education show response patterns similar to those of the college graduates in the general public and of college seniors and graduate students. There are, however, some special points of interest. High school teachers and vocational counselors are somewhat more likely (22 percent each) than other well-educated groups to see federal salaries as a motive. The two high school groups (as well as others in education) also mention the service motive and the presence of specific job opportunities somewhat more often than members of the general public do. It is also worth noting that 10 percent of the high school vocational counselors say people are apt to enter federal service because they can't succeed elsewhere.

COLLEGE TEACHERS, NATURAL AND SOCIAL SCIENTISTS, AND ENGINEERS. As a whole, the college teachers resemble most of the other highly educated groups in the motives they suggest. They refer to the service motive, however, considerably more often (19 percent) than do the two high school teacher groups (9 percent) or respondents in the general work force (4 percent). The college engineers, compared with the other college groups, mention the security and the service motives less often, and lack of ambition and initiative more often. The social scientists, with a figure of 26 percent, lead not only the college groups but also all other non-federal and federal groups in mentioning desire to serve others as a motivating factor.

GROUPS IN BUSINESS. The business groups are less likely than any other group to see the federal salary scale and an interest in the work as attracting factors. In each of the four populations, no more than 10 percent mentions the first factor, and no more than 8 percent the second. On the other hand, the figures for the business executives, natural and social scientists, and engineers on lack of ambition (16, 6, 16, and 12 percent) and on inability to work or succeed outside government service (14, 20, 18, and 17 percent) are among the highest found in any group.

There are also some differences within the four groups. Mention of the service motive is made by 21 percent of the natural scientists and 18 percent of the social scientists, and by only 10 and 9 percent of the executives and engineers. The 6 percent figure noted above for natural scientists on lack of ambition is much lower than the group average. Finally, although very large percentages of all the business groups say that concern for security is the principal motive that draws people to the federal service, the social scientists' figure of 67 percent seems almost moderate when compared with the range of 76 to 83 percent shown by the other three groups.

Federal Employee Populations

GENERAL FEDERAL EMPLOYEES. The following motives for entering government service are mentioned by small to moderate numbers of the general federal workers (usually between 5 and 15 percent): good physical environment and working conditions, desire for self-advancement and success, interest in the work, a wish to serve others, wanting to do work for which one is capable or trained, and the presence of specific job opportunities. It is worth noting that only 8 and 5 percent of the federal workers—compared with 18 and 11 percent of the general employed public—cite interest in the work and the capability-training motives. And one federal employee in every ten says that inability to work or succeed elsewhere might be a motive, a higher mention than the general public's 6 percent. Very few (2 percent) of the government employees, however, cite a lack of ambition or initiative as a reason. And again we note that the security aspects of government employment are by far the most commonly cited reasons.

Some significant variations in attitudes are revealed when educational levels are considered. Mentions of the service motive rise moderately as education increases. References to the availability of specific job opportunities climb sharply from 10 percent at the high school not completed level to 27 percent for college graduates. And respondents without a high school diploma prove a bit less likely than others to mention financial reward. The security motive declines slightly in frequency with increasing educational attainment, although the percentages are still very high at every level.

Two points on which women in the federal service differ from the men deserve special note. More women than men see financial reward (25 vs. 13 percent) and opportunities for self-advancement and progress (17 vs. 8 percent) as prominent lures of government employment. The figures on self-advancement contrast with those in the general employed public, where the percentages by sex differ hardly at all. However, federally employed men and women cite the security motive about equally, in contrast to the moderately greater emphasis given it by men in the general public.

FEDERAL EXECUTIVES, NATURAL AND SOCIAL SCIENTISTS, AND ENGINEERS. The four special federal groups tend to resemble the more highly educated of the general federal employees in the motives they specify; however, they cite interest in the work, desire to serve others, and the presence of specific job opportunities slightly to moderately more often. Their mention of specific job opportunities, ranging from 31 to 47 percent is particularly high—higher in fact than in any other group, whether federal and nonfederal, except for the college engineers' 33 percent.

Differences within the four groups are slight. The federal social scientists, however, mention being capable and qualified for the work somewhat more often (17 percent) than the other three groups (a range of 7 to 10 percent), and they also lead (47 percent) in referring to the presence of job opportunities (40, 38, and 31 percent for natural scientists, executives, and engineers). Although the figure is not significant statistically, it is worth noting that 12 percent of the natural scientists—compared to the 4 to 8 percent range of the other three special groups—cite good physical environment and working conditions. Most of these scientists obviously had the government's facilities for scientific research in mind when they volunteered this reason.

Compared with their academic and business counterparts, the four special federal groups are a little less inclined to cite desire for security and lack of ambition and initiative as motivating factors. And compared with the business groups only, they are more likely to refer to financial reward, interest in and satisfaction with the work, being capable and qualified for the work, and the presence of specific job opportunities, and less likely to cite inability to work or succeed elsewhere.

Perceived Work Activities

When respondents were asked what type of work they pictured federal civil servants and business employees doing (Tables 13-2a through 13-2g, pages 378 to 391), more than 50 percent in every group were willing to generalize about both types of employees. Among the general federal employees and the general employed public, three fourths or more willingly ventured stereotypes. In certain groups, however, large numbers refused to do so. The figures for respondents who refused vary widely from population to population—from the 4 percent of the nonfederal employees without a high school diploma who refuse to stereotype the work of civil servants, to the 47 percent of the engineers in business who would not generalize about business employees.

On the average, the nonfederal groups are more often willing to stereotype civil service work than business employee work. Among the general federal employees, this pattern is reversed somewhat, and among the special federal populations, even more so. And the more highly educated groups, both in and outside the federal service, are less willing to stereotype the work of both types of employees.

Despite these variations, the fact remains that over half the respondents in all groups do generalize about civil service and business work. The differences in their images of the tasks performed by government workers and by business workers are of special interest. In general, people are more likely to see employees of large business as managers, executives, salesmen, craftsmen, general laborers, and operatives such as machinists. And most of the groups are more likely to see civil servants as engaging in technical and scientific activities, clerical and postal work, and protective and law enforcement activities. Professional work, engineering, and office work are seen about equally in both the federal service and in business, although federal employees themselves are slightly more likely to see office work in the government.

The most-mentioned aspect of business employment is managerial, executive, or administrative work; mentioned less often are clerical, office, and sales work and the work of craftsmen and operatives. The image of the civil servant's work includes no single feature as salient as managerial work is for the image of business employment. By most groups, however, clerical and office work are singled out for the civil servant fairly often, and the less-educated nonfederal employees mention postal work with moderate frequency. Among some of the highly educated groups, the government's scientific and technical activities loom large.

Discussion of Work Activity Data

Nonfederal Populations

GENERAL EMPLOYED PUBLIC. This group generalizes readily about the work both types of employees perform—but more readily for civil service work (only 7 percent refuse) than business work (nearly 20 percent refuse).

(Text continued on page 392)

Tables 13-2a Through 13-2g

Parallel questions were asked concerning the type of work civil service employees and private business employees are perceived as doing. In this series of tables the results for each category of response are presented side by side so that direct comparison of the patterns of stereotyping for each class of employees can be made.

Table 13-2a

Highlights: Management, administrative, executive; management-level jobs.

. . . . In all populations, nonfederal and federal, management-level activities are mentioned much more often for business employees than for civil service employees. In the nonfederal populations the ratios of mention for civil service employees as compared to business employees range from roughly 1 to 2 to slightly higher than 1 to 4. In the federal populations, the ratios average about 1 to 1 1/2.

. . . . In the upper-level educational and occupational groups there is a greater tendency to mention management activities for both types of employees, but the figures for business employees are higher.

. . . . References to management activities in connection with civil service work are higher among general federal employees than in the general employed public, and frequency of mention is positively related to educational level.

Table 13-2a

The image of the federal civil servant: the kinds of work people picture
civil service employees as doing, and employees of large private business
as doing. Percentage distribution[a] of responses in each group to the
questions, "What do you picture a (federal civil service employee)
(person employed by a large private business or industry) as doing
--that is, what sort of work?"

	Number answering question about the work of:		Management, administrative, executive; management-level jobs	
	Civil service employees	Large business employees	Civil service employees	Large business employees
Nonfederal Populations				
General employed public	1139	1138	14%	38%
By sex				
Men	873	874	15	39
Women	266	264	10	35
By educational level				
High school not completed	330	330	9	30
High school completed	512	511	16	40
Some college	129	128	16	46
College graduate	138	139	17	45
Students				
High school students	359	359	12	40
College seniors	402	402	21	55
Graduate students	383	382	22	50
Groups in education				
High school teachers	283	283	16	51
Vocational counselors	80	80	23	51
College teachers	470	470	18	58
Natural scientists	121	121	17	53
Social scientists	106	105	28	52
Engineers	87	87	15	53
Groups in business				
Executives	286	285	21	50
Natural scientists	85	82	28	50
Social scientists	73	72	29	49
Engineers	90	89	24	47
Federal Employee Populations				
General federal employees	942	931	21	33
By sex				
Men	657	649	19	29
Women	285	282	26	44
By educational level				
High school not completed	190	186	16	25
High school completed	356	354	20	29
Some college	179	178	22	40
College graduate	162	160	26	43
Executives	269	273	32	43
Natural scientists	92	91	23	33
Social scientists	89	90	30	36
Engineers	98	99	21	30

Table 13-2b

<u>Highlights</u>: Professional.

. . . . Taking all groups into consideration, professional activity is somewhat more commonly mentioned in connection with the civil service than in connection with large business. The largest percentage differences favoring civil service employees occur among the groups in education and among federal executives, natural and social scientists, and engineers.

. . . . In the general employed public and among general federal employees there is a slight tendency for frequency of mention of professional activities to be positively related to educational level.

<u>Highlights</u>: Technical and scientific.

. . . . In the general employed public mention of technical and scientific activities is relatively low, but is somewhat higher in relation to civil service employees than in relation to business employees.

. . . . Mention of this category as an aspect of civil service work is especially high among natural scientists in colleges. To a lesser extent this is also true for natural scientists in business and in the government.

. . . . All groups in colleges and the federal executives, natural and social scientists, and engineers, cite these activities as more typical of civil service work than large business work.

<u>Highlights</u>: Engineering.

. . . . As one might expect, engineers--whether in colleges, business, or the government--mention engineering activities more often than do other groups; in fact, in all other groups mention is low.

Table 13-2b

The image of the federal civil servant: the kinds of work people picture civil service employees as doing, and employees of large private business as doing (cont'd.)

	Professional		Technical and scientific		Engineering	
	Civil service employees	Large business employees	Civil service employees	Large business employees	Civil service employees	Large business employees
Nonfederal Populations						
General employed public	8%	7%	7%	3%	5%	5%
By sex						
Men	8	7	7	3	5	5
Women	8	7	8	3	4	5
By educational level						
High school not completed	5	3	7	1	5	5
High school completed	8	7	6	4	5	4
Some college	12	8	7	4	5	4
College graduate	11	13	9	7	4	7
Students						
High school students	10	9	3	6	1	5
College seniors	11	11	9	10	4	6
Graduate students	12	9	17	17	4	9
Groups in education						
High school teachers	18	11	5	8	5	3
Vocational counselors	24	14	4	5	8	4
College teachers	15	11	17	9	4	6
Natural scientists	12	7	41	22	3	5
Social scientists	13	11	19	7	2	4
Engineers	21	12	31	14	25	18
Groups in business						
Executives	10	8	5	4	2	6
Natural scientists	2	4	29	26	6	9
Social scientists	11	11	7	7	3	4
Engineers	13	8	17	10	13	15
Federal Employee Populations						
General federal employees	10	10	10	7	6	5
By sex						
Men	9	10	9	7	6	5
Women	13	11	12	6	7	5
By educational level						
High school not completed	6	7	8	3	2	3
High school completed	10	12	7	7	6	6
Some college	12	12	10	5	5	5
College graduate	12	9	15	14	12	6
Executives	19	13	21	13	8	4
Natural scientists	11	8	30	15	5	4
Social scientists	20	16	30	23	7	3
Engineers	9	3	26	14	20	15

Table 13-2c

<u>Highlights</u>: Clerical work, non-sales.

. . . . High percentages of all groups, nonfederal and federal, cite
clerical activities in connection with civil service employees. Such
references in connection with business employees, while fairly high,
average 10% to 20% lower in all groups.

. . . . As one might expect, women mention clerical activities more
often than men. This is true for women in federal employment and for
those outside government, and whether they are talking about civil
service employees or business employees.

. . . . In the general employed public frequency of mention of clerical
activities as typical of civil service work is positively related to
educational level. Frequency of mention in regard to business employees
shows no such relationship. A similar pattern appears among general
federal employees.

<u>Highlights</u>: Office work, desk work, paper work.

. . . . The general employed public designates this activity in relation
to civil service employees and to business employees about equally.

. . . . Among general federal employees, mention of office work, desk
work, and paper work in connection with civil service employees is
significantly more frequent than in the general employed public.
Frequency of mention by federally employed women is especially high.

Table 13-2c

The image of the federal civil servant: the kinds of work people
picture civil service employees as doing, and employees of large
private business as doing (cont'd.)

	Clerical work, non-sales (e.g., filing, typing, secretarial)		Office work, desk work, paper work	
	Civil service employees	Large business employees	Civil service employees	Large business employees
Nonfederal Populations				
General employed public	28%	18%	15%	14%
By sex				
Men	27	16	14	14
Women	32	26	15	14
By educational level				
High school not completed	18	18	15	14
High school completed	31	16	13	15
Some college	33	23	17	14
College graduate	38	19	16	9
Students				
High school students	29	23	23	27
College seniors	41	19	27	20
Graduate students	41	22	24	12
Groups in education				
High school teachers	44	22	21	15
Vocational counselors	36	15	25	14
College teachers	37	18	22	11
Natural scientists	35	20	15	10
Social scientists	40	21	19	11
Engineers	29	21	16	5
Groups in business				
Executives	48	18	17	12
Natural scientists	38	16	19	16
Social scientists	41	24	12	8
Engineers	40	24	23	12
Federal Employee Populations				
General federal employees	35	22	20	14
By sex				
Men	31	18	18	13
Women	45	34	27	16
By educational level				
High school not completed	27	20	21	13
High school completed	38	19	24	18
Some college	38	26	16	9
College graduate	35	25	15	9
Executives	36	17	11	6
Natural scientists	33	14	16	9
Social scientists	32	13	23	11
Engineers	27	10	18	6

Table 13-2d

Highlights: Postal work.

. . . . About a fourth of the general employed public mentions postal work when asked to describe the activities of civil service employees. Attributions are negatively related to educational level; approximately one third of those at the high school not completed level mention it, whereas only 10% of the college graduates do so. A similar negative relationship with educational level prevails among the student populations.

. . . . Far fewer of the respondents in the federal populations cite postal work in connection with civil service employees. However, the negative relationship with educational level is similar to that seen in the general employed public.

Highlights: Breakdown of "postal work."

. . . . This set of figures simply shows that references to the work of mail carriers predominates among those respondents who do mention postal work as an activity of civil service employees.

Table 13-2d

The image of the federal civil servant: the kinds of work people
picture civil service employees as doing, and employees of large
private business as doing (cont'd.)

| | Postal work | | Breakdown of "postal work" (civil service employees only) | | |
	Civil service employees	Large business employees	Post-masters	Mail carriers	Mail clerks
Nonfederal Populations					
General employed public	26%	0%	4%	22%	7%
By sex					
Men	28	0	4	23	7
Women	21	0	4	16	7
By educational level					
High school not completed	32	0	6	25	11
High school completed	27	0	3	23	6
Some college	24	0	5	19	8
College graduate	10	0	2	9	2
Students					
High school students	17	0	3	14	4
College seniors	12	0	1	9	3
Graduate students	9	0	1	7	2
Groups in education					
High school teachers	12	0	1	9	6
Vocational counselors	10	0	3	5	6
College teachers	9	0	1	6	4
Natural scientists	12	0	1	7	5
Social scientists	9	0	2	6	3
Engineers	10	0	0	7	3
Groups in business					
Executives	11	0	1	6	6
Natural scientists	8	0	1	6	2
Social scientists	3	0	0	3	0
Engineers	9	0	0	6	4
Federal Employee Populations					
General federal employees	12	0	0	9	6
By sex					
Men	16	0	0	12	7
Women	3	0	0	3	2
By educational level					
High school not completed	19	0	1	13	10
High school completed	13	0	0	10	5
Some college	9	0	0	8	6
College graduate	7	0	0	6	1
Executives	3	0	0	3	1
Natural scientists	4	0	0	4	0
Social scientists	3	0	0	2	1
Engineers	5	0	1	2	2

385

Table 13-2e

Highlights: Sales work.

. . . . Significant proportions of all federal and nonfederal groups mention sales activities when asked to describe the work of business employees.

. . . . References to sales activities in connection with business employees are somewhat higher among women than men in the general employed public, and almost twice as high among women as among men in the general federal group.

. . . . Engineers have a tendency to mention sales activities somewhat less frequently than other groups.

Highlights: Protective and enforcement services.

. . . . The figures in this category simply show that protective and enforcement activities form a small but still significant part of the picture of civil service work as far as the general employed public is concerned.

Table 13-2e

The image of the federal civil servant: the kinds of work people
picture civil service employees as doing, and employees of large
private business as doing (cont'd.)

| | Sales work (e.g., selling, salesmen, sales clerks) | | Protective and enforcement services | |
	Civil service employees	Large business employees	Civil service employees	Large business employees
Nonfederal Populations				
General employed public	0%	14%	8%	0%
By sex				
Men	0	13	9	0
Women	0	16	6	0
By educational level				
High school not completed	0	13	9	0
High school completed	0	14	8	0
Some college	0	13	8	0
College graduate	0	14	6	0
Students				
High school students	0	20	4	1
College seniors	1	21	4	0
Graduate students	0	19	2	1
Groups in education				
High school teachers	0	24	6	0
Vocational counselors	0	26	10	0
College teachers	0	18	3	0
Natural scientists	1	15	3	1
Social scientists	0	13	2	0
Engineers	0	6	1	1
Groups in business				
Executives	0	19	3	1
Natural scientists	0	18	0	0
Social scientists	0	17	3	0
Engineers	0	11	4	0
Federal Employee Populations				
General federal employees	0	14	3	1
By sex				
Men	0	12	3	1
Women	6	21	4	0
By educational level				
High school not completed	0	10	5	0
High school completed	0	14	3	1
Some college	0	19	1	0
College graduate	0	16	4	1
Executives	1	17	3	1
Natural scientists	0	18	7	0
Social scientists	0	26	1	0
Engineers	0	8	0	0

Table 13-2f

Highlights: Craftsmen.

. . . . Respondents in the nonfederal populations rarely mention the
work of mechanics, machinists, carpenters, and the like, in connection
with civil service employees. For the general employed public, however, such work forms a significant part of the activity picture of
business employees. This is more true for the less educated groups
than for the well educated.

. . . . In the eyes of general federal employees, craftsmen's activities
form a significant part of the picture of both civil service work and
large business work, and in both instances there is a negative relationship with educational level.

Highlights: Operatives.

. . . . The category of operatives includes production-line activities,
such as assembly work. As one might expect, it is scarcely mentioned in
connection with civil service employment but forms a significant part
of the image of large business work, especially in the general employed
public at the lower educational levels, among federally employed men,
and at the lowest educational level among general federal employees.

Highlights: Laborers.

. . . . Laboring activities in connection with civil service employment
are rarely mentioned in the nonfederal populations. General federal
employees mention it with modest frequency, replies being concentrated
among men and at the lower educational levels.

. . . . On the other hand, in connection with the work of large business employees, a large number of federal and nonfederal groups mention
laboring activities with moderately low to moderate frequency.

Table 13-2f

The image of the federal civil servant: the kinds of work people picture civil service employees as doing, and employees of large private business as doing (cont'd.)

	Craftsmen (e.g., mechanics, machinists, carpenters)		Operatives (e.g., truck drivers, assembly line workers)		Laborers	
	Civil service employees	Large business employees	Civil service employees	Large business employees	Civil service employees	Large business employees
Nonfederal Populations						
General employed public	4%	15%	2%	18%	2%	11%
By sex						
Men	5	16	3	18	2	12
Women	4	12	1	16	2	9
By educational level						
High school not completed	7	20	4	18	2	8
High school completed	4	15	3	20	2	14
Some college	5	11	0	16	2	9
College graduate	2	10	0	12	0	10
Students						
High school students	2	11	1	12	1	10
College seniors	3	5	1	8	2	8
Graduate students	1	7	1	7	2	10
Groups in education						
High school teachers	4	6	3	9	4	11
Vocational counselors	4	10	1	12	5	10
College teachers	1	5	1	6	2	8
Natural scientists	0	3	1	7	2	7
Social scientists	1	5	1	9	4	11
Engineers	0	6	0	3	2	10
Groups in business						
Executives	2	3	0	5	1	6
Natural scientists	4	5	1	5	4	7
Social scientists	1	6	1	5	4	0
Engineers	2	9	2	9	2	8
Federal Employee Populations						
General federal employees	15	14	6	14	8	13
By sex						
Men	16	16	7	16	9	15
Women	11	9	3	6	4	8
By educational level						
High school not completed	23	22	7	20	11	17
High school completed	17	13	7	14	8	11
Some college	8	12	3	12	7	11
College graduate	5	7	4	8	3	11
Executives	8	7	4	8	5	8
Natural scientists	4	4	0	7	4	8
Social scientists	3	7	7	10	5	10
Engineers	5	3	1	8	3	7

389

Table 13-2g

<u>Highlights</u>: Refused to stereotype--explicitly rejected generalization.

. . . . Percentages in this category provide an indication of the amount
of stereotyping in the various groups concerning the work of civil
service employees as compared to the work of large business employees.
In general, it shows that the nonfederal populations reject the idea of
stereotyping more often in relation to business employees than to civil
service employees. This is especially true in the general employed
public, where the percentage ratio is roughly 1 to 2 1/2 on the side of
refusing to generalize about the work of business employees.

. . . . In the federal employee populations, on the other hand, rejection of generalization is more frequent for civil service work than for
large business work, although the differences are small among general
federal employees.

. . . . Frequency of rejection is positively related to educational
level in the general employed public and among students. This is also
true for general federal employees with respect to the work of business
employees; however, propensity to reject stereotyping about the work of
civil service employees appears to have very little relation to educational level.

Table 13-2g

The image of the federal civil servant: the kinds of work people
picture civil service employees as doing, and employees of large
private business as doing (cont'd.)

	Refused to stereotype--explicitly rejected generalization about the work of:	
	Civil service employees	Large business employees
Nonfederal Populations		
General employed public	7%	18%
By sex		
Men	7	19
Women	6	15
By educational level		
High school not completed	4	10
High school completed	6	17
Some college	6	30
College graduate	15	32
Students		
High school students	5	11
College seniors	12	15
Graduate students	27	27
Groups in education		
High school teachers	23	29
Vocational counselors	35	38
College teachers	24	30
Natural scientists	34	37
Social scientists	39	33
Engineers	24	39
Groups in business		
Executives	19	33
Natural scientists	39	38
Social scientists	34	36
Engineers	34	47
Federal Employee Populations		
General federal employees	25	21
By sex		
Men	25	23
Women	24	15
By educational level		
High school not completed	22	16
High school completed	24	20
Some college	29	21
College graduate	26	29
Executives	35	26
Natural scientists	45	37
Social scientists	39	32
Engineers	44	31

The refusals to stereotype rise markedly with education: concerning government work, from 4 percent at the high school not completed level to 15 percent for college graduates; concerning work in business, from 10 to 32 percent.

Two response categories on federal work stand out. Clerical activities and postal work are mentioned by slightly over one fourth of the general employed public. Somewhat less salient are office work (15 percent) and managerial and administrative activities (14 percent). Protective and law enforcement activities, professional work, and technical and scientific work are noted by 7 to 8 percent. Engineering activities and the work of craftsmen, laborers, and operatives are mentioned by only 2 to 5 percent. The figures for the blue-collar categories—craftsmen, operatives, and laborers—and for postal work are by and large negatively related to educational level. References to postal work, for example, descend from 32 percent among those not completing high school to 10 percent for college graduates. On the other hand, references to managerial and professional work and clerical work rise with increasing educational status.

In describing the work of large business employees, this group of respondents most frequently cites managerial, executive, and administrative activities: 38 percent of them do so, whereas only 14 percent cite these activities as typical of the work of civil servants. Of less saliency (mentioned by 11 to 18 percent) are sales, clerical, and office work, and the work of craftsmen, operatives, and laborers. The references to clerical work in business lag behind the same references for the civil service (18 vs. 28 percent), but the work of craftsmen is seen in business more than in government (15 vs. 4 percent), as is that of operatives (18 vs. 2 percent). laborers (11 vs. 2 percent), and, of course, sales work (14 vs. 0 percent).[1] The figures for office work are virtually identical in each set of responses —14 percent for business employees and 15 percent for government employees. Sex and education make little difference in the relative degree to which various activities are seen in one sector more than in the other.

HIGH SCHOOL STUDENTS, COLLEGE SENIORS, AND GRADUATE STUDENTS. As the data in Table 13-2g indicate, all but 5 percent of the high school students stereotype civil service work, and only 11 percent refuse to stereotype business work. But the refusal rates increase among the more

---

[1] Virtually no federal or nonfederal respondents attribute sales work to civil service, and, equally understandably, no respondents attribute postal work to large business employment.

advanced students—and especially among the graduate students, 27 percent of whom refuse to stereotype both kinds of work.

The pattern of responses among the student populations on civil service work tends to resemble that of respondents at different educational levels in the general employed public. Thus, the college seniors and graduate students are somewhat more inclined than the high school students to characterize government work as administrative, technical and scientific, engineering, and clerical; they are less inclined to mention postal work. On other responses there is little difference among the students. As do employees in the general public, the students often see business employees in administrative and management activities and as craftsmen, operatives, and laborers, while federal employees are seen as performing clerical work and (by graduate students) office work.

HIGH SCHOOL TEACHERS AND VOCATIONAL COUNSELORS. These two groups are considerably less willing than the college-trained members of the general public to generalize about the work of civil servants, and they are fairly similar to each other in their refusals to stereotype either type of work. Both groups are also more inclined to mention sales work for business employees and professional work for government employees; for the latter reference, the vocational counselors' 24 percent is the highest figure in any group.

In other respects, the responses of the high school teacher groups resemble those of the college graduates in the general public. The most often mentioned characteristics of federal employment are clerical work, office work, professional work, and managerial and executive activities, in that order. For business employment, managerial activities are dominant—being cited by 51 percent of each group—followed by sales, clerical, and office work.

COLLEGE TEACHERS, NATURAL AND SOCIAL SCIENTISTS, AND ENGINEERS. In some respects the special groups in higher education differ from the general employed public in their description of the work of civil servants. Although clerical work (especially) and office work receive heavy emphasis, other kinds of activities are also cited fairly often by the various special college teaching groups. Thus, 41 and 31 percent of the college natural scientists and engineers cite technical and scientific activities, and 25 percent of the engineers specifically mention engineering. Most of the groups attribute managerial, professional, technical and scientific, and engineering endeavors to federal workers more often than respondents in the general employed public do. Postal work, however, is cited by no more than 12 percent of any college teacher group, versus 26 percent in the general public, and references to federal blue-collar activities and protective services are, for the most part, also less frequent. In terms of the activities associated with the work of civil service employees compared with those of large business employees, the *relative* frequencies of mention among the special groups in education are roughly the same as those of the general employed public; for example, as in the general public, managerial work is attributed to business employees by three to four times the number of respondents that attribute it to civil servants.

GROUPS IN BUSINESS. Like their counterparts in education, the business groups stress the clerical and office work in federal employment. They also tend to give greater emphasis than the general public does to managerial, professional, technical and scientific, and engineering activities carried on in government; and less emphasis to federal postal work, blue-collar activities, and protective services. In emphasizing some activities for civil servants and others for business employees, however, the business groups display roughly the same pattern noted in the general public.

Federal Employee Populations

GENERAL FEDERAL EMPLOYEES. In contrast to the nonfederal public, these respondents are almost equally unwilling to stereotype the work of civil servants (25 percent) and business employees (21 percent). The refusal to generalize about government work varies little by educational level, but for business work it increases as the levels rise. Men are considerably more inclined than women to refuse to generalize about business work.

When the general federal employees describe civil service work, clerical work looms largest, being mentioned by 35 percent. Next are managerial activities and office work, cited by 21 and 20 percent. Mentions of postal, professional, craft, and technical and scientific activities are made by a range of 10 to 15 percent. The work of laborers and operatives and engineering activities are mentioned even less frequently—a range of 6 to 8 percent. And about 3 percent of the respondents cite protective and law enforcement activities.

Federal clerical work is mentioned most frequently by high school graduates and those with college training. The college graduates also cite technical and scientific work the most often. References to federal managerial, professional, and engineering activities all show a general tendency to rise with educational level, while references to craftsmen, laborers, and postal workers decline among the more highly educated. Office work is cited least often by the college trained.

The women respondents differ noticeably from the men on two points. They are more likely to mention clerical work (45 percent) and office work (27 percent) than men are (31 and 18 percent). But men cite the postal work of the federal service considerably more often than women, although the figures are not high in either case (16 and 3 percent).

When the descriptions of civil service work given by the two general employee groups are compared, we find some striking differences in perception. The general federal work force is somewhat more inclined than the nonfederal to list such activities as management and administration (21 vs. 14 percent) and clerical work (35 vs. 28 percent). But the federal workers are much less likely than the general public to mention postal work in government (12 vs. 26 percent). Federal workers, moreover, while still more likely to cite administrative-management activities as typical of business (33 percent) rather than of government (21 percent), see much less of a gap between the two sectors in this respect than do workers in the general public, whose figures are 14 percent for civil service vs. 38 percent for large business.

FEDERAL EXECUTIVES, NATURAL AND SOCIAL SCIENTISTS, AND ENGINEERS. Among the special federal groups, large numbers of respondents refuse to generalize about either type of work. Unlike nearly all of their nonfederal counterparts, however, they refuse to stereotype civil service work (a range of 35 to 44 percent) more often than business work (26 to 37 percent). Of all the groups interviewed, the federal natural scientists, social scientists, and engineers are the most reluctant to generalize about the work of federal civil servants. Among those who do generalize, however, the aspects cited most often (by more than 20 percent of each group) are clerical work, managerial activities, and technical and scientific work. Two other activities noted in moderately high proportions are office and professional work.

Compared with the general federal population, the special federal groups put greater emphasis on the higher-status types of federal work. They refer more often—with occasional exceptions—to professional, technical and scientific, and engineering activities. But they generally accord less notice to clerical activities, postal work, protective and enforcement services, and the blue-collar work of craftsmen, operatives, and laborers. However, none of the four special federal groups diverges appreciably or consistently in its descriptions of government work from its business and academic counterparts. Yet there are again some signs that, over all, the higher status activities in government are somewhat more frequently cited by the federal respondents.

PART THREE

PART THREE

14

The General Employed Public:
Occupational Ratings and Values

DIVIDING OUR TWO GENERAL employed population samples by sex and educational strata, as in Part Two, by no means exhausts the relevant variables which may be analytically applied to a group's responses. In this chapter the occupational ratings and stated occupational values of the respondents in the general employed public are further explored by relating them in various ways to a number of other demographic features. These include family income, occupation, age, race, region, community background, and place of residence, as well as factors that emerge from a more refined analysis of differences according to sex.

The importance of analysis in relation to this wider assortment of demographic characteristics is self-evident. We had, however, a further purpose in conducting the supplementary analysis: to go beyond these standard factors to a consideration of variables that represent attitudes or states of mind which have bearing on an individual's occupational outlook. Thus we have examined the association of occupational ratings and job values (particularly the former) to four classificatory schemes: (1) orientation to opportunity in a job versus orientation to security; (2) occupational satisfaction; (3) evaluations of civil service employees; (4) the appeal of federal employment. Since these dimensions are employed extensively in this and following chapters and since they are less obvious in nature than the demographic variables, we will explain briefly why we believed they would have bearing on the major points examined in the supplementary analysis, and how the respondents were distributed along each of the four continuums.

1. For two main reasons the measurement of orientation to opportu-

nity seemed a reasonable bet to heighten our understanding of occupational ratings and the images of federal employment and federal employees. First, although there is much present debate as to which orientation affects our society the most—the desire for job security or the desire for opportunity—it appears likely that both desires are present and of relevance to people as they view the occupational world. Second, one of the hallmarks of the image of federal employment and employees is an emphasis on security (as Part Two illustrated).

Our measure for opportunity orientation was relatively simple in technique. Respondents were placed in a three-way classification according to the ratings they assigned, on the ten-point, agree-disagree scale, to the following statement:

"It is more important for a job to offer *opportunity* than *security*." Scores were distributed rather uniformly along the ten-point scale so that the following allocations were made:

Opportunity vs. Security	Agreement Scores	Number of Cases
Low on Opportunity	1-4	340
Medium on Opportunity	5-7	368
High on Opportunity	8-10	384

While there may be some danger in basing such a classification on the reactions to a single statement, our developmental work and later analysis indicated that it was a highly discriminating measure and, when cross tabulated against other data, yielded findings in accord with theoretical expectations.

2. The satisfaction people find in their present occupations, expressed in terms of the self-anchoring occupational ladder, is one of the principal points of inquiry in our study. Customarily we use occupational satisfaction as a "dependent" variable; we are interested, for example, in how it is affected by such factors as sex, education, occupational attainments, and so on. Present occupational ratings also serve as important comparison measures—for example, when respondents are asked to indicate their past and future mobility on the occupational ladder. In our supplementary analysis, however, we also use occupational satisfaction as an "independent" variable. We will be interested, that is, in how certain matters, particularly occupational ratings other than present ones, vary according to a person's occupational satisfaction.

Our index groupings were obtained from the ratings that respondents gave their present occupations on the ten-interval self-anchoring ladder (see Chapter 4). Although the ladder scores had tended to fall into the upper half of the ladder, we obtained three fairly equal groupings of the sample, as follows:

Occupational Satisfaction	Ladder Scores	Number of Cases
Low	1-6	419
Medium	7-8	369
High	9-10	353

Because of the self-anchoring nature of these present occupational ratings, we place a good deal of confidence in them as indices of present occupational satisfaction.

3. Our study also places major emphasis on the image people have of federal employees, particularly general civil service employees. Again, we are usually interested in how this image varies according to standard demographic and social characteristics. But it seemed possible that a person's perceptions and evaluations of civil service personnel are also related to other items of concern to us, especially in regard to the attractiveness of federal employment. Therefore, we constructed an index derived from the scores assigned by respondents to civil service employees on the ten-point, high-low scale in reference to five qualities (see Chapter 12). Out of the five characteristics on which ratings were obtained, three were selected for inclusion in the index: honesty, ability, and interest in serving the public. Since ratings were made on the basis of a 1-to-10 step scale a total of 30 points was possible, with 3 points being the minimum; the higher the point total, the higher or more favorable was the evaluation. Dividing the respondents into the three most nearly equal groupings we obtained the following classification:

Evaluation of Civil Service Employees	Sum of Rating Scores	Number of Cases
Low	Under 20	349
Medium	20-24	401
High	25-30	320

Such an index by no means includes all of the relevant factors constituting a person's image of the civil service employee. Yet these components appear to be sufficiently important so that the index does serve to differentiate among the respondents.

4. Still another focus of our inquiry deals with the appeal of federal

employment for various kinds of people. In Part Two we have seen that
the degree of this appeal is unequally distributed throughout the general employed public, as well as among other populations. Hypothesiz-
ing that these variations would be a useful analytical tool in examining
such matters as occupational ratings and the image of federal employees,
we selected the reactions to the following statement as an approximate
measure of the appeal of federal work: "All things considered, working
for the federal government appeals to me." Ratings of agreement with
the statement were well distributed along the ten-point, agree-disagree
scale; thus the following divisions were constructed.

Appeal of Federal Employment	Agreement Scores	Number of Cases
Low	1-3	363
Medium	4-7	395
High	8-10	321

This measurement of appeal differs from the two other measures in
which respondents made occupational ladder comparisons between their
present jobs and working for the government, from their own viewpoints
and from the suppositional viewpoint of their families. Nevertheless, the
intercorrelations of response patterns among all three questions are similar enough to make us confident that the present measurement is a valid
expression of the appeal of federal employment.

Occupational Ratings

Present Satisfaction, Sense of Progress, and Future Expectations

In terms of the ten-point occupational ladder, most people in the general employed public profess a state of job satisfaction, with scores tending to fall in the upper ranges of the scale rather than the lower. Nevertheless, the respondent's position in life has bearing on the rating he as-
signs himself. Higher occupational status, higher income, and higher age
accompany higher occupational satisfaction. Thus, as Table 14-1 shows,
professional and managerial people who make $8,500 and over and
those who are 49 years old and over have the highest scores. On the
other hand, such demographic characteristics as geographic region and
community background (the place lived in up to the age of 15) account
for little variation in scores. The population size of the present place of

TABLE 14-1. *Ratings of Own Occupation at Present, 5 Years Ago, and 5 Years Hence, Related to Six Characteristics of the General Employed Public*[a]

Characteristics	Average Number Answering	Present Occupation	5 Years Ago	Difference: "Present" Minus "5 Years Ago"	5 Years from Now	Difference: "5 Years from Now" Minus "Present"
Occupation						
Unskilled and semi-skilled	362	6.6	6.1	+ .5	7.6	+1.0
Skilled	178	7.1	6.1	+1.0	7.8	+ .7
Clerical	161	7.3	6.2	+1.1	8.6	+1.3
Professional and managerial	284	7.7	6.7	+1.0	8.6	+ .9
Farmers	77	7.4	7.0	+ .4	7.7	+ .4
Family Income						
Under $4,000	215	6.8	6.4	+ .4	7.9	+1.1
$4,000–5,499	303	6.9	6.1	+ .8	7.8	+ .9
$5,500–8,499	311	7.2	6.5	+ .7	8.1	+ .9
$8,500 and over	226	7.7	6.7	+1.0	8.6	+ .9
Age						
Under 33	277	6.9	5.7	+1.2	8.4	+1.5
33–39	203	6.9	5.9	+1.0	8.0	+1.1
40–48	291	7.2	6.6	+ .6	8.0	+ .8
49 and older	284	7.5	7.0	+ .5	7.8	+ .3
Place of Residence Size						
Open country and urban fringe	391	7.2	6.5	+ .7	8.1	+ .9
1,000–9,999	149	7.5	6.8	+ .7	8.2	+ .7
10,000–99,999	179	7.1	6.2	+ .9	8.1	+1.0
100,000–249,999	114	7.3	6.3	+1.0	8.2	+ .9
250,000 and over	229	6.6	6.0	+ .6	7.9	+1.3
Geographic Region						
Northeast	499	7.0	6.3	+ .7	8.0	+1.0
Midwest	113	7.0	6.3	+ .7	7.7	+ .7
South	273	7.4	6.7	+ .7	8.4	+1.0
West	137	7.0	6.1	+ .9	8.1	+1.1
Community Background						
Farm	388	7.1	6.4	+ .7	7.9	+ .8
Town	343	7.1	6.4	+ .7	8.0	+ .9
Suburbs	161	7.2	6.4	+ .8	8.4	+1.2
Center city	143	7.1	6.2	+ .9	8.2	+1.1

[a] The mean ratings shown in this table and subsequent rating tables in this chapter are based on a ten-step scale.

residence similarly makes little difference—unless the population is 250,000 or more. Somewhat lower occupational and income levels probably account for the lower placements of this group.

Respondents in the general public also express a sense of occupational progress, but again there is variation. The respondents in unskilled and semiskilled jobs and the farmers feel they have advanced least in the last five years; those in skilled, clerical, and professional-managerial occupations express the most sense of progress, with few differences among the groups. The relationship between income and rate of progress is direct— those with the lowest income indicate the least movement, those with the highest income, the most. The association with age is understandably inverse; the older a person is, the less likely he is to be making the perceived kind of progress found among younger persons. Having been in the work force for a longer period of time he has presumably experienced his years of fastest acceleration. Rates of perceived progress vary little or not at all with geographic region, community background, or by size of place of residence.

Continued progress in the coming five years is also foreseen. Nevertheless, as can be seen again in Table 14-1, this is more true of some groupings than of others. The major shift occurs when age is considered. Respondents under 33 years predict an upward movement of + 1.5; those 49 and over expect to move only + 0.3. Perhaps the most striking feature here is the expectation of the youngest group; if this were to be realized, the mean score five years hence would be 8.4, a radical contrast to the 7.5 rating the oldest age group gives its present occupation. In other words, the younger people expect their advance to be considerably faster and farther than the older people's has been. The farmers make up the only other group to show little expectation of progress. Although they rank their present occupation second highest among the occupational groups (7.4), they expect to move only slightly in the next five years (to 7.7). In contrast, respondents in clerical occupations see themselves moving from the present rating of 7.3 to 8.6, a jump which would place them beside the professional-managerial group in five years.

Some of our other perspectives can also shed light on this subject (Table 14-2). What is the relationship, for example, between opportunity orientation and sense of progress? One might hypothesize that people who emphasize opportunity would have greater expectations for the future, but the data clearly show (Table 14-2) virtually no association between the factors. Opportunity-oriented respondents have only slightly higher mean scores on their present occupation ratings, feel they were at about the same point five years ago as the less opportunity-oriented, and expect to advance to approximately the same height as others five years from now.

The three other attitude measures, however, reveal sharp differences. When the occupational satisfaction index is applied, there is of course considerable difference between the three groups on their present occupational ratings (Table 14-2), since this is the measure used to establish

TABLE 14-2. *Ratings of Own Occupation at Present, 5 Years Ago, and 5 Years Hence, Related to Four Classifications of the General Employed Public*

Classifications[a]	Average Number Answering	Present Occupation	5 Years Ago	Difference: "Present" Minus "5 Years Ago"	5 Years from Now	Difference: "5 Years from Now" Minus "Present"
Opportunity vs. Security						
Low on opportunity	316	7.0	6.5	+ .5	8.0	+1.0
Medium on opportunity	341	7.1	6.2	+ .9	8.0	+ .9
High on opportunity	361	7.3	6.4	+ .9	8.2	+ .9
Occupational Satisfaction						
Low	389	4.7	4.8	− .1	6.4	+1.7
Medium	346	7.5	6.2	+1.3	8.4	+ .9
High	327	9.6	8.4	+1.2	9.7	+ .1
Evaluation of Civil Service Employees						
Low	326	7.0	6.3	+ .7	7.9	+ .9
Medium	371	7.2	6.2	+1.0	8.2	+1.0
High	299	7.2	6.6	+ .6	8.1	+ .9
Appeal of Federal Employment						
Low	342	7.6	6.6	+1.0	8.4	+ .8
Medium	365	7.1	6.3	+ .8	8.0	+ .9
High	300	6.7	6.2	+ .5	7.9	+1.2

[a] Explanations concerning the construction of these classifications are presented in the opening pages of this chapter.

the index. Of more significance is the fact that respondents with the lowest present ratings see themselves, on the average, as having gone down rather than up over the past five years. This grouping is one of the very few revealed by our analysis that shows a sense of downward mobility, which contrasts with the optimism of the respondents with medium and high scores of satisfaction, who indicate progress of over a scale point. Within the next five years, however, those of lowest satisfaction expect to go from a ranking of 4.7 to 6.4, a gain of 1.7 scale points. This rise would still place them well below the other two groups, both in present ratings and expectations for the future. It is also worth noting that people with medium levels of present satisfaction also expect to advance, but those with the highest ratings expect only a minute shift—their average present score of 9.6 leaving scant room for a show of advancement on a ten-point scale.

When the civil service employee evaluation index is applied, it makes little difference (as Table 14-2 shows) in the appraisals of present occupation or the feelings of past and future mobility. But the index that is based on the degree to which working for the government appeals to respondents proves more discriminating. There is an inverse relationship between the appeal of federal employment and present occupational rating—the more appeal, the lower the satisfaction. The relationship is seen also, though less markedly, for the estimations of progress over the past five years and over the next five.

Present Employment vs. Working for the Federal Government

Where do people think they would be on the occupational ladder if their type of work stayed the same but they were employed by the federal government? The comparisons, according to various demographic factors, between present occupation ratings and ratings of working for the government are shown in Table 14-3. For the factors of occupation, family income, and age there tends to be an inverse relationship—the higher the occupational status, income, and age, the lower is the rating for federal employment. Conversely, these groups have the highest present occupational ratings. Thus, while respondents with family incomes of less than $4,000 indicate an upward movement of from 6.8 to 7.2 (for a net gain of 0.4), those at the other extreme of $8,500 and over calculate a downward movement of from 7.7 to 5.7 (for a net loss of 2.0). The movement is similar, though less sharp, by age level. Highlighting the picture is the extreme drop expressed by the farmers (a net loss of 2.9), if they were to work for the government. This may be partly due to the farmers' difficulty in imagining their occupations placed under federal employment.

TABLE 14-3. *Ratings of Present Occupation vs. Doing the Same Work, but for the Federal Government, Related to Seven Characteristics of the General Employed Public*

Characteristics	Average Number Answering	Present Occupation	Same Occupation, but for the Government	Difference: "Government" Minus "Present"
Occupation				
Unskilled and semiskilled	386	6.6	7.0	+ .4
Skilled	181	7.1	6.8	− .3
Clerical	178	7.3	7.0	− .3
Professional and managerial	297	7.7	6.0	−1.7
Farmers	78	7.4	4.5	−2.9
Family Income				
Under $4,000	230	6.8	7.2	+ .4
$4,000–5,499	318	6.9	6.7	− .2
$5,500–8,499	324	7.2	6.5	− .7
$8,500 and over	206	7.7	5.7	−2.0
Age				
Under 33	308	6.9	6.7	− .2
33–39	207	6.9	6.5	− .4
40–48	295	7.2	6.4	− .8
49 and older	302	7.5	6.6	− .9
Place of Residence Size				
Open country and urban fringe	409	7.2	6.1	−1.1
1,000–9,999	156	7.5	7.1	− .4
10,000–99,999	188	7.1	6.6	− .5
100,000–249,999	122	7.3	7.0	− .3
250,000 and over	246	6.6	6.8	+ .2
Geographic Region				
Northeast	524	7.0	6.5	− .5
Midwest	118	7.0	5.7	−1.3
South	293	7.4	7.5	+ .1
West	142	7.0	5.6	−1.4
Community Background				
Farm	406	7.1	6.4	− .7
Town	364	7.1	6.7	− .4
Suburbs	171	7.2	6.5	− .7
Center city	148	7.1	6.7	− .4
Race				
White	978	7.2	6.3	− .9
Negro	116	6.4	7.8	+1.4

Differences in community background account for little variation, but place of residence size and geographic region do affect the measure. In general the more populated the area, the better the government looks by comparison (but not in the absolute ratings assigned—Column 3 in the table). This seems to be, not merely a function of population per se, but a consequence of the occupational structure of the areas. Geographically, respondents in the Northeast and the South give the highest absolute scores to working for the government. They likewise see the smallest difference resulting if the government became their employer—the southerners, in fact, claim a slight rise would follow. These regional variations persist when the amount of family income is controlled at under $5,500 and $5,500 and above.[1] Other cross tabulations (not tabled) showed that Protestants and Catholics, with income controlled, vary insignificantly on this measure. Similarly, strong Republicans and strong Democrats, as well as Independents, make about the same placements, although there is more response variation by income level for Republicans than for Democrats and Independents.[2]

We encountered another sharp division of opinion on the basis of the respondents' race. Predictably, present jobs are rated lower by Negro workers than by white workers. While we might reasonably expect the Negroes to rate government employment higher than the whites do, the net advantage they give it is excessive, especially when compared to the net deficit given by white employees. To be sure, the Negro group is more heavily comprised of people at the lower educational and income levels; such people favor government employment more than the upper-level groups, as we have seen. Despite this weighting we found that when occupational incomes were held constant at under $4,500 and at

[1] Statements indicating that certain factors are "being controlled" or "held constant" are common in the literature of survey analysis. Actually, of course, other factors are often not held exactly constant, respondents' sex being a classic exception. In the present case, for example, there might be considerable difference in ranges, means, or medians of family incomes above and below $5,500 in the four geographical regions. Saying that family income in controlled is thus somewhat misleading. However, unless the researcher has strong reasons to suspect that marked inner variations are occurring within one or more of his "controlled" cells, it seems legitimate and has in practice been adopted as a convention to use such expressions as "holding constant" and "controlling for." Throughout this section we will occasionally use such terms, keeping the above-stated qualifications in mind.

[2] Because we anticipated that whatever associations party identification might have with other parts of the study would be most marked among the strong partisans and Independents, all analyses by partisanship deal with strong Republicans, strong Democrats, and Independents.

$4,500 and above the differences still remained, although mitigated somewhat.

The breakdown by sex on this measure, noted earlier (Chapter 4), showed that women give a higher absolute rating to working for the government (7.4 vs. 6.3 for men). A comparison of this with their rating of present occupation resulted in a standoff, while men registered an overall net loss of 0.8. Holding such factors as education, family income, occupation, age, and community background constant in relating sex to this measure indicates that women in each case exceed men in the scores assigned working for the government. For example, according to family income and sex the mean ratings for working for the government are:

	N	Working for the Government
Under $4,000		
Men	(158)	7.0
Women	(67)	7.6
$4,000-5,499		
Men	(252)	6.5
Women	(62)	7.7
$5,500-8,499		
Men	(256)	6.3
Women	(65)	7.3
$8,500 and over		
Men	(157)	5.4
Women	(46)	6.7

It does not follow, however, that women regularly perceive the same degree of difference between present and governmental employment ratings. Among respondents at the some-college level or more, there is little difference between the sexes on net scores resulting from a comparison of the two ratings. At the two lower educational levels, however, women are considerably less anti-government than men, and actually have positive net scores for government employment. Among respondents 49 years old and over there is virtually no difference in net scores by sex, whereas at the younger age levels women produce consistently higher scores than men in favor of government employment. But perhaps the best index of the sex cleavage is provided by comparative ratings according to occupation. Over 95 percent of the women in the sample are in the unskilled and semiskilled, clerical, and professional-managerial categories; the difference scores that emerge when present employment placements are subtracted from federal employment ratings are as follows:

	N	Difference Scores
Unskilled and Semiskilled		
Men	(276)	+.4
Women	(110)	+.4
Skilled		
Men	(176)	−.4
Women[3]	—	—
Clerical		
Men	(94)	−.9
Women	(84)	+.6
Professional and Managerial		
Men	(240)	−1.7
Women	(57)	−1.5
Farmers		
Men	(76)	−2.9
Women[3]	—	—

These data leave little doubt that, in the categories occupied in substantial numbers by both men and women, it is among the clerical respondents that the great gap between the sexes appears. In sum, we may say that while women typically rate working for the government at their same job absolutely higher than do men, the comparisons between present and governmental ratings show that women of younger age, of lower education, and in clerical occupations would feel the least disadvantaged by working for the government and would, in fact, feel that government employment would be better.

Our four nondemographic factors are equally relevant to this comparison measure (Table 14-4). Despite the small difference on present occupational ratings according to the degree of opportunity orientation, there is a significant spread when the present work is pictured being done in the federal government: the less affinity toward opportunity, the higher the placement of working for the government. Consequently the net difference between the two ratings shows a perceived increment of 0.1 for those low on opportunity and a net deficit of 1.2 for those highest on opportunity; in other words, the more opportunity-oriented a person is, the more disadvantaged he feels he would be, absolutely and relatively, were he to work for the government at his same occupation.

When comparisons are made on this measure by level of occupational

[3] Too few cases to warrant entry.

satisfaction the findings prove dramatic. Although the rating assigned the occupation if it were with the federal government varies directly with the present level of satisfaction, it is in the difference scores that

TABLE 14-4. *Ratings of Present Occupation vs. Doing the Same Work, but for the Federal Government, Related to Four Classifications of the General Employed Public*

Classifications	Average Number Answering	Present Occupation	Same Occupation, but for the Government	Difference: "Federal" Minus "Present"
Opportunity vs. Security				
Low on opportunity	335	7.0	7.1	+ .1
Medium on opportunity	361	7.1	6.4	− .7
High on opportunity	379	7.3	6.1	−1.2
Occupational Satisfaction				
Low	412	4.7	5.6	+ .9
Medium	362	7.5	6.8	− .7
High	346	9.6	7.4	−2.2
Evaluation of Civil Service Employees				
Low	343	7.0	6.0	−1.0
Medium	398	7.2	6.6	− .6
High	313	7.2	7.1	− .1
Appeal of Federal Employment				
Low	354	7.6	5.6	−2.0
Medium	389	7.1	6.7	− .4
High	318	6.7	7.4	+ .7

the real significance lies. People ranking their present jobs the lowest feel their lot would be improved significantly; those who rank them highest feel they would suffer a serious occupational setback. The conclusion is inescapable—the less satisfied a person is, the higher he rates the relative appeal of government employment.

There is a moderate relationship between the evaluation of the civil servant index and the rating given working for the government: respondents having the highest estimate of the employees also upgrade working for the government. This suggests a link between respondents' perceptions of an aspect of federal employment and the attractiveness of working for the federal government. Similarly, there is a positive association between the appeal of federal employment and ratings for present occupation if it were with the government. It would, of course, be surprising if the case were otherwise; to a certain extent these two measures tap a common attitude. But the internal consistency is impressive and lends reliability to each measure.

Other findings (not tabled) based on the comparison of present versus governmental occupational ratings include the following: self-employed respondents rate working for the government lower than those not self-employed (5.0 vs. 6.8); religious preference, previous military service, and previous federal civilian employment[4] show negligible relationship to the scores. And strong Democrats, strong Republicans, and Independents differ little on the absolute score given working for the government, but the Republicans do show the greatest net loss when their scores are compared with present occupational ratings (−1.2 vs. −0.6 for the Democrats and −0.5 for the Independents.)

When respondents were asked whether they thought their families would feel a switch in employment to the government was a move up the occupational ladder, down the ladder, or would make no difference, this significant datum emerged: according to virtually every classification used in our analysis, a substantial proportion of respondents, ranging from one fourth to one half, say "no difference." Implicit here is the suggestion that the specific employer is of little relevance to many people as far as occupational ratings are concerned. This is demonstrated for occupation, income, age, and size of place of residence in Table 14-5.

But the distribution of "up the ladder" and "down the ladder" replies is important too. For the most part they parallel the pattern reported earlier; as occupational status, income level, and age rise, the percentage saying "up the ladder" declines, and conversely the percentage saying "down" increases. This disparity is most graphic in the case of family income. Of the workers with incomes under $4,000, 53 percent report moving up, and only 11 percent down. In sharp contrast, 23 percent in the highest bracket reply moving up, with almost twice that many (43 percent) saying "down."

[4] Statements on the relationship of previous federal civilian employment to various measures used here and in following chapters should be interpreted cautiously. Although 157 respondents indicated that they were in this category, the range of experiences and the time elapsed since such employment occurred were so great that it proved difficult to characterize these people as a whole or to control for various characteristics so that subanalysis could be performed. Most of our findings show few or no relevant differences between these former employees and the rest of the working force sample. However, for the above reasons we cannot say with certainty that previous federal employment makes *no* difference in the kinds of responses we obtained. It could be that it affects the outlook of some one way, some another, and exerts little or no effect on still others.

TABLE 14-5. *Responses to: "Suppose you were to change now and go to work for the U.S. government doing the same thing you are doing now, how do you think your family might feel about it? Would they feel you were moving up the ladder or down?" Related to Four Characteristics of the General Employed Public*

Characteristics	Number Answering	Up the Ladder	Down the Ladder	No Difference	Don't Know
Occupation					
Unskilled and semiskilled	388	54%	10%	35%	1%
Skilled	179	34	17	48	2
Clerical	177	44	15	41	1
Professional and managerial	290	27	32	39	1
Farmers	79	18	58	24	0
Family Income					
Under $4,000	229	53	11	36	0
$4,000–5,499	316	46	16	36	1
$5,500–8,499	324	33	20	45	2
$8,500 and over	202	23	43	32	2
Age					
Under 33	307	45	16	39	1
33–39	208	44	21	33	1
40–48	293	36	23	39	1
49 and older	297	34	25	40	1
Place of Residence Size					
Open country and urban fringe	404	30	29	39	2
1,000–9,999	159	42	17	42	0
10,000–99,999	187	43	14	41	2
100,000–249,999	120	43	19	36	2
250,000 and over	243	49	16	34	0

Occupationally, it is worth noting that skilled workers estimate less advancement than clerical personnel, and that farmers again show the least feeling of improvement and the most sense of loss if they were to switch. The major difference by place of residence size is that respondents living in the open country and the urban fringe attribute less movement up and more down than those in other population areas. Other demographic variables (not tabled) were introduced into the analysis to test suggested hypotheses. Community background, religious preference, and previous government employment show virtually no relationship with the responses to this question; however, the self-employed are much more prone than those not self-employed to say "down" and much less prone to say "up." And, again, a substantial percentage in each of these classifications falls into the "no difference" category.

Looking at the answers given by men and women in the analysis by education, family income, occupation, age, and community background confirms the findings reported earlier. Higher percentages of women almost universally indicate movement up the ladder and lower percentages indicate movement down, but the differences between men and women are more marked for some classifications than others. The divergencies are most marked among the less educated, younger, clerical, and lower-income groups. But even though women in these categories find greater attractiveness in government employment than do comparable males, these women do not necessarily have the highest absolute percentages favoring the government; for example, 56 percent of the women in unskilled and semiskilled work versus 49 percent of those in clerical jobs say "up the ladder." The point being made here is that the differences between men and women are greater in clerical occupations than in other kinds of work.

An examination of the work force in nondemographic dimensions brings additional information on the estimated views of families (Table

TABLE 14-6. *Responses to: "Suppose you were to change now and go to work for the U.S. government doing the same thing you are doing now, how do you think your family might feel about it? Would they feel you were moving up the ladder or down?" Related to Four Classifications of the General Employed Public*

Classifications	Number Answering	Up the Ladder	Down the Ladder	No Difference	Don't Know
Opportunity vs. Security					
Low on opportunity	334	44%	14%	40%	2%
Medium on opportunity	361	41	22	36	1
High on opportunity	370	32	29	38	1
Occupational Satisfaction					
Low	413	51	16	32	1
Medium	359	38	21	40	1
High	340	26	28	44	2
Evaluation of Civil Service Employees					
Low	340	31	27	41	1
Medium	391	40	23	37	1
High	312	48	15	36	1
Appeal of Federal Employment					
Low	346	19	38	42	1
Medium	388	40	17	42	1
High	317	61	9	29	1

14-6). Again the findings coincide with those cited earlier. The higher the orientation to opportunity rather than security the lower are the percentages for "up the ladder," and the higher are the percentages for "down the ladder." The differences, while not extremely large, are consistent and progressive. Level of occupational satisfaction is highly associated with the measure: 51 percent of those lowest on satisfaction say "up the ladder" compared to 26 percent of those highest on satisfaction.

A connection between imagery and appeal is demonstrated in the association between a favorable view of civil servants and perceived movement up and down the ladder. This, too, is congruent with earlier findings. The more favorably respondents view federal employees, the more likely they are to say "up the ladder," and the less likely to say "down." Finally, the higher the appeal of federal employment the more likely is "up the ladder" to be the reply. Such a relationship not only highlights the internal consistency of the measurements but also suggests that appeal is solidly rooted in the anticipation of occupational improvement in going to work for the government.

Absolute and Comparative Appeal of Federal Employment

When respondents react to the statement, "All things considered, working for the federal government appeals to me," and to a similar statement about a large private business, the pattern is a now-familiar one (Table 14-7). As occupational status and income rise, the absolute appeal of working for the government drops.[5] On the other hand age makes little difference.

When the two appeal scores are compared, a similar ordering emerges. The unskilled and semiskilled and the lowest income groups see more appeal in working for the government rather than a large business; all other occupational and income groupings show the opposite. An interesting sidelight here is again provided by the farmers. They are not overly attracted to either type of employment, but do express more interest in working for the government (5.1) than for business (4.3).

[5] Throughout this supplementary analysis it will be noted that the responses of the skilled and clerical workers do not always constitute strata of a neat linear progression anchored by professionals and managerials on one pole and the unskilled and semiskilled on the other. For many measures, the progression of data along the occupational hierarchy corresponds to the arrangement used for tabling purposes; at other times, however, the distribution would be more "symmetrical" if the clerical group preceded the skilled. For consistency, however, we have used only one tabling order.

Differences by race correspond to the earlier picture regarding the degree of occupational satisfaction respondents would feel in carrying on their present work but as civil servants. The absolute appeal of government employment is higher for Negroes than for whites; the Negroes also favor government over business—whereas white workers do the reverse. The racial differences are more pronounced at the lower levels of income than at the higher.

TABLE 14-7. *Ratings of Occupational Appeal of the Federal Government vs. Large Private Business, Related to Four Characteristics of the General Employed Public*

Characteristics	Average Number Answering	"All things considered, working for a large private business firm appeals to me"	"All things considered, working for the federal government appeals to me"	Difference: "Government" Minus "Business"
Occupation				
Unskilled and semiskilled	367	5.8	6.1	+ .3
Skilled	175	5.8	5.1	− .7
Clerical	176	6.3	5.5	− .8
Professional and managerial	287	5.6	4.6	−1.0
Farmers	76	4.3	5.1	+ .8
Family Income				
Under $4,000	210	5.6	5.9	+ .3
$4,000–5,499	310	5.8	5.6	− .2
$5,500–8,499	320	5.9	5.3	− .6
$8,500 and over	204	5.5	4.2	−1.3
Age				
Under 33	296	5.7	5.3	− .4
33–39	202	5.9	5.7	− .2
40–48	286	5.5	5.2	− .3
49 and older	288	5.8	5.3	− .5
Race				
White	947	5.7	5.2	− .5
Negro	102	6.1	6.8	+ .7

When the responses of men and women are controlled by income, occupation, age, and education, we obtain the familiar pattern. Women consistently accord higher absolute scores than men to the appeal of working for the government and also regularly favor government as an employer over the large business firm. Because of the changed emphasis, however, the inclination of women in certain occupational groupings to show more comparative favoritism to government is not as prominent or consistent here as in the previous two measures used. Nevertheless the cleavage between males and females in clerical occupations is once more in greater evidence—the women rate government appeal at 6.3, the men rate it at 4.8.

Several other social characteristics (not tabled) have some moderate association with the appeal of government work. Workers living in the open country and urban fringe are least attracted, while those in cities of 250,000 and over are most attracted. By geographic region, respondents in the West and Midwest have the lowest scores on appeal, those in the South and Northeast the highest. Strong Republicans express somewhat less attraction than strong Democrats (4.9 vs. 5.6). Finally, the self-employed record less appeal than people who work for others. These findings are quite consistent with prior measures.

Certain other features show little or no relationship, again in accordance with earlier findings. Type of community background, religious preference, former military experience, or previous federal civilian employment have negligible bearing on the degree of federal employment appeal.

In the light of previous discussion it is to be expected that the non-demographic aspects of the individual's occupational world will also be related to the degree of appeal government employment has for him (Table 14-8). On the opportunity vs. security index, the lower opportunity scores are associated with the higher absolute scores on working for the government. The lower a person's present occupational satisfaction the more likely he is to rate government high on appeal. Scores on evaluations of civil service employees are strongly and directly related to higher appeal answers. The major significance of the appeal of federal employment index lies in the extreme range of responses obtained on this item.

Comparing the scores on federal appeal with those on private business appeal produces the same ordering of data found in the absolute scores on federal appeal (Table 14-8). The comparisons are illuminating, however, because they show that the people who find government employment appealing are not likely to be the same as those who find private business appealing—since the mean scores on working for a business tend to be similar for each classification. The appeal of federal employment index is an exception: here the appeal of business rises moderately (from 5.3 to 6.4) with the rises of federal appeal; the increase is

TABLE 14-8. *Ratings of Occupational Appeal of the Federal Government vs. a Large Private Business, Related to Four Classifications of the General Employed Public*

Classifications	Average Number Answering	"All things considered, working for a large private business firm appeals to me"	"All things considered, working for the federal government appeals to me"	Difference: "Government" Minus "Business"
Opportunity vs. Security				
Low on opportunity	332	5.8	5.7	− .1
Medium on opportunity	364	5.4	5.5	+ .1
High on opportunity	374	6.0	4.8	−1.2
Occupational Satisfaction				
Low	394	5.6	5.8	+ .2
Medium	348	5.8	5.2	− .6
High	338	5.8	4.9	− .9
Evaluation of Civil Service Employees				
Low	342	5.6	4.4	−1.2
Medium	390	5.7	5.3	− .4
High	311	6.0	6.3	+ .3
Appeal of Federal Employment				
Low	360	5.3	1.8	−3.5
Medium	394	5.6	5.5	− .1
High	316	6.4	9.1	+2.7

not large, however, compared to the distribution of the index itself (from 1.8 to 9.1). Furthermore, the net difference scores for the two appeal statements are of extreme magnitude. Subtracting "business" from "government," we find that respondents with low federal employment appeal scores show a *negative* difference of 3.5 and those with high appeal scores show a *positive* difference of 2.7. In other words, the higher a person rates the absolute appeal of federal employment, the higher he also rates its comparative appeal.

To what extent is employment appeal associated with perceptions of the chance for success in a given employment? Indexes were constructed on the basis of responses to the twin statements claiming that the best chance for young men of ability to be *really successful* lies in working for (the federal government) (a large private business corporation). Responses were classified into low, medium, and high levels of agreement with the statements. The hypothesis was that the more the particular

TABLE 14-9. *Ratings of Occupational Appeal of the Federal Government vs. a Large Private Business, Related to the General Employed Public's Perceptions of Avenues to Success*

Perceived Avenues to Success[a]	Average Number Answering	"All things considered, working for a large private business firm appeals to me"	"All things considered, working for the federal government appeals to me"	Difference: "Government" Minus "Business"
Large Corporation Employment				
Low agreement	303	4.7	4.9	+ .2
Moderate agreement	380	5.5	5.4	− .1
High agreement	390	6.8	5.7	−1.1
Federal Employment				
Low agreement	337	5.5	3.8	−1.7
Moderate agreement	392	5.6	5.2	− .4
High agreement	334	6.2	7.0	+ .8

[a] These two sets of scores are derived from ratings on the ten-point agree-disagree scale assigned to the following statements: "For a young man of ability, his best chance for being *really successful* lies in working for (a large private business corporation) (the federal government)." The higher the score, the more agreement.

employment is seen as an avenue to success the higher will be the appeal of that employment for the person. Table 14-9 offers substantial confirmation of the proposition. Interestingly, the correlation is higher for the pair of statements on government employment than for the pair on private employment.

These associations between perceptions of success and employment appeal are clouded somewhat by the presence of simultaneous associations with each other. That is, those who agree most that the large corporation is an avenue to success give higher appeal ratings to *both* private business and government; the same thing happens among those agreeing most that federal employment is an avenue to success. It seems sufficient to point out that these latter associations of "unlikes" are of considerably less magnitude than the former ones of "likes." This is amply shown by subtracting the figures for business appeal from those for government appeal. As the belief in achieving success in *private employment* increases, the comparative appeal of federal work *decreases*. But as the belief in achieving success in *government* increases, the comparative appeal of federal employment also *increases*, progressively and strongly.

Occupational Values

The "Ideal" Occupation

In Chapter 5 it was shown that the general employed public's visualization of an "ideal" occupation varied extensively according to the level of education attained and the sex of the respondents. One may reasonably expect, therefore, that other features of a person's position in life will be strongly associated with the kinds of occupational values he construes as "ideal." Table 14-10 shows the relationships between family income and ten major occupational values.

The associations are not invariant—that is, the frequency with which an item is mentioned sometimes does *not* vary in direct, linear fashion with the income level. For example, the values of security, stability, etc., and physical environment and working conditions are cited by the two middle income groups somewhat more often than by the lowest and highest income groups. More typically, however, the emphasis on the values varies directly with income level. All the values in the lower half of the table show a positive association with income; these are values that embody a concern with the nontangible, ego-rewarding aspects of a

TABLE 14-10. *Attributes of the "Ideal" Occupation, Related to Family Income in the General Employed Public*

Attributes of the "Ideal" Occupation	Family Income			
	Under $4,000	$4,000– 5,499	$5,500– 8,499	$8,500 and Over
Interest, enjoyment, satisfaction, pleasure	80%	71%	69%	65%
High or good financial reward	38	48	42	43
Security, stability, protection, fringe benefits	8	20	17	9
Good physical environment and working conditions	36	46	45	34
Good *active* relations with people at work	14	17	20	27
Self-development, self-expression, and creativity	4	8	11	14
Self-determination	23	30	29	35
Challenge	1	4	6	18
Sense of achievement or accomplishment	6	6	10	11
Variety, absence of monotony and routine	3	9	12	16
NUMBER ANSWERING	(234)	(321)	(328)	(209)

TABLE 14-11. *Attributes of the "Ideal" Occupation, Related to Occupation in the General Employed Public*

Attributes of the "Ideal" Occupation	Occupation				
	Unskilled and Semi-skilled	Skilled	Clerical	Professional and Man-agerial	Farmers
Interest, enjoyment, satisfaction, pleasure	72%	72%	65%	72%	79%
High or good financial reward	45	43	47	39	32
Security, stability, protection, fringe benefits	13	20	20	13	4
Good physical environment and working conditions	43	45	53	29	38
Good relations with supervisors	14	10	20	4	1
Good *passive* relations with people at work	13	9	19	10	3
Good *active* relations with people at work	11	8	33	31	4
Self-development, self-expression, and creativity	5	8	11	17	3
Self-determination	24	25	29	35	48
Sense of achievement or accomplishment	4	12	6	13	6
Challenge	1	7	7	15	1
Variety, absence of monotony and routine	6	10	15	14	3
Do work that is worthwhile, useful, constructive	10	8	17	24	8
NUMBER ANSWERING	(392)	(185)	(179)	(301)	(79)

job. As income rises there is a corresponding increase in the saliency of such values. Perhaps the most striking difference occurs for "challenge"— 1 percent of those in the lowest bracket mention it vs. 18 percent in the highest bracket.

Occupational groupings also bring out different emphases on occupational values (Table 14-11). In general, the lower the occupational prestige, the higher the mention of the more tangible, material aspects of a job. Conversely, the higher the status, the greater is the reference to the more intrinsic, nonmaterial, and ego-rewarding attributes. However, this is a very rough generalization, for the relationships are not always progressive. If the unskilled and semiskilled are matched against professional and managerial personnel, the generalization is upheld. For example 43 percent of the unskilled and semiskilled mention good physical environment and working conditions—against 29 percent of those in professional and managerial positions; at the other extreme, only 11 percent of the unskilled and semiskilled versus 31 percent of the top group cite good *active* relations with people at work.

On the other hand, the clerical group's blend of occupational values has elements of both the higher and lower prestige groupings. They share with the blue-collar workers a greater emphasis on security, physical environment, and, to a certain extent, good relations with supervisors and superiors. Concomitantly they resemble the professional and managerial respondents in their greater mention of good active personal relations and variety in the work. Farmers, too, have a mix of occupational values. While they have the lowest percentages for such values as financial reward, security, and good relations with supervisors, they show the highest mention of self-determination. These findings are not surprising, given the nature of the farmer's work environment. They do help to illustrate, however, the differential patterning of values which make up the ideal occupation for people in various walks of life. Although this patterning tends to vary with occupational "prestige," ingredients of the work environment may produce nuances transcending the prestige structure.

Education, income, and occupation have been shown to be highly related to the structuring of the ideal occupation. Age is much less closely associated with the shape of this ideal; on only a few items does it appear to make a difference (not tabled). It shows a strong negative association with the desire for high economic reward—53 percent of those under 33 years compared to 31 percent of those over 48 cite the factor. Young workers also mention good working conditions considerably more often (48 vs. 33 percent). Younger people are somewhat more concerned than older people about self-advancement and progress, but somewhat less concerned about doing work that fits one's capacities, and doing work that is worthwhile, useful, and constructive. There is only slight support for the feeling that young people are more security conscious: of those under 33, 17 percent cite some aspect of security; between 33 and 39, 16 percent; between 40 and 48, 13 percent; 49 and older, 12 percent. These variations could be explained by sampling error even though there is a uniform direction.

We saw earlier (Chapter 5), that women and men hold some common conceptions of the ideal occupation and differ on others. Holding constant the replies by sex according to educational level, family income, occupation, and age, it was found that divergencies persist under almost every classification. Thus, men more regularly display a moderate to strong concern about having a secure job, opportunities for self-advancement, self-determination and autonomy, and challenge in the work. Women almost universally give more attention than comparable males to good relations with supervisors, good active *and* passive personal relations with people at work, and doing work that is worthwhile and useful.

Among certain categories of men and women, however, we find less persistence of a pattern by sex only. For example, the greater desire for sense of achievement on the part of men is primarily reflected by education steps; at each level this is mentioned more frequently by men than women, but the greatest disparity comes at the upper educational levels. Similarly, the general margin that men give to high financial reward stems primarily from the fact that in the professional-managerial and clerical categories women show much less concern for it than do comparable men.

In fact, one of the over-all reasons for differential concern about certain occupational values is the distribution of women in the work force. The skilled worker and farmer populations in our work force sample are composed almost entirely of males. On some values the differences by sex within the professional-managerial, clerical, and unskilled and semiskilled groupings are not great. But when all men and all women are combined for analysis, or when they are considered according to some other characteristic, the weight of the skilled worker and farmer groupings tends to highlight the intersex differences.

The "Worst" Occupation

Persons interviewed were also asked to picture the attributes that would make an occupation the worst, rather than the best. Almost invariably the response patterns parallel those for the ideal occupation. However, in absolute terms, the mention of certain values is not entirely the same for the two descriptions; rather, the distribution of such replies among the various groupings tends toward two similar profiles. For example, in structuring the ideal work world, professional and managerial workers note the *presence* of self-development, self-expression, and creativity most frequently, and farmers least frequently. In describing the worst kind of occupation, the professionals and managers cite the *absence* of this factor most frequently, and farmers again least often. The range and frequency of replies differ somewhat on the second question, but the essential pattern is similar. A few attributes highlight the differences that may accompany variations in basic demographic features, such as the following, where family income is considered:

	Under $4,000 (234)	$4,000- 5,499 (321)	$5,500- 8,499 (330)	$8,500 and Over (206)
Poor or inadequate financial reward	33%	25%	29%	22%
Bad physical environment and working conditions	52	53	49	36
Excessive work load; too hard work	18	11	12	5
Monotony, routine, lack of variety	10	17	21	37

Level of income is inversely related to the mention of poor financial reward, bad physical environment, and a dislike for excessive or too hard work; the positive association with a desire to avoid monotonous work is quite evident, however. These findings are, for the most part, in accord with the data on the ideal job. Analysis by occupation and age produced similar conclusions.

Scale Ratings of Occupational Values

Another way of ascertaining the structuring of job values lay in utilizing the agree-disagree scale ratings assigned to various statements about occupational values and orientation to work. To the extent that the scale sort items correspond to the values mentioned in describing the most ideal and least ideal occupation, the patterning of responses tends to be similar. This comparability may be seen in Table 14-12, which presents the mean scores on selected items by income breaks. Consider, for example, the item, "Work is most satisfying when there are hard problems to solve." The movement from an agreement rate of 5.6 among people with the lowest incomes to 7.7 among those with the highest incomes closely parallels, and exceeds in its progressiveness, the movement for the corresponding value of "challenge" found in describing the ideal occupation (Table 14-10 above).

Certain other items are not so directly comparable to the open-end questions but the basic attitudinal structure accompanying different in-

TABLE 14-12. *Ratings of "Occupational Value" Statements, Related to Family Income in the General Employed Public*

"Occupational Value" Statements	Family Income			
	Under $4,000	$4,000– 5,499	$5,500– 8,499	$8,500– and Over
"To me, work is nothing more than a way of making a living"	5.5	4.4	3.9	3.2
"I like the kind of work you can forget about after the work day is over"	7.5	6.9	6.7	5.6
"To be really successful in life, you have to care about making money"	6.4	6.0	5.4	5.4
"To me, it's important in an occupation to have the chance to get to the top"	7.3	7.6	8.0	8.3
"It is more important for a job to offer *opportunity* than *security*"	5.5	5.6	5.8	7.0
"It is satisfying to direct the work of others"	6.0	6.3	6.8	7.1
"Success in an occupation is mainly a matter of luck"	4.6	3.7	3.2	3.0
"Success in an occupation is mainly a matter of knowing the right people"	5.9	5.0	5.0	4.3
"Success in an occupation is mainly a matter of hard work"	7.2	7.3	7.2	7.6
"To me, it's important to have the kind of work that gives me a chance to develop my own special abilities"	7.6	7.9	8.3	8.8
"Work is most satisfying when there are hard problems to solve"	5.6	6.1	6.7	7.7
AVERAGE NUMBER ANSWERING	(210)	(312)	(323)	(204)

come levels is apparent. Low-income respondents are more inclined than those of high income to agree that work is to be viewed as "bread and butter," that it is something to be done and forgotten about, that opportunity is less important than security, and that succeeding is more a matter of luck and knowing the right people than of hard work. But the higher the income the greater is the tendency to affirm such values as being able to direct others, having a chance to get to the top, developing one's special abilities, and having more opportunity than security in the job. Thus higher income accompanies more emphasis on the ego-rewarding, self-realization aspects of the job; the lower the income, the more is emphasis given to the extrinsic, material rewards of work and to the role of luck and "pull" in being successful.

When occupational classifications are related to the occupational values ratings, in many respects the data again mirror the responses to the open-end questions, but here too the intergroup differences are somewhat clearer and more regular. If we exclude the farmers in the sample, the distributions in Table 14-13 almost universally show the unskilled and semiskilled to be on one end of the range, the professional and managerial on the other, and the skilled and clerical in the middle. The professionals and managers have higher scores on such values as being able to direct others, to carry out ideas without interference, to solve hard problems, and to have opportunity rather than security. The unskilled and semiskilled agree more that work is only a way of making a living, that work you can forget about is preferable, and that success is a matter of knowing the right people and of luck. Farmers tend to fall midway be-

TABLE 14-13. *Ratings of "Occupational Value" Statements, Related to Occupation in the General Employed Public*

"Occupational Value" Statements	Occupation				
	Unskilled and Semi-skilled	Skilled	Clerical	Professional and Managerial	Farmers
"To me, work is nothing more than a way of making a living"	5.2	4.4	3.8	3.1	4.6
"I like the kind of work you can forget about after the work day is over"	7.4	6.6	6.7	5.9	6.8
"It is more important for a job to offer *opportunity* than *security*"	5.5	5.6	5.6	6.8	5.7
"Success in an occupation is mainly a matter of luck"	4.0	3.6	3.4	2.9	4.1
"Success in an occupation is mainly a matter of knowing the right people"	5.6	5.0	4.7	4.5	5.0
"Success in an occupation is mainly a matter of hard work"	7.1	7.5	7.2	7.4	7.2
"It is satisfying to direct the work of others"	5.9	6.8	6.5	7.3	6.3
"To me, it's important in an occupation for a person to be able to carry out his own ideas without interference"	6.2	6.6	6.6	7.2	7.4
"Work is most satisfying when there are hard problems to solve"	5.7	6.7	6.7	7.4	6.3
AVERAGE NUMBER ANSWERING	(369)	(176)	(177)	(290)	(77)

TABLE 14-14. *Ratings of "Occupational Value" Statements, Related to Age in the General Employed Public*

"Occupational Value" Statements	Age			
	18–32	33–39	40–48	49 and Older
"I like the kind of work you can forget about after the work day is over"	6.7	6.6	6.6	6.9
"Work should be the most important part of a person's life"	5.0	5.5	5.5	6.3
"To be really successful in life you have to care about making money"	5.5	5.7	5.9	6.0
"A person should constantly try to succeed even if it interferes with other things in life"	5.5	5.8	6.3	6.5
"To me, it's important in an occupation to have the chance to get to the top"	8.0	7.9	7.8	7.6
"It is more important for a job to offer *opportunity* than *security*"	5.8	6.0	5.9	6.0
"To me, it's important to have the kind of work that gives me a chance to develop my own special abilities"	8.5	8.0	8.1	7.9
"Work is most satisfying when there are hard problems to solve"	6.6	6.4	6.4	6.7
"The main satisfaction a person can get out of work is helping other people"	6.7	7.0	6.9	7.2
"Work helps you forget your personal problems"	6.7	7.0	7.5	7.7
"Work is a way of being of service to God"	7.3	7.7	7.8	7.9
NUMBER ANSWERING	(298)	(204)	(286)	(289)

tween the extremes—with the exception of the importance of being able to carry out ideas without interference, where they score highest (7.4 vs. a low of 6.2 for the unskilled and semiskilled). As noted before (Table 14-11), the farmers lead all occupational groups in mentioning the comparable value of "self-determination" in describing the ideal job. According to data from many parts of the interview schedule, this feeling for autonomy and control of the immediate work situation is a hallmark of the farmers and, of course, coincides with the traditional picture of the farmer.

Does age make a difference in the stress placed upon work values and perspectives in our sample of the work force? In part it does not. On many of the items for which income and occupation classifications show high discrimination, reactions by age remain stable (Table 14-14). Differences by age level are negligible for the statements referring to forgetting about work, making money, having hard problems to solve, the importance of opportunity versus security, and being able to get to the top. The relative emphasis placed on these items, therefore, seems to be much more a function of a person's sex and educational, occupational, and financial situation rather than of age, per se, although to thoroughly document this assumption would necessitate controlling for each of these variables at each age level. However, the cumulation of findings from various questions in the interview schedule lends strong support to the notion that age, itself, is not the critical factor for these types of occupational values.

On the other hand, certain values are moderately related to advancing age; these are in the area of attitudes that involve the ethics of work. Older people agree more that work should be the most important part of a person's life, that a person should constantly strive for success, that work helps in forgetting personal problems, and that work is a way of serving God. Although the differences are not large, it also appears that older people place more importance on doing work that is worthwhile and helps other people. Older age, then, seems to be associated with a stress on the inherent goodness and primacy of work, plus some altruistic motivation.

Looking at the responses according to sex reveals over-all variations between men and women on a number of items, and most of the variations continue when education, income, age, and occupation are held constant. The strongest sex differences occur in regard to the statements on opportunity orientation and on directing others. While differences are found by each of the four variables, that by family income level is perhaps the most revealing, as the tabulation on the next page indicates. At each level there is a clear and considerable difference between men and women. Furthermore, on the opportunity versus security measure the rise by income is much larger for men than women. We can see, then, that the over-all sex contrasts may sometimes obscure the level at which the discrepancy is greatest—which in this case is the highest income level.

Other findings showing intersex differences dovetail with those found in describing the ideal occupation. Men, compared to women, regularly rate higher having the chance to get to the top, gaining the increased respect of family and friends, being able to work without interference, and having hard problems to solve. Women attach more importance to hav-

Family Income Level	N	"It is more important for a job to offer opportunity than security."	"It is satisfying to direct the work of others."
Under $4,000			
Men	(147)	5.7	6.3
Women	(63)	5.0	5.5
$4,000-5,499			
Men	(248)	5.7	6.5
Women	(64)	5.1	5.3
$5,500-8,499			
Men	(255)	6.0	7.0
Women	(68)	5.4	5.9
$8,500 and Over			
Men	(157)	7.3	7.3
Women	(47)	5.6	6.4

ing the opportunity to make friends, doing work you can forget about after the work day, and being able to help other people. Statements related to the ethics of work also show consistent variations by sex. Men, for example, almost uniformly agree more that doing a better job than the next person is important, while women show more concurrence with the idea that work helps one forget personal problems.

We tested a number of other hunches about the relationships of various population characteristics to occupational values and perspectives, using the mean ratings on relevant agree-disagree scale-sort statements. Only a few consistent differences emerge when the community backgrounds of the respondents are compared. However, those with a farm upbringing are somewhat more inclined than others to agree that success is mainly a matter of knowing the right people and of luck, and less inclined to attribute it to hard work. This is perhaps a reflection of the farmers' continual battle with nature and of a certain amount of agrarian distrust. On the other hand, they do agree more strongly that work is a way of serving God (8.0 vs. a low of 7.1 for those with suburban backgrounds). People reared in the suburbs moderately minimize the dominating importance of work; for example, they agree least that a person should try to succeed even if it interferes with other things in life (5.6 vs. about 6.1 for all others).

Size of place of residence makes some difference in the agreement expressed on various items—especially on those dealing with work ethics. Residents of cities 250,000 or larger tend rather consistently to give more support than other respondents to the somewhat cynical statements and less to statements on the virtues of work: they agree least that work is a way of serving God, that one should always do his best, and that success is mainly a matter of hard work. At the same time they concur most that success is mainly a matter of knowing the right people and of luck (4.2 vs. about 3.3 for each of the other groupings), that not wanting to work is one's own business, and that work is only a way of making a living.

In general, the value scores vary little according to geographic region. With income level controlled (at under $5,500 and $5,500 and more), however, there are a few differences of moderate magnitude. Higher-income residents in the West and the Northeast tend, more than residents in other sections, to cite opportunity as more important than security, and to reject a liking for work one can forget about after the work day. Northeasterners of both low and high income attach more importance than comparable groups to the notion that to be really successful you must care about making money, and less importance to carrying out ideas without interference. Respondents from the Northeast and the South agree more that success is mainly a matter of knowing the right people and of luck, and that whether a person works hard or not is his own business. But the southerners combine with midwesterners in giving more weight to seeing work as a way of serving God, and to expecting work to be fun. Over all, high-income westerners support the materialistic values least and the nontangible values most. In terms of work ethics, easterners and southerners are more cynical about how to succeed in an occupation, while midwesterners join the southerners in attaching more significance to certain religious and "fun" aspects of work.

Men who are self-employed put greater emphasis on self-determination (7.6 vs. 6.5) and opportunity (6.7 vs. 5.9). A footnote here is that self-employed sons of fathers who were *not* self-employed rate opportunity significantly higher than self-employed sons of fathers who *were* self-employed (7.7 vs. 6.4).

On the items selected for analysis, the factor of religious affiliation appears to have little effect. With income controlled, Catholics give slightly more support to the assertion that what matters about a job is doing something worthwhile, and (perhaps paradoxically) that one must care about making money to be really successful. Catholics also agree more that success is mainly a matter of knowing the right people (5.4 vs. 4.8

for Protestants). Significantly, Protestants and Catholics are virtually alike in their responses about the religiosity of work.

	N	"Work is a way of being of service to God"
Protestants		
Under $5,500	(385)	7.7
$5,500 and Over	(344)	7.9
Catholics		
Under $5,500	(123)	7.7
$5,500 and Over	(137)	7.6

Positive and Negative Aspects of One's Job

Asking the respondents why they rated their present jobs as low or as high as they did served to shed additional light on the kinds of occupational values people have, and to illustrate the specific sources of occupational contentment and discontentment. As suggested earlier (Chapter 7), the hierarchy of reasons is associated with sex and education in the work force. This hierarchy bears a strong resemblance to the distribution of values found in the depiction of the most and least ideal occupations and in the response patterns on the scale-sort questions. At the same time they are modified by the degree to which the occupational aspirations are being satisfied in the respondent's present occupation.

The blending of the two qualities is shown in Table 14-15 where the percentages are recorded by income level for selected values. Respondents' explanations of why they did not place their occupation lower on the occupational ladder are moderately differentiated. Generally, the higher the income level, the more frequent are references to high financial reward, doing work that fits a person's capacities, the presence of self-determination, and challenge in the work. The two middle-income groups mention the security aspects of their jobs more frequently than the extremely low or high groups. The one item on which income is negatively related in significant fashion is in seeing the job as satisfactory in comparison to other jobs, a claim that does not credit the present occupation with favorable features so much as it suggests the feeling "it could be worse." Summing up, the higher the income, the more likely is the feeling of receiving comparably more rewards of various kinds from the job and the less likely the feeling of being deprived of certain rewards in the job.

TABLE 14-15. *Positive and Negative Attributes People See in Their Own Jobs, Related to Family Income in the General Employed Public*

Attributes	Family Income			
	Under $4,000	$4,000– 5,499	$5,500– 8,499	$8,500 and Over
Positive				
High or good financial reward	23%	34%	36%	36%
Security, stability, protection, fringe benfits	8	17	14	6
Work that fits capacities and or training	9	12	13	22
Self-determination	13	13	16	23
Challenge	1	8	12	18
Sense of well being, satisfaction, fulfillment	15	13	17	20
Good job in comparison to some, many, or most others	18	11	13	7
NUMBER ANSWERING	(215)	(312)	(321)	(204)
Negative				
Poor or inadequate financial reward	47%	32%	29%	24%
Poor physical environment and working conditions	28	26	26	12
Always room for improvement	13	20	19	28
NUMBER ANSWERING	(187)	(276)	(254)	(157)

Income level differences are somewhat less marked in answers concerning the negative features of one's job, but three items stand out. Responding to "What kept you from placing it higher?" the very low income group mentions about twice as frequently as the highest income respondents (47 vs. 24 percent) the lack of adequate financial reward and the presence of poor physical environment and working conditions (28 vs. 12 percent). In contrast, the higher the income, the greater the feeling that there is always room for improvement in a job, since no job is perfect. This sentiment is not a complaint so much as a state of mind—an outlook about the work world.

Presumably the worker's state of occupational satisfaction would be highly related to the responses he gives to support why his rating is not higher or lower. The hypothesis would be that the more satisfied he is the more likely he is to point out certain positive aspects of the job, and, conversely, the less likely to suggest various negative factors. Table 14-16 presents the range of percentages by level of occupational satisfaction for the ten items most frequently mentioned in reply to "what kept you from placing it lower?"

With two exceptions the data lend general support to the hypothesis. Perhaps the strongest confirmation comes from the category of interest, enjoyment, satisfaction, and pleasure experienced in the work, where the figures run 23, 31, and 58 percent for people with low, medium, and high levels of job satisfaction, respectively. Another strong point is the distribution for the category which states that the job is considered good in comparison to "some, many, or most others," where the figures are 22, 12, and 3 percent according to low, medium, and high levels of satisfaction. As pointed out above, this response is hardly a positive endorsement of the job, so that even though the percentages run in a direction counter to the others the conclusion to be drawn is the same.

The exceptions found in the table are worth noting. First, there is no noticeable difference on high or good financial reward offered as a reason by the three groups—about a third of each group mention it. This finding does not suggest that there is no relationship between income level and occupational satisfaction (an association which, in fact, was demonstrated in the first section of this chapter). It does, however, highlight that certain noneconomic features of a job are of differential salience to people in describing the positive aspects of their jobs—that is, although in-

TABLE 14-16. *Positive Attributes People See in Their Own Jobs, Related to Occupational Satisfaction in the General Employed Public*

Positive Attributes	Occupational Satisfaction		
	Low	Medium	High
Interest, enjoyment, satisfaction, pleasure	23%	31%	58%
High or good financial reward	32	31	35
Security, stability, protection, fringe benefits	14	13	8
Good physical environment and general working conditions	17	20	29
Work that fits capacities and/or training	10	12	20
Good *passive* relations with people at work	7	14	12
Good *active* relations with people at work	9	7	18
Self-determination	10	14	22
Sense of well-being, satisfaction, fullfillment	7	16	24
Good job in comparison to some, many, or most others	22	12	3
NUMBER ANSWERING	(379)	(362)	(352)

come from the job is of equal salience no matter what the level of satisfaction, this is not true of several other characteristics. The other exception relates to the various aspects of security associated with the job.
Here the slightly negative relationship adds further support to the notion that security is not of paramount concern today, especially to those
who see themselves as doing well occupationally.

The data for the other side of the coin—"what kept you from placing
it higher?"—also either conform to expectations or do not contradict the
expectations. Table 14-17 presents the distribution for the six most frequently mentioned values. The lower the state of occupational satisfaction, the more frequent are the mentions of poor financial reward and
bad physical environment and working conditions as reasons for not

TABLE 14-17. *Negative Attributes People See in Their Own Jobs, Related
to Occupational Satisfaction in the General Employed Public*

Negative Attributes	Occupational Satisfaction		
	Low	Medium	High
Poor or inadequate financial reward	38%	30%	22%
Absence of or insufficient security, stability, protection, fringe benefits	11	6	8
Bad physical environment and working conditions	27	20	19
Dislike present job or prefer another one	12	9	12
Personal limitations or lack of choice	11	14	9
Always room for improvement	15	21	32
NUMBER ANSWERING	(415)	(365)	(129)

ranking the occupation higher. Little variation is shown for the other
three values. But 15 percent of the least satisfied, 21 percent of the moderately satisfied, and 32 percent of the most satisfied note that no job is
perfect, that there is always room for improvement. It should be pointed
out again that this category does not disparage or downgrade the job—
rather it points toward a standard or goal which many people feel can
never be attained. The 32 percent in the most satisfied group are exclusively those rating their jobs at 9 on the scale, since the question did not
apply to those with scores of 10. Some people obviously feel that perfec-
tion, in this case 10, can never be reached. Thus it is not inconsistent that
the more satisfied mention this factor more often than do the less satisfied.

15

General Employed Public: Images
of Federal Employment and Employees

HERE WE WILL DEAL with points three and four of the major foci of
the supplementary tabulations described in Chapter 14—the image of
the federal government as an employer and the image of federal employees. The prime directions of inquiry are: (1) the general employed
public's perceptions of security and mobility in government work, and
the relative advantages and disadvantages seen in having the government
for an employer; (2) the over-all picture the working public has of the
federal employee, how he is rated on five specific traits, and various attributed motives for his entering federal service. Response patterns are
again related to the demographic and the "attitude" variables employed
in Chapter 14.

Image of the Government As an Employer

Security and Mobility

In Table 15-1 three pairs of statements referring to security or mobility
aspects of employment—with the government and with a private business organization—are related to occupational and income levels of the
respondents. Absolute mean scores and difference scores are shown for
each pair.

The data about perceptions of a high degree of security being offered
in government work are tabled primarily to illustrate the ubiquity of this
sentiment. Neither income level nor occupational classification seems to
affect the prevalence of the idea: scores for each occupational and income grouping hover around 7.4 on the ten-point scale. A large private
business is viewed as offering much less security. With no exceptions

TABLE 15-1. *Ratings of Evaluative Statements About Federal and Private Employment, Related to Family Income and Occupation in the General Employed Public*[a]

Statements	Family Income				Occupation[b]			
	Under $4,000	$4,000–5,499	$5,500–8,499	$8,500 and Over	Un-skilled and Semi-skilled	Skilled	Cleri-cal	Profes-sional and Man-agerial
"Employment with the federal government offers a high degree of security"	7.5	7.4	7.3	7.4	7.5	7.2	7.5	7.2
"Employment with a large private business offers a high degree of security"	6.4	6.0	5.9	6.1	6.1	6.1	6.0	5.9
Difference: "Government" Minus "Business"	+1.1	+1.4	+1.4	+1.3	+1.4	+1.1	+1.5	+1.3
"A person who works for the federal government generally has a good chance to get ahead"	7.0	6.6	6.4	5.8	6.9	6.7	6.5	5.7
"A person who works for a large private business generally has a good chance to get ahead"	6.6	6.1	6.6	6.4	6.5	6.4	6.4	6.3
Difference: "Government" Minus "Business"	+.4	+.5	−.2	−.6	+.4	+.3	+.1	−.6
"For a young man of ability, his best chance for being *really successful* lies in working for the federal government"	5.4	4.6	4.3	3.0	5.1	4.7	4.2	3.3
"For a young man of ability, his best chance for being *really successful* lies in working for a large private business corporation"	5.9	5.4	5.2	5.3	5.5	5.6	5.4	5.2
Difference: "Government" Minus "Business"	−.5	−.8	−.9	−2.3	−.4	−.9	−1.2	−1.9
AVERAGE NUMBER ANSWERING	(210)	(312)	(323)	(204)	(369)	(176)	(177)	(290)

[a] The mean ratings shown in this table and subsequent rating tables in the chapter are based on a ten-step scale.
[b] Farmers are omitted.

all of the groupings see a difference between the two types of employer in excess of one scale point.

For another pair of items, however, homogeneity in outlook is decidedly not the case. As income and occupational levels rise there is a marked decrease in agreement that a person who works for the government generally has a good chance to get ahead, with a movement of from 7.0 down to 5.8 by income rank, and from 6.9 to 5.7 by occupational rank. Thus, the lower a person's income level and occupational status, the more likely he is to perceive government as an avenue for getting ahead. Notice, however, that agreement has much more constancy concerning a person who works for private business. Consequently, the difference scores form a ranking not unlike that for the absolute ratings of the federal government. The lower income and occupational groups give a net advantage to the government, and the higher groups (the professionals and managers in the occupational classification) give a net deficit.

An even greater disparity of opinions is found concerning the statements on "real" success. Concomitant with rising income and occupational levels is a decreasing agreement that a young man's best chance for being really successful lies in working for the government. The range is most marked by income level: those with incomes under $4,000 have a mean figure of 5.4 vs. 3.0 for those with $8,500 and more. In contrast to this spread are the relatively even scores found when the statement applies to working for a large private business corporation; only the very low income group deviates with a slightly higher mean figure. The difference scores are to the disadvantage of government for each classification, and the magnitude of the differences increases dramatically as one ascends the income and occupational hierarchy. Judged, then, either by the absolute ratings or by comparison with private business, the image of the government as a place to attain real success varies markedly with income and occupation. That the difference scores are considerably greater for this pair of statements than for the preceding pair (chance to get ahead) seems partly attributable to the more global concept "really successful," whereas having a chance to get ahead is possibly seen as only one part of the concept of success.

In various earlier chapters we have seen that women in general look more favorably than men on the government as an employer. They agree less than men that most government work is routine and monotonous, and agree more that federal employment offers a chance to get ahead, of ending up in a top-level job, and of being really successful. Our supplementary analyses indicate that these differences according to sex usually persist at various educational, income, age, and occupational strata. Yet they are more marked at some levels than others.

The inspection by educational and age levels reveals no consistent departure from the "normal" male-female differences on these items, but by income and occupational classifications there are variations. At the two lower income levels (below $5,500 annual family income) men and women are more or less alike in rating government employment in terms of getting ahead, landing a top-level job, and of being really successful; at the two higher levels ($5,500 and above), however, women place the government considerably higher than men do. On the chances of getting ahead in federal employment, women in the $5,500-8,499 bracket score 7.3 vs. 6.2 for men; in the $8,500 or more bracket, they score 6.8 vs. 5.5 for men. It appears that the ratings by men tend to drop as income advances, whereas the ratings by women are either nearly equal or irregular according to income; therefore, the divergencies between the sexes tend to increase at the upper income levels.

Occupationally, we find the greatest sex disparities in the clerical occupations, as the figures below demonstrate:

	N	Chance To Get Ahead	Chance for Being Really Succcessful
Unskilled and Semiskilled			
Men	(260)	6.7	5.1
Women	(108)	7.3	5.3
Skilled			
Men	(168)	6.7	4.7
Women	....	...	...
Clerical			
Men	(96)	6.0	3.6
Women	(80)	7.1	4.8
Professional and Managerial			
Men	(234)	5.6	3.4
Women	(53)	6.3	3.1
Farmers			
Men	(74)	6.7	4.5
Women	...	...	...

A number of other characteristics have a conceivable bearing on the image of the government as a place to work. In Table 15-2 seven variables and their accompanying mean figures are shown in relation to the declarations about the chance to be really successful in federal employment or in business. Also presented are the differences between the two scores. Considering first the absolute figures on seeing the government as the place to be really successful, the following categories express moderately higher agreement: respondents in towns between 1,000 and 10,000 population, those living in the South, those with farm backgrounds, and those working for others. Moderately lower rates of agreement come from respondents in the West, those with suburban backgrounds, and the self-employed. Age, political identification, and previous civilian employment in government have little or no relation to scores on the item. (Similar findings occur for other statements about government employment—not tabled—and in most instances the distribution ranges are not extreme. Therefore, what moderate variation might be found among these classifications is adequately expressed by the tabled figures.)

When working for the government is compared with working for a large corporation, the pattern of the resulting net scores resembles that for the absolute figures. Although every entry shows a net deficit for the government, respondents residing in small towns, living in the South, and having farm backgrounds produce the least disadvantageous scores for government. Those living in the West and those of suburban backgrounds produce the greatest negative gap between the two ratings. Additionally, people living in areas with populations of 10,000-99,999 and 250,000 and over have large minus scores. Finally, older people seem slightly more inclined than younger ones to see more negative difference betwen the government and the corporation on this measure. Political identification, previous federal employment, and presence or absence of self-employment account for little or no difference.

Turning now to the attitudinal variables, we hypothesized a relationship between people's evaluation of civil service employees and of the appeal of federal employment, on the one hand, and their image of federal employment on the other. Four key items bear this notion out. The higher the evaluation of civil servants and the appeal of working for the government, the higher is the agreement that federal government employment offers high security (Table 15-3). That some people do not consider high security a positive aspect of an occupation is beside the

TABLE 15-2. *Ratings of Chance for Success in the Federal Government vs. a Large Corporation, Related to Seven Characteristics of the General Employed Public*

Characteristics	Average Number Answering	"For a young man of ability, his best chance for being *really* *successful* lies in working for the federal government"	"For a young man of ability, his best chance for being *really* *successful* lies in working for a large private corporation"	Difference: "Government" Minus "Business"
Age				
18–32	296	4.4	5.2	− .8
33–39	204	4.2	5.1	− .9
40–48	288	4.2	5.4	−1.2
49 and older	290	4.6	5.8	−1.2
Place of Residence				
Open country and urban fringe	398	4.2	5.2	−1.0
1,000–9,999	151	4.8	5.0	− .2
10,000–99,999	180	4.2	5.8	−1.6
100,000–249,999	120	4.5	5.2	− .7
250,000 and over	237	4.4	5.8	−1.4
Geographic Region				
Northeast	516	4.4	5.6	−1.2
Midwest	114	4.2	5.1	− .9
South	278	4.7	5.4	− .7
West	142	3.9	5.2	−1.3
Community Background				
Farm	388	4.8	5.3	− .5
Town	358	4.3	5.4	−1.1
Suburbs	166	3.9	5.7	−1.8
Center city	147	4.2	5.3	−1.1
Employer (males only)				
Self-employed	183	3.8	4.9	−1.1
Not self-employed	637	4.4	5.6	−1.2
Political Identification				
Democrats	272	4.5	5.5	−1.0
Independents	176	4.1	5.2	−1.1
Republicans	113	4.1	5.4	−1.3
Previous Federal Civilian Employment				
Yes	156	4.6	5.4	− .8
No	910	4.3	5.4	−1.1

TABLE 15-3. *Ratings of Evaluative Statements About Federal Employment, Related to Evaluation of Civil Servants and the Appeal of Federal Employment in the General Employed Public*

Statements	Evaluation of Civil Service Employees			Appeal of Federal Employment		
	Low	Medium	High	Low	Medium	High
"Employment with the federal government offers a high degree of security"	6.6	7.4	8.2	6.4	7.4	8.3
"Most jobs in the federal government are routine and monotonous"	5.3	4.9	4.4	5.2	5.1	4.3
"A person who works for the federal government generally has a good chance to get ahead"	5.6	6.3	7.7	5.3	6.6	7.5
"For a young man of ability, his best chance for being *really successful* lies in working for the federal government"	3.7	4.2	5.3	2.9	4.7	5.7
AVERAGE NUMBER ANSWERING	(341)	(393)	(310)	(357)	(391)	(315)

point here. Almost certainly the respondents with higher agreement see a linkage between the perception of high security and the attractiveness of government and the people working there. In other words, for them it exerts a positive valence.

This reasoning is supported when we look at the statement that most government jobs are routine and monotonous. Very definitely the connotation is negative here; therefore those with high evaluation and appeal scores should reject it more than those with low scores. And the figures show this to be so, though the differences are not as large as those for the security item (about a scale point each for evaluation and appeal indices).

The final two items link evaluation and appeal to perceptions about the chance to get ahead in the government and to be really successful. In both instances the association is extremely strong and progressive. People having a higher evaluation of civil servants and being more attracted toward government work are much more likely than those with lower scores to see the chances as favorable for getting ahead and for being really successful in government. Thus the higher the evaluation and appeal, the more favorable the image. Taken together the data based on the four statements suggest a significant association between the evaluation of federal employees, the appeal of working for the government, and the kind of work world the government is perceived as representing.

Advantages and Disadvantages in Working for the Government

When respondents were asked what would be better and what would be worse if they went to work for the government in the same occupation they had now, the answers were a mingling of occupational values and their perceptions of government employment. Importantly, the perceptions were evaluated in terms of the individual's values and goals. Four categories were most frequently mentioned as being "better," and four, similarly, as being "worse."

Examining the replies by income level, we see the following:

"What things would be likely to be better?"	Under $4,000 (223)	$4,000- 5,499 (300)	$5,500- 8,499 (311)	$8,500 and Over (201)
High or good financial reward	48%	28%	19%	10%
Security, stability, protection, fringe benefits	45	44	41	37
Good physical environment and working conditions	21	21	14	10
Nothing would be better	12	15	23	31

Among the four features, two have a strong negative association with income level. The higher a person's income, the less likely he is to perceive financial reward and physical environment and working conditions as being better in the government. Especially interesting are the figures for financial reward. While nearly one half of those with incomes under $4,000 envisage a financial improvement in working for the government, only one tenth of those making $8,500 and over respond similarly. The percentages for the security category show smaller differences, but they are in the same direction. It is worth noting that the higher-income people, though citing security frequently, often add that for them the factor would not necessarily make working for the government more attractive; they mention security because of its saliency as a feature of government employment and as something that might be better for other people. The lower-income respondents seldom qualify their remarks about security in this fashion; for them it definitely seems to be a positive attribute of government employment.

The one category that climbs in frequency with increasing income level is the assertion that nothing would be better about working for the government. This, of course, is a negative evaluation and in its relationship to increasing income it complements the percentages for the other three categories. That nearly one third of the respondents in the highest income bracket could think of nothing which would be more advantageous is especially significant.

When the replies to what would be worse about working for the government are analyzed, once again a pattern of perceptions emerges. Now, however, there is a positive association between rising income and mention of three of the four major points:

"What things would be likely to be worse?"	Under $4,000 (223)	$4,000- 5,499 (305)	$5,500- 8,499 (325)	$8,500 and Over (205)
Poor or inadequate financial reward	4%	9%	19%	20%
Lack of self-determination	17	17	22	35
Bureaucracy, red tape, inefficiency, large size	11	12	15	27
Nothing would be worse	41	31	21	10

Not unexpectedly, the higher one goes on the income hierarchy the more likely he is to cite poor financial reward, a corollary of the trend noted above, where rising income accompanies a *decrease* in the mention of financial reward as something that would be *better* about working for the government.

Two other sentiments, related in nature, are also expressed more frequently by the higher-income groups. Approximately twice as many high-income as low-income respondents cite lack of self-determination and the presence of some unfavorable aspect of bureaucratic organization. These two attitudes seem to reflect a picture of employment wherein the individual is submerged in an organized world with loss of identity and autonomy. Rounding out the picture is the strong belief by the lower-income groups that nothing would be worse; since this is essentially a positive statement about working for the government, its negative relationship to income level is entirely congruent with the earlier findings.

It is instructive to compare the extremes of the "nothing would be better" and the "nothing would be worse" categories:

	Under $4,000 (223)	$8,500 and Over (203)
Nothing would be better	12%	31%
Nothing would be worse	41	10

Given these and other data presented above, it is clear that at least one reason why the appeal of federal employment is more pronounced among low-income respondents is that they are hard pressed to think of any negative attributes, while high-income respondents find it difficult to conceive of any positive aspects.

When the advantages and disadvantages perceived by respondents in federal employment are examined in terms of the occupational hierarchy, a pattern similar to that found by the income analysis results. Considering the unskilled and semiskilled at one end of the hierarchy and the professional and managerial at the other, the typical configuration is for those low on the hierarchy to see financial reward, security, and good physical environment as being enhanced with the government, and for those high on the hierarchy to view financial reward, self-determination and bureaucracy as being worse with the government (Table 15-4). Twice as many of the unskilled and semiskilled, compared to the professional and managerial, think their financial situation would be improved. Conversely, the highest status employees mention about two and a half times more often than those of lowest status, that self-determination would be worse.

For the most part those in skilled and clerical occupations occupy an intermediate position in the range of replies. There are some exceptions, however. Clerical personnel lead all other groupings (slightly) in pointing out the security benefits in working for the government. And skilled workers mention more than others that poor or inadequate financial reward would be a worse factor in government employment. The general antipathy of the farmers is demonstrated by the fact that 41 percent of them could visualize nothing as being better and 46 percent see self-determination as being worse.

In general, women are more inclined than men to cite economic reward as better if one worked for the government, whereas men more frequently refer to security. And men claim somewhat more frequently

TABLE 15-4. *Positive and Negative Attributes Seen in Federal Employment, Related to Occupation in the General Employed Public*

Attributes	Occupation				
	Unskilled and Semi-skilled	Skilled	Clerical	Professional and Managerial	Farmers
Better in Federal Employment					
High or good financial reward	35%	24%	27%	15%	20%
Security, stability, protection, fringe benefits	43	44	49	39	29
Good physical environment and working conditions	21	14	15	11	16
Nothing would be better	14	21	15	24	41
NUMBER ANSWERING	(373)	(174)	(169)	(286)	(75)
Worse in Federal Employment					
Poor or inadequate financial reward	10%	22%	14%	14%	5%
Lack of self-determination	12	12	22	33	46
Bureaucracy, red tape, inefficiency, large size	10	17	14	22	20
Nothing would be worse	41	28	22	13	12
NUMBER ANSWERING	(377)	(176)	(176)	(295)	(76)

than women that nothing would be better. Differences on other major categories are slight. Additional investigation suggests that these differential associations run throughout various educational, income, age, and occupational classifications. But the masculine emphasis on security is more pronounced, vis-à-vis female concern, among certain groupings. Women under 33 years mention security much less frequently than men in the same age bracket (30 vs. 47 percent); at other age levels the percentages are much closer together, and in the 33 to 39 bracket, women mention security more often than men. It is also true that women in professional and managerial pursuits mention security much less often than similar men (19 vs. 43 percent). The difference at the clerical level on security is slight (53 vs. 44 percent), suggesting again the relatively more favorable image of government employment women in clerical work seem to have. Finally, variations by sex are almost imperceptible at family income levels of under $4,000 and $5,500-8,499, but are significant in the $4,000-5,499 and $8,500 and over brackets, where the male emphasis on security is the more pronounced. It seems probable that the lack of symmetry by income level is related to such a factor as dual incomes in the family.

Turning to "what would be worse" about federal employment, men in general refer more frequently than women to lower financial return, and to the presence of bureaucracy. Women say more often that nothing would be worse. Other differences are not large. Based on further analyses it appears that these three differences by sex hold according to education, income, occupation, and age strata. The major exception lies in the response that nothing would be worse about working for the government. At the lower income levels, women volunteer this reply much more often than men; in the upper brackets men and women mention it in about equal proportions. Another exception occurs in the oldest age category, where difference by sex is negligible. Using occupational breakdowns, the main division comes in the clerical grouping:

	N	Nothing Would Be Worse
Unskilled and Semiskilled		
Men	(270)	38%
Women	(107)	47
Skilled		
Men	(170)	28
Women	. . . .	. . .
Clerical		
Men	(93)	14
Women	(83)	30
Professional and Managerial		
Men	(238)	13
Women	(57)	12
Farmers		
Men	(73)	12
Women	. . .	. . .

Both women and men in the unskilled and semiskilled trades lead the way in denying that anything would be worse. Of more concern here is the pattern of intersex relationships. While the professional-managerial respondents differ little by sex, the unskilled and semiskilled show a moderate division, and the clerical respondents an even larger one. Taking these three breakdowns together, we see that women in general are more

TABLE 15-5. *Positive and Negative Attributes Seen in Federal Employment, Related to Occupational Satisfaction and Opportunity Orientation in the General Employed Public*

Attributes	Occupational Satisfaction			Opportunity vs. Security		
				Low on Opportunity	Medium on Opportunity	High on Opportunity
	Low	Medium	High			
Better in Federal Employment						
High or good financial reward	32%	26%	18%	34%	25%	18%
Security, stability, protection, fringe benefits	51	43	31	43	40	44
Good physical environment and working conditions	23	14	9	21	16	11
Nothing would be better	13	18	30	15	22	25
NUMBER ANSWERING	(391)	(349)	(336)	(322)	(348)	(361)
Worse in Federal Employment						
Poor or inadequate fiancial reward	11%	13%	16%	12%	13%	16%
Lack of self-determination	17	21	27	19	21	25
Bureaucracy	9	22	17	10	15	21
Nothing would be worse	36	22	19	29	30	19
NUMBER ANSWERING	(399)	(357)	(343)	(324)	(357)	(374)

likely than men to say that nothing would be worse—but that the strongest such differences emanate from young and middle-aged, lower income, and the nonprofessional women, particularly in the clerical occupations.

The attitudinal factors may be expected to show a relationship to the perceived advantages and disadvantages of government work. We would predict, for example, that the more satisfied a person is with his occupation the less advantage he would see in government employment. If he is highly satisfied now, then it would be difficult to improve his lot, no matter who the employer. Estimating the direction of opinion according to the opportunity vs. security score is a bit more hazardous. However, given the security image attached to government employment, it seems probable that the more opportunity oriented the person is, the fewer advantages he is likely to see in the government.

For the most part the data in Table 15-5 bear the two hypotheses out, but much more so in regard to what would be better about government employment than what would be worse. As occupational satisfaction and opportunity orientation increase, the references to financial reward and physical environment as "better" factors decrease. This pattern also holds true, according to job satisfaction level, for the responses dealing with security advantages in the government; but such responses are mentioned in about equal frequency by each grouping in relation to the opportunity orientation index. The pattern reasserts itself for both crossbreaks on the category "nothing would be better," though again it is stronger as measured by occupational satisfaction; predictably, as satisfaction and orientation to opportunity increase so does the feeling that nothing would be better about working for the government. Dividing the respondents by sex at each level produces no consistent differences on the opportunity-security dimension. However, among the most satisfied respondents, men say much more often than women—36 vs. 16 percent—that nothing would be better. Differences at the other two job contentment levels are slight.

While there is a semblance of the same pattern in descriptions of what would be worse about working for the government, the intergroup differences are not nearly so marked. The highly satisfied and highly opportunity-oriented are only slightly more likely to mention poor or inadequate financial reward than are the less satisfied and those low on opportunity, but they are somewhat more inclined to mention lack of self-determination and some aspect of bureaucracy. Finally, the higher the satisfaction and the opportunity orientation, the less is it said that nothing would be worse in working for the government. Sex variations at each opportunity-security level again produce no consistent aberrations, but among the least occupationally satisfied, women note much more often than men—52 vs. 32 percent—that nothing would be worse. That is, among the respondents who are most dissatisfied in their present jobs, women are more likely to see no disadvantages in working for the government.

Although the primary message of Table 15-5 is clear, a word of caution is needed, since there are people on the low ends of these two continuums who see relative disadvantages in government employment, and sizable numbers at the upper limits who see relative advantages. Therefore, one must not assume that *only* the unsatisfied and the security-oriented perceive relative merits in government work in terms of their own work worlds. The blends and mixes of occupational values and perceptions are varied enough so that one-to-one correlations are rare. We are speaking here, as elsewhere, of tendencies.

Another pair of indexes—the evaluation of civil service employees, and the appeal of federal employment—would be presumed to show discrimination in the replies to the two questions. It would be surprising if positive and negative perceptions of government employment did not vary with the level of its appeal. However, because of the narrower focus of the measurement, the evaluation of civil servants might show less relationship to the replies.

The figures below leave little doubt concerning the relationship between strength of appeal and the image of government as an employer:

"What things would be likely to be better?"	Appeal of Federal Employment		
	Low (332)	Medium (380)	High (306)
High or good financial reward	16%	25%	35%
Good physical environment and working conditions	9	18	24
Security, stability, protection, fringe benefits	33	47	47
Nothing would be better	34	17	11

As the appeal scores rise so do the assertions that government would offer better financial reward, more security, and better physical conditions, while the fewer are the assertions that nothing would be better. The lesson of these proportions is that the respondents who rate government work as appealing to them are doing so, not whimsically or carelessly, but because they have concrete reasons for their choice.

The distribution for what would be worse in the government is as follows:

"What things would be likely to be worse?"	Appeal of Federal Employment		
	Low (353)	Medium (384)	High (305)
Poor or inadequate financial reward	17%	14%	11%
Lack of self-determination	28	20	16
Bureaucracy, red tape, inefficiency, large size	20	16	10
Nothing would be worse	14	25	41

Now the flow is in the opposite direction: the lower the appeal of federal work, the greater the feeling that government employment would mean less money and self-determination, but more bureaucracy, and at the same time the weaker is the sentiment that nothing would be worse.

Comparing the "nothing better" and "nothing worse" entries highlights the disparities according to the level of appeal. Of the interviewees who say that government work has little attraction for them, 35 percent respond that nothing would be *better*, while less than half that many say that nothing would be *worse*. In contrast, of those indicating high attraction toward government work, only 11 percent say that nothing would be *better*, and almost four times that many reply that nothing would be *worse*. Thus the degree of appeal seems to be firmly anchored in the individual's cognitions and evaluations of the merits and demerits of government work.

The evaluations of civil service employees prove to be less related to the replies to these two questions. There are virtually no differences on three of the four major response categories for "better"; the exception is "nothing would be better," which is cited slightly more often by those who rate civil servants lowest. Replies for "worse" are more strongly related to the evaluation index. Even here there is no difference among the respondent groupings for the financial reward category, but there is a moderate to strong tendency for those with higher evaluations to mention less frequently lack of self-determination and presence of bureaucracy as disadvantages of federal employment. Those who give federal employees higher ratings also reply more frequently that nothing would be worse about working for the government.

The Image of Federal Employees

If there are variations in the perceptions the general work force has of government employees, we may expect the differences to parallel those found for picturing the government as an employer. That proved to be the case in the primary analyses of Chapters 11 and 12. Although our supplementary data and analysis are more limited in this respect, in general the findings support the proposition. Table 15-6 shows, by income rank, the distribution of the major response categories for the question: "If you were to describe your general idea of a U.S. civil service employee, what sort of a person would that be?" The table also contains the general evaluation or tone of the entire response.

TABLE 15-6. *Over-All Tone of Responses and Characteristics Attributed to Federal Civil Servants, Related to Family Income in the General Employed Public*

Tone and Attributed Characteristics	Family Income			
	Under $4,000	$4,000– 5,499	$5,500– 8,499	$8,500 and Over
Over-All Tone				
Favorable	58%	50%	55%	34%
Unfavorable	3	6	12	22
Both favorable and unfavorable	1	2	2	4
Undeterminable	21	35	27	38
Don't know	16	7	4	2
Characteristics				
Mental ability is above average	11%	9%	12%	4%
Educational level is above average	15	11	14	6
Personality is agreeable	17	16	15	11
Good personal character	30	26	31	21
Capable of doing the work because of ability or training	14	15	19	15
Good worker	16	15	15	14
Not very ambitious, low initiative	2	5	9	21
Security conscious	6	10	15	24
NUMBER ANSWERING	(235)	(323)	(331)	(209)

It is apparent that low-income respondents, compared to those with high incomes, have a much more favorable opinion of civil service employees. Their figure for clearly favorable statements is the highest (58 percent), the lowest for clearly unfavorable (3 percent), and the lowest for unclear evaluations (21 percent). High-income people have the fewest clearly favorable replies (34 percent), the most unfavorable (22 percent), and the most undeterminable (38 percent). The two middle income groups typically fall between the two extremes. (Inasmuch as the coding specifications for this dimension were conservative—that is, the total response had to be unequivocally favorable or unfavorable to be placed in those categories, the "undeterminable" category assumes more importance. The consensus of the coding supervisors was that if less conservative coding specifications had been employed a majority of the "undeterminable" codes would have been placed in the unfavorable category rather than dividing equally.)

Concerning the substantive characterizations in Table 15-6, the figures are most significant for the disparity they show between the respondents in the very highest income bracket and those at all other levels. The people of highest income are much less inclined than others to mention the more positive aspects of the civil servant. Thus they less frequently see him as having mental ability above average, being well-educated, personable, and having good character. None of the income groups differ much on capability and presence of good workers among federal employees, but there are radical differences in the references to security consciousness and lack of ambition. References to these two qualities show a progressive increase as income level rises. Taking both the general evaluation and the attribution of specific traits into account, there is little doubt that the higher the income level, the less favorable is the opinion of civil service employees.

Rating Civil Servants on Specific Traits

The image of civil service employees held by the work force was further elicited through ratings on five specific traits: honesty; interest in serving the public; how well respected they are; drive to get ahead; and ability. Mean scores based on ratings on the ten-point high-low scale are presented for various sample groupings in Table 15-7. The data show that the ratings on "honesty" are the highest assigned to any characteristic, and are uniformly high among all groupings. On other qualities, however, ratings differ considerably.

According to income levels, we observe that people in the highest bracket consistently give lower ratings on the four other qualities than do people at the other three levels, all of whom tend to show somewhat similar scores. This pattern, of course, complements the pattern shown in Table 15-6.

Occupationally, too, a similar configuration emerges. Professional and managerial personnel are less likely than other kinds of workers to give high ratings on these four qualities. Here, however, the unskilled and semiskilled respondents form another extreme by giving consistently higher ratings (joined in some instances by farmers). The result is a rating range which runs counter to the occupational hierarchy, so that higher occupational status tends to accompany lower evaluations.

We find suggestions of patterned variations in images according to age and size of place of residence. Although the disparities are not large,

TABLE 15-7. *Ratings of Federal Civil Servants on Five Traits, Related to Six Characteristics of the General Employed Public*

Characteristics	Average Number Answering	"Honesty"	"Interest in Serving the Public"	"How Well Respected They Are"	"Drive To Get Ahead"	"Ability"
Family Income						
Under $4,000	209	7.6	6.9	7.1	6.8	7.3
$4,000–5,499	317	7.4	6.7	7.1	6.6	6.9
$5,500–8,499	326	7.8	6.9	7.2	6.9	7.1
$8,500 and over	204	7.6	6.4	6.6	6.0	6.4
Occupation						
Unskilled and semiskilled	370	7.6	7.1	7.3	7.0	7.3
Skilled	179	7.6	6.9	7.3	6.8	7.0
Clerical	177	7.6	6.7	6.9	6.5	6.9
Professional and managerial	291	7.5	6.2	6.6	6.1	6.3
Farmers	75	7.8	7.2	7.3	6.8	7.6
Age						
18–32	298	7.4	6.5	7.0	6.4	6.8
33–39	204	7.9	6.7	7.1	6.6	6.9
40–48	290	7.7	6.9	7.1	6.7	6.9
49 and older	293	7.6	6.9	7.1	6.7	7.0
Place of Residence						
Open country and urban fringe	399	7.2	6.6	6.8	6.6	6.9
1,000–9,999	154	7.9	7.3	7.3	6.9	7.3
10,000–99,999	182	7.9	6.9	7.4	6.7	7.1
100,000–249,999	118	7.4	6.8	6.9	6.8	6.8
250,000 and over	241	7.8	6.7	7.0	6.3	6.8
Political Identification						
Strong Democrats	270	7.7	6.9	7.3	6.7	6.9
Independents	178	7.7	6.7	7.0	6.5	6.8
Strong Republicans	116	7.6	6.5	6.5	6.2	6.8
Previous Federal Civilian Employment						
Yes	155	7.7	6.9	7.0	6.8	7.0
No	918	7.6	6.7	7.0	6.6	6.9

the mean scores of the youngest age bracket are consistently lower than those for the other three levels. And persons living in the open country and urban fringes show a slight tendency to rate federal employees lower, while small-town respondents have a slight inclination to rate them higher. Again the differences are small and not entirely consistent. Geographically (not tabled) there appear to be few if any differences, except that persons in the Far West give slightly lower ratings.

That women in general are disposed to rate federal employees higher than men do has been demonstrated previously (Chapter 12). More refined analyses suggest that this tendency persists for women, regardless of income, education, or occupation; men, however, give significantly lower ratings as the income, educational, and occupational hierarchies ascend. The divergencies by sex are thus most pronounced at the upper strata of these hierarchies, with the result that women with family incomes of $5,500 and over, those in clerical and professional-managerial positions, and those of higher educational attainments rate civil servants markedly higher than do comparable men.

Of the two variables associated with government and politics—political party identification and previous federal employment—only the first seems to be associated with the mean scores. Strong Democrats exhibit a slightly more favorable attitude toward federal employees than do strong Republicans. The differences are most marked concerning respect and drive to get ahead.

Presumably a person's image of the civil servant would be conditioned by (or at least related to) his perceptions and evaluations of the government as a place to work. In Table 15-8 the mean scores assigned federal employees on the five qualities are shown in relation to (1) the extent

TABLE 15-8. *Ratings of Federal Civil Servants on Five Traits, Related to the General Employed Public's View of Federal Employment As a Way to Success and the Appeal of Federal Employment*

Traits	Federal Employment As an Avenue to Success			Appeal of Federal Employment		
	Poor	Fair	Good	Low	Medium	High
"Honesty"	7.3	7.5	7.9	7.3	7.5	8.1
"Interest in serving the public"	6.2	6.7	7.4	6.2	6.8	7.4
"How well respected they are"	6.7	6.9	7.5	6.6	6.9	7.7
"Drive to get ahead"	6.0	6.6	7.3	6.0	6.6	7.3
"Ability"	6.4	6.9	7.5	6.5	6.9	7.6
AVERAGE NUMBER ANSWERING	(338)	(391)	(332)	(357)	(390)	(315)

to which a respondent sees federal employment as an avenue to success, and (2) the measure of appeal which federal employment has for him.

Without exception, the more government employment is perceived as an avenue to success and the greater its appeal, the higher are the ratings assigned civil servants on the five traits. The greatest discrepancies between low and high ratings occur on interest in serving the public, drive to get ahead, and ability; scores move more than one scale point in each instance. Differences are least, though still statistically significant and in linear progression, for ratings on honesty and respect. These figures point toward a convergence and reinforcing of perceptions and appeal of federal employment and employees.

Reasons for Becoming a Civil Servant

As a third approach to the image held of federal employees, respondents were asked to explain why a person would become a federal employee instead of something else. Viewing a selection of the response categories according to family income results in an ordering quite similar to that found by educational attainment (Chapter 11):

	Under $4,000 (234)	$4,000- 5,499 (323)	$5,500- 8,499 (330)	$8,500 and Over (208)
Security, stability, protection, fringe benefits	47%	55%	65%	68%
High or good financial reward	29	24	18	11
Self-advancement and desire for success	15	8	9	9
Lack of ambition and initiative; desire for easy work	4	5	8	12
Unable to work or succeed elsewhere	3	6	7	9

Variations by income proved to be small for such factors as capability and qualifications, working conditions, and job opportunities. For the categories presented above, however, the relative emphasis by income groupings indicates that respondents with lower incomes, compared to those with higher, cite financial reward moderately more often and self-advancement and progress slightly more often. Higher-income people refer with greater regularity to the security factor, lack of ambition and initiative, and inability to work elsewhere.

Among other characteristics not tabled, age appears to be only slightly related to the explanations offered. Approximately 15 percent of the interviewees under 33 years, compared to about 8 percent over 33, mention self-advancement and desire for success. The oldest respondents and the youngest are together most inclined to mention financial remuneration; these two groupings are also similar in citing the desire for security least. According to place of residence size, we find that as the size increases there is a rise in the references to the security factor, with a range from a low of 50 percent for those in the open country and urban fringe to 68 percent for those living in cities of 100,000 or more population.

Finally, it seemed possible that people who had worked previously for the government might have a picture of motives differing from those who had not. Actually, only two meaningful contrasts emerged, one of them involving small percentages: (1) 71 percent of the respondents with previous federal experience vs. 57 percent of those without it give the security factor as a prime motive; (2) 5 percent of those with previous experience vs. 11 percent without it mention capabilities and qualifications. As pointed out in Chapter 14, our generalizations about the effect on members of the general employed public of previous federal employment are made very tentatively. However, these present findings at least suggest that former work experience with the government is unlikely to result in large-scale differences in the motives that are perceived for becoming a civil servant.

16

General Federal Employees: Occupational Ratings and Values

OUR SUPPLEMENTARY WORK with the sample of the general employed public proved fruitful in highlighting other correlates of occupational ratings and values. In this chapter the responses of the general federal employee sample will be similarly explored in relation to a number of variables other than education and sex. And here our supplementary analysis includes a measurement according to federal grade classification, a variable which proved to have great utility in discriminating among federal employees.

Approximately 94 percent of the 2,400,000 full-time federal employees are grouped within one or another of three pay systems.[1] About 42 percent are in general schedule positions, commonly referred to as "GS," with the grade level numeral following. (Since the basic structure for the system is provided for in the Classification Act of 1949, as amended, these employees are also termed "classified personnel.") Salary ranges for the various grades are fixed by congressional act. Most employees under the general schedule system hold "white-collar" positions.

The second largest grouping, 27 percent, works under the wage board system (WB). These employees receive remuneration in accordance with prevailing wage rates for comparable positions in the geographical area. Virtually all of them are "blue-collar" employees.

The third system, known as the Postal Field Service, covers nearly all

[1] All employee figures in this paragraph are as of 1961, and are based on *Summary Analysis of the President's Proposal for Reform of Federal Statutory Salary Systems* (prepared by the U.S. Civil Service Commission), House Committee on Post Office and Civil Service, 87th Cong., 2d sess. (March 1962).

postal workers and includes 25 percent of all federal employees. Congress also sets the salary schedules for this group.

To conduct supplementary analysis based on these three general systems seemed important, because they encompass three disparate kinds of work environments and occupational endeavors. We concluded that all postal employees in our sample could be grouped together for analysis, because of sample size and because over 80 percent of them fall into three adjoining steps in the postal pay system. There were also a priori reasons for assuming a moderately high degree of homogeneity on relevant matters within the group. But with the general schedule and wage board employees, the great range of positions appeared to call for finer distinctions, and the samples were of sufficiently large size that such distinctions could be made. Therefore we established four echelons of grade ranges for the general schedule or white-collar employees. The wage board or blue-collar employees, because of lack of comparability in prefixes and numbering systems, were divided into two subgroups, one of which included the unskilled and semiskilled, the other the skilled and supervisory. The resulting seven-fold classification is as follows:

	Number of Cases[2]
Wage Board	
Unskilled and semiskilled	128
Skilled and supervisory	114
Postal Service	106
General Schedule	
GS 2-4	180
GS 5-7	170
GS 8-11	145
GS 12 and above	90

It is fairly obvious that unskilled and semiskilled wage board employees form the lower end of the federal grade hierarchy, while GS 12 and above employees comprise the other. But it is also true that there is a two-way break within the wage board system and a four-way split in the general schedule system. We are handling two separate hierarchies as well as an over-all structure; all GS positions are by no means "higher" than all WB positions. Postal service employees are cast between the other two types because empirically they seem to resemble workers in

[2] These are the number of cases before the sample was brought into balance by weighting procedures. See Chapter 3, pp. 37-39.

both other systems in some respects and to constitute a unique grouping in others.

Aside from its general usefulness, this classification scheme has two special advantages, especially when comparisons are made with the occupational classification consisting of the four standard components—unskilled and semiskilled, skilled, clerical, and professional-managerial.

1. By separating out the postal service employees, we "purify" the clerical category, since the majority of postal employees are classified occupationally as performing clerical work. Such a division means that we can concentrate on this sizable segment of the federal population as a group which is basically different occupationally from the employees found in the more heterogeneous clerical grouping. The bulk of clerical workers who are not postal employees are found in the GS 2-4 groupings and, to a lesser extent, in the GS 5-7.

2. By establishing GS 8-11 and GS 12 and above groupings, we have essentially broken the professional and managerial classification into two subdivisions. A large majority of such employees are found in these grades, and there are very few people in these grades who do not fit the designation of professionals or managers.

OCCUPATIONAL SATISFACTION LEVEL, an attitudinal characteristic used in the examination of the general employed public, is also employed here for the general federal employees. Three other factors of particular relevance for the analysis of federal employees are used. These include length of government employment; present plans to continue with or leave the government; and past considerations of leaving government work. Length of employment is an important variable because it represents a combination of several factors: indirectly it measures satisfaction with the work, the degree of commitment, and how much of himself the employee has "invested" with the government; it is also a partial reflection of age and experience, and so on. It seemed highly probable that length of employment would be reflected in occupational ratings, in selected types of occupational values, and in the images of the government as a place of work and of federal workers. Many of the same indications are provided by past and present intentions of staying with or leaving federal employment—especially past and present states of relative dissatisfaction with government work.

Occupational Ratings

Present Satisfaction, Sense of Progress, and Future Expectations

A major finding of Chapter 4 was that occupational satisfaction and sense of past and future mobility are remarkably similar for general federal employees and for the general employed public. By education, however, we saw that members of the general public vary considerably more in this respect than federal employees. Our supplementary analysis of the federal population indicates that other variables show greater association with occupational satisfaction and feeling of mobility than education shows.

Dealing first with present job satisfaction, we find that in general satisfaction levels rise in company with increased occupational income, occupational rank, federal grade level, and age (Table 16-1). A comment is in order, however, to clarify these relationships in regard to the occupational and federal grade classifications. First, as in the general work force, for various measures used in this study employees in the skilled and clerical occupations typically fall midway between those in unskilled and semiskilled work and those in professional and managerial endeavors. Although clerical jobs are placed above skilled work on the occupational hierarchy—primarily because "white-collar" jobs normally command more prestige than "blue-collar" jobs—the status distance between the two is not regularly reflected in marked differences on many of our measures of occupational ratings, values, and images. A prime reason for this is that clerical workers in postal service constitute around one fourth of the total clerical grouping. In Table 16-1 we see, for example, that the present occupational mean rating of clerical employees dips below that of skilled workers; this is partially accounted for by the rating from the postal clericals, which is lower than that of clerical employees as a whole. Thus postal employees "drag down" the over-all clerical ratings of present occupation.[3]

---

[3] Further, the clerical group may be expected to show aberrations if compared with the clerical group in the nonfederal populations, on the basis of various findings presented in this and the next two chapters. For example, the sex ratio of the clerical group in the general work force is approximately equal, with men in a slight majority, while in the federal work force it is 3/2, with women in the majority. And the clerical males in federal work are predominantly postal employees (a fairly homoge-

TABLE 16-1. *Ratings of Own Occupation at Present, 5 Years Ago, and 5 Years Hence, Related to Four Characteristics of General Federal Employees*[a]

Characteristics	Average Number Answering	Present Occupation	5 Years Ago	Difference: "Present" Minus "5 Years Ago"	5 Years from Now	Difference: "5 Years from Now" Minus "Present"
Occupation						
Unskilled and semiskilled	114	6.5	6.0	+ .5	7.9	+1.4
Skilled	152	7.1	6.3	+ .8	8.1	+1.0
Clerical	333	6.6	5.7	+ .9	7.8	+1.2
Professional and managerial	294	7.7	6.7	+1.0	8.5	+ .8
Federal Grade Level						
Wage board						
Unskilled and semiskilled	120	6.8	6.0	+ .8	8.1	+1.3
Skilled and supervisory	111	7.2	6.4	+ .8	8.3	+1.1
Postal service	103	6.2	5.5	+ .7	7.3	+1.1
General schedule						
GS 2–4	165	6.9	6.5	+ .4	8.2	+1.3
GS 5–7	159	7.1	5.9	+1.2	8.4	+1.3
GS 8–11	140	7.6	6.2	+1.4	8.4	+ .8
GS 12 and over	85	7.7	7.0	+ .7	8.5	+ .8
Occupational Income						
Under $4,500	171	6.7	6.1	+ .6	8.1	+1.4
$4,500–5,499	264	6.6	5.8	+ .8	7.9	+1.3
$5,500–6,999	245	7.1	6.0	+1.1	8.0	+ .9
$7,000–9,999	143	7.5	6.5	+1.0	8.4	+ .9
$10,000 and over	72	8.0	7.5	+ .5	8.6	+ .6
Age						
Under 33	136	6.8	5.1	+1.7	8.3	+1.5
33–39	191	6.8	5.8	+1.0	8.2	+1.4
40–48	295	6.8	6.2	+ .6	7.7	+ .9
49 and older	269	7.4	6.8	+ .6	8.3	+ .9

[a] The mean ratings shown in this table and subsequent rating tables in the chapter are based on a ten-step scale.

neous group). The upshot is that the federal and nonfederal clerical categories are more unalike than we might anticipate.

It is also true that unskilled, semiskilled, and skilled workers and non-postal clerical employees in government are relatively "better off" than others in government because in most cases their salaries and fringe benefits are equal to or better than those of their outside counterparts. This is not true of federal professional and managerial personnel. Such differences may well result in intergroup variations on measures of occupational satisfaction and of occupational values and images.

All strata of occupation, grade level, income, and age groupings report a feeling of occupational progress over the past five years. By job income levels this is lowest for the least and for the most affluent respondents— for different reasons, of course. Those making $10,000 or more record relatively high ratings for five years ago (7.5) so that there is less room for them to progress; those with incomes under $4,500 had relatively low ratings (6.1) so that there was sufficient space for them to move up, even though they report next to the lowest present satisfaction. Occupationally, the unskilled and semiskilled indicate the least progress, the professional and managerial the most (+5 vs. +1.0). But what stands out when this five-year change is analyzed by our federal grade level scheme is that the two middle strata in the classified service, GS 5-7 and 8-11, report the most progress while the lowest group, the GS 2-4, estimates the least. Notice that postal employees, who have the lowest present rating, also feel that they were least well off five years ago. By age brackets, ratings and sense of progress move in the anticipated direction and in progressive manner, with the youngest people calculating a move of +1.7 vs. the oldest group's +0.6.

All strata also expect to advance moderately in the next five years. There is remarkably little variation in the level most respondents expect to reach—between 8.0 and 8.5—at least by the variables used in Table 16-1; only the postal employees depart from this norm with an anticipated future rating of 7.3. While the absolute anticipations tend toward similarities, the amount of gain over present ratings necessarily varies considerably. Those who are least satisfied now, i.e., have the lowest occupational rating scores, have room to make bigger jumps than those possessing the highest scores. Thus, those with smaller incomes, lower occupational status, occupying lower grade levels, and being younger in age predict the most precipitous climbs.

Analysis of job ratings by other demographic and personal features of the sample produce few differences of any significance. Scores were found to vary little according to geographic region, community background, whether or not either parent was foreign born, political party identification, or the incidence of previous military service. Whites tend to assign slightly higher ratings than Negroes, and respondents from center cities are inclined to score lower than those from other backgrounds, especially rural. We had thought that location within or outside the Washington, D.C., area might reflect somewhat higher satisfaction for those in the Washington area; however, very few differences showed up, especially when federal grade level is held constant.[4] The only meaningful difference found was that GS 2-7 respondents in the Washington area report somewhat more advancement within the last five years than their non-Washington colleagues (+1.4 vs. +0.6).

As noted earlier (see Chapter 4, Table 4-1), men and women federal employees in the aggregate show quite similar feelings of occupational satisfaction, sense of progress, and expectations of future advancement. Further analysis indicates that this resemblance continues, regardless of educational, financial, occupational, federal grade, and age classifications. There is, however, suggestive evidence that the present occupational satisfaction of women at the very lowest income and federal grade levels is somewhat higher than that of comparable men. But since men occupy an overwhelming majority of the highest income and grade classifications, and because such incumbents register higher levels of satisfaction, the over-all difference between men and women is only 0.2 of a scale step on the occupational ladder. Another moderate difference occurs by age groupings—women between 40 and 48 years register a slightly higher figure than similar males (7.5 vs. 6.6). The only noticeable variation by sex regarding past or future progress is that males of the youngest age category claim a much sharper gain over the last five years than comparable females (as well as men and women at all other age levels); their net increase is 2.1 versus that of 0.7 for the females.[5]

The other special variables which we hypothesized would have a rela-

[4] The distribution of Washington, non-Washington employees was as follows (the distribution being that before weighting—see footnote 2 above):

	Number of Cases in	
	Washington Area	Non-Washington Area
GS 2-7	83	267
GS 8 and Above	54	181
Other (mainly wage board employees)	28	320
Total	165	768

[5] A possible explanation for the lack of symmetry is that the young women are more probably noncareer types who plan to work for a short time only, have been in the work force for a shorter period of time, and, unlike their male counterparts, feel no strong psychological need for occupational progress.

tionship to occupational satisfaction, sense of past progress, and expectation of advancement are presented in Table 16-2. They include length of government service, present intentions of staying with the government, past considerations of leaving, and occupational satisfaction.

According to length of federal employment, those respondents longest employed by the government rate their present occupation somewhat higher (7.4) than those with the shortest length of service (6.6). To determine the incidence and surety of intentions to remain in federal employment, interviewees were asked whether they planned to leave or continue working for the federal government and how sure they were of these intentions.[6] Three analytical groupings were derived from the questioning—those planning to leave, those fairly sure about continuing, and those very sure about continuing (by far the largest number). Those planning to leave have the lowest occupational ratings, 6.0, those fairly sure about staying, 6.2, and those very sure about continuing, the highest rating, 7.3. Thus, the more sure a person is of continuing, the higher his present satisfaction.

Next, a related series of questions ascertained whether the respondents had ever considered leaving the government in the past, and if so, when.[7] Three more analytical categories emerged—those who had never thought of leaving (the largest number), those who had considered leaving over five years ago, and those who had considered departing within the past five years. Although employees in the first two categories have nearly identical job satisfaction scores (7.1 and 7.0), those who thought of leaving within the past five years yield a lower average (6.3). Alternatively, we may say that the more recently a person has thought of leaving the government, the lower he rates his occupation. Finally, the mean scores by occupational satisfaction given in Table 16-2 are derived from the occupational ratings. Their only importance here is to reveal the spread of occupational placements and the mean score at each level—low, medium, and high.

As to progress made in the past five years, the longer a person has been with the government, the less is his feeling of recent progress. This inverse relationship is partly a function of the age of the respondents. The older a person is, the less likely he is to report recent rapid progress

[6] For the exact wording, see Items 17 and 19 of the Federal Employee Questionnaire, Appendix B.
[7] For the exact wording, see Items 20 and 21 of the Federal Employee Questionnaire, Appendix B.

TABLE 16-2. *Ratings of Own Occupation at Present, 5 Years Ago, and 5 Years Hence, Related to Four Classifications of General Federal Employees*

Classifications	Average Number Answering	Present Occupation	5 Years Ago	Difference: "Present" Minus "5 Years Ago"	5 Years from Now	Difference: "5 Years from Now" Minus "Present"
Length of Government Employment						
Under 5 years	152	6.6	5.0	+1.6	8.1	+1.5
5–9 years	246	7.0	6.1	+ .9	8.1	+1.1
10–19 years	385	7.0	6.3	+ .7	8.1	+1.1
20 years and over	113	7.4	7.1	+ .3	7.7	+ .3
Present Plan for Leaving or Continuing in Government						
Plan to leave	58	6.0	5.4	+ .6	7.7	+1.7
Plan to continue						
Fairly sure	159	6.2	5.6	+ .6	7.7	+1.5
Very sure	648	7.3	6.3	+1.0	8.2	+ .9
Considered Leaving Government						
Within last 5 years	174	6.3	5.3	+1.0	7.6	+1.3
Over 5 years ago	185	7.0	6.3	+ .7	7.9	+ .9
Never	536	7.1	6.3	+ .8	8.3	+1.2
Occupational Satisfaction						
Low	302	4.6	4.6	0.0	6.5	+1.9
Medium	367	7.6	6.3	+1.3	8.6	+1.0
High	227	9.6	8.2	+1.4	9.8	+ .2

(as shown in Table 16-1). And since length of service is moderately correlated with age, we should expect a similar relationship. What the figures do suggest, however, is that new federal employees feel they are experiencing strong upward mobility on the occupational ladder, their average advance being from 5.0 to a present 6.6. Although the differences are not large, there is also a progressive association between intentions of remaining with the government and perceived progress, running from +0.6 for those planning to leave to +1.0 for those very sure about staying. The differences according to previous thoughts about leaving are minor. Level of occupational satisfaction, on the other hand, is distinctly related to a sense of improvement. Respondents with the lowest levels of satisfaction report, on the average, no upward movement at all over the past five years.[8] Contrasting with that maintenance of the status quo are the scores of those with medium and high levels of satisfaction, who estimate their advance at well over one step on the occupational ladder.

Finally, we find that the estimates of advancement in the next five years also vary. Respondents with the government under five years expect to advance 1.5 steps on the occupational ladder, whereas those employed by the government twenty years and over expect an upward movement of only 0.3. Age is again a critical factor here, but significantly those employed the longest do not predict as high an *absolute* rating five years hence as do employees employed for fewer years. Additionally, if the employees in each length-of-employment bracket were to achieve their predicted five-year climb, they would be well beyond the mean scores for the next higher bracket. Optimism seems to be the keynote of the more recently employed, who are also typically younger people.

Employees most certain of remaining with the government have the highest absolute expectations about where they will be five years hence, but their relative gain is exceeded by those planning to leave and those who are only fairly sure about continuing with the government. Similarly, respondents who never thought of leaving have somewhat higher absolute expectations. Finally, the lower the level of satisfaction, the more relative advancement a person expects in the future but the lower his absolute figure will be. Given the nature of the ten-step occupational ladder it would be impossible for those with very high scores—9 or 10—to show much relative advancement. Without doubt the most fascinating portion of the series is the anticipated improvement of the least satisfied. Even though they remained stable over the past five years, they predict an upward movement of nearly two ladder steps (from 4.6 to 6.5) during the coming five years.

Government and Nongovernment Employment Compared

The respondents were asked to consider that they retained their present occupation but in nongovernment employment, and then to indicate where they thought they would be on the occupational ladder. The prime interest here is not so much the absolute scores assigned to out-

[8] Concealed beneath this static situation is a variation by sex. Men estimate a slight gain of 0.2 whereas women signify a net loss of 0.4. That women hope to recoup this loss is indicated by their expectation of future mobility, which results in a net advantage of 2.4 over their present score vs. a figure of 1.8 for comparable men.

TABLE 16-3. *Ratings of Present Occupation vs. Doing the Same Work, but Outside the Federal Government, Related to Three Characteristics of General Federal Employees*

Characteristics	Average Number Answering	Present Occupation	Same Occupation but Outside the Federal Government	Difference: "Outside" Minus "Present"
Occupation				
Unskilled and semiskilled	118	6.5	5.1	−1.4
Skilled	160	7.1	6.1	−1.0
Clerical	344	6.6	5.8	− .8
Professional and managerial	305	7.7	7.2	− .5
Federal Grade Level				
Wage board				
Unskilled and semiskilled	127	6.8	5.3	−1.5
Skilled and supervisory	112	7.2	6.4	− .8
Postal service	101	6.2	5.5	− .7
General schedule				
GS 2–4	174	6.9	5.9	−1.0
GS 5–7	168	7.1	6.5	− .6
GS 8–11	142	7.6	7.1	− .5
GS 12 and over	88	7.7	7.8	+ .1
Occupational Income				
Under $4,500	184	6.7	5.5	−1.2
$4,500–5,499	270	6.6	5.8	− .8
$5,500–6,999	252	7.1	6.2	− .9
$7,000–9,999	146	7.5	7.1	− .4
$10,000 and over	73	8.0	7.8	− .2

side employment, but rather the comparison between nongovernment and present employment scores. We expect, and the data confirm, that the kinds of people who rate their present jobs the highest also rate outside employment higher than do other respondents (Table 16-3).[9] Of more interest is the *difference* the respondents see between present and outside employment, which indicates how well off they feel relative to other employment possibilities.

Examination of Table 16-3 leaves little doubt as to which groups feel they would be most penalized by a shift to nongovernment employment.

[9] For some remarkable contrasts, these data may be compared with those in Table 14-3 of Chapter 14, where the pattern within the general employed public is the reverse; i.e., the *higher* the present rating, the *lower* the rating assigned to government work.

By occupational income, federal grade level, and occupational classification, the data plainly show that the lower a person's rank in these hierarchies the worse off he feels he would be if he were no longer working for the government. Conversely, the higher his position in these hierarchies the smaller is the difference he sees for himself whether in government or nongovernment employment. In fact, respondents at the GS 12 and over level estimate a minute rise on the ladder of 0.1. Recording the largest drop are wage board workers in the unskilled and semiskilled category. They say their difference would be from a present of 6.8 down to 5.3 outside the government.

Two other classifications (not tabled) deal with race and political party preference. Although data for the general employed public indicated that federal employment appeal was much greater for Negroes than whites, this is not true among federal employees. By race, there is very little variation in the difference scores, even with income controlled. Similarly, political partisanship makes little difference, but Democrats do envisage a slightly greater decline than Independents and Republicans; these differences persist when a control of occupational income is introduced.[10] Other analyses revealed that little variation occurs in the comparison of the two ratings by age, geographic region, location in or outside the Washington area, and presence of previous military service. Respondents with suburban backgrounds are slightly less inclined to feel they would be worse off.

Women in general feel slightly more than men that they would experience a loss by changing employers, the net decrease being 1.1 for women and 0.7 for men. Even though this minor intersex difference is found at

---

[10] For the party identification by income break the number of respondents in each cell is sufficient to warrant measures of statistical significance. In the case of race by income, however, the number of Negroes in the upper-income bracket is rather small, as these figures (from the unweighted sample) illustrate:

	White Employees	Negro Employees
Under $5,500	321	142
$5,500 and Over	436	37
Total	757	179

Strictly speaking, then, when we say that differences persist with income controlled, we are referring primarily to comparisons between whites and Negroes with occupational incomes under $5,500. Even here it may be that the average income of the Negroes is below that of whites, so that the term "controlled for" may be more approximate than is usually the case. As purely *descriptive* statements the differences between races are still worth pointing out, even if the differences are only products of such factors as income and education.

TABLE 16-4. *Ratings of Present Occupation vs. Doing the Same Work, but Outside the Federal Government, Related to Four Classifications of General Federal Employees*

Classifications	Average Number Answering	Present Occupation	Same Occupation but Outside the Federal Government	Difference: "Outside" Minus "Present"
Length of Government Employment				
Under 5 years	166	6.6	5.5	−1.1
5–19 years	252	7.0	6.3	− .7
10–19 years	391	7.0	6.1	− .9
20 years and over	118	7.4	6.8	− .6
Present Plan for Leaving or				
Continuing in Government				
Plan to leave	64	6.0	6.0	0.0
Plan to continue				
Fairly sure	166	6.2	5.9	− .3
Very sure	663	7.3	6.2	−1.1
Considered Leaving Government				
Within last 5 years	180	6.3	6.0	− .3
Over 5 years ago	185	7.0	6.3	− .7
Never	560	7.1	6.1	−1.0
Occupational Satisfaction				
Low	314	4.6	4.6	0.0
Medium	378	7.6	6.8	− .8
High	236	9.6	7.5	−2.1

nearly all educational, income, federal grade, and age levels, it is most marked among the more elite groups—the higher educational, income, and occupational levels. Illustratively, men in the professional and managerial brackets predict a drop of only 0.3 in contrast to a 1.7 figure for comparable women. By age, it is women in the two mid-age categories who see a more significant decline than men: between the ages of 33 and 39 the net scores are −1.1 for women and −0.7 for men; between 40 and 48, −1.3 vs. −0.6. The more successful women employees probably see certain difficulties in maintaining and enhancing their status outside federal work; such feelings would seem to be justified in view of the barriers women face in many high-status occupations.

Other factors are also associated with perceptions of how well federal employees think they would fare outside government (Table 16-4). Thus, people who have been with the government twenty years or more tend to estimate a smaller loss than those who have worked for the government less than five years. Among those planning to leave the government, the average feeling is that there would be no difference; those very sure about staying see a drop of 1.1 steps down the ladder. People who have never thought of leaving the government perceive more difference than their colleagues who had ideas of leaving sometime in the last five years. There is also a strong negative relationship between occupational satisfaction and the estimated effect of a nongovernment employer. Respondents with lower job satisfaction foresee no rise on the ladder; those with medium level occupational ratings see a moderate drop of 0.8; and employees with the highest level of satisfaction predict a precipitous downward plunge of 2.1.

Another question designed to probe into the self-perceived occupational well-being of federal employees concerned what they thought their families would think if they went to work outside the government: would they be going up the ladder, down the ladder, or would there be no difference? The hypothesis would be for an ordering of responses similar to that found in the preceding analysis.

According to the data of Table 16-5, this is precisely the case. As income, occupational status, and federal grade level rise, so does the belief that families would see the employees as moving up the ladder. However, as these strata rise, the belief that families would see a movement *down* the ladder decreases. Also, movements up these hierarchies are accompanied by growing expectations that there would be no perceived difference if the employer changed. This "no difference" score is significant because it seems reasonable to expect a certain amount of inertia or resistance to change. That the "no difference" scores vary directly with the level of income, occupation, and grade level indicates that, despite this built-in resistance, the occupants of higher-level positions still see less possibility that their families would forecast a downward movement.

A close look at two polar groupings under the federal grade heading illustrates the disparities in outlooks. Among the respondents classified as unskilled and semiskilled, predictions of family thinking are as follows: only 8 percent say moving up, a whopping 63 percent say moving down, and 28 percent say no difference. Sharply juxtaposed against these figures are the following for the GS 12's and above: 29 percent, moving up,

TABLE 16-5. *Responses to:* "*Suppose you were to change now and go to work outside the federal government doing the same thing you're doing now; how do you think your family might feel about it? Would they feel you were moving up the ladder or down?*" *Related to Four Characteristics of General Federal Employees*

Characteristics	Number Answering	Up the Ladder	Down the Ladder	No Difference	Don't Know
Occupation					
Unskilled and semiskilled	112	8%	65%	26%	1%
Skilled	155	16	49	35	0
Clerical	344	18	47	35	0
Professional and managerial	301	23	35	41	1
Federal Grade Level					
Wage board					
Unskilled and semiskilled	122	9	63	28	1
Skilled and supervisory	108	22	44	34	0
Postal service	100	21	51	28	0
General schedule					
GS 2–4	176	10	55	34	1
GS 5–7	165	14	39	45	1
GS 8–11	140	17	23	60	0
GS 12 and over	87	29	18	51	2
Occupational Income					
Under $4,500	179	8	59	33	0
$4,500–5,499	267	18	47	34	0
$5,500–6,999	246	16	47	36	1
$7,000–9,999	145	26	37	37	0
$10,000 and over	74	29	22	46	2
Race					
White	731	17	42	40	2
Negro	174	18	62	19	2

18 percent, moving down, and 51 percent, no difference.

Variations according to race and party identification are now sharper than by previous measures. There is little difference in the percentages for moving up the ladder, but for moving down the ladder Negroes far outstrip whites and (not shown) Democrats outdistance Independents and Republicans. Congruent with this, fewer Negroes and Democrats see no difference. Again, the variations hold when income is held constant.

Three other divisions of the sample also bear a relation to the patterning of responses. Respondents presently planning to leave the government, those having considered leaving in the past five years, and those with low and medium occupational satisfaction ratings are most likely to say that their families would feel they were moving up the ladder, and least likely to say the opposite (Table 16-6). Conversely, those very sure about staying, those who never thought of leaving, and those with the highest occupational satisfaction predict less upward movement and more downward movement. Answers of "no difference" are approximately the same for all respondent categories.

Other analyses (not tabled) suggest again that age makes only a slight difference in these comparative evaluations, although younger employees, compared to older ones, do predict somewhat more upward and less downward movement. Length of government employment makes only slight and inconsistent difference in the replies. Over all, more men than women say their families would see the change as a movement up the ladder (20 vs. 10 percent), and women reply more often that there would be no difference (41 vs. 34 percent), while the replies for down the ladder are only 3 percentage points apart. Further analysis yields a

TABLE 16-6. *Responses to:* "*Suppose you were to change now and go to work outside the federal government doing the same thing you're doing now; how do you think your family might feel about it? Would they feel you were moving up the ladder or down?*" *Related to Three Classifications of General Federal Employees*

Classifications	Number Answering	Up the Ladder	Down the Ladder	No Difference	Don't Know
Present Plan for Leaving or Continuing in Government					
Plan to leave	61	34%	38%	28%	0%
Plan to continue					
Fairly sure	166	25	36	37	1
Very sure	651	13	51	36	0
Considered Leaving Government					
Within last 5 years	179	26	40	32	1
Over 5 years ago	188	22	44	34	0
Never	544	14	48	38	0
Occupational Satisfaction					
Low	310	20	47	33	0
Medium	367	21	41	37	1
High	235	9	52	39	0

general confirmation of the findings reported in the previous section: sex variations are most evident among higher-status employees and the 33 to 48 age grouping, with women giving more of an edge to government employment.

Absolute and Comparative Appeal of Federal Employment

Another measure of occupational satisfaction, both absolute and relative, was provided by having the federal employees indicate on the ten-point, agree-disagree scale their reactions to the statements, "All things considered, working for (the federal government) (a large private business firm) appeals to me." Two things are of concern here: the absolute appeal of the government as an employer and the comparative appeal in relation to a large private business (not tabled).

According to income, federal grade, occupation, and age the scores vary only slightly to moderately. In general, the absolute appeal scores hover around 8.0 on the scale and the comparative scores show the government having a net score of around +3.5 to +4.0. One of the few large variations occurs by federal grade level, where postal employees express the lowest absolute appeal and also the lowest comparative appeal (+2.9 vs. +4.3 for the GS 2-4 grouping, for example). Age comparisons show that the youngest workers give slightly lower absolute and comparative ratings, while the very oldest employees are somewhat higher on both counts. On the average, women employees signify more absolute and comparative attraction to government employment at all levels of income, occupation, federal grade classification, and age.

By region, midwesterners have slightly lower absolute and comparative appeal figures, their net difference score being about a scale point higher than that for southerners. One of the few distinctions according to Washington, non-Washington residency occurs on this measure, and even here the discrepancy is not far-reaching. Employees at the GS 8 or above level in Washington rate the absolute and comparative appeal of government about one scale point higher than their counterparts in the field. This suggests that upper-level Washington respondents may have more attachment to government work, per se, even though they rank their present occupations no higher than do their non-Washington counterparts.

Employees with small to medium-sized town backgrounds find more absolute and comparative appeal in government, especially in contrast to those with suburban backgrounds. Negligible differences emerge according to race and incidence of previous military service. Finally, Democrats and Republicans show slightly higher absolute and comparative preference for government employment than do Independents.

The data on the absolute and comparative appeal of government are primarily suggestive. In most instances the differences cited are not large, even though many are statistically significant.

More dramatic relationships are seen in Table 16-7, where the distribution of mean ratings according to three measures of federal employment commitment are presented. On the straightforward rankings of government appeal, the more committed the person is now and was in the past to staying with the government and the higher his job satisfaction score, the greater is the appeal of federal employment to him. To a certain extent these are internal validation measures, but the range of scores suggests a confluence of commitment, appeal, and satisfaction. When the appeal of federal and of private business employment are compared the relationships become even more pronounced. This is because the employ-

TABLE 16-7. *Ratings of Occupational Appeal of the Federal Government vs. Large Private Business, Related to Three Classifications of General Federal Employees*

Classifications	Average Number Answering	"All things considered, working for a large private business firm appeals to me"	" All things considered, working for the federal government appeals to me"	Difference: "Government" Minus "Business"
Present Plan for Leaving or Continuing in Government				
Plan to leave	65	4.9	6.7	+1.8
Plan to continue				
Fairly sure	166	5.1	7.6	+2.5
Very sure	668	4.2	8.3	+4.1
Considered Leaving Government				
Within last 5 years	181	4.9	7.2	+2.3
Over 5 years ago	188	4.9	8.1	+3.2
Never	560	4.2	8.2	+4.0
Occupational Satisfaction				
Low	314	4.6	7.4	+2.8
Medium	382	4.4	8.2	+3.8
High	236	4.3	8.7	+4.4

ees with the least present and past intentions of staying in government and with lower satisfaction ratings give slightly higher scores to the appeal of business, and the net differences thus become enlarged.

An additional note here is that as job satisfaction increases, differences on the basis of sex decrease, as the following tabulation shows:

Occupational Satisfaction	N	Absolute Appeal of Government	Comparative Appeal of Government
Low			
Men	(218)	7.2	+2.5
Women	(96)	8.0	+3.6
Medium			
Men	(279)	8.1	+3.5
Women	(103)	8.6	+4.7
High			
Men	(152)	8.6	+4.5
Women	(83)	8.9	+4.3

It is apparent that the appeal of government employment covers a wider range, by both absolute and comparative scores, for men than for women. Since women in general signify more attraction to government work than do men, the contrast between the men and women who manifest least satisfaction helps account for much of the greater disaffection toward government employment shown by men.

Occupational Values

The "Ideal" Occupation

In Chapter 5, data on the characteristics of the "ideal" occupation gave us a fairly detailed notion of the kinds of occupational values which are most salient to federal employees. Here we will apply additional analyses to the responses given.

Table 16-8 will serve as the basis of discussion. It presents, according to federal grade classification, the distribution of the major categories of respondents' descriptions of an "ideal" occupation. A striking feature of the data is the lack of sharp and consistent differences by grade level for some of the categories. For the first six listed—interest in the work, security, physical environment, relations with supervisors, and active and passive personal relations—the distribution is either fairly homogeneous or somewhat erratic. Even here, however, general schedule workers stand apart from wage board workers in paying more attention to active and passive personal relations; the upper-level GS employees also express somewhat less concern than other respondents about a good physical environment and working conditions.

Beginning with the value of self-advancement and progress the disparities become more pronounced. In general, these last nine factors are cited less frequently by wage board and postal service employees than by those on the general schedule. Within the WB and GS subhierarchies, respondents at the lower end are less likely to mention them than those at the upper extreme. These values for the most part form a cluster which focuses on the ego-rewarding, self-realization aspects of the job, whereas most of those in the upper half of the table are more material, physical, and extrinsic in nature—active personal relations being an exception.

Consider, for example, the category "responsibility for making decisions." The figures range from lows of 5 percent for postal service and for the unskilled and semiskilled, and of 7 percent for GS 2-4 respondents to a high of 21 percent for those at GS 12 and above. Providing the most extreme polarities is the "challenge" category. Only 7 percent of the unskilled and semiskilled mention this value, but a total of 41 percent of the GS 12's and over cite it. Similar patterns (although not always as significant) are found for the other "self-realization" categories.

The distribution of replies according to income and occupational classifications are not tabled because for the most part the pattern tends to follow the either explicit or implicit pattern in the data by federal grade level. In general, there is relatively small variation for those values dealing with the more physical and extrinsic elements of work, but much more for the ego-rewarding, nontangible aspects. The higher the income and occupational status, the more frequent are the responses of the latter type. Some of the differences are less pronounced, some more pronounced, than by federal grade level; nearly all, however, assume the general ordering discussed above.

Other variables are less associated with the image of the ideal job (not shown). By age groupings, the very oldest respondents exhibit less concern about high financial reward: 32 percent mention it, in comparison to 41 to 45 percent for other age levels. They are also the least concerned about working conditions, although a healthy 38 percent of them

TABLE 16-8. *Attributes of the "Ideal" Occupation, Related to Federal Grade Level of General Federal Employees*[a]

Attributes of the "Ideal" Occupation	Wage Board		Postal Service	General Schedule			
	Semi-skilled and Un-skilled	Skilled and Super-visory		GS 2–4	GS 5–7	GS 8–11	GS 12 and Above
Interest, enjoyment, satisfaction, pleasure	72%	73%	68%	76%	69%	70%	74%
Security, stability, protection, fringe benefits	19	23	22	18	17	19	21
Good physical environment and working conditions	51	43	47	44	45	32	38
Good relations with supervisors	19	26	19	26	20	14	18
Good passive relations with people at work	27	15	16	34	31	15	29
Good active relations with people at work	23	17	29	26	36	21	22
Self-advancement and progress	7	16	8	12	19	17	26
Recognition for one's work	6	4	6	9	9	10	23
Self-development, self-expression, and creativity	15	21	14	15	24	26	29
Self-determination	16	24	27	17	22	26	30
Responsibility for making decisions	5	9	5	7	13	10	21
Challenge	7	12	9	10	15	19	41
Sense of achievement or accomplishment	9	19	9	15	15	22	24
Variety, absence of routine or monotony	13	12	10	17	19	20	22
Do work that is worthwhile, useful, constructive	15	10	12	18	27	24	29
NUMBER ANSWERING	(127)	(114)	(106)	(179)	(170)	(145)	(90)

[a] As noted earlier, "federal grade level" denotes our sevenfold classification of federal employees within the three pay systems.

still refer to that feature. Frequency of other responses varies insignificantly by age groupings. Length of government employment likewise
bears little relationship to the configuration of the ideal job; however,
there is a small but regular decline in the mentions of financial reward
and working conditions and a small but regular increase in references to
desire for a sense of achievement as length of service increases. Interestingly, by both age and length of employment, the most junior and senior
groupings refer most often to the element of security, while the next to
oldest group and the next to longest employment group mention it least.
In each case, however, the percentage difference between the extremes
is modest.

Because occupational satisfaction ratings originate from a complex
blend of values, expectations, and perceptions, we found virtually no relationship between levels of job satisfaction and constructs of the ideal
occupation.[11] As with the nonfederal employed public, most of the more
than trivial variations between men and women in picturing the ideal
job exist at all levels of education, occupation, age, and, in the case of
federal employees, federal grade.

With few exceptions the distribution of replies by grade level, income,
and occupation in response to the question of what would constitute the
very worst sort of occupation—the least ideal—assumes the pattern seen
in descriptions of the ideal occupation. That is, if a respondent group
more frequently mentions certain features they would want in an ideal
occupation, they are likewise inclined to mention more often the *absence*
of such features in describing the least ideal job. But certain values which
are only slightly or moderately discriminating or which are very infrequently mentioned on the first question are more manifest with the second.

Six of these are presented, according to rate of occurrence by federal
grade level, in Table 16-9. Here the relationships between grade and
concern about the physical environment, passive relations with people,
self-determination, and too much routine on the job are more strongly
set forth than in the ideal job descriptions. The higher the grade level
within WB and GS subhierarchies, the less is the concern about physical

---

[11] This is not to say that people at each level of satisfaction have the same values.
If, for example, we were to control for education, income, occupation, or the like,
we would be almost assured of finding different structures of occupational values
operative within and between different levels of job satisfaction.

TABLE 16-9. *Attributes of the "Worst" Occupation, Related to Federal Grade Level of General Federal Employees*

Attributes of the "Worst" Occupation	Wage Board		Postal Service	General Schedule			
	Semi-skilled Un-skilled	Skilled and Super-visory		GS 2–4	GS 5–7	GS 8–11	GS 12 and Above
Bad physical environment and working conditions	58%	55%	49%	46%	45%	38%	33%
Bad passive relations with people at work	23	14	14	32	27	22	18
Lack of self-determination	6	12	14	14	14	20	29
Too much routine in the work, monotonous	14	25	25	24	39	42	56
Too much pressure or tension	6	7	7	17	12	8	2
Excessive work load; hard work	9	2	9	15	11	2	3
NUMBER ANSWERING	(127)	(112)	(106)	(178)	(170)	(145)	(87)

environment and passive relations, but the greater is the interest in having self-determination and variety in one's work. Two categories infrequently volunteered in depicting the ideal occupation assume more prominence here: white-collar workers make less reference as grade level increases to fears about too much pressure or tension on the job, and the lowest in each subhierarchy of both blue-collar and white-collar workers are more inclined to mention an excessive work load and hard work as undesirable traits. Examination of the answers to this question in terms of income and occupational classifications reveals similar trends.

Scale Ratings of Occupational Values

Another way of eliciting the patterning of occupational values was to present the respondents with prepared statements and ask them to indicate their feelings about them in terms of the ten-point agree-disagree scale. For most of the populations in this study the correlation between the *patterning* of values uncovered through each type of questioning (free-response and scaling) is quite high. Additionally, by using the scale device, we can inquire into attitudes about the work world which are usually not elicited by the questions on the most and least ideal kinds of work, especially in regard to work ethics and orientations to the work world.

The data show a negative association between income level and the agreement scores on the first three items (Table 16-10). As income increases there is less agreement that work is nothing more than a way of making a living, about liking the kind of work you can forget about, and that to be really successful you must care about making money. All of these items connote values of a materialistic, nonintrinsic nature.

Other values cluster around interests in the more ego-rewarding, status enhancing, and nonextrinsic dimensions. Now the relationships to income level are in the positive direction; the higher the income, the more agreement there is that money is not all-important, that opportunity is more important than security, that work is most satisfying when accompanied by hard problems, that directing others is satisfying, and that carrying out one's own ideas without interference is important. Higher income is also associated, though somewhat irregularly, with greater agreement on the status-related item that one's family should have the things that others have. The magnitude of the differences between low and high income groups on these items is large, ranging from 1.1 to 2.1 steps on the ten-point scale. Of particular relevance in this instance is the discrepancy of scores on the two "money" statements. The higher the income, the lower is the agreement that caring about money is essential to being successful. Complementing this, the higher the income, the more pronounced is the agreement that, given a necessary minimum, making more money isn't important. Taken together, the two items illustrate the broader, less tangibly centered value structure accompanying rising income levels.

When we divide respondents according to their grade ranking, the picture is similar to that by income levels. Within the blue-collar and white-collar subhierarchies, increasing rank is accompanied by lower agreement on the tangible, materialistic values and by higher agreement on the ego-rewarding, high-achievement traits (Table 16-11). The postal

TABLE 16-10. *Ratings of "Occupational Value" Statements, Related to Occupational Income of General Federal Employees*

"Occupational Value" Statements	Occupational Income				
	Under $4,500	$4,500– 5,499	$5,500– 6,999	$7,000 9,999	$10,000 and Over
"To me, work is nothing more than a way of making a living"	3.7	3.7	2.9	3.1	2.1
"I like the kind of work you can forget about after the work day is over"	6.7	6.5	6.0	5.6	4.9
"To be really successful in life, you have to care about making money"	5.5	5.2	4.6	4.5	4.3
"After you are making enough money to get along, then making more money in an occupation isn't very important"	4.5	4.3	4.9	5.6	5.5
"I would like my family to be able to have most of the things my friends and neighbors have"	6.7	7.2	7.4	7.2	7.6
"It is more important for a job to offer *opportunity* than *security*"	5.2	5.4	5.6	6.6	7.3
"Work is most satisfying when there are hard problems to solve"	6.5	7.0	7.3	8.2	8.3
"It is satisfying to direct the work of others"	6.5	6.8	7.3	7.7	7.7
"To me, it's important in an occupation for a person to be able to carry out his own ideas without interference"	6.0	6.2	6.6	6.9	7.1
AVERAGE NUMBER ANSWERING	(179)	(274)	(254)	(147)	(74)

service employees are somewhat paradoxical; on some items they resemble the GS 2 to GS 7 people, while on others they are more akin to either the unskilled and semiskilled or the skilled employees. Once again there seem to be factors which mark postal workers as a unique group.

In Table 16-11, three items not used in the analysis of Table 16-10 shed additional light on the panorama of values. GS workers on the higher levels to a much greater extent than their colleagues on the lower levels, and higher-level WB employees to a slightly greater extent than the

TABLE 16-11. *Ratings of "Occupational Value" Statements, Related to Federal Grade Level of General Federal Employees*

"Occupational Value" Statements	Wage Board		Postal Service	General Schedule			
	Semi-skilled and Un-skilled	Skilled and Super-visory		GS 2–4	GS 5–7	GS 8–11	GS 12 and Above
"I like the kind of work you can forget about after the work day is over"	6.9	5.9	6.2	6.7	6.2	5.6	4.6
"To be really successful in life you have to care about making money"	6.1	5.1	5.0	4.8	4.5	4.6	4.0
"It is more important for a job to offer *opportunity* than *security*"	5.3	5.4	5.3	5.5	5.7	6.7	7.5
"It would be hard to live with the feeling that others are passing you up in your occupation"	6.0	6.6	5.9	6.2	6.8	6.7	7.0
"To me, it's important in an occupation to have the chance to get to the top"	8.4	8.8	8.4	7.5	8.1	8.3	8.8
"To me, it's important to have the kind of work that gives me a chance to develop my own special abilities"	8.5	8.8	8.3	7.9	8.8	8.7	9.0
"Work is most satisfying when there are hard problems to solve"	7.0	7.6	6.5	6.6	7.7	7.8	8.7
"It is satisfying to direct the work of others"	6.5	7.9	7.0	6.2	7.0	7.6	8.0
"To me, it's important in an occupation for a person to be able to carry out his own ideas without interference"	6.6	6.9	6.1	5.6	6.0	7.1	7.4
AVERAGE NUMBER ANSWERING	(122)	(113)	(105)	(174)	(169)	(145)	(89)

lower-level ones, attach importance to not being passed up by others, having the chance to get to the top in an occupation, and developing one's special abilities in an occupation. These scores suggest (when combined with other data) not so much a concern about the material rewards accompanying advancement, but rather a desire to achieve goals which are valued in and of themselves. Whereas the lower-level employees emphasize the "bread-and-butter" aspects of these values, the workers of higher status seem to want the self-fulfillment such advancement and development afford.

If the respondents are grouped by the standard occupational categories (not tabled), patterns paralleling those found by income and grade level emerge. However, there is a tendency for skilled workers to resemble professional and managerial personnel, and for the clerical workers to share some of the attitudes of the unskilled and semiskilled. For many discriminating items about occupational values, then, the rates of agreement would vary either upward or downward with the order of an occupational hierarchy which is ordered as unskilled and semiskilled, clerical, skilled, and professional and managerial.

Age shows little or no association with the kinds of values highly related to income, grade level, and occupation. Apparently certain value clusters of a skilled worker, for example, do not vary significantly with his age. On the other hand, there are some values or perspectives which do vary with age, primarily those regarding belief in the importance and value of work (as the tabulation on the following page demonstrates). As age rises there comes a corresponding increase in seeing work as the most important part of a person's life and opportunity as slightly more important than security, in trying to succeed at all costs, and viewing work as an aid in forgetting personal problems. On the other hand, older people agree least that if a person doesn't want to work hard, it's his own business. Whether because of generational changes, or not, older employees evidently feel that work and getting ahead are more vital in a person's life. A substantial reiteration of these findings by age is found in terms of length of government employment.

There is some evidence that past considerations of withdrawing from government employment are related to occupational value structures. Those who have earlier considered leaving express slightly to moderately greater affirmation for these propositions: work is most satisfying when accompanied by hard problems; it would be hard to live with the feel-

	Under 33 (148)	33-39 (193)	40-48 (296)	49 and Older (289)
"Work should be the most important part of a person's life"	5.0	5.5	5.8	6.3
"It is more important for a job to offer *opportunity* than *security*"	5.5	5.6	5.7	5.9
"A person should constantly try to succeed at work, even if it interferes with other things in life"	5.9	6.4	6.7	6.9
"If a person doesn't want to work hard, it's his own business"	4.9	4.5	4.4	3.9
"Work helps you forget your personal problems"	6.2	7.1	7.2	7.5

ing that others are passing you up; it is important to carry out one's own ideas without interference; opportunity in a job is more important than security; and it is satisfying to direct the work of others. They also agree more that success is mainly a matter of knowing the right people and less that success is mainly a matter of hard work. Most of these statements lie in the cluster of intrinsic, nonmaterial work values. In most instances the disparities between the two groupings—respondents who had earlier contemplated leaving and those who had not—are moderate; hence our declaration that the evidence is only suggestive. It appears, however, that on the average those who once felt most inclined to leave are among the more dynamic, ambitious, and problem-solving present employees.

When we examine the present-day intentions of remaining with the government and their surety, there is some coincidence of response patterns to those found according to past intentions of remaining or leaving. For example, respondents intending to leave and those only fairly sure of staying rate opportunity vs. security somewhat higher than those very sure of staying. On the other hand, those intent on staying put more stock in doing work that is worthwhile to society. On the whole, the associations by this breakdown are much less conclusive than those dealing with past intentions of continuing or leaving government work.

Positive and Negative Aspects of One's Job

When the interviewees were asked why they did not rank their occupations higher and why not lower, the answers provided clues to what they considered the negative and positive aspects of their jobs. The variations in responses according to federal grade classification are not extreme for the "why not higher" replies. For three of the leading response categories—low or inadequate financial reward, lack of self-advancement and progress, and the feeling that there is always room for improvement —there is little if any difference. Postal service employees and unskilled and semiskilled workers refer to bad physical environment and working conditions the most frequently, whereas respondents in GS 12 and over positions cite the lack of sufficient equipment and wherewithal most often. The higher the grade level, the more is reference made to the lack of self-determination (3 percent for the unskilled and semiskilled vs. 17 percent for the GS 12's and above). Finally, postal employees and the GS 12's and above mention personal limitations or lack of choice less often than others.

When we look at the positive attributes people see in their jobs, two groupings stand out in contrast to the others. Postal employees refer less often than others to interest, enjoyment, and satisfaction in their work, the feeling of self-development, self-expression, and creativity on the job, and experiencing a sense of challenge, but 44 percent of them mention the security aspects of their job, in contrast to about 20 percent of the other employee classes. Top-echelon GS people are significant for referring less often to good physical environment and working conditions and more often to self-development, self-expression, and creativity. White-collar employees in general cite more frequently than WB workers the presence of self-determination, having responsibility and authority, and a sense of challenge; and these percentages tend to be higher as the general schedule hierarchy climbs.

The patterning of answers to this pair of questions, when examined in the light of income and standard occupational groupings, resembles the general contour found by grade level. By age groupings, only three findings stand out: employees between 40 and 48 years mention more frequently than others the lack of self-advancement and progress as negative aspects; the youngest employees refer with more regularity to work that does not fit their capacities as a negative attribute; and the very oldest grouping more often cites a sense of well-being in the job as a positive factor.

By length of service, those least experienced cite poor economic reward slightly more often; those with the government twenty years or more mention lack of wherewithal to do the job, and cite their own personal limitations as reasons for not ranking their jobs higher. Those with the government the longest less often mention low economic rewards and working conditions as negative attributes, and also mention with greater frequency as positive aspects the challenge and responsibility their work involves, and the sense of well-being associated with it.

Thus the response pattern to these two questions by social characteristics is somewhat irregular and not always differentiated. But when the answers are broken down according to level of occupational satisfaction, we find a different picture (Table 16-12). As the occupational ratings rise, the percentages descend for bad physical environment, bad superiors, lack of advancement and progress, and (not shown) too much routine in the work. Significantly, satisfaction level is virtually nonrelated to the mention of poor financial reward. We find that higher occupational satisfaction accompanies the feeling that there is always room for improvement; this is not inconsistent with the other findings, since this feeling essentially represents a state of mind about an ideal to be attained in a job, rather than a criticism of the job being rated.

By the same token, the most satisfied personnel express the more positive sentiments about not rating their occupation lower (Table 16-12). Compared with others, they are more interested in their work, have a greater general sense of fulfillment and well-being, are more likely to think they have good supervision, good personal relations at work, and a high degree of self-determination; they also have a greater sense of doing a worthwhile job. They are much less inclined than others to say that their jobs are good only in comparison to others, a basically nonpositive response. On the negative aspects of the job ("What kept you from placing it higher?"), the major differences in respondents' answers involve matters primarily of a more tangible, extrinsic nature.

One other related analytical variable has a parallel association with the replies to these two questions about the negative and positive features of one's work. Dividing the employees into those planning to leave the government, those fairly sure of staying, and those very sure of staying, we find that those planning to leave are much more likely than others to cite as justifications for not placing their jobs higher on the oc-

TABLE 16-12. *Negative and Positive Attributes General Federal Employees See in Their Own Jobs, Related to Their Occupational Satisfaction*

Attributes Seen in Own Jobs	Occupational Satisfaction		
	Low	Medium	High
Negative			
Poor or inadequate financial reward	23%	26%	19%
Bad physical environment and working conditions	20	17	10
Bad superior, supervisor, boss	22	14	9
Lack of self-advancement and progress	22	13	4
Always room for improvement	12	22	27
NUMBER ANSWERING	(317)	(386)	(111)
Positive			
Interest, enjoyment, satisfaction, pleasure	30%	42%	55%
General sense of fulfillment, well-being	5	8	28
Good superior, supervisor, boss	12	16	22
Good physical environment and working conditions	19	25	25
Good personal relations with people at work	20	29	39
Self-determination	7	15	14
Do work that is worthwhile, useful, constructive	6	5	11
Relative merits of job or occupation	23	12	13
NUMBER ANSWERING	(300)	(384)	(241)[a]

[a] The reason more of the highly satisfied replied to this question than to the previous one dealing with negative attributes is that all respondents who rated their occupations at 10 on the occupational ladder were not asked for the negative aspects of their jobs ("What kept you from placing it higher?").

cupational ladder: low economic rewards; lack of self-determination; inadequate responsibility for decisions; doing work that does not fit one's capacities; and poor working conditions. On the other hand, they mention less often the matters of personal limitations and the possibility of room for improvement. Even though the number of cases does not warrant broad generalization (sixty-one employees were planning to leave), these data point toward the kinds of factors which may be operating to make government work unattractive to some employees.

17

General Federal Employees: Images of Federal Employment and Employees

Ascertaining the images that members of the general government work force have of federal employment and of civil servants is particularly fascinating, since to a large extent these are self images, involving considerable introspection. Here we will relate various aspects of the two images (as treated in chapters of Part Two) to independent variables such as occupation, federal grade level, income, age, occupational satisfaction, and present and past thoughts of leaving government employment.

Image of the Government As an Employer

Characterization of the Work Performed

In Chapter 13 we contrasted the image which members of the federal service hold of the kind of work they perform with the image held by other populations. It was shown that variations by sex and level of education as well as occupational specialties were related to that image. Certainly we would predict that such characterizations would be related to a person's grade level in the federal service, inasmuch as this classification is an indicator both of rank and of the kind of work performed.

Looking at the response patterns by federal grade level to the question, "What do you picture a federal civil service employee as doing—that is, what sort of work?", we find that they vary with the type of work people at different levels are most acquainted with and exposed to. Thus postal employees mention postal work of some type much more frequently than do other respondents—35 percent vs. 3 to 8 percent for other groupings. Similarly, wage board workers refer to crafts and craftsmen and laboring or laborers considerably more often than do other types of employees. White-collar workers show higher percentages for management, professional, technical and scientific, engineering, and clerical work than do the blue-collar and postal workers. And the higher the rank of the GS personnel, the more likely they are to cite the prestige activities such as management, professional work, and so forth. Finally, office work in general is referred to by about 20 percent of the employees at each level, except by those at the GS 12 and above level where the figure is 11 percent.

When the replies to the question are viewed according to income brackets and occupational classifications, the same basic ordering prevails. The higher the income and occupational status, the more the image consists of higher status types of endeavors. And, again, certain activities such as clerical work and office work are mentioned with almost equal frequency by nearly all groupings.

Length of employment appears to be related to the image perceptions also, but in a somewhat different manner. As the length of service increases, the more references there are to work of managerial, professional, technical and scientific, engineering, clerical, craft, and laboring nature. The reference to such a variety of endeavors suggests that length of employment may have an effect on perceptions independent of one's own work level. Quite probably the longer a person has worked with the government the more he knows about the diverse nature of government work.

Finally, even with grade classification held constant, the Washington area employees exceed employees outside the area in characterizing the work as managerial, professional, technical, and clerical, but they fall below the outside respondents in mentioning postal, crafts, and laboring endeavors. In general the Washington area responses relate government work to higher status activities than do non-Washington descriptions.

Security and Mobility

We gain further information on the federal employee's view of his employer when we consider the mean ratings on preformulated statements.

Characteristics	Average Number Answering	"Employment with the federal government offers a high degree of security"	"A young man of ability who starts work in the federal civil service has a good chance of ending up in one of the top-level jobs"	"For a young man of ability, his best chance for being *really successful* lies in working for the federal government"
Occupation				
Unskilled and semiskilled	114	8.6	8.0	5.6
Skilled	160	8.0	7.8	4.7
Clerical	351	8.3	6.6	4.1
Professional and managerial	307	7.7	6.7	4.0
Federal Grade Level				
Wage board				
Unskilled and semiskilled	122	8.5	7.9	5.6
Skilled and supervisory	113	8.0	7.9	4.8
Postal service	105	8.5	6.4	4.2
General schedule				
GS 2–4	174	8.1	7.1	4.4
GS 5–7	169	8.1	7.0	3.7
GS 8–11	145	7.5	6.6	4.1
GS 12 and above	89	7.3	6.5	3.7
Occupational Income				
Under $4,500	179	8.4	7.4	5.1
$4,500–5,499	274	8.3	7.1	4.2
$5,500–6,999	254	8.2	7.0	4.5
$7,000–9,999	147	7.5	6.8	4.2
$10,000 and over	74	7.5	6.6	3.6
Age				
Under 33	148	8.1	6.5	4.2
33–39	193	8.4	7.2	4.2
40–48	296	8.0	7.0	4.3
49 and older	289	8.1	7.3	4.6
Length of Government Employment				
Under 5 years	167	8.5	7.0	4.4
5–9 years	250	8.1	7.1	4.4
10–19 years	392	8.0	7.1	4.6
20 years and over	122	7.7	7.1	3.8

[a] The mean ratings shown in this table and subsequent rating tables in the chapter are based on a ten-step scale.

490

There tends to be an inverse association between occupational income, federal grade level, and occupational classification on the one hand, and the ratings given government employment on three key factors on the other. As income, grade level, and occupational level go up, there is less agreement that federal employment offers high security, that a young man can wind up in one of the top-level jobs, and that a person's best chance for being really successful lies in working for the government (Table 17-1). The disparities are greatest on being really successful, next largest on ending up in a top-level job, and least, though still on the order of about 1 scale point, for security. The data by federal grade level are particularly interesting; they not only provide the most extreme polarity between the unskilled and semiskilled and the GS 12 level and above, but also show that blue-collar or wage board workers tend to have higher mean scores than counterpart white-collar groups (GS 2-7).

Age and length of employment are of less relevance here. Younger people are less inclined to feel that federal employment provides a good chance of ending up in a top-level job, and people who have worked for government less than twenty years see a greater degree of security than do the veterans of twenty years or more. This latter group also agrees less that government offers the best chance for being really successful.

With one exception we discovered virtual unanimity between Washington and non-Washington employees in their reactions (not tabled) to the preformulated statements: the GS 8 and above respondents in the Washington area are more disposed than their field counterparts to agree that a person who works for the federal government generally has a good chance to get ahead (7.3 vs. 6.5); Washington employees occupying GS 2-7 grades, however, rate the government slightly lower than do comparable field personnel (6.2 vs. 6.7).

In the preceding chapter it was shown by at least one measure that Negroes feel they would be more disadvantaged than whites if they were to start working outside the government. The figures that follow on the next page suggest some of the reasons for this state of mind. For each of the three factors, Negroes rate the government as high as whites do, or higher. But for each of the same three factors as applied to private business the Negro ratings are lower than the white ratings. The net result is a considerable gap between the two groupings in the difference scores, so that the Negro scores are more favorable to government.

	White (749)	Negro (173)
"Employment with the federal government offers a high degree of security"	8.1	8.1
"Employment with a large private business offers a high degree of security"	4.9	4.1
Difference: "Government" Minus "Business"	+3.2	+4.0
"A person who works for the federal government generally has a good chance to get ahead"	6.7	6.7
"A person who works for a large private business generally has a good chance to get ahead"	6.3	5.3
Difference: "Government" Minus "Business"	+ .4	+1.4
"For a young man of ability, his best chance for being *really successful* lies in working for the federal government"	4.3	4.8
"For a young man of ability, his best chance for being *really successful* lies in working for a large private business corporation"	5.2	4.5
Difference: "Government" Minus "Business"	− .9	+ .3

Negroes also see more absolute and relative chance of ending up in a top-level job in government than in corporate work (not tabled). These findings leave the distinct impression that Negroes have a more favorable image of government as an employer, absolutely and relatively; this remains so when race differences are controlled for occupational income.

Is a person's state of satisfaction with government employment related to his image of government employment? The hypothesis would be that the higher his satisfaction, the more positive his evaluations of significant facets of government employment. The data bear this out with remarkable clarity. As present satisfaction ratings increase there is much more agreement that government work offers a chance to get ahead, of ending up in one of the top-level jobs, and of being really successful (Table 17-2). Unquestionably then, job satisfaction is highly related to positive perceptions of government as a place of work.

Examining the mean scores for three comparable statements about private business (Table 17-2), we see that job satisfaction has only a small relation to this set of figures. When the scores for the three pairs of statements are compared, the relative positive image of the highly satisfied and the relative negative image of the much less satisfied are brought into sharp focus. Those with lowest levels of satisfaction rate private busi-

TABLE 17-2. *Ratings of Evaluative Statements About Federal and Private Employment, Related to Occupational Satisfaction of General Federal Employees*

Statements	Occupational Satisfaction		
	Low	Medium	High
"A person who works for the federal government generally has a good chance to get ahead"	6.0	6.9	7.6
"A person who works for a large private business generally has a good chance to get ahead"	6.1	6.0	6.2
Difference: "Government" Minus "Business"	−.1	+.9	+1.4
"A young man of ability who starts work in the federal civil service has a good chance of ending up in one of the top-level jobs"	6.6	7.0	7.8
"A young man of ability who starts work in a large private business corporation has a good chance of ending up in one of the top-level jobs"	7.0	7.1	7.1
Difference: "Government" Minus "Business"	−.4	−.1	+.7
"For a young man of ability, his best chance for being *really successful* lies in working for the federal government"	4.1	4.2	5.0
"For a young man of ability, his best chance for being *really successful* lies in working for a large private business corporation"	5.4	4.7	4.9
Difference: "Government" Minus "Business"	−1.3	−.5	+.1
AVERAGE NUMBER ANSWERING	(315)	(382)	(233)

ness as the equal of government on providing a chance to get ahead, but as better on providing a chance for top-level jobs and achieving real success; employees who are the most satisfied see government as better on all three counts. Another striking feature is that the ordering of the relative position of government as an employer is exactly the same for all three levels of job satisfaction. Government comes off best in offering a chance to get ahead, next on providing an opportunity for a top-level job, and least well as a way for being really successful. In short, a person's possibilities for forging ahead are viewed as reasonably bright but considerably less promising for reaching the pinnacle of success.

Since attachment and commitment to a job are at least partly a product of the employee's image of his employer, we may expect that the presence of past considerations of leaving the government will be related to the nature of these perceptions. Dividing the respondents according to (1) those who have never thought of leaving, (2) those who considered it over five years ago, and (3) those who have considered it within the past five years, we find that the positive evaluation of government decreases as we move from the first group to the third. This holds true, for example, in ratings of government for its security, opportunity for a top-level job, and chance for being really successful (Table 17-3). Those who have never thought of leaving also think that government jobs are less routine and monotonous.

TABLE 17-3. *Ratings of Evaluative Statements About Federal and Private Employment, Related to General Federal Employees' Past Thoughts of Leaving Government*

Statements	Considered Leaving Government		
	Within Last 5 Years	Over 5 Years Ago	Never
"Employment with the federal government offers a high degree of security"	7.5	8.1	8.3
"Employment with a large private business offers a high degree of security"	5.0	4.7	4.7
Difference: "Government" Minus "Business"	+2.5	+3.4	+3.6
"A young man of ability who starts work in the federal civil service has a good chance of ending up in one of the top-level jobs"	6.3	7.0	7.3
"A young man of ability who starts work in a large private business corporation has a good chance of ending up in one of the top-level jobs"	7.4	6.8	7.1
Difference: "Government" Minus "Business"	−1.1	+.2	+.2
"For a young man of ability, his best chance for being *really successful* lies in working for the federal government"	4.1	4.1	4.6
"For a young man of ability, his best chance for being *really successful* lies in working for a large private business corporation"	5.2	5.2	4.9
Difference: "Government" Minus "Business"	−1.1	−1.1	−.3
AVERAGE NUMBER ANSWERING	(180)	(189)	(558)

Comparing the scores for private business vs. those for government on the factors of security, gaining a top-level job, and attaining success sheds further light on the differential evaluations. Employees who never thought of leaving rank government employment higher on all three, and tend to place private business slightly lower than do those who have thought of leaving within the past five years. (The pattern is irregular for those who thought of leaving more than five years ago.) Consequently, the comparative rankings of government are more extreme than the absolute rankings. In sum, the chances are that if a person has considered leaving the government he will be less positive in his absolute and relative evaluations of government as an employer in terms of its security and mobility offerings. Furthermore, if he has thought of leaving in the recent past, he will be less positive than those so inclined in the more remote past, although in this instance there are some irregularities.

If past considerations of leaving are related to the image, present state of mind should also be related. Portioning the sample in terms of those

TABLE 17-4. *Ratings of Evaluative Statements About Federal Employment, Related to General Federal Employees' Present Plans To Stay with or Leave the Government*

Statements	Plan To Leave	Plan To Continue	
		Fairly Sure	Very Sure
"Most jobs in the federal government are routine and monotonous"	4.9	4.3	4.0
"Employment with the federal government offers a high degree of security"	7.9	7.9	8.3
"A person who works for the federal government has a good chance to get ahead"	5.3	6.0	7.0
"A young man of ability who starts work in the federal civil service has a good chance of ending up in one of the top-level jobs"	6.3	6.9	7.2
"For a young man of ability, his best chance for being *really successful* lies in working for the federal government"	2.7	4.2	4.7
AVERAGE NUMBER ANSWERING	(58)	(159)	(648)

who are very sure of continuing, those who are fairly sure, and those who plan to leave, the supposition is confirmed (Table 17-4). Those presently planning to leave, of whom there are only fifty-eight, rate the government higher on routine and monotony, but lower on its security, opportunity for getting ahead, the chances of a top-level job, and the prospect of being really successful. Conversely, those definitely planning to stay see less routine and monotony and more of the other qualities.

It is worth comment that the differences in evaluations are least on the routine and security statements, and greatest on the statements dealing with advancement and success. This suggests that a determination to leave may be oriented around disappointments about opportunity for achievement rather than concern about the security advantages or the degree of boring work. On the other hand, it could be a "sour grapes" reaction by those who have been frustrated in some respect. In Chapter 18 the incidence of present and past intentions of leaving and the reasons for such intentions will be explored more deeply.

Advantages and Disadvantages in Working Outside Government

Federal employees were also asked what would be better and what would be worse if their occupations stayed the same but they were to work outside government. Answers to the two questions can be evaluated in relation to the degree to which the individual's structure of occupational values and aspirations is being achieved or not in working for the government.

When a person points out something which would be improved if he worked outside the government, he is citing, in effect, a "negative" aspect that he sees in government employment. The five categories mentioned most frequently are financial reward, self-advancement and progress, self-determination, less bureaucracy—and the declaration that nothing would be better, clearly an answer different in nature and affect than the other four. Although there are minor inconsistencies, the tendency is very strong for those in the upper echelons of the income, grade level, and occupational hierarchies to see the four substantive features as being improved upon outside the government much more than do lower levels of these hierarchies (Table 17-5).

Financial reward, the category referred to most often by all groupings, highlights the variation most vividly. A substantial 31 percent of those making under $4,500 estimate that financial reward would be improved outside of government—but the figure for those in the highest bracket is more than double that—65 percent. The percentages for self-advancement and progress are somewhat irregular. There seems to be a slight tendency for the mid-level income and grade classification employees to most anticipate more advancement. Forming a logical and symmetrical obverse to the percentages on the four substantive categories are those for the response that nothing would be better. The lower the level of the employee, the greater is the likelihood of his insisting that his lot would not be improved in any way if he worked outside the government. The differences are large and progressive, with the lowest levels having percentages two and three times as high as those in the topmost level. By occupation, for example, 41 percent of the unskilled and

TABLE 17-5. *Positive Attributes Seen in Nonfederal Employment, Related to Three Characteristics of General Federal Employees*

Characteristics	Number Answering	Better in Nonfederal Employment				
		High or Good Financial Reward	Self-Advancement and Progress	Self-Determination	Less Bureaucracy	Nothing Would Be Better
Occupation						
Unskilled and semiskilled	114	32%	3%	2%	4%	41%
Skilled	157	41	12	7	7	28
Clerical	336	34	15	5	5	28
Professional and managerial	299	51	13	9	11	17
Federal Grade Level						
Wage board						
Unskilled and semiskilled	122	34	6	4	3	39
Skilled and supervisory	110	38	14	6	4	26
Postal service	100	36	15	2	5	34
General schedule						
GS 2–4	171	35	10	7	4	27
GS 5–7	163	39	18	4	9	19
GS 8–11	140	50	14	9	10	16
GS 12 and above	87	62	8	18	16	8
Occupational Income						
Under $4,500	180	31	9	3	6	35
$4,500–5,499	265	34	12	5	3	31
$5,500–6,999	245	43	12	5	10	22
$7,000–9,999	144	46	18	8	7	20
$10,000 and over	71	65	5	18	12	11

semiskilled vs. 17 percent of the professional and managerial give this response.

One would predict that employees who have considered separating from government work in the past would more often cite these major factors than employees who have not. It might be further hypothesized that those who had thought of leaving most recently would mention such factors more often than those who thought of leaving more than five years ago. The data lend only mild, though consistent, support to both propositions. Those who have thought of departing do mention more often such features as higher economic rewards, more self-advancement, and less bureaucracy.[1] At the same time, fewer of them claim that nothing would be better. The more recent waverers occupy the extreme positions on these statements. Most of the differences are, however, not great, and even though statistically significant should not be overly stressed; it is their congruence with logical expectations and other correlative findings which makes them meaningful.

There are similar, though less conclusive associations between levels of satisfaction and present intentions of staying with the government on the one hand, and perceptions of what would be better outside the government on the other. Respondents who presently plan to leave, and those only fairly sure about staying speak more frequently of advantages and less often say that nothing would be improved than do those very sure of staying. Differences according to level of job satisfaction on the rating ladder are primarily in the anticipated direction—the greater the satisfaction, the less advantageous seems outside work.

If the lack of exceptionally strong relationships suggested by the foregoing analysis seems surprising, it must be remembered that satisfactions and commitments cut across the strands of education, income, occupation, and grade level. The unequal importance attached to certain occupational values by different groupings within those hierarchies sometimes cancel each other when they are "mixed" together in measures reflecting satisfaction and commitment to government employment.

It is reasonable to expect that relationships will also be found between some of these variables and estimates of what would be *worse* out-

---

[1] Although there are only forty-eight mentions of "relative emphasis on merit" in the entire sample, it is worth noting that 2 percent of the respondents who never thought of leaving vs. 7 percent of those who have say that work outside the government would emphasize recognition of merit more.

TABLE 17-6. *Negative Attributes Seen in Nonfederal Employment, Related to Three Characteristics of General Federal Employees*

Characteristics	Number Answering	Worse in Nonfederal Employment				
		Poor or Inadequate Financial Reward	Less Security and Protection	Poor Physical Environment and Working Conditions	Excessive Work Load; Hard Work	Less Leisure, Vacation, Leave
Occupation						
Unskilled and semiskilled	119	24%	68%	29%	11%	30%
Skilled	158	13	70	31	6	29
Clerical	348	22	68	13	4	28
Professional and managerial	306	14	59	16	4	22
Federal Grade Level						
Wage board						
Unskilled and semiskilled	126	22	73	27	9	34
Skilled and supervisory	111	16	71	29	7	31
Postal service	102	15	69	14	4	22
General schedule						
GS 2–4	178	31	68	15	5	30
GS 5–7	168	23	63	15	5	30
GS 8–11	143	7	59	16	0	21
GS 12 and above	89	8	55	19	1	20
Occupational Income						
Under $4,500	186	32	67	20	9	25
$4,500–5,499	273	21	67	18	4	30
$5,500–6,999	251	14	69	21	5	26
$7,000–9,999	146	8	66	15	1	25
$10,000 and over	74	8	46	25	7	17

side the government. The five major response categories for the question are poor or inadequate financial reward; less security; bad physical environment and working conditions; excessive work load; and relative lack of leisure, vacations, and time off. In nearly every instance the respondents on the lowest levels of the income, grade level, and occupation hierarchies mention these features more often than the respondents at the other extreme of the hierarchies (Table 17-6). The variations between the extremes are usually in the anticipated direction, but some inconsistencies do occur.

Some of the categories deserve special notice. Physical environment factors are cited much more often by blue-collar workers than white-collar workers. This can be seen in the figures for both grade level and occupational classifications but tends to be buried in those for income. On the other hand, it is the skilled workers and the professional and managerial personnel who least feel that financial reward would be worse.

The very high figures referring to security factors also warrant comment. An inspection of Table 17-6 shows that the primary drop in mention of this feature comes with the higher extremes of each of the three hierarchies—respondents making $10,000 or over, those at the GS 8 level and above, and those classified as professionals or managers. The differences among other strata are minimal. We have not tabled the distribution for the five components of this global category of security—security unspecified, job security, financial security, retirement security, and other protective benefits. The distribution indicates, however, that the divergence of the upper groups lies primarily in their much less frequent references to miscellaneous protective benefits, and especially sick leave. For example, 53 percent of the WB unskilled and semiskilled workers, as contrasted with 19 percent of the classified GS 12 and above mention these types of benefits. Other security aspects are cited with nearly equal frequency by all groups; in fact, job security is mentioned by upper-level employees slightly more often than by lower-level workers.

Answers to what would be worse about outside employment form no strong regular pattern according to present and past intentions of remaining with the government, or according to occupational satisfaction. As a rule, employees who have formerly thought of leaving, those less committed to staying now, and those having lower levels of satisfaction are somewhat less likely than others to mention the five major items referred to above. An exception is lower economic reward: here there is either little difference in opinion or the response is given more frequently. And, within the over-all security response, the lack of job security is more often referred to by these classes of respondents. Thus, 33 percent with low satisfaction vs. 22 percent of those with high satisfaction and 34 percent of those who have thought of leaving vs. 26 percent of those who have not mention job security as worse outside government. Again, it should be pointed out that socioeconomic and personal factors cross-cut these indicators, thereby introducing cancellation effects and reducing the possibility of strong relationships.

The Image of Federal Employees

Since asking federal employees for their impressions of the federal employee is asking for a collective self image, we may expect the image to vary among different kinds of employees (as we saw according to educational levels and occupational attainments in Chapters 8 and 9, Part Two). When responses are analyzed according to federal grade classification, there emerges a moderate discrepancy in the portrayal. Employees of higher grade are more inclined to cite, on one hand, work capability and sincerity in trying to do a good job and on the other security consciousness and lack of ambition; at the same time they tend to speak less

TABLE 17-7. *Characteristics Attributed to Federal Civil Servants, Related to Federal Grade Level of General Federal Employees*

Characteristics Attributed to Civil Servants	Wage Board		Postal Service	General Schedule			
	Un-skilled and Semi-skilled	Skilled and Super-visory		GS 2–4	GS 5–7	GS 8–11	GS 12 and Above
Good personal character	33%	35%	36%	34%	36%	26%	28%
Capable of doing the work because of ability or training	8	11	7	14	12	12	20
Good worker	34	28	24	37	36	28	27
Sincere and conscientious worker—*tries* to work well	15	12	11	13	19	19	27
Personality is agreeable	35	22	19	32	31	18	14
Security conscious	11	8	24	10	13	27	21
Ambitious, high initiative	6	5	6	10	12	10	6
Not very ambitious, low initiative	5	4	11	2	5	9	11
Serves or wants to serve others	7	11	16	18	18	13	18
NUMBER ANSWERING	(127)	(112)	(104)	(179)	(169)	(145)	(89)

frequently of good workers and agreeable personalities (Table 17-7). There are only slight differences in pointing out the civil servant's good personal character, but GS respondents note his orientation to service more frequently than do WB workers. Over all, there is some indication that the higher the grade level, the lower is the mention of characteristics which connote a "positive" image.

Findings according to income and occupational level (not tabled) correspond to these. By income level, for example, 32 percent of those making under $4,500, compared with 14 percent of those making $10,000 and over, mention agreeable personality; and while 11 percent in the lower income bracket describe the civil servant as security conscious, twice that many in the highest bracket picture him that way. Undoubtedly the images conveyed are in part reflections of a respondent's own way of looking at his environment and the people there; thus, some things are more important and salient to him than others. Even so, however, the differences in images and conceptions *are* present and most probably have consequences for the employee's evaluation of and satisfaction with his job.

An employee's commitment to staying with his employer, it would be hypothesized, is related to the image he has of his fellow workers. Although the distinctions are not apparent for all response categories, some of the percentages suggest that this is indeed the case. Dividing the respondents according to their intentions of staying or of not staying with the government, we find the following distribution on three key categories:

	Plan To Continue		*Plan To*
	Very Sure (675)	*Fairly Sure* (168)	*Leave* (65)
Good personal character	36%	32%	16%
Security conscious	15	16	26
Not very ambitious	5	11	14

Thus, the more sure a person is of staying, the more he describes the employee as having good personal character, and the less he pictures him as being security conscious, and unambitious. Similar findings appear when the sample is grouped according to past thoughts of leaving. Those who have thought of departing within the last five years attribute fewer positive, and more negative, qualities than those who have never thought of leaving.

Workers in the Washington area contribute, on the average, more favorable comments about the government employee than do non-Washington workers. They more often tag the civil servant as having an agreeable personality, being sincere, and as a good worker. They less often note his security consciousness and lack of ambition. To be sure, some of the differences are not statistically significant. Yet they coincide with the distributions found for other categories and point toward a more favorable outlook on the part of the Washington employees. Because the largest Washington, non-Washington discrepancies occur among the upper-level GS employees, the variations are apparently not an artifact of the higher proportion of blue-collar WB workers in the field.

Rating Civil Servants on Specific Traits

When the ratings assigned to general civil servants on five traits are related to selected characteristics of general federal employees, we find the ratings universally high in regard to honesty, with scores averaging more than 8.0 on the ten-point scale (not tabled). But for the four other items—ability, how well respected, drive to get ahead, and interest in serving the public (Table 17-8)—not only are placements lower, but also there is a negative relationship between income, grade level, and occupation, on the one hand, and the assigned ratings on the other. Thus, the more money a person makes, the higher his grade ranking, and the more prestigious his occupation, the lower the score assigned the general federal employee.

Significantly, the direction is reversed somewhat by age groupings, as Table 17-8 shows. The older a person is, the more likely is he to assign a higher rating. The most pronounced shift comes with the 6.6 mean score given by those under 33 years vs. the 7.5 score of those over 48 in evaluating the respect given civil servants. Intentions of remaining with the government and job satisfaction are also positively associated with the ratings. Employees who considered leaving within the last five years assign lower ratings than those who thought about it over five years ago, but both are exceeded in favorable judgments by employees who never thought of leaving. A similar pattern prevails according to satisfaction; the lower a person rates his job, the lower he rates the employees.

TABLE 17-8. *Ratings of General Civil Servants on Four Traits, Related to Six Characteristics of General Federal Employees*

Characteristics	Average Number Answering	"Ability"	"How Well Respected They Are"	"Drive To Get Ahead"	"Interest in Serving the Public"
Occupation					
Unskilled and semiskilled	115	7.9	7.8	8.0	8.1
Skilled	160	7.7	7.3	7.3	7.7
Clerical	351	7.4	7.2	7.1	7.5
Professional and managerial	308	7.2	6.7	6.9	7.3
Federal Grade Level					
Wage board					
Unskilled and semiskilled	123	7.8	7.6	7.7	7.8
Skilled and supervisory	113	7.7	7.1	7.5	7.7
Postal service	105	7.4	7.4	6.7	7.6
General schedule					
GS 2–4	176	7.6	7.4	7.7	7.5
GS 5–7	169	7.4	7.2	7.4	7.5
GS 8–11	144	7.1	6.7	6.9	7.2
GS 12 and above	90	7.1	6.2	6.6	7.3
Occupational Income					
Under $4,500	181	7.7	7.5	7.7	7.7
$4,500–5,499	276	7.6	7.5	7.3	7.7
$5,500–6,999	253	7.4	7.0	7.1	7.3
$7,000–9,999	148	7.3	6.7	6.6	7.3
$10,000 and over	75	7.2	6.7	6.7	7.5
Age					
Under 33	148	7.2	6.6	7.0	7.1
33–39	195	7.5	7.3	7.4	7.5
40–48	295	7.5	7.2	7.0	7.6
49 and older	290	7.6	7.5	7.3	7.8
Considered Leaving Government					
Within last 5 years	181	7.2	6.7	6.9	6.9
Over 5 years ago	189	7.5	7.1	7.2	7.6
Never	562	7.6	7.4	7.3	7.7
Occupational Satisfaction					
Low	317	7.1	6.9	6.8	7.1
Medium	381	7.5	7.1	7.1	7.5
High	237	8.0	7.6	7.9	8.2

Reasons for Becoming a Civil Servant

When the interviewees are asked what would cause a person to become a civil service employee instead of something else, sharp differences in the responses do not emerge. What variations do occur stem pri-

TABLE 17-9. *Motives Seen Causing a Person To Become a Federal Civil Servant, Related to Federal Grade Level of General Federal Employees*

Motives	Wage Board		Postal Service	General Schedule			
	Un-skilled and Semi-skilled	Skilled and Super-visory		GS 2–4	GS 5–7	GS 8–11	GS 12 and Above
Interested in, satisfied with, enjoys, or desires that type of work	14%	7%	7%	7%	5%	9%	16%
High or good financial reward	16	11	8	23	20	16	22
Self-advancement and desire for success	7	17	4	12	18	10	6
Security, stability, protection, fringe benefits	71	77	84	75	75	74	58
Serves or wants to serve others, society, or certain parts of society	7	9	6	7	9	11	17
Presence of job opportunities	11	15	7	12	15	16	26
Chance, circumstances, or fate	6	5	1	6	4	11	17
NUMBER ANSWERING	(127)	(114)	(103)	(178)	(169)	(143)	(90)

marily from the upper-echelon positions. The distribution by federal grades classifications (Table 17-9) is representative. Employees at the GS 12 and above level offer somewhat more often as reasons: interest in the work, presence of job opportunities, desire to serve others, and chance or circumstances. They mention security factors much less frequently. Postal employees stand out for suggesting the security motive most often (84 percent) and for low frequencies on other categories. It should be stressed, however, that the differences are usually not extreme.

The findings by income and occupation (not tabled) tend to parallel this outline. Few variations occur by age and length of time in government employment, although older people and those longest in service cite the retirement aspects of security more often than do younger employees and those with shorter years of service. Employees in the Washington region differ from non-Washington respondents in pointing out somewhat more often such reasons as the service-to-others motive, self-advancement, financial reward, interest in the work, working conditions, and sheer chance. Percentage differences are most pronounced at the GS 8 and over levels, just as they were in the general description of the federal employee.

TABLE 17-10. *Ratings of Top-Level People in Federal Service and in Private Business on Their Interest in Serving the Public, Related to Four Characteristics of General Federal Employees*

Characteristics of General Federal Employees	Average Number Answering	"Interest in Serving the Public"		
		People in Top-Level Jobs in the Federal Civil Service	People in Top-Level Jobs in Private Business	Difference: "Federal" Minus "Private"
Occupation				
Unskilled and semiskilled	115	8.2	7.8	+ .4
Skilled	160	8.1	7.3	+ .8
Clerical	351	7.9	7.3	+ .6
Professional and managerial	308	8.0	6.8	+1.2
Federal Grade Level				
Wage board				
Unskilled and semiskilled	123	8.0	7.7	+ .3
Skilled and supervisory	113	7.9	7.2	+ .7
Postal service	105	8.1	7.4	+ .7
General schedule				
GS 2–4	176	7.8	7.3	+ .5
GS 5–7	169	8.1	7.4	+ .7
GS 8–11	144	8.0	6.8	+1.2
GS 12 and above	90	8.0	6.2	+1.8
Occupational Income				
Under $4,500	181	7.7	7.5	+ .2
$4,500–5,499	276	8.0	7.5	+ .5
$5,500–6,999	253	8.0	7.1	+ .9
$7,000–9,999	148	7.9	6.7	+1.2
$10,000 and over	75	8.3	6.8	+1.5
Age				
Under 33	148	7.6	6.5	+1.1
33–39	195	8.0	7.2	+ .8
40–48	295	8.0	7.3	+ .7
49 and older	290	8.1	7.6	+ .5

Our primary attention here has been on the image of the general civil service employee. As reported in Chapter 11, respondents were also asked to rate other kinds of employees, including occupants of top-level jobs in the federal civil service and of top-level jobs in private business. In the ratings assigned to these two types, one of the greatest disparities appeared for judgments about their interest in serving the public. The mean score for top-level civil servants was 8.0 vs. one of 7.2 for top-level businessmen.

The data in Table 17-10 show that there are variations in these evaluations, although ratings of top civil servants tend to be similar by occupation and grade level, and show only a slight and irregular rise according to advancing income and age. It is for the top-level businessmen that the differentiation occurs. Generally speaking, the higher the income, grade level, and occupation of the respondents, the lower is the private business employee rated on his interest in serving the public. But by age the reverse is true—the more age, the higher the rating.

We find that the comparative difference scores in the table all favor top-level civil servants, but it is apparent that the degree of comparable favorableness varies. Higher income, upper grade levels, younger age, and skilled and professional-managerial occupations are all associated with a more favorable comparative image. However, when comparisons are made on other trait ratings, the pattern is not so strong; nevertheless there are still indications that respondents in the three upper-level hierarchies consider top-echelon people in government at least equal and, in some cases, superior to comparable people in private business.

18

Federal Employees:
Further Attitudes and Values

MOST OF THE QUESTIONS INVOLVED in our discussion of federal employees in the two preceding chapters were also used in the investigation of the nonfederal working force. However, several special questions were addressed to the federal employees alone, because of the focus of this study. The responses to these questions shed further light when related to the three dimensions of our supplementary analysis—occupational satisfaction, occupational values, and the comparative image of the government as an employer.

Present Intentions To
Continue in or Leave Federal Employment

The first question in the special series was: "Now, returning to your present situation, do you plan to continue working for the federal government, or do you think you might leave it?" Respondents replying "continue" or "leave" (only a small fraction replied "don't know") were asked, as a follow-up, how sure they were of staying or leaving—very sure, fairly sure, or not sure. A distribution of combined replies from the two questions is shown in Table 18-1. Looking first at the total column of those planning to continue, it is obvious that the great bulk of the employees do plan to remain with the government. But it is also apparent that the intention, while identical for men and women, shows a moderate drop for the college graduate among the general federal employees and for the natural scientists; the drop is even more prominent for the social

TABLE 18-1. *Present Intentions of Federal Employees To Continue in or Leave the Federal Service, and the Degree of Certainty Felt by Those Planning To Continue*

Federal Groups	Number Answering	Plan To Leave	Plan To Continue				
			Not Sure	Fairly Sure	Very Sure	Total	Don't Know
General Federal Employees	948	7%	2%	16%	72%	90%	4%
By sex							
Men	661	7	1	16	72	90	4
Women	287	8	2	16	72	90	2
By educational level							
High school not completed	192	5	2	17	75	94	1
High school completed	357	6	1	15	72	89	5
Some college	180	7	0	16	72	89	4
College graduate	163	12	2	17	63	83	5
Executives	273	3	2	25	69	95	2
Natural Scientists	92	10	2	23	59	84	6
Social Scientists	90	18	1	30	48	79	3
Engineers	99	15	3	29	40	73	12

scientists and engineers. It is of more than passing interest that the executives show the highest percentage of any grouping for expecting to continue with the government. This high figure seems to be directly related to the long length of federal service on the part of most of the executives. The corollary to intentions of continuing with the government is found in the "plan to leave" column. General federal employees who are college graduates, the natural and social scientists, and the engineers exhibit the greatest intentions of departure, though the figures are all well below 20 percent.

Table 18-1 also shows the surety of intentions to continue with the government. Based on the proportions of respondents planning to continue or leave, we would hypothesize that the groupings showing the highest expectations of remaining would also be the most certain about this intention. The data indicate that this is precisely the case. General federal employees and executives are more sure of remaining than the natural and social scientists and engineers. And in the general federal work force those who have less than a college degree are more sure than the college graduates. The engineers present an extreme of potential disaffection: their percentages are the lowest for planning to continue and for being very sure of continuing, the highest for not knowing whether they will continue, and next to the highest for presently planning to leave.

Summing up, we can say that, according to the present thinking expressed by federal employees, the people least intent on staying in the government come from the ranks of those for whom governmental shortages are most likely to be critical—the highly educated and specialized personnel. Executives constitute an exception to this rule.

Supplementary Analysis

Since 90 percent of the general federal employees interviewed expect to continue with the government, it is unlikely that large-scale variations in these intentions will occur according to the standard sorts of population classifications used. This is in fact the case when the employees are considered on the basis of income, grade classification, occupation, race, and community background. However, there are two interrelated factors which are associated with such determinations—age level and length of government employment.

	N	Plan To Continue	Plan To Leave	Don't Know
Age				
Under 33	(150)	73%	16%	11%
33–39	(196)	89	9	2
40–48	(300)	92	5	3
49 and older	(296)	96	3	1
Length of Government Employment				
Under 5 years	(170)	78	16	6
5–9 years	(254)	90	6	4
10–19 years	(401)	93	5	2
20 years and over	(122)	95	3	3

Although large majorities in each age and employment-length category plan to continue, there is little doubt that such expectations increase directly with older age and longer length of service. By the same token, plans to leave and uncertainty of intentions show a progressive drop as age and length of service climb. Finally, there is a barely perceptible relationship (not shown) between level of job satisfaction and plans to continue, with the range being from 86 percent for those with the lowest level of satisfaction to 93 percent for respondents with the highest level.

TABLE 18-2. *Certainty of Continuing in Government Employment, Related to Age, Length of Employment, and Occupational Satisfaction of General Federal Employees*

Characteristics	Number Answering	Certainty of Continuing		
		Very Sure	Fairly Sure	Not Sure
Age				
Under 33	110	72%	24%	4%
33–39	174	76	21	3
40–48	276	80	19	1
49 and older	283	87	12	1
Length of Government Employment				
Under 5 years	133	81	15	4
5–9 years	224	76	22	2
10–19 years	373	81	18	1
20 years and over	117	89	10	1
Occupational Satisfaction				
Low	273	71	26	4
Medium	351	83	16	1
High	223	90	9	0

How firmly convinced are those who plan to continue? Again, few if any differences emerge by such standard hierarchies as income, occupation, or grade level. Approximately four fifths of each subgrouping in these hierarchies are very sure of continuing and up to a fifth or more are fairly sure or not sure. But age, length of employment, and degree of job satisfaction do make a difference in the certainty of planning to remain. The older the person is and the higher he rates his present job, the more positive he tends to be about continuing (Table 18-2). These people, then, not only plan to continue in greater proportions but also are much surer of continuing. Note, too, that those with five to nine years of service seem the least certain of staying, while the twenty-year veterans are the most certain.

Reasons for Continuing

After respondents indicated whether they planned to leave or continue federal employment, they were asked, "Why? What are the main things that make you feel that way?" Given the fact that a preponderant majority of general federal employees and executives, and a sizeable

TABLE 18-3. *Major Reasons Mentioned by Federal Employees for Continuing with the Government*

Federal Groups	Number Answering	Security Factors						Length of Time and Experience in Government	Lack of Other Job Opportunities
		Not Further Specified	Job Security	Financial Security	Retirement Security	Other Benefits	Total		
General Federal Employees	850	14%	20%	5%	42%	23%	70%	31%	13%
By sex									
Men	594	16	22	5	43	23	71	33	13
Women	256	10	13	2	40	26	67	28	13
By educational level									
High school not completed	181	9	28	8	40	27	71	32	13
High school completed	320	13	19	4	45	25	72	36	12
Some college	162	20	15	4	33	19	66	33	12
College graduate	134	18	13	2	44	17	62	33	18
Executives	256	8	11	2	47	10	61	44	15
Natural Scientists	77	10	10	4	34	10	52	29	9
Social Scientists	68	7	6	2	32	13	46	25	24
Engineers	72	7	13	1	38	25	60	35	13

Federal Groups	Interest, Enjoyment, Satisfaction in the Work	High or Good Financial Reward	Self-Advancement and Progress	Good Physical Environment and Working Conditions	Good Personal Relations	Leisure, Vacation, Leave
General Federal Employees	27%	19%	11%	11%	9%	18%
By sex						
Men	25	17	11	12	8	17
Women	36	25	12	9	10	19
By educational level						
High school not completed	21	18	5	11	9	20
High school completed	25	20	10	12	10	20
Some college	32	16	20	8	7	15
College graduate	38	21	17	13	9	9
Excutives	45	17	16	4	11	6
Natural Scientists	46	27	18	9	17	9
Social Scientists	59	15	21	6	13	7
Engineers	44	13	14	4	4	13

majority of the natural and social scientists and engineers plan to continue working for the government, it is enlightening to examine the explanations offered. This kind of analysis serves to portray the occupational values which people feel are maximized in government employment. The replies may be considered indicative of the relative strength
of various retention factors that government employment exerts on people presently in the federal service. However, they should not be construed as depicting the relative strengths of recruiting or inducement
factors.

It is worthwhile to note in passing the general direction of findings
applying to the 7 percent who plan to *leave* federal work. Referring to
a given factor's lack or shortage within the government, or to its presence
or greater occurrence outside government, these respondents offer three
major reasons for planning to leave: financial reward and self-advancement are each cited by approximately one third; self-determination, by
about one fifth. (Personal and domestic reasons, not related to job content, per se, are noted by about a third.) Among the executives, natural and social scientists, and engineers there are only a handful who
plan to depart from the government; therefore general statements cannot be made as to the reasons for departure. It is noteworthy, however,
that economic reward and self-advancement and progress receive high
attention here also.

Returning to the reasons for continuance in the federal service, we
find that responses are usually cast in terms of positive attributes of the
job or of federal employment; occasionally, however, the respondents
may speak of negative features of nonfederal employment. Both kinds of
replies are essentially positive reasons, either absolutely or relatively, for
planning to continue with the government.

Table 18-3 presents the main reasons volunteered by the general and
special federal populations. The most frequently given reply concerns
the various security factors afforded by federal employment. This applies to the general employees regardless of sex and educational level
and to three of the four special groupings. (For the social scientists, references to the interest and enjoyment found in the work go ahead of security.) The reply is also large in absolute terms; it is given by 70 percent
of the general employees, and variations are insignificant by sex and only
marginal by educational level. The percentage is not much higher than
the figures for executives and engineers, though it does substantially exceed those for the natural and social scientists.

Of the major components of the security factor, retirement security benefits are easily the most often cited by all groups. Ranking second (though well below) for most classes of respondents are various other protective benefits, among which the sick leave provision is most often mentioned. The only component to show a systematic difference among the groupings is job security: the general employees cite it somewhat more frequently than the four special populations, men moderately more so than women, and the less-educated slightly more often than the well-educated. "Financial" security is mentioned infrequently, and some respondents in all classes merely say "security" without specifying further.

Two other response categories shown in Table 18-3 are somewhat related to security aspects. Many respondents point out their extensive length of service or the seniority or status they have attained. The main thrust here is the respondent's feeling of having invested so much in government employment that he cannot "afford" to leave. The other category involves the belief of some respondents that they could not obtain jobs elsewhere, either because of the *lack* of qualifications (as in the case of older age) or, less often, because of the *presence* of qualifications and interests which could not be applied and satisfied elsewhere.

Over one fifth of each grouping cites the length of time and experience factor; federal executives have the highest figure at 44 percent. Men are slightly more inclined than women to mention the factor, and respondents who have not completed high school cite it less often than those with more education. Lack of other job opportunities is referred to by slightly over one tenth of the general employees. In the special groups, the social scientists outdistance the others with a proportion of almost one fourth. A third type of reply given by some 5 percent of the various groupings (not tabled) indicates wariness or fear about changing jobs and unwillingness to upset the status quo. This is a further hint of the emphasis attached to security.

We said earlier that the categories of length of service and lack of other opportunities were somewhat related to the security response as reasons for continuing with the government. This is so, in that they, like security, represent reasons which are only tangentially associated with the particular kind of work being done and the satisfactions inherent in the work itself. The main emphasis of such responses is not on the benefits flowing directly from the work itself, particularly the nonmaterial and intrinsic kinds of rewards.

Of the six other prime reasons for staying with government shown in Table 18-3, the category of interest, enjoyment, satisfaction, and pleasure found in the work is the second most frequently mentioned among all groupings except for social scientists, who rank it first. It is noted by 27 percent of the general employees, but distribution by sex and educational level is unequal: the response is more common among women than men, and is more frequent the higher the educational level. The four special populations have the highest percentages of all, with the social scientists' 59 percent representing the extreme.

Financial reward is offered as a reason by nearly one fifth of the general employees, with women having a slightly higher percentage than men. Differences by educational attainment are negligible. Although the executives, natural and social scientists, and engineers do not diverge appreciably from the general employees, it is worth noting that the natural scientists' 27 percent is the highest figure of all and the engineers' 13 percent the lowest.

The self-advancement and progress category is cited by about one eighth of the general employees. Men and women differ little on this, but respondents in the two higher strata of education have larger percentages than those in the two lower levels—especially those not completing high school. Frequencies of mention tend to run slightly higher for the four special groupings than for the general employees, and the engineers are again the least inclined to cite the factor.

From previous data (Chapter 5) we know that good physical environment and working conditions and good personal relations with people on the job are important occupational values for federal (as well as other) workers. Table 18-3 indicates that these two factors are also important reasons for staying with the government. About one tenth of the general employees cite them; sex and educational level account for little or no difference in the proportion. The four special groups mention physical environment and working conditions slightly less often than the general employees, and engineers stand out for their particularly low reference (4 percent) to good personal relations.

The final response category shown in Table 18-3 consists of the leisure, vacation, leave, recreation, and time off afforded by government employment. References to annual leave or vacations, especially in terms of how much a worker has come to be entitled to over the years, fairly well dominate this explanation. Worthy of note is that the general employees allude to this reason almost exactly as often as they do to financial reward. Of equal importance is the fact that the response is more common among general employees—nearly one fifth of them give it—than among the special populations. Correspondingly, those at the lower educational levels offer it more frequently than those of higher educational attainments.

A number of other reasons for continuing with the government were cited, but none of them frequently. Less than 5 percent of the general federal work force volunteered the following factors: prestige of the work; recognition for one's work; self-development, self-expression, and creativity; self-determination; sense of challenge; having responsibility and authority; sense of achievement; doing work that is worthwhile, useful, and constructive; and having variety in the work. The special populations also, for the most part, showed low figures for these factors; on self-determination, however, the natural scientists were a notable exception with a figure of 16 percent, and on work that is worthwhile the social scientists diverged with a figure of 15 percent. We know, from replies to open-end and scale-sort questions, that these factors are of concern and importance to many respondents as occupational values—yet they were seldom offered as justifications for staying in government work.

Does this mean that they are of concern and importance in the abstract, but not in a concrete situation? We believe the answer is "no." The data suggest that their *saliency* becomes somewhat subordinate to such values as security, interest in the work, financial reward, time off, self-advancement and progress, working conditions, and personal relations when the issue is posed in terms of the few major factors which act to keep a person in federal employment. It is possible that the infrequently-cited values are not being maximized in a respondent's present work with the government; it is also possible that within the specific framework of choosing between government and nongovernment employment their priority is seen as lower for the time being.

Further Analysis of Reasons for Continuing in Government

We have seen that references by the general federal work force to good physical environment and to good personal relations on the job as reasons for continuing in government employment were rather uniformly distributed throughout the population. Several other major reasons, however, received unequal attention. The next three tables deal with these according to five characteristics of the sample—income, grade level, age, length of employment, and job satisfaction.

As noted before, the reply most frequently given concerned the elements of security that federal employment affords the worker. A glance

TABLE 18-4. *References to Security As a Major Reason for Continuing with Government, Related to Five Characteristics of General Federal Employees*

Characteristics	Number Answering	Security Factors					Total
		Not Further Specified	Job Security	Financial Security	Retirement Security	Other Protective Benefits	
Federal Grade Level							
Wage board:							
Unskilled and semi-skilled	117	13%	22%	6%	39%	24%	77%
Skilled and supervisory	100	7	17	7	44	24	66
Postal service	95	20	29	8	37	24	71
General schedule:							
GS 2–4	156	10	15	1	44	33	69
GS 5–7	156	14	17	3	42	22	68
GS 8–11	134	18	16	3	42	16	68
GS 12 and over	79	17	11	3	57	17	68
Occupational Income							
Under $4,500	157	11	22	4	35	34	68
$4,500–5,499	254	18	23	6	38	26	72
$5,500–6,999	235	11	21	6	44	19	72
$7,000–9,999	136	17	12	2	50	18	67
$10,000 and over	66	12	7	3	53	15	58
Age							
Under 33	108	15	24	0	30	30	65
33–39	175	19	31	5	34	25	72
40–48	278	16	19	5	42	26	69
49 and older	284	9	12	5	53	17	70
Length of Government Employment							
Under 5 years	133	21	34	4	20	26	72
5–9 years	224	18	22	5	34	26	67
10–19 years	375	11	15	5	50	24	69
20 years and over	117	9	13	5	60	13	76
Occupational Satisfaction							
Low	274	15	24	7	40	26	73
Medium	350	14	17	4	44	22	68
High	225	14	19	3	41	22	68

at the "Total" column in Table 18-4 demonstrates only mild variation within each population division. These figures, however, conceal rather striking differences in the components. Notice, for example, that job security is more frequently offered as a reason among the younger and newer workers, postal employees, and respondents in the three lower income brackets. In contrast, the security stemming from retirement benefits is mentioned considerably more often by older people, by respondents with longer service and higher incomes, and by those in the upper reaches of the general schedule classification. Finally, references to other kinds of fringe benefits (primarily sick leave) come least from people of older ages, longest employment, higher incomes, and the upper grade levels. A noteworthy finding is that the response pattern by job satisfaction level varies hardly at all for any of the security components.

Another frequently-cited reason is the length of time spent as a government employee. Mentions of this are of more generous proportions among respondents of higher incomes and higher grade ranking, those 33 years and over, and those having served the longest. The most positive relationship is found on the length of service dimension. It is informative to examine the distribution by length of employment and by age.

	N	Reason for Continuing: Length of Time in Government
Age		
Under 33	(108)	16%
33–39	(175)	30
40–48	(278)	35
49 and over	(284)	35
Length of Government Employment		
Under 5 years	(133)	6
5–9 years	(224)	20
10–19 years	(375)	42
20 years and over	(117)	51

Employees under 33 years of age give this reason roughly half as often as do those of all older age brackets. At the older age levels length of employment as a retentive factor is accorded about equal prominence. The association by actual length of employment is positive and of considerable strength; the jump of 22 percent between the "5-9 years" and the "10-19 years" groupings is particularly striking.

Age and length of employment also show fairly strong relationships to the emphasis attached to the lack of jobs elsewhere, or the difficulty of finding or obtaining them as a reason for staying in government. While the variations by income level, occupation, and federal grade are slight and inconsistent, age and length of employment show a fairly definite positive relationship to such matters. Only 5 percent of those under 33 years, vs. 20 percent of those 49 and older, mention this reason, while the figure for those who have been with the government less than five years is 6 percent compared to 16 percent for those employed twenty years or more.

Frequency distributions for four other leading response categories are presented in Table 18-5. Three features stand out in reference to the interest, etc., category. First, this item is most closely associated with level of job satisfaction; the more satisfied the person is, the greater the probability of his using this global value as a reason for continuing. Second, postal employees advance this reason less frequently than any other grouping; their 18 percent is more than doubled by the 37 percent of the GS 12 and over echelon. Third, there seems to be no *consistent* association with income, age, and length of employment, though the data hint that the very highest income group considers this value somewhat more important than do people with lower incomes.

Examining the financial reward category, we find one rather ironical situation. This is given as a reason for staying by respondents with the very lowest incomes about twice as often as by people of other income levels; obviously, differential expectations and evaluations play some part here. And both those who are younger and those who have been with the government the shortest time are much more likely to mention this value. The third response—self-advancement and progress—is again emphasized far the most by the younger respondents and those with the least time in government. There also appears to be a slight tendency for the GS 8-11 and the $7,000-9,999 respondents to emphasize self-advancement and progress more than their fellows do. The greater stress placed on financial reward and self-advancement by younger people and by those of shorter government service is significant. It indicates, in respect to two important occupational values, that the government is meeting the needs and aspirations of the younger and newer employees, at least to the extent that they offer these values as grounds for staying with the government.

The fourth response category—vacation, leave, leisure, etc.—is referred to, for the most part, with decreasing frequency as income, grade level,

TABLE 18-5. *References to Interest, Financial Reward, Self-Advancement, and Leisure Time As Reasons for Continuing with Government, Related to Five Characteristics of General Federal Employees*

Characteristics	Number Answering	Interest, Satisfaction, Pleasure in the Work	High or Good Financial Reward	Self-Advancement and Progress	Leisure, Vacation, Leave
Federal Grade Level					
Wage board					
Unskilled and semiskilled	117	25%	21%	9%	21%
Skilled and supervisory	100	27	15	9	17
Postal service	95	18	18	10	18
General schedule					
GS 2–4	156	28	26	8	24
GS 5–7	156	34	15	15	21
GS 8–11	134	34	21	20	10
GS 12 and over	79	37	11	17	11
Occupational Income					
Under $4,500	157	25	31	10	26
$4,500–5,499	254	24	16	10	21
$5,500–6,999	235	30	18	13	15
$7,000–9,999	136	23	15	15	13
$10,000 and over	66	43	14	9	5
Age					
Under 33	108	32	29	25	30
33–39	175	26	31	14	18
40–48	278	21	15	13	21
49 and older	284	34	11	4	10
Length of Government Employment					
Under 5 years	133	28	28	20	19
5–9 years	224	28	26	13	21
10–19 years	375	26	13	9	18
20 years and over	117	29	11	6	10
Occupational satisfaction					
Low	274	16	19	13	17
Medium	350	30	20	11	19
High	225	40	16	10	17

age, length of service, and occupational satisfaction advance. Income level provides the most striking example of this tendency: 26 percent of those making under $4,000, compared to 5 percent of those making $10,000 and over, mention this value.

In sum, we can say that the supplementary analysis of general federal employees shows that income, grade level, age, and length of employment bear moderate to strong relations, both positive and negative, to nearly all the major reasons extended for remaining with the government. Job satisfaction is highly associated with only one of the major categories, but it is the important one of interest in and enjoyment of the work.

Past Considerations
of Leaving Federal Employment

The data depicting federal employees' present intentions of leaving or staying in the federal service have clearly demonstrated that most civil servants do expect to continue with the government. One would guess, however, that large numbers of present employees have considered leaving in the past, and then decided to stay. To gain a clearer notion as to how extensive these past considerations were, the reasons for them, and why the decision was finally against leaving, we asked a series of further questions. These are important in and of themselves, but they also offer comparative data with the analysis of present intentions and the "whys" thereof.

Interviewees were first asked: "Thinking now about the past. Was there ever a time when you thought fairly seriously of leaving the United States government, and then didn't?" The distribution of replies appears in Table 18-6. A number of things stand out. First, as expected, the number of employees who once thought of leaving far exceeds the proportion who expect to leave at present; for example, only 7 percent of the general workers presently expect to leave (see Table 18-1), contrasted with 39 percent who thought seriously of doing so in the past. Second, these past considerations are higher among the four special populations than among the general employees, much more pronounced among men than women, and increase significantly among general employees as educational level rises. In the special populations, the executives display the highest proportions (63 percent), while the natural and social scientists and the engineers trail somewhat (around 50 percent for each group). In general, the kinds of respondents who thought of leaving in the past are the ones who are the least sure of presently staying (see Table 18-1), but there are two notable exceptions to this. Whereas men and women general employees register virtually no difference on present intentions, men are more likely to have considered leaving in the

TABLE 18-6. *Responses of Federal Employees to: "Thinking now about the past. Was there ever a time when you thought fairly seriously of leaving the United States government, and then didn't?"*

Federal Groups	Number Answering	No	Yes
General Federal Employees	948	61%	39%
By sex			
Men	661	58	42
Women	287	70	30
By Educational Level			
High school not completed	192	75	25
High school completed	357	58	42
Some college	180	58	42
College graduate	163	49	51
Executives	273	37	63
Natural Scientists	92	49	51
Social Scientists	90	52	48
Engineers	99	48	52

past. And while the federal executives have the highest percentage for presently planning to stay of all four special populations, they also outrank the three other special groups in saying they thought of leaving in the past.

Further Analysis of Past Plans To Leave Government

Sharper and no less intriguing differentiations were derived from relating past thoughts of leaving to other characteristics of general federal employees. The higher the income and grade level, the longer the time of service, and the lower the job satisfaction, the more likely is the respondent to have considered separation in the past (Table 18-7). The exact converse is also true. These findings are not surprising, inasmuch as the longer an employee has been with one employer and the higher his income and grade level, the more he has probably been exposed to the pull of other jobs and been in demand. And the lower his job satisfaction, the more likely it is that he will have considered other employment that might raise his satisfaction level.

A number of factors (not tabled) appear to be unrelated to this phenomenon. They include age, geographic region, race, and party identification. Surprisingly, the only deviation which does occur according to

TABLE 18-7. *Past Thoughts of Leaving Government, Related to Four Characteristics of General Federal Employees*

Characteristics	Number Answering	Considered Leaving	
		No	Yes
Federal Grade Level			
Wage board			
Unskilled and semiskilled	128	67%	33%
Skilled and supervisory	114	59	41
Postal service	106	61	39
General schedule			
GS 2–4	180	72	28
GS 5–7	170	65	35
GS 8–11	145	46	54
GS 12 and over	90	43	57
Occupational Income			
Under $4,500	187	72	28
$4,500–5,499	279	64	36
$5,500–6,999	256	58	42
$7,000–9,999	148	49	51
$10,000 and over	76	53	47
Length of Government Employment			
Under 5 years	170	68	32
5–9 years	254	68	32
10–19 years	401	57	43
20 years and over	122	49	51
Occupational Satisfaction			
Low	319	55	45
Medium	386	63	37
High	242	67	33

age is among the oldest employees—fewer of them say they thought of leaving than do respondents in other age brackets.

Reasons for Past Thoughts of Leaving

The respondents who said that they had considered leaving federal work were asked, "What were the main things that caused you to think fairly seriously about leaving the federal government?" (In examining the allocation of response categories for this question, it should be borne in mind that the number of respondents in each of our various standard groupings is reduced, in some instances by one half or more, from the number usually found in the tables. Therefore, the data should be interpreted somewhat cautiously and conservatively.) The replies were coded according to both the "sources" and the substantive content of the reasons. (The substantive coding will be discussed later.) The "source" of a reason may be the negative aspects of the current government job, job opportunities outside government, or the interworking of both of these factors; there may also be personal and domestic sources, unrelated to work.

Table 18-8 indicates that for the general federal employees negative aspects of their own jobs, that is, various factors which made their work unsatisfying to them, constitutes the most prevalent single source. Over 50 percent of the general group respond in this fashion, with differences according to sex and education being slight. But the four special populations present a far from uniform picture. Natural scientists are somewhat more extreme than the general employees in citing this source, while the engineers come rather close to the figure of the general group. But social scientists single out negative aspects somewhat less often, and the executives much less often, than the general workers.

TABLE 18-8. *General Sources of Reasons Cited by Federal Employees in Response to: "What were the main things that caused you to think fairly seriously of leaving the federal government?"*

Federal Groups	Number Answering	Negative Aspects of the Work	Definite or General Work Opportunities Elsewhere	Negative Aspects Plus Definite or General Work Opportunities Elsewhere	Other Sources
General Federal Employees	377	57%	21%	16%	5%
By sex					
Men	291	56	24	16	3
Women	86	61	10	16	12
By educational level					
High school not completed	45	60	14	17	8
High school completed	148	62	19	15	5
Some college	76	55	25	15	5
College graduate	87	53	27	20	0
Executives	170	35	38	24	2
Natural Scientists	47	68	11	17	4
Social Scientists	43	44	42	14	0
Engineers	51	61	20	18	2

About one fifth of the general employees locate the source of their reasons in definite or general work opportunities outside the government. Although the frequencies of mention vary minimally by educational stratum, men make such a reply more than twice as often as do women. Among the four special groupings, the engineers' figure is nearly identical to that of the general employees, but only 11 percent of the natural scientists cite this source. Again, however, executives and social scientists diverge by having particularly high figures (38 and 42 percent).

The responses in the third category of Table 18-8 make it quite clear that distasteful aspects of the current job and the lure of outside employment operated simultaneously to cause some employees to consider leaving the government. The figures demonstrate that from 15 to 20 percent of each grouping (except executives, whose figure is 24 percent) cite both sources. Sources other than those related to the government or outside work world are indicated by a small proportion of both the general employees and the special populations. It is interesting to note, however, that men make such reference less often than women, and the highly educated less often than the less educated.

When the *total* percentage of respondents referring to negative aspects (columns 1 and 3) is compared to the *total* percentage noting outside opportunities (columns 2 and 3) we see that mentions of negative aspects exceed those of outside opportunities by a ratio of 7 to 4 among the general employees; by 3 to 1 among natural scientists; and by 2 to 1 among engineers. In contrast, the sources are almost evenly balanced among the executives and social scientists. These ratios do not necessarily mean that executives and social scientists actually had more outside opportunities available at the time of consideration; they do suggest, however, that unfavorable characteristics of their work and the existence of outside opportunities were of equal salience to the executives and social scientists, whereas for the other groupings the negative factors were of much greater salience than outside opportunities.

As noted earlier, the reasons offered for a past contemplation of withdrawal from federal service were also coded on the basis of their substantive content. The respondents cast their replies in terms which implied or definitely stated either that certain features about their jobs at that past time were poor or that certain characteristics were good or adequate in nongovernment employment. In either case federal employment is being viewed as *relatively* worse, in regard to specific factors, than other employment. For the most part, we may regard the reasons as occupational values which the employees feel were not, comparatively speaking, being adequately realized in their work.

Only three replies are offered by more than 10 percent of the general employees (Table 18-9). Two of these stand out from the third: financial reward, mentioned by 31 percent, and self-advancement and progress, 25 percent. Then there is a drop to the 14 percent mention of aspects of relations with supervisors, the third main reply. It seems significant that the two most frequently given answers both relate to "getting ahead" and "improving one's lot." It is the relatively poorer performance of government as an employer in these regards that most readily leads people to think of quitting the government.[1] This finding confirms an earlier one in this chapter which suggested that considerations of economic reward and self-advancement and progress were the major work-related reasons offered by employees who are *presently* planning to leave the government. In view of the occupational concern federal employees have about relationships with their supervisors (see Chapter 5), it is also important to note the finding here that the inadequate realization of this concern constitutes the third most important reason given for thinking of leaving.

A host of other reasons (not tabled) are volunteered by smaller numbers of the general employees. From 5 to 10 percent of the population mention: interest, enjoyment, satisfaction, and pleasure in the work; self-development, self-expression, and creativity; self-determination; physical environment and working conditions; variety and lack of routine; security factors; the prospect of losing one's job; and personal and domestic reasons. These minor features suggest that the reasons for thinking of leaving the government are varied and highly dispersed. Nevertheless, they also heighten the importance assigned to the major causes of financial reward, self-advancement and progress, and relations with supervisors.

In general, the federal executives, natural and social scientists, and engineers do not diverge appreciably from the general employees in the patterning of their replies (Table 18-9). While the general and special group employees do not differ appreciably from each other in mentioning financial reward, there is an inner variation by sex among the general

---

[1] Throughout this discussion it is necessary to realize that the people who offered these reasons are those who only *thought* of leaving, not those who actually did. Also, the caution given in regard to the data of Table 18-8 should be recalled for Table 18-9: the number in each group is smaller, and therefore interpretation of the data should be conservative.

TABLE 18-9. *Major Substantive Reasons Cited by Federal Employees for Past Thoughts of Leaving Federal Employment*

Federal Groups	Number Answering	Seen as Poor Inside Government or Good Outside		
		Financial Reward	Self-Advancement and Progress	Relations with Supervisors
General Federal Employees	377	31%	25%	14%
By sex				
Men	291	35	26	12
Women	86	13	22	21
By educational level				
High school not completed	45	37	8	12
High school completed	148	33	27	18
Some college	76	26	32	11
College graduate	87	30	29	11
Executives	170	39	26	15
Natural Scientists	47	38	34	11
Social Scientists	43	28	28	12
Engineers	51	33	29	12

employees. Men indicate more dissatisfaction then women with the financial reward of government work as a reason for thinking of leaving. Again, the general and special groups have about the same percentage of references to self-advancement and progress, but within the general group those of the three upper educational strata have strikingly higher figures than those of the lowest level—around 30 percent for the former vs. 8 percent for the latter. Finally, the similarity between general and special employee populations is repeated on the topic of supervisor relations. But women are more likely than men to cite this factor, and employees who have completed high school register a somewhat higher figure than respondents at other educational levels.

Subjecting the data on the general federal respondents to additional scrutiny by income, grade level, occupation, and age revealed few systematic differences about the *source* of reasons for considering departure. There is, however, some indication that the GS 8-11 bracket and the middle-income groups were tempted more than others by outside opportunities and that clerical personnel, especially the lower echelons, were less affected by such possibilities.

Somewhat stronger associations prevail according to other factors. The less time a person has been with the government the more likely he is to cite only negative aspects of the job, and the less likely to mention only outside opportunities. Those with the government from five to twenty years are slightly more likely to mention both negative aspects and outside possibilities as combined factors. Dividing the respondents according to those who thought of leaving within the past five years and those who pondered it more than five years ago shows that the former cite only negative aspects of the work more often, and opportunities on the outside a little less often.

Level of occupational satisfaction produces the strongest associations. Of those rating their occupations lowest, 67 percent mention only negative aspects of their work, compared to 51 percent of those with medium ratings, and 47 percent of those with highest ratings. The three divisions have similar percentages on "only outside opportunities," but the higher the satisfaction, the more likely is the mentioning of negative aspects *and* outside chances. In other words, those who are most dissatisfied point out negative factors of their work more often and more often single out *only* these shortcomings as reasons for past thoughts of leaving; at the same time they less frequently talk about outside opportunities.

The distribution of the major substantive reasons for considering separation from the government was also investigated further. By occupation, we found that professional and managerial employees offer self-advancement and progress as grounds for leaving somewhat more often than other groups do and (along with skilled and supervisory personnel) relations with supervisors somewhat less. The allocation of such responses by two other hierarchies is as follows:

	N	Financial Reward	Self-Advancement and Progress	Relations with Supervisors
Length of Government Employment				
Under 5 years	(51)	28%	29%	20%
5–9 years	(83)	26	22	13
10–19 years	(178)	32	25	14
20 years and over	(65)	40	24	9
Thought of Leaving Government				
Within last 5 years	(183)	27	33	19
Over 5 years ago	(192)	35	18	9

By length of employment, those with the government twenty years or longer mention financial reward somewhat more frequently but reference to supervision decreases with length of service. Finally, employees who thought of leaving within the past five years, compared to those who considered it earlier, refer a bit less often to financial reward, but moderately more often to relations with supervisors and to self-advancement and progress. Tying in with this relationship, there is a strong hint that the more sure a person presently is of staying the less likely is he to mention self-advancement (not shown).

The findings by income, grade level, age, and job satisfaction prove rather inconclusive. It appears that the lowest income level is slightly less affected by financial considerations, and that the GS 8-11 grade level bracket is more affected. The youngest age group, in comparison to others, mentions self-advancement and progress somewhat more frequently.

Reasons for Deciding To Remain in the Federal Service

After explaining why they considered leaving the government in the past, respondents were asked this question: "What were the main things that caused you to stay in the federal government?" Again, the responses were coded according to the sources of the reasons and according to the actual substance of the reasons. Five main sources are cited by respondents: real or potential improvement in their job with the government; reconsideration of their own position and work; outside opportunities falling through; re-evaluation and re-appraisal of outside opportunities; and various other sources not integral to the job situation, primarily personal and domestic factors. (It should be noted that point three—outside opportunities falling through—is both a source and an actual substantive reason.)

It is apparent from the data presented in Table 18-10 that the two major sources of reasons for staying with the government are the perceived real or potential improvements in the job and a reconsideration of the position or the work. Each of these sources, which are for the most part mutually exclusive, are referred to by one fourth to over one half of every grouping. Of most striking interest, however, is the relative attention given the two sources by different kinds of respondents. Among general employees as a whole, reconsideration of their jobs or positions is cited by moderately more people than the real or potential improvement of their jobs. Men and women vary only slightly in their responses, but by educational level there is a tendency, particularly prominent at the lowest echelon, for the less-educated to give less emphasis to the betterment of the job and more to the reconsideration of the job. Thus, among employees with less than high school completed, 26 percent mention improvement in the job vs. 60 percent who refer to reconsideration of their work; the corresponding figures for employees who are college graduates are almost identical—46 and 45 percent.

The ratio among the college graduates is a tip-off to the ratios found among the four special populations. The executives, natural and social scientists, and engineers, in contrast to the general federal workers, in no instance refer to job reconsideration more than job improvement. To generalize, the more highly educated and occupationally situated respond-

TABLE 18-10. *General Source of Reasons Cited by Federal Employees in Response to: "What were the main things that caused you to stay in the federal government?"*

Federal Groups[a]	Number Answering	Real or Potential Improvement of Job	Reconsidered Own Position and Work	Outside Opportunities Fell Through	Outside Opportunities Re-evaluated	Other Sources
General Federal Employees	376	36%	50%	11%	18%	12%
By sex						
Men	291	35	51	12	19	13
Women	85	42	50	7	10	11
By educational level						
High school not completed	45	26	60	9	13	9
High school completed	148	35	49	9	18	16
Some college	75	34	53	16	23	12
College graduate	87	46	45	12	14	10
Executives	171	44	42	9	28	8
Natural Scientists	47	53	38	0	36	8
Social Scientists	43	51	40	7	28	7
Engineers	50	44	38	8	18	6

[a] Percentages do not add to 100% in each group due to multiple replies.

ents are more likely than others to say they secured a real or potential improvement in their work situation, and are more likely to cite this source as often or more often than the source of their own reconsideration and reappraisal of their jobs.

References to outside opportunities falling through as a source of reasons for staying in the government are noted by around one tenth of all groupings except the natural scientists, none of whom mention it. Reevaluating outside opportunities enjoys somewhat greater attention; nearly one fifth of the general work force notes it, men having a moderately higher figure than women. Figures tend to run somewhat higher among the special groups (especially natural scientists), with the exception of the engineers. Finally, nonwork-related sources are referred to by 12 percent of the general employees and by slightly lower percentages of the special populations.

Turning now to the actual substantive reasons for remaining with the government, if the reply deals with occupational values, per se, the respondents typically broach their answers in one of two ways. They often cite some feature or aspect of their work world as being good or satisfactory or in the process of being improved upon. These are reasons internal to their work environment at the time. Alternatively they comment about certain aspects of outside employment as being poor, unsatisfactory, or becoming worse; these are reasons external to their work environment. In either instance, however, the *relative* advantage is with government. Consequently, whether a respondent says, "My pay went up, so I stayed" (internal) or "The jobs on the outside did not pay enough" (external), he is in both cases signifying that the relative favorableness of income in his government job was a reason for staying.

Among the reasons advanced which bear directly on occupational values, the following are mentioned by more than 5 percent of the general federal employees and, with a few exceptions, of the executives, natural and social scientists, and engineers: interest and enjoyment in the work; financial reward; self-advancement and progress; various aspects of security; long service career; work that fits one's capacities and training; and location of work. But of these, only the first four are mentioned by over 10 percent of the general and special populations. The percentage distribution for these four categories is shown in Table 18-11.

Unquestionably the most popular reason advanced for staying by general federal employees is the cluster of values that includes security, stability, protection, and fringe benefits. It is interesting, however, that while 32 percent of the general population mention these values the reply is given over twice as often by men as women, and more often as educational levels descend. Responses among the four special populations resemble those of the more highly educated general employees in the lower notice given the security factors. But even here (with the exception of natural scientists) over 20 percent of each group mention the feature. Some aspect of the security theme was also the reason most frequently offered by general employees for *present* plans to continue with the government. In other words, the factor which seems to be most important in presently retaining general federal employees is the same one that most influenced people who once thought of leaving the government to change their minds.

Among the other replies, the cluster of interest, enjoyment, satisfaction, and pleasure found in the work—that is, the relative lack of these qualities outside government—is cited by 12 percent of the general group. Even though this response is nonspecific in nature, it does refer to the intrinsic aspects of the work rather than the extrinsic. Significantly, there

TABLE 18-11. *Four "Occupational Value" Replies Given by Federal Employees as Reasons for Staying with Government After Having Considered Leaving*

Federal Groups	Number Answering	Seen As Good Inside Government or Poor Outside			
		Interest, Satisfaction, Pleasure in the Work	Financial Reward	Self-Advancement and Progress	Security, Protection, Fringe Benefits
General Federal Employees	376	12%	18%	14%	32%
By sex					
Men	291	12	17	14	36
Women	85	16	21	17	16
By educational level					
High school not completed	45	7	25	7	41
High school completed	148	11	19	11	35
Some college	75	14	16	23	30
College graduate	87	18	16	18	26
Executives	171	19	15	23	23
Natural Scientists	47	19	23	17	13
Social Scientists	43	28	21	33	23
Engineers	50	16	16	12	22

is a moderate but distinct positive association between such responses and educational level. As a retaining factor, then, the inherent interest and enjoyment of the work is of considerably more salience as educational level rises. Adding confirmation to this finding are the figures for the four special populations: their percentages resemble those for the more highly educated general employees rather than those for the less educated.

The presence of good or adequate financial reward inside the government or the absence of it outside government is noted as a reason by around one fifth of all groupings (Table 18-11). Self-advancement and progress receives attention from 14 percent of the general federal work force, with virtually no difference in the percentages for men and women. By education, respondents in the two lower strata cite the value somewhat less often than those in the two higher levels. The picture for the four special groups is irregular; the engineers have a low figure of 12 percent, compared to the social scientists' high of 33 percent.

In terms of the over-all ordering of the four major occupational value categories the replies of the general employees clearly peak around the cluster of security factors, whereas among the special groups the distribution tends to be more even. By sex, men definitely refer to security more often, while women have a more stable ordering and, in fact, give financial reward the most attention. According to education, respondents on the two lower levels concentrate mainly on security and financial reward while those on the two upper levels have a more balanced set of explanations.

Three other substantive reasons for deciding not to leave the government are advanced with moderate frequency by the respondents (Table 18-12). These are not concerned per se with the values or aspects of work. The first refers to the retention of a job that had seemed in jeopardy or to securing another federal position (either when the current job was jeopardized or for other reasons). The second notes that outside opportunities fell through or that the respondent was unable to locate a "suitable" outside job. The third deals with extraneous personal and domestic factors.

Just under one fifth of the general employees give the first reason, with men and women varying only slightly from each other. According to education, there is a modest increase in responses of this nature as educational attainments rise. The four special groupings equal or exceed the general population in citing the retention or securing of a job; the figure for the natural scientists is particularly high (36 percent). Further

TABLE 18-12. *Three "Nonoccupational Value" Replies Given by Federal Employees as Reasons for Staying with Government After Having Considered Leaving*

Federal Groups	Number Answering	Retained Job or Secured Another One	Outside Opportunities Fell Through or Unable To Locate Outside Job	Personal and Domestic Reasons
General Federal Employees	376	18%	14%	22%
By sex				
Men	291	16	16	22
Women	85	27	7	21
By educational level				
High school not completed	45	12	16	24
High school completed	148	17	14	24
Some college	75	16	17	22
College graduate	87	24	12	15
Executives	171	27	9	14
Natural Scientists	47	36	2	11
Social Scientists	43	19	7	14
Engineers	50	20	10	8

analysis (not shown) indicates that among general employees the ratio of securing another job when the present one was in jeopardy to securing another one when there was no jeopardy is about 1 to 5. Comparable ratios among the special populations are much higher, running to as high as 1 to 20. A similar pattern prevails by educational level among the general employees—the more highly educated are more likely to mention transfers when jeopardy was not a factor. The conclusion to be drawn is that when employees with higher educational and occupational attainments, as compared to other persons, decided to stay in government on the basis of securing another job, this was much more likely to be a case in which their current job was not in jeopardy.

In the references to jobs outside of government, it is interesting to note that the general employee group mentions somewhat more frequently than the special groups that the potential outside opportunities fell through or that they were unable to locate a nonfederal position. There is a tendency for men to offer this reason slightly more often than women.

Finally, that over one fifth of the general employees say that various personal and domestic factors caused them to stay in government is worth noting. A respondent's health, age, loyalties, his family's preferences and general condition, and a host of other matters are included among the reasons. Evidently such matters are of equal salience to men and women as reasons for staying, but the data hint that as educational and occupational attainments rise the reasons assume less prominence.

When we subjected the responses of the general employees to various further cross-tabulations, there were few exceedingly strong variations in the response patterns, as far as the general sources of reasons cited for remaining were concerned. But some of the associations are of more than passing interest. Among the respondents who more often noted actual or potential improvement in their jobs are professional and managerial workers, those at upper-income levels, those with higher-grade positions, older employees, and (perhaps surprisingly) the unskilled and semi-skilled among the blue-collar workers. Others include people who have been with the government from five to nine years, those who are presently fairly sure of continuing in it, those who thought of leaving over five years ago, and people with the highest degree of job satisfaction.

The obverse of this distribution tends to appear for the replies which indicate that the person decided to stay after giving further thought to his own job. That is, the groupings listed above are generally less likely to say that they re-evaluated their own positions. Conversely, those who cite improvement in their jobs least often tend to mention reconsideration, though there are some irregularities here. Of special interest are the high percentages for the postal employees, two thirds of whom cite re-evaluation. Generally speaking, then, the more successful and satisfied employees refer more frequently to real or potential betterment of their jobs as a reason for staying, whereas the less successful and less satisfied more often say they reconsidered their jobs.

No clear picture emerges for the category of outside opportunities being re-evaluated or falling through. Responses are fairly evenly distributed throughout all groupings, with re-evaluation being advanced more often than "falling through" for virtually all classifications. Sources external to the work world, primarily personal and domestic reasons, are referred to less frequently by those at the very highest income and grade levels and by those who have thought seriously of leaving within the last five years.

The pattern of the substantive reasons for deciding to remain with the government is again rather mixed, but a few suggestive findings do come forth (not tabled). Whether the replies reflect what is deemed to be good about government employment or poor about outside employment, the relative advantage is with the government. References to the interest and enjoyment of the work come most often from the professional and managerial classes, the higher income levels, and those most satisfied with their jobs; they are particularly rare from the postal employees. Financial reward is cited in fairly even proportions, but aspects of security are mentioned somewhat more frequently by nonprofessional and nonmanagerial workers, especially postal employees, by people over 33, and by those showing least occupational satisfaction. Self-advancement and progress are referred to slightly more often by people with professional and managerial jobs, those having higher incomes and grade levels, and those with medium and high levels of job satisfaction.

Reasons other than occupational values are also differentially distributed, though the variations are not large. Having retained the federal job or secured another is mentioned about equally by all occupational groups, but somewhat less frequently by the very low and the very high income groups, less often by those who had considered leaving within the last five years, and less often by those reporting low job satisfaction. The category of outside opportunities falling through or the inability to locate outside jobs comes most frequently from the skilled and clerical workers and the lowly satisfied, and least from the highest income group. The pattern for domestic and personal reasons is irregular, but respondents of the highest income and federal grade levels seem to attach less significance to such matters.

Parts of the Private Economy Federal Groups See as Better for Employment

The series of three questions treated here was designed to elicit from federal employees whether or not they perceived certain parts of the private economy as being better for employment than others and, if so, what parts they had in mind, and why.[2] The first question read: "Again suppose for the moment that a person in your line of work *did* go

[2] The questions parallel three that were asked of nonfederal employees. See Chapter 10.

TABLE 18-13. *Responses by Federal Employees to: "Again suppose for the moment that a person in your line of work did go to work outside the federal government. Are there any particular kinds of employment or businesses that would be better to be in than others, from your point of view?"*

Federal Groups	Number Answering	Yes	No	Don't Know
General Federal Employees	947	56%	26%	17%
By sex				
Men	660	57	27	16
Women	287	54	24	22
By educational level				
High school not completed	192	45	36	19
High school completed	356	54	27	19
Some college	180	62	21	17
College graduate	163	71	16	12
Executives	273	84	11	5
Natural Scientists	91	82	9	9
Social Scientists	89	83	15	2
Engineers	99	86	13	1

to work outside the federal government. Are there any particular kinds of employment or business that would be better to be in than others, from your point of view?" Replies were tabulated in the categories of "Yes," "No," and "Don't know" (Table 18-13).

Knowledge of Differentiation

We find that 56 percent of the general employees responded "Yes," indicating that they differentiate certain parts of the private economy as being better than others for someone in their line of work; 26 percent of them say "No," and only 17 percent, "Don't know." Although sex accounts for no perceptible differences, the same cannot be said for educational levels. The higher the education, the much more likely is the reply to be "Yes." Conversely, the better-educated are much less inclined to respond in the negative. Among the four special populations the percentages saying "Yes" are much higher—all of them being over 80 percent—than among the general employees. This means, of course, that the "No" and "Don't know" responses are lower than for the general employees.[3]

[3] A comparison of Table 18-13 with Table 10-1 in Chapter 10 reveals that the

Statements of Preference

All respondents who signified that certain kinds of nonfederal work would be preferable to others were then asked: "What particular kinds of employment or business would be better?" The replies presented a problem in classification. Many employees mentioned specific firms, others specified a type of business or industry; still others described a kind of activity as well as a specific employer or kind of employer they had in mind. We finally decided to classify the responses in seven general categories: five grouped under business and industry—size unspecified, large business firm, small business firm, business of one's own, and total business and industry; and two other groupings—professional firm or private professional practice, and college or university.

Table 18-14 indicates that the general employees overwhelmingly (74 percent) cite some kind of work in business or industry. Of those who give any indication of size, by far the largest proportion mentions a large business (28 percent vs. 5 for small business). A professional firm or private professional practice is the only other category receiving substantial attention (20 percent).

Men and women differ perceptibly on two response categories. Men more often than women cite some aspect of business and industry as being preferable to other nonfederal work, whereas women more often single out a professional firm or private professional practice. By education there is a strong positive relationship between level of schooling and mention of professional employment. Although the number of references to colleges and universities is small, it is congruent with expectations that such comments are greatest among college graduates. Finally, references to some aspect of business or industry fall off perceptibly among college graduates (60 percent vs. around 80 for the three other strata). It is particularly interesting that the percentages referring to a business of one's own decline from a high of 14 percent among the least-educated federal employees to a low of 3 percent among the best-educated.

The figures for the executives almost perfectly parallel those for general employees, with a similar strong emphasis on business or industry, especially on large business, followed by a moderately high figure for pro-

---

respondents in the general employed public are far less apt to differentiate between parts of the government as being better than are general federal employees to differentiate between parts of the private sector. This disparity is somewhat less true of comparisons between the special federal and nonfederal populations.

TABLE 18-14. *Kinds of Private Employment Mentioned As Being Better for Them by Federal Employees Who Had Stated That Certain Parts of the Private Economy Would Be Better To Work in Than Others, and Named One or More*[a]

| Federal Groups | Number Answering | Business and Industry | | | | | Professional Firm or Private Practice | College or University |
		Size Unspecified	Large Firm	Small Firm	One's Own Business	Total		
General Federal Employees	559	43%	28%	5%	7%	74%	20%	2%
By sex								
Men	404	43	28	5	9	78	17	2
Women	155	42	24	5	3	64	31	1
By educational level								
High school not completed	88	50	19	6	14	80	5	1
High school completed	194	42	32	5	8	81	16	0
Some college	116	47	30	6	5	77	20	2
College graduate	122	33	24	2	3	60	40	8
Executives	230	44	30	1	4	77	22	5
Natural Scientists	75	37	16	0	1	53	33	32
Social Scientists	74	27	28	3	4	60	35	31
Engineers	85	39	33	1	1	68	35	2

[a] Percentage base=number of respondents answering in each group. Percentages add to more than 100 in some groups due to multiple replies. Some general employee totals do not reach 100 because the percentages for "miscellaneous" have not been tabled.

fessional firm or private practice, and a low figure for college or university. Natural scientists depart from this pattern; slightly over one half of them choose business or industry, about one third a college or university, and one third a professional firm or private practice. Figures for the social scientists closely parallel the natural scientists. Engineers, on the other hand, show a distribution more like that for the executives and general employees, except for a greater emphasis on professional employment.

Reasons for Preferences

Those who identified the kinds of private employment they considered better for them than others were then asked: "Why do you think that?"[4] The major reasons federal employees gave in response are shown in Table 18-15. The responses are very heavily concentrated in the first two categories shown, both of which are fairly general. Most common (except among women) is the reply that the preferred sector of the private economy offers work that fits the individual's capacity or training. Also prominent is the reply dealing with the interest, enjoyment, and satisfaction that might be found in the work.

Among the general employees, women tend more than men to mention the interest and enjoyment of the work, but the opposite prevails for work that fits one's capacities. The executives stand out among the special populations for their lower citing of interest and enjoyment and (along with the engineers) for their higher mention of work that fits one's capacities.

In general, then, federal employees are not highly specific in designating the occupational values they feel would be more satisfied by one sector of the private economy than by another. However, some of the few replies that *are* more specific (shown in the table) are of considerable interest. Of these, the most frequent among the general employees is financial reward; about one fifth of this group makes this reply. It will be recalled that financial reward was frequently cited as a factor which would be better about nonfederal employment (Chapter 8). A smaller but still significant proportion (13 percent) of the general group advances occupational security as a reason. Again, this conforms with earlier data which showed that security factors were seen as being worse in nonfederal employment; the conformity lies in the relative saliency which security has for federal employees as they view the work world.

Other reasons offered by approximately one tenth of the general employees include opportunity for self-advancement and progress; opportunity for self-development, self-expression, and creativity; the high standards set by the preferred employment; and the factor of active personal relations. The figures for two other categories (not shown) are important because they indicate that few federal employees mention that segments of the economy would provide work which is (1) worthwhile and useful or (2) significant for others. It is instructive to compare the singularly low figures for the latter category—5 percent or less for all groupings—with the moderately high percentages of some groups in the

[4] To compare the data for federal employees on this question to data for nonfederal employees on a parallel question, see Tables 10-3a through 10-3d in Chapter 10.

TABLE 18-15. *Reasons for Selecting As Better for Employment a Certain Kind of Nonfederal Employment or Business Given by Federal Employees Who Had Named a Selection and Answered the Question: "Why do you think that?"*

Federal Groups[a]	Number Answering	Interest, Enjoyment, Satisfaction in the Work	Work That Fits Capacities or Training	High or Good Financial Reward	Self-Advancement and Progress
General Federal Employees	560	24%	38%	22%	9%
By sex					
Men	405	21	41	23	9
Women	155	32	26	17	6
By educational level					
High school not completed	89	20	37	24	4
High school completed	194	24	35	24	11
Some college	116	17	37	18	9
College graduate	122	26	50	15	11
Executives	230	20	52	15	10
Natural Scientists	75	37	35	15	1
Social Scientists	74	37	39	8	5
Engineers	85	37	48	13	14

Federal Groups[a]	Security, Stability, Fringe Benefits	High Standards (e.g., demand high skill; interested in progress)	Active Personal Relations (e.g., meet stimulating people; good contacts)	Self-Development, Self-Expression, and Creativity
General Federal Employees	13%	9%	8%	9%
By sex				
Men	14	9	6	8
Women	13	9	13	11
By educational level				
High school not completed	13	10	4	5
High school completed	18	8	11	8
Some college	13	9	8	11
College graduate	4	7	4	11
Executives	7	11	5	7
Natural Scientists	4	5	7	15
Social Scientists	4	11	10	11
Engineers	9	13	5	5

[a] Percentage base = number of respondents answering in each group. Percentages do not add to 100 in each group due to multiple replies.

nonfederal work force who see certain parts of the government as better for them because of the significance to others of the work (see Table 10-3d, Chapter 10).

For the most part, men and women in the general federal work force do not differ significantly on the specific reasons. Similarly, the differences by education are slight, but it is notable that the college graduates cite security factors far less often than people with less education (4 percent vs. 13 to 18 percent). The four special groups resemble the general group in the kinds of specific reasons offered. Natural and social scientists, compared with the executives and engineers, cite self-advancement and progress slightly less often, and self-development, self-expression, and creativity more often.

19

Student Populations:
Occupational Ratings and Values

THUS FAR THE STUDENT POPULATIONS have not been subjected to analysis beyond their classifications as high school students, college seniors, and graduate students. These straightforward comparisons have demonstrated that there are important distinctions among the groups, but have not shown what kinds of internal variations there are within a given student population or how such variations compare with those within another student population. In this and the following chapter, six variables are introduced which we hypothesized might reflect significant relationships with occupational ratings, occupational values, the image of the federal government as an employer, and the image of federal employees. The variables are sex, family income, grade average, college major, party identification, and inclination to start work with the federal government.

Occupational Ratings

In Chapter 4 the gross differences between high school students (juniors and seniors), college seniors, and graduate students were considered in relation to the occupational expectations and ratings of the various groups. The more advanced the present level of schooling, the higher was the expected starting point on the occupational ladder, although the groups differed little on where they expected to be five years later. High school students in general rated government employment much higher than college seniors and graduate students did. This section highlights the variations within the three levels and makes some cross-level comparisons of comparable groupings.

Occupational Expectations

First let us consider where the students think they will start out on the ten-step occupational ladder, where they expect to be five years later, and where they would be at the start if they worked for the federal government. The occupational ratings presented here reflect descriptions which the students had given of factors or values that would constitute for them the "ideal" and the "worst" occupation. The ratings are thus self-anchored. In Table 19-1 the ratings are related to sex and to family income differences.

Looking at the sex variables first, it is apparent that females, in terms of their own occupational value orientations, at all three schooling levels expect to start out at a higher level than males do. The discrepancy is greatest at the college stage. Females also expect to reach a higher level than males five years hence, with about the same distance existing between them and males as at the start; consequently, the net gain is approximately the same for both sexes at each level.

A new theme is introduced when the students estimate where they would be if they started for the government. Girls in high school and college feel they would be starting out considerably higher than do boys, while the difference between male and female graduate students, although in the same direction, is minimal. Comparing the federal rating with where they actually expect to start reveals that the females expect, on the average, slightly less disadvantage than do the males at the high school and college level, but among graduate students there is no discernible intersex difference. It should be noted that there is a slight indication that high school girls estimate on the average that they would be starting out a little higher if they began with the government instead of their "actual" prospective employer.

As reported earlier (Chapter 4), level of income is highly related to occupational ratings for the sample of the general work force. The data for the high school and college students, however, prove inconclusive in this regard. (And see footnote b in Table 19-1.) First, family income as such bears virtually no relationship to any of the scores among college seniors. In this sense we may think of college as something of a leveler of assessments which might otherwise be expected to vary according to income. For high school students the expectations of the starting point are irregular according to income. Although students coming from homes where the income is $8,500 and over expect to begin at the highest level

TABLE 19-1. *Ratings of Own Occupation at the Start, 5 Years Later, and Starting Out for the Federal Government, Related to Students' Sex and Family Income*[a]

Student Characteristics	Average Number Answering	Expect To Be at Start	Expect To Be 5 Years Later	Difference: "5 Years Later" Minus "Start"	Same Occupation at Start, but for the Federal Government	Difference: "Federal" Minus "Start"
Sex						
High school students						
Males	237	5.4	7.8	+2.4	5.3	− .1
Females	121	5.8	8.3	+2.5	6.1	+ .3
College seniors						
Males	266	6.0	8.0	+2.0	4.9	−1.1
Females	138	6.7	8.5	+1.8	6.1	− .6
Graduate students						
Males	299	6.8	8.4	+1.6	5.7	−1.1
Females	82	7.1	8.7	+1.6	5.9	−1.2
Family Income[b]						
High school students						
Under $4,000	38	5.6	8.0	+2.4	5.9	+ .3
$4,000–5,499	94	5.1	7.9	+2.8	5.3	+ .2
$5,500–8,499	103	5.5	7.8	+2.3	5.6	+ .1
$8,500 and over	95	6.0	8.1	+2.1	5.7	− .3
College seniors						
Under $5,500	93	6.2	8.1	+1.9	5.2	−1.0
$5,500–8,499	112	6.5	8.2	+1.7	5.4	−1.1
$8,500 and over	177	6.2	8.2	+2.0	5.3	− .9

[a] The mean ratings shown in this table and subsequent rating tables in the chapter are based on a ten-step scale.

[b] Family income data for graduate students lack comparability because of the high proportion of married graduate students who reported their *own* incomes. Therefore, data on family income for this group are omitted from this table and subsequent discussion.

(6.0), the next highest expectation is from the lowest ranking bracket, while the lowest figure of all four comes from the second income level. Predictions of where they will be five years from now hover around 8.0 on the ladder for students of all income levels, but in terms of the net increase this means that the students with family incomes between $4,000 to 5,499 expect to make the biggest jump. Finally, there is a slight progression of less favorable net differences for the government as income levels rise. Only with the highest level, however, does the score represent a negative score for starting out with the government.

Considering the respondents on the basis of their scholastic grade av-

TABLE 19-2. *Ratings of Own Occupation at the Start, 5 Years Later, and Starting Out for the Federal Government, Related to Students' Grade Averages and College Majors.*

Student Characteristics	Average Number Answering	Expect To Be at Start	Expect To Be 5 Years Later	Difference: "5 Years Later" Minus "Start"	Same Occupation at Start, but for the Federal Government	Difference: "Federal" Minus "Start"
Grade Average						
High school students						
A	51	6.2	8.2	+2.0	6.2	0.0
B	142	5.5	8.0	+2.5	5.6	.1
C and below	164	5.3	7.9	+2.6	5.3	0.0
College seniors						
A	90	6.6	8.2	+1.6	5.7	− .9
B	204	6.2	8.1	+1.9	5.4	− .8
C and below	106	6.2	8.1	+1.9	5.0	−1.2
Graduate students						
A	153	7.1	8.5	+1.4	5.7	−1.4
B and below	205	6.5	8.3	+1.8	5.6	− .9
College Major						
College seniors						
Engineering	38	6.2	8.0	+1.8	4.8	−1.4
Natural sciences	73	6.5	8.4	+1.9	5.5	−1.0
Social sciences	73	6.0	7.9	+1.9	5.2	− .8
Humanities	53	6.1	7.9	+1.8	5.5	− .6
Graduate students						
Engineering	63	6.8	8.3	+1.5	5.3	−1.5
Natural sciences	93	7.1	8.6	+1.5	6.0	−1.1
Social sciences	75	6.4	8.3	+1.9	5.5	− .9
Humanities	31	7.1	8.3	+1.4	5.9	−1.2

erages indicates that in general the higher the grade the higher the student expects to be at the start of his occupation (Table 19-2).[1] High school students show the greatest range in this respect, college seniors the least. At "five years later," however, the gap narrows. "A" students still have the highest scale score but only by a slight and inconclusive margin. As a result, in terms of how much gain they expect to make in their first five

[1] We approached analysis according to academic grades with considerable trepidation, since there are many sources of unreliability in the measure. The unreliabilities associated with the grading process, per se, were in our case compounded by variability in standards from one high school and college to another, and by the fact that we had to rely on students' reporting of their own grades. Despite these limitations, there emerged a strong pattern of association between the academic grades and occupational ratings and values.

years, the "B" and "C" students lead the way. As with where they expect to be at the start, the "A" students in high school and college place their starting point if it is with the government higher than the students with lower grade averages. The difference at the graduate level is minute. But comparing anticipated ratings at the start with starting with the government produces little or no difference by grade average among high school and college students. In the latter case the "C" students feel they would be dropping slightly more than do "A" and "B" students. Among graduate students, on the other hand, the "A" students see the greatest net loss.

The ratings of the college seniors and graduate students were also allocated according to those majoring in engineering, natural sciences, social sciences, and the humanities.[2] Although the variations are not sharp, it appears that majors in the natural sciences at the college level and in the natural sciences and humanities at the graduate level expect to be slightly better off at the start than do majors in other fields. Similarly, natural science majors at both levels anticipate, by a slim margin, the highest level five years later. Whereas college seniors in the four fields expect to make about the same degree of progress in their first five years, graduate students show one variation—the graduate social science majors envision a little faster climb than other majors. What stands out about the ladder scores in regard to starting with the government is the somewhat greater aversion of the engineering majors at both college and graduate levels. This appears in the absolute score for starting out with the government as well as when this figure is compared with where they actually expect to start.

The scores were also examined in two other ways: the students' political party identification and degree of inclination to begin their work careers with the government (Table 19-3). For the party identifications we find only minor variations. The figures suggest, however, that at the high school and graduate stages Democrats and Independents, as compared with Republicans, think they will be starting out slightly higher; at the college level this is reversed and the Republicans have a slightly higher score. This ordering carries over, though with even less strength, to where the respondents expect to be five years from now. Differences in expected rates of advancement are minor. Contrary to what might be anticipated, occupational ratings under conditions of starting with the government vary only slightly by party identification, both in absolute

[2] The analysis was confined to these four majors because of the presence of comparable specialties in the academic, industrial, and federal samples. Humanities majors are utilized for comparative purposes.

terms and when compared to the "actual" expected starting level. It is significant, despite the small differences involved, that among high school students the only party identifiers who, on the average, see themselves as starting a bit higher with the government are the Republicans. Graduate students show a corresponding tendency, with the Republicans seeing themselves as taking less of a drop than do Democrats and Independents.

When the students were asked outright if they had in mind beginning their work careers with the government, at the high school and graduate student levels there is, as Table 19-3 shows, little difference between those answering yes or no and the place at which they expect to start on the occupational ladder.[3] For college seniors, however, those who reply "No" predict they would start out higher than those who reply "Yes" (6.4 vs. 5.6). Estimates of ladder ratings five years hence again reveal virtually no inner divergencies among high school and graduate students, and consequently in how much net progress is anticipated in that five years. College seniors considering government employment think they will advance somewhat more rapidly, but on expectations for five years later they are still behind those not considering government work.

Turning now to the ladder placements made on the assumption that the student was starting out with the federal government as employer, it should be noted that for students who have government work in mind this placement is automatically the same as that made for where they expect to be at the start. It would seem reasonable that students considering government work would rate starting out with the government (i.e., their "expect to be at start" scores in Table 19-3) higher than students not considering it. Nevertheless, this does not hold for high school students, where scores are virtually identical for those inclined and not inclined to start with the government.[4] Perhaps of even greater interest is the fact that the students not inclined to start work with the government do not, on the average, envision that they would be starting out any lower if they began with the government rather than a nongovernment employer.

---

[3] For the exact wording of the question and the percentage distribution of the replies, see tabulation on p. 554.

[4] The scores of those having the government in mind may be deflated somewhat by lower scores of some high school boys who feel that they will be "employed" by the government in the form of military service. Interviewers were instructed to make sure that respondents were thinking only of nonmilitary federal service, but on occasion this objective was not met.

TABLE 19-3. *Ratings of Own Occupation at the Start, 5 Years Later, and Starting Out for the Federal Government, Related to Students' Party Identification and Inclination To Start Work for the Government*

Student Characteristics	Average Number Answering	Expect To Be at Start	Expect To Be 5 Years Later	Difference: "5 Years Later" Minus "Start"	Same Occupation at Start, but for the Federal Government	Difference: "Federal" Minus "Start"
Party Identification						
High school students						
Democratic	112	5.8	8.2	+2.4	5.7	− .1
Independent	80	5.8	7.9	+2.1	5.8	.0
Republican	96	5.2	7.6	+2.4	5.6	+ .4
College seniors						
Democratic	151	6.2	8.1	+1.9	5.4	− .8
Independent	139	6.2	8.2	+2.0	5.2	−1.0
Republican	90	6.6	8.3	+1.7	5.6	−1.0
Graduate students						
Democratic	120	6.9	8.5	+1.6	5.7	−1.2
Independent	138	6.9	8.5	+1.6	5.7	−1.2
Republican	101	6.5	8.2	+1.7	5.7	− .8
Inclination To Start Work for the Federal Government						
High school students						
Yes	48	5.5	8.0	+2.5	5.5	.0
No	256	5.6	8.0	+2.4	5.6	.0
College seniors						
Yes	61	5.6	7.9	+2.3	5.6	.0
No	323	6.4	8.2	+1.8	5.2	−1.2
Graduate students						
Yes	61	7.0	8.6	+1.6	7.0	.0
No	305	6.8	8.4	+1.6	5.5	−1.3

On the other hand, the college seniors and graduate students who are disposed toward government, contrasted with those who are not, give a higher absolute rating to federal employment; the differences are especially noticeable at the graduate level. The absolute scores of those not considering federal employment are not only lower than the absolute scores of the other group, but they are also over 1.0 steps lower on the ladder than the "actual" expected starting points. Thus college seniors and graduate students not having federal employment in mind would expect to be disadvantaged by starting with the government; among comparable high school students no difference is seen in government versus nongovernment starting points.

Appeal of Federal Employment

The federal government's drawing power (or lack of it) is also shown by the students' degree of agreement on the ten-point scale to the following statements: "All things considered, working for the (federal government) (a large private business) appeals to me." Of primary interest here are the absolute ratings assigned to the appeal of federal employment and the comparison of this appeal with that of private business. There are, of course, other employment possibilities, especially for college seniors and graduate students, many of whom plan to become teachers, engage in private practice, etc. But our comparison will show

TABLE 19-4. *Ratings of Occupational Appeal of the Federal Government vs. Large Private Business, Related to Students' Sex and Family Income*

Student Characteristics	Average Number Answering	"All things considered, working for a large private business appeals to me"	"All things considered, working for the federal government appeals to me"	Difference: "Government" Minus "Business"
Sex				
High school students				
Males	234	5.7	5.4	− .3
Females	120	5.5	5.9	+ .4
College seniors				
Males	266	5.3	5.0	− .3
Females	134	4.8	5.6	+ .8
Graduate students				
Males	298	5.1	5.0	− .1
Females	82	4.0	5.2	+1.2
Family Income				
High school students				
Under $4,000	36	5.4	6.1	+ .7
$4,000–5,499	94	5.5	5.6	+ .1
$5,500–8,499	102	5.5	5.7	+ .2
$8,500 and over	94	5.7	5.3	− .4
College seniors				
Under $5,500	92	4.8	5.2	+ .4
$5,500–8,499	112	4.9	5.2	+ .3
$8,500 and over	174	5.2	5.2	0.0

the relative appeal of two large-scale employers, and signify the attractiveness of government vs. one of its stiffest competitors.

Females at all three educational strata show more absolute favor toward the government than do males (Table 19-4). The margin is not large, but is consistent. When the scores are compared to the absolute scores for private business, the disparities become more marked. In each instance females register a positive pull toward government, while males are slightly negative. Males differ little by educational level on the comparison scores; with females, the higher the level the more positive is the relative attraction of government.

The amount of family income is unrelated to the absolute appeal of the government at the college level, but does seem to be at the high school stage. Both of these findings parallel the pattern noted in student estimates of where they would be on the occupational ladder if they started their work careers with the government. High school students coming from homes where the income is under $4,000 rate the appeal higher than those from homes with incomes $8,500 and over. This difference is carried over in the comparison with private business appeal: respondents with least family income have the highest net *positive* score for government; those with the highest incomes have the highest (and only) *negative* score. There is a slight tendency in the same direction among college seniors.

Considering the students by their grade averages (Table 19-5) produces only one consistent trend in the absolute appeal of government: among high school students the higher the grade average, the higher is the rating given to government appeal, but differences are slight and irregular among college seniors and graduate students. "A" high school students consider government somewhat more appealing compared to a large business, while "B" and "C" students view it as about the same as business. The "A" and "B" college seniors give government a modest edge, whereas the "C" students depart radically from this by considering government far less appealing (a difference score of −1.1). Graduate student figures are in the same direction, though the variations are small.

One of the most discriminating factors affecting the expressed attractiveness of government employment is the college major. At both college and graduate levels the social science majors clearly display the highest absolute government appeal scores (Table 19-5). Among college seniors, engineering majors register a moderately lower appeal figure than other majors. The private business scores provide something of a contrast to this ordering: seniors with engineering majors score its appeal much higher than do the other majors (6.7 vs. close to 5.0). The pattern has more gradation among graduate students, but here again the engineering majors have the highest business appeal scores.

The net differences between the appeal of government and private business scores bring out some remarkable disparities. In both populations the engineering majors—especially among college seniors—register a substantial negative score for the government. Social science majors in both groupings yield a substantial score in the government's favor (and are joined at the graduate level by the humanities majors). Over all, the ab-

TABLE 19-5. *Ratings of Occupational Appeal of the Federal Government vs. Large Private Business, Related to Students' Grade Averages and College Majors*

Student Characteristics	Average Number Answering	"All things considered, working for a large private business appeals to me"	"All things considered, working for the federal government appeals to me"	Difference: "Government" Minus "Business"
Grade Average				
High school students				
A	51	5.3	5.9	+ .6
B	142	5.7	5.6	− .1
C and below	160	5.6	5.4	− .2
College seniors				
A	88	4.7	5.0	+ .3
B	202	4.8	5.3	+ .5
C and below	106	6.0	4.9	−1.1
Graduate students				
A	154	4.6	4.9	+ .3
B and below	205	5.2	5.1	− .1
College Major				
College seniors				
Engineering	38	6.7	4.5	−2.2
Natural sciences	72	4.8	5.1	+ .3
Social sciences	73	4.7	5.8	+1.1
Humanities	52	5.0	5.2	+ .2
Graduate students				
Engineering	63	5.6	4.7	− .9
Natural sciences	92	5.3	4.9	− .4
Social sciences	75	4.5	5.5	+1.0
Humanities	31	3.9	4.9	+1.0

TABLE 19-6. *Ratings of Occupational Appeal of the Federal Government vs. Large Private Business, Related to Students' Party Identification and Inclination To Start Work for the Government*

Student Characteristics	Average Number Answering	"All things considered, working for a large private business appeals to me"	"All things considered, working for the federal government appeals to me"	Difference: "Government" Minus "Business"
Party Identification				
High school students				
Democratic	110	5.5	5.3	− .2
Independent	80	5.5	5.1	− .4
Republican	94	5.5	5.9	+ .4
College seniors				
Democratic	150	4.7	5.5	+ .8
Independent	139	5.3	5.0	− .3
Republican	88	5.3	5.0	− .3
Graduate students				
Democratic	118	4.5	5.3	+ .8
Independent	138	4.7	4.8	+ .1
Republican	101	5.4	5.1	− .3
Inclination To Start Work for the Federal Government				
High school students				
Yes	47	6.0	8.0	+2.0
No	253	5.5	5.0	− .5
College seniors				
Yes	59	5.0	7.9	+2.9
No	322	5.0	4.6	− .4
Graduate students				
Yes	61	4.8	7.3	+2.5
No	304	4.9	4.5	− .4

solute and comparative appeal of government scores for natural science and humanities majors in the colleges fall between the engineering and social science extremes. This pattern is less distinct among graduate students.

The appeal scores according to the political party identification of the students are marked by inconsistency between the populations (Table 19-6). Among college seniors and graduate students the Democratic identifiers agree somewhat more to the statement about government's appeal; among high school students, it is the Republicans who do. In none of the cases are the differences large. This inconsistency persists in

the comparative scores: Democratic identifiers see government as relatively better at the two upper educational levels; the Republicans do so
at the high school level. (The "aberration" of the high school Republicans
was presaged somewhat by their more favorable to government occupational ladder scores; see Table 19-3.) Distinctions between Democrats
vs. Republicans and Independents are more marked among college and
graduate students, with the range in both cases being from + 0.8 for the
Democrats to − 0.3 for the Republicans (joined by the college senior Independents).

Finally, we analyzed the mean scores based on whether the person
has in mind starting out with the government (Table 19-6). The hypothesis was that those so inclined would evidence much greater pull toward
the government. This is emphatically the case. For each student population, those considering government work rate its appeal about 3.0 steps
higher on the scale than do those not considering it. Similarly, the comparative scores show that pro-government students give the government
an advantage of at least 2.0, while those not thus oriented have a negative difference of around 0.5. The contrast is most pronounced among the
college seniors. Results contrary to these would be surprising. Nevertheless, the findings indicate internal validity and consistency of the measuring instruments and demonstrate as well that considerations of working with the government are anchored in the basic appeal of such employment, especially vis-à-vis the appeal of private business.

We sought in additional ways to obtain an approximation of the appeal of federal employment. One question (referred to in connection
with Table 19-3 above) asked of students was: "Returning now to when
you start out, did you have in mind starting out working for the federal
government—that is, the United States government?" The replies were as
follows:

	N	Yes	No	Nothing Particular in Mind
High School Students	(359)	19%	71%	10%
Males	(238)	21	69	10
Females	(121)	16	75	9
College Seniors	(404)	16	80	4
Males	(266)	14	82	4
Females	(138)	21	75	4
Graduate Students	(383)	17	80	3
Males	(300)	16	81	3
Females	(83)	18	77	5

For the totals at each stage there is only slight variation, with just under 20 percent in each population saying that they are considering the government as the first employer. If these percentages seem large—and certainly the government does not need, nor is it likely to receive, such a high number of novitiates—it should be noted that the question does not suggest that the student must be *planning* to enter federal employment in order to reply affirmatively; it merely seeks out those who are considering such employment. Thus, we may think of a "yes" reply as indicating that government has not been excluded as a potential first employer. Sex differences affect the replies very little; a few more high school boys, a few more college women, and a shade more graduate women respond "yes." The inflation of the male percentage at the high school level is possibly due to the boys' thoughts about military service.

We also tried to determine less manifest feelings about working for the government. Those students who indicated they were *not* thinking of the government as a starting place were asked: "Suppose your first occupation was with the U.S. government. Would this be better or worse from your point of view?" Here are the answers:

	N	Better	Worse	No Difference
High School Students	(289)	38%	29%	32%
Males	(187)	33	36	29
Females	(102)	46	18	36
College Seniors	(337)	12	55	33
Males	(229)	11	62	27
Females	(108)	13	41	46
Graduate Students	(317)	9	61	30
Males	(249)	9	62	28
Females	(68)	9	56	35

The responses reveal that the high school group diverges widely from the other two groups. Nearly two fifths of the high schoolers think government would be better, vs. around one tenth of the other two populations. Since about one third of each group thinks it would make no difference, the proportions saying "worse" also show a dramatic cleavage. Over half the college seniors and graduate students reply "worse," compared with slightly less than one third of the high school students. Viewed another way, 70 percent of the high school students, 45 percent of the college seniors, and 39 percent of the graduate students feel that starting with the government would at least not be worse than where they plan to start.

Males and females among graduate students vary minimally on this, but there are some striking differences in the high school and college populations. A larger proportion of high school girls think a start in government employment would be better or offer no difference, whereas a smaller proportion of them think it would be worse. At the college level a much greater proportion of the males consider that government would be worse, while more of the females foresee no difference.

Occupational Values

The "Ideal" Occupation

Although they are not yet part of the full-time work force, students have rather definite notions about what they desire in an occupation. These ideas are not invariably the same for the three populations. Some features of a job are of approximately equal salience to them, but others differ with each educational step. It also seems reasonable to expect variations within levels; we would not expect all high school students, for example, to show the same concern about various clusters of occupational values.

Such suppositions are borne out when we examine, according to respondents' sex, descriptions of what would make an occupation ideal (Table 19-7). In each student population the males evince more concern about financial reward, stability and security, self-advancement and progress, self-determination, and (except for high school students, where there is no difference) having responsibility for decisions. Females give more thought to doing interesting and satisfying work (as teachers), having good passive and active relations with people at work, and doing work that is worthwhile. A few values are peculiar to each student population. Among college seniors, for example, coeds refer to physical environment and working conditions more often, as well as variety and the absence of routine. But over all, here, as in other places where the sex variable is introduced, comparisons between the student populations and the adult working force are instructive and, especially at the high school level, remarkable for their convergencies.

Descriptions of ideal occupation factors vary also by grade averages (Table 19-8). (In summarizing these relationships, we exercise some

TABLE 19-7. *Attributes of the "Ideal" Occupation, Related to Students' Sex*

Attributes of the "Ideal" Occupation	High School Students		College Seniors		Graduate Students	
	Males	Females	Males	Females	Males	Females
Interest, enjoyment, satisfaction						
Not further specified	29%	17%	26%	27%	23%	13%
In a specific field	53	55	38	28	30	28
Through teaching	8	19	19	24	26	36
Through research	4	3	7	10	22	22
High or good financial reward	47	32	42	37	38	25
Security, stability, protection, fringe benefits	14	7	15	10	8	4
Good physical environment and working conditions	41	37	23	35	20	27
Good *passive* relations with people at work	14	15	17	25	14	16
Good *active* relations with people at work	26	48	35	50	31	47
Self-advancement and progress	15	9	20	9	11	5
Self-determination	17	8	32	22	43	34
Responsibility for making decisions	3	3	20	9	10	7
Variety, absence of routine, monotony	13	11	14	25	16	10
Do work that is worthwhile, useful, constructive	22	34	37	47	37	39
NUMBER ANSWERING	(238)	(121)	(266)	(138)	(300)	(83)

license in including a few minor or statistically insignificant variations found among a given population so that the general sweep of the findings may be pictured.) The "A" students in all groups express more concern about enjoyment and satisfaction in their work (through teaching and through research), work that fits one's capacities, self-determination on the job, opportunities for self-development, self-expression, and creativity, *active* relations with people at work, and work that is worthwhile and constructive. They are less concerned than students with lower grades about the physical environment and working conditions, having good *passive* relations at work, and (with the exception of graduate students) high financial rewards. At the college level, "A" students also mention self-advancement and progress less frequently. Regardless of grade average, approximately equal emphasis is placed on security and related features.

All the differences referred to are not linear, that is, they do not vary directly with grade average. There tends to be more distance between "A" and "B" students in high schools and colleges than between "B" and "C" students. And there is less difference among graduate students than among the other two groups. The weight of the data, however, lies in the direction of moderate to strong associations by grade average. Summing up, the cumulative findings indicate that the higher the grade av-

TABLE 19-8. *Attributes of the "Ideal" Occupation, Related to Students' Grade Averages*

Attributes of the "Ideal" Occupation	High School Students			College Seniors			Graduate Students	
	A	B	C and Below	A	B	C and Below	A	B and Below
Interest, enjoyment, satisfaction								
Not further specified	31%	25%	23%	22%	27%	31%	21%	21%
In a specific field	39	49	63	36	33	35	34	27
Through teaching	20	18	4	27	22	14	34	22
Through research	6	4	3	14	7	6	23	19
High or good financial reward	31	43	44	33	40	45	36	35
Security, stability, protection,								
fringe benefits	6	13	12	12	14	11	7	8
Good physical environment and								
working conditions	24	40	45	16	32	28	20	23
Do work that fits one's capacities								
and/or training	24	16	10	20	16	18	16	13
Self-advancement and progress	12	13	13	7	18	21	11	9
Good *passive* relations with								
people at work	8	15	16	18	21	20	12	16
Good *active* relations with people								
at work	41	33	31	47	39	38	35	34
Self-determination	20	15	12	32	28	26	46	36
Self-development, self-expression,								
and creativity	18	15	12	37	32	25	34	32
Do work that is worthwhile, use-								
ful, constructive	37	28	21	50	37	38	42	34
NUMBER ANSWERING	(51)	(143)	(164)	(90)	(204)	(106)	(154)	(206)

erage the more likely is the concern with the ego-rewarding, nontangible values of an occupation and the less likely the saliency of the more tangible, physical, and passive features.

Although the number of cases involved is not large, there are strong suggestions that notions of the best kind of occupation assume disparate forms according to college major (not tabled). For instance, among college seniors the engineering majors are less likely to cite enjoyment and pleasure in a job (through teaching), good active relations with people, and work that is worthwhile. Humanities majors are inclined to mention worthwhile work, a sense of achievement, and (via teaching) interest and satisfaction.

Among graduate students, the engineers show least concern about wanting to teach, but are among the foremost in desiring research. The humanities majors cite financial reward less frequently and teaching more frequently, while social science majors are highest on positive *active* relations with people at work and work that is worthwhile.

Values and Features of Importance

Fairly regular relationships are found between various factors within each student population and the kinds of occupational values they cite in describing the ideal occupation. When the reactions to the standardized statements dealing with occupational values and orientations are studied, additional insights are provided into these relationships (Table 19-9).

In each population males show higher agreement with items noting the importance of money if one is to be really successful; having a chance to get to the top; doing a better job than the next person; getting recognition; and having more opportunity than security. Females agree more than males that the main satisfaction of work lies in helping others and that work helps one forget personal problems, and is a way of serving God. From these findings it seems that males attach more importance than females to "succeeding" in an occupation, and that females emphasize altruistic and personal goals somewhat more than do males.

Although these differences persist for all three groups, they are more pronounced at some levels than others. Illustratively, work is credited with helping a person forget problems to only a slightly greater extent by high school girls, moderately more so by college girls, and extremely

TABLE 19-9. *Ratings of "Occupational Value" Statements, Related to Students' Sex*

"Occupational Value" Statements	High School Students		College Seniors		Graduate Students	
	Males	Females	Males	Females	Males	Females
"To be really successful in life, you have to care about making money"	4.7	3.7	4.2	3.1	3.6	3.3
"It's important to do a better job than the next person"	7.0	5.1	6.5	5.2	6.1	5.3
"To me, it's important in an occupation to have the chance to get to the top"	8.2	7.2	8.0	7.2	7.5	6.6
"Getting recognition for my own work is important to me"	7.3	6.3	7.8	7.4	7.7	7.5
"It is more important for a job to offer *opportunity* than *security*"	5.7	5.2	7.4	6.7	7.8	7.0
"The main satisfaction a person can get out of work is helping other people"	7.8	8.5	7.5	8.1	7.1	8.1
"Work helps you forget your personal problems"	6.1	6.2	5.8	6.6	5.9	7.2
"Work is a way of being of service to God"	7.8	8.2	6.5	7.5	6.3	6.6
AVERAGE NUMBER ANSWERING	(235)	(119)	(265)	(135)	(298)	(82)

more so by women in graduate school. On the other hand, high school males and females are further apart on believing that getting recognition is important than are the college seniors, who are slightly further apart than graduate students. It may be that self-selection and the education process bring the sexes closer together on some values and draw them further apart on others. In general, these findings strongly resemble the clustering of responses derived from descriptions of the ideal occupation (see Table 19-8).

Grade averages are also associated with the agreement scores given certain values (Table 19-10). As grade averages climb within each population, there is less agreement on items that represent a more extrinsic, materialistic orientation to work: that work is only a way of making a living; that one likes the kind of work one can forget about at the end of the day; and that to be really successful one must care about making money.

TABLE 19-10. *Ratings of "Occupational Value" Statements, Related to Students' Grade Averages*

"Occupational Value" Statements	High School Students			College Seniors			Graduate Students	
	A	B	C and Below	A	B	C and Below	A	B and Below
"To me, work is nothing more than a way of making a living"	1.8	3.1	2.8	1.8	2.1	2.4	1.9	2.2
"I like the kind of work you can forget about after the work day is over"	3.6	5.0	5.3	3.4	3.9	4.1	3.3	3.8
"To be really successful in life, you have to care about making money"	3.9	4.1	4.7	3.4	3.5	4.7	3.2	3.9
"After you are making enough money to get along, then making more money in an occupation isn't very important"	5.3	5.4	4.6	6.5	6.1	4.9	6.7	6.3
"Work is most satisfying when there are hard problems to solve"	8.0	7.1	6.5	8.3	7.9	7.6	8.3	8.1
"It is more important for a job to offer *opportunity* than *security*"	6.5	5.6	5.1	7.4	6.9	7.4	8.0	7.4
"To me, almost the only thing that matters about a job is the chance to do work that is worthwhile to society"	7.2	6.5	6.2	6.9	7.1	6.3	6.6	6.8
"The main satisfaction a person can get out of work is helping other people"	8.7	8.2	7.8	7.6	7.9	7.3	7.3	7.4
AVERAGE NUMBER ANSWERING	(51)	(142)	(161)	(89)	(203)	(105)	(153)	(205)

On the other hand, higher grades are positively associated with a cluster of values more oriented toward the ego-rewarding intrinsic values. In general (with occasional irregularities), the higher the grade average, the greater the affirmation that after a given minimum of money is achieved, making more is not very important; work is most satisfying when there are hard problems to solve; opportunity is more important than security; doing work that is worthwhile to society is important; and the main satisfaction in work is helping other people.

The major exceptions to the grade average-agreement score relationship occur in the college senior population. "B" students here are slightly higher than the "A" students on work that is worthwhile and work that helps others, and slightly lower than both "A" *and* "C" students on putting opportunity ahead of security. It is also apparent that with each rise in the educational hierarchy the divergencies by grade averages narrow —that is, students with different grade averages differ more on items at the high school level than at the college level, and more there than at at the graduate stage. To some extent this is a reflection of the increasing homogeneity of composition, exposure, and experiences accompanying higher educational pursuits.

We noted above that college majors might have an impact on students' occupational values and perspectives. This possibility is further suggested by the responses to several of the value statements shown in Table 19-11. Among college seniors, the engineering and humanities majors represent the extremes on several of the items. Engineering majors agree more and humanities majors less on the need to care about money to be really successful; having a chance to get to the top; not wanting others to pass you up; doing a better job than the next person; having opportunity, rather than security; and directing the work of others. Conversely, the humanities majors put more stress, and engineering students less, on doing work that is worthwhile to society and helps other people, and on seeing work as a way of serving God. The natural and social science majors tend to fall between these two polarities, though not invariably. In any case, the engineering and humanities majors more consistently highlight the differences in occupational perspectives shown by the four classifications. These perspectives run from the more advancement-oriented, high-achievement syndrome of the engineering majors to the more altruistic emphasis of the humanities majors.

A similar though less distinct pattern emerges from the responses of the graduate students. There are indications that the graduate humanities majors attach more importance, and engineering students less, to the altruistic-religious aspects of work, but the sharp cleavages marking the college seniors are not present here. As with grade averages, so with college majors: divergencies within the educational groupings diminish as the level ascends.

TABLE 19-11. *Ratings of "Occupational Value" Statements, Related to College Majors Among Students*

"Occupational Value" Statements	College Seniors				Graduate Students			
	Engineering	Natural Sciences	Social Sciences	Humanities	Engineering	Natural Sciences	Social Sciences	Humanities
"To be really successful in life, you have to care about making money"	4.2	3.9	3.6	2.9	3.6	3.5	3.2	3.0
"To me, it's important in an occupation to have the chance to get to the top"	8.6	7.6	7.8	6.8	7.3	7.2	7.4	7.4
"It would be hard to live with the feeling that others are passing you up in your occupation"	7.2	6.3	6.8	6.4	6.3	6.4	6.4	5.1
"It's important to do a better job than the next person"	6.5	6.2	6.0	5.3	5.7	5.9	5.9	5.1
"It is more important for a job to offer *opportunity* than *security*"	8.3	7.0	7.2	7.1	7.9	7.5	7.6	7.5
"It is satisfying to direct the work of others"	8.2	7.2	7.4	7.0	7.7	6.7	7.0	6.8
"To me, almost the only thing that matters about a job is the chance to do work that is worthwhile to society"	6.5	6.9	6.9	7.2	5.9	6.6	7.0	6.3
"The main satisfaction a person can get out of work is helping other people"	6.9	7.9	7.1	8.3	6.6	6.9	7.7	7.7
"Work is a way of being of service to God"	6.2	6.9	6.0	7.3	6.1	6.0	5.1	7.5
AVERAGE NUMBER ANSWERING	(38)	(72)	(73)	(52)	(63)	(92)	(75)	(31)

Reasons for Occupational Choice

Further insights into students' structuring of occupational values were gained when interviewees were asked what occupation they hoped to follow after leaving school, and then queried as to what caused them to favor that work instead of some other. The fourteen major response cate-

TABLE 19-12. *Reasons Given by Students for Favoring the Occupation They Plan To Enter*

Reasons	High School Students	College Seniors	Graduate Students
Interest, enjoyment, satisfaction			
In specific field	51%	31%	32%
Through teaching	7	14	15
Through research	0	7	9
Total	56	47	49
High or good financial reward	14	11	8
Security, stability, protection, fringe benefits	5	4	2
Good physical environment and working conditions	8	6	6
Leisure, vacation, recreation, time off	2	6	7
Work that fits one's capacities and/or training	25	30	31
Self-advancement and progress	16	11	8
Good active personal relations with people at work	21	32	21
Self-development, self-expression, and creativity	5	19	24
Self-determination	4	7	12
Sense of challenge	4	16	12
Sense of achievement or accomplishment	5	6	13
Variety in the work	5	7	8
Do work that is worthwhile, useful, constructive	18	31	29
NUMBER ANSWERING	(343)	(395)	(374)

gories shown in Table 19-12 may be considered the prime occupational values that students see as being maximized in their preferred occupations.

On several of the values, differences among the populations are negligible. These include security or some aspect thereof, good physical environment and working conditions, leisure time provisions, the presence of variety in the work, and work that fits one's capacities. None of these categories, except the last, was mentioned frequently by any of the populations. Other reasons, volunteered more often by at least one of the populations, show more variation. The interest, enjoyment, etc., derived from the work easily exceeds all other responses. While the total proportions of students citing this category vary only slightly from one level to the next, figures for the specific components do diverge. Thus, college seniors and graduate students prove much more likely than high school students to mention teaching and research as avenues for enhancing this interest and enjoyment. But high school students cite other specific fields much oftener.

On the two related categories of financial reward and self-advancement and progress there is a slight but consistent inverse relationship between school level and frequency of mention. High school students cite these more often than college seniors, and college seniors more often than graduate students. On other values we find the college seniors and graduate students grouping together in their differences from the high school students. They are more prone than the high schoolers to refer to the advantage of an occupation that offers self-development, self-expression, and creativity; self-determination; a sense of challenge; and an opportunity for worthwhile work. The college seniors, however, separate themselves from the other two groups by showing moderately higher regard for good *active* personal relations.

In sum, the order of the findings from this question differs little in principle from that obtained through students' descriptions of the ideal occupation or their reactions to various key statements about the work world. With each elevation in education, more emphasis tends to be given to the less tangible, more ego-rewarding, and more socially purposeful values. The demarcation between the high school level and the two upper levels seems especially significant in explaining why a particular occupation has been chosen.

20

Student Populations: Images of Federal Employment and Employees

FURTHER ANALYSES OF the three student populations were also pursued in relation to their perceptions of the federal government as a place of work and to their perceptions of federal employees. For the image of federal employment, we will here direct attention toward the degree of routine, security, and mobility thought to exist in government work, and toward the advantages and disadvantages seen in government vs. nongovernment employment. For the image of federal employees, the main focus will be on the over-all picture of the civil service employee, but some attention will also be given to the ratings of employees on character traits, and to attributed reasons for becoming civil servants.

Image of the Government As an Employer

We noted in Part Two that high school students are more disposed than college seniors and graduate students to view the government favorably as an employer (see Chapters 8 and 9). But, just as various segments of the general work force differ in their image of the government as an employer, so too we may expect the individual student populations to show internal variations.

Routineness, Security, and Mobility

Students were asked to react to preformulated statements about government employment and private business employment in reference to the presence of routine in the work, the degree of security, and the opportunities for getting ahead, reaching a top-level position, and achieving real success. By grade averages and sex the differences are not sizable or invariant, although females at each level tend to take a slightly more positive view of government employment than males, especially in comparison with private business. Similarly, there is an occasional hint that "A" students in high school are a bit more positive in their evaluation of government and that "C" college seniors are a bit more negative. But again, these findings are more suggestive than definitive.

A look at the students from other vantage points, however, suggests that their images are not undifferentiated. By family income level, the lower-income high school students are less likely to see government work as routine and monotonous and more inclined to agree that it offers a high degree of security, whereas college seniors show no appreciable difference on these features. With the mobility statements concerning advancement and success possibilities, however, the relationships become more regular and apply to both high school and college populations, especially the former (Table 20-1). The higher the family income, the lower is the agreement that government employment offers a chance to get ahead, of ending up in a top-level job, and of being really successful.

The difference scores on government employment vs. a large private business indicate the same trend. High school students from lower-income families tend, in fact, to give "plus" scores to government when comparisons are made, and, while government fares less well in the college population, it comes off best among seniors who also are from low-income families. Consequently, we find that, in both an absolute and comparative sense, higher family incomes accompany lower ratings for the government on these advancement-success features.

The four college majors also illuminate the image of government as employer (Table 20-2). Although the major makes only a slight difference in the degree to which government is seen as offering high security and as being mainly routine and monotonous, the variations are stronger on the advancement and success possibility items, particularly when government is compared to private business in this regard. The views of the groups are fairly similar on the chances of ending up in a top-level job and of being really successful in government employment, although the social science majors tend slightly to perceive government more favorably than the other majors.

Perceptions of the mobility opportunities offered by a large private business, however, vary significantly according to college major. Both in college and in graduate school, engineering majors are more positive in their private business ratings than are other majors; as a result their comparative scores show the largest net disadvantage for government. Majors in the social sciences at the graduate level tend to have the best net scores for the government, so much so that on the comparison of

TABLE 20-1. *Ratings of Evaluative Statements About Federal and Private Employment, Related to High School and College Students' Family Income*[a]

Statements	High School Students				College Seniors		
	Under $4,000	$4,000-5,499	$5,500-8,499	$8,500 & Over	Under $5,500	$5,500-8,499	$8,500 & Over
"A person who works for a large private business generally has a good chance to get ahead"	6.6	6.5	6.4	6.5	5.9	6.2	6.3
"A person who works for the federal government generally has a good chance to get ahead"	7.4	6.9	6.6	6.1	5.9	5.9	5.6
Difference: "Government" Minus "Business"	+.8	+.4	+.2	−.4	0.0	−.3	−.7
"A young man of ability who starts work in a large private business corporation has a good chance of ending up in one of the top-level jobs"	7.0	7.0	7.1	6.9	6.2	6.6	6.5
"A young man of ability who starts work in the federal civil service has a good chance of ending up in one of the top-level jobs"	7.3	6.6	6.1	5.9	6.0	6.1	5.8
Difference: "Government" Minus "Business"	+.3	−.4	−1.0	−1.0	−.2	−.5	−.7
"For a young man of ability, his best chance for being *really successful* lies in working for a large private business corporation"	4.5	4.9	4.9	4.7	4.8	4.8	5.2
"For a young man of ability, his best chance for being *really successful* lies in working for the federal government"	5.1	5.0	4.2	3.7	3.7	3.7	3.5
Difference: "Government" Minus "Business"	+.6	+.1	−.7	−1.0	−1.1	−1.1	−1.7
AVERAGE NUMBER ANSWERING	(37)	(94)	(101)	(94)	(92)	(112)	(174)

[a] The mean ratings shown in this table and subsequent rating tables in the chapter are based on a ten-step scale.

TABLE 20-2. *Ratings of Evaluative Statements about Federal and Private Employment, Related to Students' College Majors*

	College Seniors				Graduate Students			
Statements	Engineering	Natural Sciences	Social Sciences	Humanities	Engineering	Natural Sciences	Social Sciences	Humanities
"A young man of ability who starts work in a large private business corporation has a good chance of ending up in one of the top-level jobs"	7.2	6.4	5.8	6.5	6.8	6.6	5.8	6.0
"A young man of ability who starts work in the federal civil service has a good chance of ending up up in one of the top-level jobs"	5.8	5.7	5.7	5.7	5.6	5.9	6.0	5.3
Difference: "Government" Minus "Business"	−1.4	−.7	−.7	−.1	−.8	−.7	+.2	−.7
"For a young man of ability, his best chance for being *really successful* lies in working for a large private business corporation"	6.3	4.3	4.8	5.2	5.6	4.9	4.5	3.9
"For a young man of ability, his best chance for being *really successful* lies in working for the federal government"	3.1	3.4	3.7	3.4	3.3	3.2	3.9	3.3
Difference: "Government" Minus "Business"	−3.2	−.9	−1.1	−1.8	−2.3	−1.7	−.6	−.6
AVERAGE NUMBER ANSWERING	(38)	(73)	(72)	(53)	(64)	(92)	(75)	(31)

chances offered by government and private business for ending up in a top-level job they give the government a small net plus score. College seniors who are social science majors are also among the more positively inclined.

Presumably those students who are thinking of working for the government will have a more favorable image than those who are not. The data in Table 20-3 bear this out. In each population, those who are considering the federal civil service are less inclined to agree that a government job is routine and monotonous and more disposed to view it as offering high security. These students also agree more than others that the federal service offers a good chance to get ahead, an opportunity to end up in a top-level job, and a chance for being really successful. On these three items the difference in ratings is substantial and approximately the same within each student population, with most of the disparities being at least 1.0 or more on the agree-disagree scale.

In judging the government on the prevalence of routine and monotony and on offering security, however, college seniors and graduate students stand apart from high schoolers. Among the latter, those who are considering federal work, compared to those who are not, rate government only slightly, if at all, lower on the routine and monotony item,

TABLE 20-3. *Ratings of Evaluative Statements About Government Employment, Related to Students' Inclination To Start Work for the Government*[a]

Statements	High School Students		College Seniors		Graduate Students	
	Yes	No	Yes	No	Yes	No
"Most jobs in the federal government are routine and monotonous"	4.2	4.3	4.2	5.2	4.3	5.5
"Employment with the federal government offers a high degree of security"	8.7	7.2	7.8	7.6	8.1	7.8
"A person who works for the federal government generally has a good chance to get ahead"	8.0	6.4	6.8	5.4	6.4	5.3
"A young man of ability who starts work in the federal civil service has a good chance of ending up in one of the top-level jobs"	7.1	6.2	6.7	5.7	6.5	5.7
"For a young man of ability, his best chance for being *really successful* lies in working for the federal government"	5.3	4.2	4.7	3.4	4.0	3.3
AVERAGE NUMBER ANSWERING	(46)	(252)	(60)	(320)	(61)	(304)

[a] Students were asked: "Returning now to when you start out, did you have in mind starting out working for the federal government—that is, the United States government?"

whereas they give government a much higher score (8.7 vs. 7.2) on security. College seniors and graduate students, on the other hand, vary only slightly on the security proposition, but show at least one scale point difference on routine and monotony.

These contrasting figures, when combined with our previous findings, suggest that the security image is more pervasive among college seniors and graduate students than among high schoolers. The figures also indicate that college seniors and graduate students considering government employment, compared to like-minded high school students, have a more favorable impression of government work itself. Over all, the linkage between a positive image of government as an employer as measured by these five features and the disposition to enter government service is widespread within each school population.

By political party identification (not tabled) students do not vary as much as might be expected. Democrats, Republicans, and Independents at each level have nearly the same scores concerning monotony and routine and security in government employment. The advancement and success possibilities in government tend to be most favorably viewed by Republicans among the high school and graduate students—but least favorably by Republicans among college seniors. A partial explanation for this discrepancy is that GOP partisans at the high school and graduate stages are also more bullish about advancement and success in working for a large business or in being self-employed. It is only the Republican college seniors that complement their comparatively less favorable ratings of government with comparatively higher ratings for business and self-employment. Indeed, only among college seniors is there any consistent inclination for Republican identification to be associated with a more negative view of government employment (at least in terms of advancement and success opportunities).

Advantages and Disadvantages of Federal Employment

To discover what students thought would be better and what worse about working for the government, they were asked to imagine that their first job was with the government. In Chapter 8, college seniors and graduate students were shown to be more adept at singling out "worse" features, whereas high school students excelled in citing "better" features. As we apply further analyses to these answers, it must be kept in mind

TABLE 20-4. *Positive and Negative Attributes Seen in Federal Employ-ment, Related to Students' Sex*

Postive and Negative Attributes	High School Students		College Seniors		Graduate Students	
	Males	Females	Males	Females	Males	Females
Better in Federal Employment						
High or good financial reward	31%	34%	16%	28%	14%	30%
Security, stability, protection, fringe benefits	50	35	51	28	40	31
Interest, enjoyment, satisfaction	9	7	12	22	13	20
Travel	4	10	7	22	11	15
Nothing would be better	4	9	12	8	17	16
Worse in Federal Employment						
Poor or inadequate financial reward	23%	13%	32%	14%	28%	13%
Lack of self-advancement and progress	17	8	21	10	15	5
Lack of self-determination	20	12	32	22	35	28
Lack of emphasis on merit in promotion	3	3	16	8	15	6
Bureaucracy, red tape, ineffi-ciency, large size	9	6	24	18	26	41
Lack of drive	0	0	8	4	13	2
Nothing would be worse	16	27	3	7	6	16
NUMBER ANSWERING	(230)	(117)	(262)	(134)	(296)	(82)

that they represent a mixture of the student's occupational values, his ex-pectations, and his image of the kind of employer the government is. For example, a student may feel that security aspects are better in govern-ment than in nongovernment employment, but he may not say so if, in his own hierarchy of values, security occupies a low position.

Analyzing the replies according to sex and grade averages yields the most discriminating response patterns (Tables 20-4 and 20-5), a mild switch from the ratings in which family income and college major provided the best cutting edges (Tables 20-1 and 20-2). In citing what would be *better* about government work, the females in each student population tend more frequently than the males to mention financial reward; the interest, enjoyment, and satisfaction afforded by the work; and the pos-sibilities of travel. The only exception to this trend occurs among high school students, where slightly more males than females mention the interest, etc., aspects of the work. Males in each population lead in only one "better" feature—the security aspects of government work. In general, the sexes are closest in their response patterns at the high school level.

However, for what would be *worse* if the first occupation were with the federal government, the response pattern now shows the masculine side with higher frequencies on virtually all of the response categories. Thus males, more often than females, cite poor or inadequate financial reward; lack of self-advancement and progress; absence of self-determination; less emphasis on merit in promotion; and the lack of drive found in federal employment and employees. Only for the prevalence of bureaucracy, etc., category is there an exception to this tendency; in this instance, graduate student coeds stress this more as a disadvantage. That more females than males say nothing would be worse is in accord with the general direction of the findings since it indicates that the females are less negative in attitude and the males more negative.[1] If the general tenor of the findings on the "worse" factors for the two sexes in the non-federal work force are recalled (Chapter 8), these male-female divergencies in the student populations come as no surprise. Furthermore, they suggest that the differentiated view of government employment held by the two sexes in our society begins at a fairly early stage and well before actual entry into the labor force.

Although academic grade averages are associated with the perceptions of what would be better or worse about government employment (Table 20-5), the consistency across the three educational levels is not nearly as strong as in the case of sex. Among the three sets of high school respondents, "A" students are least inclined to see financial reward and good physical environment and working conditions as better in government, and most inclined to mention the opportunity to do worthwhile and useful work. Students of all three grade averages see the security advantages and good personal relations in about equal strength. Perhaps most outstanding is the degree to which the "A" students cite the service possibilities of government employment: 22 percent of them versus 5 and 8 percent of the "B" and "C" students.

---

[1] The higher percentages for females on this category also help explain why their proportions are lower on the other categories. Since virtually all respondents who said nothing would be worse give no further replies and since more females than males replied in that fashion, it is almost inevitable that female percentages will lag behind male proportions in other categories.

As for college seniors, we find little difference between the grade groups on financial reward, physical environment and working conditions, and the chance to do worthwhile work as "better" in government. However, the lower the grade average, the more frequently noted are the security factors and the less frequent is the reply that nothing would be better. The "B" students more often volunteer that personal relations on the job would be better in government. ("B" high school students also use this category more frequently.)

Among graduate students, the divergencies between "A" and "B and

TABLE 20-5. *Positive and Negative Attributes Seen in Federal Employment, Related to Students' Grade Averages*

Positive and Negative Attributes	High School Students			College Seniors			Graduate Students	
	A	B	C and Below	A	B	C and Below	A	B and Below
Better in Federal Employment								
High or good financial reward	22%	35%	33%	18%	21%	21%	17%	16%
Security, stability, protection, fringe benefits	46	48	43	35	45	49	35	42
Good physical environment and working conditions	6	10	14	6	10	9	4	4
Good personal relations with people at work	8	12	6	7	17	6	9	8
Do work that is worthwhile, useful, constructive	22	5	8	10	10	9	11	5
Nothing would be better	2	4	8	15	10	8	18	14
Worse in Federal Employment								
Poor or inadequate financial reward	18%	21%	18%	19%	24%	36%	27%	26%
Bad or inadequate personal relations with people at work	4	2	1	15	10	8	8	7
Lack of self-advancement and progress	16	11	15	10	17	24	14	13
Lack of self-determination	27	16	17	36	28	23	37	28
Lack of emphasis on merit in promotion	6	3	2	9	13	17	15	13
Bureaucracy, red tape, inefficiency, large size	12	6	8	26	25	14	35	26
Nothing would be worse	16	18	23	1	5	5	3	11
NUMBER ANSWERING	(50)	(138)	(158)	(89)	(197)	(106)	(153)	(203)

below" students are either imperceptible or slight for the response categories. But the percentages hint that "B and below" students, compared with the "A" students, more often perceive security as an advantage, while the "A" students more frequently consider the worthwhile nature of government work.

When asked what would be worse about starting out with the government, high school students vary only slightly by grade average, but the "A" students lead in frequency of mention on all main attributes, except one, and also say least often that nothing would be worse. The disparity is especially strong for lack of self-determination (27 percent of the "A" students vs. 16 and 17 percent of the "B" and "C" students).

Differences are more marked among the college seniors. Here the "C" students mention with greater regularity poor or inadequate financial reward, absence of self-advancement and progress possibilities, and lack of emphasis on merit in promotion—all of which are aspects of getting ahead and gaining material rewards. Standing in moderate contrast are the "A" students, who put less emphasis on the three foregoing points but devote more attention to the perceived lack of self-determination, poor personal relations at work, and (with the "B" students) the elements of bureaucracy found in the government—categories that stress the ego-enhancing and the less material aspects of the job.

Graduate students vary almost not at all, except on two items. The "A" students cite both the lack of self-determination and the bureaucratic nature of government work more often than students with lower averages, a finding convergent with that for high school students (where the differences are small) and for college seniors.

We observed earlier that a proclivity for emphasizing somewhat opposing clusters of values existed on the part of high school and college "A" students at one extreme and the "C" students at the other. It is not without significance that each grouping of students according to grade average finds government deficient with respect to those occupational values to which they attach the most importance. This suggests that at least two different sets of values are found wanting in the government— one set by the students with high averages, the other by the students with low averages.

Although family income and college major do not bear the striking relationships that sex and grade average do to the positive and negative attributes seen in government employment, there are nevertheless some provocative findings (not tabled). In citing what would be better about government work, lower-income high school students prove somewhat more likely to mention financial reward and physical environment and working conditions, while comparable college seniors more often cite self-advancement and progress. Looking at what would be worse about federal work, the high school students from higher-income families refer more frequently to low financial reward and to lack of self-advancement and progress; they also claim less often that nothing would be worse. College senior income groups differ little in these respects.

By college major the picture is complex, but several features stand out. For college seniors, financial reward, interpersonal relations, interesting work, self-advancement and progress, prestige of the job, and wherewithal to do the work are seen as "better" in government slightly to moderately less by the engineering majors, and slightly more by the social science and humanities majors. But engineering majors, joined here by the natural scientists, lead in mentioning security as a positive factor, though this reply was often volunteered in a way which suggested that security had little appeal. A similar pattern holds among graduate students. One important finding is that natural science majors in both college senior and graduate populations (21 percent in each case) call attention more often than the other majors to the wherewithal and facilities to carry out the work.

In reference to the negative features of government work, engineering majors in both college and graduate school rank among the leaders in citing poor financial reward, lack of self-advancement and progress, and lack of self-development, self-expression and creativity. They are also by far the most likely to cite the lack of emphasis on merit. While all majors show high frequencies for the lack of self-determination category, the proportions are particularly high among social and natural science majors in graduate school (44 and 37 percent). It is important to remember that the variations among college majors are usually not large for these "better" and "worse" questions, and that the patterns are by no means clear cut.

To inquire more deeply into the nature of the students' positive images of government work, we asked all of those who thought they might start their working careers in a government job why they were considering this. Since the group included only sixty-nine high school students, sixty-five college seniors, and sixty-four graduate students, the answers to our question are only suggestive.

High school students give four major kinds of replies: some aspect of security benefits, 28 percent; interest, pleasure, or satisfaction in the work, 26 percent; opportunity for self-development, 20 percent; and self-advancement and progress, 19 percent. The three most frequently mentioned reasons from college seniors are: interest, enjoyment, satisfaction in the work, 40 percent; some aspect of security benefits, 31 percent; and self-advancement and progress, 25 percent. Among the graduate students only one category is mentioned by more than 20 percent: the interest, enjoyment and satisfaction which the work offers; this was volunteered by 58 percent of them.

Thus, the higher the level of the student population, the more frequently is interest in the work cited as a reason for considering government employment. And the reason is not as ambiguous as it might seem, for the students often made reference to specific work which is peculiar to government. Additionally, graduate students are less inclined than other students to offer security and self-advancement and progress as reasons, but more inclined to mention their expectation of having the necessary equipment and facilities on the job and of doing work that fits their capacities. That less than 15 percent of each student group cites high financial reward as a reason shows that in general students recognize that government is not a place of lucrative salaries.

Some of the responses to this question pointed to specific places in the government where students wished to be or thought they would be. For high school students, the leading response of this type indicated that the student was interested in being a member of the armed forces or felt that he would have to be. This answer is given by 30 percent of the highschoolers—primarily boys—but receives only token attention among the college seniors and graduate students. These latter two populations tend to center on specific jobs or agencies in the domestic federal service or some aspect of overseas or State Department work. It must be reiterated that, given the relatively small absolute number of students involved, all of these findings are tentative at best.

The Image of Federal Employees

Data presented in Chapter 12 indicated that the high school, college, and graduate school populations held differentiated impressions of civil servants. In general, high school students saw them in the most favorable light, graduate students least favorably. Our supplementary analysis suggests that differences in images also exist within each student population, and that the sex of the respondent is a major factor associated with this differentiation. When the students were asked to describe their general idea of a civil service employee, the responses tended to show a consistent, though sometimes small, cleavage between males and females within each population.

Considering the over-all tone of the descriptions, we find that at each educational level females are more likely to express a favorable opinion than males. The difference is most pronounced among college seniors, where 44 percent of the females, vs. 28 percent of the males, have favorable impressions (Table 20-6). Complementing this distribution, males at each echelon also have the highest percentages for unfavorable images and for the responses which do not safely permit allocation to either favorable or unfavorable categories. Sex is least related to over-all tone of response among graduate students and most related among college seniors.

If we consider the major substantive statements made about the civil

TABLE 20-6. *Over-All Tone of Responses and Characteristics Attributed to Federal Civil Service Employees, Related to Students' Sex*

Over-All Tone and Characteristics	High School Students		College Seniors		Graduate Students	
	Males	Females	Males	Females	Males	Females
Over-All Tone[a]						
Favorable	60%	71%	28%	44%	25%	30%
Unfavorable	8	4	27	19	33	30
Both favorable and unfavorable	1	2	10	6	1	1
Undeterminable	24	16	34	29	41	38
Characteristics						
Personality is agreeable	19	28	7	12	6	5
Capable of doing the work	16	20	10	17	9	10
Security conscious	8	7	29	15	31	29
Not very ambitious, low initiative	6	3	20	7	20	14
Poor or mediocre worker	1	2	16	5	13	10
NUMBER ANSWERING	(238)	(120)	(263)	(138)	(299)	(79)

[a] Percentages on over-all tone do not total 100 in some cases because replies of "Don't know" are included in the percentage base.

servant in response to the question, the source of this attitude variation becomes apparent. Descriptions of the employee as being personable, having good character, and possessing capability emanate more frequently from females. Characterizations of him as being security-conscious, lacking ambition, drive, and initiative, and being a poor worker spring more often from male respondents. While the individual differences between the sexes on a given category may not be large, the cumulative weight of the responses points in the direction of less favorable impressions being held by males than by females. Again, the difference is most noticeable among college seniors and least among graduate students.

Supporting evidence for the male-female divergency comes from the students' reactions to a number of prepared statements asking for ratings of general civil servants on five qualities—honesty, ability, interest in serving the public, drive to get ahead, and how well respected they are. Virtually no differences in mean scores emerge between high school boys and girls. At the college senior and graduate levels, women rate the employees higher than men do on each of the traits. Most of the differences do not exceed 0.6 on the ten-point high-low scale but they are fairly prevalent. Furthermore, they seem not to be functions of any tendency for females to rate people higher in general; in the ratings assigned other position-incumbents (such as top-level business men and government appointees) females often lag behind males in the ratings given. Rather, the more favorable view complements the general thesis that females are more positively disposed toward federal employment and employees in general.

Other findings add still more weight to the sex divergencies. When asked to explain why a person would become a civil servant instead of something else, males in each student population mention more frequently than females the security the work offers, the person's lack of ambition, and his inability to work elsewhere. Females are more inclined to mention the possibilities for self-advancement and progress, a person's interest in doing a specific kind of work, and the presence of job opportunities. Once more differences in attitudes between the sexes are most marked among college seniors.

Dividing the students according to their grade averages and their college majors does not produce any strong evidence of conflicting viewpoints about government employees. However, there are a few undertones worth noting. There is a slight but persistent tendency for lower grade averages to be associated with higher ratings of civil service employees in regard to their honesty, ability, interest in serving the public, drive to get ahead, and how well respected they are. This leaning appears to be independent of any proclivity of students with lower grade averages to rate other position-incumbents higher also. Second, students majoring in engineering consistently rate federal employees lower than do other majors and this is true for both college seniors and graduate students. Again, we would not stress these variations too much in and of themselves, but they do conform to the general picture of the engineering majors' attitudes about government work and workers.

21

College and High School Teachers

GIVEN THE MAJOR FOCUS of our study and the nature of the populations, we surmised that college teachers and high school teachers would
emerge as two of the more homogeneous populations surveyed. Nevertheless, it seemed possible that certain variables might be associated
with aspects of job ratings, occupational values, images of the federal
service as employer, and images of federal employees. The four factors
of age, sex, political party identification, and religious preference were
selected as having potential relationships with select portions of the data.
As the next few pages demonstrate, we found that strong relationships
are rare.

College Teachers[1]

Occupational Ratings

College teachers in general rate their present occupations quite high
on the occupational ladder; they also have a definite sense of progress
in the past and, even though their present ratings are high, expect to advance still further in the future. Our supplementary analysis reveals virtually no difference between men and women in terms of their present
ratings, how much progress they think they have made, or how much
more they expect to make in the next five years. By age groupings, we
obtain the familiar pattern of older age being associated with higher

[1] The college teacher population analyzed here consists of the entire sample of college teachers, including the natural and social scientists and engineers who were used
as subgroups in Part Two.

present satisfaction, and younger age being related to a feeling of more past progress, with even more to come in the future.

When teachers were asked where they thought they would be if their occupation stayed the same but was carried on for the federal government, men report a slightly lower absolute score than women, and the mid-age group a somewhat lower figure than the very youngest and very oldest groups. This ordering also holds when the present occupational rating is compared with that found in working for the government:

	N	Present Occupation	Same Occupation, but for the Federal Government	Difference: "Federal" Minus "Present"
Men	(679)	8.7	7.0	−1.7
Women	(222)	8.8	7.4	−1.4
Under 40	(323)	8.5	7.2	−1.3
40-49	(271)	8.7	6.7	−2.0
50 and Over	(244)	9.1	7.4	−1.7

Even though both men and women rate government employment lower than their present occupations, women are a bit less extreme than men. Similarly, the mid-age group registers the most difference while the youngest group shows the least. The tenuous nature of the sex differences was indicated, however, when the teachers were asked about the reaction of their families toward a change to government employment. There are no perceptible intersex differences in the percentages who say that their families would think they were moving up the occupational ladder or down, or that it would not make any difference. But the mid-age group again expresses the least favorable view of government employment by responding least often in terms of moving up the ladder.

Asked to consider the statement: "All things considered, working for the federal government appeals to me," women teachers, and respondents under 40 years of age have slightly higher scores on the ten-point agree-disagree scale (Table 21-1). When the appeal scores of working for a large private business are compared to these scores, however, both men and women give government an almost equal small net advantage. For teachers 50 years and over the appeal of government employment is matched by that of private business, but for the two younger age groupings government employment has a small plus. In terms of party identification, the difference is negligible on the absolute appeal of government, but the comparison with private business demonstrates that the score of

TABLE 21-1. *Ratings of Occupational Appeal of the Federal Government vs. Large Private Business, Related to Three Characteristics of College Teachers*[a]

Characteristics	Average Number Answering	"All things considered, working for a large private business appeals to me"	"All things considered, working for the federal government appeals to me"	Difference: "Government" Minus "Business"
Sex				
Males	372	4.3	4.6	+.3
Females	91	4.5	4.9	+.4
Age				
Under 40	174	4.7	5.1	+.4
40–49	146	4.1	4.4	4.3
50 and over	131	4.3	4.3	0.0
Party Identification				
Democratic	184	4.0	4.7	+.7
Independent	162	4.3	4.5	+.2
Republican	103	5.2	4.8	−.4

[a] The mean ratings shown in this table and subsequent rating tables in this chapter are based on a ten-step scale.

the Republicans (with their higher pull toward private business) is favorable to private business at one extreme, and that of the Democrats is favorable to the government at the other extreme.

Occupational Values

The supplementary analysis indicates that age apparently bears little or no regular relationship to the kinds of occupational values and aspirations the college teacher holds. As with other populations, however, distinctions do exist on the basis of sex (Table 21-2). Thus male teachers attach more importance to opportunities for reaching the top occupationally, recognition for one's own work, and viewing work as the most important part of a person's life. While female teachers do not necessarily eschew these values, they put more emphasis than their male colleagues on making friends through an occupation, doing work that is worthwhile and of service to God, seeing work as a way of forgetting personal problems, and viewing work as a builder of character. Women, therefore, highlight the ethical and personal rewards of a job more than

TABLE 21-2. *Ratings of "Occupational Value" Statements, Related to College Teachers' Sex*

"Occupational Value" Statements	Males	Females
"I like the kind of work you can forget about after the work day is over"	3.4	4.0
"Work should be the most important part of a person's life"	5.6	4.5
"Getting recognition for my own work is important to me"	7.7	7.1
"To me, an important part of work is the opportunity to make friends"	7.0	7.8
"To me, it's important in an occupation to have the chance to get to the top"	7.3	6.5
"To me, almost the only thing that matters about a job is the chance to do work that is worthwhile to society"	7.0	8.0
"Work helps you forget about your personal problems"	6.6	7.4
"Work is a good builder of character"	7.2	8.1
"Work is a way of being of service to God"	6.9	8.4
AVERAGE NUMBER ANSWERING	(372)	(94)

men, and men place more stress on the values of advancement and recognition.

Another social characteristic associated with the teachers' occupational values is religious preference. Comparing the Protestant and Catholic teachers on the basis of their agree-disagree scores for occupational value statements produced definite patterns of outlooks on the occupational world (Table 21-3). Protestants agree more than Catholics that to be really successful in life you must care about making money; work should be the most important part of a person's life; it may be right to lose friends to get ahead; and it's important to do a better job than the next person. Catholic teachers show considerably higher agreement than Protestants that work is a builder of character and a way of serving God, while disagreeing more that if a person doesn't want to work it's his own business. Protestants, then, seem to put more emphasis than Catholics on the primacy of work and getting ahead in the world. And Catholics attach more importance to the moral and ethical qualities of work. Although the teachers who signify preference for the Jewish faith are too few to permit general comparisons with the former two groups, there is suggestive evidence that they attach less importance than others to the primacy of work in one's life, and to the moral and ethical virtues of work. It should be noted that a roughly similar pattern emerges according to the religious preferences of businessmen (see Chapter 22).

TABLE 21-3. *Ratings of "Occupational Value" Statements, Related to College Teachers' Religious Preferences*

"Occupational Value" Statements	Protestant	Catholic
"To be really successful in life, you have to care about making money"	3.7	2.9
"Work should be the most important part of a person's life"	5.7	5.0
"Sometimes it may be right for a person to lose friends in order to get ahead in his work"	4.3	3.7
"It is more important for a job to offer *opportunity* than *security*"	7.7	7.4
"It's important to do a better job than the next person"	6.6	5.9
"If a person doesn't want to work hard, it's his own business"	5.0	4.3
"Work is a good builder of character"	7.4	8.1
'Work is a way of being of service to God"	7.0	9.0
AVERAGE NUMBER ANSWERING	(246)	(152)

Image of the Government As an Employer and Image of Federal Employees

Age, sex, and political party identification account for little or no difference in the ratings which college teachers assign to either general or top-level civil servants on the five qualities of honesty, ability, interest in serving the public, drive to get ahead, and how well respected they are. These three factors likewise show no apparent relationship to the degree that government employment is perceived as a way of getting ahead in the world and as offering chances for advancement. There is an inkling that women, older people, and Democrats view government employment and employees in a shade more favorable light, but the numerous inconsistencies and the small magnitudes make general statements about these relationships unwarranted.

High School Teachers

Occupational Ratings

In many respects high school teachers resemble college teachers in their homogeneity of occupational orientations. Female teachers are a bit more satisfied than their male counterparts with their present occupation (8.6 vs. 8.2 for males on the ten-point ladder), and males feel they have made slightly more recent advancement and expect to achieve more in the future, though even this increase will not bring them up to the absolute level that women expect to achieve (9.1 for women, 8.9 for men). As with college teachers, the older high school teachers rate their occupation highest, feel they have (almost necessarily) experienced less advancement in the last five years, and predict least progress in the next five.

When high school teachers compare their present occupation with what it would be like if carried out for the government, women score the government slightly higher than men (7.7 vs. 7.4). But when their present occupational ratings are subtracted from the government ratings, both sexes give government a net disadvantage of 0.9. This similarity stands in some contrast to the male-female difference in the general employed public, where women feel they would not be dropping nearly as much as men do (Chapter 4). By age groups, those under 40 give the lowest absolute ladder score to working for the government, but those 50 and older (because of their higher present occupational rating) see the greatest difference between present and government employment, with a net score of -1.1 as compared with the mid-age group's -0.6.

In terms of what their families would think if they changed to working for the government, men and women have virtually identical proportions under each of the three alternatives. By age, however, those between 40 and 49 indicate least that their families would consider this a movement up the ladder: only 19 percent of the group say "up the ladder," vs. 31 percent of the youngest group and 28 of the oldest group. At the same time, the mid-age group has the lowest percentage responding "down the ladder" (10 percent)—a finding consistent with the comparison score related above. The apparent discrepancy is explained by the finding that this group is the most inclined to say that a change to government employment would make no difference to their families.

Rounding out the high school teacher picture of occupational appeal of federal employment are the reactions to statements that working for the government or for a large private business appeals to the respondent (Table 21-4). Here we encounter one of the few instances where men, more often than women, say that government work appeals to them. In the general work force, in the federal work force, and in the student populations we have seen that females indicate more often than males that government employment appeals to them. Women high school teachers

TABLE 21-4. *Ratings of Occupational Appeal of the Federal Government vs. Large Private Business, Related to Three Characteristics of High School Teachers*

Characteristics	Average Number Answering	"All things considered, working for a large private business appeals to me"	"All things considered, working for the federal government appeals to me"	Difference: "Government" Minus "Business"
Sex				
Males	154	4.5	5.5	+1.0
Females	124	4.2	4.8	+ .6
Age				
Under 40	134	4.6	5.6	+1.0
40–49	74	4.1	4.8	+ .7
50 and over	70	4.3	5.0	+ .7
Party Identification				
Democratic	118	4.6	5.4	+ .8
Independent	63	3.7	5.3	+1.6
Republican	76	4.5	4.7	+ .2

not only express less absolute attraction toward government work, but also give it less of an advantage in comparison to the appeal of large business. The reasons for this reversal may lie partly in the greater career commitments of women high school teachers and partly in the male teachers' feeling that government work would offer a more useful or dramatic investment of their talents.

By age level, teachers under 40 express the highest absolute appeal for federal employment and also give the government a slightly higher plus score in comparison to business. Political party identification also shows a moderate relationship to the "appeal statements": Democrats and Independents have higher absolute and comparative scores than Republicans do, a finding not divergent from that for the general work force.

Occupational Values and Images of the Government

Analysis of the high school teachers according to sex and age suggests that these two factors are not associated with differences in occupational values and perspectives. This population, in fact, appears to be even more homogeneous in outlook than the college teacher population. Religious preference does, however, affect the reactions to a limited number of occupational value statements: Catholic teachers subscribe more to work being a way of serving God (8.8 vs. 7.5 for Protestants) and to the importance of doing work that is worthwhile to society (7.7 vs. 6.7). In regard to the image of government employment and of employees, although our analyses are limited, we found no appreciable differences by sex, age, or party identification.

22

Business Executives

WHILE ALL BUSINESS EXECUTIVES might seem to be alike in the general nature of their occupational pursuit, it seemed probable to us that variations would be found to exist within the population in relation to aspects of occupational ratings and values, and perceptions of government employment and of government employees. Therefore, our supplementary analysis considered the association of educational level, occupational income, age, political party identification, and religious preference to these points of inquiry.

Occupational Ratings

Business executives as a group are optimistic about their present occupational standing, but there are some rather striking variations among them on the basis of education level, income, and age (Table 22-1). When they are gauging their present stage on the occupational ladder, higher income and older age are positively related to higher placement. Educational level appears to make little difference, except for those who have had more than four years of college; such respondents rate themselves somewhat lower than others. At first glance this ordering seems at variance with our customary finding that higher education is related to higher occupational satisfaction. However, this highly educated business group is composed predominantly of younger executives who, because of their shorter time in the work force, rate themselves less favorably than older executives do.

However, as the table shows, these well-educated people feel they have been more upwardly mobile over the last five years, making more

TABLE 22-1. *Ratings of Own Occupation at Present, 5 Years Ago, and 5 Years Hence, Related to Three Characteristics of Business Executives*[a]

Characteristics	Average Number Answering	Present Occupation	5 Years Ago	Difference: "Present" Minus "5 Years Ago"	5 Years from Now	Difference: "5 Years from Now" Minus "Present"
Educational Level						
Less than college	76	8.3	7.3	+1.0	8.8	+ .5
Some college	72	8.1	6.8	+1.3	8.9	+ .8
4 years college	74	8.3	7.0	+1.3	9.0	+ .7
Over 4 years college	47	7.6	5.8	+1.8	8.9	+1.3
Occupational Income						
Under $15,000	132	7.6	6.1	+1.5	8.6	+1.0
$15,000 and over	115	8.6	7.4	+1.2	9.2	+ .6
Age						
Under 40	77	7.6	5.6	+2.0	8.8	+1.2
40–49	83	8.1	6.7	+1.4	9.1	+1.0
50 and over	108	8.4	7.7	+ .7	8.9	+ .5

[a] The mean ratings shown in this table and subsequent rating tables in the chapter are based on a ten-step scale.

of a net gain than is recorded by their fellows. The movement according to age is even more extreme. The net gain of 2.0 registered by executives under 40 years represents one of the sharpest climbs observed among any of the populations studied.

Occupational income is the only one of the three variables that accounts for noticeable differences in where the executives expect to be on the occupational ladder five years hence. Those making $15,000 or more have a mean score of 9.2, vs. 8.6 for those making under $15,000. Nevertheless, different *rates* of mobility anticipations are found; in general, the more highly educated, the youngest, and those with lowest incomes predict the greatest net gain during the next five years.

On the question of the attractiveness of the federal service, it is to be expected that most business executives would foresee a marked decline in their occupational satisfaction if they were to work for the government. But, according to Table 22-2, the disparity is greater for some executives than for others. Those with "some college," with higher incomes, of older age, and with Protestant affiliations all show the highest negative scores when their present occupational placements are compared with federal employment.

TABLE 22-2. *Ratings of Present Occupation vs. Doing the Same Work but for the Federal Government, Related to Four Characteristics of Business Executives*

Characteristics	Average Number Answering	Present Occupation	Same Occupation, but for the Federal Government	Difference: "Federal" Minus "Present"
Educational Level				
Less than college	80	8.3	5.7	−2.6
Some college	76	8.1	4.9	−3.2
4 years college	77	8.3	6.0	−2.3
Over 4 years college	48	7.6	5.5	−2.1
Occupational Income				
Under $15,000	138	7.6	5.9	−1.7
$15,000 and over	120	8.6	5.1	−3.5
Age				
Under 40	78	7.6	5.5	−2.1
40–49	84	8.1	5.3	−2.8
50 and over	118	8.4	5.7	−2.7
Religious Preference				
Protestant	123	8.4	5.4	−3.0
Catholic	65	7.9	5.6	−2.3
Jewish	68	7.7	5.5	−2.2

Estimates of family reaction to changing to government employment are not altogether consistent with the above findings. Here are the replies, in the context of the occupational ladder, according to the executives' education, income, and age:

	N	Up the Ladder	Down the Ladder	No Difference	Don't Know
Less Than College	(78)	15%	37%	44%	4%
Some College	(75)	12	49	39	0
4 Years College	(78)	9	46	45	0
Over 4 Years College	(45)	9	60	29	2
Under $15,000	(131)	18	37	44	1
$15,000 and Over	(123)	7	55	36	2
Under 40	(77)	10	49	40	0
40-49	(83)	11	51	36	2
50 and Over	(114)	12	43	43	2

Income level is still the most discriminating variable, as it was in relation to occupational rating of government employment. But age makes only a slight difference, and variations by educational level indicate in general that the higher the educational level the greater the inclination to report less movement up and more movement down. In contrast to the pattern in Table 22-2, then, it is those with more than four years of college, rather than those with "some college" who downgrade government employment the most. While strong reliance should not be placed on differences such as these because of the relatively small numbers of cases, it is possible that in this instance the most highly educated respondents are more concerned about the expectations of an important reference group—the family—than are the other executives. They may feel that the family will expect "better" things of them, given "all that education" they have experienced.

Finally, when we examine the agree-disagree scores on statements about the general appeal of working for a large private business and for the government, we find that level of education and income make scant difference in the appeal of business, with the absolute scores hovering just over 7.0 on the occupational ladder (Table 22-3). However, among older respondents, Republicans, and both Protestants and Catholics (compared to Jews) the absolute appeal of working for business is apt to be higher. These relationships are altered somewhat when the absolute appeal of government employment is considered. Again education and age make only a slight difference, but respondents earning over $15,000 show considerably less interest in government employment than their less affluent colleagues. Though the differences are not large, Republicans evince less interest than Democrats and, especially, Independents. Protestants record considerably lower scores than Catholics and Jews.

Comparing the two sets of mean scores gives an indication of the relative appeal of federal employment vs. the kind of employment toward which most of the executives would be expected to be thoroughly sympathetic. Thus all the "difference" scores show a huge net disadvantage for government (from -2.6 to -4.6 scale points). But here again the interest is in the range within this generally negative situation. We find, for example, that education is not invariantly related to these scores. Executives in the two middle educational strata give government employment the worst comparative score, whereas both the least and the most educated groups give it the best, albeit still heavily on the minus side. By age, the scores offer another case of asymmetry. It is the mid-aged group (those between 40 and 49), which exhibits the lowest abso-

TABLE 22-3. *Ratings of Occupational Appeal of the Federal Government vs. Large Private Business, Related to Five Characteristics of Business Executives*

Characteristics	Average Number Answering	"All things considered, working for a large private business appeals to me"	"All things considered, working for the federal government appeals to me"	Difference: "Government" Minus "Business"
Educational Level				
Less than college	76	6.9	3.6	−3.3
Some college	73	7.3	3.2	−4.1
4 years college	75	7.3	3.3	−4.0
Over 4 years college	48	7.0	3.5	−3.5
Occupational Income				
Under $15,000	135	7.2	3.9	−3.3
$15,000 and over	118	7.2	2.9	−4.3
Age				
Under 40	78	6.7	3.5	−3.2
40–49	80	7.0	3.1	−3.9
50 and over	112	7.6	3.6	−4.0
Party Identification				
Democrat	67	6.9	3.4	−3.5
Independent	56	6.8	3.7	−3.1
Republican	134	7.5	3.2	−4.3
Religious Preference				
Protestant	122	7.5	2.9	−4.6
Catholic	62	7.4	3.9	−3.5
Jewish	62	6.1	3.5	−2.6

lute and net scores for federal employment. By income, not unexpectedly, the higher-paid executives give government the greatest net disadvantage, as Republicans also do. By religious preference, Protestants see federal employment least favorably, the Jews most favorably, with the Catholics approximately midway between the extremes. The net difference score of −4.6 among Protestants is the worst single showing for the government in Table 22-3, and the Jewish executives' −2.6 is the best.

Occupational Values

The sample of business executives was too small to provide productive analysis by further subgroupings on the open-end questions designed to ascertain conceptions of the best and worst occupational worlds. However, we knew that the configuration emerging from responses to predetermined scale-sort items tends to resemble the pattern for the unstructured questions. In addition, the scale-sort items contain references to perspectives on work which would not ordinarily be elicited by the free-answer questions.

When we examine the scale item scores of the business executives according to certain demographic features, we find that the business executives are by no means homogeneous in respect to the importance of select types of occupational values (Table 22-4). Educational attainment, for example, is related to the importance attached to a number of statements dealing with work. Although there are irregularities, higher education tends to accompany a greater orientation to opportunity, interest in doing work that is worthwhile to society, and the belief that it is a person's own business to decide whether or not he wants to work hard. On the other hand, education tends to be inversely related to the view that success stems primarily from hard work and to the belief that work is a builder of character and a way of serving God. Interestingly, the executives do not diverge appreciably on the statement that caring about money is essential to real success.

TABLE 22-4. *Ratings of "Occupational Value" Statements, Related to Business Executives' Educational Level*

"Occupational Value" Statements	Educational Level			
	Less than College	Some College	4 Years College	Over 4 Years College
"To be really successful in life, you have to care about making money"	5.7	5.8	5.7	5.5
"It is more important for a job to offer *opportunity* than *security*"	7.1	7.8	7.9	8.3
"If a person doesn't want to work hard, it's his own business"	4.9	5.1	5.5	5.9
"Success in an occupation is mainly a matter of hard work"	7.8	7.2	6.9	6.4
"To me, almost the only thing that matters about a job is the chance to do work that is worthwhile to society"	5.1	5.7	6.2	5.8
"Work is a good builder of character"	8.5	8.4	8.1	7.6
"Work is a way of being of service to God"	7.3	7.2	6.9	6.0
AVERAGE NUMBER ANSWERING	(76)	(73)	(74)	(48)

This patterning of responses strongly resembles that found by educational level among the larger samples of the general employed public and the general federal work force. The data on the business executives become especially significant in the light of this similarity of patterning, since one would have expected the executives, as a more homogeneous population, to show certain common orientations which might conceivably override the discriminating influence of formal education. As was the case with the larger working force samples, the major differences for the executives often come at the extremes. We found, for example, that executives with the least formal training were significantly more inclined to record a liking for work they could forget about at the day's end, to agree more that work is only a way of making a living, and to affirm more readily that work helps one forget personal problems.

By occupational income, the ratings of agreement to most of the scale-sort items reveal little variation when the respondents are dichotomized into those making under $15,000 and those earning that figure or more. On four items the scores were suggestive, however. Executives with higher incomes agreed more than those with lower incomes on the importance of opportunity rather than security in a job (8.2 vs. 7.3). And there was also a difference on the perceived paths to success, as this tabulation shows:

	Under $15,000 (133)	$15,000 and Over (119)
"Success is mainly a matter of hard work"	7.1	7.4
"Success is mainly a matter of knowing the right people"	4.1	3.2
"Success is mainly a matter of luck"	3.4	2.6

While all hands render the highest agreement to the sentiment that success comes from hard work, the most affluent concur in this a bit more fully, and, more importantly, agree much less on the importance of knowing the right people and luck. This resembles the findings for higher-income people in the general work force (Chapter 14).

The variable of the executives' age is typically related, not so much to views on the substantive qualities of an occupation, but rather to those on work ethics and how work interacts with and affects the person's life away from the job (Table 22-5). As age advances, so does the degree of concurrence on such assertions as it's important to do a better job than

TABLE 22-5. *Ratings of "Occupational Value" Statements, Related to Business Executives' Age*

"Occupational Value" Statements	Age		
	Under 40	40–49	50 and Over
"A person should constantly try to succeed in work, even if it interferes with other things in life"	5.6	6.5	6.6
"To me, gaining the increased respect of family and friends is one of the important rewards of getting ahead in an occupation"	7.5	7.6	8.3
"It's important to do a better job than the next person"	6.9	7.5	8.3
"Success in an occupation is mainly a matter of hard work"	6.9	6.8	7.7
"Success in an occupation is mainly a matter of knowing the right people"	4.4	3.6	3.5
"Work should be the most important part of a person's life"	4.7	5.1	6.3
"Even if you dislike your work, you should do your best"	7.6	8.5	8.7
"If a person doesn't want to work hard it's his own business"	5.7	5.2	5.1
"Work helps you forget your personal problems"	6.9	7.1	7.7
"Work is a good builder of character"	7.4	8.1	8.9
"Work is a way of being of service to God"	5.6	6.7	8.0
"To me, almost the only thing that matters about a job is the chance to do work that is worthwhile to society"	4.9	5.3	6.4
AVERAGE NUMBER ANSWERING	(77)	(81)	(112)

the next person; success stems mainly from hard work; work helps you forget personal problems; work is a way of building character and of serving God; and doing worthwhile work is the only thing that matters about a job. Since most of the statements are couched in a positive sense, most of the scores move upward as age advances.

We may note, however, that this type of progression is not attributable to any general tendency of older people to agree more to statements per se: executives under 40 give higher scores to the statements that success is mainly a matter of knowing the right people, and that not wanting to work hard is one's own business. Thus, the clear force of the response pattern is in the direction of older age being associated with an upgrading of the moral, ethical, and altruistic aspects of work as well as its essential importance to the individual. But, when dealing with age as a social variable, we cannot (without extensive analyses) say whether the differences found underscore intergenerational changes, reflect shifts

TABLE 22-6. *Ratings of "Occupational Value" Statements, Related to Business Executives' Religious Preferences*

"Occupational Value" Statements	Religious Preference		
	Protestant	Catholic	Jewish
"I like the kind of work you can forget about after the work day is over"	4.1	5.1	5.4
"Sometimes it may be right for a person to lose friends in order to get ahead in his work"	4.2	3.2	4.4
"It is more important for a job to offer *opportunity* than *security*"	8.2	7.5	7.1
"Success in an occupation is mainly a matter of hard work"	7.3	7.8	6.6
"Success in an occupation is mainly a matter of knowing the right people"	3.5	3.2	4.7
"Success in an occupation is mainly a matter of luck"	2.9	3.0	3.7
"Work should be the most important part of a person's life"	5.8	6.2	4.4
"Even if you dislike your work, you should do your best"	8.8	8.1	7.7
"If a person doesn't want to work hard, it's his own business"	5.2	4.5	6.1
"Work is a good builder of character"	8.3	8.5	7.9
"Work is a way of being of service to God"	7.7	8.0	5.2
"To me, almost the only thing that matters about a job is the chance to do something worthwhile to society"	6.0	6.2	4.8
AVERAGE NUMBER ANSWERING	(120)	(62)	(65)

which occur with advancing age, or result perhaps from a blending of both factors. Whatever the explanation, the conclusion is inescapable that the perspectives on work and occupational endeavors held by business executives vary significantly by age.

The kinds of dissimilarities in the occupational values of Protestant and Catholic college teachers (along with a suggestive indication of how Jewish teachers fit into the pattern) are found again among the businessmen (Table 22-6). Although the cases are not numerous when allotted according to Protestant, Catholic, and Jewish preferences, the variations are marked and consistent, and run parallel to the findings for college teachers.

As with age, the majority of these divergencies occur on statements referring to the ethical, moral, and altruistic elements of the work world.

Thus Protestants and Catholics, far more than Jews, attach importance
to doing worthwhile work, to work as the most important part of a person's life, and to work as a way of serving God. But the Protestants stand
apart somewhat from the other groups in placing less emphasis on forgetting about work after the day is over, ranking opportunity higher than
security, and doing your best even if you dislike the work. Those with a
Jewish preference are more disinclined to view success as a matter of
hard work, and more inclined to see it resulting from luck and knowing
the right people.

In sum, the findings suggest that Protestant and Catholic businessmen, compared with Jewish businessmen, put moderately greater emphasis on the moral and ethical, yet work-centered and upward-striving
aspects of an occupation. Again, the existence of a range of values and
perspectives among people of different religious views is perhaps not so
surprising as that, given a sample having some major characteristics in
common, differences of such magnitude are obtained.

Images of the Government As an Employer and of Federal Employees

Our subanalysis of the way business executives perceive the federal
government as an employer and how they see civil servants was confined to the scale-sort statements. For the most part the images are not
sharply differentiated within the population, although this is less true for
government than for the civil servants.

Regardless of education, income, age, or party the executives perceive
about the same high level of security in government employment. They
also differ little in evaluating government jobs as routine and monotonous, but there are two exceptions here. Respondents with more than
four years of college and those under 40 years are less inclined to agree
to this than their colleagues and, at the same time, a bit more inclined
to see most jobs in private business as routine and monotonous.

All of the businessmen see the chances for getting ahead, landing a
top-level job, and being really successful as more possible in private employment than with the government, yet there are minor variations on
the theme (Table 22-7). The less-educated executives, those making
over $15,000, and the two older groups all express more agreement than
others that a young man of ability has a good chance of ending up in a
top-level job in a large corporation, and their net difference scores put

TABLE 22-7. *Ratings of Evaluative Statements About Federal and Private Employment, Related to Four Characteristics of Business Executives*

Characteristics	Average Number Answering	"A young man of ability who starts work in a large private business corporation has a good chance of ending up in one of the top-level jobs"	"A young man of ability who starts work in the Federal Civil Service has a good chance of ending up in one of the top-level jobs"	Difference: "Government" Minus "Business"
Educational Level				
Less than college	76	7.4	5.8	−1.6
Some college	72	7.4	5.3	−2.1
4 years college	73	7.1	5.2	−1.9
Over 4 years college	47	6.6	5.9	− .7
Occupational Income				
Under $15,000	132	6.9	5.6	−1.3
$15,000 and over	117	7.6	5.6	−2.0
Age				
Under 40	77	6.3	5.0	−1.3
40–49	80	7.2	5.5	−1.7
50 and over	110	7.8	5.9	−1.9
Party Identification				
Democratic	67	6.8	5.1	−1.7
Independent	56	7.2	6.0	−1.2
Republican	131	7.2	5.5	−1.7

the civil service at more of a disadvantage. Thus, the executives who are most educated, have lower incomes, and are younger give government employment a better *relative* rating than do their colleagues. They are joined, not by executives identifying with the Democratic party as we might expect, but by the Independents.

Executives differ only slightly in their ratings of civil servants. On the five qualities used in the scale-sort statements—ability, honesty, interest in serving the public, desire to get ahead, and how well respected they are—ratings tend to dip slightly as educational and income levels ascend and to rise somewhat as age advances. But these are slight trends, even though fairly consistent, and undue emphasis should not be attached to them.

23

Federal Executives

THE PREVIOUS CHAPTER DEMONSTRATED that certain differential patternings exist within the business executive population, especially in regard to occupational ratings and occupational values. Although civil
service executives would seem to constitute an even more homogeneous
group than the businessmen, we hypothesized significant inner-group
variations for them, with respect to age, educational attainment, and
party identification. We were also interested in the variables of length
of government service, past considerations of leaving the service, and
location in or outside of the Washington, D.C., area.

Occupational Ratings

We have seen that federal executives rate their present occupations
rather high on the occupational ladder, believe they have made substantial progress within the last five years, and expect more advancement in
the five years to come (Chapter 4). Our further analysis reveals certain
nuances in these occupational ratings. Because the federal executive
sample is highly homogeneous these differences are ordinarily not of the
magnitude found for the sample of general federal employees, but for
the most part they follow the general direction of findings for that larger
sample.

Considering first the placement these upper-level civil servants give
to their present occupation, we find that the differences by the various
subcategories are not large (Table 23-1). By educational level and according to location in or outside of Washington, there is virtually no dif-

TABLE 23-1. *Ratings of Own Occupation at Present, 5 Years Ago, and 5 Years Hence, Related to Five Characteristics of Federal Executives*[a]

Characteristics	Average Number Answering	Present Occupation	5 Years Ago	Difference: "Present" Minus "5 Years Ago"	5 Years from Now	Difference: "5 Years from Now" Minus "Present"
Educational Level						
Less than 4 years of college	115	8.2	7.2	+1.0	9.0	+ .8
4 years or more of college	147	8.0	6.9	+1.1	8.8	+ .8
Age						
Under 40	38	7.6	5.0	+2.6	8.8	+1.2
40–49	113	7.9	7.2	+ .7	8.9	+1.0
50 and over	112	8.2	7.5	+ .7	9.0	+ .8
Location						
Washington area	131	8.1	7.3	+ .8	8.9	+ .8
Non-Washington area	131	8.0	6.8	+1.2	8.9	+ .9
Length of Government Employment						
Under 10 years	33	7.8	5.9	+1.9	9.1	+1.3
10–19 years	104	7.8	6.7	+1.1	8.8	+1.0
20 years and over	125	8.3	7.6	+ .7	8.9	+ .6
Considered Leaving Government						
Within last 5 years	48	7.7	6.4	+1.3	9.1	+1.4
Over 5 years ago	114	8.0	7.1	+ .9	8.9	+ .9
Never	96	8.1	7.2	+ .9	8.9	+ .8

[a] The mean ratings shown in this table and subsequent rating tables in the chapter are based on a ten-step scale.

ference. Since educational level is usually a standard cutting device for occupational satisfaction, the negligible difference here is probably a function of the generally high educational attainments of the executives. Only 13 percent have not had at least some college training. Other variables reveal more common findings—older age and longer employment are both associated with somewhat higher occupational satisfaction. Finally, those respondents who have thought of leaving government within the last five years show a slightly lower job rating than those who thought of it more than five years ago or those who never considered it.

A feeling of upward mobility over the past five years is most marked for the executives under 40 years of age and for those who have worked with the government less than ten years (to a certain extent these are the same people). The 2.6 escalation score for the youngest grouping is one of the highest found among the several populations in the study and compares quite favorably with the +2.0 that business executives of the same age bracket give to their sense of progress in their employment milieu. Expectations of mobility in the coming five years follow a similar pattern: the youngest age group and the group with shortest government service expect to advance the most. It is also worth noting that executives who most recently thought of leaving also expect to climb the most.

When the executives are asked to rate their occupation on the assumption that they worked outside government, very few meaningful differences appear. Those with less than four years of college training think they would be somewhat better off than do their more highly educated colleagues (8.1 vs. 7.6), and this is the greatest difference the analysis produced. Similarly, a comparison of their present ratings with those projected if they worked outside the government reveals little variation, with one exception. Looking at the respondents in terms of their past considerations of leaving government service yielded the following results:

Considered Leaving	N	Present Occupation	Same Occupation but Outside the Government	Difference "Outside" Minus "Present"
Within Last 5 Years (50)		7.7	8.0	+.3
Over 5 Years Ago (114)		8.0	8.0	0.0
Never (98)		8.1	7.6	−.5

Clearly, those who have thought about leaving do not see themselves disadvantaged by nonfederal employment in the way that those who have never considered departure do. And the more recent the thought of departure, the more likely is the executive to see outside employment as representing a gain on the occupational ladder. Therefore, it appears that the pull of outside employment has not completely worn off for those who at some time thought of leaving. But the executives who have never considered leaving seem even more unlikely to consider it in the future, since they rate their present employment a full half scale point better than comparable outside employment.

Asking a respondent what his family would think if he worked outside the government puts a different slant on the relative standing of federal employment. While the distribution of responses is a bit ambiguous, the general nature of the findings proves suggestive (Table 23-2). On the response that families would view the switch as a move up the

TABLE 23-2. *Responses to: "Suppose you were to change now and go to work outside the federal government doing the same thing you're doing now; how do you think your family might feel about it? Would they feel you were moving up the ladder or down?" Related to Six Characteristics of Federal Executives*

Characteristics	Number Answering	Up the Ladder	Down the Ladder	No Difference	Don't Know
Educational Level					
Less than 4 years of college	115	31%	28%	41%	0%
4 years or more of college	145	30	17	51	2
Age					
Under 40	38	37	10	53	0
40–49	108	26	24	49	1
50 and over	114	33	23	42	2
Location					
Washington area	127	34	21	43	2
Non-Washington area	133	28	22	50	1
Party Identification					
Democratic	107	40	19	39	2
Independent	92	28	23	48	1
Republican	57	19	25	56	0
Length of Government Employment					
Under 10 years	33	27	9	64	0
10–19 years	99	30	20	48	2
20 years and over	128	32	26	41	1
Considered Leaving Government					
Within last 5 years	48	38	12	50	0
Over 5 years ago	113	37	26	35	2
Never	96	21	21	57	1

occupational ladder, we see that the greatest incidence occurs among those under 40, those who have considered leaving the government, and those identifying with the Democratic party.

The pattern for those reporting "down the ladder" is not a perfect complement to the "up" estimate because nearly half of the respondents choose to say "no difference." Nevertheless, estimates of downward movement are greatest among executives with less than four years of college, those 40 years and over, those who have ten years or more in government service, and (though the cases are few) those who have never thought of leaving government or considered it in the more remote past. Location in or outside of the nation's capital apparently makes little difference in this measure of occupational satisfaction.

It is noteworthy that the "no difference" responses, with only two exceptions, account for the largest proportion of replies for each grouping. In sum, there is some evidence that the executives who would feel the least disadvantaged, according to their families' attitudes, are the more highly educated, the youngest in age and in length of service, Democrats and Independents, and those who have recently considered separating from the government.

Another index of the attractiveness of federal employment for upper-level civil servants comes from their ratings on the pair of statements dealing with the appeal of working for a large private business and for the government (Table 23-3). There is only slight variation on each statement by educational level, location of work, and party identification. But age, length of federal service, and past thoughts of leaving the government do bear on the extent to which executives agree with the two items. For the absolute appeal of federal employment there is only a slight difference by age, but the appeal level increases with length of government service. And those who have never considered leaving government rate its appeal higher than those who have, especially those who thought of doing so within the past five years. When the scores for the two state-

TABLE 23-3. *Ratings of Occupational Appeal of the Federal Government vs. Large Private Business, Related to Three Characteristics of Federal Executives*

Characteristics	Average Number Answering	"All things considered, working for a large private business appeals to me"	"All things considered, working for the federal government appeals to me"	Difference: "Government" Minus "Business"
Age				
Under 40	38	5.4	8.8	+3.4
40–49	113	4.6	8.9	+4.3
50 and over	120	4.9	8.5	+3.6
Length of Government Employment				
Under 10 years	34	5.0	8.4	+3.4
10–19 years	105	5.0	8.6	+3.6
20 years and over	132	4.7	8.9	+4.2
Considered Leaving Government				
Within last 5 years	50	5.0	8.1	+3.1
Over 5 years ago	117	4.7	8.7	+4.0
Never	102	4.9	9.0	+4.1

ments are compared, this relationship is again found by length of service and past thoughts of leaving. Additionally, executives between 40 and 49 stand out as giving the government the largest net advantage over private business.

A final measure of the executives' attachment to and satisfaction in federal employment comes from this question: "Now, returning to your present situation, do you plan to continue working for the federal government, or do you think you might leave it?" A follow-up question ascertained the certainty of the intention to leave or remain. The replies according to length of employment with the government are:

	Under 10 Years (34)	10-19 Years (105)	20 Years and Over (134)
Plan To Continue	70%	100%	98%
Plan To Leave	15	0	1
Don't Know	15	0	1

Quite obviously, if the executive has been with the government for at least ten years the probabilities are almost 100-1 that he intends to continue there. Extreme caution should be used in judging the replies of those with less than ten years service, since the number of persons involved is small; given this qualification, however, the data suggest that this group is somewhat less intent on remaining, though even here a large majority signifies intention to stay. It appears that the more seasoned administrators are not "looking over the fence" for other jobs, but some of the newer administrators may be doing so. It is from this latter group, of course, that the government must be expected to draw its future mature, experienced executives.

The potential problem with the younger administrators is heightened in view of the responses to the follow-up question for those who said they planned to continue with the government: "How sure are you that you will continue in the federal government—very sure, fairly sure, not sure?" According to length of service the distribution is:

	Under 10 Years (24)	10-19 Years (104)	20 Years and Over (131)
Very Sure	63%	64%	81%
Fairly Sure	29	33	18
Not Sure	8	3	1

About three fifths of the executives with less than ten years of service (but again the small number of cases should be noted as a caution) and between ten and twenty years who say they intend to stay also say they are quite certain of staying. This compares with approximately four fifths of those who have served for twenty or more years. Length of service, then, is positively related both to the prospect of staying with the government and the surety of this intention. Had the sample been larger, we could have established a more precise "turning point" for the commitment to remaining with government. Nevertheless, the *intention* of continuing is virtually unanimous beyond the ten-year mark, and the *certainty* of continuing is almost a foregone conclusion at the twenty-year mark.

Occupational Values

Few systematic revelations about wide variations in occupational values and perspectives among the federal executives were shown by the supplementary analysis. When the scale-sort statements about the work world are related to education, age, length of service, and considerations of leaving government, we find only slight to moderate differences in the respondents' rating patterns.

For example, owing in part to relatively high educational attainments, the federal executives show few dramatic differences when they are considered by two levels of formal schooling. Nevertheless, there is a moderate association between having four or more years of college training and agreeing more that a person is entitled to expect his work to be fun, that after an adequate income is assured making more money isn't important, and that it's a person's own business if he doesn't want to work hard.

These findings are consistent with findings for other populations, just as the tendency of executives with less than four years of college to agree more that work is a way of building character and of serving God parallels the value patterns of less-educated groups in other samples. But among the federal executives these relationships are the exception, whereas in the general federal working force they are the rule. A much higher level of education and other social achievements among the executives and the socializing forces accompanying their particular kind of occupational endeavor seem to make for in-group similarities rather than dissimilarities. As we have seen, other elite groups, both in and out of government, show a similar tendency.

By age, executives under 40 years attach somewhat more importance to seeing work as a way of serving God, believing that one can expect his work to be fun, and wanting to do work that helps other people. In contrast, the executives of 50 and above place slightly more emphasis on work as the most important part of one's life, and on doing a better job than the next person. However, there is virtually no difference by age on the importance of opportunity vs. security in a job.

The most interesting aspect of the federal executive scores according to age is the strong contrast they make with the profile of the business executive scores. The contrast is most apparent for statements dealing with work's primacy and its ethical and altruistic factors (Table 23-4). Looking at the first two statements in the table, which deal with work primacy and obligation, we see that among federal executives there is only a slight rise by age in agreeing that work should be the most important part of one's life; for the second statement, there is a slight drop by age. Among the business executives, however, there is in each instance a sharp rise in agreement as age climbs.

For the next two statements, dealing with moral and ethical aspects of work, little difference is found among the federal respondents on viewing work as a character builder, but as age advances they agree decidedly less that work is a way of serving God. Again the businessmen

TABLE 23-4. *Ratings of "Occupational Value" Statements, Related to Age of Federal and Business Executives*

"Occupational Values" Statements	Federal Executives			Business Executives		
	Under 40	40–49	50 and Over	Under 40	40–49	50 and Over
"Work should be the most important part of a person's life"	5.0	5.1	5.6	4.7	5.1	6.3
"Even if you dislike your work, you should do your best"	9.3	9.1	8.9	7.6	8.5	8.7
"Work is a good builder of character"	8.0	8.1	7.8	7.4	8.1	8.9
"Work is a way of being of service to God"	8.3	7.6	7.0	5.6	6.7	8.0
"The main satisfaction a person can get out of work is helping other people"	7.6	6.9	7.1	6.2	6.5	7.3
"To me, almost the only thing that matters about a job is the chance to do work that is worthwhile to society"	6.4	6.4	6.3	4.9	5.3	6.4
AVERAGE NUMBER ANSWERING	(38)	(113)	(121)	(77)	(81)	(112)

differ radically from this pattern: there is substantially more ratification of both statements with advancing age. On the final two statements, concerning altruistic and social aspects of work, among the federal executives the differences by age are either minor or in fact show the younger executives placing more importance on helping other people. But the picture among the businessmen is one of increasing subscription to the altruistic statements as age climbs.

Some care should be exercised in interpreting these data because of the relatively low number of federal executives under 40 years. However, even if each of the two executive populations were dichotomized into groups of under 50 years and 50 years and over, the direction of the findings would remain the same. In addition, the pattern of other ratings on items of a similar nature distinctly resembles that found for the six statements in Table 23-4. The general conclusion to be drawn is that among federal executives, age makes far less difference than it does among business executives in the ratings assigned to statements stressing the primacy and duty of work, its ethical and religious qualities, and its altruistic aspects. There is even suggestive evidence that, whereas the subscription to these values and orientations increases among business executives as age rises, there may be a slight decrease by age on some of the same sentiments among federal executives.

Two other findings are also of importance. According to length of employment, the federal executives with less than ten years of service agree more than others that opportunity is more important than security, and that it is important to have a chance to get to the top in an occupation. It is also worth noting that the executives who have considered leaving the government within the last five years give more stress to wanting the chance to reach the top, and to the feeling that it is distressing to know that other people are passing you in your occupation. There is, consequently, some tentative evidence that federal executives with a short service period and those who have recently considered leaving are more ambitious than their colleagues.

Image of the Government As an Employer

How the federal executives perceive the government in the role of employer appears to have little or no relationship to educational at-

TABLE 23-5. *Ratings of Evaluative Statements About Federal and Private Employment, Related to Federal Executives' Age and Length of Employment*

Statements	Age			Length of Government Employment		
	Under 40	40–49	50 and Over	Under 10 years	10–19 Years	20 years and Over
"For a young man of ability, his best chance for being *really successful* lies in working for a large private business corporation"	4.2	4.5	5.0	4.4	4.5	4.8
"For a young man of ability, his best chance for being *really successful* lies in working for the federal government"	4.2	3.8	3.7	4.1	3.9	3.7
Difference: "Government" Minus "Business"	0.0	−.7	−1.3	−.3	−.6	−1.1
AVERAGE NUMBER ANSWERING	(38)	(113)	(121)	(34)	(105)	(133)

tainment. Distinctions do exist, however, on the basis of age, length of government service, past thought of leaving the government, and, to a slight extent, political party identification. Thus younger executives, those with the least amount of service, and those who have considered leaving the service are all less inclined to see government as offering a high degree of security. At the same time, the younger executives and those with least government service are a bit more optimistic about the possibilities of getting ahead, reaching a top-level position, and having the chance to be really successful. As Table 23-5 indicates, the older the respondent is and the longer he has been with the government, the lower is his agreement that federal employment offers the best chance for real success. Concomitantly, rises in age and seniority are accompanied by more affirmation that the best chance for success is in a large private business. Consequently the net difference scores between the two avenues for success reveal a marked movement by age and length of employment, with the relative position of government employment growing worse rather than better. Although, as observed earlier, the younger and the least-experienced executives are the least sure about continuing in government, they are at the same time more sanguine about the opportunities for success in government, especially vis-à-vis a large business.

Party identification proves not to be highly associated with the ratings assigned government employment in terms of opportunities to get ahead, landing a top-level job, or achieving maximum success (Table 23-6). But Independents and, especially, Republicans rate private business employment much higher on these three aspects than do Democrats. When the scores for government and business are compared, we find the Democrats giving the government significantly better relative scores than do Independents and Republicans, with the difference being most marked on the statements dealing with obtaining real success. These distinctions by party preference are much more pronounced among the upper-level civil servants than in the general federal work force.

TABLE 23-6. *Ratings of Evaluative Statements About Federal and Private Employment, Related to Party Identification of Federal Executives*

Statements	Party Identification		
	Democratic	Independent	Republican
"A person who works for the federal government generally has a good chance to get ahead"	7.3	6.8	7.4
"A person who works for a large private business generally has a good chance to get ahead"	5.9	5.9	6.8
Difference: "Government" Minus "Business"	+1.4	+ .9	+ .6
"A young man of ability who starts work in the federal civil service has a good chance of ending up in one of the top-level jobs"	7.7	7.1	8.0
"A young man of ability who starts work in a large private business corporation has a good chance of ending up in one of the top-level jobs"	6.6	6.8	7.6
Difference: "Government" Minus "Business"	+1.1	+ .3	+ .4
"For a young man of ability, his best chance for being *really successful* lies in working for the the federal government"	4.0	3.5	3.8
"For a young man of ability, his best chance for being *really successful* lies in working for a large private business corporation"	4.3	4.6	5.3
Difference: "Government" Minus "Business"	− .3	−1.1	−1.5
AVERAGE NUMBER ANSWERING	(113)	(95)	(59)

TABLE 23-7. *Positive Attributes of Nonfederal Employment, Related to Federal Executives' Past Considerations of Leaving Government*

Positive Attributes	Considered Leaving Government		
	Within Last 5 Years	Over 5 Years Ago	Never
Better in Nonfederal Employment			
High or good financial reward	53%	68%	51%
Having the wherewithal to do the job	20	19	12
Recognition for one's own work	18	6	3
Self-advancement and progress	14	8	13
Self-determination	33	27	16
Less bureaucracy	29	17	13
Nothing would be better	6	5	13
NUMBER ANSWERING	(49)	(115)	(97)

Another aspect of the view that top-level civil servants take of their employer emerges from the question concerning what would be better and what would be worse about working outside the government, assuming that their work stayed the same. Table 23-7 shows the "better" factors, according to whether the respondent had considered leaving government, and if so, how recently. Although there are some irregularities, the evidence suggests that those who have considered leaving say more frequently that financial reward, wherewithal to do the job, recognition, self-determination, and less bureaucracy would be advantages of outside employment. And those who have never thought of leaving say more often that nothing would be better.

The responses for what would be worse outside government do not add up to as clear a picture (not tabled). There tends to be more unanimity on what would be worse, with some aspect of less security and protection being mentioned by 60 percent of those who never have thought of departing, 57 percent of those who considered leaving more than five years ago, and 52 percent of those thinking of it in the last five years. Buried in those totals is the fact that while 40 percent of the first two groups specifically mention *job* security, only 18 percent of those who recently considered leaving do so. Conversely, only about 20 percent of the first two groups vs. 36 percent of the third cite *fringe benefits* as being worse. Thus, those who have most recently thought of leaving the government—and among them are more younger than older executives—

are not particularly concerned about job security on the "outside," but they still see the fringe benefits of government employment as being superior to what they would receive outside government.

The Image of Federal Employees

For the most part, perceptions of civil servants vary little among federal executives. On the five traits by which they rate general civil servants—ability, honesty, desire to get ahead, interest in serving the public, and how well respected they are—the executives with lower education and those who are Democrats are more inclined to assign somewhat higher scores than executives with more education and of other political leanings. There is a slight tendency for those with longer federal service to give higher scores, but age shows no relationship to the ratings. These latter trends are minor, however, and mainly fall short of statistical significance. And there is virtually no difference among the executives in the ratings given occupants of top-level positions in the civil service for the same five qualities.

Finally, a moderate amount of evidence indicates that executives who have considered leaving government within the last five years downgrade both the general civil service employee and the top-level employee. There is a certain irony in the finding that executives who thought of leaving the service more than five years ago often rate federal employees higher than do those who never thought of leaving. The picture emerging from the more negative ratings by those who most recently thought of leaving is supported by the replies to the open-end question that seeks out the general description of the civil service employee. This group of recent waverers makes the fewest favorable comments about civil servants as well as the most numerous unfavorable comments. They refer *less* to above-average mental ability, personableness, service motivation, honesty, and interest in the work, and *more* to lack of ambition, acceptance of routine, and a noncreative personality. This does not mean, however, that the executives who have recently considered leaving have an unfavorable image of government employees, because the data indicate that, over all, the image is favorable. But it is less positive than the image held by those who have never thought of leaving and by those who thought of leaving in the more distant past.

In sum, perhaps the most important findings in this chapter are the strong relationships—both positive and negative—which age, length of employment, and past considerations of leaving government service have to occupational satisfaction, feelings of mobility, evaluations of outside employment, the image of government as a place to succeed, and the image of the kinds of people who are federal employees. Important also is the showing on the lack of (or slightly negative) relationship between the age of federal executives and their subscription to statements stressing the obligatory, ethical, and altruistic aspects of work; this stands in marked contrast to the positive relationships found among business executives according to age.

24

Natural Scientists, Social Scientists, and Engineers

THE SMALLEST SAMPLES in our study are those of the three specialist groups—the natural and social scientists and engineers in colleges, business, and government. In various chapters of Part Two, it was shown that these specialists are to a moderate extent homogeneous on such matters as occupational values, but appear more heterogeneous in reference to comparative occupational ratings and the image of federal vs. non-federal employment. Despite the small size of the samples, we considered it worthwhile to test the possibilities of variations within each of the special groupings in each sector of employment.

Natural and Social Scientists and Engineers in Colleges

Our supplementary analysis of these groups in the sample of college teachers was confined primarily to a consideration of age, dividing the group into those who are under 40 and those 40 and over. Given the relative homogeneity of academic specialists in general and the limited sample size, age was thought to be a factor which might discriminate among the specialties better than other social variables.

Occupational Ratings

The older teachers in each field rate their present occupations higher than do their younger colleagues, who in turn think they have made more progress in the last five years and expect more in the next five years. The one exception to this occurs among the engineers: both age groups report a net improvement of 1.0 over the past five years. When teachers are asked to judge where their occupation would be on the ladder if their work stayed the same but was done for the federal government, the absolute scores for federal employment differ little by age.

	N	Present Occupation	Same Occupation, but for the Federal Government	Difference: "Federal" Minus "Present"
Engineers				
Under 40	(44)	7.9	6.8	−1.1
40 and over	(42)	9.0	7.1	−1.9
Natural Scientists				
Under 40	(46)	8.5	7.1	−1.4
40 and over	(70)	8.9	6.9	−2.0
Social Scientists				
Under 40	(48)	7.7	6.6	−1.1
40 and over	(52)	8.7	6.6	−2.1

Comparing this score with the present occupational rating, however, we see that in each academic specialty the older people perceive the largest net loss in working for the government.

On the query of what their families would think about such a change of employer, the responses are significant primarily for the large proportion—over 50 percent—of each age grouping in each speciality area reporting that their families would perceive no difference. And, except for the natural scientists, there is no clear inclination for younger teachers to report more frequently "up the ladder" and less frequently "down the ladder."

Reactions to statements about the general appeal of employment in government and in a large business add another perspective by age. The absolute attractiveness of working for the federal government is slightly less for the older engineers and natural scientists, but moderately more for the older social scientists. Although these differences are not extreme and the cases none too many, there is a suggestion here that subtle intergenerational changes may be at work in a differential manner among academic specialists. Comparing the government and business appeal scores highlights the differences between the engineers and the natural and social scientists. Both engineer age groups show a net disadvantage for government employment, and the older engineers more so than the younger. In marked contrast, both age levels among the natural scientists show a moderate positive advantage for government work of 0.6, while the social scientists, especially the older ones, record still higher favorable scores for the government.

	N	"All things considered, working for a large private business firm appeals to me"	"All things considered, working for the federal government appeals to me"	Difference: "Government" Minus "Business"
Engineers				
Under 40	(44)	5.0	4.5	− .5
40 and over	(43)	5.2	4.2	−1.0
Natural Scientists				
Under 40	(46)	4.4	5.0	+ .6
40 and over	(72)	3.9	4.5	+ .6
Social Scientists				
Under 40	(48)	3.9	4.7	+ .8
40 and over	(56)	4.2	5.4	+1.2

Occupational Values

When we consider occupational values, the most arresting finding is the similarity of the divergencies by age among these academic specialists to the variations in other populations surveyed. Although some of the reactions to occupational value statements according to age show stronger variations within one academic group than another, the distinctions are almost universally in the same direction (Table 24-1).

Older age is associated with more agreement that the feeling that others are passing you by would be hard to live with; opportunity is more important than security; a person should constantly try to succeed; work should be uppermost in importance; and doing a better job than the next person is important. All of these statements stress the key role of work in one's life and the importance of getting ahead. But the older teachers also agree more on the intangible benefits of work: that work helps one forget personal problems, builds character, is a way of serving God, and that it is important to do work that is worthwhile to society. Older teachers thus put more emphasis than their younger colleagues on both the importance of doing well in an occupation and the inner and societal importance of work.

TABLE 24-1. *Ratings of "Occupational Value" Statements, Related to Age of College Engineers, Natural Scientists, and Social Scientists*[a]

"Occupational Value" Statements	Engineers		Natural Scientists		Social Scientists	
	Under 40	40 and Over	Under 40	40 and Over	Under 40	40 and Over
"It would be hard to live with the feeling that others are passing you up in your occupation"	6.1	6.3	6.2	6.6	5.8	6.9
"I would like my family to be able to have most of the things my friends and neighbors have"	6.8	6.7	7.2	6.5	6.0	7.0
"It is more important for a job to offer *opportunity* than *security*"	7.2	8.2	7.1	7.8	7.3	7.5
"A person should constantly try to succeed at work, even if it interferes with other things in life"	4.8	6.2	5.5	6.3	4.6	5.9
"It's important to do a better job than the next person"	6.0	7.0	5.8	6.2	5.1	6.2
"Work should be the most important part of a person's life"	5.3	5.8	5.0	5.8	5.0	5.8
"Even if you dislike your work, you should do your best"	8.8	8.4	8.2	8.9	7.1	7.9
"Work helps you forget your personal problems"	6.2	7.0	6.9	7.6	5.4	6.8
"To me, almost the only thing that matters about a job is the chance to do work that is worthwhile to society"	6.9	7.0	6.2	7.5	6.3	7.1
"Work is a good builder of character"	7.2	8.0	7.5	7.7	5.6	7.0
"Work is a way of being of service to God"	6.3	7.0	6.6	7.2	5.0	6.3
AVERAGE NUMBER ANSWERING	(44)	(42)	(46)	(73)	(48)	(56)

[a] Mean ratings shown in this table and subsequent rating tables in the chapter are based on a ten-step scale.

While this theme of associations by age does run through the three teacher populations, certain suggestive differences between the groups on the basis of age should not be ignored. On the whole, for example, social scientists appear to diverge the most and natural scientists and engineers the least. This means that older social scientists, compared to the older engineers and natural scientists, agree more than their younger colleagues on not liking to be passed up occupationally; the importance of doing better than the next person; wanting their families to keep up with the neighbors; seeing work as a way of serving God; and seeing work as a character builder.

It is also significant that the greater emphasis given by older teachers to the two related items—opportunity being more important than security, and the need to try constantly to succeed even at the expense of other things—is somewhat more noticeable among the engineers. And the older natural and social scientists both concur more than their younger colleagues that even if you dislike your work, you should do your best. The situation is reversed, however, among the engineers, with the younger ones showing the higher agreement score.

Image of the Government As an Employer and Image of Federal Employees

Additional investigation according to age categories of the image of government as an employer yielded few or no meaningful differences. The academic specialists, whatever their age, tend to respond almost identically to the scale-sort items concerning the nature of government employment. But the case is different in regard to their picture of general civil servants. Upon being asked to rate them on five traits—honesty, ability, drive to get ahead, interest in serving the public, and how well respected they are—the older teachers within each discipline score the employees higher than do the younger (Table 24-2). The engineers di-

TABLE 24-2. *Ratings of General Civil Servants on Five Traits, Related to Age of College Engineers, Natural Scientists, and Social Scientists*

Age Groups	Average Number Answering	"Honesty"	"Ability"	"Drive To Get Ahead"	"Interest in Serving the Public"	"How Well Respected They Are"
Engineers						
Under 40	44	7.0	5.3	4.9	5.7	5.3
40 and over	43	7.7	6.4	6.0	6.4	6.5
Natural Scientists						
Under 40	46	6.7	5.9	5.5	6.1	5.9
40 and over	72	7.7	6.4	5.5	6.2	6.1
Social Scientists						
Under 40	48	7.1	6.0	5.3	6.0	5.1
40 and over	55	7.8	6.2	6.2	6.2	6.2

verge the most in this regard and natural scientists the least. Not only do the ratings as a whole tend to be fairly low, but the situation seems unlikely to change toward higher ratings because the younger academics are less favorable than the older ones. Similar, though less marked, distinctions by age level are also found in the ratings given top-level people in the civil service.

Natural and Social Scientists and Engineers in Business

Two major variables were examined in the further analyses of the three special groups in business. As with their college counterparts we divided the groups into two age categories. And, on the basis of their work descriptions, we allocated them into two other categories: activities that seemed primarily professional, and activities that seemed mainly managerial.[1] The latter dichotomy was rather crude, but it proved to be a discriminating factor in analyzing these special populations.

Occupational Ratings

Again, older age is associated with higher ratings of present occupation, but with the difference for all three groups being less than one scale point on the occupational ladder. Similarly, younger age is associated with a sense of more progress in the past five years and projections of more rapid advancement in the coming five years. The professional-managerial split yields less distinct disparities. Managerial personnel have slightly higher present occupational satisfaction, but the feelings of past mobility and expectations for the future are irregular and the differences negligible.

Assuming that their work stayed the same but their employer was the government, the older respondents give a slightly higher rating to government than do their younger fellows (Table 24-3). And the professionals among engineers and natural scientists place government employment higher than do the managers, but for the social scientists a slight reversal occurs. The comparative scores tend to reinforce this picture.

---

[1] Classifications were made on the basis of replies to these questions: (1) "Where are you employed—I don't mean the name of the place but what kind of a place is it?" (2) "What *exactly* do you do there?" (3) "What is your title?"

Although all of the groups, by age or work activity, register a large negative score for government employment, the older respondents and the managers are usually the more negative. Again there are exceptions, one within the professional-managerial break among social scientists, another one by age brackets of the natural scientists. The internal differences by age are neither quite as large nor as consistent as those found among comparable groups in colleges.

Predictions about what their families would think of a switch to government employment throw little additional light on the general order of relationships. Regardless of age level, all of these respondents are much more inclined than their college counterparts to say their families would think they were moving down the occupational ladder. However, those under 40 are less inclined to say "no difference" and somewhat more prone to say "down the ladder."

TABLE 24-3. *Ratings of Present Occupation vs. Doing the Same Work but for the Federal Government, Related to Age and Major Work Activity of Business Engineers, Natural Scientists, and Social Scientists*

Age and Major Work Activity	Average Number Answering	Present Occupation	Same Occupation, but for the Federal Government	Difference: "Federal" Minus "Present"
Age				
Engineers				
Under 40	24	7.5	5.4	−2.1
40 and over	64	8.3	5.6	−2.7
Natural scientists				
Under 40	42	7.7	5.6	−2.1
40 and over	38	8.2	6.1	−1.9
Social scientists				
Under 40	40	7.6	5.2	−2.4
40 and over	32	8.5	5.5	−3.0
Major Work Activity				
Engineers				
Professional	50	8.0	5.7	−2.3
Managerial	40	8.2	5.4	−2.8
Natural Scientists				
Professional	44	7.7	6.3	−1.4
Managerial	37	8.4	5.2	−3.2
Social scientists				
Professional	49	8.0	5.3	−2.7
Managerial	22	8.1	5.5	−2.6

TABLE 24-4. *Ratings of the Occupational Appeal of the Federal Government vs. Large Private Business, Related to Age and Major Work Activity of Business Engineers, Natural Scientists, and Social Scientists*

Age Groups and Major Work Activity	Average Number Answering	"All things considered, working for a large private business appeals to me"	"All things considered, working for the federal government appeals to me"	Difference: "Government" Minus "Business"
Age				
Engineers				
Under 40	25	7.4	2.6	−4.8
40 and over	64	7.7	3.3	−4.4
Natural scientists				
Under 40	42	6.8	3.6	−3.2
40 and over	39	6.8	4.2	−2.6
Social scientists				
Under 40	40	6.8	3.8	−3.0
40 and over	29	7.3	4.4	−2.9
Major Work Activity				
Engineers				
Professional	50	7.5	3.4	−4.1
Managerial	40	7.8	2.7	−5.1
Natural scientists				
Professional	45	6.4	4.0	−2.4
Managerial	37	7.1	3.5	−3.6
Social scientists				
Professional	46	7.0	3.7	−3.3
Managerial	22	6.9	4.7	−2.2

Illustrating the cross currents which seem to be operating in judging the occupational appeal and attractiveness of government employment are the response patterns to the pair of items dealing with the appeal of working for the government and for a large private business (Table 24-4). By age level, the more senior in each group express more positive pull toward federal employment than the junior respondents. And the relative appeal of government, when compared with business employment, is also slightly greater in the older group. More accurately, because the negative scores are universal and high, the disadvantageous government score for those 40 years and over is lower than for those under 40.

The picture by professional-managerial classification is more complex. While the professionals among the engineers and natural scientists express moderately more attraction toward government employment, among the social scientists it is the managers who have the higher appeal score. Furthermore, when the appeal score for business is subtracted from the government score the cleavages become more marked. (The peculiarity of the social scientists was presaged in the data of Table 24-3, which showed the social science managers giving higher absolute and relative scores to government work than the professionals did. However, the size of the samples and the relative approximations of the professional-managerial classification make these findings more incidental than definitive.)

Occupational Values

Here again we find that age seems to have an impact on the importance attached to certain occupational values (Table 24-5). And the differences, as before, usually refer to the higher concern of the older respondents with the centrality of work in their lives, the significance of doing well in an occupation, and the ethics and moral goodness of work. Younger respondents do place slightly more emphasis on having a chance to get to the top. Older people also agree more that having a chance to do worthwhile work matters greatly and that there are limitations on the importance of money.

Significantly, there appear to be some moderate divergencies by age level among the three groups. Thus, *older* natural scientists, compared with younger ones, put more stress on the availability of opportunity rather than security in a job (8.6 vs. 7.7). *Younger* social scientists and engineers, however, give more support to the importance of opportunity than their older colleagues. Also, while older natural and social scientists subscribe much more than their younger fellows to wanting their families to keep up with the neighbors, there is only a minute difference between younger and older engineers on the same item. It is also worth noting that, although the older respondents in all three groups agree more that work should be the most important part of a person's life, and that it's important to do a better job than the next person, such differences tend to be more pronounced among natural and social scientists than among engineers.

To a moderate extent the findings by age are paralleled in the professional-managerial classification. The managers tend to resemble the respondents who are 40 and over, particularly on items related to the ethics of work. They are also more inclined than the professionals to see success as mainly a matter of hard work and less inclined to attribute success to

TABLE 24-5. *Ratings of "Occupational Value" Statements, Related to Age of Business Engineers, Natural Scientists, and Social Scientists*

"Occupational Value" Statements	Engineers		Natural Scientists		Social Scientists	
	Under 40	40 and Over	Under 40	40 and Over	Under 40	40 and Over
"After you are making enough money to get along, then making more money in an occupation isn't very important"	4.7	5.4	5.1	6.3	5.0	5.4
"To me it's important in an occupation to have the chance to get to the top"	9.3	8.7	8.2	7.8	8.5	8.2
"I would like my family to be able to have most of the things my friends and neighbors have"	7.6	7.5	6.6	7.5	6.4	7.9
"It is more important for a job to offer *opportunity* than *security*"	8.6	8.3	7.7	8.6	8.2	7.9
"A person should constantly try to succeed at work, even if it interferes with other things in life"	5.7	6.4	5.5	6.7	5.0	6.4
"Work should be the most important part of a person's life"	5.8	6.0	5.3	6.7	4.4	5.5
"It's important to do a better job than the next person"	7.4	7.7	6.8	7.2	6.8	7.6
"Success in an occupation is mainly a matter of luck"	4.2	3.3	2.5	2.8	3.2	2.3
"Work helps you forget your personal problems"	6.4	7.3	5.3	6.8	6.0	7.0
"To me, almost the only thing that matters about a job is the chance to do work that is worthwhile to society"	5.3	6.4	5.8	6.7	5.7	6.7
"Work is a good builder of character"	7.2	8.4	7.4	8.6	6.7	8.0
"Work is a way of being of service to God"	5.6	6.8	5.5	6.4	5.2	6.0
AVERAGE NUMBER ANSWERING	(25)	(63)	(42)	(39)	(40)	(29)

luck and knowing the right people. Managers seem slightly more ambitious and eager to advance, though the opportunity-security score reveals virtually no difference between the two groups. Oddly, managers do not concur more that directing the work of others is satisfying. All in all, the differences in occupational values stemming from the professional-managerial dichotomy are not overwhelming and lack the strength and regularity from group to group that the age break produces.

Image of the Government As an Employer and Image of Federal Employees

For these three groups the variations in perceptions of the federal service are small to moderate according to both age and type of work activity. Younger respondents indicate slightly higher agreement that most jobs in the federal government are routine and monotonous and also agree less strongly about the opportunities for getting ahead, achieving a top-level position, and attaining high success. Such differences are not great, but they are fairly consistent and are in sympathy with the age differentials for other populations.

In the case of the professional-managerial division, the managers are more inclined to type government jobs as routine and monotonous. Ratings on the chances government employment offers for a top-level job

TABLE 24-6. *Ratings of Evaluative Statements About Federal and Private Employment, Related to Major Work Activity of Business Engineers, Natural Scientists, and Social Scientists*

Statements	Engineers		Natural Scientists		Social Scientists	
	Profes-sional	Mana-gerial	Profes-sional	Mana-gerial	Profes-sional	Mana-gerial
"A young man of ability who starts work in a large private business corporation has a good chance of ending up in one of the top-level jobs"	6.9	7.7	6.8	7.2	6.7	7.3
"A young man of ability who starts work in the federal civil service has a good chance of ending up in one of the top-level jobs"	5.5	4.9	5.7	5.1	5.5	5.7
Difference: "Government" Minus "Business"	−1.4	−2.8	−1.1	−2.1	−1.2	−1.6
"For a young man of ability, his best chance for being *really successful* lies in working for a large private corporation"	6.1	6.9	5.0	6.0	5.3	6.1
"For a young man of ability, his best chance for being *really successful* lies in working for the federal government"	2.8	2.7	2.9	2.5	3.0	3.0
Difference: "Government" Minus "Business"	−3.3	−4.2	−2.1	−3.5	−2.3	−3.1
AVERAGE NUMBER ANSWERING	(50)	(40)	(45)	(37)	(47)	(22)

TABLE 24-7. *Ratings of General Civil Servants on Five Traits, Related to Age of Business Engineers, Natural Scientists, and Social Scientists*

Age Groups	Average Number Answering	"Honesty"	"Ability"	"Drive To Get Ahead"	"Interest in Serving the Public"	"How Well Respected They Are"
Engineers						
Under 40	25	6.8	5.1	4.5	4.8	5.0
40 and over	63	7.9	6.0	5.0	5.7	5.9
Natural Scientists						
Under 40	42	7.3	5.5	4.9	5.7	5.4
40 and over	39	7.7	6.2	5.4	6.3	6.5
Social Scientists						
Under 40	39	7.2	5.6	4.4	5.3	5.3
40 and over	30	7.8	5.4	5.0	5.8	5.7

and for being really successful vary little between the two types of respondents. But when these ratings are compared to ratings for large corporate employment, the managers clearly put government at more disadvantage than do the professionals (Table 24-6). The disparities are greatest for engineers and natural scientists, least for social scientists.

Turning to the image of federal employees, we find that in nearly every case the older respondents rate the civil servant higher on the five standard traits (Table 24-7). This relationship conforms to a similar tendency for older personnel to have a slightly more positive image of government as an employer, and to the patterns shown for other populations. Differences by age are greatest among engineers. Similarly, older respondents (especially among engineers) give slightly higher ratings to people in the top-level civil service positions. That these higher scores are not the result of any proclivity of older people to rate everybody higher is demonstrated by the mean scores on the ratings assigned people in the top-level positions in private industry: here there is either no difference by age or the *younger* respondents assign the higher ratings.

Natural and Social Scientists and Engineers in Government

The three special groups in government came under more extensive supplementary analysis than their counterparts in colleges and business for several reasons. To begin with, these elite groups represent one of the more pressing problems the government has in terms of recruitment and retention. Further, there are a greater number of relevant variables which we hypothesized would distinguish among them. At the same time we may expect some of the relationships found in the counterpart college and business groups to hold here also. Primary attention is devoted to the factors of age, grade level in the classified service, percentage of the work which is administrative, and past thoughts of leaving the government service.[1]

Occupational Ratings

For each of the three groups estimations of where they are on the occupational ladder at present vary moderately and consistently according to age, grade level, and (with the exception of the social scientists) whether their work consists of 50 percent or more of administrative duties (Table 24-8). Since these factors all reflect or are correlated with higher job standing and classification and are to some extent interrelated, the findings are not surprising. Again we have the recurrent pattern, with a sense of mobility in the past and expectations of advancement in the future being higher among younger respondents, those below GS 12, and (for the most part) those whose work consists of less than 50 percent administration.

While these findings may by now seem monotonously repetitive, they assume an importance in a comparative framework. If, for example, it turned out that the younger and less-advanced engineers, natural scientists, and social scientists in government employment visualized only slightly more past and future mobility than their older and higher level colleagues, or if this feeling of progress were markedly less than that enjoyed by the comparable groups in the academic and business worlds— this would be cause for concern on the government's part. Actually, it appears that the younger members of each federal group have much greater feelings of mobility than the older, and a comparison of age groups reveals that younger people in government service vary only slightly from those in colleges and business in terms of past progress and expectations about the future.

[1] The administrative percentage utilizes respondents' answers to the following: "About what percentage of your work is administrative work (e.g., supervising, planning, organizing, coordinating, reporting, delegating, etc.)? Would you say it is closest to: 100%, 75%, 50%, 25%, 0%?"

TABLE 24-8. *Ratings of Own Occupation at Present, 5 Years Ago, and 5 Years Hence, Related to Three Characteristics of Federal Engineers, Natural Scientists, and Social Scientists*

Age, Grade Level, and Percent of Administrative Work	Average Number Answering	Present Occupation	5 Years Ago	Difference: "Present" Minus "5 Years Ago"	5 Years from Now	Difference: "5 Years from Now" Minus "Present"
Age						
Engineers						
Under 40	49	7.3	5.7	+1.6	8.4	+1.1
40 and over	41	8.0	7.0	+1.0	8.5	+ .5
Natural scientists						
Under 40	42	7.8	5.7	+2.1	8.8	+1.0
40 and over	44	8.0	7.2	+ .8	8.6	+ .6
Social scientists						
Under 40	31	7.3	5.3	+2.0	8.8	+1.5
40 and over	54	8.0	7.1	+ .9	8.8	+ .8
Grade Level						
Engineers						
Below GS 12	31	7.2	5.2	+2.0	8.4	+1.2
GS 12 and above	59	7.9	6.8	+1.1	8.5	+ .6
Natural scientists						
Below GS 12	34	7.5	5.2	+2.3	8.7	+1.2
GS 12 and above	51	8.2	7.2	+1.0	8.7	+ .5
Social scientsts						
Below GS 12	23	7.5	5.5	+2.0	8.9	+1.4
GS 12 and above	62	7.8	6.8	+1.0	8.8	+1.0
Percent of Administrative Work						
Engineers						
Under 50%	32	7.4	6.2	+1.2	8.5	+1.1
50% or more	58	7.7	6.6	+1.1	8.4	+ .7
Natural scientists						
Under 50%	61	7.7	6.0	+1.7	8.6	+ .9
50% or more	25	8.5	7.7	+ .8	8.9	+ .4
Social scientists						
Under 50%	38	7.8	6.1	+1.7	8.8	+1.0
50% or more	47	7.6	6.8	+ .8	8.8	+1.2

In general, these respondents in scientific and engineering positions in the government consider that doing the same kind of work outside the government would place them only slightly lower on the occupational ladder (from −0.1 for the engineers to −0.5 for the natural scientists) than where they locate their present occupation. Among the natural and social scientists, older age, higher grade level, and longer government service are slightly related to higher negative net differences on the comparison; for engineers the differences are almost imperceptible.

According to whether respondents have considered leaving government service, there is no meaningful variation except among the social scientists: those who never thought of leaving and those who considered it over five years ago see the difference between the present occupation and the same occupation outside the government as −0.5 and −0.4. But among those who more recently considered departing, the net score changes to +0.4; in other words, they see outside employment as somewhat better than their present government employment. Hence these particular social scientists resemble their counterparts among federal administrators, who also rated outside employment higher (Chapter 23).

The breakdowns by age, grade level, length of employment, and percentage of administrative work also yield little intragroup variation when the respondents are asked to speculate on what their families would think of a change to a nonfederal employer. A noticeable difference does emerge, however, when the responses are classified according to past considerations of leaving government:

Thought of Leaving	N	Up the Ladder	Down the Ladder	No Difference
Engineers				
Within last 5 years	(24)	46%	12%	42%
Over 5 years ago	(25)	16	24	60
Never	(45)	27	9	64
Natural Scientists				
Within last 5 years	(22)	46	9	46
Over 5 years ago	(23)	52	22	26
Never	(44)	25	30	46
Social Scientists				
Within last 5 years	(21)	33	24	43
Over 5 years ago	(19)	21	42	37
Never	(45)	22	22	56

Although the small number of cases limits the extent of generalization, it is clear for all three groupings that those who had thought of leaving in the more recent past are far more likely to respond "up the ladder" than those who had never thought of it.

An examination of the mean ratings given the appeal of working for

TABLE 24-9. *Ratings of Occupational Appeal of the Federal Government vs. Large Private Business, Related to Three Characteristics of Federal Engineers, Natural Scientists, and Social Scientists*

Characteristics	Average Number Answering	"All things considered, working for a large private business appeals to me"	"All things considered, working for the federal government appeals to me"	Difference: "Government" Minus "Business"
Age				
Engineers				
Under 40	56	5.4	7.9	+2.5
40 and over	42	5.1	8.3	+3.2
Natural scientists				
Under 40	44	4.3	8.4	+4.1
40 and over	46	4.0	8.3	+4.3
Social scientists				
Under 40	33	4.8	7.9	+3.1
40 and over	57	4.0	8.6	+4.6
Grade Level				
Engineers				
Below GS 12	38	5.4	7.7	+2.3
GS 12 and above	60	5.2	8.4	+3.2
Natural scientists				
Below GS 12	38	4.3	8.3	+4.0
GS 12 and above	53	4.0	8.4	+4.4
Social scientists				
Below GS 12	24	4.8	8.0	+3.2
GS 12 and above	66	4.1	8.5	+4.4
Percent of Administrative Work				
Engineers				
Under 50%	37	5.8	7.8	+2.0
50% or more	61	5.0	8.2	+3.2
Natural scientists				
Under 50%	66	4.0	8.3	+4.3
50% or more	25	4.4	8.3	+3.9
Social scientists				
Under 50%	41	3.9	8.3	+4.4
50% or more	49	4.6	8.4	+3.8

the government or for a large private business highlights anew some moderate differences among such relatively homogenous groups as these (Table 24-9). According to age, the younger respondents agree slightly more than older ones that working for a large business appeals to them. With the exception of the natural scientists, the findings are reversed concerning the appeal of government employment, for there the older persons render the higher scores. Comparing the two sets of scores shows that the older respondents in all three groups give government a greater positive advantage than do the younger, but the scores vary from the slight 0.2 point difference found among younger and older natural scientists to the substantial 1.5 point difference among comparable social scientists. The above pattern also holds according to a break by grade level, as shown in Table 24-9.

The results from the analysis by percentage of administrative work yield a different picture, however. In terms of the difference scores, we see from Table 24-9 that the comparative advantage of federal appeal is considerably higher among "administrator" engineers than among the other engineers. The reverse is true for the natural and social scientists; the respondents doing less than 50 percent administrative work give government the better net score. To sum up, we may say that among federal engineers older age, higher grade levels, and doing mainly administrative work are all positively related to more advantageous scores for the relative appeal of federal work. Among social scientists and natural scientists the same pattern holds true by age and grade level, but it is particularly strong for social scientists and noticeably slight for natural scientists.

Ratings on the appeal items are also related to previous thoughts of leaving the government:

Thought of Leaving	N	"All things considered, working for a large private business appeals to me"	"All things considered, working for the federal government appeals to me"	Difference: "Government" Minus "Business"
Engineers				
Within last 5 years	(25)	5.8	8.2	+2.4
Over 5 years ago	(25)	5.3	8.2	+2.9
Never	(48)	5.1	8.0	+2.9
Natural Scientists				
Within last 5 years	(22)	4.8	8.4	+3.6
Over 5 years ago	(24)	3.8	8.6	+4.8
Never	(44)	3.9	8.1	+4.2
Social Scientists				
Within last 5 years	(21)	5.5	7.7	+2.2
Over 5 years ago	(21)	4.0	8.4	+4.4
Never	(47)	4.0	8.6	+4.6

Respondents who have pondered leaving recently rate the appeal of business employment higher than those who never considered leaving or considered it over five years ago. For the engineers and natural scientists there exists only a small internal difference in the scores assigned the appeal of government, but among the social scientists, those who recently considered leaving rate government's appeal noticeably lower. What stands out when the business and government appeal ratings are studied together is that in all three of the special groups the employees who most recently thought of leaving give the government lower net scores than do the other two categories. Most acute in their variations are the social scientists, while the engineers are more nearly alike. The data definitely imply that recent thoughts of leaving have left a pull toward outside employment which is still strong enough to lower the relative appeal of government for these respondents.

The respondents were also asked whether they presently planned to remain with the government or if they thought they might leave. We saw earlier (Chapter 18) that the engineers and the natural and social scientists are less definite than the general federal employees and the federal executives about continuing with the government. A likely hypothesis would be that the longer a person has been with the government the more inclined he is to stay there—and this proved to be the case for the general federal employees and the excutives.

To test this notion for the three special groups, and to show the magnitudes involved, we divided our scientific and engineering samples into those who have been with the government (1) under ten years and (2) ten years and over. The proportions involved are as follows:

Length of Government Employment	N	Plan To Continue	Plan To Leave	Don't Know
Engineers				
Under 10 years	(49)	55%	26%	18%
10 years and over	(50)	90	4	6
Natural Scientists				
Under 10 years	(41)	73	15	12
10 years and over	(51)	92	6	2
Social Scientists				
Under 10 years	(37)	62	32	5
10 years and over	(53)	91	8	2

Because of the relatively small number of cases involved, we do not emphasize the demonstrated differences. But these percentages would seem to be a sure sign that the longer a person has been a government employee the more likely he is to continue in that capacity, and the less likely to think of leaving or to feel undecided (represented by the "don't know" column).

If the hypothesis holds true, we would expect that, among those planning to stay, the certainty of this intention would be greater among the longer-employed personnel. This, too, is borne out by the data.

Length of Government Employment	N	Certainty of Continuing: Very Sure	Fairly Sure	Not Sure
Engineers				
Under 10 years	(27)	44%	48%	7%
10 years and over	(45)	62	36	2
Natural Scientists				
Under 10 years	(30)	60	40	0
10 years and over	(47)	77	19	4
Social Scientists				
Under 10 years	(23)	39	56	4
10 years and over	(48)	71	29	0

Those with ten years or more of government service have higher proportions who are "very sure" of staying, while those with less than ten years show more only "fairly sure" replies. It is patent that present plans—and the surety of them—to remain with the government are related to the length of government employment. For analytical purposes, we set the dividing line at ten years, although the most critical period probably comes somewhere before this mark. At any rate, there seems to be little question that many engineers, natural scientists, and social scientists are by no means committed to government employment at or before the ten-year point; after that point, the odds seem high on retaining these specialists.

Occupational Values

Like their counterparts in colleges and business, the engineers and scientists in government vary little among themselves in regard to occupational values. Nevertheless, there are nuances of relationships worth singling out.

Dividing the respondents according to those under 40 and those 40 and over, we find that the engineers and natural scientists are virtually indistinguishable in the mean ratings they assign the scale-sort items referring to occupational values. But among the social scientists some of the usual associations between age and values are found, although the differences are not large: younger persons assign less emphasis to work as a way of serving God, to doing your best even if you don't like the work, and to the importance of doing work which will help other people. They also score somewhat higher on having an opportunity to get to the top of an occupation, doing better than the next person, and believing that if a person doesn't want to work hard it's his own business.

The associations by length of employment prove to be more consistent and numerous. Engineers and social scientists with the government less than ten years attach more importance to such values and perspectives as wanting to do work without interference; being able to direct the work of others; believing that success comes mainly from hard work (this is a departure from the usual relationship obtained according to *age*); and maintaining that not wanting to work hard is a person's own business. Natural scientists present a different ordering. Those with the government less than ten years give less emphasis to statements indicating that work is a way of serving God and of developing character; that it is important to do better than the next person; that work is the most important part of a person's life; that opportunity is more important than security; and that they would like to be able to direct the work of others.

The different patterning of emphasis between the engineers and social scientists on one hand and the natural scientists on the other runs through several of the breakdowns carried out. Due to the limited sample size we cannot rely too much on these differences. There is, however, some indication that younger, less-experienced, and lower-ranking natural scientists in government depart from their older, more-experienced, and higher-ranking fellows in a fashion that is not seen among the engineers and social scientists. Such variances were not common among the academic or business natural scientists.

Other relationships in the patterning of occupational values were explored. Differences according to whether the respondents are under GS 12 or at and above that grade level are rare, and only slightly more frequent according to percentage of administrative work. The most important finding according to considerations of leaving government service is that those who have thought of departure within the past five years attach somewhat higher importance to opportunity rather than security, and believe more in doing a better job than the next person.

Despite the variations alluded to above, it is clear that on the great bulk of items related to the values of and attitudes toward work there is a paucity of distinctions within each of the three federal subpopulations on the basis of the analysis performed. For such values as challenge in the job, self-development, helping other people, gaining the respect of others, getting recognition for one's own work, seeing the results of one's work, and the more material aspects of work, the picture is monolithic. The variations become apparent primarily in regard to items involving the ethical approach to the work world and some aspects of self-determination, but even here they are not large.

Image of the Government As an Employer and Image of Federal Employees

The responses of the three special groupings to the scale-sort items dealing with the federal government and federal employees show few subvariations. Surprisingly, a respondent's thoughts of leaving the government, either recently or longer ago, bear little relationship to his appraisal of government as an employer. But there are some differences by age, length of service, and grade level. A slight to moderate tendency exists among engineers and social scientists for those who are younger, those who have been in federal service a shorter length of time, and those who occupy a lower GS level to see the government less favorably than their opposites. This is seen especially when the absolute ratings for government and private business are compared.

The largest such variations occur among the engineers (Table 24-10). Taken together with other data about engineers, they add further weight to the notion that the engineering population, especially the younger group, is less wedded to government employment than are the other federal populations studied. The natural scientists, continuing the pattern noted above in the section on occupational values, differ from the engineers and social scientists in terms of the breakdowns applied. In this instance, for example, natural scientists show almost no difference according to age, length of employment, and grade level. But, for what few differences there are, it is actually the younger, less-experienced, and lower-grade personnel who rate government employment *higher,* both absolutely and comparatively. Again we caution that the small samples preclude making general statements with surety, but at the least there is the suggestion that the newer crop of natural scientists are more positive about federal employment, especially when these data are related to occupational satisfaction findings, than are comparable engineers and social scientists.

TABLE 24-10. *Ratings of Evaluative Statements About Federal and Private Employment, Related to Three Characteristics of Federal Engineers*

Statements	Age		Years of Government Employment		Federal Grade Level	
	Under 40	40 and Over	Under 10	10 and Over	Under GS 12	GS 12 and Over
"A young man of ability who starts work in the federal civil service has a good chance of ending up in one of the top-level jobs"	6.4	6.5	6.3	6.6	5.9	6.8
"A young man of ability who starts work in a large private business has a good chance of ending up in one of the top-level jobs"	6.6	6.1	6.7	6.2	7.3	5.9
Difference: "Government" Minus "Business"	−.2	+.4	−.4	+.4	−1.4	+.9
'For a young man of ability, his best chance for being *really successful* lies in working for the federal government"	3.8	4.3	3.9	4.2	4.1	4.0
"For a young man of ability, his best chance for being *really successful* lies in working for a large private business corporation"	4.7	4.8	4.8	4.6	5.1	4.5
Difference: "Government" Minus "Business"	−.9	−.5	−.9	−.4	−1.0	−.5
AVERAGE NUMBER ANSWERING	(56)	(42)	(49)	(49)	(38)	(60)

The image of government employees accords more or less with the depiction of government as an employer. Engineers and social scientists show a sameness by age level in rating general civil servants on ability, honesty, interest in serving the public, how well respected they are, and on drive to get ahead, with the older respondents giving slightly higher scores than the younger. Again, however, the younger natural scientists return slightly but consistently higher ratings than the older ones do. Ratings of top-level civil servants on these five characteristics are virtually identical by age break for all three groups.

A pattern similar to that found by age holds for length of government employment. While the engineers and social scientists with longer service give slightly higher ratings to the general civil servants, the opposite tends to be true among natural scientists. The differences are not large; they are, however, regular and in agreement with the general pattern for the sample of natural scientists. For all three groups, evaluations of the top-level civil service people show no perceptible patterns of variation.

Further attesting to the homogeneity of opinion among these groups are the analyses according to grade level and proportion of administrative work; differences in employee images for all three groupings are exceedingly meager and irregular by both measures. A final null association concerns past thoughts of leaving the federal service. The hypothesis might be that that who recently considered leaving would rate civil servants lower than would those who considered it more than five years ago or never. Actually, contrary to the pattern often seen before, the responses indicate no consistent or large variations by this classification.

APPENDIXES

I. Occupational Values and American Society

Early Views of Occupational Values

SOME OF THE EARLIEST INSIGHTS into Americans' views of their work came from perceptive foreign visitors to the United States. Not all of them liked what they saw. Charles Dickens, after his first visit to the United States in 1842, wrote scornfully of the "national love of trade":

> The love of trade is assigned as a reason for that comfortless custom, so very prevalent in country towns, of married persons living in hotels, having no fireside of their own, and seldom meeting from early morning until late at night, but at the hasty public meals. The love of trade is a reason why the literature of America is to remain for ever unprotected: "For we are a trading people, and don't care for poetry:" though we *do*, by the way, profess to be very proud of our poets: while healthful amusements, cheerful means of recreation, and wholesome fancies, must fade before the stern utilitarian joys of trade.[1]

A number of other critics were repelled by what they regarded as the excessive commercialism of American life, but one aspect of the early American attitude toward work was beyond dispute. At the time of which Dickens wrote, the gospel of hard work held sway in the United States; except in the ante-bellum South, there were no notions of work as a badge of dishonor, something belonging to a lower caste while the elite cultivated the mind or the graces of living. Hard work was set forward as the prime economic virtue, not only by the successful, or the soon to be successful, bourgeois but also, as Max Lerner has pointed out, in the great folk myths of America. The stories of Paul Bunyan and Mike Fink, of Casey Jones and John Henry are all myths of mighty workers and their prowess.

[1] Charles Dickens, *American Notes and Pictures from Italy* (Oxford University Press, 1957), p. 246.

Freshly wrested from the frontier wilderness, the American land was a living reminder of the relation between work and survival; and as America grew in wealth it was a reminder also of the relation of work to its immediate rewards."[2]

Attention was also drawn to the nation's work ethic by American men of letters who turned critical eyes on certain kinds of occupations that began to flourish in the nation after the Civil War.

Occupational Prestige Studies

As technological innovation gradually transformed the relationship of the worker to the machine and to his job, systematic studies of selected aspects of American occupational values began to appear. Attempts to measure the prestige enjoyed by various occupations were among the first such investigations. In 1925, George S. Counts asked a group of students to rank some 45 occupations in terms of how well regarded they were.[3] There followed a whole series of studies refining Counts' methods and elaborating his basic findings: that in the United States there is a fairly widely agreed hierarchy of occupational prestige, with occupations such as physician and Supreme Court Justice ranked at the top, policemen and railroad conductors enjoying an intermediate prestige, and jobs such as street sweeper and janitor at the bottom.[4]

In recent years, evidence has accumulated that this hierarchy prevails in other economically developed countries as well—a finding that stemmed from analysis of the prestige enjoyed by various occupations in several different industrial societies. Alex Inkeles, the author of one such study, has declared:

> The scattered data in hand suggest that there are definitely some common values about the occupational realm shared not only within particular countries but in all modern, large-scale, more or less industrial societies, without much differentiation in the population by occupational group. Inkeles and Rossi located and analyzed the relative standing of lists of occupations in six industrial countries. To an extraordinary degree the occupa-

[2] Max Lerner, *America as a Civilization* (Simon and Schuster, 1957), p. 238.
[3] George S. Counts, "The Social Status of Occupations: A Problem in Vocational Guidance," *School Review*, Vol. 33, (January 1925), pp. 16-27.
[4] See, for example, Maethel E. Deeg and Donald G. Paterson, "Changes in Social Status of Occupations," *Occupations*, Vol. 25, (January 1947), pp. 205-208; Paul K. Hatt, "Occupation and Social Stratification," *American Journal of Sociology*, Vol. 55, (May 1950), pp. 533-543; National Opinion Research Center, "Jobs and Occupations: A Popular Evaluation," in Reinhard Bendix and Seymour M. Lipset, eds., *Class, Status and Power: A Reader in Social Stratifications* (Free Press, 1953), pp. 411-426; Richard L. Simpson and Ida H. Simpson, "Correlates and Estimation of Occupational Prestige," *American Journal of Sociology*, Vol. 66 (September 1960) pp. 135-140; and Mapheus Smith, "An Empirical Scale of Prestige Status of Occupations," *American Sociological Review*, Vol. 8 (April 1943) pp. 185-192.

tions were ranked in the same order. More important for us, they found very little variation in the evaluation of these occupations from one subgroup of the population to another. In other words, whether a worker or a professor does the rating, both place the doctor, lawyer, and engineer very near the top of the list, the ordinary worker about two-thirds of the way down, and the shoe-shine boy or garbage man at the bottom. This seems to be true for all countries, although there are some interesting variations which cannot be gone into here.[5]

Studies of Employee Productivity, Morale, and Job Satisfaction

Studies made in the United States of employees' attitudes and behavior on the job (many of which were motivated by an interest in finding ways to increase worker productivity) provide another source of information about occupational values. From Frederick W. Taylor's early time-and-motion studies to the most recent work of Elton Mayo, the American concern with "scientific management" and "human relations in industry" has been among the nation's most distinctive contributions to the art of management.

In the famous experiments at the Western Electric Company's Hawthorne plant, Mayo and his associates made the extremely important finding that the interest shown by the investigators in the workers and their jobs far outweighed the importance of externally introduced changes in the work environment as a stimulus to productivity. They also suggested that a precondition for this increase in productivity may have been the opportunity given the employees to participate in decisions affecting their own working conditions.[6] In later studies conducted under Mayo's guidance, the emphasis of the analysis shifted

---

[5] Alex Inkeles, "Industrial Man: The Relation of Status to Experience, Perception, and Value," *American Journal of Sociology*, Vol. 66, (July 1960), p. 8. The article cited in the quotation is: Alex Inkeles and Peter H. Rossi, "National Comparisons of Occupational Prestige," *American Journal of Sociology*, Vol. 61 (January 1956), pp. 329-339.

[6] The Hawthorne experiments are summarized in F. J. Roethlisberger and W. J. Dickson, *Management and the Worker* (Harvard University, Graduate School of Business Administration, 1934). See also Elton Mayo, *The Human Problems of an Industrial Civilization* (Macmillan, 1933), and F. J. Roethlisberger, *Management and Morale* (Harvard University Press, 1942).

In one of the Hawthorne experiments—that in the bank wiring room—there was no increase in productivity, despite the same investigator interest in the work and the employees. Though some have disputed their viewpoint, Conrad Arensberg and others have suggested that this was because the bank wiring room operated *inside* the ordinary channels of supervision and management, whereas the employees in the other studies, as part of the experimental procedure, helped make the decisions about their own working conditions. For a penetrating study of the whole problem, see Daniel Bell, *Work and Its Discontent* (Beacon Press, 1956).

from the individual to the group. These investigations pointed up the importance of group norms and standards as determinants of attitudes and behavior on the job.[7]

The work of this "human relations in industry" school was soon supplemented and expanded by other studies of employee morale on the job. Most of these have been based on interviews in a particular plant, business firm, or agency. The variety of approaches that can be taken are reflected in the diversity of their findings: some have related the job satisfaction of a firm's employees to employee turnover;[8] others have attempted to identify the factors that contribute to high or low morale;[9] still others have tried to determine what type of person likes or dislikes his job.[10]

Another kind of inquiry has involved comprehensive examination of a single factor felt to be important in motivating people on the job. Whole books have been written about the role of money, both in attracting competent personnel and in stimulating them to perform more effectively. There have also been studies of the effect of general working conditions and of other incentives on employee morale and productivity.[11]

Choosing an Occupation

The way in which people choose their occupation has concerned a number of researchers. In one such study the jobs selected by Missouri high school graduates in the 1920's were compared with the occupational choices made by graduates of similar schools in 1939-40. The major finding was the marked drop in the proportion of high school graduates going into teaching or farming, with a pronounced shift toward clerical, professional, and other forms of

---

[7] Elton Mayo, *The Social Problems of an Industrial Civilization* (Routledge and Kegan Paul, 1949), and A. Zaleznik, C. R. Christensen, and F. J. Roethlisberger, *The Motivation, Productivity, and Satisfaction of Workers* (Harvard University, Graduate School of Business Administration, 1958).

[8] Ian C. Ross and Alvan Zander, "Need Satisfactions and Employee Turnover," *Personnel Psychology*, Vol. 10 (Autumn 1957), pp. 327-338.

[9] Mason Haire and Josephine S. Gottsdanker, "Factors Influencing Industrial Morale," *Personnel*, Vol. 27 (May 1951), pp. 445-454.

[10] Remsen J. Cole, "A Survey of Employee Attitudes," *Public Opinion Quarterly*, Vol. 4 (September 1940) pp. 497-506. For a sampling of other job satisfaction studies, see Frederick Herzberg, Bernard Mausner, Richard O. Peterson, and Dora F. Capwell, *Job Attitudes: Review of Research and Opinion* (Psychological Service of Pittsburgh, 1957).

[11] See Robert B. Fetter and Donald C. Johnson, *Compensation and Incentives for Industrial Executives* (Indiana University Press, 1952); John W. Riegel, *Administration of Salaries and Intangible Rewards for Engineers and Scientists* (Bureau of Industrial Relations, University of Michigan, 1958); George A. Peters and Max Lees, "Better Incentives for Scientific Personnel," *Personnel*, Vol. 34 (January-February 1958), pp. 59-62.

white-collar employment.[12] Another study compared the occupations college students said they intended to enter with the occupations in which they were actually engaged a number of years later. For the college students studied, the correlation between the jobs they intended to enter and the jobs they actually obtained was substantial.[13]

Probably the most comprehensive investigation of the way people choose an occupation has been made by Eli Ginzberg and his associates. This study, a collaborative effort involving an economist, a sociologist, a psychologist, and a psychiatrist, sought to define the successive stages by which an individual decides upon his eventual job. The authors made the presuppositions underlying their investigation clear:

> We did not find much merit either in the psychoanalytic formulation, which holds that one's occupational choice is determined by early unconscious needs, or in the position of the environmentalists, who hold that the key to the problem is in "such commonplace things as the nature of the jobs available in the community." The psychiatrists explain too much, too simply; the environmentalists explain too little, too patently. . . . Our basic assumption was that an individual reaches his ultimate decision, not at any single moment in time, but through a series of decisions over a period of many years; the cumulative impact is the determining factor.[14]

Ginzberg identified three distinct stages through which the individual passes in choosing an occupation. For given individuals, to be sure, there are important variations in behavior within this general framework. The different times at which different children come to a definitive choice is a case in point. Some individuals exhibit an extraordinary singleness of purpose at a very young age. Their special talents come to the surface early; they soon feel certain what they want to do; and they carry out this preference. Other individuals, by contrast, have broad and ill-defined areas of interest; for them the eventual choice of an occupation is a much slower process.

But whether the final decision is made early or late, the cumulative effect of the earlier decisions made at each stage in an individual's development gradually narrows his actual freedom of choice. As Ginzberg and his associates put it:

> . . . occupational choice is a process; the process is largely irreversible; compromise is an essential aspect of every choice. . . . The second element of our theory, the irreversibility of the choice process, grows out of the reality pressures which introduce major obstacles to alterations in plans. A student in the second year of medical school will not easily decide to

[12] C. T. Pihlblad and C. L. Gregory, "Changing Patterns in Occupational Choice," *Journal of Teacher Education*, Vol. 6 (December 1955), pp. 286-292.

[13] Edward K. Strong, Jr., "Validity of Occupational Choice," *Educational and Psychological Measurement*, Vol. 13 (Spring 1953), pp. 110-121.

[14] Eli Ginzberg, "Toward a Theory of Occupational Choice," *Occupations*, Vol. 30 (April 1952), pp. 491-494. The quotation is from p. 492.

change his career plans. In addition, there are serious emotional barriers to a shift in plans because such a shift can so easily take on the quality of failure and present a threat to self-esteem. . . . But in seeking an appropriate choice, [an individual] must weigh his opportunities and the limitations of the environment, and assess the extent to which they will contribute to or detract from his securing a maximum degree of satisfaction in work and life.[15]

Surveys by Business Firms and Commercial Polling Organizations

Some of the most revealing analyses of occupational values probably reside in the file cases of leading American corporations. Such studies, based on social survey data, are frequently undertaken either by the firm itself or by a commercial research organization, to determine what is needed in the corporation's "public image" in order to sell the firm's stock, to advertise its products, and to attract high quality personnel to the corporation's staff. The results are usually not made available to the general public. If they were, they would provide revealing insights into not only the occupational values of the nation's future business executives but also the attitudes toward work of the firms' other employees.[16]

Such surveys were made possible by the existence of public opinion polling organizations in the United States, a development of the last thirty years that ranks among the nation's chief contributions to the social sciences. By the mid 1930's, several major organizations of this kind were functioning, and it was not long before they began to ask questions that probed into the public's occupational preferences. In 1948, for instance, a sample of young men between 18 and 25 were asked: "What are you planning for a career?" The answers revealed that the group as a whole had a wide variety of occupational plans. The responses ranged from the 44 percent who wanted a business career and the 21 percent preferring one of the professions, to the 4 percent planning government or social work and the 3 percent planning a career in the armed forces.[17]

[15] *Ibid.*, pp. 492-493.
[16] For samples of studies that bear on corporation recruitment programs, see Clifford E. Jurgensen, "What Job Applicants Look for in a Company," *Personnel Psychology*, Vol. 1 (Winter, 1948), pp. 433-445, and "Attracting Future Executives: What Bait Are You Using?" *Dun's Review and Modern Industry*, Vol. 70 (September 1957), pp. 51-53.
[17] Roper Fortune Survey #71 (October 1948). Data for this citation and those that follow (in footnotes 18-22) obtained from the Roper Public Opinion Research Center, Williamstown, Mass.

In a 1947 survey, a cross-section of Americans were given a list of seven notable occupations and asked to indicate their preference. The answers to the question, "Assuming you had the ability and that you had your choice of any of these jobs—which one would you prefer?" make interesting reading. The desire to be "a big basketball star" led the desire to be a "United States senator" 21 percent to 11 percent; becoming the "president of a large company" outranked being "a movie star" by 28 percent to 11 percent.[18] This question may have seemed unrealistic to many of the respondents, but other such surveys have had a more practical orientation. A sample of women between 20 and 35, for example, was asked in 1943: "If you had your choice, what kind of work would you like to do?" Answers ranged from the 22 percent for "office work" and the 11 percent for "factory work," to the 8, 6, and 2 percent for nursing, teaching, and social work, respectively.[19]

Most of the questions used in polling surveys have been asked only once. In a few cases, however, the same question has been repeated in a later survey, thus providing trend data that point up actual changes in public attitudes over time. A 1937 survey, conducted under the lingering shadow of the Great Depression, sought to measure people's optimism or pessimism about their chances for self-advancement: "Do you think the opportunities for getting ahead today are greater, or not so great as they were in your father's day?" The answers showed that after years of sustained mass unemployment many people were rejecting the pervasive optimism of the American dream. Although 41 percent of the men interviewed said that their chances were greater than those of their fathers, 40 percent said they were not so great.[20] The response constituted one of the most pessimistic poll results concerning prospects for self-advancement and progress ever obtained in the United States.

This question was not repeated, but in 1939 another question, similarly designed to measure the public's confidence or pessimism, was used: "Do you think your opportunities to succeed are better than, or not as good as, those your father had?" This question was asked again in 1946. The results (Table A-1) suggest that as memories of the depression receded American men had grown markedly more optimistic about their chances to get ahead. (Apparently, not even the Great Depression destroyed the conviction of the American woman that things had improved for her during the last generation. On all three surveys, women were considerably more likely than men to feel that their opportunities to get ahead were better than in their father's day.)

Results obtained by the commercial polling organizations have been useful and informative. They constitute a basic fund of knowledge on the distribution

[18] Gallup Poll Survey #400 (July 1947).
[19] Roper Fortune Survey #35 (May, 1943).
[20] Gallup Poll Survey #95 (August, 1937).

TABLE A-1. *Percentage of American Men Who Felt Their Opportunities To Succeed Were Better Than, or Not As Good As, Those Their Fathers Had, 1939 and 1946.*[a]

Year Survey Taken	Number Interviewed	Per Cent Who Felt Opportunities Were:			No Answer; Don't Know; All Other Answers
		Better	Worse	Same	
1939	2,631	56%	24%	14%	6%
1946	1,755	70	13	13	4

[a] Data obtained in the Roper Fortune Survey #13, December 1939, and Roper Fortune Survey #56, September 1946. In both surveys the question was phrased, "Do you think your opportunities to succeed are better than, or not as good as, those your father had?"

of attitudes and values in the population, and provide data that can be used by those engaged in further studies of long-term trends in American society.

Nonetheless, the opportunity for assembling comparative trend data has yet to be adequately exploited. When a question is asked more than once by the same polling organization, it has often, on the second survey, been put to a sample of a different group in the population, a change that makes it impossible to compare the results of the two polls. When different polling organizations have asked the same question, the detailed breakdowns of the data obtained have frequently been based on different classification schemes. Sometimes an organization has changed its own breakdowns over the years. Moreover, a question designed to probe into the same general attitudes may have had its wording changed in a way that radically changes its meaning; even a modest change in wording can cause an enormous change in the public's response.

Two questions designed to probe into the public's concern with job security offer a case in point. In 1943, 1946, and 1948, a survey asked:

> Here are three different kinds of jobs. If you had your choice, which would you pick? A job which pays quite a low income, but which you were sure of keeping? A job which pays quite a good income but which you have a 50/50 chance of losing? A job which pays an extremely high income if you make the grade but in which you lose almost everything if you don't make the grade?

The responses suggested that the proportion of people who would prefer the low-paying job with extreme security declined between 1943 and 1948: in 1948, well under half of those interviewed opted for the most secure alternative.[21] Yet just six months later, in April 1949, when a question with a

[21] Roper Fortune Survey #35 (May, 1943); Roper Fortune Survey #56 (September 1946); and Roper Fortune Survey #71 (October 1948).

different wording was asked of a cross-section of people, the response was sharply different. The new question was phrased:

Some people would prefer a job which pays very well even though it may not be secure. Other people prefer a steady job even though it may not pay so much. Which would you prefer, a steady job or a better paying job?

To this query, 81 percent of those interviewed replied that they would prefer the steady job.[22]

In all likelihood, the dramatic shift in the answer stemmed not from any basic change in the public's attitude between 1948 and 1949 but from the change in the question wording. That the second question gave the interviewees only two alternatives probably had an especially important effect on their responses. Those who use poll data regularly would find nothing unusual in these results. Two different questions were asked, and two different responses were obtained. But if basic trend data that reveal actual changes in public attitudes are to be obtained, something more is required. Identically worded questions must be asked of samples of identical groups in the population, and the results must be analyzed in terms of identical breakdowns of the data. If these elements of comparability could be built into some of the operations of the major commercial polling organizations, the benefits to all those who have an interest in the analysis of long-term changes in the nation's social institutions would be substantial.

The use of differently worded questions to probe into the same general area of public attitudes has been extremely helpful, of course, in revealing nuances of sentiment on a particular issue and in highlighting the profound differences in the responses that can be given to differently worded questions. What is argued here, however, is that there is a need for a more frequent repetition of identically worded questions if actual changes in public attitudes over time are to be identified and analyzed.

Studies of the Variety and Distribution of Occupational Values

In recent years many studies have been made which point up the extraordinary variety and complexity of men's attitudes toward their work. Some of these have compared the distribution of occupational values among different groups in the American population. The attitudes of men and women toward their work have frequently been compared, as have the occupational values

[22] Gallup Poll Survey #441 (April 1949).

of the rich and the poor, the highly educated and the uneducated, and the old and the young.[23]

To cite one example, the question of whether the American tradition of wanting to get ahead is shared by low social status groups has been the subject of a lively debate. One group of researchers holds that it is not. A. B. Hollingshead has concluded that lower-class youngsters "have limited their horizons to the class horizon, and in the process they have unconsciously placed themselves in such a position that they will occupy the same levels as their parents."[24] Other investigators, however, contend, either explicitly or implicitly, that the low-status groups have adopted this tradition, and that the American dream of "getting ahead" is shared even by those now farthest from the top.[25]

In a 1947 survey that took a different tack, Elmo Roper explored some of the characteristics that American factory workers felt were important in a job. Special stress was laid on the provision of security for old age, but to this Roper added four other elements that counted for the workers: whether the job overworked them, whether merit was rewarded, whether there was a chance for advancement, and whether they found the job "interesting."[26] In an earlier poll, Roper queried a cross-section of people to determine the degree of interest they had in their jobs. The results showed two out of three (64.7 percent) finding them "really interesting," the rest either lukewarm or apathetic. A breakdown of the results found that men were more satisfied than women, whites more than Negroes, city workers more than those in the small towns and on farms, professional and executive people more than wage earners, and the prosperous more than the poor (87 and 48 percent).[27]

Other studies have explored in greater detail the full range of occupational values shared by members of a particular group in American society. Morris Rosenberg, for example, analyzed the relationship between college students' values and their occupational preferences. The college years, he pointed out,

[23] See, for example, Carl Dickinson, "The Relative Importance of Job Factors to College Graduates and to Employers," *Journal of College Placement*, Vol. 14 (October 1953), pp. 25-31; Nancy C. Morse and Robert S. Weiss, "The Function and Meaning of Work and the Job," *American Sociological Review*, Vol. 20 (April 1955), pp. 191-198; Waino W. Suojanen and G. C. Hoyt, "Differences in Motivation Among White-Collar Workers," *Personnel*, Vol. 34 (September-October 1957), pp. 26-31; John P. Troxell, "Elements in Job Satisfaction, A Study of Attitudes Among Different Occupational and Status Groups," *Personnel*, Vol. 31 (November 1954), pp. 199-205; Howard M. Vollmer and Jack A. Kinney, "Supervising Women is Different," *Personnel Journal*, Vol. 34 (December 1955), pp. 260-265.

[24] A. B. Hollingshead, *Elmtown's Youth* (Wiley, 1949), p. 285.

[25] LaMar T. Empey, "Social Class and Occupational Aspiration: A Comparison of Absolute and Relative Measurement," *American Sociological Review*, Vol. 21 (December 1956), p. 703.

[26] "The Fortune Survey," *Fortune*, May 1947, pp. 5-12, and June 1947, pp. 5-10.

[27] The results of this poll are summarized in Max Lerner, *op. cit.*, p. 246. Most of the data were reported in "The Fortune Survey," *Fortune*, January 1947, p. 10.

are a particularly good time to study the impact of values on the occupational selection process:

> At college, the student's ideas about work are still relatively undistorted by the special conditions of the job situation in which he will eventually find himself; it is therefore easier to observe the influence of certain abstract factors, such as values, attitudes, personality structure, and images, as they bear on the decision process.[28]

In another detailed examination, Robert Guest drew a vivid picture of the occupational values and job aspirations of workers in an automobile plant:

> Certain themes ran through the hundreds of qualitative remarks of these assembly line workers. The most prominent ones covered were aspirations for children, hopes for an independent business future, immediate desire to get out of the present line of work, no plans or aspirations for the future, and income and security of the present.
>
> Workers spoke at length about their children's future. In general the man on the assembly line wanted his children to get a better education, and to avoid factory work. Most of these comments were in the nature of vague hopes with little indication of specific planning.
>
> These comments reveal a persistent jockeying back and forth on the verbal level between wishful thinking and reality. The men yearned for the freedom which they thought a "little business of my own" would give, but they knew that to make the step would involve too much capital and not enough personal security.[29]

One thinks here of Eugene O'Neill's *The Iceman Cometh*, with its depiction of men haunted by a yawning gap between illusion and reality, and of their need for pipe dreams to bridge that gap.

General Studies of Occupational Values

Detailed studies of the work ethic of particular segments of the American population have been supplemented by works that generalize more broadly about the occupational values of major groups in American society. In one of the most widely read books of the 1950's, William H. Whyte described "the organization man."[30] And C. Wright Mills has written of the occupational values of what he termed the new American middle class—white-collar people on salary. The attitudes and values of this group, Mills contended, differ in a number of vital respects from those of the middle class of an earlier day. The

[28] Morris Rosenberg, *Occupations and Values* (Free Press, 1957), p. 4.
[29] Robert H. Guest, "Work Careers and Aspirations of Automobile Workers," *American Sociological Review*, Vol. 19 (April 1954), pp. 161-162.
[30] William H. Whyte, Jr., *The Organization Man* (Doubleday, 1957).

old middle-class entrepreneurs were in business for themselves, and this had a profound impact on their attitudes toward work. According to Mills, they retained the "secularized gospel of work as a compulsion," whereas the members of the new middle class of modern American society have not:

> To understand the significance of this gospel and its decline, we must understand the very spirit of twentieth-century America. That the historical work ethic of the old middle-class entrepeneurs has not deeply gripped the people of the new society is one of the most crucial psychological implications of the structural decline of the old middle classes. The new middle class, despite the old middle-class origin of many of its members, has never been deeply involved in the older work ethic, and on this point has been from the beginning non-bourgeois in mentality.[31]

One of the most penetrating general analyses of occupational values—drawn from interviews with a national cross-section of American men—appeared in *Americans View Their Mental Health*. The primary focus was on people's feeling of adjustment in their jobs, in terms of their satisfaction and feeling of adequacy and in terms of the frequency with which they encountered problems in the work situation. The authors drew a useful distinction between the ego-centered factors (such as interest in the work and opportunities for self-expression or responsibility) and the extrinsic factors (such as money, job security, and working conditions) cited as reasons for satisfaction and dissatisfaction on the job.

The authors found that a concern with ego gratification was much more common among people in high-status jobs than among those in lower-status jobs. The former were more involved in their work and had a higher degree of job satisfaction, for their positions usually enabled them to fulfill their ego-oriented values through their work. Occupants of low-status jobs tended to get much less self-fulfillment from their job, but they also asked less of their job to begin with. Consequently the lack of opportunities for self-fulfillment in the lower status jobs "is less often experienced as a problem than one might have expected it to be."[32]

Other scholars have attempted to pool and synthesize the available material on occupational values. Edward Gross's *Work and Society* is a good example of a work of this kind, as is Theodore Caplow's *The Sociology of Work*.[33] The logical extension of these studies of differences in occupational values among various groups within American society is to compare the occupational values of various groups in other societies as well. In recent years, steps have been taken in this direction.

[31] C. Wright Mills, *White Collar* (Oxford University Press, 1951), pp. 219-220.

[32] Gerald Gurin, Joseph Verloff, and Sheila Feld, *Americans View Their Mental Health* (Basic Books, 1960), p. 173.

[33] Edward Gross, *Work and Society* (Crowell, 1958); Theodore Caplow, *The Sociology of Work* (University of Minnesota Press, 1954).

In a paper of extraordinary interest, Alex Inkeles has suggested that the variations in occupational values found in American society can also be found, in more or less identical fashion, among different socioeconomic groups in several other industrially developed societies:

> From country to country, we observe a clear positive correlation between the over-all status of occupations and the experience of satisfaction in them. This seems to hold, as well, for the relation between satisfaction and the components of the job, such as the pay, but the evidence is thinner here. We may expect that the relationship will hold for other components, such as the prestige of the job and the autonomy or independence it affords. Job situation appears also to pattern many values germane to the occupation realm, such as the qualities most desired in the job and the image of a good or bad boss.[34]

This paper by Inkeles followed an earlier research project of his in which the relative prestige enjoyed by various occupations in different societies was analyzed; here, too, Inkeles found striking similarities in the distribution of occupational values throughout a number of different industrialized societies:

> These results suggest the possibility of developing a social psychology of industrial society with substantial predictive power. They also give us a firmer basis for assessing the possibility that as institutional patterns around the world become more homogeneous we may be moving toward a homogenized "world culture" at the level of individual opinion and value orientation.[35]

[34] Inkeles, *op. cit.* (see footnote 5 above), p. 12.

[35] To this statement, Inkeles added a cautionary note: "But many additional studies, particularly studies designed to meet the special methodological problems of cross-national comparison, must be undertaken before firm conclusions will be possible." See Inkeles, "Occupation as a Reference Group: Toward a Social Psychology of Industrial Society," abstract of a paper delivered before a panel of the American Association for Public Opinion Research, Proceedings of the Fourteenth Annual Conference, *Public Opinion Quarterly*, Vol. 23 (Fall 1959), p. 421.

II. Studies and Evaluations of the Federal Service

FROM 1789 TO 1964 the federal service has grown from a simple administrative machine that could be manned by a few hundred individuals to one of the largest and most complex public services in the world. During the same period the ways in which the federal service has been studied and evaluated have also undergone a radical change. Early appraisals of the role of the public servant in American society came mostly from two main sources. Again, it is to visitors from abroad who came for a firsthand look at the United States— such observant and articulate men as Alexis de Tocqueville, Charles Dickens, and James Bryce—that we owe some of our most perceptive insights into the nature of our public service in its formative years.[36] The other source consists of the comments and observations of Americans themselves—both those who had an intimate involvement in public affairs and those who did not. Their legacy, also, constitutes a rich fund of information upon which students of American administrative institutions have been able to draw.

Most of the contemporary documentary sources illuminate specific aspects of the role of the public servant, yet, taken together, they provide a basis for an evaluation of the early federal service. From some of these comments one can derive a vivid picture of the relative appeal of public service in comparison with other occupations in the early years of the Republic. To Alexander Hamilton, private employment was preferable to holding a public position. As he wrote to a relative in Scotland:

> Public office in this country has few attractions. The pecuniary emolument is so inconsiderable as to amount to a sacrifice to any man who can employ his time with advantage in any liberal profession. The opportunity of doing good, from the jealousy of power and the spirit of faction, is too small in any station to warrant a long continuance of private sacrifices. The enterprise of party had so far succeeded as materially to weaken the necessary influence and energy of the executive authority, and so far diminish the power of doing good in that department, as greatly to take away the motives which a virtuous man might have for making sacrifices. The pros-

[36] See Alexis de Tocqueville, *Democracy in America*, 2 vols. (Vintage Books, 1958); Charles Dickens, section dealing with the United States in *American Notes and Pictures from Italy* (Oxford University Press, 1957); and James Bryce, *The American Commonwealth*, 2 vols. (Macmillan, 1888). Dickens' *American Notes* first appeared in 1842; de Tocqueville's *Democracy in America* in 1835.

pect was even bad for gratifying in future the love of fame, if that passion was to be the spring of action.[37]

Other leading citizens of the day, however, took a more sanguine view of the rewards of public service. For some, the chief question was whether it was preferable to take an administrative post in the executive branch of the government or to seek elective office. On January 19, 1798, Representative Robert Goodloe Harper argued on the floor of the House for elective office, as reported in *Annals of Congress*:

> In some countries, indeed, office conferred power, and was therefore sought by ambitious men as a means of obtaining power. Office there gave patronage, authority, and influence, and was therefore eagerly pursued. But in this country, he said, the case was different. Offices here gave a scanty maintenance, much labor, and no patronage or influence, and, therefore, ambitious politicians did not desire them. That House was the place for such men to appear. There and there alone they had a conspicuous theater for the display of their talents; there and there alone could they acquire fame, popularity, and political enforcements; there and there alone could they make a strong impression on the country and the government, give way to their own opinions, and force their own system into activity. There, of course, they would desire to remain and not to undertake offices, which though respectable, were not brilliant, imposed much labor, but conferred neither splendor nor authority.[38]

More than a century later, El Bie K. Foltz described some of the advantages of federal employment in a vocational guide for people who might be considering a lower-level position in the federal service.

> Not only is tenure of office and income secure under the government during good behavior, but the services performed are surrounded with a dignity not seen in private life. The government employee has the added advantages of earning a comfortable living, congenial work, short hours, long vacation, ample provision against sickness, a chance to educate himself and his family and, most important of all, time to live. The worries and haste to succeed, common in commercial life, are entirely absent.[39]

Early in the nineteenth century, the government itself began making internal reviews of the national public service. Originating sometimes in the Executive branch and sometimes in Congress, these reviews covered a wide range of subjects; as the service grew in size and complexity, their number increased. As early as 1839, Secretary of the Navy James K. Paulding complained that "the great increase of public records and documents renders all reference to the past more embarrassing."[40]

In the late 1840's and the early 1850's several congressional discussions of

---

[37] Hamilton to —— Hamilton, May 2, 1797, quoted in Leonard D. White, *The Federalists*, p. 318.

[38] Quoted in White, *ibid.*, pp. 317-318.

[39] El Bie K. Foltz, *The Federal Civil Service as a Career* (Putnam's, 1909), p. 229.

[40] Quoted in White, *The Jacksonians*, pp. viii-ix.

governmental efficiency were held which led to the institution in 1853 of an examination requirement for appointment to clerical positions in Washington. Individual departments and agencies also conducted reviews of their own operations which produced analyses of the problems and activities of particular parts of the government. With the report in 1912 of the President's Commission on Economy and Efficiency in the Government Service, a series of more comprehensive analyses of the functioning of the federal service was begun. In 1937 came the report of the President's Committee on Administrative Management, and in 1949 and 1955 the Hoover Commission reports.

In examining the government's operations, both congressional investigators and members of the Executive branch have relied heavily on the testimony of experts—people who were or had been actively involved in the type of governmental activity under study, and also individuals in private organizations with experience and problems similar to those of the government. In recent years, however, as the search for expertise has widened, extensive use has also been made of professional consulting firms, research institutes, and university personnel. Thus, the hearings of the Jackson Subcommittee on National Policy Machinery in 1960 included testimony from such diverse sources as Eugene Wigner, professor of mathematical physics at Princeton University, Crawford Greenewalt, the president of Du Pont de Nemours and Company, Marion Folsom, formerly Secretary of the Department of Health, Education, and Welfare and at the time of the hearings a director and management adviser of the Eastman Kodak Company, and John J. Corson, then manager of the Washington office of McKinsey and Company, a management consulting firm.[41]

The writings and other statements of private individuals and groups with an interest in the improvement of the public service form another major source of information about the American federal service. During the agitation that led to the Pendleton Act in 1883 much of this literature was polemical. When President Garfield's assassin, Guiteau, was found to be a disappointed office seeker, the advocates of civil service reform seized upon the event to belabor the spoils system. A widely circulated cartoon in Puck pictured Guiteau brandishing a pistol and demanding, "An office or your life!" Shortly after Garfield died, Dorman B. Eaton, another of the reformers, declared:

> With marvellous promptness and unanimity, hardly less in foreign countries than among ourselves, the source and significance of Guiteau's acts have been found in our spoils system of administration. . . . From a thousand pulpits the great fact, with solemn admonition, has been proclaimed. On the myriad pages of our journals, of every section and class, the truth has been daily uttered in words of mingled anxiety, shame and detestation.[42]

[41] *Organizing for National Security,* Hearings Before the Subcommittee on National Policy Machinery of the Senate Committee on Government Operations, 86th Cong., 2d sess. (1960), Parts 2 and 3, pp. 237-544.

[42] Quoted in Paul Van Riper, *History of the United States Civil Service* (Row, Peterson, 1958), p. 89.

Once the Pendleton Act became law, the focus of the reformers shifted gradually from a concentration on the more blatant evils of the spoils system to a broader concern with the issues affecting the quality and performance of the public service. Today a whole series of publications, some the lineal descendants of the reformers' early tracts, provide an outlet for materials concerning the federal government. The National Civil Service League publishes its own pamphlet, *Good Government*, regularly, and a number of journals in the field of public administration, among them the *Public Personnel Review*, *Public Administration Review*, and *Personnel Administration*, have been established.

The preparation of statistical profiles of the federal work force represents another way in which the public service has been studied. Two such analyses, *The Executive Civil Service of the United States* and *Statistics of Employees*, published by the U.S. Census Bureau in 1904 and 1908, provide a wealth of data about the social composition of the federal bureaucracy, including breakdowns in terms of age, sex, marital status, veterans status, and a number of other variables. Modern counterparts of these are the two reports on the occupations of federal white-collar and blue-collar workers issued by the Employment Statistics Office of the U. S. Civil Service Commission in 1958 and 1959, which give detailed breakdowns of the distribution of different kinds of government occupations. The Commission now plans to maintain detailed information on the background, training, and current occupations of a 10 percent sample of all federal civilian employees. This project will provide the most reliable and useful information yet assembled on the character of the federal work force.

The first attempt to forecast the future manpower needs of the government as a whole appeared in a report completed by the Civil Service Commission in 1960.[43] This survey, which was based on a collection and analysis of anticipated needs reported by the various parts of the government, covered only selected types of scientific and technical manpower. More comprehensive estimates of future needs are currently underway, covering most of the kinds of positions the government will need to fill, and relating these projections to estimates of the number of people with the requisite skills who are likely to be available.

In recent years, a number of specialized studies of particular aspects of the federal service have been made by social scientists in and outside of government. Marver Bernstein, for example, has explored the nature of the federal executive's activities and the government's problems in obtaining and developing effective executives; Paul David and Ross Pollock have also looked into the problems involved in staffing the highest echelons of the federal public

[43] U. S. Civil Service Commission, "The Growing Demand for Scientific and Technical Manpower in the Federal Service" (pamphlet, October 1960).

service.[44] The examination by Reinhard Bendix of the social background of senior civil servants was a pioneering study of the groups in society from which America's top-level career administrators are drawn.[45]

The extensive research in the field of industrial psychology and sociology that has been carried out since World War II, although not primarily focused on public administration, has had an impact on government procedures. Studies concerning worker productivity, labor-management relations, the effects of automation, and interpersonal relations on the job have all had implications, not only for large-scale private organizations, but also for the agencies of government.[46]

Within the last generation, systematic attempts to probe basic attitudes toward government employment have also been made. Some of the studies have been focused on the morale of people currently in government work, others have been much broader in scope. For example, the attitudes of Americans regarding politics, politicians, and federal officeholders have been probed in a variety of public opinion polls, with equally varied results.

In a 1947 poll the National Opinion Research Center found that several specific governmental positions were ranked at or near the top of a list of 100 occupations or positions by a national sample of people who were asked to indicate "your own personal opinion of the general standing such a job has."[47] Among the positions on the list were U. S. Supreme Court Justice, state Governor, Cabinet member in the federal government, diplomat in the U. S. Foreign Service, mayor of a large city, and member of Congress.

The ratings made it clear that one who held this top-level kind of govern-

---

[44] Marver H. Bernstein, *The Job of the Federal Executive* (Brookings Institution, 1958); Paul T. David and Ross Pollock, *Executives for Government* (Brookings Institution, 1957).

[45] Reinhard Bendix, *Higher Civil Servants in American Society* (Boulder: University of Colorado Press, 1949).

[46] For examples of the vast number of studies dealing with these and related problems, see Daniel Katz, Nathan Maccoby, Gerald Gurin, and Lucretia G. Floor, *Productivity, Supervision and Morale Among Railroad Workers* (Survey Research Center, Institute for Social Research, University of Michigan, 1951); Daniel Katz, Nathan Maccoby, and Nancy C. Morse, *Productivity, Supervision and Morale in an Office Situation*, Part I (Survey Research Center, . . . University of Michigan, 1950); Nancy C. Morse, *Satisfaction in the White Collar Job* (Survey Research Center, . . . University of Michigan, 1953); Waino W. Suojanen and G. C. Hoyt, "Differences in Motivation Among White-Collar Workers," *Personnel*, Vol. 34 (September-October 1957), pp. 26-31; Raymond H. Van Zelst, "Worker Popularity and Job Satisfaction," *Personnel Psychology*, Vol. 4 (Winter 1951), pp. 405-412; Howard M. Vollmer and Jack A. Kinney, "Age, Education, and Job Satisfaction," *Personnel*, Vol. 32 (July 1955), pp. 38-43; A. Zaleznik, C. R. Christensen, and F. J. Roethlisberger, *The Motivation, Productivity, and Satisfaction of Workers* (Harvard University, Division of Research, Graduate School of Business Administration, 1958).

[47] National Opinion Research Center, "Jobs and Occupations: A Popular Evaluation," in Reinhard Bendix and Seymour Martin Lipset, eds., *Class, Status and Power: A Reader in Social Stratification* (Free Press 1953), pp. 411-426.

ment position enjoyed a reputation with the public that placed him near the pinnacle of prestige in American society. Yet the findings did not indicate how the public regarded the holders of lower-level political positions. And evidence that politics, as such, had a negative connotation for many Americans appeared to be forthcoming from a later survey which asked respondents whether they agreed with the statement that it was almost impossible for a man to stay honest if he went into politics. Some 48 percent of those interviewed said they agreed.[48]

Perhaps the most frequently cited question bearing on attitudes toward politics has been asked by the National Opinion Research Center and by Dr. Gallup's American Institute of Public Opinion. In 1943, a national cross-section was asked the following question: "If you had a son just getting out of school would you like to see him go into politics as a life's work?" In 1944, 1945, 1953, 1955, and 1962 a similar question was asked in five other surveys. As Table A-2 shows, on all six occasions only a relatively small minority said "yes" to the question (see page 658).

The studies and polls concerned with the politician have been paralleled by analyses of the public's attitudes toward the nonelective government service; undertaken by individual scholars, by organizations, and by the government, these have dealt both with the prestige of public employment and with more general attitudes toward government employment. The pioneering effort in this field was made by the University of Chicago's Leonard D. White.[49] His 1929 study focused on public attitudes toward the municipal public service, rather than the federal service, and only in Chicago. Even so, White's work is a landmark of enduring importance for research on the occupational appeal of all levels of government; it was the first systematic attempt to probe into the public's attitude toward government service by using social survey techniques, and it uncovered broad patterns of attitudes toward public employment which continue to prevail today.

Other studies followed the course White had charted. In 1954, Morris Janowitz and his associates examined the prestige of public employment in Detroit as a part of a larger study of attitudes toward government in a metropolitan community.[50] Meanwhile government itself had begun to undertake research in this area. In a 1947 report the President's Scientific Research Board

[48] The question was phrased: "It has been said that it is almost impossible for a man to stay honest if he goes into politics. Do you agree or disagree?" See William C. Mitchell, "The Ambivalent Social Status of the American Politician," *Western Political Quarterly*, Vol. 12 (September 1959), p. 690.

[49] Leonard D. White, *The Prestige Value of Public Employment in Chicago* (University of Chicago Press, 1929).

[50] Morris Janowitz, Deil Wright, and William Delany, *Public Administration and the Public—Perspectives toward Government in a Metropolitan Community* (Bureau of Government, Institute of Public Administration, University of Michigan, 1958).

TABLE A-2. *Percentage of Adult Americans Who Would and Who Would Not Like To See Their Son Go Into Politics As a Life's Work When He Gets Out of School, 1943–1962*[a]

Year Survey Taken	Would Like Their Son To Make Politics His Life's Work	Would Not Like Their Son To Make Politics His Life's Work	Don't Know; No Opinion; All Other Answers	Number Interviewed
1943	17%	71%	12%	2,560
1944	21	68	11	3,060
1945	24	65	11	1,258
1953	21	69	10	1,548
1955	27	60	13	1,274
1962	23	68	9	1,616

[a] The data in this table were obtained in the following surveys: National Opinion Research Center Survey #217, November 1943; The Gallup Survey #338, December 1944; National Opinion Research Center Survey #239B, November 1945; The Gallup Survey #516K, May 1953; The Gallup Survey #543, February 1955; and a Gallup Survey undertaken for the Brookings Institution in January 1962. The question used in the 1943 and 1945 surveys was phrased, "If you had a son just getting out of school, would you like to see him go into politics as a life's work?" In the other four surveys the question was phrased, "If you had a son, would you like to see him go into politics as a life's work when he gets out of school?"

explored the attitudes of scientists toward a career in government; a year later, the Personnel Policy Committee of the first Hoover Commission analyzed the views of college students concerning a career in the public service.[51]

The authors of these studies—particularly those viewing the occupational standing of the federal service from the standpoint of its impact on the government's recruiting programs—have frequently expressed dissatisfaction with the

[51] The President's Scientific Research Board, *Administration for Research*, Vol. 3: *Science and Public Policy*, A Report to the President by John R. Steelman, Chairman (1947); Commission on Organization of the Executive Branch of the Government, *Task Force Report on Federal Personnel*, Appendix A (1949).

For additional studies that examine various aspects of the occupational standing of the federal service, see The American Assembly, *The Federal Government Service: Its Character, Prestige, and Problems* (Graduate School of Business, Columbia University, 1954); Paul H. Appleby, "A Reappraisal of Federal Employment as a Career," *Public Administration Review*, Vol. 8 (Spring 1948); Lyle G. Belsley, "'Why Bureaucracy is Belittled," *Personnel Administration*, Vol. 9 (January 1947); George P. Bush, *Engineering Students and Federal Employment* (American University, 1951); W. Richard Lomax, "Prestige Values in Public Employment in the United States and Canada," *Personnel Administration*, Vol. 12 (January 1950); William C. Mitchell, "The Ambivalent Social Status of the American Politician," *Western Political Quarterly*, Vol. 12 (September 1959); National Civil Service League, "Survey of Business and Industry Executives with Government Administrative Experience" (mimeographed; National Civil Service League, 1952); John A. Perkins, "Staffing Democracy's Top Side," *Public Administration Review*, Vol. 17 (Winter 1957); Syracuse University, Maxwell Graduate School of Citizenship and Public Affairs, *Attitudes of Scientists and Engineers About Their Government Employment*, Vol. 1 (1950).

standing of public employment in American life. Yet none has produced evidence that is fundamentally at variance with the broad general findings published by White more than thirty years ago. White found that among different segments of the population there were marked variations in the prestige of the public service. The prestige of municipal employment was higher among women than among men, and lower among older people than among younger people. The higher a person's level of education, the more negative his attitude was likely to be. Professional and technical personnel accorded public employment a low prestige rating; skilled and unskilled workers regarded it more highly. The foreign-born and Negroes had a more favorable attitude than did other major groups in the population.[52]

There were individuals, of course, whose attitudes differed sharply from the dominant view of most people in their group. But the general trend was plain. The higher a person's social or economic status was, the less prestige was likely to attach to public employment.

In a 1932 study, based on responses to a questionnaire by residents of ten cities, White established that there was a hierarchy of prestige for municipal, state, and federal employment. "The prestige ratings," he reported, "give the federal employee the highest position, the state next, and the city lowest."[53] In 1956, Janowitz and Wright pointed out that, in Detroit, an individual's evaluation of the prestige value of public employment also varied with his conception of what constituted the proper sphere for government activities. People who favored an expansion of the government's social service functions tended to rate public employment higher than those who did not.[54]

One of the most penetrating analyses of attitudes toward federal employment was reported in 1961 by William Jasper of the United States Naval Laboratories in California. This study explored the attitudes of senior engineering students at UCLA and Stanford and of young scientists and engineers who had already chosen to work for the Naval laboratories in California. Among other techniques, a focused group interview was used, in which ten to fifteen people discussed informally a prescribed pattern of topics. Throughout the discussions, participants were encouraged to discuss the pros and cons of government employment in their own words.

Jasper summarized the views of the engineering students as follows:

> It appeared to be the general feeling of the group that there was a stigma attached to government employment. . . .
> The students pictured the engineer working for the government as being primarily interested in security and [felt] that employees hired by the govern-

[52] White, *op. cit.*, pp. 139-156.
[53] Leonard D. White, *Further Contributions on the Prestige Value of Public Employment* (University of Chicago Press, 1932), p. 33.
[54] Morris Janowitz and Deil Wright, "The Prestige of Public Employment: 1929 and 1954," *Public Administration Review*, Vol. 16 (Winter 1956), p. 21.

ment are generally mediocre in ability. They also felt that the inflexible salary schedule stifles initiative and results in a promotional system that relies primarily on seniority for advancement. . . .

Some of the students equated government employment with postal and clerical work and did not appear to differentiate between kinds of occupations within the Federal service. The job satisfactions that these students sought were not in harmony with the image that they possessed of government employment. The primary motivating factors in job choice was the interesting and challenging nature of the job and whether the job allows for individual initiative and adequate recognition of accomplishments. Government employment was generally not looked upon as meeting these prerequisites for a career choice. The opinion seemed to be among the prospective new graduates that the Federal government is a good way to get a start in an occupation and should be regarded only as a temporary stopover before going into private industry.[55]

The California study and most of the other surveys cited above were based on interviews of special segments of the population, living or working in certain parts of the country. Some of the national polling organizations, however, have obtained information about the appeal of public employment for the adult population of the United States as a whole. A few of the questions used in

TABLE A-3. *Percentage of Adult Americans Who Would Prefer the Government to Private Business As an Employer, 1939–1962*[a]

Year Survey Taken	Would Prefer Government Employment	Would Prefer Private Business Employment	Don't Know; No Opinion; All Other Answers	Number Interviewed
1939	39%	50%	11%	5,216
1946	27	61	12	3,538
1962	26	63	11	1,616

[a] The data in this table were obtained in the Roper Fortune Survey #13, December 1939, the Roper Fortune Survey #56, September 1946, and a Gallup Survey undertaken for the Brookings Institution, January 1962. On all three occasions, the question was phrased "Would you prefer the Government or private business as an employer?"

these surveys have had the added advantage of being repeated at a later date, and have thus provided trend data that reveal changes over time in the public mood. One such question was asked by the Roper Fortune Survey in December 1939 and September 1946: "Would you prefer the Government or private business as an employer?" As Table A-3 indicates, from 1939 to the end of World War II, there was a considerable drop in the proportion of people who would prefer public employment to working for a private business.

[55] William Jasper, "Attitudes Toward Federal Employment as Measured by Group Interview and Questionnaire Techniques," paper for the 69th Annual Convention of the American Psychological Association, September 1961 (mimeographed), p. 4.

APPENDIX B

The Questionnaires

Questionnaire for Employed, Nonfederal
Adult Populations

WE ARE DOING A SURVEY for a major research foundation to find out something about how people feel about various ways of making a living. Most of the questions I will ask you are related to this general topic. I am sure you will find the questions interesting. Please answer them just as frankly and completely as you can.

1. First, I would like you to think about what really matters most to you in your own life. Tell me what kind of a way of earning a living would be ideal for you—that is, the very best way of doing it from your point of view. Maybe no occupation could fit your ideal. But just let yourself dream a bit and tell me the various things *about* an occupation which would make it *absolutely ideal* for you. I'm not asking for the name of a specific occupation, but for the *kinds of things about* an occupation which would make it *absolutely ideal* for you. (USE "Anything else" PROBES)

(Has R. described *things about* an occupation, rather than just given names of occupations?)

2. Now, about the worst sort of occupation. What *kinds of things* about an occupation would make it the worst or least satisfying to you? (USE "Anything else" PROBES)

(Has R. described things about an occupation, rather than just giving names of occupations?)

3. (HAND RESPONDENT CARD SHOWING LADDER) Here is a picture of a ladder.[1] Suppose we say at the *top* of the ladder (POINTING) is the *very best*, the absolutely ideal sort of occupation you have just described. At the *bottom* is the *very worst* sort of occupation. Where on this ladder (MOVING FINGER RAPIDLY UP AND DOWN LADDER) would you put your present occupation, that is, what you are doing now?

    ENTER STEP NUMBER

[1] The ten-step ladder is shown in Chapter 2.

4. Now think of what you were doing five years ago. Where on this ladder would you put what you were doing as an occupation five years ago?

ENTER STEP NUMBER

Not working 5 years ago

5. Thinking now of your occupational future. Where on the ladder do you expect to be five years from now?

ENTER STEP NUMBER

Not rated because will be retired

Other (SPECIFY)

(INTERVIEWER: NOTE PARTICULARLY THE STEP NUMBER YOU RECORDED UNDER Q. 3. THEN ASK EITHER Q. 6 OR Q. 7 WHICHEVER APPLIES AND EITHER Q. 8 OR Q. 9 WHICHEVER APPLIES—THAT IS, THERE MUST BE TWO QUESTIONS ANSWERED ON THE NEXT PAGE.)

6. (FOR THOSE WHO ANSWERED Q. 3 WITH A "9" OR A LOWER NUMBER) Returning now to the present, that is, to the rating marked here in red (POINT TO Q. 3 RATING) which you gave your present occupation—what *kinds of things* about your present occupation kept you from placing it higher on the ladder? (USE "Anything else" PROBES)

7. (FOR THOSE WHO ANSWERED Q. 3 WITH A "10") Returning now to the present, that is, to the rating marked here in red (POINT TO Q. 3 RATING) which you gave your present occupation—what *kinds of things* about your present occupation caused you to place it at the top? (USE "Anything else" PROBES)

8. (FOR THOSE WHO ANSWERED Q. 3 WITH A "2" OR A HIGHER NUMBER) What *kinds of things* about it kept you from placing it lower? (USE "Anything else" PROBES")

9. (FOR THOSE WHO ANSWERED Q. 3 WITH A "1") What *kinds of things* about it caused you to place it at the bottom? (USE "Anything else" PROBES)

10. Suppose your work or occupation stayed the same but you worked for the Federal government—that is, the United States government—how much better or worse would that be? Show me on the ladder, please. The place you pointed to before is marked in red.

ENTER STEP NUMBER

(Q'S. 11 AND 12 ARE TO BE INTERCHANGED. IF SAME STEP OR A HIGHER STEP IN Q. 10 THAN IN Q. 3, ASK Q. 11 FIRST AND THEN Q. 12. IF A LOWER STEP IN Q. 10, ASK Q. 12 FIRST AND THEN Q. 11.)

11. What things would be likely to be better? (USE "Anything else" PROBES)
12. What things would be likely to be worse? (USE "Anything else" PROBES)
13. Suppose you were to change now and go to work for the U. S. Government doing the same thing you're doing now, how do you think your family might feel about it? Would they feel you were moving up the ladder or down?

Up

Down

No difference

14. Again suppose for the moment that a person in your line of work *did* go to work for the United States Government. Are there any particular branches

or parts of the government that would be better to be in than others, from your point of view?

Yes

No

Don't know } (SKIP TO Q. 17)

15. (IF "YES" TO Q. 14) What particular branches or parts of the Government would be better?

16. Why do you think that?

(INTERVIEWER: BE SURE TO SHUFFLE SMALL CARDS WELL)

17. Now, I have some small cards here, each of which has a statement on it saying something about jobs or occupations. I also have this large card (SHOW LARGE SCALE CARD) which says "AGREE" on the top and "DISAGREE" on the bottom and has these spaces (MOVE HAND UP AND DOWN) in between.[2] Please take the small cards and place each one in turn on the large card according to how much you agree or disagree with the statement on it. You have ten different positions available to you. There are, of course, no right or wrong answers. Now, let's take the first small card, where would you place it? Now, just go on from there, please, as quickly as you can. We are just interested in your first impressions.[3]

1. A person has a right to expect his work to be fun

2. There are a lot of problems in this country that the federal government ought to step in and do something about

3. Employment with a large private business offers a high degree of security

4. Whenever the federal government steps into something, it just makes things worse

5. To be really successful in life, you have to care about making money

6. Work is most satisfying when there are hard problems to solve

7. After you are making enough money to get along, then making more money in an occupation isn't very important

8. To me, it's important in an occupation to have the chance to get to the top

9. It's important to do a better job than the next person

10. A person who works for the federal government generally has a good chance to get ahead

11. Success in an occupation is mainly a matter of hard work

12. Success in an occupation is mainly a matter of luck

13. All things considered, working for a large private business firm appeals to me

14. All things considered, working for the federal government appeals to me

15. Most people who work for the federal government do their best to serve the public

16. Even if you dislike your work, you should do your best

17. If a person doesn't want to work hard, it's his own business

18. Work is a good builder of character

19. It is satisfying to direct the work of others

20. Work is a way of being of service to God

21. To me, a very important part of work

---

[2] The ten-point "agree-disagree" scale is shown in Chapter 2.

[3] Each statement of the fifty-five that follow was printed on a separate small card, which the interviewee picked at random, *not* in the order given here. The numbers used here appeared on the back of the cards, for interviewers' use in recording. The cards were shuffled between interviews to insure random presentation.

is the opportunity to make friends

22. The main satisfaction a person can get out of work is helping other people
23. Work should be the most important part of a person's life
24. I would like my family to be able to have most of the things my friends and neighbors have
25. It is more important for a job to offer *opportunity* than *security*
26. To me, work is nothing more than a way of making a living
27. Most jobs in the federal government are routine and monotonous
28. Most jobs in private business are routine and monotonous
29. To me, it's important in an occupation for a person to be able to carry out his own ideas without interference
30. It would be hard to live with the feeling that others are passing you up in your occupation
31. Work helps you forget about your personal problems
32. To me, it's important in an occupation that a person be able to see the results of his own work
33. Getting recognition for my own work is important to me
34. The United States government interferes in a lot of things it should stay out of
35. Success in an occupation is mainly a matter of knowing the right people
36. To me, it's important to have the kind of work that gives me a chance to develop my own special abilities
37. A young man of ability who goes into politics has a good chance of becoming a United States Senator or Representative
38. Once a person has shown what he can do by working a number of years, he ought not to have to take a special examination to get a job
39. If I had a son just getting out of school, I would like to see him go into politics as a life's work
40. To stay honest in politics, you have

to have wealth or a different occupation to fall back on

41. If I had a son who wanted to go into politics, I would want him to learn some other occupation first
42. A young man of ability who starts work in the Federal Civil Service has a good chance of ending up in one of the top level jobs
43. A young man of ability who starts work in a large private business corporation has a good chance of ending up in one of the top level jobs
44. For a young man of ability, his best chance for being *really successful* lies in going into politics
45. For a young man of ability, his best chance for being *really successful* lies in working for the federal government
46. For a young man of ability, his best chance for being *really successful* lies in working for a large private business corporation
47. For a young man of ability, his best chance for being *really successful* lies in setting up his own business
48. Sometimes it may be right for a person to lose friends in order to get ahead in his work
49. If I had a son who became a United States Senator or Representative, I would be proud of him
50. To me, almost the only thing that matters about a job is the chance to do work that is worthwhile to society
51. A person who works for a large private business generally has a good chance to get ahead
52. A person should constantly try to succeed at work, even if it interferes with other things in life
53. I like the kind of work you can forget about after the work day is over
54. To me, gaining the increased respect of family and friends is one of the most important rewards of getting ahead in an occupation
55. Employment with the federal government offers a high degree of security

18. Now, a somewhat different type of question. If you had a son just getting out of school, would you like to see him go into politics as a life work?

    Yes

    No

    Don't know

19. Why? (PROBE)

20. Suppose he did become a United States Senator or Representative. How would you feel about that?

21. Now let's think about one particular kind of person in the Federal government. If you were to describe your general idea of a United States civil service employee, what sort of a person would that be?

22. What do you picture a Federal civil service employee as doing—that is, what sort of work?

23. What do you suppose would cause a person to become a United States civil service employee instead of something else?

24. On the whole, who would be likely to be most satisfied with civil service employment—men or women?

    Men

    Women

    No difference

    Don't know (SKIP TO Q. 26)

25. Why do you say that?

26. What is the top salary per year in the United States Civil Service—that is, not the salaries of elected and appointed officials, but the highest salary anyone in the regular United States Civil Service can get? (IF "DON'T KNOW," ASK: Well, what would you guess is the highest salary? IF GUESS, MARK "GUESS")

    $_____ per year

    Cannot even guess

27. What do you think the highest salary per year *should be* for people who hold the top level jobs in the United States Civil Service? (IF "DON'T KNOW," ASK: Well, about what do you think it should be?)

    $_____ per year

    Cannot even guess

28. Turning away from government people for a moment, how about a person employed by a large private business or industry. If you were to describe your general idea of such a person, what would that be?

29. What do you picture a person employed by a large private business or industry as doing—that is, what sort of work?

30. Now, I'm going to ask you to think a little bit more about some of the other kinds of people in our government. If you were to describe your general idea of a United States congressman, what sort of a person would that be?

31. What do you suppose would cause a person to become a congressman instead of something else?

32. Now we've talked about two different kinds of United States government people—those who are elected like congressmen, and those who are in civil service. There is a third kind—those people who are quite high in the United States Government and who are appointed to their positions. When you think about these appointed positions, which one comes to mind? Any others?

33. For talking purposes here, let's say that the appointed positions we are concerned with are mainly the administrative or executive positions together

with their assistants. If you were to describe your general idea of an appointed person, what sort of person would that be?

34. Now, here is a different set of cards. Each of these cards asks you to consider a particular group of people. They are described in red at the top of the card. Below you are asked to rate those people on some particular thing about them. Here is a card (SHOW LARGE SCALE CARD) which says "EXTREMELY HIGH" at the top and "EXTREMELY LOW" on the bottom and has these spaces (MOVE HAND UP AND DOWN) in between. Please take these small cards and place them on the large card, according to how you rate the people described, on the point made about them. This "point" is always underlined for your convenience. Now, let's take the first card. You see, it says (READ RED WORDS). Those are the people you are to consider. Then here it says (READ BLACK WORDS). Now, how would you rate them on that point? Place the card to indicate your rating. Now, just go on from there, please, as quickly as you can. We are just interested in your first impressions.[4]

1. Consider: People who are appointed to top level jobs in the United States Government
   On the average, how would you rate them on their *interest in serving the public?*
2. Consider: People in the top level jobs in private business
   On the average, how would you rate them on their *interest in serving the public?*
3. Consider: Federal Civil Service empolyees in general
   On the average, how would you rate them on their *interest in serving the public?*
4. Consider: Federal Civil Service employees in general
   On the average, how would you rate them on *honesty?*
5. Consider: Federal Civil Service employees in general
   On the average, how would you rate them on their *drive to get ahead?*
6. Consider: People who are appointed to top level jobs in the United States Government
   On the average, how would you rate them on *honesty?*
7. Consider: People in the top level jobs in the Federal Civil Service
   On the average, how would you rate them on their *drive to get ahead?*
8. Consider: Members of the United States House of Representatives
   On the average, how would you rate them on *ability?*
9. Consider: People in the top level jobs in private business
   On the average, how would you rate them on *honesty?*
10. Consider: Members of the United States House of Representatives
    On the average, how would you rate them on *honesty?*
11. Consider: Federal Civil Service employees in general
    On the average, how would you rate them on *ability?*
12. Consider: Federal Civil Service employees in general
    On the average, how would you rate them on *how well respected they are?*
13. Consider: Members of the United States House of Representatives
    On the average, how would you rate

[4] Each of the thirty items that follow was on a separate card, numbered on the back. The first part of each item, "Consider:" (etc.), was printed in red, the second part in black. The ten-point "extremely high-extremely low" scale is not shown in Chapter 2, but is the same as the "agree-disagree" scale except for the wording at top and bottom. The cards were shuffled between interviews.

them on their *interest in serving the public?*

14. Consider: People in the top level jobs in the Federal Civil Service

On the average, how would you rate them on their *interest in serving the public.*

15. Consider: Members of the United States House of Representatives

On the average, how would you rate them on *how well respected they are?*

16. Consider: People in the top level jobs in private business

On the average, how would you rate them on *ability?*

17. Consider: People in the top level jobs in private business

On the average, how would you rate them on *how well respected they are?*

18. Consider: People in the top level jobs in private business

On the average, how would you rate them on their *drive to get ahead?*

19. Consider: Members of the United States House of Representatives

On the average, how would you rate them on their *drive to get ahead?*

20. Consider: People in the top level jobs in the Federal Civil Service

On the average, how would you rate them on *ability?*

21. Consider: People in the top level jobs in the Federal Civil Service

On the average, how would you rate

them on *honesty?*

22. Consider: People in the top level jobs in the Federal Civil Service

On the average, how would you rate them on *how well respected they are?*

23. Consider: People who are appointed to top level jobs in the United States Government

On the average, how would you rate them on their *drive to get ahead?*

24. Consider: People who are appointed to top level jobs in the United States Government

On the average, how would you rate them on *how well respected they are?*

25. Consider: United States Senators

On the average, how would you rate them on *ability?*

26. Consider: United States Senators

On the average, how would you rate them on their *interest in serving the public?*

27. Consider: People who are appointed to top level jobs in the United States Government

On the average, how would you rate them on *ability?*

28. Consider: United States Senators

On the average, how would you rate them on their *drive to get ahead?*

29. Consider: United States Senators

On the average, how would you rate them on *how well respected they are?*

30. Consider: United States Senators

On the average, how would you rate them on *honesty?*

CLASSIFICATION DATA: Now I need some information about you, so that, after we have completed all of our interviews, we'll be able to find out such things as whether men have different ideas than women, whether people who live in the country have different ideas from city people and so on.

35. First, where were you born—in the United States or in some other country?
    United States
    Other country

36. In what kind of place did you live most of the time while you were growing up (that is, up to age 15)? Would you say:

On a farm or ranch

In a town or towns under about 50,000 population

In the suburbs of a city or cities larger than 50,000 population

In the more central part of a city or cities

37. Where was your father born—in the United States or in some other country?

United States

Other country

38. What was the last grade of school your father completed?

Less than high school

High school

College—less than 4 years

College—4 years

College—more than 4 years

Trade school, nursing, etc.

39. Where was your mother born—in the United States or in some other country?

United States

Other country

40. What was the last grade of school your mother completed?

Less than high school

High school

College—less than 4 years

College—4 years

College—more than 4 years

Trade school, nursing, etc.

41. Have you yourself ever served in the United States Armed Forces—that is, in the Army, Navy, Air Force, or other branch?

Yes

No

42. Aside from military service, have you ever worked as a *civilian* for the federal government?

Yes

No (SKIP TO Q. 45)

43. (IF "YES") For how long?

Less than 6 months

6 months to 1 year

More than 1 year but less than 5 years

5 years or more

44. (IF "YES") What was the last year you worked for the federal government?

45. Now, about your present occupation. Are you now self-employed or do you work for somebody else?

Self-employed

Work for somebody else

46. Where are you employed—I don't mean the name of the place but what kind of a place is it?

47. What *exactly* do you do there?

48. What is your title?

49. (IF R. IS TEACHER, ASK:) What subject or subjects do you teach?

50. Now about your father's *principal* occupation. Was he self-employed or did he work for somebody else?

Self-employed

Work for somebody else

51. Where was he employed—I don't mean the name of the place but what kind of place was it?

52. What *exactly* did he do there?

53. What was his title?

(ASK QS. 54 THROUGH 60 IF R. IS NOT HEAD OF HOUSEHOLD, OTHERWISE, SKIP TO Q. 61.)

54. Is the head of household *now* self-employed or working for somebody else?

Self-employed

Work for somebody else

Unemployed (SKIP TO Q. 58)

55. At what kind of a place is (he) (she) employed?

56. What *exactly* does (he) (she) do there?

57. What is (his) (her) title?

58. Has head of household ever worked, as a *civilian,* for the federal government?

Yes

No (SKIP TO Q. 61)

59. (IF "YES") For how long?

Less than 6 months

6 months to 1 year

More than 1 year but less than 5 years

5 years or more

60. (IF "YES") What was the last year he worked for the federal government?

61. Getting back now to you, what was the last grade of school you completed?

Less than high school

High school

College—less than 4 years

College—4 years

College—more than 4 years

Trade school, nursing, etc.

62. What general kind of course did you take in high school?

Academic, college preparatory

Commercial

Vocational, agricultural

Other (SPECIFY)

63. (IF ANY COLLEGE EDUCATION IN Q. 61) What was your college major?

64. How old are you?

65. Generally speaking, do you usually think of yourself as a Republican, a Democrat, an Independent, or what?

Republican } (ASK Q. 66)
Democrat }

Independent (SKIP TO Q. 67)

Other (SPECIFY)

No choice (SKIP TO Q. 68)

66. Would you call yourself a strong (Republican) (Democrat) or a not very strong (Republican) (Democrat)?

Strong (Republican) (Democrat)

Not very strong (Republican) (Democrat)
No choice (SKIP TO Q. 68)

67. Do you think of yourself as closer to the Republican or Democratic Party?
Closer to Republican party
Closer to Democratic party
No choice

68. What is your religious preference or affiliation?
Protestant
Catholic
Jewish
Other (SPECIFY)
None

69. Present marital status:
Single
Married
Widowed
Divorced
Separated

70. Referring now to *your* occupation, the one you described for me earlier. Would you point out for me on this card the group which includes the amount of yearly income you receive before taxes, as wages or salary (including commissions and bonuses) from your present occupation. (HAND RESPONDENT INCOME CARD)

INCOME CARD

Weekly	*Yearly*
1. Under $20	Under $1,000
2. $20-$38	$1,000-$1,999
3. $39-$57	$2,000-$2,999
4. $58-$76	$3,000-$3,999
5. $77-$86	$4,000-$4,499
6. $87-$96	$4,500-$4,999
7. $97-$106	$5,000-$5,499
8. $107-$115	$5,500-$5,999
9. $116-$134	$6,000-$6,999
10. $135-$163	$7,000-$8,499
11. $164-$192	$8,500-$9,999
12. $193-$288	$10,000-$14,999
13. $289 and over	$15,000 and over

71. Which group on the card contains the amount of your *total family income?*

INTERVIEWER: ENTER FROM OBSERVATION

72. Sex:
Male
Female

73. Race:
White
Negro
Other non-white

74. Socio-economic:

Answered Q. 74:

  By observation

  Used card

    A

    B

    C

    D

INSTRUCTIONS FOR Q. 74

—circle code for Q. 74 from observation when you are interviewing respondents in *their homes.*

—present card provided for Q. 74 to respondent and have (him) (her) select a category when you are interviewing respondents in any place other than their homes.

Card presented to respondent

THINK OF THE COMMUNITY IN WHICH YOU LIVE:

Select "A" to represent your family if:

  —live in nicest section or neighborhood

  —have a relatively large, well-kept home

  —generally considered well-to-do

  —able to have a good many luxuries

  —head of house might be professional man, high business executive, owner of own business, or equivalent

Select "B" to represent your family if:

  —live in above average section or neighborhood

  —have a nice home, but not as large as some

  —generally considered to have a comfortable income

  —able to have some luxuries but not all

  —head of house might be minor or junior executive, a better paid white collar worker, owner of a neighborhood store, a plant official, or equivalent

Select "C" to represent your family if:

  —live in just about the average section or neighborhood

  —have a modest home, about average size

  —generally considered to have an adequate income, but comparatively little reserve

  —able to have few luxuries, if any

  —head of house may be clerical worker, an average white collar worker, better paid factory worker, or equivalent

Select "D" to represent your family if:

  —live in the poorest section or neighborhood

  —have a comparatively poor home, often in bad repair

  —generally considered to have an absolutely minimum income

  —able to have only the necessities of life

  —head of house might be a day laborer, less well paid factory worker, or equivalent

Questionnaire for Federal Populations

WE ARE DOING A SURVEY for a major research foundation to find out something about how people feel about various ways of making a living. Most of the questions I will ask you are related to this general topic. I am sure you will

find the questions interesting. Please answer them just as frankly and completely as you can. Right now we are talking to a representative group of
Federal employees, just as we talked earlier to a representative group of
persons in private industry. Could you tell me, first, whether you are employed
full-time or part-time by the Federal government?

1-9. [Same as questions 1-9 in the Nonfederal Adult Questionnaire.]
10. Suppose your work or occupation stayed the same but you no longer
worked for the U. S. government—that is, suppose you continued in your
present occupation, but went to work outside the Federal government—how
much better or worse would that be? Show me on the ladder, please. The
place you pointed to before is marked in red.

    ENTER STEP NUMBER

(Q's. 11 AND 12 ARE TO BE INTERCHANGED. IF SAME STEP OR A HIGHER STEP IN
Q. 10 THAN IN Q. 3, ASK Q. 11 FIRST AND THEN Q. 12. IF A LOWER STEP IN
Q. 10, ASK Q. 12 FIRST AND THEN Q. 11.)
11. What things would be likely to be better? (USE "Anything else" PROBES)
12. What things would be likely to be worse? (USE "Anything else" PROBES)
13. Suppose you were to change now and go to work outside the Federal
government doing the same thing you're doing now, how do you think your
family might feel about it? Would they feel you were moving up the ladder
or down?

    Up
    Down
    No difference

14. Again suppose for the moment that a person in your line of work *did* go
to work outside the Federal government. Are there any particular kinds of
employment or businesses that would be better to be in than others, from your
point of view?

    Yes
    No
    Don't know } (SKIP TO Q. 17)

15. (IF "YES" TO Q. 14) What particular kinds of employment or businesses
would be better?
16. Why do you think that?
17. Now, returning to your present situation, do you plan to continue working
for the Federal government, or do you think you might leave it?

    Continue
    Leave
    Don't know (SKIP TO Q. 20)

18. (IF "CONTINUE" OR "LEAVE" TO Q. 17) Why? What are the main things
that make you feel that way? (PROBE FOR REASONS, PRO OR CON)
19. How sure are you that you will (continue in) (leave) the Federal government—very sure, fairly sure, or not sure at all?

    Very sure
    Fairly sure
    Not sure

20. Thinking now about the past. Was there ever a time when you thought

fairly seriously of leaving the United States government, and then didn't?

 Yes

 No   } (SKIP TO Q. 24)

 Don't know}

21. (IF "YES" TO Q. 20) About how long ago was that? (RECORD NUMBER OF YEARS AGO TO NEAREST YEAR THE LAST TIME RESPONDENT THOUGHT FAIRLY SERIOUSLY OF LEAVING THE UNITED STATES GOVERNMENT AND THEN DIDN'T)

 ——————— YEARS AGO

22. (IF "YES" TO Q. 20) What were the main things that caused you to think fairly seriously about leaving the Federal government? (VERBATIM)

23. (IF "YES" TO Q. 20) What were the main things that caused you to stay in the Federal government? (VERBATIM)

24-41. [Same as questions 17-34 in the Nonfederal Adult Questionnaire.]

CLASSIFICATION DATA: Now I need some information about you, so that, after we have completed all of our interviews, we'll be able to find out such things as whether men have different ideas than women, whether people who live in the country have different ideas from city people, and so on.

42-48. [Same as questions 35-41 in the Nonfederal Adult Questionnaire.]

49. Have you ever worked outside the Federal government—that is, have you ever had a private employer or been self-employed?

 Yes

 No (SKIP TO Q. 56)

50. (IF "YES") For how long?

 1 year or less

 More than 1 year, but less than 5 years

 More than 5 years, but less than 10 years

 More than 10 years, but less than 20 years

 20 years or more

51. (IF "YES") What was the last year you worked outside the Federal government?

52. Thinking back to the time when you last worked outside the Federal government, were you self-employed or did you work for somebody else?

 Self-employed

 Worked for somebody else

53. Where were you employed—I don't mean the name of the place but what kind of a place was it?

54. What *exactly* did you do there?

55. What was your title?

(ASK EVERYBODY)

56. Now about your present occupation with the Federal government. What is the grade of your position—that is, is it something like GS-9, WB-5, PFS-7 or something else? (ENTER GRADE RESPONDENT GIVES. IF NO GRADE GIVEN, ENTER DESCRIPTION OF GRADE LEVEL.)

57. For what major Federal government department or branch are you now working?

 Agriculture Department

 Commerce Department

 Defense: Office of the Secretary

Air Force Department
Army Department
Navy Department
Health, Education, and Welfare Department
Interior Department
Justice Department
Labor Department
Post Office Department
State Department
Treasury Department
Federal Aviation Agency
General Services Administration
Veterans Administration
All other (SPECIFY)

58. Within the (ANSWER IN Q. 57), for what bureau or major subdivision are you now working?

59. What exactly do you do here?

60. What is your title?

61. Is this the official title which your personnel office uses for your position?
Yes (SKIP TO Q. 63)
No (ASK Q. 62)
Don't know (SKIP TO Q. 63)

62. What is the exact title for your position used by your personnel office? (ASK EVERYBODY)

63. About what percentage of your work is administrative work (e.g., supervising, planning, organizing, coordinating, reporting, delegating, etc.)? Would you say it is closest to:
100%
75%
50%
25%
0%

64. How long have you worked for the Federal government?
1 year or less
More than 1 year, but less than 5 years
More than 5 years, but less than 10 years
More than 10 years, but less than 20 years
20 years or more

65-68. [Same as questions 50-53 in the Nonfederal Adult Questionnaire.]

69. Did either of your parents ever work for the Federal government for a period of 3 years or more?
Yes, father did
Yes, mother did
Yes, both did
No, neither
Don't know (SKIP TO Q. 71 OR Q. 78 WHICHEVER IS APPLICABLE)

70. (IF "YES") Was this during the time when you were growing up and living at home, or was it some other time?

Time when growing up and living at home
Some other time
(ASK Q'S. 71 THROUGH 77 IF RESPONDENT IS NOT HEAD OF HOUSEHOLD. OTHER-
WISE SKIP TO Q. 78.)
71-77. [Same as questions 54-60 of the Nonfederal Adult Questionnaire.]
78. Getting back now to you, what was the last grade of school you completed?
    Less than high school
    High school
    College—less than 4 years
    College—4 years
    College—more than 4 years
    Trade school, nursing, etc.
79. What general kind of course did you take in high school?
    Academic, college preparatory
    Commercial
    Vocational, agricultural
    Other (SPECIFY)
80. (IF ANY COLLEGE EDUCATION IN Q. 78) What was your college major?
81. (IF TWO OR MORE COLLEGE MAJOR SUBJECTS GIVEN IN Q. 80) In which *one*
of these subjects did you do the most work?
82-89. [Same as questions 64-74 in the Nonfederal Adult Questionnaire.]

Questionnaire for Student Populations

WE ARE DOING A SURVEY for a major research foundation to find out something
about how people feel about various ways of making a living. Most of the
questions I will ask you are related to this general topic. I am sure you will
find the questions interesting. Please answer them just as frankly and completely as you can.

1-2. [Same as questions 1-2 in the Nonfederal Adult Questionnaire.]
3. (HAND RESPONDENT CARD SHOWING LADDER.) Here is a picture of a ladder.
Suppose we say at the *top* of the ladder (POINTING) is the *very best*, the
absolutely ideal occupation you have just described. At the *bottom* is the *very
worst* sort of an occupation. Now, thinking of the time when you start to work
at a regular occupation, where on this ladder (MOVING FINGER RAPIDLY UP
AND DOWN LADDER) do you think you are apt to be when you start?
    ENTER STEP NUMBER
4. How about five years after you start? Where on this ladder do you expect
to be then?
    ENTER STEP NUMBER
5. Returning now to when you start out, did you have in mind starting out
working for the Federal government—that is, the United States government?
    Yes (ASK Q. 6)
    No
    Nothing particular in mind } (SKIP TO Q. 7)

6. (IF "YES") Tell me more about what you had in mind. Why the Federal Government? (PROBE FOR AS MUCH DETAIL AS POSSIBLE)

    (NOW SKIP Q'S. 7 & 8 AND ASK Q'S. 9 & 10 IN THAT ORDER)

7. Suppose your first occupation was with the U. S. government. Would this be better or worse from your point of view?

    Better

    Worse

    No difference

8. How much (better) (worse)? Show me on the ladder. The place you felt you might start out is marked in red.

    ENTER STEP NUMBER

(QUESTIONS 9 & 10 ARE TO BE INTERCHANGED. IF RESPONDENT ANSWERED "WORSE" TO Q. 7, Q. 10 SHOULD BE ASKED FIRST. IF RESPONDENT ANSWERED "BETTER" OR "NO DIFFERENCE" TO Q. 7, Q. 9 SHOULD BE ASKED FIRST.)

9. What things would be likely to be better? (USE "Anything else" PROBES)

10. What things would be likely to be worse? (USE "Anything else" PROBES)

11. Let's talk for a moment about what you are actually doing and planning. In what year of school are you now?

High school	11
	12
College	1
	2
	3
	4
Graduate school	1
	2 or over

12. About what has been your grade average in school this year?

13. Do you have any plans for further education? What are they?

(CIRCLE CODE AND GIVE RESPONDENT'S OWN WORDS HERE)

    No, stop before completing high school

    Just complete high school

    Take college work, but less than 4 years

    4 years college, no more

    4 years college and master's degree

    4 years college and doctorate or more

       (incl. medical, law schools, etc.)

    No accredited college, but special training—nursing, art school, secretarial school, trade school, etc.

14. (FOR HIGH SCHOOL STUDENTS) What general kind of course are you taking in high school?

    Academic, college preparatory

    Commercial

    Vocational, agricultural

    Other (SPECIFY)

15. (FOR COLLEGE STUDENTS) What is your college major?

16. What occupation do you hope to follow after you leave school? (CIRCLE CODE AT RIGHT AND GIVE RESPONDENT'S OWN WORDS HERE)

Professional—doctor, lawyer, etc.
Scientist—physicist, chemist, etc.
Engineering—civil, chemical, mechanical
Business or business management
Teaching of any kind
A skilled trade—carpenter, welder, etc.
Farmer or farming, other agricultural   } (SKIP TO Q. 18)
Military
Social or welfare work
Clerical—secretary, bookkeeper, etc.
Sales
Art, architecture, etc.
Government or politics (ASK Q. 17)
Don't know (SKIP TO Q. 19)

17. (IF "GOVERNMENT OR POLITICS" IN Q. 16) When you say that, what do you mean?

18. What are the main things that cause you to favor that line of work instead of some other?

19-36. [Same as questions 17-34 in the Nonfederal Adult Questionnaire.]

CLASSIFICATION DATA: Now I need some information about you, so that, after we have completed all of our interviews, we'll be able to find out such things as whether men have different ideas than women, whether people who live in the country have different ideas from city people, and so on.

37-46. [Same as questions 35-44 in the Nonfederal Adult Questionnaire.]

47. Now about your father's *principal* occupation. Is he self-employed or does he work for somebody else?

   Self-employed
   Work for somebody else

48. Where is he employed—I don't mean the name of the place but what kind of place is it?

49. What *exactly* does he do there?

50. What is his title?

51. Has your father ever served in the United States Armed Forces—that is, in the Army, Navy, Air Force or other branch?

   Yes
   No

52. Has your father ever worked *as a civilian* for the Federal government?

   Yes
   No (SKIP TO Q. 55)

53. (IF "YES") For how long?

   Less than 6 months
   6 months to 1 year
   More than 1 year but less than 5 years
   5 years or more

54. (IF "YES" TO Q. 52) What was the last year he worked for the Federal government?

55-60. [Same as questions 64-69 in the Nonfederal Adult Questionnaire.]

61. Would you point out for me on this card the group which includes the amount of your family's total yearly income before taxes. (HAND RESPONDENT INCOME CARD)[5]

(INTERVIEWER: ENTER FROM OBSERVATION)

62. Sex
　　　Male
　　　Female
63. Race:
　　　White
　　　Negro
　　　Other non-white
64. Socio-economic: (PRESENT CARD)[6]
　　　　A
　　　　B
　　　　C
　　　　D

[5] See question 70 of Nonfederal Adult Questionnaire.
[6] See question 74 of Nonfederal Adult Questionnaire.

APPENDIX C

Supplemental Profiles

Various descriptive profiles of the populations surveyed in this study were presented in Chapter 3. The tables that follow here are designed to supplement the tables of that chapter.

TABLE C-1. *Education, Income, and Age Distributions in the Samples of the General Employed Public and General Federal Employees*

Characteristics	General Employed Public (N=1,142)	General Federal Employees (N=948)
Education		
High school not completed	29%	24%
High school completed	45	39
Some college—less than four years	11	18
College—four years	6	7
College—more than four years	6	7
Other (trade, nursing, etc.)	3	5
Occupational Income		
Under $3,000	19	1
$3,000–$4,999	36	31
$5,000–$6,999	27	47
$7,000–$9,999	9	13
$10,000–$14,999	4	7
$15,000 and over	4	0
Median Income	$4,700	$5,500
Age		
Under 20	2%	0%
20–24	8	3
25–34	22	18
35–44	29	37
45–54	25	27
55 and over	13	15
Median age	40 Years	42 Years

TABLE C-2. *Age, Income, and Father's Education Level in the Sample of College Teachers*

Characteristics	College Teachers (N=470)
Occupational Income	
Under $5,000	5%
$5,000–$6,999	27
$7,000–$9,999	36
$10,000–$14,999	25
$15,000 and over	6
Median income	$8,300
Age	
Under 35	22%
35–44	30
45–54	31
55 and over	17
Median age	43 Years
Father's Educational Level	
High school not completed	34%
High school completed	23
College—less than four years	15
College—four years	11
College—more than four years	15
Other (trade, nursing, etc.)	1
Don't know	1

TABLE C-3. *Age and Occupational Income Distributions of Executives, Natural and Social Scientists, and Engineers in Business*

Age and Income	Executives (N=287)	Natural Scientists (N=85)	Social Scientists (N=73)	Engineers (N=90)
Age				
Under 35	15%	26%	36%	11%
35–44	26	39	39	37
45–54	35	22	21	26
55 and over	23	13	4	26
Median age	46 years	39 years	38 years	44 years
Occupational Income				
Under $7,000	13%	7%	8%	6%
$7,000–$9,999	19	21	21	15
$10,000–$14,999	21	38	22	31
$15,000 and over	47	34	49	49
Median income	$14,300	$12,800	$14,700	$14,800

TABLE C-4. *Age and Occupational Income Distributions of Executives, Natural and Social Scientists, and Engineers in Government*

Age and Income	Executives (N = 273)	Natural Scientists (N = 92)	Social Scientists (N = 90)	Engineers (N = 99)
Age				
Under 35	6%	34%	21%	40%
35–44	29	36	37	30
45–54	42	16	27	17
55 and over	23	14	16	12
Median age	48 years	39 years	43 years	38 years
Occupational income				
Under $7,000	0%	22%	10%	16%
$7,000–$9,999	21	34	34	31
$10,000–$14,999	68	42	51	48
$15,000 and over	12	2	5	4
Median income	$12,000	$9,600	$10,600	$10,300

TABLE C-5. *Education and Occupation of Fathers of High School Junior and Senior, College Senior, and Graduate Student Samples*

Education and Occupation of Students' Fathers	High School Juniors and Seniors (N = 359)	College Seniors (N = 404)	Graduate Students (N = 383)
Fathers' Education			
High school not completed	30%	28%	26%
High school completed	37	30	32
College—less than four years	14	13	15
College—four years	9	12	10
College—more than four years	7	15	16
Other (trade, nursing, etc.)	3	2	1
Fathers' Occupation			
Manager, proprietor, and official	26%	31%	29%
Professional, technical, and kindred worker	15	24	23
Farmer and farm manager	5	3	5
Clerical and kindred worker	3	4	3
Sales worker	7	8	7
Craftsman, foreman, and kindred worker	24	19	18
Operative and kindred worker	10	4	5
Service worker	5	3	3
Household, farm laborer and foreman, and laborer	5	3	2
Not in labor force	1	1	5